PALEOANTHROPOLOGY

PALEO-ANTHROPOLOGY

MILFORD H. WOLPOFF

University of Michigan

ALFRED A. KNOPF • *New York*

THIS IS A BORZOI BOOK
PUBLISHED BY ALFRED A. KNOPF, INC.

First Edition
987654321
Copyright © 1980 by Alfred A. Knopf, Inc.

Library of Congress Cataloging in Publication Data

Wolpoff, Milford H. Paleoanthropology.

Bibliography: p.   Includes index.
1. Human evolution.   I. Title.
GN281.W6416   573.2   80-443
ISBN 0-394-32197-9

Manufactured in the United States of America

Book design: Lorraine Hohman

Introduction

As we are increasing phenomenally our formulated knowledge of the particular part of space occupied by the earth, in its revolutions around its sun, through our astronauts' travelling to the moon and probing the planets of the solar and galactic systems to which this earth belongs, so too we are becoming cognizant that the biological persistence of our earthly human species is utterly dependent upon the thoroughness and speed with which the totality of that species come to comprehend their phylogenetic past and adapt themselves intelligently, in its light, to the planet that produced all the other forms of life upon it, as well as the form called sapient man.

Raymond A. Dart, 1973

Paleoanthropology is the study of our origins. I view it as more than a history or a simple narrative of past events. The subject is a *science* and not a *history* because there are reasons for what happened in the past, explanations for why a certain course of events occurred, and some of the theories offered in explanation of our origins can be proven wrong. Historically, the idea of human evolution has been a controversial one. For many, the controversy centers on whether there is any reality to the concept at all. Within the disciplines that study human evolution (anthropology and paleontology), the idea is universally accepted, but its specific applications are debated.

The proposal that humans might have descended from something that was *other* than human seemed to contradict certain aspects of the philosophical and religious thinking in the Western world. Yet most now find the general concept acceptable. This is no small accomplishment in a cultural framework with a biological folk-knowledge that still refers to "mixed blood" in offspring of mixed parentage and retains the belief that there are things called "germs" that cause everything from mouth odors to diseases.

Controversy within the disciplines has a rather different basis. Three things contribute to what often appear to be fundamental differences in how the course of human evolution is best interpreted. These are basic differences in the philosophy of science, the scarcity of large samples of human fossil material, and the inability to fully prove any contention about what might have happened in the distant past.

Philosophical differences are often not recognized among the scientists themselves. Yet these contribute to the differences in approach that allow the same data to be viewed in very different ways. One might think of the main difference in approach as reflecting the difference between induction and deduction.

An inductive approach is practiced explicitly by many scientists. It is implicit in the so-called "scientific method" taught in most secondary schools. The approach involves gathering data, using these data to suggest hypotheses, and testing the hypotheses to determine whether they can be proven correct. An example of how hypothesis testing might be applied to fossil data is provided in a recent paper by D. Pilbeam and J. R. Vaišnys. These authors propose that conditional probabilities be calculated for competing hypotheses and that these be compared to decide which hypothesis is most likely.

The deductive approach differs from the inductive because of the contention that hypotheses can never be proven correct. As developed by Popper, it is argued that certainty lies only in the disproof, or refutation, of hypotheses. Consequently, scientists using this approach attempt to disprove the simplest explanatory hypothesis tested or be tentatively accepted.

As an example of how these approaches differ, let us consider an evolutionary event that occurred in East Africa some 1.5 million years ago. A new human species called *Homo erectus* appeared for the first time in fossil-bearing deposits east of Lake Turkana in Kenya. The paleontological question is: Where did this new species come from? All workers recognize that no completely definitive answer can ever be given. A scientist using the inductive approach might list the most credible hypotheses and derive probabilities for them. These possibilities would include migration from another area, evolution from the smaller of the australopithecine species living in the Turkana area earlier in time (variously called *Homo habilis*, *Australopithecus habilis*, *Homo africanus*, or *Australopithecus africanus*), evolution from the more robust australopithecine form present earlier in time (variously called *Zinjanthropus boisei*, *Australopithecus boisei*, *Paranthropus boisei*, *Paranthropus robustus*, or *Australopithecus robustus*), or evolution from a different earlier form perhaps only poorly represented in this region. A scientist using the deductive approach would pick what appeared to be the simplest of these hypotheses and attempt to find evidence to disprove it. Because of the morphological similarities, the simplest hypothesis would probably be the second of those listed above (evolution from the smaller earlier australopithecine form). Disproof could be accomplished by finding an even more similar ancestral species, by showing that *Homo erectus* could be found earlier than the first appearance of the proposed ancestral species, or by demonstrating that the amount of evolutionary change that took place could not have happened over the timespan allowed for it.

These approaches may not result in the same conclusion. Moreover, discourse between scientists using the different approaches may be misleading, since the same words and concepts can be used in very different ways. Another factor that has similar effects on scientific discourse is the fact that the currently accepted synthesis of evolutionary theory is barely forty years old. Evolutionary biology underwent a scientific revolution with the publication of the *Synthetic Theory of Evolution* in the early 1940s, and the resulting changes in interpretive framework have spread persistently but slowly.

The second source of paleontological controversy is the scarcity of fossils. Even if fossil remains were thousands of times more plentiful, they would represent only the smallest proportion of once living populations. Thus there are two aspects to this problem. First, events that took millions of years and involved billions of individuals must be reconstructed and interpreted from a handful of specimens. Second, these specimens may not represent the time or area where important changes were taking place, and they may not even accurately reflect the normal characteristics of the populations they come from. The second problem is more serious than the first since the expanding fossil record has seemed to fill in most of the gaps that once appeared in human evolutionary history. There is no longer a search for a "missing link" in human evolution. The contemporary problems result from the fact that there are many links (some would say too many) and involve the related questions of how these might best be put together and what underlies the pattern that results.

Finally, the third source of paleoanthropological controversy results from the inability to prove completely any interpretation of the fossil record. This uncertainty is intertwined with the other problems discussed above. Because it is universal, it is often forgotten. Yet underlying any attempt to make sense out of human evolution is the possibility that the best efforts could be completely wrong. Some would say that this makes the whole endeavor hopeless and the attempts to find new data or interpret the evidence more accurately meaningless. Others, however, find that this makes paleoanthropology more challenging and interesting.

I have attempted to accomplish three things in preparing this basic introduction to human evolution. I have presented what I believe is a consistent framework for understanding the course of human evolution. My approach is deductive, and consequently the framework I propose is the simplest one that I believe cannot be disproved at the present time. I have tried to demonstrate the process of interpretation, relating the known data to this framework by showing how questions have been asked in a way that is testable rather than speculative. Finally, I have presented the fossil evidence for human evolution as I understand it to fit within the framework of evolutionary theory. It is my hope that this presentation will allow more than a memorization of dates and events, but rather will lead to an understanding of process and an appreciation of how much basic research and experimentation remains to be done in the field of human paleontology.

The book, of course, is written from my own viewpoint. It expresses the framework from which I view the human evolutionary process. I have tried to make this framework as explicit as possible, since I believe that a framework is not something that can be eliminated in order to provide "objectivity." In my view, "objectivity" does not exist in science. Even in the act of gathering data, decisions about what data to record and what to ignore reflect the framework of the scientist. The approach I follow provides for the existence of a framework, and suggests that progress best be made by attempting to disprove it.

However, lest the reader come to believe that the framework and interpretations I suggest are the only ones possible, I have also provided a "State of the Art" section at the end of each chapter. The purpose of this is to discuss one of the issues raised in the chapter and analyze other positions that have been taken regarding it. These sections act as both a further discussion and an indication of where major points of disagreement lie in the field today.

I have also provided two bibliographies. At the end of the chapters are briefly annotated references to the materials discussed. These are picked on the basis of their simplicity, accessibility, and balanced discussion of the topics. Whenever possible, they are discussions rather than descriptions. At the end of the book is a more general bibliography, arranged by topic. Here the reader may pursue points and issues raised in the text and find both original research and descriptions and original statements of position taken by scientists.

Whenever possible, I have based my observations and conclusions on studies of the original fossil materials. I am deeply indebted to a number of individuals, and their institutions, for permission to work on the fossil remains, as well as for the hospitality and encouragement I received all over the world. The community of human and primate paleontologists is small, and it has been gratifying to discover that the communication, interest, and cooperation within this community transcends geographic and political boundaries. I would like to acknowledge particularly my gratitude and indebtedness to the following individuals and institutions:

P. Andrews   *British Museum (Natural History)*

C. Stringer

H. Bach   *Schiller Universität*

C. K. Brain   *Transvaal Museum*

E. Vrba

E. Voigt

Y. Coppens   *Musée de l'Homme*

J.-L. Heim

V. Correnti   *Universita di Roma*

I. Crnolatac   *Geološko-Paleontološki Muzej*

M. H. Day   *St. Thomas' Hospital Medical School*

H. Delporte   *Musée des Antiquities Nationales de Saint Germain-en-Laye*

L. deBonis   *Laboratoire de Paléontologie Vertèbrès et de Paléontologie Humaine, Université Paris*

B. Vandermeersch

A.-M. Tillier

M.-A. and H. deLumley   *Laboratoire de Paléontologie Humaine et de Prehistoire, Université de Provence*

R. Feustel   *Museum für Ur- und Frühgesichte Thüringens*

F. Fulep   *Magyar Nemzeti Muzeum*

F. C. Howell   *Department of Anthropology, University of California at Berkeley*

W. W. Howells   *Peabody Museum, Harvard University*

T. Jacob   *Projek Penelitian, Paleoanthropologi National, Universitas Gadjah Mada*

J. Jelinek   *Anthropos Institute, Moravske Museum*

K. Valoch

H. E. Joachim   *Rheinisches Landesmuseum*

D. C. Johanson   *Cleveland Natural History Museum*

D. Kadar   *Museum Geologi Bandung*

G. H. R. von Koenigswald   *Natur-Museum und Forschungs-Institut Senckenberg*

M. Kretzoi   *Magyar Allami Foldtani Intezet*

M. D. Leakey   *National Museums of Kenya*

R. E. F. Leakey

A. Leguebe   *Institut Royal des Sciences Naturelles des Belgique*

C. O. Lovejoy   *Department of Sociology and Anthropology, Kent State University*

M. Malez   *Geološko-Paleontološki zbirka i laboratorij za krs, JAZU*

J. Radovčić

D. Mania   *Landesmuseum für Vorgesichte*

J. Melentis   *Geological and Paleontological Institute, University of Thessalonika*

E. Sergi-Naldini   *Instituto Italiano di Paleontologia Umana*

B. A. Ogot   *The International Louis Leakey Memorial Institute for African Prehistory*

R. Protsch   *Goethe Universität*

J. Szilvassy   *Abteilung Anthropologie, Naturhistorisches Museum Wien*

A. G. Thorne   *Research School of Pacific Studies, Australian National University*

P. V. Tobias   *Department of Anatomy, University of the Witwatersrand*

A. Hughes

T. Toth   *Természéttudományi Muzeum*

A. Walker   *John Hopkins University Medical School*

Woo Ju-Kang   *Institute of Vertebrate Paleontology and Paleoanthropology, Academia Sinica*

Wu Xin-zhi

Dong Xing-ven

U. T. Yakimov   *Department of Anthropology, Moscow State University*

I deeply appreciate the advice and encouragement provided by the Random House Personnel, especially the Executive Editor, B. Fetterolf, and the Acquiring Editor, P. Metcalf. Finally, a number of workers reviewed and helped revise this manuscript during various stages of its preparation. I am grateful for help provided by G. Conroy, B. Sigmon, F. Szalay, R. Tuttle, and C. Weitz. I am expecially indebted for the substantial efforts of E. Delson, M. Russell, and E. Trinkaus. However, the time and effort given by D. W. Frayer were truly monumental. I owe Dr. Frayer my most sincere gratitude.

Support for the research on the human and primate fossils was provided by the National Academy of Sciences, the Rackham fund at the University of Michigan, and the National Science Foundation (grants BNS 76-82729, BNS 76-04894, BNS 75-21756, and GS-38607.

FURTHER READINGS

Dart, R. A. 1973. Recollections of a Reluctant Anthropologist. *Journal of Human Evolution* 2:417–428

A wide-ranging essay combining philosophy and history in the search for human origins

Kuhn, T. S. 1970. *The Structure of Scientific Revolutions*, 3rd ed. University of Chicago Press, Chicago.

Probably the best description of how scientific revolutions take place and effect scientists.

PILBEAM, D., and J. R. VAIŠNYS. 1975. Hypothesis Testing in Paleoanthropology. In *Paleo-anthropology: Morphology and Paleoecology*, ed. R. Tuttle. Mouton, The Hague, pp. 7–18.
    The paper, and the discussion following it (included in the page reference), provide a clear statement of the inductive approach.

POPPER, K. R. 1961. *The Logic of Scientific Discovery*, Science Editions, New York.
    The philosophical foundations of the deductive approach.

Milford H. Wolpoff
Hoof 'N' Paw Farm 1979

Contents

PART ONE
THE BASIS FOR HUMAN EVOLUTION

PART TWO
THE APPEARANCE OF THE FIRST HUMANS

CHAPTER FOUR Hominid Features   65

CHAPTER FIVE Why Are There Hominids?   88

PART THREE
DEVELOPMENT OF THE HOMINID PATTERN

PART FOUR
THE EVOLUTION OF MODERN PEOPLE

TABLE OF FIGURES

TABLE OF SPECIMENS FIGURED

TABLE OF MAPS

TABLE OF TABLES

PALEOANTHROPOLOGY

THE BASIS FOR HUMAN EVOLUTION

CHAPTER ONE

Background for Studying the Past

The study of human evolution focuses on the explanations for a particular sequence of events that eventually led to the appearance of living people. These events occurred far in the past, and the only records left to us are the fossil remains of once living organisms, preserved artifacts suggesting their behavior, and some evidence of the habitat in which they died. Paleoanthropology is mainly concerned with the first of these, although data resulting from the other two (archaeological, paleoecological, geological, and taphonomic) are critically important. The fossils are studied in a variety of contexts, with very different questions in mind. Comparisons are made of their form, and scientists usually attempt to determine behavioral and genetic analogies from the once living populations that they (inadequately) represent. Since the evolutionary process involves the average changes in the characteristics of these populations over time, determining their temporal sequence is crucial.

This chapter begins with a discussion of what fossils are and how they are formed, followed by the more difficult problem of determining their age.

The fossils that exist in museums are such an extraordinarily small proportion of the creatures that once lived on our planet that the circumstances surrounding their preservation could result in a biased sample. Moreover, problems in dating fossils are so great that even now the age of most human fossils cannot be determined with any degree of precision. Thus a study of human evolution should begin with a discussion of the problems posed by the preservation and aging of fossils.

What Are Fossils?

The fossil evidence for human evolution is limited, fragmentary, and generally incomplete. Yet this evidence provides the only secure framework for charting prehistorical events. Fossils are the remains or imprints of once living organisms. But only a very small number of organisms are preserved as fossils; it has been estimated that the total weight of all the organisms that have ever lived on earth would equal the weight of the planet itself!

3

Fossils can be formed in several different ways. The most common is the preservation of certain portions of the organism. When an organism dies, a combination of physical, chemical, and biological processes may quickly lead to its destruction. This can be prevented only if the organism is enclosed in a medium that protects it from these processes. This would generally require burial, which could occur in streams or lakes; in caves; in peat, mud or tar; or more rarely in ash falls resulting from volcanic eruptions. However, the organism may have already been partially altered or destroyed before burial (see Figure 1.1). Most human fossils are preserved in deposits resulting from water action (along streams or lakes) or in caves, except for those rare individuals who were intentionally buried as the result of human activities.

These facts place certain limitations on which organisms became fossils. Fossilization is accidental, and which organisms become fossils may seem a matter of blind luck, but this is not completely true. Those that lived in or near water had a much better chance of being buried and preserved. Fortunately for the human fossil record, people have been dependent on drinking large quantities of water for some time, and there is much evidence from the archaeological record of human activity that they often lived near water. Early in human evolution people did not live in caves, but caves often form where there is a flow of water, allowing accidental burial of the animals and people who died in the vicinity. Later, caves were regularly occupied, and even more cave deposits contain human fossils. Paleontologists dealing with more ancient human ancestors or relatives have less fossil evidence to work with. The fossil history of the living apes, especially over the last 10 million years, is very poorly known. Ancestors of apes living during this period apparently occupied forests, generally away from bodies of water. Conditions in a tropical forest lead to rapid decomposition, so there are very few fossil remains because of the combination of rapid deterioration, scavenging, and rareness of burial.

Many body tissues are partially composed of inorganic (noncarbon) minerals. These are the so-called "hard tissues," bones and teeth. Such tissues are already on the way to becoming fossils because of their high mineral content, while the remaining "soft tissues" are almost never preserved for long

periods of time. However, fossilization is not the simple preservation of the mineralized portions of the body. Elements in the soil such as silica, calcium carbonate, and calcium phosphate can replace the organic as well as the mineral content of bones and teeth. But usually, the more minerals in a tissue, the more readily it can be preserved. Teeth, which are over 90 percent mineral in content, are the most common fossils, and harder bones such as the skull are preserved much more commonly than softer bones such as ribs.

The condition of a fossil often depends on what happens to the organism before the bones are buried. Taphonomy is the study of this process, and taphonomic studies have revealed that deposits of fossilized bone are rarely a random sample of the once living organisms. For instance, if scavengers

FIGURE 1.1   *Different conditions of fossil preservation for humans and apes. Photo A is the best possibility, a perfectly preserved foot of a female Neandertal from the French site of La Ferrassie. This individual was buried about 50,000 years ago. Photos B and C are an 18-million-year-old fossil ape skull from Rusinga Island, Kenya, attributed to Proconsul africanus. The entire back of the skull is missing. Note the very irregular shape of the left eye socket, the result of crushing. Photos D and E are an even more distorted specimen, a 2-million-year-old skull of a juvenile from the South African australopithecine site of Swartkrans. The faceless skull shows both plastic distortion and direct breaks; the plastic deformation results in curves and angles that did not exist during life, while the visible breaks are augmented by the fact that the entire face is broken off. The lower jaw shown in Photo E is that of a leopard, also from Swartkrans. C. K. Brain, director of the Transvaal Museum in Pretoria, has demonstrated that the projecting canines of this leopard's jaw fit exactly into two holes at the back of the skull. He hypothesizes that a leopard killed the Swartkrans youth and carried the body up into one of the trees that grew about the mouth of the cave (with its lower jaw grasping the skull as shown). As the leopard ate its kill, or perhaps later, part of the skull fell from the tree into the cave. While some of the breaks are due to the cat, others come from the weight of the accumulating soil on top of the skull.*

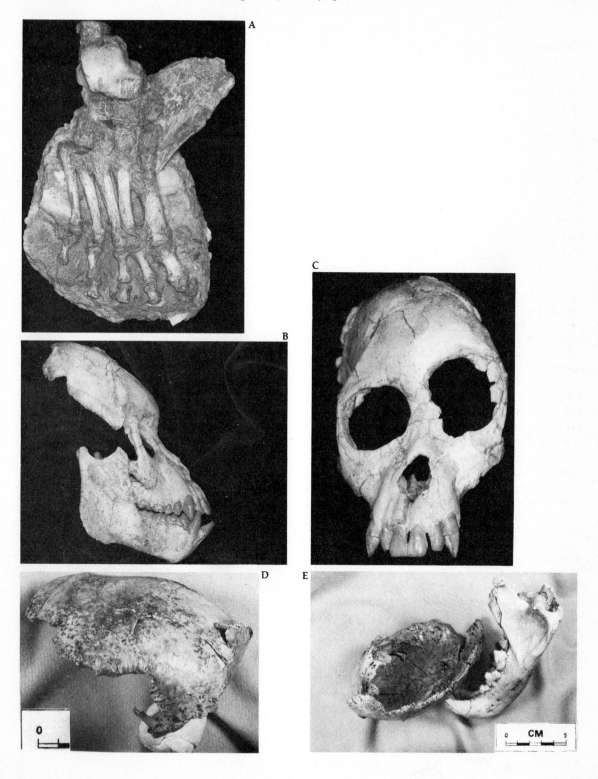

have eaten a carcass, only certain parts will remain. If bones are disturbed by water before fossilization, lighter, less dense bones will separate from the heavier, denser ones. Bones may be trampled by animals or cracked and broken by the drying heat of a tropical sun.

Although the "hard tissues" are most often preserved, there are other possibilities. Under certain chemical conditions, the mineral content of bones may dissolve while the softer organic content remains. The bones may then undergo "plastic distortion," bending and twisting into new shapes. Another possibility is the disintegration of the original bone, leaving an open space or mold of its exact form. This mold may then fill with material, leaving a fossil cast.

Since the process of fossilization depends on local ground conditions, its speed can vary greatly from place to place. In one area fossilization may occur in only a few thousand years, while in another significant mineral replacement may literally take millions of years. Thus the age of a fossil cannot be determined from how mineralized it has become.

In sum, the process of fossilization is rare, and the conditions surrounding death and burial are usually so traumatic that only parts of the original organism become fossilized. Yet the fossils themselves, interpreted in an evolutionary and ecological framework, provide the primary data for the study of human evolution.

Dating Past Events

One of the most important things that can be known about a fossil is when the organism lived. For instance, the overlap in size and form between various fossil human groups is so great that isolated portions of skeletons—jaws, teeth, leg bones, and so on—sometimes cannot be identified taxonomically until their age is known.

There are many ways to tell how old something is. The methods used depend on what information is available. Generally, we can divide dating procedures into two types: those that give the absolute date in years and those that give a relative age in comparison with something else. The latter can be very important when the former is not possible.

RADIOACTIVE DECAY

Today our most accurate technique for absolute dating is called "radiometric"—an age in years (metric) based on radioactive decay (radio). There are various forms of radiometric dating, all depending on the fact that certain elements, or their isotopes (chemically identical but atomically different forms of the element), are naturally unstable. This means that the atoms making up the element regularly break apart into several smaller atoms of what are then different elements—for instance, the gradual decay of uranium into lead. Every time an atom breaks apart, small high-energy atomic particles shoot off. This is the radioactivity that accompanies such decay. The amount of decay occurring at any time (i.e., the number of atoms that break apart) can be measured by the amount of radioactivity.

The probability of *any* atom decaying at a given moment is constant for a given element or isotope. Therefore, the *number* of atoms of an element or isotope decaying depends on the number of atoms present. For instance, if there are 10,000 atoms present, and if the probability of decay in a given second is .001, then the number that probably will decay in that second is

$$10,000 \times .001 = 10$$

The probability of decay is different for every element and isotope. Moreover, in any specific element the *number* of atoms that decay varies over time. Using the above example, in the next second we cannot again expect that ten atoms will decay, because there are no longer 10,000 atoms present. Instead, there are 9,990 atoms. Each second there will be fewer atoms decaying.

After a given length of time, only half of the original atoms will remain. This length of time is called the "half-life." After one half-life, the rate of decay, or the amount of radioactivity, is also halved. After the span of another half-life, half of the remaining atoms will be present (¼ of the original), and after yet another half-life only half of these will remain (⅛ of the original). This property of radioactive decay allows its use in dating past remains.

ERROR

All forms of radiometric dating are subject to error. Some errors result from contamination of the object being dated, but others are the direct result of the fact that the technique is based on probability. It depends on the average behavior of atoms over a *long* period of time as measured in a laboratory over a *short* time span. The short-term result may not be the same as the long-term average. This is similar to what may happen if one flips a coin. Many tries will always result in heads an average of 50 percent of the time and tails 50 percent of the time. However, if the coin is flipped just three times, it is possible (and not especially rare) to have three heads in a row. Predicting the long-term average from such a short-term sample could be very misleading.

Consequently, all radiometric dates have an associated probability range and they are always reported with this range. The range may be as small as 1 or 2 percent, or as large as 50 percent. The probability statement means that the date most likely falls within the reported range. Thus, for instance, two fossils may be dated 25,000 ± 200 BP (before present). This means the organisms lived between 24,800 and 25,200 years ago. While they may possibly have lived at exactly the same time, they may instead have lived as much as 400 years apart. Generally, this error factor increases when the age of the specimen or object is extremely ancient or recent.

DETERMINING DATES DIRECTLY

There are a number of both direct and indirect techniques for determining the absolute age of a specimen. The most important direct determination is through the decay of radiocarbon (carbon 14). In the upper atmosphere, nitrogen, the most common gas in our atmosphere, is transformed into carbon 14 (an unstable form of carbon) as the result of bombardment by cosmic rays. The carbon 14 filters down into the lower atmosphere, where it mixes with normal carbon 12 and is absorbed by all living things. As a result, the amount of carbon 14 (in proportion to carbon 12) in a living organism is the same as that in the atmosphere. When the organism dies, however, no new carbon is introduced, and the proportion of carbon 14 becomes less and less as the result of radioactive decay. Therefore, the amount of carbon 14 in proportion to carbon 12 in once-living material can be used to determine how long it has been since the organism died.

There are two limitations to this technique. One is that the half-life of carbon 14 is only 5,568 years. If a bone is 55,680 years old, ten half-lives have elapsed and only 1/1024th of the original carbon 14 remains. This amount is so small that it is difficult to measure accurately, and carbon 14 dating is not accurate for bones much older than 50,000 years. The other disadvantage is that there is not that much carbon 14 in bone tissue to begin with. The dating method requires the destruction of bone to determine how much regular carbon is present. This means that the older the bone, the more of it must be destroyed to determine its age, and there is a natural reluctance to destroy large portions of ancient human remains.

Certain other new dating techniques can also be applied directly to bone for an age in years. At present, however, other radiometric techniques, mainly based on uranium decay, have not proved successful in dating bone because uranium can be absorbed from the surrounding soil, making it impossible to determine how much was originally present. Certain techniques not using radioactivity seem more promising. One of these, which depends on natural changes that take place in amino acids (part of the organic content of bone), is useful when the fossil bone has a history of constant temperature, such as in a cave. The technique appears to be good over at least 200,000 years, and it has been used to date some important specimens. However, the procedure and the assumptions it is necessary to make about the pre- and post-excavation history of the specimen provide many opportunities for error.

INDIRECT TECHNIQUES

Indirect absolute dates result from a direct determination of the age of the *deposit* in which the fossil was found. The techniques discussed above can be used to date bones of other animals, and carbon 14 dating can be particularly accurate when it is applied to charcoal. Another radiometric technique that has been extremely useful since the 1960s is the potassium-argon (K/A) method of dating. The isotope potassium 40 decays into the inert gas argon. In many types of rocks the argon gas is trapped and can accumulate as the potassium decays. If these rocks are carefully analyzed with regard to eliminating contamination, the ratio of potassium 40 to argon 40 will tell how long it has been since the argon began to accumulate. The hitch is that the "date" is not necessarily the age of the rock or the age of the deposit, but only the length of time since the argon began to accumulate. Therefore, for this method to be used in determining the age of a deposit, there must be some event which links the beginning of argon accumulation with the deposit. The most common possibility is a volcanic eruption. If potassium-bearing rocks or ash results from such an eruption, all of the argon accumulated earlier will have escaped if the rock was sufficiently heated. And argon will begin to accumulate again when the rock cools. If the rock was deposited when solidifying, the age of the rock will be the age of the deposit. The K/A technique is useful wherever there are volcanic eruptions and has provided the first dates for many really ancient hominid fossils. Coincidentally, it has been useful for dating in many other circumstances (it was the technique used to determine the age of the moon craters).

The half-life of the potassium-argon decay process is very long, about 1.3 billion years, and unlike carbon 14 it can be used to date rocks that were heated billions of years ago. The disadvantage of this long half-life is that it takes argon a considerable time to accumulate. When little time has elapsed since accumulation began, not enough argon is present to date the rock accurately. While carbon 14 dating cannot be used on specimens that are too old, the K/A technique cannot be used when the deposits are too young. Although many recent dates have been claimed for the K/A technique, it does not yet seem accurate on deposits younger than about 400,000 years.

Numerous other radiometric techniques can be used in indirect absolute dating. All of these, however, must depend on an event which relates the age of the object to the age of the deposit. Fission track dating can be used to date many crystal structures with a uranium content because of the tracks made in the crystal by high energy particles. The

fission track dating

technique dates the last time that the rock was heated, and the potential time range is very great. The most important use of this technique is the dating of small, smooth, and often teardrop-shaped glassy rocks called tectites, which are probably of meteoric origin.

The accuracy of these indirect absolute dates is a step removed from the dating procedure itself, since they depend on how certainly the specimen can be associated with the dated deposit. Moreover, when dating depends on a correlation with other deposits, there is a further reduction in accuracy. In sum, while absolute dating procedures give an age in years, we must not forget that this is an estimate, and not a birthday.

Relative Dating Techniques

A different series of problems affects the accuracy of relative dating procedures. Relative dates relate the age of a fossil to the age of something else, such as other fossils, paleolithic cultures, or geologic events. Relative dating is used when absolute dating is impossible. Moreover, it is an integral part of indirect absolute dating procedures.

LOCAL DATING

Relative dating is primarily used in relating a fossil to the deposit in which it is found. Such dating is generally chemical, and depends on the fact that when bones are buried, they gradually absorb certain elements from the soil. The longer the bones are buried, the more they absorb. These chemicals can then be measured and the amounts in different bones compared. For example, if human fossils have been in the ground as long as the surrounding fossil fauna, the percentages of the various elements will be the same in the two. On the other hand, if the human bones were buried into a more ancient layer, or otherwise became mixed with older fauna, then the human bones will have less of the various elements.

It is common to use several different elements for this dating procedure. The earliest analyses were based on fluorine. At the turn of the century, Gorjanović-Kramberger, a Croatian paleontologist, first used fluorine to show that the human fossils at the

Neandertal site of Krapina were contemporary with the extinct fauna also found at the site. It is unfortunate that the same technique was not used in western Europe to discredit the antiquity of the Piltdown cranium until over 50 years later. Other elements commonly used include nitrogen and uranium. Chemical dating depends completely on local soil conditions and cannot be extended to compare one site with another even if they are near each other. Depending on the local conditions, chemical dating may not work consistently, or may work so poorly that it is useless. Yet it is particularly important in considering human fossils because of the practice of burial, which became common during the last 100,000 years.

WIDESPREAD DATING

A secondary use of relative dating determines the position of the fossil-bearing deposit in the local stratigraphic sequence, archaeological sequence, or sequence of animal evolution. This is done by determining the order of events that occurred locally and then relating the deposit to this order. Such a sequence may depend on a local series of distinct volcanic lavas or tuffs (ash from eruptions), a series of climatic fluctuations (wet/dry, or warm/cold), a sequence of evolving animal species, or local trends in cultural evolution. In the last case, the appearance of new tools or frequency changes in the tools may be used in conjunction with relative stratigraphic position to determine a cultural sequence.

There are many examples of relative dating. In the 2-million-year-old deposits of East Lake Turkana, in Kenya, the stratigraphic positions of hominids many miles apart can be related to each other by tracing the volcanic tuffs through their exposures from one area to another. The relative positions of many European Neandertals can be determined only by the sequence of temperature oscillations local to western Europe. These can be determined from the fauna, as well as from the composition of ancient soils and other geologic features affected by temperature.

Dating by use of a cultural sequence is the most difficult of these techniques. The evolution of human technology has been characterized more by the addition of new tools than by the discarding of old ones. People living today have been seen using

the most primitive-looking pebble tools, comparable to the earliest tools recognized, to butcher an animal so that it could be conveniently carried away. If we judged solely from the presence of very simple tools, we might be tempted to date an event that actually happened recently to millions of years ago. On the other hand, a steel axe head would clearly show that a site was very recent. Only the tools that appear most advanced can be used in defining the position of a site in a local cultural sequence. Moreover, the activities at the site must also be considered, since a site where an animal was butchered may have very different tools from an area where people lived. The same principle is used when analyzing the position of a site in a sequence of faunal evolution. Only the most modern appearing species are important.

The same techniques can be used to locate the position of a fossil-bearing site in a wider-scale sequence of geologic, cultural, or faunal changes. However, the wider the area considered, the greater the potential for error. For instance, almost every important human technological innovation appears today throughout the inhabited world. This is probably the result of both diffusion and parallel independent invention. Consequently, cultural changes in various areas need not have taken place at the same time.

Relative dating by fauna depends on evaluating and recording the evolution and spread of wide-ranging species. The earliest appearance of certain species in an area can be used to date it, under some circumstances. The beginning of the Pleistocene epoch (the period of ice ages) itself was until recently defined by the appearance of modern genera of horses, elephants, and cattle. Other useful animal groups include hyenas and other carnivores, as well as pigs.

The more local the attempt, the more accurate faunal dating can be. One recent development has been the use of microfaunas (very small animal species such as mice) for comparisons. There are promising possibilities for relating small species of rodents over wide areas which are just beginning to be explored. Yet the inaccuracies of faunal dating and the problems that occur when different habitats are involved present difficulties in many comparisons which cannot always be overcome. One effect of this has been the attempt to use other sorts of widely occurring phenomena to establish relative dates.

pluvial
interpluvial

The Pleistocene Glaciations

Most of the other attempts to use widespread phenomena for dating are based on the sequence of Pleistocene glaciations and the effects of these glaciations on temperature, moisture, and the level of bodies of water. The original work on glaciations was done in the European Alps in the mid-nineteenth century. Studies of local stratigraphic sequences led to the idea that four main glaciations had occurred during the Pleistocene, and there was evidence of a fifth earlier one. Beginning with the most recent, the names given to the Alpine glaciations are Würm, Riss, Mindel, Gunz, and Donau. The periods between these glaciations were called "interglacials." In western Europe the names generally used to correspond to the Alpine interglacial sequence are:

Eemian	Riss-Würm
Hoxnian	Mindel-Riss
Cromerian	Gunz-Mindel
Tiglian	Donau-Gunz

stadial
interstadial

Later it was discovered that each of the glaciations was actually a sequence of distinctly colder periods (stadials) separated by warmer periods, or "interstadials." As they were recognized, the stadials and interstadials were also given specific names.

Evidence for alternating warm and cold periods was found all over the world. In some areas there was direct evidence of glaciations. In others, where glaciations did not occur, different events were used to determine the glacial sequence because of the *effects* of glaciations. For instance, during a glaciation the sea level becomes lower because much of the water from the oceans ends up as ice deposited on the land. During periods of low sea level, beaches were formed that are now under water. On the other hand, during the interglacials the sea level was somewhat higher than it is today, because the water now "locked" in the ice of existing glaciers and ice sheets was deposited in the oceans. Beaches formed during the interglacials are higher than the beaches of today. Detailed studies have attempted to determine the sequences of beach formation and relate them to the periods of glaciation.

River terraces are also used for this purpose. When the sea level is lowered, rivers flow faster because they have further to drop before they reach the sea. Since they flow faster, they tend to cut deeper. During the interglacials, when the sea level was higher, the rivers did not have as far to drop and thus flowed more slowly. Instead of downcutting, they formed broad terraces, which can presumably be related to the glacial sequence. Finally, a continent-wide series of wet and dry periods was thought to have been identified in Africa. These were respectively called "pluvials" and "interpluvials" and were theorized to result from a greater moisture content in the atmosphere during the glaciations.

Definitions of the Pleistocene, and the divisions within it, were at one time based completely on the Alpine glacial sequence. The Pleistocene itself was defined as the period of ice ages and was broken into three portions: Lower (or early), Middle, and Upper (or late). These were defined as follows:

Lower	Donau and Gunz glaciations
Middle	Gunz-Mindel interglacial to Riss glacial
Upper	Riss-Würm interglacial and Würm glacial

The Recent, or Holocene, is the post-Würm period which begins slightly more than ten thousand years ago.

With a distinguishable sequence of worldwide events, it seemed possible to relate deposits in widely separated areas or on different continents by using pluvials, beach or river terrace sequences, or direct evidence of glaciation. It is one of the great tragedies of human paleontology that it doesn't work!

There are a variety of reasons why it doesn't. The "worldwide associated phenomena" turn out to be neither worldwide nor particularly well associated. For instance, sequential beaches or river terraces may be the results of different events in different areas, and cannot always easily be correlated with one another. It is not even certain that the river terraces on the Rhine, Danube, Somme, and Thames can be correlated at all. Considerable evidence shows that there were no continent-wide wet and dry periods in Africa; again, local sequences cannot be correlated.

What mainly underlies these problems was discovered during studies of borings taken out of ocean floors. A drill is used to take a long core containing a sequence of sediments from the ocean floor. The water temperature at the time of sedimentation can be closely estimated by determining the ratio of the oxygen 18 isotope to "normal" oxygen 16. Oxygen 18 is chemically the same as oxygen 16, but it is slightly heavier. When the water is colder (less molecular activity), more ^{18}O settles to the bottom while more ^{16}O evaporates. As a result, the ratio of the isotope to regular oxygen is higher in inorganic compounds such as calcium carbonate as well as in the carbon-based compounds in the shells of marine animals. When the water is warmer, less of the isotope is available and the ratio is lower. This fact allows detailed sequences of ancient water temperatures to be determined and compared from area to area. It was discovered that the sequences of temperature changes in widely scattered areas seem to correlate with one another, and it has been suggested that this sequence directly corresponds to the amount of ice on the continents.

According to the Ewing-Donn hypothesis, glaciations during the Pleistocene resulted from the alternate freezing and thawing of the Arctic Ocean, greatly changing the evaporation of moisture over this area. One result of this alteration was widespread differences in the major ocean currents and resulting changes in water temperatures. It seems likely that the sea cores do provide a record of past continental glaciations. If they are interpreted this way, the problem with correlating the various continental events discussed becomes understandable because it is apparent that there were at least nine worldwide cold stages *before* the Upper Pleistocene and at least five more distinct stages associated with the Upper Pleistocene. The record of *major* cold stages extends to at least 800,000 years ago, and the cold stages vary in length from 18,000 to 67,000 years, while the intervening warmer periods range from 23,000 to 73,000 years. Furthermore, the sea core data show that the intensity of the cold stages differed from place to place. With so many distinct cold stages and differences of intensity, there is no reason to expect that four recognized cold stages in one area would necessarily correspond to four stages found in another. The problem is multiplied when cold stages are defined by river terraces in one area and glacial deposits in another. Four glaciations recognized in the Alps may be completely different events from the sea level changes that resulted in the Thames terraces.

The problems of correlation with the Alpine gla-

ciations are not insurmountable, but they do increase considerably with antiquity. Correlations on the same continent with the Würm stages, and perhaps even with the later portions of the Riss, may be fairly accurate if a sufficiently detailed sequence is available in the areas correlated. Much earlier than this, however, the correlations often become close to useless.

Paleomagnetism and Pleistocene Chronology

A very different worldwide sequence of events has proven to be extremely useful in dating. This is the sequence of changes in the earth's magnetic field. A number of times in the past, the direction of the earth's magnetic field has changed, or "reversed." During such a reversal, the end of a compass that points north today would point south. The reason for the magnetic changes is not known for certain, and the evidence suggests that the reversal process takes no longer than 5,000 years, during which time the magnetic field does not disappear but rather drops to 20 to 40 percent of its normal value. Since the direction of the magnetic field is recorded in many different types of rocks that contain iron compounds and the magnetic field has reversed many times, it is possible to determine a sequence of paleomagnetic "reversed" and "normal" intervals (epochs). This sequence has been very accurately dated by K/A techniques, and paleomagnetic dating is commonly used as an addition to potassium-argon absolute dating.

A detailed paleomagnetic stratigraphy has been determined for the past five million years (see Table 8.1, p. 160), and the various periods of normal and reversed paleomagnetism, as well as the specific magnetic events within these periods, all are named and accurately dated. The method can be extremely valuable, since under some circumstances it can give dates more accurately than absolute methods. This occurs when there is a potassium-argon date combined with a paleomagnetic stratigraphy.

For instance, if two sites are dated to approximately 0.9 million years ago with the K/A technique, and if there is an approximately 10 percent error to the dates, these sites could be as much as 180,000 years apart. However, if they both are paleomagnetically normal (i.e., the magnetic field is the same as today), they would have to be within 60,000 years of each other (in this case) because a well-dated normal was known to occur at this time, interrupting a long period of reversed polarity (Table 8.1). This is a considerable improvement in accuracy. On the other hand, without the absolute dates the sites would be much more difficult to relate. In the absence of any other information, there would be no way to correlate them at all. However, faunal comparisons might show that they were both in the vicinity of a million years old, in which case the paleomagnetic data would be useful. Paleomagnetism can be extremely helpful, allowing very high accuracy, but only when there is additional information about the dates.

One problem that has become apparent over the past few years stems from the fact that there were more changes in the magnetic field than previously thought, and many of these were of very short duration. The problem is that if a short reversal or normal period is recognized in one area but not another, it can throw comparison "out of phase." Furthermore, since the sequence involves only two types of events, a "normal" or "reversed" magnetic field, fitting one paleomagnetic sequence to another is impossible without absolute dates showing where at least part of the sequences fit together. Thus paleomagnetic reversals must be used with caution, and with as much corroborating evidence as possible.

Morphological Dating of Hominids

Morphological dating of hominids (humans and all their ancestors back to the time that the human line diverged from the ape line) might be thought of as a special form of faunal dating. The process involves using the morphology (form) of hominid specimens (the remains of humans and their ancestors back to the time when the lines leading to humans and apes split). In the morphological dating of faunal collections, the most modern appearing species are used to relate one collection to a series of others. Morphological dating of a single species, in this case hominids, involves using the morphological features of a sample of hominids to suggest the approximate date of the sample. Used incautiously, it can simply be a form of circular reasoning. Morphological dating has been greatly misused in the past, particularly in attempts to establish

great antiquity for humans in the Americas by claiming that certain crania were very "primitive" looking. In reaction to the misuse, the idea of morphological dating has fallen into disrepute. The reaction is probably too extreme. Morphological evolution did occur, and on the average, samples from different times can be distinguished from one another. The better we come to understand the course of human evolution, the easier it should be to apply morphological dating to help date human fossil material. It is interesting that if there were no known dates at all, the human evolutionary sequence that could be built up on entirely morphological grounds would not be significantly different from the sequence we recognize from other dating evidence.

Perhaps the main point to remember is that morphological dating can really be accurate only for samples. The larger the sample, the better the estimate. Dating individuals by their morphology is a more risky business because there is a great amount of variation in humans at any given time. There is no doubt that the technique should be used when appropriate; it is part of the total body of evidence for dating fossils.

Geologic Time

One result of the new dating techniques is that a fairly accurate time scale for the major events in the earth's history can be constructed. The number of years represented by the age of the planet is beyond imagination. It is easy to write down the numbers, but difficult to comprehend what they mean. Most people find it difficult to form a mental image of six or seven distinct objects, let alone millions of years. Try to imagine a row of seven distinct apples!

Figure 1.2 is a time scale for the earth's history, beginning with the origin of the planet about 4.5 billion years ago. While life appeared within a

FIGURE 1.2   A time scale for the major events in the earth's history, based on absolute dates. The scale gives dates in millions of years, and additional dates for the eras and the periods within the eras. The times of appearance for various life forms, and specifically for primates, are shown.

Date in Millions of Years (Varying scale)	Era	Period	Series = Epoch	Appearance of Life Forms
— 0 —	CENOZOIC	QUARTERNARY	PLEISTOCENE	*Homo sapiens*
			2 ±.5	*Homo erectus*
			PLIOCENE	Australopithecines
			6 ± 1	Appearance of many modern animal genera
— 10 —		TERTIARY	MIOCENE	Possible early hominids
				Eurasian fossil apes
				African fossil apes
— 20 —			25 ± 2	
— 30 —			OLIGOCENE	Earliest apes (*Aegyptopithecus*)
			38 ± 2	First higher primates (Anthropoidea)
— 40 —			EOCENE	Major carnivore radiation
— 50 —				Prosimians
			55 ± 2	Rodents
— 60 —			PALEOCENE	Rodent-like primates
				Small ungulates
			65 ± 2	Grasses
— 100 —	MESOZOIC		CRETACEOUS	Primates
				Opossum-like marsupials
			135 ± 5	Insectivores
				Placental mammals
			JURASSIC	Flowering plants
				Birds
				Snakes
			190 ± 5	Lizards
— 200 —			TRIASSIC	
			225 ± 5	Earliest mammals
	PALEOZOIC		PERMIAN	Dinosaurs
				Turtles
			270 ± 5	
— 300 —			CARBONIFEROUS	Amphibians
				Conifers
			340 ± 10	
			DEVONIAN	Modern fish
				Modern ferns
— 400 —			400 ± 10	Sharks
			SILURIAN	
			430 ± 10	
			ORDOVICIAN	Fish
— 500 —			500 ±	
			CAMBRIAN	Invertebrates
— 600 —			600 ±	
— 800 —	PROTEROZOIC			Metazoa (simple multiple-celled organisms)
— 1000 —	ARCHEOZOIC			Eucaryotic cells (cells with walls, capable of division)
— 2000 —				Bacteria
				Algae
— 3000 —				Oldest fossils (simple cells, lacking distinctive walls)
— 4000 —				

Origin of earth

"mere" billion years, the evolution of most of the diversified forms occurred within a small segment of the entire span.

If the entire age of the earth if likened to a 24-hour day, with the earth's origin at midnight, each second of the day would be equal to about 50,000 years, and each minute to 3 million years. By this scale:

Earth originates	midnight
earliest fossils	5:45 a.m.
earliest vertebrates	9:02 p.m.
earliest mammals	10:45 p.m.

earliest primates	11:37 p.m.
earliest higher primates	11:48 p.m.
possible earliest hominids	11:56 p.m.
australopithecines	11:58 p.m.
Homo sapiens	6½ seconds before midnight

Recorded history could not be measured on this scale. In terms of the history of our planet, the appearance of humans is a very recent happening. Human evolution occurs mostly in the Quaternary period, although the earliest human ancestors appear toward the end of the Tertiary, in the Miocene epoch.

SUMMARY

Because the process of fossilization depends on burial, fossils are not a random sample of past life. The conditions surrounding fossilization must be kept in mind when fossils and their apparent environments are analyzed. Age determination of fossil remains depends on the conditions of their preservation. Determinations can be based on radioactive decay; in this case, they result in an absolute age in years (and an associated probable error). Decay may occur in elements within the bone, or elements in the surrounding deposit. Other procedures are used to relate human fossils to the fossil fauna (or flora) surrounding them, and to relate stratigraphic, faunal, or cultural elements among different sites. These result in ages relative to one another and can be used to build up a sequence, although not an absolute time scale, for evolutionary events. While many supposed worldwide phenomena such as continental glaciations, reversals of the magnetic field, or widespread faunal or floral changes have been used in dating, these have almost inevitably been found less accurate or widespread than once thought. The absolute time scale that is available shows that the appearance of humans and their earliest distinct ancestors is very recent when viewed in the context of the full history of life on earth.

STATE OF THE ART

In spite of the application of modern technology to fossil hominid age determination, and the potential for using different techniques, serious problems abound at many of the most important hominid sites. One good example is in the area east of Lake Turkana (formerly Rudolf) in northern Kenya. The site is actually over 700 square miles of badlands—like deposits at the northeast end of the lake. Interspaced through the deposits are a series of volcanic ash layers (tuffs) from a yet-to-be-discovered vol-cano. These tuffs were dated radiometrically through the potassium/argon technique. In the early 1970s it was felt that a few main tuffs could be traced over the entire area.

One specific tuff, the KBS (named after Kay Behrensmeyer), quickly became the source of a problem. K/A provided a consistent date of 2.6 million years for the tuff. When a large-brained hominid (ER-1470) was found below it, the effects on paleo-anthropology were dramatic since this was a very early date for a hominid with a large brain size. Moreover, the earliest dated stone tools are within the tuff layer. At about this time, the evolution of several faunal species was also under study. In analyzing the fossil fauna, comparisons were naturally made with a site called Omo at the north end of the lake, no more than 50 miles away. There, an even larger sequence of tuffs had been dated and similarly both hominids and other fauna were found. The immediate problem was that fauna appearing below the KBS tuff at Turkana first appeared below much younger tuffs at the nearby Omo deposits. The fauna suggested that a Turkana tuff dated at 2.6 million years represented the same evolutionary stages as an Omo tuff dated at 1.8 million years. This difference was much larger than the margin of error for the dates. If the fauna evidence was correct, one of the dates was wrong. If the dates were correct, it took the faunal species ¾ of a million years to spread 50 miles.

One approach to resolving the problem was to make comparisons with a third site having dated tuffs and similar fauna. The closest was Olduvai Gorge, in Tanzanya, hundreds of miles to the south. The dated Olduvai fauna supported the Omo sequence.

A second approach was to use different radiometric techniques for dating the KBS tuff. A modification of the K/A technique was applied by two different geologists working through two different laboratories. One resulted in a date of 2.4 million years, while the other yielded dates of 1.6 and 1.8

million years from two different areas at east Turkana. The latter stimulated a geological reappraisal of the situation which ultimately demonstrated that several different tuffs had been identified as KBS. All of the geological correlations were thrown into doubt.

A third approach was to use a totally different dating technique. Fission track dating was applied several times, and the results indicated a date of about 2.2 million years. However, it is not clear whether a fission track date can be compared directly with a K/A one. These techniques may result in internally consistent but noncomparable dates, and the problem of which, if either, is "correct" may be unanswerable.

What then is the date of the KBS tuff? As is so often the case when problems are examined in detail, there is no clear answer. Many workers, including myself, accept the more recent radiometric determinations since these agree with the dated fauna from two other sites. Others, however, accept one of the other dates because of their confidence in the particular technique involved. The fact is that there is no *a priori* reason to believe that one of the techniques will be more accurate than another, so that if one of the dates is accepted, it is *not* because the others have been shown incorrect. Finally, still others propose that we will never know the date of the tuff, and that one is limited to the statement that it is probably no older than 2.6 million years or younger than 1.6 million years.

FURTHER READINGS

BEATY, C. B. 1978. The Causes of Glaciation. *American Scientist* 66:452–459.

While favoring one composite theory, this is an excellent introduction to the many theories of glacial origins that have been proposed.

BEHRENSMEYER, A. K. 1976. Taphonomy and Paleoecology in the Hominid Fossil Record. *Yearbook of Physical Anthropology* 19:36–50.

This is one of the best presentations of how natural processes determine which animals and which portions of animals have the best chance of becoming preserved as fossils. The discussion concentrates on areas where early humans once lived.

BISHOP, W. W., and J. A. MILLER, eds. 1972. *Calibration of Hominoid Evolution.* Scottish Academic Press, Edinburgh.

A technical but up-to-date survey of most procedures currently used for dating fossil remains. Techniques are summarized in a series of papers discussing the state of the art, and the references are invaluable.

BRAIN, C. K. 1972. An Attempt to Reconstruct the Behavior of Australopithecines: The Evidence for Interpersonal Violence. *Zoologica Africana* 7:379–401.

A discussion of cave deposits and the particular problems of how early hominids and other fauna got into caves and what effects this had on their preservation and appearance as fossils.

BUTZER, K. W. 1977. Environment, culture, and Human Evolution. *American Scientist* 65:572–584

A fairly introductory account of past environments, how they have been determined, and what effect they had on human adaptation.

CORNWALL, I. W. 1970. *Ice Ages: Their Nature and Effects.* Humanities Press, New York.

An easy-to-read introduction.

EWING, M. 1971. The Late Cenozoic History of the Atlantic Basin and Its Bearing on the Cause of the Ice Ages. In *Late Cenozoic Glacial Ages,* ed. K. Turekian. Yale University Press, New Haven, pp. 565–574.

A well-referenced summary of the most popular explanation for the Pleistocene glaciations.

FLINT, R. 1971. *Glacial and Quaternary Geology.* Wiley, New York.

The "source book" on Pleistocene glaciations, their causes and effects.

HALLAM, A. 1974. *A Revolution in the Earth Sciences.* Clarendon, Oxford.

A historical introduction that relates continental drift, past climates, and paleomagnetism in an attempt to trace the current understanding of plate tectonics.

OAKLEY, K. P. 1964. *Frameworks for Dating Fossil Man.* Aldine, Chicago.

An introductory but complete summary of dating techniques.

RALPH, E. K., and H. N. MICHAEL. 1974. Twenty-five Years of Radiocarbon Dating. *American Scientist* 62:553–560.

A summary of radiocarbon dating.

ROMER, A. S. 1974. *The Vertebrate Story.* University of Chicago Press, Chicago.

Probably the best simple presentation of the vertebrate fossil record, providing the essential context for more detailed presentations of mammalian, primate, and ultimately human origins.

SMITH, F. H. 1977. On the Application of Morphological "Dating" to the Hominid Fossil Record. *Journal of Anthropological Research* 33:302–316.

A thoughtful discussion of the advantages and pitfalls of this procedure, using some specific and very problematic examples.

CHAPTER TWO

The Process of Evolution

I f fossils are the remains of evolutionary events, and dating is the means of determining their sequence, it is the process of evolution that provides the _explanation_ of what happened. This chapter presents the basic concept of evolution, beginning with a definition of the term. Then the four basic causes of evolutionary change are discussed in some detail. This is followed by an examination of some of the more generalized effects of evolution, and finally by a discussion of how evolutionary relationships are determined.

Evolutionary theory provides the key to understanding both the history of organisms on our planet and their present diversity. Its discovery in the last century surely ranks with the great conceptualizations in the physical sciences, since it has come to be the paramount unifying concept of biological studies. This chapter is meant to serve as a simple introduction to evolution; it by no means explores all of the detailed ramifications that have come to characterize the results of applying a profoundly simple insight to the incredible complexity of life.

The Meaning of Evolution

The theory of evolution is probably the most simple and yet the most important biological concept ever discovered. _Evolution is the change in the genetic makeup of populations from generation to generation_. It is no more complex than that!

The "theory" part of the theory of evolution is concerned with _how_ these changes in genetic makeup occur, and _what effect_ they have on living populations. There is really no question about whether evolution actually exists. _For there to be no evolution, every generation would have to be exactly the same genetically as the previous generation._

EVOLUTION AS GENETIC CHANGE

For evolution to take place, all that is required is genetic change from generation to generation. Evolution occurs whether that change is "good" or "bad," "advantageous" or "disadvantageous" for the population, because evolution is defined as the process of change itself, regardless of its direction. The idea is analogous to the concept of speed. A moving car has a speed regardless of what direction it is moving in.

What do we mean by "the genetic makeup of a population"? The genetic material itself is made of a very special molecule known as DNA. This molecule has two critical features: the ability to carry information by means of the exact sequences of chemical units (bases) that attach to it, and the ability to accurately reproduce itself. There are only four bases to carry the information of inheritance, just as there are only 26 letters in the English alphabet. Similarly to English, these bases (letters) form words, which describe the actual information, but unlike English, the genetic words are always only three letters long. This is more than sufficient to handle a potentially infinite amount of information because of the second level of information transmission.

Each DNA "word" (three base "letters") codes for a specific amino acid. The proteins and enzymes may be thought of as "sentences"; their production is the main activity of most cells. Like English sentences, the protein or enzyme sentences can be of any length. Consequently, the finite information at the DNA level is ultimately transformed into a potentially limitless number of biological messages, just as the finite number of letters in the alphabet can be used to produce a limitless number of English messages. In this context, the genetic material is the DNA, and a "gene" may be thought of as a basic structural unit of the DNA molecule, such as a 3-base word. While other definitions of "gene" have also been used, the basic concept of the gene as a unit of genetic material is sufficient for an understanding of "genetic change."

The "population" in our definition of evolution is a group of organisms (human or otherwise) that regularly breed together. All of the genes in a population are referred to as its "gene pool." Evolution, then, is *change in a gene pool from generation to generation*.

How does a gene pool change? The simplest and easiest to understand change is the introduction of new genetic material, or a new gene. After all, if a new gene appears, then the gene pool is different because it includes something that was not there before. However, the vast majority of gene pool changes are not the result of introducing new genes. Instead, they are the result of changing frequencies of genes already present. The frequency of a gene is a simple measure of how often it occurs. It can be thought of as the proportion of individuals that carry the gene. If in a classroom of 50, five people have blond hair, the *frequency* of blond hair is:

$$\frac{\text{number with blond hair}}{\text{total number in the class}} = \frac{5}{50} = \frac{1}{10} = 0.1$$

and the proportion of people with blond hair is simply the frequency multiplied by 100, or:

$$0.1 \times 100 = 10\%$$

Gene frequencies in a gene pool are calculated the same way, and if the frequency of a gene changes from one generation to another, no matter why that change happened and no matter how small it might be, evolution has occured. Almost all evolutionary changes that can be observed in the present or past are the result of gene frequency changes. Therefore, *the actual course, or direction, that evolutionary change takes depends in part on the genes already in the gene pool*. It also depends on the cause of the gene pool change.

The Causes of Evolution

Anything that causes a gene pool to change from generation to generation is a cause of evolution. One might think there is a very long list of such causes, but fortunately there are only four general categories: selection, mutation, migration, and drift. These will be discussed separately, but they often work in combination.

SELECTION

Selection is the result of individuals' having differing numbers of offspring survive to parent the next generation. If some individuals have more surviving offspring than others, their genes are represented in higher frequency in the next generation. This results in a gene frequency change, which by definition is evolution. Differing numbers of surviving offspring can result from both differential fertility (how many offspring are born to individuals during their lifespan) and differential survivorship (how many of those offspring survive to adulthood in order to have offspring of their own). These two concepts are combined in the definition of selection as differential contribution to the gene pool of the next generation, or *differential reproduction.*

There are many reasons for differential reproduction. Presumably, if the reasons are "natural," it is "natural selection," while if they are "artificial," it is "artificial selection." "Natural" and "artificial" can be hard to distinguish, however, and it is better simply to use the word "selection" to refer to all cases when differences in contribution to the next generation within the population result in changes in the gene pool.

In the past, the concept of selection was closely tied to the idea of "survival of the fittest." With the gradual acceptance of Darwin's ideas in the nineteenth century, one widespread interpretation of his writings was that only the strongest and most able survived to have offspring. The idea occurred in sources varying from biology textbooks to political tracts such as Hitler's *Mein Kampf*. "Survival of the fittest" sounds right, since the most "fit" should be the ones with the most surviving offspring. Yet the idea reminds me of a story told by the eminent evolutionist G. G. Simpson. Two adult stags with enormous antlers were battling over who was to receive the attentions of a nearby doe. During this epic battle, a third stag, smaller and younger, found the doe and left with her. Which was the fittest? "Conventional wisdom" tells us it was one of the large stags, but in terms of evolution it was the stag with the doe. The point is that "survival of the fittest" can be an accurate definition of the selection process if "fittest" means those with the most surviving offspring. These may or may not be the strongest or the most powerful, but whatever features they have will be present in higher frequency in the next generation.

The real lesson that has been learned about selection is that it is not usually a "life or death" or an "all or none" effect. Selection can be extremely effective without being either dramatic or pronounced. Most often it is a slight reproductive advantage that results in gene pool changes, and not a "struggle" for existence in which the better adapted have all the offspring while the more poorly adapted have none. The slightness of the reproductive advantage is reflected in the fact that even the most rapid-appearing evolutionary changes turn out to be very slow when examined closely. This can be easily exemplified by the evolution of cranial capacity in hominids.

In the course of recent human evolution, one of the most pronounced changes occured in the size of the brain. Within an evolutionary sequence over considerable time, brain size is related to intelligence. The cause of brain size increase in our ancestors is related to the fact that one unique human adaptation is to rely on intelligence for survival. If intelligence is important for survival, it follows that increases in intelligence will be advantageous and should be favored by selection. That is, individuals with more intelligence would be expected to have a better chance of surviving to adulthood and of having more surviving offspring. This may not be true for every individual, but it should represent an average trend. In looking at the human fossil record, it is apparent that some features change rapidly, while others change slowly, and still others do not change at all. (The fact that different features may change at different rates is called "mosaic evolution.") In the course of human evolution, brain size has been one of the most rapidly changing features, and compared with evolution in other organisms, it is one of the most rapid changes that can be found.

Yet how fast is this change? To use round figures, the average cranial capacity of human ancestors two million years ago is about 500 cc, ("cc" means cubic centimeters, a volume measure in the metric system). A liter (approximately one quart) is 1,000 cc, so two million years ago humans had half-quart brains. Today, again using round figures, average cranial capacity is about 1,500 cc, or one and a half quarts. The rapid increase, then, is 1,000 cc in two million years—a tripling of capacity. On the average the increase per year is 1,000/2,000,000, or only 1/2,000th of a cc. If the average length of a generation is 20 years, the "rapid" change is 1/100th of a cc per generation! 1/100th of a cc is about the volume of a fingernail clipping. The change per generation is so small that if it is still in progress today, it could not be measured.

The point to all this is that even a very rapid change over long periods of time results from a phenomenally small change per generation. Selection does not have to result in much change at any time in order to have significant effects because of the immense periods of time involved in the evolutionary process.

One of the key points in understanding the action of selection is that selection can act only on the variation already present. The basis of selection is genetic difference. All organisms in a population are different from one another, and it is the *combinations* of different features that make some better adapted. If there were no genetic differences, then differential reproduction could produce no change. Differences, then, are a crucial aspect of the evolutionary process (See Figure 2.1). Populations that maintain differences in many features can continue to survive and adapt to a changing world, while populations that lose their variation cannot. There are many genetic mechanisms that help maintain variation within populations, the main factor being the action of selection itself.

How can new, or novel, features occur in the evolutionary process? The appearance of novelties usually results from new *combinations* of genes, rather than the appearance of new genes (or new genetic material). Consider the analogy of evolution and a poker game. In the analogy, the cards are the genes, each chromosome has only one gene, and the hands dealt in a game represent the variations of one individual feature present in each player's genotype (an individual's genes). Shuffling the deck and redealing it represents the independent assortment of chromosomes in each generation. Let us imagine that in this poker game the losing hands are all returned to the deck, but the winning hand is reproduced before it is returned (this would increase the size of the deck, which is irrelevant for this analogy). If the winning hand was four aces and a deuce, then eight aces and two deuces would be returned. This would simulate the process of selection because the frequency of the cards (genes) in the winning hand (best adapted features) would increase in the deck (gene pool) each shuffle (generation). What would such a game be like and what would be the effect on the card deck (gene pool)? One might expect the frequency of the higher cards to increase, but if by chance the first few games were won by three or four of a kind of a low card, the frequency of those low cards would increase. Then, as the game continued, the chances of getting multiples of those low cards would be greater, and more winning hands might increase their frequency even further. This is what is meant by the statement that evolutionary change depends in part on the features already present in a population.

What about new features? At the beginning of the game, there are a large number of different cards, although only four of each type. At first, no hand of five kings can occur. Later in the game, if the frequency of kings increases, a hand of five kings becomes possible. This is a novel feature. It is the result of different frequencies of cards already present, and not of the appearance of a new type of card. The analogy suggests how most novel features appear in real populations. They result from new combinations made possible by differing frequencies of genes already present. Once a new feature occurs, selection may act to increase its frequency by increasing the frequency of genes which, in combination, produce it.

The card game is a simple but useful analogy because most features (equivalent to poker hands) are polygenic (poly - many, genic - genes). That is to say, their development and final form are influenced by a combination of many genes (or cards). Polygenic features are usually polymorphic (morphic - forms).

The many possible gene combinations result in different forms of the feature in a population, but genes are not the only determinant of the final form of a feature, because virtually every characteristic can also be influenced by environment. In general, the following holds for most features:

$$\text{Phenotype} = \text{genotype} + \text{environment}$$

where the phenotype is the final physical form, the genotype is the particular combination of genes that an individual has, and the environment refers to any aspect of the surroundings, habitat, or behavior that affects the development of the phenotype. The relation holds for all physical features, from blood type to relative limb length, and there is increasing evidence that it holds for certain aspects of behavior as well. Consequently, selection does not act directly on the gene pool. Selection is the result of the relation of the phenotype to the environment, but it only influences the gene pool insofar as the differences in the genotype are reflected by differences in the phenotype. The relation between the genetic and environmental components of the variation that occurs for a feature within a population is measured by the herita-

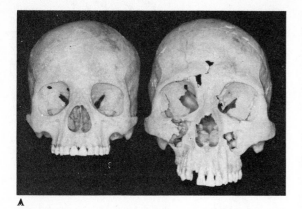

A

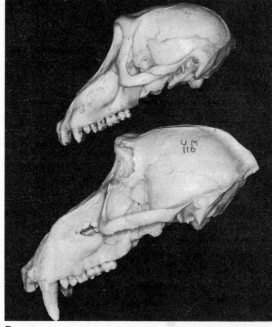

FIGURE 2.1   *The critical factor of variation. Variation, providing the basis for evolutionary change, is present in all species. In many primates, one important cause of variability is found in the presence of consistent sex differences. Photo A is a male cranium (right) and a female cranium (left) from a recent American Indian site, and Photo B shows crania of a male baboon (bottom) and a female baboon (top) from a single population in Kenya.*

B

bility. This concept is similar to a proportion of the genetic contribution and the environmental contribution to the final form of a characteristic, although the derivation is complex. Actually, the square of the heritability (a number between 0 and 1) measures the percent of phenotype variation that is the direct result of genetic variation. Needless to say, the higher the heritability figure, the more important the genetic contribution to the final form of a characteristic. The amount of heritability for various features (or for one feature at different times) can differ greatly, but as long as there is some genetic component, evolution can occur. The higher the genetic component, the more rapidly change in the gene pool can take place.

In sum, selection results in changes in the gene pool by changing the frequencies of various genes. The genes of individuals with more surviving offspring are more frequent in the next generation, while the genes of those with fewer surviving offspring are less frequent. Changing gene frequencies within a population results in changing frequencies of morphological characteristics. Since most characteristics are polygenic, and their final form is influenced by the action of many genes, new frequencies can actually result in novel charac-

teristics through combinations that could not occur before.

The action of selection is limited by two things. First, the speed with which it can cause change in a characteristic depends partly on the heritability of the characteristic. The genetic component contributing to the heritability is a compromise between genetic adaptation and individual adaptability. On the one hand, characteristics with a high genetic component cannot rapidly respond to short-term (within an individual's lifespan) changes in the environment through immedate modification. On the other hand, characteristics with a low genetic component can respond rapidly to immediate environmental changes but cannot easily respond to permanent differences in selection.

The second limitation is in the genetic variation present in a population, since selection can only promote existing variants. The amount of variation present in populations is also a compromise, since great variation usually means that only some individuals will be extremely well adapted, while little variation is an evolutionary dead end because it limits the potential for further evolutionary change.

Selection is not the only cause of evolutionary change, but it is the most important and probably

[margin handwritten notes: (x observed variation from generation to generation due to recombination of genetic material)]

accounts for most changes that can be observed in living populations or in the fossil record. The rate of change due to selection is usually very small each generation, but small changes can have great results when they proceed in the same direction for long periods of time.

MUTATION

Mutation is the direct change of genetic material resulting from physical or chemical alteration. Radiation, chemicals, and temperature extremes can cause mutations. All of these mutagens (phenomena that cause mutations) are part of the normal environment, and mutations appear constantly in all species. The changed genetic material can then be inherited.

[margin handwritten notes: mutagens: phenomena / or mutations]

Mutations are random. One cannot predict what mutations will occur, or what changes mutations might result in. However, this does not mean that one cannot predict their *effects* on organisms. A person tuning a car might make many different random changes, but the effect of most would be the same: the car would not run well, if at all. A mutation randomly alters part of what is usually a very complicated process—the interrelated steps that lie between the genetic code for a characteristic and the actual development of that characteristic. The most likely effect of a random change in a complicated process is that the process will work imperfectly, or not work at all. Think of how a cake might be affected if one of the ingredients were picked at random instead of according to the recipe. Thus the effect of most mutations is not random even though the mutations are. The most likely consequence is disadvantageous: who would want to eat that cake?

[margin handwritten notes: mutations random: can't predict as to when or what effects]

However, not all mutations are disadvantageous. Some cause an effect so small that it makes no difference in the survival of the organism, and a very occasional few are actually advantageous.

Mutations were once thought to be the most important cause of major evolutionary change, since it was believed that really new features could arise only as the result of mutation. This was called the "hopeful monster" theory: while most mutations were disadvantageous (monsters), the very occasional advantageous one (hopeful monster) led to significant evolutionary change. With the development of the modern theory of evolution, this idea became difficult to support. It was soon realized that most of the variation that could be observed

[margin handwritten notes: hopeful monster]

from generation to generation was due to recombination of the genetic material, especially pronounced in its effect on polygenic traits, and not due to mutations. The discovery that traits were polygenic itself created difficulties for the hopeful monster theory, because it became apparent that major changes were not likely to be caused by a single mutation. Finally, the problem of what organisms a hopeful monster would be able to interbreed with successfully, and what the offspring would look like, proved insurmountable. The hopeful monster explanation for major evolutionary change was replaced by the explanation of gradual change in polygenic characteristics leading to the appearance of new features by new combinations.

Mutations are now thought to play two roles in the process of evolution. First, mutations are the source of all new genetic material. Without mutations, the variation of all organisms would be limited by changes in frequency and new combinations of existing genetic material. While the *possible* variation is great, it is much less than the variation that actually occurs. Mutation introduces new genetic material into gene pools at a very slow rate. The maximum rate of mutation estimated for humans is about five per generation for each individual. The vast majority of these are lost by accident over a number of generations, since in each generation there is a chance that the mutated gene will not be part of the genetic material passed on to the next generation. Selection against harmful mutations accounts for the loss of even more. Only an extremely small proportion of mutations are added to the gene pool, and usually as neutral rather than as particularly advantageous genetic changes.

[margin handwritten notes: mutation play 2 roles]

Thus the number of mutations permanently added to a population is extremely small and generally results in no observable difference in either the average or the variation of particular characteristics. Yet this new material ultimately provides the basis for future evolutionary change.

The second role thought to be played by mutation may be more direct. Some scientists have suggested that it can orient the direction of evolutionary change. This can happen only under a specific set of circumstances. Mutations, as we have seen, are usually disadvantageous because they more likely than not stop a complex developmental process from occurring correctly. Actually, the most likely effect that a random change will have on such a process is to stop it completely at some point. The probable effect of most mutations is the reduction, or incomplete development, of the characteristic controlled by the mutated genetic material. Of course, reduction is a likely consequence only *if* the characteristic is polygenic and *if* its growth involves a complex series of steps, each of which is dependent on the previous steps proceeding correctly. Many, although not all, characteristics that have evolutionary importance fit this description.

Stopping the growth or reducing the complexity of a feature is disadvantageous if the feature is necessary for survival or propagation. However, what if the feature is no longer under selection? What if the selection for the feature is relaxed, so that it no longer matters whether or not the characteristic is present in the organism? Under these conditions, mutations causing reduction will not be selected against. Because reduction is the consequence of a large number of mutations, and because in a polygenic trait mutations in most of the many genes will have the same effect of reduction, *reduction of the characteristic is the likely consequence of mutation when there is relaxed selection*. This has been called the "probable mutation effect" by C. L. Brace. There are three things to remember about the probable mutation effect. First, it occurs only when there is no selection for or against a characteristic. Otherwise, selection will be the cause of whatever change takes place. Second, it occurs only in polygenic traits. In traits that are influenced by only a few genes, there is not enough genetic material to mutate and result in reduction. The effect works because the consequence of most mutations is the same, mainly to hamper if not stop a developmental process, and if there are many places for mutations to happen, enough can occur and accumulate in a population over long periods of time to result in the eventual reduction of the characteristic. Third, even under the above restrictions, reduction is not the only possible result. It is not inevitable, but only likely.

The reduction of complex features in the absence of selection has been suggested for a variety of different species. While the mechanism is still considered controversial, one of the most compelling cases is the loss of eyes that occured in cave fish. A similar process has been used in interpreting structural reduction and structural loss in features of species ranging from termites to humans.

In the case of genetically simple characteristics,

mutation accumulation does not lead to reduction, although in the absence of selection the genetic changes can still accumulate. This phenomenon has been used in studies of genetically simple characteristics of blood, and the reaction of the body's immunological system to differences in these simple characteristics. Varying degrees of immunological reaction among species have been taken to indicate the amount of neutral differences that have accumulated due to mutations. This, in turn, can be used to measure the degree of relationship among the species. For instance, the reaction of a gorilla's immunological system to human blood is much less than the reaction to blood from a dog. The implication is that gorillas and humans are more closely related than gorillas and dogs, a contention supported by most other evidence. Immunological reaction has been further used to calibrate a time scale for when the species with known immunological differences diverged. However, attempts to determine how long gorillas and humans, or gorillas and dogs, have been separate species have met with great difficulties, and at present many workers feel that little if any useful information has resulted from these attempts to calibrate a time scale for the evolutionary divergence of living species.

In sum, the one certain role of mutation in evolution is the origin of new genetic material. In its second role, according to some, evolutionary change due to accumulating mutations in features not under selection is a common although not very rapid course of evolutionary events. The reduction of complex structures in human evolution may be more frequent than in the evolution of other species because of the progressive replacement of morphological features by behavior and technology that has characterized our evolutionary history. However, even if mutation accumulation can result in reduction, the fact remains that mutations are only one of the causes of reduction in human evolution, and the relative importance of reduction due to mutation, as opposed to selection, is yet to be determined.

MIGRATION

Migration is the third factor that can cause gene pool change. When new individuals enter (immigrate) or leave (emigrate) a population, they introduce new genetic material or remove genetic material.

Migration usually acts in conjunction with selection or drift, which we will discuss in the next section. Selection and migration work together in two ways. First, the genetic changes introduced into a small population as the result of new individuals entering it are subject to the selection process. Those that are advantageous will usually be maintained in later generations, while those that are disadvantageous will be discarded. However, if the number of migrants is very large, a change need not be advantageous to be retained. New genetic material that is not really disadvantageous, or perhaps is idiosyncratic, may be retained by the population. Second, when individuals leave a population, the reasons for their leaving might result in selection for certain characteristics in the migrating group. For instance, many of the migrants might be better adapted to a warmer (or cooler) climate because of average physiological differences.

punctuated equilibria concept One evolutionary model that emphasizes the importance of migration is the punctuated equilibria concept. According to this model, most important evolutionary changes are not the result of gradual evolutionary processes in species (phyletic gradualism). Instead, it is argued that most species undergo little change over long periods of time (i.e., they are in equilibrium). But occasionally, at the extremes of the species range where the habitat is least desirable, the increased intensity of selection and the relative isolation of a peripheral population results in a new, better-adapted species. This species may spread and rapidly replace the older species over its full range and then remain in relative equilibrium until the process happens again.

The punctuated equilibria model thus suggests that some evolutionary change is the result of the appearance of new species and their subsequent replacement of the parental species through migration. Because the fossil record is very incomplete for most species, there has been a great deal of debate over how important this process may have been in evolutionary history. The less evidence we have, the easier it is to support alternate interpretations. In those cases where a fairly complete evolutionary sequence is known, many workers have argued that gradual evolutionary change within species is a more convincing interpretation. However, the issue is far from resolved.

The relative importance of migration in human evolution is unknown. This is partly because the effects of migration can be difficult to distinguish from the effects of selection. Certainly, the habitation of new areas must be the result of migration. For instance, the ancestors of the Amerinds (American aborigines) entered North America over a landbridge between Siberia and Alaska. In this case, migration and selection worked together, since only groups that could adapt to Arctic conditions were able to cross the landbridge. The environmental conditions acted as a filter, passing only populations with the requisite cultural and biological adaptations. However, as the Americas were populated, local adaptation proceeded, and today only the most northern populations remain Arctic adapted. Yet this "filter effect" may account for certain features shared by all modern Amerinds.

Migration can best be established as an important force in human evolution when there is both archaeological and morphological evidence of the arrival of new people. For instance, people from New Guinea migrated to Australia long after the continent was inhabited. They brought a new technology and also a new physical form; both spread over much of the continent. Migration is clearly responsible for this evolutionary change. However, this is one of the few instances where a past migration can be distinguished from selection.

Migration was an evolutionary force of some importance throughout the Pleistocene, since at its beginning humans were found only in Africa, while by its end they had spread throughout the world. Possibly its most important single effect was the continuance of the gene flow throughout the range of the human species. There was almost always enough gene flow to prevent reproductive isolation from being established for long enough to allow speciation.

DRIFT

The fourth cause of evolutionary change is genetic drift. Drift is a random change not due to selection, mutation, or migration. One way to look at drift is by a comparison with sampling. The gene pool of a sample from a population is not always identical to the gene pool of the population itself. Think, for instance, of a population of 100 individuals with an average height of 5½ feet. If a sample of three is drawn at random from the population, the chances are that the average height of this sample will *not* be exactly 5½ feet. The difference between the population and the sample is a potential example of drift. If a larger sample, say ten, is drawn from the population, the average height of the sample has a better chance of being 5½ feet, and if the sample is 50, the chances are extremely good that its average will be identical to that of the population.

Drift, then, is a phenomenon of small samples. The sample may be the result of migration from a larger population (over space), or it may be the next generation of that population (over time). In either case, if the sample is small, the chances are that its gene pool will not be exactly the same as the gene pool of the parent population. The difference is due to drift. Because it is a genetic difference, the result is evolution.

One might expect that evolutionary change due to drift would be completely random. However, while the *process* is random, the *result* of the process may not be. The effect of drift is the fluctuation of gene frequencies. One result might be to eliminate genes that appear in low frequency. In a population of 100, each generation is actually a small sample and will differ from the previous generation because of drift. A gene at low frequency may vary upwards and downwards in its frequency of appearance, but if it ever varies to nothing, it is then eliminated from the population. For instance, a gene may be held by only two people. There is a chance that all of their offspring will carry it, and an even greater chance that at least some of their offspring will carry it. However, there is also a chance that none of their offspring will carry it. When this occurs, the gene is lost to the next generation. This is the way that most neutral mutations are lost, although a very few may become widespread through the same process.

One potentially important effect of drift may occur during the process of species formation. If a new species is formed as the result of isolation of a small population, many of the common characteristics of the new species may be the result of drift (random sampling) from the parent species. Bearing in mind that the direction of subsequent evolution partially depends on the variation already present, the consequences of drift may allow the new species to evolve in a very different direction from its parent species. Thus the role of purely probabilistic change in evolution may be significant. In the long-term evolution of a group of animals, such as the living primates, it is legitimate to question how many of the established features thought to be the result of selection may actually have resulted from random processes expressed as drift.

One visible effect that drift seems to have had on the human fossil record is the recognition of what might be thought of as idiosyncratic similarities in populations. Small populations tend to develop many "look-alikes" because of the genetic variation lost by drift. This becomes especially apparent in the Upper Pleistocene, where the remains of individuals from the same population can be compared.

Another common effect of drift is to increase variability between populations. Because of the randomness of the process, different genetic material is lost in various groups subject to drift.

Evolution as a Process

Evolution is a process: an ongoing phenomenon that continually changes the genetic makeup of populations and ultimately results in their continued success or eventual failure. While some of the causes of evolutionary change are random, *the results of evolution are not*. In viewing the incredible variety of life on earth, and in tracing its past history, there are some generalizations regarding the process of evolution that seem to be as valid in understanding human prehistory as they are in understanding the evolution of other organisms.

SPECIES AND LINEAGES

Evolution is a process that applies to populations rather than to individuals. It is the population, and not the individual, that evolves. The population is not the only unit of evolution, however, because genetic change can spread from population to population if they are in the same species. Different species are often thought of as different "types" of organisms. In any particular area this is quite accurate. One cannot confuse dogs with cats or with squirrels. At each locality the species are usually represented by populations that are very distinct from one another. However, the "type" idea of species does not apply when broader geographic regions are considered. Instead, populations of a species, although similar, are seen to differ from each other. If populations are widespread, these differences can be quite great because of differences in environment and adaptation. This is readily apparent in humans when we look at populations from different parts of the world. Which, then, would be the "type" of the species?

The question is unanswerable, and species actually has a very different definition. *A species is a group of populations that can actually or potentially interbreed and produce fertile offspring, and which are reproductively isolated from populations in other species.* The species is the main unit of evolution because genetic change can spread anywhere within a species, but cannot spread from one species to another.

Species, of course, existed in the past, and past species can be related to present ones through ancestry. *A lineage is a group of ancestral-descendent species that is reproductively isolated from other lineages.* Looking at these definitions another way, a species is a lineage at a particular point in time.

Because the definition of species is reproductive rather than morphological, a species can include much more variation than the older "type" concept allowed. Animals once considered to be in separate species, such as dogs and wolves, are now known to be in the same species since they regularly interbreed and produce fertile offspring when they are in contact. Species such as these which show marked differences between populations are called polytypic (poly - many, typic - types). Species without great differences between populations are monotypic (mono - single).

SPECIATION

All new species must originate from other species. This can happen in only two ways: through the evolution of one species into another along the same lineage, or by the splitting of one lineage into two.

The evolution of one species into another along the same lineage is called anagenesis, or phyletic evolution (see Figure 2.2 opposite). Phyletic evolution is not associated with any particular event. Rather it is a matter of definition and convenience. When enough change over time has occured along a lineage, it is convenient to divide the lineage into time segments and give the segments different species names. This is because giving the entire lineage a single name, if carried to the extreme, would lead to placing the earliest form of life and living humans in the same species! Phyletic evolution is a real phenomenon, but the division of a lineage into temporal species is somewhat arbitrary and depends as much on the history of fossil discoveries as on the fossils themselves (see the discussion in Chapter 10). Phyletic evolution is the main form of speciation in the humans of the Plio-Pleistocene (Pliocene and Pleistocene epochs, see Figure 1.2), and will be discussed in more detail later.

Cladogenesis is the splitting of one lineage into two (see Figure 2.2). In this form of speciation, one ancestral species becomes two (or more) descendent species. The splitting takes some time to occur and can happen only when populations are geographically, or spatially, isolated from each other. When there is a geographic separation, it is possible for differences in selection or drift to result in true reproductive isolation. The reproductive isolation may be genetic (interbreeding no longer produces fertile offspring), morphological (interbreeding is no longer physically possible), or behavioral (interbreeding no longer occurs because of different mating seasons or different signals for recognizing sexually receptive mates). Whatever the case, speciation has not occurred until reproductive isolation is complete, and gene pools can become reproductively isolated from each other only when descendent populations are not in physical contact.

It is more difficult for cladogenesis to occur in wide ranging populations than in narrow ranging ones for two reasons. First, wide ranging populations are generally more often in contact with each other. There are fewer sources of geographic isolation. Second, wide ranging species often utilize many different resources, so that when physical isolation does occur, it takes a long time for reproductive isolation to result. Humans are a good example of a wide ranging species, and many authors feel that cladogenesis has rarely characterized human evolution.

One of the common misunderstandings about cladogenesis comes from the observation of living species. Since members of living species can be clearly distinguished by their morphology (form), it is often thought that the morphological difference is the cause of the speciation. Actually, this is the

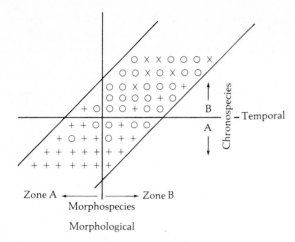

Zone A ← | → Zone B
Morphospecies

Morphological

FIGURE 2.2 *Diagrammatic representation of the process of speciation. Shown above is anagenesis, or phyletic evolution. Consider the "+," "x," and "o" to represent genetic variation within the species. The figure shows the evolution of species A into species B, and indicates two different definitions of species that may be applied to the process. The lineage may be divided into* **morphospecies** *on the basis of morphological characteristics. This is indicated by the vertical line. As such, identification of each member of the species is quite clear, since the determination is morphological and irrespective of the date of the specimen. However convenient, the definition leads to the biological problem of having two different species alive at the same time, but able to interbreed (if this was not assumed, we would be dealing with two lineages instead of one). On the other hand, the lineages can be divided into* **chronospecies,** *with an arbitrary date representing the species division. This is represented by the horizontal line. In this case, identification of members of a species depends almost completely on the date of a specimen, largely irrespective of its morphology. Biologically, this a more meaningful definition since at any one time only one species is present, which after all is the meaning of a single lineage. The process of cladogenesis is shown below. Reproductive isolation can occur only with spacial separation. Notice that the "genetic frequencies" of "+" and "o" are about the same in A, as well as in the early members of B and C. In later members of B, "+" becomes more common while "o" is lost. In C, "o" becomes more common and a new variant, "x," appears, replacing "+." While these changes could appear within a species, really great population differences could only accumulate after speciation.*

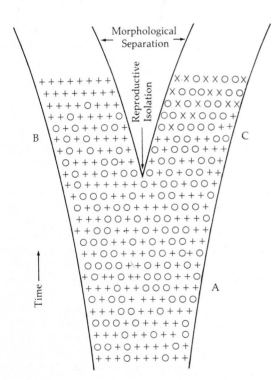

tion. They are a consequence, rather than a cause, of speciation. Generally during and just after the process of speciation, populations of the two species are virtually indistinguishable.

OPPORTUNISM

One of the most important generalizations is that evolution is opportunistic. Populations take advantage of all the resources available that they can utilize. Evolutionary change is always occurring either as new resources become available or because resources already present can be utilized for the first time. The process of evolution should not be thought of as a passive response to environmental change, because much evolutionary change occurs

reverse of what happens. Great morphological differences between populations can only evolve after speciation, and therefore after reproductive isola-

as populations develop the ability to use resources that are already present, or more efficiently take advantage of resources already in use.

For example, the earliest adaptive change that can be recognized in human evolution is an adaptation to the African grasslands, or savanna. The grasslands existed long before early humans adapted to them, but a savanna adaptation could occur only when these primates developed characteristics which allowed them to take advantage of the available resources and survive under the new conditions. The point is that this adaptation did not necessarily happen because the primates were "forced" to readapt due to a climatic or ecological change. Of course, changes in the environment result in either successful evolutionary change or extinction, but the converse does not follow. All evolutionary change is not necessarily due to changes in the environment. Many, perhaps even most, evolutionary changes result from new potentials evolved by the species itself, which in turn result in change because of the opportunistic nature of evolution.

ROMER'S RULE AND "PREADAPTATION"

"Preadaptation" refers to an old and probably invalid idea that species are in some manner "predesigned" to meet the requirements of their habitat. Yet, like so many of the older evolutionary ideas, the concept holds some validity if viewed a different way. Romer's rule, named after the eminent vertebrate paleontologist, outlines the role of preadaptation in evolution, although the "rule" is really only a generalization of a sequence of events that often takes place.

Romer's rule states that new adaptations are often allowed by changes which initially better adapt a species to its old way of life. The changes appear to be "preadapted" to the new adaptation in retrospect, but to believe the changes took place *in order to allow* a new adaptation is to put effect before cause. Romer's rule is actually a special case of opportunism.

A good example can be drawn from one interpretation of early hominid evolution. At one point, hominids or perhaps prehominids shifted from a forest to a grasslands adaptation. On the African savanna, food resources are particularly hard to obtain during the dry season, when animal herds have dispersed and much of the plant life is dry and dormant. Adaptation to the grasslands was not possible until a consistent dry season food resource could be obtained. Many of the dormant plants store considerable food resources underground during this season as roots and tubers, but roots and tubers are unavailable to most primates because they have nails rather than claws on their digits and these are unsuitable for digging. Thus the development of a simple digging stick, such as some living chimpanzees use, was probably one of the most important factors that allowed these early hominids to adapt to the grasslands.

One could say that the invention of the digging stick "preadapted" the early hominids to a grasslands habitat. However, they probably did *not* invent the digging stick *in order to* change their adaptation from forest to grasslands. Instead, this invention almost surely was used to improve the forest adaptation just as it is used by chimpanzees today. Chimps manufacture sticks of a certain length, diameter, and suppleness. Some populations use them for collecting termites while others use them for digging up ant nests. In both cases modified sticks are used as a regular part of the subsistence technology, improving the forest adaptation by providing access to foods during certain times of the year. If this can be taken as a parallel to the early hominids, digging sticks became a useful part of the hominid forest adaptation *before* any shift to a grasslands habitat during the dry season became possible. According to this interpretation, some early hominid populations opportunistically moved into this new habitat, taking advantage of the then-utilizable resources.

In sum, "preadaptation" is a word with many meanings. I understand it to refer to an adaptation that *allows* occupation of a new habitat, and not an adaptation that evolved *in order for* a new habitat to be occupied. As such, it becomes an important part of the concept that evolutionary change is opportunistic and that the process of evolution is primarily active rather than a basically passive response to changing conditions.

ADAPTIVE RADIATION

When a population of a species enters a new habitat, opportunities for adapting to a new set of resources abound. This is especially true during the initial occupation, when there is a little competition from similar species (see pp. 32–33). Under these conditions, one common response is a rapid population growth, population splitting, and the development of different adaptive patterns. This results in a multiplication of species through cladogenesis called an adaptive radiation. An adaptive radiation is an example of evolution above the species level, since the result is an increase in the number of species. While the descendent species share many characteristics with the parental species which first occupied the new habitat, subsequent adaptations to more narrow portions of the habitat can result in the rapid appearance of a wide variety of differences among a group of closely related species.

Adaptive radiations seem to have been common in evolutionary history. For instance, marsupial mammals reached Australia before the much better-adapted placental mammals. In the absence of competition from placental mammals, the marsupials evolved many species that parallel placental forms, such as the dog-like Tasmanian wolf, along with species that have no real parallel among the placentals, such as the kangaroo. Although the Tasmanian wolf looks and behaves much more like a dog than like a kangaroo, numerous anatomical details show its relations are with the latter instead of the former. Several different adaptive radiations have characterized primate evolution, and at least one occurred among hominids.

GROUP SELECTION

A controversy exists as to whether selection is best considered a populational or an individual phenomenon. Proponents of the latter point out that the direct cause of gene frequency change is the ability of individuals to survive and have surviving offspring. Yet the concept of frequency change necessarily applies to a population, and numerous studies of human populations have shown that it is common for the best populational adaptation to be different from the best individual adaptation for all, or even many, members of the population. The question of which level selection acts upon becomes particularly important in the analysis of behaviors such as altruism in which behavior beneficial to a group may be harmful to an individual, or in the analysis of the role of human behavior in limiting population size.

The concept of group selection is based on the survival and differential success of interrelated groups, and consequently can best be applied to social animals. As stated in perhaps its most extreme form by V. C. Wynne-Edwards, group survival is related to individual survival through the evolution of population limiting behaviors in which animals "voluntarily" help control population size through reduced survivorship and fertility. Much of the debate over these ideas has centered on models which attempt to show how behaviors disadvantageous to individuals might be advantageous to the group. These models tend to view altruism as a population limiting device.

Yet other models have emphasized the importance of population competition and replacement in polytypic species. It seems likely that differences in population success underlie the establishment of numerous social behaviors, which when considered by themselves would seem to confer little advantage, if not actual disadvantage, on many social animals within the population.

BEHAVIOR AND EVOLUTION

Behavior is the ultimate interface between morphology and environment. The evolutionary importance of behavior cannot be overstated; indeed, in most cases it is likely that morphological changes must follow changes in behavior. Evidence has shown that there is a genetic component to behavioral variability and that the genetics of behaviors are subject to the forces of evolution. However, a great gulf separates the demonstration of a genetic component to behavior from models indicating a genetic basis for particular behaviors.

Recent works in sociobiology, defined by E. O. Wilson as the "study of the biological basis of all social behavior," have utilized relatively simple "genes cause behaviors" models in attempting to explain the evolution of behavior from the simplest to the most complex social creatures. Wilson, for instance, even explains the marked variability among human social organizations in terms of "genes promoting flexibility." It is argued that behaviors can be understood through an analysis of how they affect the genetic makeup of the next

inclusive fitness

generation. An important concept utilized by these models is "inclusive fitness," a characterization of how much of an individual's genetic material is passed on to the next generation through the survival of a relative. For instance, an offspring has about one-half of each parent's genetic material and about one-fourth of a sibling's. Behavior which enhances the survival of a sibling increases the probability of an additional genetic contribution (albeit indirect) to the next generation, and consequently adds to the inclusive fitness. Sociobiologists have attempted to demonstrate that the evolution of genetically based behaviors always acts to maximize inclusive fitness.

Yet such models ignore the fundamentally structural aspects of social behavior in humans (see Chapter 4) as well as in many other social mammals, and numerous other models suggest that only the deep underlying structural bases for behavioral classes respond to some degree of genetic control (such as the common underlying logic for all human language grammars). This distinction creates two very different types of models of the underlying basis for behavioral evolution in the hominid lineage.

The approach currently suggested by sociobiology relates selection for behavioral changes to the specific advantages gained by individuals. In contrast, the structural approach is an example of what E. Mayr calls an "open behavioral program," one which is modifiable during life. The unique aspect of human behavioral evolution, in this view, is the development of a species-specific structural element in what became an increasingly complex array of behaviors. Such elements act both to limit the range of possible structures and to provide a common basis for the necessary logical ordering within structures. This ordering allows behaviors to be interpreted within and between human groups. That such elements have a genetic component to their variation makes them subject to evolution. The action of selection, however, is *not* on specific behaviors (such as a language) or on specific behavioral structures (such as a language grammar).

Thus disagreement with ideas expressed by some sociobiologists need not mean opposition to the hypothesis that in some sense behavior has a genetic component and consequently can evolve. Hominid behavioral evolution, however, can probably best be understood in terms of the appearance and increasing complexity of the *structural aspects* underlying the behavioral systems which are expressed as language, kinship systems, and so on. This contrasts with one sociobiology model which suggests that specific behavioral changes are caused by specific gene frequency changes. In the former model, behavioral evolution is most likely the result of selection acting at the population level.

Phylogeny, Taxonomy, and Taxa

One consequence of the evolutionary process is the concept of relationship. Indeed, awareness of the fact that some species are more closely related than others considerably predates the development of evolutionary theory. Closeness of evolutionary relationship, like relationship in genealogical studies, depends on the recentness of common ancestry. In a formal sense, evolutionary, or phylogenetic, relationships are the secondary data of human paleontology. A phylogeny is a hypothesis about how fossil and living species are related. Without an idea of the relationships among species, no study of evolution is possible.

Systematics, the science concerned with the diversity of organisms and the relationships among them, provides the basis for determining phylogenetic relationships, while taxonomy is concerned with the theory and practice of classifying organisms once these relationships are known. How taxonomy and phylogeny are (or should be) related has become a controversial topic among evolutionists in recent years. One school of thought contends that no relationship should exist and that organisms should be classified solely on the basis of their morphological similarities. A variant of this approach admits the use of phylogenetic relations but retains the concept that phylogenetic or taxonomic affinity is measured through morphological and metric similarity. A second school of thought is cladistic. According to this approach, relationships are defined by branch points that occur when an ancestral species splits into two sister species. The degree of relationship between two taxa (formal units in a taxonomy) is measured by the number of derived features they share. Finally, a third approach and that used by this author makes classifications based on both the resemblances and differences of taxa in an evolutionary framework.

Features correlated with each other or features with a low genetic input to their variation are considered less important, and whenever possible the total functional (or morphological) patterns made up of many individual features are compared as a whole.

Hominid taxonomy reflects our current understanding of hominid phylogeny. This understanding is fluid, changing with time as more fossil material is discovered and more information is gleaned from the specimens already at hand.

TAXONOMIC NAMES

In discussing fossils, the technical language is very important. Unfortunately, there has often been confusion between the names of organisms represented by fossils and the names of the taxa to which they belong.

Every fossil specimen has its own name, usually in the form of a museum number. For instance, the fifth hominid found at Olduvai Gorge is called OH (the catalogue abbreviation for Olduvai hominid) 5. But a fossil may also have another name. In the case of OH-5, the massive jaw and teeth of the specimen led to the nickname "Nutcracker man." Quite distinct from the name of the fossil specimen is the name of the species to which it belongs, and the place of this species in a general classification of animals.

A taxon, according to G. G. Simpson, is a group of organisms recognized as a formal unit, at any level of a hierarchic classification. Examples (from higher to lower) are phylum, class, order, family, genus, and species. Each taxon may be modified by super-, sub-, and infra-. A genus is made up of species, a subfamily is made up of genera, etc.

Taxa are determined by inference from samples. However, the taxon is not the same as the sample. OH-5, for example, was placed originally in the genus *Zinjanthropus* and the species *boisei*. A genus consists of a group of species more closely related to one another than to any other species group. The term *Zinjanthropus* refers to all specimens that ever lived thought to belong to that category. The characteristics of the genus are the combined characteristics of all its member species. Since they were not all fossilized, and since those that were fossilized will not all be found, these characteristics must be determined from the known sample. The smaller the sample, the less accurate the determi-

nation. Similarly, *Homo erectus* refers to all members of the genus *Homo* in the species *erectus* that ever lived. It is represented in the fossil record by a very small sample of this total from which the characteristics of the taxon must be inferred.

POPULATIONS AND SAMPLES

There are some important limitations to evolutionary studies based on the fossil record. To begin with, a collection of fossils is usually not a sample of a single population. With few exceptions, each fossil specimen probably represents a different biological population. The problem is that evolutionary relationships are not between individuals but between populations, and it is rarely possible to identify populations among fossils. Therefore, the species is the lowest *taxonomic* level that can be compared and is thus the cornerstone for evolutionary studies.

THE INTERBREEDING CONCEPT AND FOSSILS

Because the definition of species is based on reproductive behavior, a second problem is that fossil species can never be determined with certainty because reproductive behavior cannot be directly observed in fossils.

Ultimately, it is the lineage rather than the species that takes on evolutionary significance: each lineage evolves separately from all others and has its own unique evolutionary tendencies. At a given time, the members of a lineage form a species. However, the concept of lineage is a more realistic description of the evolutionary process.

The problem comes from the fact that identifying lineages depends on an interpretation. Does there appear to be reproductive isolation? This is what it boils down to. Reproductive isolation, of course, cannot be seen in fossils; it can only be inferred—by analogy with living species or by a reconstruction of ecology.

Analogy can be used in two ways to help infer reproductive behavior. First, variation within a fossil sample (see Figure 2.3, p. 32) can be compared with variation known to occur within one closely related living species. Second, variation between

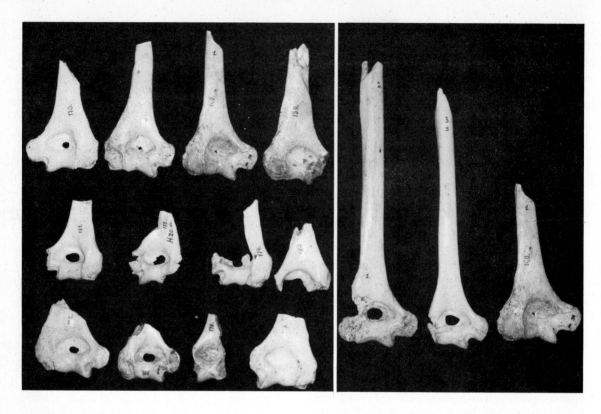

FIGURE 2.3   *Variation within a large sample is normal in hominids (among others) whenever more than a few individuals are found. This figure shows all of the distal (furthest from the body) humerus (upper arm bone) ends from the Croatian Neandertal site of Krapina. Some of the features, such as the size of the bone and prominence of the large projection at the end of the bone, reflect genetic variation. Other characteristics, such as whether or not there is a hole through the bone in the position of the elbow joint, are purely a function of how old the individual was when death occurred.*

useful in defining lineages only when the morphology indicates reproductive isolation.

two fossil samples can be compared with the known variation between two closely related living species. The variation within a living species suggests how much morphological difference can be expected within a single gene pool, while the variation between closely related species suggests the morphological differences that distinguish separate gene pools. Morphological criteria, however, are

ECOLOGY AND COMPETITIVE EXCLUSION

As was pointed out earlier, the species in a particular area (sympatric species) usually cannot be confused with one another. It was this observation that led to the idea that species were different "types" of organisms, an idea that proved to be of little use when the geographic variation of populations within a species was discovered. However, the underlying basis for the fact that species in a limited area are generally distinct points to an important consequence of competition among species, one which helps us identify lineages in the fossil record.

Species occupy limited portions of the environment in terms of space, resources used in survival, position in the ecosystem, and so on. The portion of the environment used by a species is called its "niche." Species populations within a given area all have their own unique niches. To some degree the niches overlap, causing the populations to compete for resources. In many cases, this competition has no important consequence. Several species of leaf-eating monkeys, for example, can coexist in the same tree as long as there is enough food for all.

Some aspects of a niche, however, act to limit the number of individuals in a population. These are called limiting factors; they vary from population to population but include such things as food supply, predators, physical space, and disease. When there is niche overlap between two species and competition over limiting factors, one of three things occurs:

1. One of the populations leaves the area to avoid competition.
2. One or both of the populations changes its adaptation to eliminate the competition.
3. One of the populations is more successful and prevails while the other becomes extinct.

The fact that these are the only three consequences possible when there is niche overlap in limiting factors is called the "competitive exclusion principle."

Because of this principle, the surviving species in a given area are usually quite distinct from one another and are not in competition for limiting factors. In an area where many similar species coexist, the selection leading to the similarities does not involve part of the niche that is a limiting factor. For instance, in the case of several species of leaf-eating monkeys occupying the same tree, food supply is not a limiting factor for them although it was very important in selecting for their particular morphological adaptations.

The importance of species competition was recognized by Darwin, who suggested that limitation due to competition were as effective as limitations resulting from climatic adaptations, and possibly more so. The competition, however, need not be dramatic. Moreover, it may not even be visible between living species since the present niche divergence could be the result of competition in the past.

Competitive exclusion can be helpful in interpreting past evolutionary history from the fossil record by providing an adaptive framework. If samples thought to represent closely related lineages are continually found together, they would be expected to become more and more different over time. The exact differences that accumulate give important insight into the area of competition and can be used to help reconstruct the differences in adaptation.

SPECIALIZED AND GENERALIZED

The words "specialized" and "generalized" often lead to confusion because they are used in two different ways by authors describing the evolutionary process. The words are sometimes used in the adaptive sense. A specialized species is one which is specifically adapted to a limited set of resources, whereas a generalized species is adapted to a wide range of resources. Both types of adaptation have been successful, and both can be found in primates. Some of the African monkeys, for instance, are particularly specialized for leaf eating both in their dentition and in compartmentalization of their stomachs, allowing a very efficient digestion of leaves without a great amount of chewing. Other African monkeys are generalized, eating a wide range of foods. If the two types of monkeys are in the same area and compete over leaves, the specialized species "wins" the competition and the generalized species eats something else. However, the more generalized monkeys can live in leaf-poor areas where the specialized species cannot survive, while the specialized forms can subsist on mature leaves which the more generalized monkeys cannot easily digest.

But these words are also used in a very different sense—"specialized" to mean "derived," or different from the ancestral condition, and "generalized" to mean "primitive," referring to a feature similar to the ancestral condition. For instance, even the most ancient primates had five digits on their hands and feet, so the appearance of five digits in humans is generalized in this phylogenetic sense, although they allow adaptively specialized behavior. The same ancient primates, however, had very small brains, so the large brains of modern humans are specialized in the phylogenetic sense. Yet the behavior of our species is very wide ranging and adaptively generalized. The two sets of meanings have no relation to each other.

The problem becomes particularly acute when

the term "overspecialization" is used. The European Neandertals, for instance, are sometimes said to be "extinct because they were overspecialized." What does this mean? If specialization is used in the first sense, it would have to mean that the Neandertals became specifically adapted to one environment and could not readapt when that environment changed. In the second sense it would have to mean that their characteristics were very different from those of their ancestors, and if the characteristics of living people are more similar to the Neandertals' ancestors (more generalized), the Neandertals "could not" have evolved into modern humans. Neither of these interpretations appears to be defensible. The first because the Neandertal "specializations" were mostly cultural and therefore easy to change without any genetic change at all, and the second for two reasons: living people are not more similar to the ancestors of Neandertals than the Neandertals themselves, and even if they were, it is not completely true that evolution cannot be reversed (see below).

The characterization of features as "primitive" or "derived" has recently been used as the cornerstone of the Hennigian (or cladistic) approach to phylogeny. According to this approach, relationships between species are determined solely from derived features. The more shared derived features, the closer the relationship. Differences in derived features imply taxonomic differences. Ancestry, to the extent that it is hypothesized at all, is determined by the substitution of derived for primitive characteristics in the descendent. A supposed ancestor cannot have a derived form of a characteristic if the supposed descendent has a primitive form. In considering this approach, we must take up the question of whether evolution can reverse itself because this bears on the problem of whether "primitive" characteristics can ever be identified.

IRREVERSIBILITY OF EVOLUTION

The idea that evolution cannot be reversed is both true and not true. It is true on the level of the species. Once a species becomes extinct, it can never evolve again. This is because the genetic basis for its evolution is gone; the ancestors themselves are extinct. However, the concept does not work on the level of individual characteristics. These may disappear and reappear—if selectively advantageous—any number of times during the evolution of a lineage.

Consider, for instance, the browridge, a thick structure of bone over the eyes. One of the few known fossil ape crania does not have this ridge and instead the forehead is smooth (Figure 1.1). This particular specimen, known as *Proconsul africanus* (the genus and species), is about 18 million years old. Some authors have argued that since the specimen does not have a browridge and living people generally do not have browridges, it may be an ancestor of humans. It would follow that modern humans are generalized (primitive) in their lack of a browridge (like the ancestral form). However, the Neandertals and *Homo erectus* have browridges and are therefore specialized (derived) in their morphology. Since "evolution cannot reverse itself," in this case go from the absence of a browridge to a browridge and then return to the absence of a browridge, according to one viewpoint the Neandertals and *Homo erectus* are "too specialized" to be human ancestors. Actually, this is exactly the way "irreversibility of evolution" *does not apply*. Individual features like the browridge, the size of the canine tooth, and others, are known to change and "reverse" over the course of evolution, and cannot be used to decide which fossils may or may not be human ancestors.

GRADE AND CLADE

A final pair of concepts that are often confused contrast two different reasons for the sharing of features between populations. Grade features are shared because of a common level of organization, while clade features are shared because of common descent. In living humans, large brains are a grade feature shared by all populations, while prominent noses are a clade feature that is common among Europeans and their ancestors. The use of the term "Neandertal" is a classic case in which this confusion has led to a considerable amount of debate at cross-purposes. The term is usually used to describe a European clade with a near-modern grade of characteristics. Unfortunately, some authors (including myself) have used it as a grade term, arguing that Neandertals represent a worldwide evolutionary stage. The question of whether Neandertals represent a European version of a grade common throughout the world was thus potentially confused with the question of whether this grade should be called "Neandertal," as well as with the question of whether the European Neandertals can represent the ancestors of modern populations throughout the world.

EVOLUTION IS MOSAIC

One of the things that becomes apparent from the previous discussion is that different characteristics may evolve at very different rates. G. G. Simpson called this "mosaic evolution." To take the extreme, it is obvious that in the course of human evolution the size of the brain has changed dramatically, while the number of eyes has not changed at all. Selection can act on individual characteristics with very different intensity and in very different ways. While this may seem obvious, the implications of mosaic evolution are sometimes forgotten.

In the nineteenth and earlier twentieth centuries, much time was spent in the search for a "missing link" between humans and apes (in spite of the fact that humans did not descend from apes but rather both evolved from a common ancestor). This "missing link" was envisioned as being literally halfway between ape and human, and its features were conceptualized by taking the midpoint between human and ape features. Consequently, when the real "missing link" was discovered, it was not recognized. The first australopithecines were found to have human teeth and an ape's brain size. But scientists were looking for a creature with teeth and brains halfway between those of humans and apes. Since the australopithecines did not fit this description, most authors originally considered them "aberrant apes." As it turns out, the australopithecines are human ancestors and may well be halfway between living people and the common ancestors of apes and humans in time. However, they are not halfway between apes and humans in morphology. The brain size is very similar to that of apes while the bipedal (two-legged) locomotion is identical to that of humans. Neither is midway between. Moreover, the posterior teeth (molars and premolars) are like neither humans nor apes, and they are not anywhere between them. Relative to body size, these teeth are larger than the posterior teeth of both humans and apes.

The australopithecines were generally not recognized as the "missing links" when they were found because the mosaic nature of evolution was not considered. The morphology of the australopithecines cannot be fully explained as that of an apelike creature evolving into a human. Their unique set of characteristics results from the successful adaptation of a species to its environment.

SUMMARY

The process of evolution is a universal phenomenon, affecting all life forms through genetic changes in populations. Four factors cause genetic change: selection, mutation, migration, and drift. Of these, selection appears to be the most important, causing frequency changes in gene pools through relative differences in fertility and survivorship. The main role of mutation seems to be the gradual introduction of new genetic material, although some believe it can result in structural simplification and reduction in the absence of selection. Migration as an evolutionary force can be particularly important in conjunction with selection or drift. Some evolutionary models suggest that migration and rapid replacement may be a major cause of large evolutionary changes. Finally, drift acts mainly to introduce an element of randomness to the process, although another effect is to eliminate rare genetic variants.

The evolving entity is the species, or when considered over time the lineage, since the boundaries of the species (or lineage) are the permanent barriers to gene flow and the spread of genetic change. Speciation occurs when such barriers appear, almost always with the requirement of spatial isolation. Speciation is also considered to have taken place when sufficient change occurs in the evolution of a lineage; in this case, the species boundaries are arbitrary.

Evolution is an active opportunistic process and not simply a passive response to environmental change. "Breakthroughs" often occur because of newly developed abilities of species to utilize resources already present in their environments. Such breakthroughs sometimes allow species to utilize previously unoccupied niches, resulting in a rapid multiplication of closely related forms called an adaptive radiation.

Behavior is no less subject to evolutionary change than morphological features. One model of behavioral evolution relates changes to the advantages they confer on the survival of groups. The genetic models for behaviors are complex, and in many cases the genetic influence may be on the logical ordering and interrelationships of behavioral classes rather than on specific behaviors.

A phylogeny is a hypothesis concerning how species seem to be related. The taxonomic names given to species reflect this hypothesis. Phylogeny is difficult to determine for fossil samples because populations are almost never represented, and species (or lineage) determinations must depend on inferences about reproductive barriers. The competitive exclusion principle can be helpful when closely related species are sympatric since competition over limiting factors will result in extinction, population movement, or character displacement. Another interpretive tool that can be used in suggesting relationship is the comparison of derived features. Since evolution is mosaic and characteristics in a lineage do not change at the same time or rate, equivalent features in two species that differ from the condition in the common ancestor can be helpful in ascertaining their degree of relationship.

Evolution applies to humans as surely as it applies to other organisms. The evolutionary history of our species has been unique. No organism with the potential of humans has ever evolved before. The goal of this book is to try to understand how and why this happened.

STATE OF THE ART

Many of the topics discussed in this chapter are the subject of controversy and ongoing research. The relative importance of the four causes of evolution has not been definitively established. Selection, for instance, normally occurs with so low a magnitude that it is difficult to establish in living populations. Conversely, many observable causes of differences in mortality and fertility seem unrelated to one another and to any long-term evolutionary trend. Attempts to speed up the process of change due to selection under laboratory conditions result in magnitudes of selection which rarely if ever occur in nature, and there is some evidence that the response of populations to high magnitudes of selection is quantitatively different from the long-term response to the much lower levels that occur normally. If evolutionary studies cannot directly observe changes due to low levels of selection in nature, and if laboratory studies do not accurately duplicate the natural process, it is legitimate to question how much is actually known (in contrast to hypothesized) about the importance of selection.

Similarly, the role of mutation continues to be debated. Some workers cling to the concept of the macro-mutation, pointing out that mutational effects early in ontogeny (individual development) could have dramatic consequences in the adult organism. The question of whether mutations can actually accumulate (i.e., become established at high frequency through drift) in the genome (genetic basis) of structures subject to reduced or relaxed selection has been under continued debate. Again, the slow rate of change does not allow a significant contribution from the study of living organisms. In instances of structural reduction in fossil lineages, there are unresolved arguments as to whether the structure in question was truly under relaxed selection or whether there was an advantage to the observed reduction or simplification.

Interpretation of the evolutionary process has been no less problematic. The punctuated equilibrium model seems to have high explanatory power in certain instances. Yet uncertainties in dating, even at a single site, usually make it extraordinarily difficult to determine whether observed changes were gradual or "sudden." Samples said to be geologically contemporary may actually span hundreds of thousands of years. Thus the question of whether observed changes in the fossil record are "too sudden" to be the result of gradual frequency changes cannot be answered. Two examples of this in the hominid fossil record are the "sudden" appearance of *Homo erectus* between 1.6 and 1.5 million years ago in east Africa (Chapter 8) and the "sudden" appearance of anatomically modern-looking populations in Europe between 50,000 and 30,000 years ago (Chapter 12).

It follows from the above that reconstructions of phylogeny, and the resulting taxonomy, are the subjects of ongoing (and often heated, especially if hominids are involved) discussions. The simple temporal positioning of one sample after another may look like an ancestral-descendent relationship but it is not *proof*. The fact is that *there is no proof of such a relationship*. In spite of attempts to provide an objective basis for determining phylogenetic relationships, studies remain as much an art as a science. The problem is complicated by different philosophical approaches to how science should be conducted. A logical positivist attempting to determine relative probabilities for competing hypotheses may emphasize very different data and arrive at dramatically different conclusions from a Popper-

ian attempting to disprove what appears to be the simplest explanatory hypothesis. The approaches are as different as induction and deduction.

Yet in spite of this there is a certain stability and rationality to evolutionary studies that stems from a complete acceptance and recognition of the evolutionary process itself. The difficulties and problems mentioned above are not evidence of an endeavor whose main paradigm (the synthetic theory of evolution) has failed, but rather of one whose paradigm has proven to be encompassing and long lasting. It is important not to miss the forest for the trees. Patching together out-of-context quotes by eminent workers which question specific causes and processes cannot hide the fact that evolutionary biology is here to stay. Its condition can best be described as vigorous health. The continued controversies result from ongoing research, and I would suggest that its progress not be judged by how many problems it has raised, but rather by how many it has settled.

FURTHER READINGS

BARASH, D. P. 1977. *Sociobiology and Behavior*. Elsevier, New York.

One of the best-written fairly simplified introductions to sociobiology and general aspects of behavioral genetics.

BRACE, C. L. 1963. Structural Reduction in Evolution. *American Naturalist* 97:39-49.

The classic paper on the probable effect of accumulating mutations when selection is relaxed.

CLARKE, B. 1975. The Causes of Biological Diversity. *Scientific American* 233 (2):50-60.

An excellent introduction to the evolutionary factors that maintain biological diversity.

DELSON, E., N. ELDREDGE, and I. TATTERSALL. 1977. Reconstruction of Hominid Phylogeny: A Testable Framework Based on Cladistic Analysis. *Journal of Human Evolution* 6:263-278.

Application of the Hennigian approach to hominid relationships, and an excellent introduction to cladistic methodology.

DIAMOND, J. M. 1978. Niche Shifts and the Rediscovery of Interspecific Competition. *American Scientist* 66:322-331.

A thoughtful essay on the history and current status of competition between species and the competitive exclusion principle.

DOBZHANSKY, T. 1970. *Genetics of the Evolutionary Process*. Columbia University Press, New York.

Probably the best comprehensive survey of population genetics and its relation to the evolutionary process.

ELDREDGE, N., and S. J. GOULD. 1972. Punctuated Equilibria: An Alternative to Phyletic Gradualism. In *Models in Paleobiology*, ed. J. Schopf. Freeman and Cooper, San Francisco, pp. 82-115.

A technical account of the punctuated equilibrium model for evolutionary change.

GINGERICH, P. D., and M. SCHOENINGER. 1977. The Fossil Record and Primate Phylogeny. *Journal of Human Evolution* 6:483-505.

Besides an effective counterbalance to the cladistic approach, this paper emphasizes the importance of stratigraphic position in several critical areas of hominoid evolution.

HUTCHINSON, G. E. 1978. *An Introduction to Population Ecology*. Yale University Press, New Haven.

This is an introduction written by one of the founders and most insightful contributors to modern ecological theory, presenting an in depth analysis of most issues raised in this chapter and many others.

KING, J. L., and T. H. JUKES. 1969. Non-Darwinian Evolution. *Science* 164:788-798.

A technical discussion of non-oriented evolutionary changes due to mutation.

MAYR, E. 1960. The Emergence of Evolutionary Novelties. In *The Evolution of Life*, ed. S. Tax. University of Chicago Press, Chicago, pp. 349-380.
One of the best discussions of how truly novel characteristics originate, explained within the Darwinian framework.

————. 1976. *Evolution and the Diversity of Life*. Belknap, Cambridge.
A series of wide-ranging essays on most of the important issues in evolutionary studies.

RAUP, D. M. 1977. Probabilistic Models in Evolutionary Paleobiology. *American Scientist* 65:50-57.
An excellent presentation of the role of drift in the evolutionary process.

SAVAGE, J. M. 1977. *Evolution*, 3rd ed. Holt, Rinehart, and Winston, New York.
A paleontologically oriented basic introduction.

SIMPSON, G. G. 1953. *The Major Features of Evolution*. Columbia University Press, New York.
A more technical and detailed account of the evolutionary process than the preceding.

————. 1963. The Meaning of Taxonomic Statements. In *Classification and Human Evolution*, ed. S. L. Washburn. Aldine, Chicago, pp. 1-31.
An excellent, fairly detailed account of the evolutionary process.

————. 1975. Recent Advances in Methods of Phylogenetic Inference. In *Phylogeny of the Primates*, eds. W. P. Luckett and F. S. Szalay. Plenum, New York, pp. 3-19.
A balanced discussion of the several current approaches that relate taxonomy to phylogeny.

SMITH, J. M. 1975. *The Theory of Evolution*, 3rd ed. Penguin, Baltimore.
A well-written basic introduction, especially strong in its emphasis on behavior.

STERN, C. 1973. *Principles of Human Genetics*, 3rd ed. Freeman, San Francisco.
Probably the best introduction to human genetics available.

TATTERSALL, I., and N. ELDREDGE. 1977. Fact, Theory, and Fantasy in Human Paleontology. *American Scientist* 65:204-211.
An application of Hennigian procedure to hominid systematics bringing out, perhaps inadvertently, both the strong and weak points of the approach.

CHAPTER THREE

Trends in
Primate Evolution

3 directions' primate studies

A s our closest living relations, primates deserve more than glancing attention. Typically, primate studies have had one of three orientations. Primates are often studied for their own sake. They represent an interesting group whose behavior, morphology, and evolution present a series of unique problems. A rather different orientation is the study of primates as surrogate humans. While this may have the least direct relevance to more evolutionarily directed research, its obvious application to medical science has resulted in funding more research in this area than any other dealing with primates. A third orientation is the study of primates to develop a context for a better understanding of human evolution.

Living primates have been used as models for how early humans and their ancestors may have adapted and behaved. Studies of primates have also helped distinguish what is unique in our heritage from what is shared with our nearest relatives. Finally, studies of fossil primates provide evidence concerning when, where, and why humans emerged as a distinct lineage.

The first section of this chapter provides some basic information about the distribution and variation of living primates. The next section discusses the major trends that have been shared in the evolution of most primate lineages. These trends are general, shared adaptive tendencies resulting from a combination of similar genetic material (common ancestry) and similarities in adaptation. The last section presents a brief review of primate origins and some of the basic changes that occured in their early evolution. More detailed attention is paid to the origin of the higher primates and to the emergence and evolution of the ape-like forms that were ancestral to the earliest humans.

Overview of the Primates

Modern people are a particular type of mammal called a primate. Primates is an order of mammals. *primate, order, mammals* The living primates are more closely related to each other than they are to mammals in other orders. That they are placed together in an order implies

[handwritten margin notes: "2 suborders / Anthropoidea / Prosimii"]

that most primates have features in common not usually found in other mammals. However, all primates do not share one specific set of features, so that it is impossible to make up a list of characteristics which "define" what a primate is. This problem occurs in most orders of mammals. For instance, the order Carnivora includes many familiar species: dogs, cats, bears, raccoons, and so on. One would think that meat eating, or carnivorous behavior, would be a distinguishing feature of this order, but although it is characteristic of most of the species in the order, there are exceptions, such as the giant panda, whose diet is purely vegetarian. Yet it certainly is true that an adaptation to meat eating characterizes the evolutionary development of modern carnivore species; even the giant panda is a descendant of meat-eating ancestors. Probably the best way to characterize the order Carnivora is in terms of the adaptive trends visible in its evolutionary history. In general, the carnivores are a group of related species for which meat eating has been a primary adaption over most of its evolutionary history.

Similarly, no single feature or group of features uniquely characterizes all primates. However, there are three adaptive trends in our order; two of these apply to all primates and the third mainly applies to humans and the species most similar to humans (monkeys and apes). These three adaptations are:

1. Adaptation to living in trees (arboreal).
2. Maintenance of dietary plasticity (the ability to eat many different kinds of foods).
3. Investing large amounts of parental care in a very small number of offspring.

An understanding of features shared by primates, especially those most closely related to humans, provides a necessary background for discussing human origins and evolution. A surprising number of features and abilities widely considered to be uniquely human are actually part of our primate heritage. The important questions in human evolution center about the origin of derived (or specialized) features.

THE LIVING PROSIMIAN PRIMATES

The order Primates is usually divided into two groups, or suborders. These are often referred to as

the higher primates and the lower primates, although the formal names for the suborders are Anthropoidea and Prosimii (see Figure 3.1). The Prosimii are the ancestors of Anthropoidea in a general sense; of course the living prosimians are not the ancestors of the living higher primates, but between 30 and 40 million years ago the first higher primates evolved from a prosimian ancestor.

Living prosimians are generally not characterized by the third primate trend (marked parental investment in a few offspring). Moreover, many of the arboreal features are not as well developed in some prosimian species and a number of primitive (early mammal-like) features are retained. The four infraorders of prosimians are each believed to include as much variation as all of Anthropoidea.

The tree shrews (Tupaiiformes) are the most primitive of the prosimians. Most workers do not even consider them primates. Whether they are primates or primate-like members of a different order (Insectivora), they give insight into the most primitive primate condition. The several forms of tree shrew are small, quick moving creatures. They are distributed over most of Southeast Asia, living in low forest growth and rarely climbing high above the ground. Their main dietary staple is insects, although they also eat fruits and seeds. Insects are generally caught on the forest floor and are seized with the front teeth. Unlike in most primates, the snout is very long and the orbits (eye sockets) face to the side of the cranium. The hands and feet have claws on all digits, and grasping ability is poorly developed.

Loris and loris-like prosimians (Lorisiformes) inhabit forested areas in both Africa and Southeast Asia. The Lorisidae are larger, slow moving primates whose main activity takes place at early dawn and late dusk (crepuscular) or at night (nocturnal). Because they are active when light is dim, their eyes are large. The orbits face more forward than those in the tree shrews and there is some degree of visual overlap (the ability to see the same object in both eyes), which is a prerequisite for three-dimensional vision. The snout is short, and as with most other prosimians there is an external, wet nose (moist rhinarium). All the digits have nails except for the second toe, which has an elongated claw used for cutting through rotten wood or vegetation and for grooming. The first digit (thumb, big toe) is offset in its direction from the remaining digits, allowing some grasping ability.

[handwritten margin notes: "no single / feature / in / primates"; "3 adaptive / trends in / primates"]

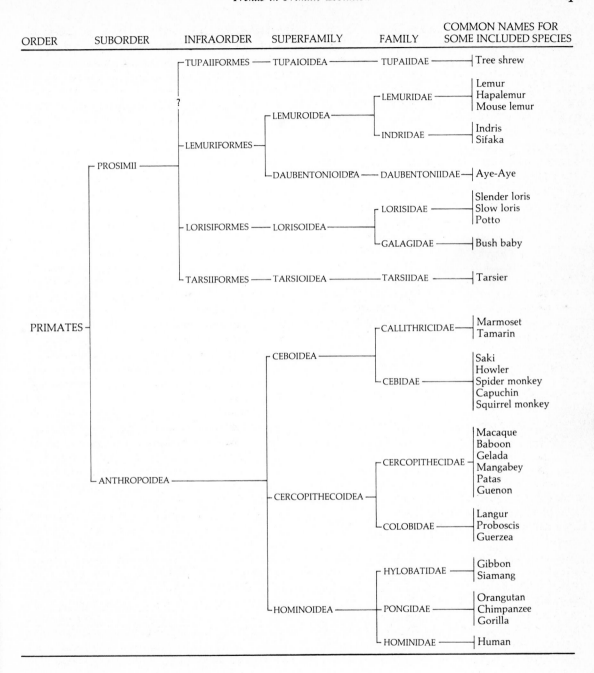

FIGURE 3.1   *A taxonomy of the living primates.*

Diet includes lower forest canopy insects as well as higher level fruits and leaves. Insects are seized with the hands or tongue.

Galagos (Galagidae, or bushbabies) are small, quick moving crepuscular Lorisiformes restricted to African forest and brush. They are largely insectivorous, stalking their prey and seizing it with their hands.

The third prosimian infraorder is the tarsiers (Tarsiiformes). Many consider these the most anthropoid-like of the living prosimians. The tarsiers are small and are restricted to islands in Southeast Asia (Indonesia, Borneo, and the Philippines). The orbits face forward, the snout is short, and the external rhinarium is dry and small in the living members of *Tarsius* (see Figure 3.2). When in the trees, the tarsier clings vertically to upright branches. The skull is consequently better balanced on the neck vertebrae in this vertical position. Like the loris, the tarsier's activity is mainly nocturnal and the eyes are extraordinarily large. The hind limbs are modified to allow jumps of up to six feet—a remarkable distance for a creature the size of a small kitten. Tarsiers are carnivorous, eating mainly insects, frogs, snakes, and other small amphibians and reptiles.

The final group of prosimians is the lemurs (Lemuriformes). These primates are now restricted to the island of Madagascar, where they lived without competition from higher primates until humans arrived within the last 10,000 years. Over this brief period, many of the Malagasy prosimians became extinct. In the absence of competition with higher primates, the Lemuriformes underwent an adaptive radiation; living species inhabit a much wider range of habitat than all the other prosimians combined, and in many ways they have come to parallel the higher primate adaptations, although some forms are unique. The Lemuridae are mainly omnivorous and arboreal, although some extinct species may have lived on the ground. Only some share the nocturnal adaptations of the other prosimians. In the trees they are generally quadrupedal, and in many ways they parallel the African monkeys, although their behavior is much less complex, their sense of smell is more strongly emphasized (living species have an external wet nose), and they retain sensitive facial hairs (vibrissae). Like the *Loris* species, all of the digits have nails except the second toe. Also resembling many *Loris* species, lemurs have an unusual dental adaptation

known as a tooth comb. The incisors and canines of the lower jaw are of similar size and form, and are set horizontally across the front of the mouth. The apparatus resembles a comb and is used for grooming.

Indriidae are larger and generally higher canopy Lemuriformes with relatively longer hindlimbs. Resembling the tarsier, they cling vertically to upright trunks and branches. Leaping from branch to branch is an important part of their locomotion. They are mainly leaf-eaters. The third Malagasy form, the aye-aye (*Daubentonia*), is closely related to the indriids. Its dental anatomy is strikingly rodentlike. This primate has two expanded anterior teeth (the central incisors) in the upper jaw which grow constantly during life, wearing to a chisel-like edge. The incisors are used for gnawing and opening hard-shelled fruits.

HIGHER PRIMATES

The suborder Anthropoidea comprises monkeys, apes, and humans. A higher-level taxonomic division favored by many authors is into New World (i.e., the Americas) and Old World forms. These are the New World platyrrhines, so named because their nostrils face to the side (Ceboidea), and the Old World catarrhines with downward-facing nostrils (Cercopithecoidea, Hominoidea). A consistent dental difference is the loss of a premolar (one on both sides of each jaw) in the living catarrhines, while other distinctions range from the anatomy of the external edge of the bony ear opening to the use of the tail during locomotion in some New World forms. Most catarrhines show more complex social behavior in their more intricate role relations and more elaborate parental investment in offspring.

The New World monkeys are divided into the true monkeys (Cebidae) and the marmosets (Callithricidae). In many respects, the latter are American parallels to the prosimians, with claw-like nails on all of their digits except the first toe. The Cebidae are represented by a wide range of living species, varying from the fruit-eating spider monkeys, which represent the closest New World parallel to the apes, to leaf- and insect-eating forms which are like the Old World monkeys in many respects. Only one New World species is nocturnal. In contrast to the Old World forms, no ground dwelling

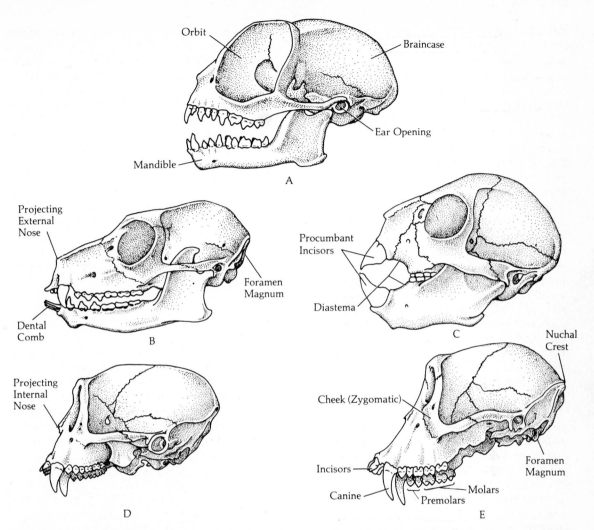

FIGURE 3.2   *Cranial forms in some living primates, from Schultz (1969). The crania compared include three prosimians and representatives of the Anthropoidea from the New and Old Worlds. These are (A) a tarsier, (B) a lemur, (C) an aye-aye, (D) a New World cebus monkey, and (E) an Old World macaque. The skulls are drawn to the same approximate size and are not to scale.*

form has evolved in the Americas. The Cebidae are larger than the marmosets, ranging up to the 20-pound howler monkey (a leaf-eater with powerful jaws and large teeth for grinding down this difficult-to-chew food source). The Cebidae share numerous features with the other higher primates,

including forward-facing orbits, the complete loss of claws, absence of the external wet nose, and the appearance of certain features of the brain associated with complex behavior.

Old World monkeys (Cercopithecoidea) are represented by a leaf-eating subfamily (Colobinae) and a more generalized omnivorous form (Cercopithecinae). The distribution of the living animals suggests that the former might have evolved in Southeast Asia (only one living genus is African) and the latter in Africa (only one living genus is outside of Africa). The Colobidae have evolved large subdivided stomachs, allowing them to digest leaves without prolonged chewing.

The Cercopithecinae are more widely adapted and behaviorally complex than their leaf-eating

Cebidae share → some
r & primates

relatives. Were it not for humans, they would be considered the most successful of the living primates. Most living forms are characterized by cheek pouches for storing food, a thickening on the buttocks (ischial callosities) for sitting, and a basically quadrupedal (four legged) form of locomotion with their palms facing down. Many of the species are adapted for living on the ground, and the family includes the only primate species besides humans (and some gorilla groups) that are fully terrestrial as well as the only other living primate species with successful adaptations to temperate habitats.

The smaller-sized species include the mainly arboreal mangabeys and guenons and fully terrestrial patas. The latter is among the few primate species adapted to dry, open country. A group of larger species form a closely related set. These include the baboons and the baboon-like forms (geladas, mandrills, and macaques). Mandrills are adapted to the forest floor, while baboons and geladas range from open woodlands to extremely dry areas. The behavior of baboons is probably the best studied of all primate behaviors; many anthropologists feel that the grasslands adaptations of the baboons and the closely related geladas parallel adaptations in earlier humans. Their social behavior is extraordinarily complex and acts as a critical part of their adaptation to habitats sparse in trees. The extra-African macaques have been extremely successful in adapting to humans and the conditions they create. Their numbers may well be larger now than in the recent past.

Hominoidea includes apes and humans. We seem to be more closely related to the chimpanzees and gorillas of Africa than to the Southeast Asian large ape (the orang) or to the Asian lesser apes (gibbon, siamang). In fact, humans and the African apes seem more closely related than the African apes are to their Asiatic relatives.

The Hylobatidae (gibbons and siamangs) are the smallest and most arboreally adapted of the apes. Their form of arm-over-arm locomotion, or brachiation, is developed to a fine art. Some of the anatomical consequences include relatively long arms and shortened lower trunks. These apes are largely fruit- and insect-eaters. The intolerance of adults to other adults of the same sex results in small "family" groups. Their social structure, along with the delicate form of their crania and the fact that when terrestrial they walk bipedally (on their

hind legs), led some earlier workers to believe they held a special relation to humans.

The Asian form of the Pongidae is the orangutan (*Pongo*) a much larger ape restricted today to the forests of Borneo and Sumatra. *Pongo* is a rapidly diminishing taxon; fossil evidence shows that orangs once ranged widely across Southeast Asia and China. When arboreal, these large apes use all four limbs in a form of slow locomotion that allows them to reach the outermost branches for the fruits that they favor. Their terrestrial locomotion involves using the first (closest to the body) of the three finger bones on their hands for weight support; they literally walk on their fists. Recent field studies of orangs have dispelled many of the earlier conceptions regarding their behavior. It has been discovered that males spend a large amount of time on the forest floor. While formerly thought to be solitary, it appears that males actually control fairly large territories that include the territories of several females. The females and accompanying young are almost always arboreal. There is an interesting contrast between orangs and gibbons in the expression of sex differences (sexual dimorphism). Apart from features directly concerned with reproduction, male and female gibbons barely differ in size, while orangutan males are much larger than females and also differ in a number of features, including having large projecting canines and the development of strength-related features.

The African apes are closely related to each other and to humans. The chimpanzees (*Pan*) and gorillas (*Gorilla*) provide a contrast and an enigma, since they seem to share the same potentialities for complex behavior but differ markedly in how these are expressed.

The gorilla is the largest of the living primates. Today populations are found in two regions of West Africa about 700 miles apart. To the west are lowland gorillas, while in central Africa gorillas live in mountainous areas. Both are primarily terrestrial (few trees can safely hold an adult). Gorilla groups consist of a few adults and offspring. Females are about half the size of males. Gorillas spend large portions of the day eating stems and leaves of secondary growth plants, which are relatively low in nutritional value. The normal locomotion is quadrupedalism of a special form called "knuckle-walking"; the arms are used in support, with the weight resting on the backs of the middle digits of the fingers. In terms of behavior, nothing could be more misleading than the "King Kong" image for gorillas. While their large size provides protection from most carnivores (except humans), aggressive behaviors are only rarely observed.

Chimpanzees are less than half the size of gorillas and differ from them in the virtual lack of size differences between males and females. With gorillas, they share the enlarged brain size, prolonged maturation of the young, flexibility in thumb motions, and a number of other anatomical features normally associated with the primate arboreal adaptation, and specifically with brachiation. Like gorillas their locomotion is neither primarily brachiating nor are they usually arboreal; they spend most of their waking hours on the ground, although in the afternoon and again at night they may build nests and sleep in trees. When terrestrial, they generally knuckle-walk. Although bipedal locomotion is common, chimps are rarely bipedal for more than a few steps.

Chimpanzee social behavior appears to be more complex and structured than the social behavior of gorillas. Moreover, comparisons of troops living in open woodlands (the species ranges as far east as Tanzania) with forest-adapted troops indicates an ecological component to behavioral differences within the species. The composition of groups varies from fairly stable to fluid, but internal structures are always female oriented. Mothers seem to maintain fairly close social relations with their offspring (especially female offspring).

Chimpanzee diet is omnivorous, including fruits, leaves, insects, and meat. Organized hunting has been observed, with cooperation among several adults in trapping and capturing the prey (which is often a red colobus monkey). Meat is shared among both adults and children. Various elements of chimpanzee behavior impinge on what was once considered to be uniquely human. Chimpanzees make tools and use them for a variety of tasks, including gathering water and various foods. Captive chimps have been taught American Sign Language and seem to be able to communicate at a basically human level, although a lower magnitude of information is communicated. Other experiments seem to confirm their ability to understand and use symbols.

Apart from the fascination and interest most people have for this most human-like of the primates, the chimpanzee offers an entirely different perspective to our own evolution. Why did humans carry these abilities to their present levels of complexity and importance? Moreover, why are chimpanzees, in contrast to the humans with which they share so much, amongst the *least* successful of the higher primates?

Primate Arboreal Adaptation

The primate adaptation to trees is not the only arboreal pattern that leads to success. Animals as diverse as squirrels and birds share only a few features with primates and yet are equally well adapted to life off the ground. Why does the primate adaptation differ?

NAILS INSTEAD OF CLAWS

One of the most important limitations which has guided the specific pattern of primate arboreal adaptation is the replacement of claws by nails on the digits. Claws are semicircular in cross-section, tapering to a thin, pointed, and structurally strong tip. The primate nail is broad and flat and has little strength. It cannot be used to adhere to trees while climbing. Instead, the advantage conferred by nails seems tied to the presence of large, flat, sensitive tactile surfaces on the underside of the digits. It is the touch sensitivity allowed by these tactile pads that seems to have been the object of selection; the broad underside of the digits required a flat broad nail on the opposite side. In primate evolutionary history, it is possible that selection for these tactile pads came before arboreal adaptation, and that the subsequent adaptation to the trees was accomplished with characteristics that were already present in the earliest primates. Whatever the case, the lack of gripping claws limited the nature and direction of arboreal adaptation in the primates.

FREE MOBILITY OF THE DIGITS

It is quite possible that the loss of sharp claws and their replacement by nails in the early primates resulted in the development of freely mobile digits as an alternative means of climbing trees. Another hypothesis is that early primates were initially under selection for grasping as part of a hand-to-eye coordination pattern also including tactile pads. This pattern presumably arose as part of an adaptation to catching insects and small mammals. Whatever the case, primates today share digital mobility and the ability to grasp. This has become a central part of their arboreal adaptation. In most cases, primate digits are relatively long and prehensile. Their mobility results from the segmentation of digits into two or three terminal bones (phalanges). Moreover, in the course of primate evolution, there is a trend to further refine grasping ability through the development of thumb and big toe opposability. When the axis of motion of the thumb and big toe are offset from the axis of motion of the other digits, opposability is possible. By itself, this allows significantly greater grasping and manipulatory ability. In living prosimians and New World monkeys, as well as in some fossil apes, the thumb morphology allows very limited rotation as well as opposability, making possible an even greater range of grasps and grips. The combination of full rotation and opposability in hominoid thumbs allows use of the so-called precision grip (what you do when you turn a screwdriver with your thumb and forefinger), although this grip is difficult for the great apes because of elongation of the other digits. If the rotatable thumb evolved in the common ancestor of the apes and humans, which is the most likely hypothesis, this might have occurred before extensive adaptation to brachiation (the arm-over-arm locomotion of the living apes) reduced the value of this morphological change to the pongids, whose short thumbs relative to finger length limit the grasping advantages of this complex.

A parallel development occurred in the big toe of many primates. In some species, this digit is also opposable, but never truly rotatable. The loss of toe opposability in humans and mountain gorillas is a relatively recent evolutionary change.

GENERALIZED LIMB STRUCTURE

As part of the arboreal adaptation, primates have retained most of the separate limb bones characteristic of the early placental mammals (see Figure 4.2, p. 74). For instance, all primates retain the clavicle (collar bone), although this has been lost in many other mammal species. The clavicle allows unusually great mobility of the forelimb, making it par-

ticularly capable of resisting forces applied in certain directions. Its action can be felt when the hand is placed behind the head—a motion impossible in most nonprimates. Mobility of the forelimb is furthered by having the scapula (shoulder blade) in a lateral position, away from the midline of the body. The shoulder joint, where the humerus (upper arm bone) articulates with the scapula, is thus angled more outward than downward. The clavicle also acts as a strut, preventing medial (toward the midline) motion of the laterally (away from the midline) positioned shoulder. In addition, primates have retained two separate bones in the lower part of the forearm, the radius and ulna. This allows a much greater flexibility in turning the hand (pronation and supination). This flexibility is especially well developed in the living Hominoidea, where the hand articulates only with the radius, rather than with both radius and ulna (which occurs in most other primates). Only the ulna articulates directly with the humerus, so the rotation of the radius about the ulna allows an extreme amount of hand rotation. All these features are clearly the result of selection for locomotion in the three-dimensional world of tree branches. The especially free mobility for rotation at the wrist in the Hominoidea is most likely an adaptation to brachiation and arm hanging. Its presence in people suggests a brachiating stage in human ancestry.

Primates have maintained functionally distinct vertebrae: cervical (neck), thoracic (rib-bearing), lumbar (lower back), sacral (behind the pelvis), and caudal (tail). The most important adaptive variations occur in the lumbar region. For instance, lumbar shortening has occurred in brachiators, whereas the greatest number of lumbar vertebrae occur in primates that spring or leap from branch to branch. Living Old World brachiators have also lost all functional caudal vertebrae. The reduction of the lumbar segment in brachiators acts to reduce mobility of the lower spine, to shorten the trunk, and to raise the center of gravity. These are useful adaptations for brachiation, since a brachiator in many ways approximates a pendulum. A short trunk allows use of the legs to control the pendulum motion: extended legs slow the swing while bent legs accelerate it. The relatively small number of lumbar vertebrae in modern humans also suggests a brachiating ancestry, although it is interesting that the only early hominid vertebral column known has six lumbar vertebrae, in contrast to the normal human number of five (although within the normal human range).

VISUAL ADAPTATIONS

An important aspect of primate arboreal adaptation is found in the sensory developments; vision is improved and elaborated while the other senses become less important. In the primate adaptation to trees, sight has become the most important sense (although there is a problem of cause and effect here since one hypothesis suggests that the improvements in vision may precede the arboreal adaptation and instead be part of an earlier insect-catching adaptation discussed above). Whatever the original cause, the advantage of vision is that it allows the greatest amount of sensory discrimination in a three-dimensional world.

Two major developments have occurred in primate evolution: the elaboration and refinement of the mammalian cone-type retina and the progressive overlap of the visual fields. The cone-type retina, with its central fovea, allows both fine discrimination and color vision. This greatly increases the amount of information obtained through vision. The overlapping of visual fields results in binocular vision and the ability to see in three dimensions (to gauge depth). This ability is allowed by sighting a single object with both eyes, and is of obvious adaptive importance to arboreal creatures. The sense of hearing, however acute, cannot play the same role as vision in gaining information from the environment. Determining direction from sound is limited to the horizontal plane (or specifically to the plane between the ears since this can be changed by tilting the head). While this is adequate for creatures that live on the ground, it cannot serve as well when up and down become important dimensions of existence.

In primate evolution, the orbits (eye sockets) have come to face increasingly forward, widening the range of the visual field that can be seen through both eyes. This makes stereoscopic vision possible. This trend has gone further in the living anthropoids than it has in the living prosimians. As a result of this trend, exposing the lateral (outside) edge of the orbit, there is a concomitant development of a bar of bone on the outside of the orbit

for all living primates, and complete post-orbital closure of the orbit by bone in the living anthropoids (see Figure 3.2).

REDUCTION OF THE SENSE OF SMELL

As the sense of vision became more important in primate evolution, the sense of smell became less so. Many of the morphological and physiological features providing for high discrimination in detecting different smells that appear in most mammals have been progressively lost in the primates. In addition, to some extent reliance on the sense of smell became less important with the development of complex grasping and manipulative ability. Primates can examine by touch rather than smell. In all, the combination of stereoscopic vision and manipulation seems a more advantageous way of exploring the environment for primates. Decrease in the importance of smell has not developed equally among living primates. For example, lemur and loris species still retain an external wet nose (moist rhinarium), this is lost in higher primates.

There is also a reduction in the size of the external nose. Primitive anthropoids such as the Oligocene genus *Aegyptopithecus* have a projecting external nose along with a very large snout (middle and lower face). In the living great apes, the snout is much shorter. Even so, the nose does not project beyond it, indicating significant reduction in the internal surface area of the air passageway where the chemical reactions of the sense of smell take place. With a few exceptions, the nose does not project beyond the large snout of early hominids. Modern people, with further snout reduction, have a projecting external nose. The nose is apparently maintained at this minimal size to retain its effectiveness in smell, and in some cases warming and moistening the inspired air, while the snout continued reducing.

The general reduction of the size of the snout (or muzzle) in primate evolution is associated with the decreasing importance of the nose and the reduction of structures involved in the sense of smell. On the other hand, long snouts are not necessarily associated with an increased importance of smell. In the cercopithecoids, especially baboons, mandrills, and geladas, snout expansion has secondarily evolved in response to the development of very

incisors
canines
premolars
molars

large canines and to a lesser degree expanded incisors. To some extent this has also occurred in the pongid lineage. Modern pongids have undergone front tooth expansion compared with the ancestral condition, while in hominids continued snout reduction seems related to decreasing use of the front teeth.

TRUNK UPRIGHTNESS

Development of the ability to function with the trunk in an upright position is the last facet of arboreal adaptation to be discussed. Tree-dwelling provides grasping species with numerous opportunities to hold the trunk in this position: vertical clinging, sitting, and so on. With the evolution of hanging and brachiation as common postures in the apes, the ability to maintain the trunk in this position gained importance. Although equivalent opportunities for prolonged vertical trunk orientation are rare for a primate terrestrial quadruped, even these primates have retained the ability to hold the trunk in an upright position, where it functions to allow an increased visual range and limited carrying, and plays a role in certain socially defined gestures. Consequently, a number of morphological correlates to truncal uprightness have evolved in the primates. These provide an important preadaptation to the bipedalism of chimpanzees and hominids.

The most important is a rearrangement of the viscera and diaphragm to allow support when the trunk is in a vertical position. In addition, the articulation of the neck and head changes its position from the very back of the head in early terrestrial mammals to a position more forward and underneath the head in the later appearing primates. In humans, with trunks always held in the upright position, this articulation is completely underneath the skull, at its approximate center.

Dietary Plasticity

The single most important factor in the primate ability to utilize widely different foods has been the retention of another primitive feature: different types of teeth. Early mammals have four functionally distinct types of teeth: incisors, canines, premolars, and molars. These are shown in Figure 3.3. The teeth are used for different purposes, and the presence of different tooth types allows a wide range of possible dental functions in both diet and environmental manipulation.

If a line is drawn down the middle of the upper or lower jaw, one side is the same as the other. That is, there is bilateral (two sided) symmetry. Usually, although not always, either jaw gives the same dental pattern, or the number of teeth of each type. This pattern is conveniently written as a formula: incisors/canines/premolars/molars. In the earliest mammals, the dental formula is usually considered 3/1/4/3, although recent discoveries suggest that early mammals may have had five rather than four premolars. From the former interpretation, the total number of teeth would be 44 (3 + 1 + 4 + 3 = 11 × 4), while according to the more recent interpretations, this number might be 48. The course of primate evolution is characterized by a reduction in the total number of teeth, but with only a few exceptions, no tooth *type* has been lost.

The maintenance of four different types of teeth is a reflection of the adaptability primates have in both diet and manipulation. Few primates have a truly specialized diet compared with specializations which have occurred in other mammals (for instance, the horse). While primate species may intensively utilize one food resource seasonally, naturalistic studies have almost always shown that a wide range of foods is eaten over the year. No primate dietary specialization has resulted in dental specializations that preclude using a wide range of food resources. Similarly, most primates use their teeth to some degree as an extension of their grasping ability, to manipulate (explore and modify) their environment. The major changes in primate dental evolution must be interpreted within this general context.

There are two types of dental change which have occurred in primate evolution: reduction of the number of teeth and morphological change (change in the form of a tooth). *2 f. dental f*

CHANGE IN TOOTH NUMBER

Prosimian dental formulas show some differences from the primitive mammalian pattern. Of

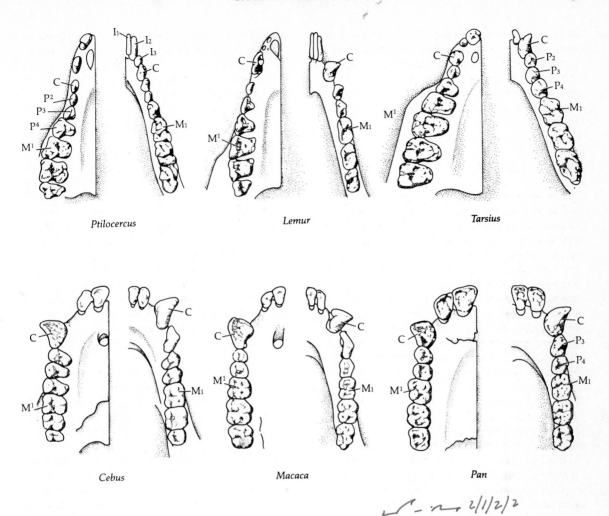

Ptilocercus   Lemur   Tarsius

Cebus   Macaca   Pan

FIGURE 3.3 *Upper and lower dentitions of prosimians (above) and higher primates (below), after Schultz (1969, figure 44). In all cases, the lower dentition is to the right. Note the retention of three incisors in the tupaiiform (upper left), the lower dental comb in the lemur, and the reduction to two premolars in the Old World higher primates (macaque, chimpanzee).*

all living primates, only the tree shrews (if primates) have retained the third incisor. With a few exceptions, most prosimians have a 2/1/3/3 dental formula, as do most New World monkeys (Ceboidea). In the higher primates of the Old World (monkeys, apes, and humans), a further reduction has occurred and the usual dental formula is 2/1/

2/3. In modern humans this is sometimes 2/1/2/2 since a number of people never develop their third molars (wisdom teeth).

Tooth numbering can be confusing and should be explained. Each type of tooth is numbered, starting with the tooth closest to the midline (the point between the central incisors). Generally, this number is written as a subscript if the tooth is in the lower jaw (mandibular) and a superscript if the tooth is in the upper jaw (maxillary). The tooth abbreviations are I (incisor), C (canine—usually written without number since there is only one), P (premolar), and M (molar). Thus, M^3 refers to the upper third molar (widsom tooth). There are two M^3s, right and left. The incisor lost in primate evolution is the third one, so the remaining incisors are

P₁ vvv
lost

numbered one and two. The problem comes in the premolars. It is thought that the premolar lost in prosimians and New World monkeys is the most forward one, so the premolars of these forms are numbered two, three, and four. The premolar lost in the Old World higher primates is thought to be the next forward one, so the remaining premolars are numbered three and four (one and two are missing). Thus, it is a paleontological convention to number living people's mandibular premolars P_3 and P_4.

The orthodontic and dental literature usually numbers these teeth one and two, and refers to them as "bicuspids." This dental convention is not used by paleontologists for two reasons. First, it does not reflect evolutionary history. If we were to name the most forward premolar P_1, this tooth would not be *homologous* (derived from the same structure in the common ancestor) for a New World and an Old World primate. With the pale-ontological system, the P_3 of a baboon is *homologous* with the P_3 of a spider monkey, while it is *analagous* with the P_2 of a spider monkey. Second, while the premolars of humans have two cusps (are *bicuspid*), this is not true of the premolars for many other primates, including some early hominids.

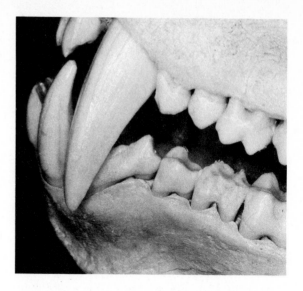

FIGURE 3.4   *An extreme form of the canine cutting complex is shown in this baboon with a partially opened jaw. The* back *edge of the upper canine shears against the sharpened* front *edge of the most forward lower premolar (P_3 in this case) as the jaw closes. To a lesser extent there is also a shear of the back edge of the* lower *canine against the front edge of the upper one. The canine projection of each jaw requires an empty space in the opposite jaw for the tooth to fit. This space, called a* diastema, *appears between the canine and incisor of the upper jaw, and the canine and premolar of the lower jaw.*

CHANGE IN TOOTH FORM

Relatively little morphological change has oc-curred in the evolution of the incisors. The upper incisors tend to be broad and spade-like (spatulate) in most higher primates. In the prosimians, smaller peg-like incisors generally occur, excepting the ro-dent-like specialization of the aye-aye. In many prosimians, the lower incisors, along with the ca-nines, form a large procumbant dental comb, used in grooming and feeding. Primates that feed with their hands tend to have reduced incisors, unless these teeth are used extensively in food prepara-tion. Hominid incisors are generally thought to be reduced from a more pongid-like (e.g., chimpanzee) condition. However, fossil apes also have small in-cisors; the modern pongid condition may be the result of incisor size increase from the ancestral condition.

pongid
↳ ↙ in
incisor

Canine size varies remarkably in primate evolu-tion. However, only three significant morphological variants occur. The usual primate canine form is that of a conical, pointed tooth with a sharp back

edge. This sharpened back (distal) edge occludes with the front (mesial) surface of the adjacent tooth in the opposite jaw to form a shearing complex (see Figure 3.4). Thus the back edge of the lower canine shears against the front edge of the upper canine. The most important action is the sharp distal edge of the upper canine against the sharp mesial edge of the lower premolar (the first in sequence). This canine cutting complex is an important part of both dietary adaptations and other behaviors. Cutting can play a part in obtaining foods as well as in preparing them for grinding between the molars and premolars. In other aspects of primate adapta-tion, the canines can be used for threats and for defense against other species, while in some of the higher primates, the canines (and gestures using them) have become important in dominance behavior and other aspects of role definition.

A second canine variant is the participation of the lower canines in the prosimian dental comb (Figures 3.2 and 3.3). Finally, the third variant is the hominid canine form. Hominid canines function as incisors and have become incisiform (shaped like incisors). They usually do not project beyond the tooth row; wear takes place only at the top (occlusal surface) and not along the distal surface. Although hominid canines are shaped like incisors, they are somewhat thicker. Their roots are much larger, suggesting that in the past the crowns were also larger and subject to forces which no longer occur. It is very likely that the hominid canine morphology evolved from canines like those of most other primates.

Canines in many higher primate species have extreme sexual dimorphism (size and form differ between males and females). In dimorphic species, female canines are quite small, barely projecting beyond the tooth row, while the males have much larger dagger-like canines. Even in modern humans, the canine shows the most sexual dimorphism of any tooth. Sexual dimorphism in canines is probably the result of other functions for the tooth than food gathering, preparation, and mastication. In the known terrestrial cercopithecoids, such as baboons, the canines play a role in maintaining male dominance both in fights and in displays that expose the front teeth, such as the snarl. In addition, canines are used in troop defense by males.

The general evolutionary trend in primate premolars is to increase the number of cusps. Cusps are the raised surfaces on top of molars and premolars. In many mammals they function in shearing by meeting cusps on the corresponding tooth on the opposite jaw with alternating sharp edges, similar to the way the upper canine and the most anterior lower premolar shear against each other. In most higher primates, the cusps do not function this way, although the ridges between the cusps in some cercopithecoid molars approximate this function. Generally, the cusps seem more important in spacing and aligning the teeth during chewing, especially before the dentition is fully erupted. They help guide the teeth of the opposing jaw into their proper position. This is particularly critical in higher primates, given the trend for a prolonged period of maturation, since this results in a long

period during which the dentition is not complete. Excepting the anterior lower premolar, the other premolars of the higher primates are molarized (become more like molars) and are bicuspid.

In the nonhuman higher primates, the anterior lower premolar has maintained the primitive single-cusped form. This cusp is large and canine-like; the front edge is sharp, occluding with the upper canine for shearing and cutting. Since the cross-section of the crown is more or less circular and the tooth is used for cutting, this premolar form is called "sectorial." Dentitions with two different premolar forms are "heterodontic" (different teeth). In recent hominids, the canines function like an incisor. Consequently, the anterior lower premolar, which no longer shears against the canine, has also changed its form. This tooth is bicuspid, like the other premolar, and the dentition is therefore called "homodontic" (same teeth).

Molar evolution is probably better understood and more often studied than the evolution of any other body part. This is largely because teeth are more often preserved as fossils than bones, and the molars are found more often than other teeth. Molar cusps all have specific names, and variation in the pattern that the cusps and fissures between them form is distinctive between certain groups of primates. For instance, the molar cusp pattern distinguishes some primates with the same dental formula, such as Old World monkeys and apes. In other cases, such as when comparing chimpanzees and humans, the molar cusp pattern is the same.

In the primates, there has been surprisingly little change in molar cusp pattern when compared with some other orders, although changes in specific features can be observed. Generally, primate molar evolution involves only little modification from the primitive mammalian form: mainly, the addition of [a cusp] a single cusp in the upper molars and the addition of two or three cusps in the lower molars along with the subsequent loss of one of the original cusps. The relative stability of the molars and premolars reflects their continued importance in grinding and crushing foods. The greatest modification in form can be found in those primates which eat grasses, a food that requires a particularly great amount of molar shearing during chewing. Various primate species have adapted to diets requiring an especially great amount of force during chewing by evolving larger teeth. While this might be considered a specialization in the adaptive sense, it actually makes the species more general-ized, since larger teeth do not prevent the species from eating foods that only require small teeth.

Parental Investment

The higher primates are characterized by a third trend that can best be described in terms of paren-tal investment. Parents spend more time in raising fewer children. The primate offspring learn more, and the chances for individual survival are greater. Some of the consequences of this trend can be seen in the reduction of litter size to normally single births, the reduction of female teats to two, and so on. In terms of behavior, living primates reflecting this trend almost always live in social groups. How-ever, the trend is probably best summarized as the evolution of intelligence. While living humans rep-resent the extreme for this trend, to varying de-grees it appears in all of the higher primates.

ELABORATION OF THE BRAIN

The elaboration of the brain in primate evolution is related to three evolving behavioral complexes: (1) increasing complexity and speed of learning, and the associated aspects of behavioral adaptabil-ity; (2) the evolution of complex social behavior and substantial role differences between members of primate societies; (3) the development of supe-rior forms of vision, including binocular and color, and improved hand-to-eye coordination.

The specific changes in primate brains related to these behavioral complexes involve both size and form. Turning first to size, generally prosimians have about the same brain size as other mammals of similar body size, whereas in the higher primates brain size is larger than in other mammals of simi-lar body size. This relative expansion of size is an important aspect of brain evolution, and is almost certainly connected to the increasing complexity of behaviors in higher primates. It does not seem to be related to the first trend (arboreal adaptation). This can be seen from the lack of brain size expan-sion in the living Malagasy prosimians, which oth-erwise parallel the higher primate adaptations.

The second aspect of brain evolution is the change in form (see Figure 3.5). Two different types

of change can be observed. First, primate evolution is characterized by different changes in various parts of the brain. For instance, with the increasing importance of vision, those portions of the brain associated with the input and recognition of visual signals expanded in size, while portions associated with hearing and smell contracted. The intregration of information required by three-dimensional and color vision led to the development of new cir-cuitries. In some higher primate species, whole new areas of the brain developed and expanded during the course of evolution. An "association area," where inputs from the various senses can be di-rectly brought together, appeared and expanded in the hominoids.

A second aspect of change in brain form is more difficult to observe. This change involves the ways in which brain cells are connected. The only direct indication is the increase in surface complexity. Size expansion alone requires more complex con-nections between the cells, but the trend goes be-yond this. The tendency in higher primates has been to prestructure the logical elements underly-ing certain class behaviors. This makes the behav-iors much easier to learn, and more importantly allows them to be learned quickly. Moreover, it re-sults in the ability of members of different popula-tions in the same species to correctly interpret one another's complex behaviors. A good example of prestructuring is the language ability of humans and chimpanzees. Language in these species is not learned through a Skinnerian "trial and error" pro-cess. Instead, the logic underlying all grammar seems to be prestructured when language is learned. The individual learns the particular gram-mar variants and vocabulary for its language, but since this learning involves "plugging into" a logi-cal structure already present, a very complex be-havior is learned quickly. Similar prestructuring may underlie all complex social interactions involv-ing numerous role differences.

GESTATION AND THE PLACENTA

Primate evolution is marked by a progressive in-crease in the efficiency of the placenta. Increasing the efficiency of providing nutrition for the fetus allows for lengthening the period of gestation, an-other primate trend. These developments are ad-vantageous in an order reducing the frequency of

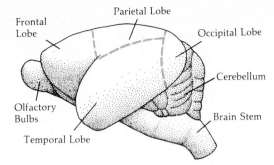

Frontal Lobe · Parietal Lobe · Occipital Lobe · Cerebellum · Brain Stem · Olfactory Bulbs · Temporal Lobe

Microcebus (primitive prosimian)

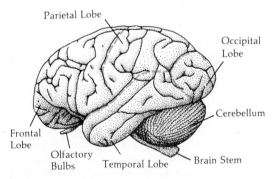

Frontal Lobe · Parietal Lobe · Occipital Lobe · Cerebellum · Brain Stem · Olfactory Bulbs · Temporal Lobe

Cebus (platyrrhine monkey)

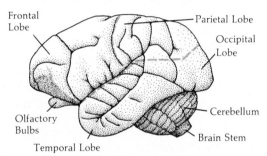

Parietal Lobe · Occipital Lobe · Cerebellum · Frontal Lobe · Olfactory Bulbs · Temporal Lobe · Brain Stem

Pan troglodytes (chimpanzee)

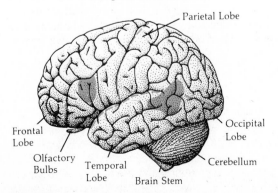

Parietal Lobe · Occipital Lobe · Cerebellum · Frontal Lobe · Olfactory Bulbs · Temporal Lobe · Brain Stem

Homo sapiens

FIGURE 3.5 *Comparison of the brain (in side view) in four living primate species, after Jolly and Plog (1976). In a general way, this represents an evolutionary sequence:* Microcebus, Cebus, Pan troglodytes, *and* Homo sapiens.
Note the relative expansion of the temporal, parietal, and frontal lobes and the increased complexity of the surface. The olfactory bulbs decrease in size. The four brains are drawn to the same size. Some of the areas believed important for the production of speech and language in humans are situated on the left cerebral hemisphere and are shown in Homo sapiens.

multiple births and relying more on learned behavior. There is clearly a trend in primate evolution to invest increasing amounts of time and energy, both prenatally and postnatally, in a smaller number of offspring. Many mammals give birth to a large number of offspring at a time, letting the environment select the best-adapted phenotype from the array of possibilities. Such a strategy is usually characteristic of species that do not greatly modify the behavior of their offspring through learning. The strategy which has developed in primate evolution is as opposite as possible. Higher primate species are generally characterized by single births. The survival potential of the offspring is enhanced through parental molding and modification of behavior. Given the evolution of this strategy, a prolonged period of fetal development is advantageous.

It is possible that the increasing placental efficiency and prolonged gestation period have had another effect on primate evolution, particularly in Anthropoidea. There is some evidence that the more intimate mingling of blood systems of the mother and fetus, over a long period of time, affects the survival of mutant proteins by increasing the effectiveness of maternal antibodies. This would result in fewer surviving mutant proteins and thus might act to slow down the rate of evolutionary change in a species, all other factors being equal, because the rate of change depends in part on genetic variability. One possible result is to decrease the rate of genetic differentiation under conditions of geographic isolation, and consequently to prolong the time necessary to establish reproductive isolation in geographically isolated populations. In other words, the effect could be to slow down the rate of speciation.

PROLONGED LIFE PERIODS

Another aspect of this trend is the lengthening of postnatal life periods. As Table 3.1 shows, this trend, as most of the others discussed, is more pronounced in the higher primates and has its greatest expression in the hominids. The table breaks the total lifespan into three periods. Lengthening in the period of child dependency on the mother, the infantile phase, extends the time of learning. The evolutionary trend is to increase the amount of learned behavior—a primate survival strategy already discussed.

The lengthened juvenile phase corresponds to the period marked by the time between full parental dependency and the expectation of adult behavior. For primates, this is a period of play, which functions as a way of practicing adult behavior. Lengthening of this period results from both an increased amount of learned behavior and the progressive elaboration of social behavior and role differentiation that characterizes primate evolution. For instance, in baboon society, many different adult behaviors can be appropriate, depending both on the circumstances and the social status of the individual. Both of these factors change considerably during a normal baboon's lifespan.

Finally, there is an increase in the adult phase of the lifespan. It is reasonable to believe that this increase is the result of the adaptive advantages of learned behavior, and to some extent this is true. However, the increase is also likely a result of the trend for decreasing the frequency of multiple births. Giving birth to fewer offspring at a time selects for a longer reproductive span, increasing the total number of offspring born.

One result of these changes, not shown in the table, is the lengthening of the average period between births. Excepting humans, primate females generally do not mate while they still have a dependent infant. This prolongs the period between births, especially in the hominoids, and consequently helps select for a longer lifespan to increase the total number of births. Prosimian births are generally spaced one year apart, baboon births two to three years apart, and chimpanzee births four to five years apart. My work suggests that early hominid births were spaced only about three to four years apart. In modern humans this reversed trend has been continued as the result of social behavior, changing roles, and different expectations during the period of infant dependency. Human births can be spaced as little as two years apart, although most living groups average wider birth spacing. In combination with the long lifespan of humans, this change has led to the expansion of human populations and has contributed to our past evolutionary success. Some scientists believe that shortened birth spacing may be intimately connected with hominid origins.

A Brief Review of Primate Evolution

The fossil history of primates is complete enough to be confusing. This may seem to be a contradiction, but it is really an inevitable consequence of the problems involved in interpreting the fossil record. When only a few fossil primates were known, it was easy to relate these to one another and provide a relatively simple picture of primate phylog-

TABLE 3.1 Comparison of primate life periods, modified after Napier and Napier (1967). Since body size can affect these figures, the best comparisons are between the small gibbon and the macaque and lemur, and between the chimpanzee and the modern human.

	Fetal Phase (days)	Infantile Phase (years)	Juvenile Phase (years)	Adult Phase (years)	Total Lifespan (years)
Lemur	126	0.8	1.8	11+	14+
Macaque	168	1.5	6	20	28
Gibbon	210	2	6.5	20+	30+
Chimpanzee	225	3	7	30	40
Modern human	266	6	9	50+	65+

TABLE 3.2   Taxonomic description of what many believe to be the first primate adaptive radiation, the superfamily Plesiadapoidea. Whether any of the later primates evolved from this group is questionable. From Jolly and Plog (1979).

Groups in Superfamily Plesiadapoidea	Description	Time	Range
Family Plesiadapidae 5 genera, including *Plesiadapis*	Medium-sized vegetarians with large incisors; some specialized for powerful gnawing.	Paleocene-Eocene	Europe North America
Family Carpolestidae 3 genera	Mouse- to rat-sized omnivores, with large incisors and an enlarged premolar for slicing.	Paleocene	North America
Family Paromomyidae 6 genera, including *Purgatorius*, possibly the earliest known primate	A diverse group of mouse- to rat-sized animals, including some very primitive forms. One genus with long, tweezer-like incisors.	Late Cretaceous-Eocene	North America Europe
Family Picrodontidae 2 genera	Two tiny, mouse-sized animals with very specialized teeth; perhaps fed on nectar and insects.	Paleocene	North America

eny. With more fossil material, and renewed interest in comparative studies ranging from gross form to biochemistry, a number of important questions can be asked of the fossil record for the first time, and many of these simply cannot be answered yet.

PRIMATE ORIGINS

The time, place, and reasons underlying the origin of the primates provide a good example of the state of primate paleontology. The classic explanation of primate origins comes as a result of comparative anatomy. Since elements of the arboreal adaptation are shared by virtually all living primates, it is argued that arboreal adaptation must represent the ancestral condition and therefore the cause of primate origins. An alternative explanation, suggested by M. Cartmill, credits the development of certain primate features to an adaptive stage preceding an arboreal adaptation, thus limiting the directions that the subsequent arboreal adaptation could take. This explanation envisions primates as initially small, shrub-layer predators, developing hand-to-eye coordination, grasping, binocular vision, and so on, in this habitat. The fossil record does not provide clear evidence for ei-

ther explanation, partially because it is not obvious which early fossils are actually primates.

ANCIENT AND MODERN PROSIMIANS

According to one school of thought, the earliest primates originated before the Cenozoic era, which is known as the age of mammals (Figure 1.2). During the latest portion of the Mesozoic era, some of the small insect-eating mammals may have shifted their diet to a greater use of fruits and vegetal foods. One of these, *Purgatorius* (first represented by a single molar from Montana), may be an early primate.

In the earliest Cenozoic epoch, the Paleocene, the ecological changes accompanying and perhaps causing the extinction of so many reptiles provided new habitats and opportunities for the emerging mammals. Some of these, represented in both North America and Europe (which were then a single continent) have been identified as primates. Four different families have been recognized, all in the extinct superfamily Plesiadapoidea (see Table 3.2). It is possible that none of these is ancestral to later primates (Figure 3.6, p. 56). The best known of the Paleocene forms is *Plesiadapis* (see Figure 3.7, p. 57). About the size of a small cat, this genus shows

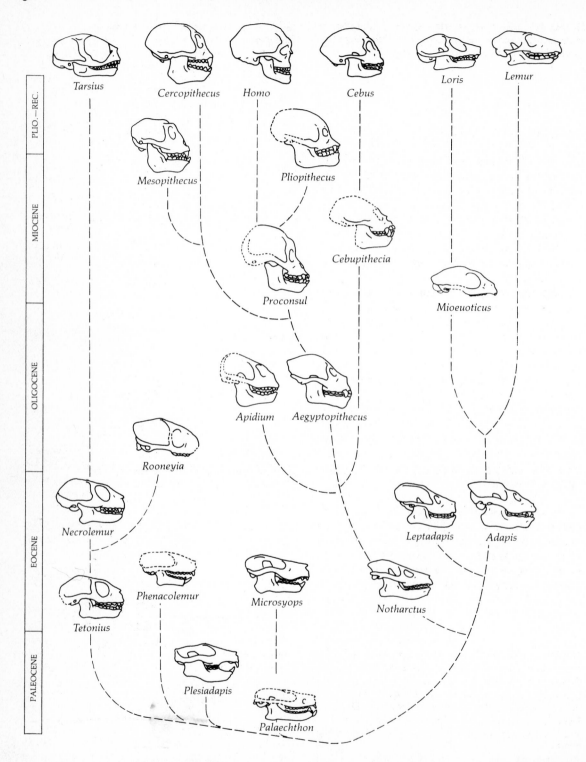

FIGURE 3.6   *(left) A phylogenetic diagram of fossil and living primate relations, after Gingerich and Schoeninger, reference Chapter 2. All relations are considered tenative.*

almost none of the later primate adaptations, and with its loss of the canine and some premolars, it appears to have been evolving in a different direction. *Plesiadapis* is superficially very rodent-like, with its very large central incisors. The digits retain claws, the orbits face to the side and are not surrounded by bone, the snout is long, and the brain very small. Besides the clear adaptations to arboreal life found in the limbs and feet, only a few details of the molars and the bony portion of the ear suggest it might be a primate.

While the Plesiadapoidea survive into the Eocene epoch, this period also sees the appearance of true prosimians (see Table 3.3, p. 58). North America and Europe separated during this time, and the primate forms on these continents became increasingly divergent. Another important development is the appearance of true rodents; these probably outcompeted many of the rodent-like Plesiadapiformes, and replaced them. The Eocene prosimians appeared before the northern continents separated, and almost surely reached Africa from Europe when these continents connected later in the Eocene. The best represented of the early prosimians are the lemur-like *Adapis* and *Notharctus* (Figure 3.7). In comparison with the *Plesiadapis*, the orbits are more forward and surrounded by bone, the ancestral condition of the canines and premolars is retained, the digits have nails and are relatively elongated and mobile, and the brain size is larger. Evidence suggests that these are arboreally adapted genera, broadly ancestral to the living Lemuri-

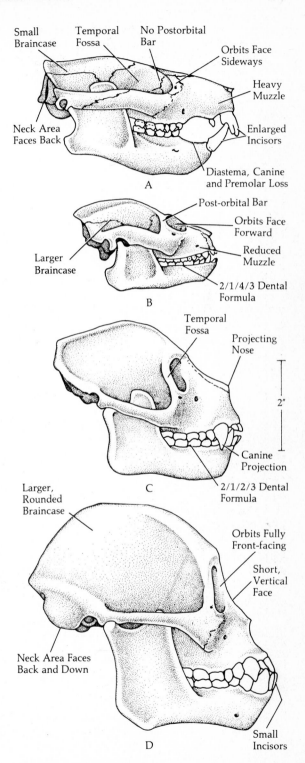

FIGURE 3.7   *(right) Skulls of primates representing the Paleocene, later Eocene, Oligocene, and Miocene forms: (A) Plesiadapis; (B) Adapis parisiensis, Eocene lemuriform primate; (C) Aegyptopithecus zeuxis, Fayum catarrhine (drawn from a cast of partly reconstructed skull); (D) female Proconsul africanus, early Miocene pongid (after a reconstruction by Davis and Napier). (Figure from Jolly and Plog, 1976.)*

TABLE 3.3   The genera of the "second wave" of primate evolution, the Lemuriformes and Tarsiiformes of the Eocene. Note that some families but no genera of this radiation are common to North America and Europe, showing that the major split between them occurred in the Paleocene, and that the two faunas were now evolving independently on either side of the widening Atlantic. From Jolly and Plog (1979).

Taxon	Description	Time	Geographical Distribution
Infraorder Lemuriformes Superfamily Adapoidea	The lemur branch of the prosimians. Early lemurs.		
Family Adapidae Several genera, including *Notharctus*	A diverse family of medium-sized lemurs; includes several robust vegetarians and some small, large-eyed (nocturnal ?) forms.	Eocene-Oligocene	North America Europe
Infraorder Tarsiiformes	The tarsier branch of the prosimians.		
Family Tarsiidae Several genera	Small, tarsier-like hoppers, close to ancestry of modern *Tarsius*, but less insectivorous, more omnivorous.	Eocene-Recent	Europe Asia
Family Anaptomorphidae Several genera	American tarsier-like primates. Mostly mixed diets; some nocturnal forms. May have included ancestors of anthropoids.	Eocene-Miocene	North America Europe Asia
(Uncertain Taxonomic Status) *Poncaungia, Amphipithecus*	Several fragments, may be early anthropoids.	Eocene	Burma

formes now restricted to Madagascar. The fact that their ancestry among the earlier Plesiadapiformes cannot be clearly established suggests to some that these are the first true primates, and that their adaptations are due to an earlier (as yet unidentified) shrub-layer predator stage.

The other modern prosimian infraorder that can be identified in the Eocene is Tarsiiformes. Whether the higher primates evolved from a lemuriform or a tarsiiform ancestor is one of the important unresolved questions in fossil primate studies (Figure 3.6). Living tarsiiforms seem more similar to higher primates than living lemuriforms. However, the fossil record shows some striking morphological links between Eocene adapids and the earliest Oligocene Anthropoidea.

HIGHER PRIMATES

The earliest Old World Anthropoidea are dated to the Oligocene epoch (Figure 1.2), and all come from a single area in Egypt, the Fayum. During the Oligocene, the Fayum was a warm, swampy region.

This was fortunate because it provided rare circumstances for the preservation of arboreal forms (it is unlikely that primates lived on the floor of what was then a swamp), but unfortunate in that it samples only one of the many possible habitats that Oligocene higher primates may have lived in.

E. L. Simons, who has done most of the recent work with the Fayum primates, divided them into two subfamilies: the Parapithecinae and the Dryopithecinae. The former retains three premolars, while there are only two premolars in the latter. In Simons' view, the parapithecines are ancestral to living Old World monkeys, while living apes and humans (i.e., hominoids) find their ancestry in the Oligocene dryopithecines.

The parapithecine forms (*Parapithecus, Apidium*) are about the size of small monkeys. Relative tooth size in *Apidium* suggests a howler monkey-like adaptation to leaf eating, while *Parapithecus* appears more generalized. Both of these are represented by jaws and teeth, with a cranial (frontal) bone thought to represent *Apidium*.

The dryopithecine genera (in order of ascending size *Oligopithecus, Aeolopithecus, Propliopithecus,* and

Aegyptopithecus) range up to the size of a large cat. Of these, only *Aegyptopithecus* is represented by more than jaws and teeth. A virtually complete cranium (Figure 3.7) allows comparison with later fossil apes. *Oligopithecus* is the earliest and most primitive of the forms (some authors suggest it may not be an anthropoid). The late appearing *Aeolopithecus* is represented by a single very worn mandible with large canines. *Propliopithecus* and *Aegyptopithecus* probably represent an ancestor-descendant sequence. Recent discoveries suggest that the ancestors for this lineage may be represented in the Eocene in Burma.

Aegyptopithecus was once described as a "monkey with an ape's teeth." Actually, brain size is relatively small, the snout is much longer than that of most living monkeys (except terrestrial baboons), and there was a prominent external nose, suggesting that the sense of smell was still adaptively important. In spite of this, some features are remarkably ape-like, including the apparent organization of the brain as seen by studies of the inside of the cranium. The incisors are quite small, while the postcanine teeth (behind the canine, i.e., premolars and molars) are large and retain an extra shelf of enamel on their sides (the lingual, or tongue, side of the upper teeth and the buccal, or cheek, side of the lowers) called a cingulum. The canines are large and projecting; the uppers form a cutting edge against the lower premolars. Interestingly, *Aegyptopithecus* might have had a tail.

The available evidence suggests that *Aegyptopithecus* is probably an ancestor of later fossil apes as well as of humans (Figure 3.6). Its anatomy suggests that it was a generalized hand-feeding omnivore. Unfortunately, with the lack of parapithecine skulls and clearly associated postcranial skeletons for any of these primates, little is understood of the reasons for cercopithecoid-hominoid divergence. (While the Fayum deposits have yielded many postcranial remains, it is difficult to establish their taxonomic affinities.)

MIOCENE FORMS

The cercopithecoids were not especially successful until quite recently. In the Miocene epoch, hominoid descendants of *Aegyptopithecus* initially inhabited forests in Africa, and later a wider variety of habitats all over the tropical regions of the Old World. Cercopithecoids were rare for most of this

period, although toward the end they become much more common and seem to replace most of the fossil apes.

It would appear that the Miocene fossil apes underwent an early adaptive radiation, which for the most part was proven unsuccessful by the end of the epoch. From this adaptive radiation evolved a number of forms that parallel the living monkeys; others parallel the living apes. And one of the Miocene hominoids evolved into hominids. Hominids are the only really successful branch of the entire radiation.

The earliest dryopithecine genus of Miocene fossil hominoids is *Proconsul*. Remains of *Proconsul* species are known from approximately 19-13 million years BP in East Africa. While this region is characterized by dry open grasslands today, during the early and part of the middle Miocene it was a high area, sloping downward toward the west and virtually completely forest covered.

Although the taxonomy is not completely clear, there may have been a small (pygmy chimpanzee sized or smaller) and medium (chimpanzee sized) *Proconsul* species, with a larger (small gorilla sized) species evolving later. An alternative explanation is that only one species with marked sexual dimorphism occurs at some sites. It is not clear whether in this case it is the same species that is present at each site. One factor that makes the *Proconsul* taxonomy difficult to interpret is that the fossil remains only sample the fringes of a total distribution that likely extended through West Africa. Besides these *Proconsul* species a related genus (*Limnopithecus*) included even smaller gibbon-like apes. *Proconsul* is represented almost entirely by jaws and teeth. The dentitions of the various species differ only in size. They all agree in an expression of dramatic sexual dimorphism; males appear to have had much larger canines and probably weighed about twice as much as females. As in *Aegyptopithecus*, the incisors were small compared with the postcanine teeth and a cingulum was retained.

Cranial material, as well as a partial postcranial skeleton, is known for only females of the smallest species (*Proconsul africanus*); neither of the two crania known is complete, and the skeleton is subadult. The female skull (Figures 3.7 and 1.1) had a moderate snout and lacked the bony ridges (browridges) that appear over the eyes of living pongids and many fossil hominids. Both of these features

[handwritten marginal note: start / separation of + ape lineage]

are feminine for small pongids; the males and the larger *Proconsul* species may have had browridges and much larger snouts.

The postcranial skeleton is of great importance because it demonstrates that *Proconsul* was not a brachiator. While it may have hung by its arms during feeding, the main form of arboreal locomotion seems to have been climbing and quadrupedal walking on branches. The skeleton lacks many of the specific adaptations held in common by living apes and humans. For instance, the forearm and wrist were not as mobile and the thumb could not

be fully rotated. These data strongly imply that *Proconsul* represents a stage before the separation of the human and ape lineages.

This separation is a critically important topic, since it involves the origin of hominids. For this reason it has become a very controversial topic in evolutionary studies. Before becoming immersed in the controversy, it is first necessary to identify those characteristics that are unique to hominids, in the hope that these will help in identifying the earliest hominids and provide insight into why they diverged and evolved in a different direction.

SUMMARY

The living primates are characterized by a limited degree of diversity. Restrictions in their range and adaptations result from the common expression of distinct evolutionary trends for the order. Two of these, an arboreal adaptation and dietary plasticity, are common to all members of the order. The third, expanded parental investment, mainly distinguishes the higher primates. The results of these trends have generally limited the evolutionary potential of primate taxa. In terms of numbers and diversity, most of them have not been extraordinarily successful. A few, however, have met with marked success. These have almost always been higher primates, and some amount of terrestrial adaptation characterizes their habitat usage.

Primates may have been more successful in the past. Earlier forms in the Paleocene and Eocene were widespread and are common in fossil assemblages. Early prosimians of modern aspect have been found on every continent except South America, Australia, and Antarctica. Higher primates originated by at least the beginning of the Oligocene, but no forms have been found outside of Africa until the middle Miocene. Hominoidea seems to have been the more successful group midway

through primate evolution; Oligocene and Miocene hominoids occupied habitats which today are utilized by Cercopithecoidea. The cercopithecoid radiation replaced most of the hominoids in the later Miocene. All of the living hominoid taxa except ourselves are relict populations that will likely soon become extinct.

The early and middle Miocene hominoids that are ancestral to living humans and apes are known only from East Africa. The several known species differed mainly in size. They were arboreally adapted, utilizing a quadrupedal form of locomotion possibly combined with arm hanging. There seem to have been marked size differences between males and females of the same species. These forms are best known from their dental remains, which differ from both living humans and apes in their combination of small incisors, cutting canines, and posterior teeth which expand in size toward the rear of the tooth row. The few cranial remains suggest snout elongation compared with living apes and a better developed sense of smell. While brain size relative to body size is unknown, studies suggest that the organization of the brain does not differ from that of the living apes.

STATE OF THE ART

One of the more vexing problems inherent in the material discussed in this chapter is concerned with the origin of Anthropoidea. The earliest of the

higher primates are found in the early Oligocene deposits of the Fayum, at the very northeast corner of Africa. Two different groups seem to be present

[handwritten note at bottom: Fayum - NE Africa]

before the beginning of the Oligocene, distinguished by the number of premolars. This is known because the ancestral condition (for these primates) is three premolars, and the earliest Oligocene form (*Oligopithecus*) has only two while others retain all three. Consequently, the division between the two Oligocene groups took place before the earliest Fayum deposits. Since both are in Anthropoidea, the implication is that Anthropoidea appeared before their division.

Identifying the origin of these primates is problematic for several reason. First, very little is actually known of the early and middle Oligocene forms. They are mainly represented by jaws, teeth, and unassociated postcranial remains. Moreover, they only sample swamp forest adapted species on a continent which has the most dramatic diversity of primates known today. Without more detailed knowledge of the early Oligocene Anthropoidea, both from the Fayum and from other preserved habitats, it is difficult to reconstruct what their immediate ancestry may have been like.

Second, although the earliest known higher primates are restricted to Africa, the inference that Anthropoidea originated there in the later Eocene is problematic. Only one relevant Eocene fossil has been discovered on the African continent, and this species, which may not even be primate, clearly has nothing to do with the origins of Anthropoidea. With no earlier African fossils to consider, the search focuses on the late Eocene of other continents. In this case, there is some success since one taxon that has been regarded as a possible ancestor of Anthropoidea is *Amphipithecus* of Burma. This taxon was initially represented by a single lower jaw fragment, and its affinities to other primates have long remained unclear (Table 3.3). However, very recently new material was discovered in Burma that may resemble *Aegyptopithecus*. The new

specimens, mainly jaws and teeth, have not yet been described, but the affinities eventually determined for them will be of great interest and importance with regard to the issues discussed here.

Apart from this material, there remain only indirect approaches to determine the probable ancestry of Anthropoidea. Consequently, it is no surprise that the question of which prosimian infraorder holds the taxon ancestral to Anthropoidea is a matter of controversy. The classic view based on comparative anatomy of living forms is that Tarsiiformes is the ancestral infraorder. The living species have the closest resemblances to Anthropoidea. However, some workers have argued that the fossil Lemuriformes represent a more credible ancestor. These arguments are based mainly on dental similarities between fossil Lemuriformes and the Oligocene Anthropoidea.

Needless to say, the whole problem simply cannot be resolved given the present lack of direct evidence. Each of the morphological arguments is internally consistent; since they rely on different evidence, it is impossible to choose between them. Moreover, the more basic problem of *why* Anthropoidea arose is yet to be addressed, let alone resolved. The few dental differences between the Oligocene forms and later Eocene prosimians from Eurasia provide little basis for understanding what behavioral or habitat differences may have been involved. A study of the endocast (an impression of the inside of a cranium) of a later Oligocene taxon, *Aegyptopithecus*, suggests an almost pongid level of basic neural organization. This strongly indicates an early behavioral distinction for the suborder, but what this may have been remains unknown.

In sum, the origin of the higher primates remains an open topic from the theoretical perspective, the perspective of data analysis, and the perspective of data collection.

FURTHER READINGS

BRAMBLETT, C. A. 1976. *Patterns of Primate Behavior*. Mayfield, Palo Alto.

A balanced introduction to primates, emphasizing behavior and ecology and presenting both a broad survey of many primates and specific field studies for some.

CARTMILL, M. 1975. *Primate Origins*. Burgess, Minneapolis.

The "alternative" theory of primate origins, suggesting that a truly arboreal adaptation may not have been the factor that initially separated primates from their closest relatives.

GAVAN, J. 1977. *Paleoanthropology and Primate Evolution*. Brown, Dubuque.

A simple introduction to the basics of primate evolution.

JOLLY, A. 1972. *The Evolution of Primate Behavior*. Macmillan, New York.

A well-organized, simple introduction to primate behavior.

LE GROS CLARK, W. E. 1966. *History of the Primates*, 5th ed. Phoenix, Chicago.

A basic introduction to primate paleontology. While this is now somewhat out of date, it is the best presentation of the classic approach to primate origins and evolution.

————. 1971. *The Antecedents of Man*. 3rd ed. Quadrangle, Chicago.

The more technical version of the preceding reference. This book is organized by adaptive system rather than by species and consequently is particularly useful for a further understanding of primate trends.

LENNEBERG, E. H. 1971. Of Language, Knowledge, Apes, and Brains. *Journal of Psycholinguistic Research* 1:1–29.

A reasonably understandable analysis of the structural basis for chimpanzee communication as it was understood in the late 1960s.

LINDEN, E. 1974. *Apes, Men and Language*. Dutton, New York.

A simple introduction to the chimpanzee communication studies.

NAPIER, J. R., and P. H. NAPIER. 1967. *A Handbook of Living Primates*. Academic Press, New York.

This is a handbook of basic data and references for all primates.

PREMACK, D. 1976. Language and Intelligence in Ape and Man. *American Scientist* 64:674–683.

A review of what was perhaps the most comprehensive attempt to teach a chimpanzee a form of human language.

RADINSKY, L. B. 1975. Primate Brain Evolution. *American Scientist* 63:656–663.

An introduction to the basic structural aspects of brain evolution in the primates, emphasizing what can be directly determined from fossil endocasts.

SCHULTZ, A. H. 1969. *The Life of Primates*. Universe, New York.

A simple but comprehensive introduction to comparative primate morphology.

SIMONDS, P. E. 1974. *The Social Primates*. Harper & Row, New York.

A particularly useful introduction to social behavior, emphasizing the higher primates.

SIMONS, E. L. 1967. The Earliest Apes. *Scientific American* 217(6):28–35.

A review of the Oligocene primates of the Fayum.

————. 1972. *Primate Evolution*. Macmillan, New York.

This is the most up-to-date source book available for primate paleontology.

————, P. ANDREWS, and D. R. PILBEAM. 1978. Cenozoic Apes. In *Evolution of African Mammals*, eds. V. J. Maglio and H. B. S. Cooke. Harvard University Press, Cambridge, pp. 120–146.

The most up-to-date statement of the phylogenetic affinities of the Miocene apes, according to one school of thought.

PART TWO

THE APPEARANCE OF THE FIRST HUMANS

CHAPTER FOUR

Hominid Features

In the context of primate evolution, and the particular trends that are common to Anthropoidea, only a relatively few morphological and behavioral complexes are distinctly different in humans and their ancestors. Following a general discussion of how morphology and behavior can be related in fossil samples, this chapter outlines the three morphological complexes that distinguish our lineage. These are associated with behavioral changes, and the nature and details of these behavioral changes are also discussed. It is in this intricate relation of behavior and morphology that the process of evolution can be seen most clearly, translating the activities of once living populations into permanent inherited gene pool changes.

The Living and the Dead

A discussion of human origins presupposes an understanding of exactly what it was that originated.

From the preceding chapter, it should be clear that human origins did *not* involve the appearance of grasping hands or binocular vision; these are features common to all higher primates and almost surely were attributes of prehuman primates. There are three morphological complexes that have come to characterize the hominid line (humans and human ancestors back to the last common ancestor with apes). None of these is truly unique. Each represents an extension or elaboration of developments that appear in at least some of the higher primates. Moreover, each represents a complex interplay between form and behavior. The three hominid complexes are (1) the development of complex structured behavior that is learned and the evolution of associated changes in the brain, (2) the development of bipedal locomotion, and (3) changes in the masticatory system (the jaws and teeth). The last involves a functional change in the canine from a cutting and slashing tooth to one used for gripping and holding, and the development of postcanine teeth especially adapted for eating foods that require prolonged or powerful chewing.

[handwritten margin notes: "3 hominid complexes" and "functional in canine"]

65

FORM AND FUNCTION

Understanding these morphological complexes requires an analysis of how form relates to function in fossil remains. This relation can sometimes be determined by analogy with living populations. When form and function can be related in living primates, there is a logical basis for inferring function *from* form in fossils. One good example involves the large orbits of some fossil primates. In this case, the large orbits indicate large eyes. In living primates, this morphology is inevitably an adaptation to frequent activity when the light is dim, and it is logical to assume that the same interpretation applies to the fossils in question.

GENETICS AND THE ENVIRONMENT

Relating form and function in fossil bones raises the immediate question of what factors are responsible for the final bone form. To what extent is this form the result of inheritance, and to what extent is it the result of how the bone was used during growth and development? There is increasing evidence that bone can be significantly altered during growth, and even after most growth has ceased, by the forces that normally act on it. These forces come from the muscles attaching to bones, from the body weight, and in the case of the jaws also from the load between the teeth during chewing. Bone is known to respond to forces, in both size and form, according to three "laws":

Wolff's Law—The external form and internal trabecular structure of the bone are related to its function.

Roux's Law—Bone is so made as to obtain the maximum strength by means of the minimum amounts of material.

Pauwels' Law—The motor system is so made as to maintain the bending stress (the force of bending on bone) as small as possible.

The three "laws" are really generalizations about the final form that bone takes in a living body. They state, in effect, that bone will be adapted to do what it normally does, provide strength, and resist the action of the forces that act on it.

How does bone end up being so well adapted to the functioning of an organism during its life? Ex-

perimental evidence shows that differences in diet or the removal of muscles can strongly influence the final size and form of bone. During life, bone is strained (or deformed) by the normal activities of an organism. This deformation stimulates the growth process in the affected area, and results in changes in form that leave the bone better adapted to resist the same forces in the future.

The particular pattern of strain (deformation due to force) in human bones has been analyzed under varying conditions, and the form of the bone seems to be responsive to the normal forces acting on it. The converse is of great interest, because it implies that from the particular form of human fossil bones, it might be possible to determine the normal forces that once acted on them. A demonstration that these forces differed from the forces known to occur today would give insight into behavioral and adaptive differences between living people and their ancestors.

Yet it is clear that there is a genetic basis to bone form that must also be taken into account. The problem is that selection would be expected to cause exactly the same changes in a bone as would changes in function. Bone will always develop to adapt itself to the way it is used, which is just what one would expect genetic change due to selection to result in. This is a paradox in analysis that cannot always be directly solved. The *speed* of change may be a key. A developmental change due to change in function can occur within a generation of the functional change. Something like this seems to have happened in recent human evolution. The introduction of the knife and fork rapidly changed the forces acting on the mandible during chewing. Less chewing was required, and the immediate result was a reduction in mandible size; with less muscle and dental force acting on the mandible, it did not grow as large. The teeth apparently have a higher inheritance factor and did not reduce in size. The result is familiar to many of us: there is often not enough room in the reduced mandible for the last molar (wisdom tooth) to erupt. Without modern dentistry, this could result in genetic change through selection acting on the teeth. Individuals with the greatest imbalance between adult jaw and tooth size might, on the average, have fewer surviving offspring because of infection (and its effects) due to impacted or partially erupted third molars. Individuals with small teeth would have a better chance of surviving, and the net result would be a

interplay √ behavior, morphology etc
" " developmental + genetic changes

reduction of tooth size over time. This example serves to demonstrate two different things: the interplay between behavior (use of the knife and fork) and morphology, and the interplay between developmental (in the mandible) and genetic (in the dentition) changes.

RECONSTRUCTING BEHAVIOR

Reconstructing behavior from fossil remains is another level of abstraction and requires information about more than one portion of the organism as well as about its environment. For instance, the arm bones in many early fossil humans are unusually thick, and the bone itself is structured to resist forces of bending and compression. A simple analogy could be made with the African apes. When these primates are quadrupedal, their arms support part of their body weight. Because of the additional forces acting on them, the arm bones are thick and structured to resist bending and compression. Thus one might suppose that the evidence of the arms shows that the early humans were quadrupedal.

However, this is not borne out by other evidence. Two things are particularly relevant here. First, body weight provides only a portion of the force acting on bone—more is provided by the muscles. Second, the pelvic remains of these same early humans show that they were bipedal during locomotion and that they could no more easily walk on all four limbs than you or I. This additional information makes it seem likely that forelimb form and thickness was a response to muscle use, showing that these early humans were far more powerful and active than any humans today and probably could be compared in their strength to chimpanzees of similar size. This tells us that muscular strength was an important part of early human adaptation, and contrasts with the much lower levels of strength required of any living people on a day-to-day basis. The real significance with reference to human evolution is found more in the decreasing importance of strength than in the resultant changes in the form of the arm.

Finally, to go a step further, we may wonder what particular activities required these powerful arms. There is no simple or single answer to this because a wide range of behaviors could benefit from muscular power. One behavior which might have been of particular importance, however, was the practice of clubbing or bludgeoning prey and predators before projectile weapons were developed. To be *effective*, bludgeoning requires power, which could be maximized through either speed or force. But to be *safe*, it is important to maintain the greatest possible distance between bludgeoner and bludgeonee. Long arms could help provide this distance; being hurt by a thrashing or biting animal is something like falling off a cliff—either it happens or it doesn't and for prevention an inch is as good as a mile. In possible confirmation of this speculation, it is interesting that the only known hominid skeleton with both arm and leg bones from the Pliocene has arm bones which are extremely powerful and proportionately longer than those in any living humans.

proportionately longer arms.

HOMINID VERSUS MODERN HUMAN

The discussion above leads to one final comment concerning hominid features. What is typically hominid is not necessarily the same as what is typically human today. Some features that have characterized most of hominid evolution do not appear in living people, as in the case of long, powerful arms associated with bipedalism. During most of human evolution, the postcanine teeth were much larger relative to body size that those of either the living African apes or of living humans. One might suppose from studying living species that no unique hominid adaptation appears in relative postcanine tooth size, but the earlier members of our lineage show otherwise. Taking another example, a dramatic difference in size between males and females seems to have been common in humans until quite recently.

Where this distinction becomes especially important is in the interpretation of hominid origins and recognition of the earliest hominids. The first members of our lineage may be more *hominid-like* than their pongid contemporaries without necessarily being more *like living humans*.

Features Associated with Intelligence

Intelligence, and the features associated with it, would seem to be the most evident if not the most important hominid characteristic. The hominid complex is an elaboration of a trend in all of the higher primates; and the initial developments in the hominid line must have been based on features and capabilities already present.

The evolution of intelligence in our lineage is marked by changes in relative brain size, as well as in the structure or organization of the brain. Analysis of these changes can be approached by comparison of living species, but some additional information can be gained by studies of the impression that the brain leaves on the inside of the cranium. A cast of the inside of a skull (an *endocast*) can occur naturally during fossilization or can be made artificially if the cranium is partially intact. Some of the surface features that are visible on endocasts can be related to behavioral capabilities of the brain.

BRAIN SIZE AND INTELLIGENCE

One obvious characteristic of human brains is their size. In terms of absolute size, the human brain is one of the largest of all living animals'. Yet human intelligence cannot be completely attributed to the absolute size of the structure since very large mammals, such as elephants or sperm whales, have brains with absolute sizes that are even larger. In these species the large brain is not associated with a human level of intelligence. But if one turns to the explanation that their large brains are simply a consequence of the requirements of running their massive bodies, there remains the fact that some of the extinct dinosaurs, such as the 5,000-pound stegosaur, survived many times longer than elephants or whales have to date with a brain the size of a grapefruit. Absolute brain size alone is, at best, an ambiguous indicator of intelligence.

Perhaps the size of the brain relative to body size provides a better indication. In this case, humans contrast with the large-brained mammals. For instance, while the human brain is about 1/50 the weight of the body, this ratio is 1/6000 for the sperm whale. However, at the other end of the size scale, some of the smaller prosimians have an even higher ratio of brain-to-body weight than humans. One might explain the lack of human-like intelligence in prosimians by the argument that their absolute brain size is too small to sustain the necessary level of complexity. Yet porpoises have brains which are both absolutely and relatively

larger than those of humans, and although their intelligence has yet to be clearly determined or validly compared with ours, one suspects that if a human level of intellectual activity was present, it would have been discovered. Simply put, the relation of either measure of brain size to intelligence is not clear.

This is not meant to deny that there is *some* relation between the expansion of brain size and the evident increase in intelligence in our lineage. However, the picture is more complex than a simple direct relation of brain size and intelligence. There are clearly some structural differences between hominid brains and the brains of our closest relatives which account for the dramatic differences in behavioral complexity.

A MODEL OF HUMAN BRAIN FUNCTION

There are two classic models of how the human brain functions. These can be thought of as localized and generalized. In the localized model, specific areas of the brain are thought to control specific functions. The basic data supporting this model come from studies of accidental injuries in which areas of the brain were destroyed and specific behaviors were altered. In the generalized model, it is thought that there is little or no difference in function between various areas of the critical tissue of the brain. Data supporting this model stem from the obvious integration of vastly different inputs or outputs in most normal behaviors, and the fact that functions lost by accident victims with brain damage can sometimes be regained. Both of these models are extreme, and both are contradicted by experimental evidence.

Recently, a number of authors have suggested a rather different model combining elements of the two classic models discussed above. This new model is based on an analogy with holography. In holography, a three-dimensional image is formed by the interference patterns between light waves. The pattern of interference between the waves bears no direct relation to the regular form of the waves themselves, just as the interference patterns between waves made by several rocks thrown into a pond do not look like the individual regular wave fronts that combine to make the pattern.

In a normal photograph, there is a one-to-one relation between the points stored on the negative and the points on the image. In a holographic "negative," there is a many-to-one relation *since it is the waves forming the interference pattern that are stored.* Thus the information defining one point on the image is spread throughout many points when recorded. The holographic model helps resolve many of the contradictions between the classical models. Moreover, it helps explain the enormous storage capacity of the brain since *regularity* in what is stored (analogous to regular waves) allows a simplified coding for unique and complex interference patterns.

Experimental evidence seems to show that as data are received through the senses, specific functional areas in the cortex are activated. However, the recording of the data occurs over broad areas, just as the waves forming a hologram spread the information defining an image over broad areas.

What do we mean by the idea of storing information in the brain? Obviously everything experienced in the environment is not stored away; what information *is* stored represents only part of the sensory input. This is because recognizing patterns requires the selective destruction of information. It is these patterns that represent the mind's interpretation, or "picture," of the physical world. The brain functions to recognize patterns by disregarding less relevant information. Such patterns can then either be reconciled with similar patterns already stored in the brain, or be stored themselves for future reference. The process of reconciliation involves a comparison between the newly perceived patterns and the stored patterns. The outcome of these comparisons determines how sensory input is processed, and whether the preexisting neural models of "reality" (whether or not inherited) will be modified.

The storage of patterns depends on the actual configuration of connections between brain cells. Some of these connections are established by the genotype, initially or during the later growth of the cells. Others, however, are established and subsequently modified by the experiences of the living organism. In a real and direct sense, neural structures are both under genetic control (and therefore subject to the evolutionary process) and subject to modification through perception *and* behavior.

It is the genetically determined preexisting connections that are of special interest to us; these are actually neural models of unexperienced sensory relationships. The more of these that exist, and the more complex they are, the easier it is for the individual to "learn" the relationships involved. This brings us to one of the primary distinguishing characteristics of human brains, *the inheritance of numerous complex neural models.* These models delimit the nature of "reality" as perceived by the mind, while at the same time they provide the basis for rapidly learning and dealing with an incredibly complex amount of related information. They clearly take up a large amount of room in the brain, and because they are inherited, these models are subject to evolutionary change. It is their evolution that largely accounts for the brain size expansion that characterizes the human lineage.

What are these neural models about? In humans, prestructured relationships appear over a wide range of behaviors that are characterized by rapid learning, marked complexity, and broad similarity in all human cultures. Examples include the structural aspects of language grammars, the "grammars" of kinship, and religious and other aspects of social behavior. Other examples range from skilled hand-to-eye coordination to abstract mathematical ability. Some of these neural models show marked variation within populations while others show little, if any.

STRUCTURAL ASPECTS OF HUMAN BRAIN FUNCTION

The initial recognition of patterns depends on connections between areas of the brain which process sensory input. The complexity that the patterns can attain would seem to depend on how complex and extensive these connections are. Moreover, the process of comparing new patterns with preexisting neural models multiplies in difficulty as the patterns increase in complexity, and ultimately these comparisons come to require a large processing unit in the brain. Many of these structural aspects of function can be recognized in the brain; some can be recognized from endocasts. This allows evolutionary studies to depend on more than comparisons of living humans with closely related primates.

To begin with, there are primary areas on the cortex, or outer layer of the brain, which directly process information from the environment gathered by each sense. There are also primary areas for the motor functions, controlling output. In the higher primates, there is a tendency for these to become surrounded by association areas, in which the functions of the primary areas are modulated. In humans, destruction of an association area usually results in loss of the ability to recognize objects, although they are still sensed.

In most mammals, the connections between the sensory (input) and motor (output) areas pass through the limbic system of the brain. This is the portion of the brain, located above the stem (see Figure 3.5), which is responsible for emotional control. As a consequence, when patterns are learned relating certain sensory inputs to certain motor outputs, there is a corresponding emotional association. Moreover, outside of some primates there are no direct connections between the various sensory association areas. Without such direct connections there are severe behavioral limitations. For instance, object naming would be impossible since this requires a connection between visual and auditory input.

However, human and other higher primate behavior utilizes sensory integration and is far removed from these simple conditioned learning sequences. This is because of the evolution of an area in the lower parietal lobe of the brain called the "parietal association area." In this area, sensory inputs can connect directly with one another without passing through the limbic system. Moreover, motor output can be controlled without limbic involvement. This allows the formation of complex patterns without any emotional association, directly merging information from different senses (cross-modal transfer). In addition, cross-modal association gives the ability to develop neural models of reality which associate relationships beyond those immediately perceivable in the sensory fields. Many scientists believe that this ability provides the basis for conceptualization, and underlies the appearance of symbolic behavior in humans and the great apes.

Recognition and comparison of these complex patterns requires the development of a processing unit, apparently located in the frontal lobes of the brain. It would appear that several functions of these lobes are unique to humans and chimpanzees. One of these is the ability to treat elements in a sequential order and to separate the relevant from the irrelevant. This ability is related to sensory inputs through the evolution of connections between the frontal lobes and the various associ-

ation areas. Another development of particular importance involving different parts of the brain is the appearance of a verbal-auditory association area, a motor-speech area, and a tract of neural fibers connecting them. These have yet to be found in living nonhuman primates, although their rudimentary appearance in chimpanzees has been suggested as the result of both behavioral and anatomical studies. Finally, there is a tract of fibers connecting the parietal association area with this processing unit in the frontal lobes in humans. Thus the frontal lobes act in integrating, sorting, and ordering during the development of a neural pattern from sensory input, and later they act in the comparison with preexisting neural models and the decision as to how the input will be treated. Another function is in relation to the speech areas, since the processing unit provides the connection between sensory input and the areas that process the information and control the motor production of speech.

LANGUAGE AND LATERALIZATION

The human brain is made up of two almost symmetrical halves, or hemispheres. Each half is concerned with the sensory input from, and the motor control of, the opposite side of the body. This pattern, crossing the sensory and motor pathways inside the brain, occurs in all mammals. The hemispheres are connected with each other through a thick series of nerve fibers called the corpus callosum. Thus information from one hemisphere is transmitted to the other, and the two hemispheres are functionally integrated. However, they can also operate independently. It is through experiments with brains that have been split (i.e., the corpus callosum cut) that the separate functioning of the hemispheres can be determined. Input can be given to only one hemisphere in a split brain and the characteristics of that hemisphere can be studied.

Experiments have shown that in most mammals the two hemispheres are usually almost perfect mirror-images of each other. Each has all of the capabilities and potentials of the other, and memory storage is duplicated in both. They differ mainly in that they deal with the sensory and motor functions of opposite sides of the body. This is a redundant system which may use more storage space than is necessary, but it also allows normal functions to continue if there is damage to one side of the brain. In the course of human evolution there has been some amount of hemispheric specialization. This seems to involve mainly the language and motor speech production areas, which appear on the left side of the brain, and corresponding areas which are concerned with manipulative ability and geometric perception on the right side. An extraordinary amount of *secondary* information (compiled input such as a 3-dimensional image) is passed through the corpus callosum, since hemispheric specialization requires much more communication between the hemispheres when functions are integrated and associated during normal behavior. The result of hemispheric specialization in hominids was a great increase in both the memory capacity of the brain and its ability to integrate different inputs without significant increase in size. Of course, the aspect of double storage and redundancy was lost, but for humans *culture has largely taken the place of redundant information storage.*

The evolution of language seems tied to the lateralization of language functions through hemispheric specializations. In experiments with humans whose hemispheres have been surgically disconnected, it has been shown that the larger so-called dominant (usually left) hemisphere alone is capable of producing relatively normal language behavior. Yet all of the brain functions associated with language do not occur uniquely in the dominant hemisphere (see Table 4.1). The right (nondominant) hemisphere is responsible for the analysis of spatial relationships and the recognition and reproduction of complex visual patterns. While by itself the right hemisphere shows little or no response to spoken language or information in the left visual field, it is capable of written response. In one interesting experiment with an individual with disconnected hemispheres, the subject could not verbally name an object presented to the right visual field, but could write its name with the left hand. In sum, the full range of language-related behaviors involves specializations of both hemispheres.

Thus the functioning of the human brain in language production is dependent on cross-modal transfer and the lateralization of specific functions. The evolution of cross-modal transfer is a prerequisite for combining language and manipulative functions. It may not be necessary to have cerebral dominance in order to have a human-like vocalized

TABLE 4.1 Some hemispheric differences in human brain function, from Laughlin and D'Aquili (1974).

Left (dominant) Hemisphere	Right (nondominant) Hemisphere
Auditory	Auditory
Speech sounds	Melody recognition
Processing of consonant syllables	Vocal nonspeech sounds (coughing, laughing, crying)
Symbol translation and analysis	Steady-state vowels
Recall of auditory images of visual objects	
Visual	Visual
Perceptual recognition of conceptual similarity	Drawing, building models from a picture
	Two- and three-dimensional space relations
	Perceptual recognition of identity
Tactile and Motor	Tactile and Motor
Contralateral motor control	Contralateral motor control
	Tactile pattern recognition
Fine-hand motor skills	
Hand gestures during speech	
Conceptual	Conceptual
"Logical-analytical" operations on perceptual material	"Gestalt-synthetic" operations on perceptual material
Temporal sequential ordering	

language, but these developments are tied together in the hominid line. It may be that the association is a necessary one; perhaps complex linguistic behavior required a degree of connectivity (circuitry between the neurons) that even in a hominid-sized brain could occur only if the cerebral hemispheres had specialized rather than redundant functions. Evidence supporting this possibility is found in another aspect of lateralization. With lateralization comes the appearance of a connecting tract between the motor-speech area and the frontal in the left hemisphere. This tract provides a pathway for information to reach the motor-speech area. The integration of these features suggests that they evolved together. It would appear that the evolution of the structural basis for human language is closely tied to the evolution of lateralization and hemispheric dominance.

HANDEDNESS

A second phenomenon tied to the appearance of hemispheric dominance and ascertainable from the fossil record is handedness. However, this topic is somewhat problematic, since the traditional assumption that the control of hand preference is in the dominant hemisphere has been questioned. Nonetheless, the fact that hand preference and speech seem to appear at the same time in the developing child, and the close association of these with the dominant hemisphere, suggest that they are controlled by overlapping neurological models. The demonstration of hand preference through asymmetric arm development provides indirect evidence of hemispheric dominance, a condition possibly present in the early hominids.

A STRUCTURAL MODEL OF CULTURAL BEHAVIOR.

A. F. C. Wallace suggests a simple model for understanding the combination of structural and individual elements in cultural behavior. His model provides insight into how the structural aspects of cultural behavior may reflect the neural models discussed above. Wallace introduces the concept of *equivalence structure* for describing the simplest possible cultural interactions. An example of a primary equivalence structure is shown in Figure 4.1, part 1. In this representation, "a" represents the act(s) of individual A, and "b" the acts of individual B. The arrow means "is followed by." Thus, in the simplest possible relationship, whenever A does a_1, sooner or later B will do b_1, and vice versa.

The next most simple relationship is shown in Figure 4.1, part 2. This is a secondary equivalence structure and demonstrates how more complex interactions might be structured. An action of A (a_1) is followed by an action of B (b_1), which in turn is followed by a second action of A (a_2). Conversely, the sequence might be initiated by B; or in another variant, a_1 may be followed by b_1, which in turn is followed by a repeat of a_1, and then finally by b_2. All of these possible interactions are described by the secondary structure.

The equivalence structures describe the interaction. Clearly, the individuals involved enter into the interaction with the expectation that their acts will lead to the interaction described. What Wallace

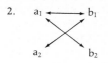
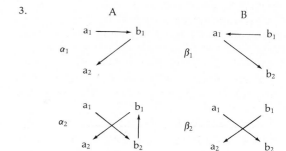
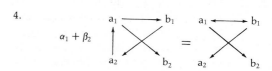

FIGURE 4.1 *Equivalence structures and cognitive maps for simplified cultural interactions, after Wallace (1961). Parts 1 and 2 show the primary and secondary equivalence structures described in the text; part 3 shows some of the cognitive maps for A and B which can combine to form the secondary equivalence structure. These maps can be defined as follows:*

α_1 *A knows that whenever a_1 is performed, B will respond with b_1 and then A will perform a_2.*

α_2 *A knows that whenever a_1 is performed, B will respond with b_2 and then b_1, and A will then perform a_2.*

β_1 *B knows that whenever b_1 is performed, A will respond with a_1 and then B will perform b_2.*

β_2 *B knows that whenever b_1 is performed, A will respond with a_2 and then a_1, and B will then perform b_2.*

Finally, part 4 gives an example of how these maps combine to form the secondary equivalence structure. All four possible combinations result in the same interaction.

demonstrates is that A's and B's understanding of the interaction need not be the same for the expectation to be valid.

He refers to the individual's understanding of the interactions as the "cognitive map." Several possible cognitive maps of the secondary equivalence structure are shown for A and B in Figure

4.1, part 3. The important point is that every possible combination of these maps results in the same equivalence structure. This demonstrates that cognitive sharing (individuals sharing the same understanding of an interaction, or having the same cognitive map) is not necessary for stable social interaction. In fact, Wallace goes a step further, arguing that human societies *require* that at least some interactions be based on cognitive maps that are not shared. And indeed it is possible that the non-sharing of maps underlies the successful functioning of any human or human-like society in which there are role differences. The main requirement is that the maps be complementary.

Relating these concepts to the neural models discussed above leads to a more explicit idea of how cultural behaviors may be inherited and subjected to the forces of evolution. Clearly, individual cognitive maps are not inherited; they are practiced and learned by individuals. Yet in a functioning society these maps must be complementary, and it is this aspect that is shared within the species through inheritance. The inherited aspect, then, involves the underlying logical structure of whole sets of maps that are mutually complementary, with the individual maps to be learned just as the particular grammatical rules of a language are.

Selection could work on these sets of complementary maps by changing the logical characteristics of a set and thus defining a new complementary set, or by adding to the complexity of the logic and thus expanding a set to allow more combinations that would result in the same equivalence structure. Selection could not be expected to change the cognitive maps themselves, or to increase the likelihood that individuals would learn some maps within a set more readily than others. This model shows how Culture can respond to the forces of evolution, while *a* culture cannot; only the structural aspects common to all cultures are under genetic control.

THE PONGID CONDITION

Recent evidence has made it clear that almost every element of human neural structural organization has its counterpart in observable pongid variation. It has been suggested that there may be no significant difference in the functional capability of the frontal lobes in living chimpanzees and humans; the corresponding areas appear to be the same relative size. With respect to the parietal association area, the best evidence comes from behavioral experiments, which indicate a rudimentary capability for cross-modal transfer, as well as the ability to utilize symbols, in chimpanzees and orangs. In sum, conditions made it advantageous for hominids to develop these already existing structures, resulting in a functional complex underlying the marked success of the lineage.

Human Locomotion

Humans have been called the "featherless bipeds," and although they are not the only creatures without feathers that use their hindlimbs alone for moving about, there are certain aspects of human locomotion that are unique. The human form of bipedalism is not an adaptation to speed; most animals of similar body size can outrun a human— even a chimpanzee running bipedally is faster. C. L. Brace likes to place human running in an adaptive perspective by painting the following picture in words:

> Imagine a suburban housewife chasing a cat down the alley. Now, shrink the housewife down to the size of a 50 pound early hominid, pump the alley cat up to the size of a sabre-toothed tiger, and reverse the chase!

The real advantages of human bipedalism are twofold. First, the consistent use of the hindlimbs alone for locomotion frees the hands for carrying and for manipulating the environment. Second, humans have evolved a particularly low-energy form of locomotion called striding, which allows them to cover long distances without developing a great deal of metabolic heat and thus without expending a great amount of energy. *Why* bipedalism evolved in our lineage is surely tied to these advantages. *What* bipedalism evolved from is more of a problem. We can use the African apes as a model for the ancestral condition, but it is probable that this model is not correct in all details.

PONGID LOCOMOTION

While the African pongids are typically considered "brachiating apes," field studies have shown that gorillas and chimpanzees spend most of their waking hours on the ground. When on the ground, these apes are generally quadrupeds, although they can be bipedal (discussed below). African pongid quadrupedalism is characterized by a unique form of forelimb support called "knuckle-walking," in which weight rests on the backs of the middle digits of the fingers, and the wrist is maintained in a fairly straight position. Whether knuckle-walking preceded bipedal locomotion in hominids is a problem that simply cannot be answered at present. For this reason, the use of living pongids as a model of what bipedalism may have evolved from will concentrate on the hindlimb, where the changes are straightforward.

In a simplified sense, a quadruped moves because of the forward force provided by the hindlimbs. The forelimbs act more as struts to support the body weight and the forces resulting from forward motion; they also act to guide the direction of motion. Two main groups of muscles act on the hindlimb to produce motion. Their actions can be determined by their position relative to the joints between the limb bones since these joints are the only places where motion can take place. Muscles that act in front of the hindlimb joints can only produce a bending motion toward the head. At the hip this motion brings the femur (see Figure 4.2) upward and forward, closing the angle at the joint (*flexion*). At the knee this brings the tibia in the same direction, but it opens the angle between the femur and tibia and is called *extension*. At the ankle, muscles that act in front of the joint close the angle, causing flexion. Similarly, muscles acting behind the joints cause the opposite motion. At the hip and ankle this is extension, while at the knee it is flexion.

In the quadrupedal pongid (see Figure 4.3, pp. 76–77), the *quadriceps* group (especially *rectus femoris*) and *sartorius* are powerful muscles that swing the leg forward when it is off of the ground. Their leverage is obtained by the angle of the pelvis; because the pelvis is tilted forward, the pelvic attachment of these muscles lies far in front of the hip joint (at the acetabulum, or hip socket, of the pelvis). After this limb touches the ground, and the forward motion of the trunk brings it into the approximate position shown in Figure 4.3, the hip extensors begin to contract. In the pongids, these extensors are mainly in the hamstrings muscle group. The same forward tilt of the pelvis positions

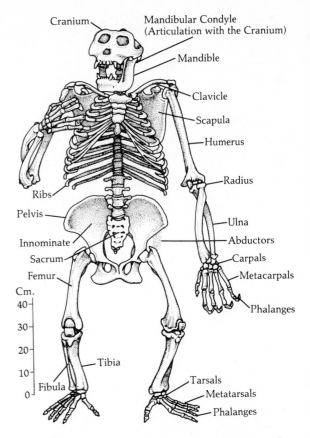

FIGURE 4.2   *A bipedal gorilla in frontal view, showing the names of the bones. The condyle of the mandible and the position of the abductor muscles are also shown. Drawing is after Schultz (1969).*

the hamstrings well behind the acetabulum, providing for their leverage. The hamstrings also have an attachment at the back of the femur, and their fibers merge with the *tensor fasciae latae* muscle, passing to the side and front of the knee. Thus while they extend the hip, they also extend the knee, adding to the forward acting force on the trunk.

Pongids can walk bipedally for long periods of time, although they rarely do. To maintain this gait, they must use the extensors and flexors in the same manner. Maintaining leverage for both these muscle groups is accomplished by continuing the same tilted relation of pelvis to femur in the bipedal position (see Figure 4.4, p. 78). This is done by flexing the knee and maintaining the hip flexion. For these muscles to retain their leverage, the hindlimb is not in a stable position; other muscles must be used and it is the inefficiency of this locomotion that seems to limit bipedalism in the pongids.

Another area in which pongid bipedalism is less than efficient is in trunk balance. During bipedal locomotion there is only one supporting leg. If the center of gravity of the body is not directly over this leg, the trunk would tend to fall toward the unsupported side. The abductor muscles, acting to the side of the hip, are in a position to prevent this motion. However, in pongids the abductors do not have a good lever arm because their attachment on the pelvis is not far to the outside of the acetabulum position. Consequently, when a pongid walks bipedally, it must shift its trunk from side to side to keep the center of gravity over the supporting limb. In sum, African pongids can regularly walk bipedally, but it is a muscularly inefficient form of locomotion for them.

DEVELOPING HOMINID BIPEDALISM

The evolution of hominid bipedalism can be understood from the preceding discussion of the problems facing a bipedal pongid. Selection for human bipedalism involved making the locomotion consistent and efficient in terms of muscular expenditure through changes in the morphology of the pelvis, and to a lesser degree of the femur. Much of our understanding of these changes is based on the work of C. O. Lovejoy and his colleagues.

Beginning with the leverage problem, hominids maintain leverage for their hip flexors and extensors while at the same time maintaining lower limb stability. Instead of flexing at the hip and knee, the lower limb can be straight in hominids because of changes in the pelvis that provide leverage. Considering the flexors, the verticality of the pelvis over the straightened limbs in hominids minimizes their leverage. In compensation, hominids evolved two projections on the front face of the pelvis to attain an advantageous position for these muscles in front of the hip joint. These are the anterior (front) spines: the anterior superior (upper) for *sartorius* and the anterior inferior (lower) for the pelvic attachment of *rectus femoris* (see Figure 4.5, p. 79).

Leverage for the extensors involved a different solution. A bipedal chimpanzee with limbs in a hominid-like configuration has no leverage for the hamstrings to bring the limb backward. Evolving a projection at the rear of the pelvis is awkward for a variety of reasons, and instead hominids evolved a "solution" which solved both this problem and another as well. In hominids, the hamstrings do not provide forward force during locomotion. Instead, the *gluteus maximus* provides this force when necessary. This was accomplished by bringing the top rear portion of the pelvis backward and downward (Figure 4.3); positioning the *gluteus maximus* behind the hip instead of to its side. The backward extension of the top-rear creates a notch, called the greater sciatic notch, between this area and the more vertically oriented lower portion. With the decreasing importance and changed orientation of the hamstrings, the lower rear portion of the pelvis where they attach, called the ischium, becomes shorter. At the same time, this backward and downward change *decreased* the effects of weight shifts in the upper body on balance at the hip by bringing the sacrum (the back of the pelvis, joining it to the spine) closer to the acetabulum.

The abductor leverage, already less than efficient in bipedal pongids, is worsened by these changes. Moreover, Lovejoy suggests that additional pelvic broadening is required by the need to support the lower viscera during the upright stance. Together, these changes move the hip joints farther apart and *decrease* the leverage for the abductors. The compensation evolved in hominids is to swing the top of the pelvis dramatically outward (Figure 4.5), maintaining if not extending the distance between the abductor attachment and the hip joint. This outward or lateral, flare of the hips is more prominent in living human females than males because female pelvic inlets must be broader in order to give birth to large-brained children.

These are not the only pelvic changes involved in the evolution of hominid bipedalism. For instance, with the widened distance between the legs, special features had to evolve which provided for the ability to swing the leg toward the midline of the body during locomotion. However, the major changes discussed above are the most dramatic, and the most easily interpreted from fossil remains of the pelvis.

Associated changes in the femur, while less marked, are still clearly observable. The *gluteus maximus* attachment shifts from the side of the bone to its rear. There is a flattening of the femur's

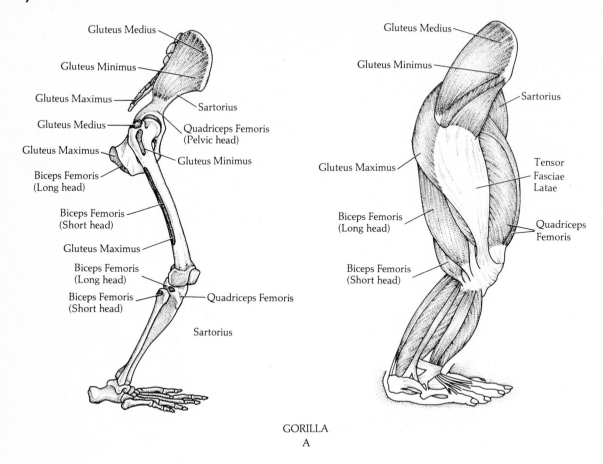

GORILLA
A

FIGURE 4.3   Bones and muscles of the hindlimb in (A) a
gorilla and (B) a human, adapted from Napier (1967). The
gorilla limb is shown in its quadrapedal position, while the
human limb is in its bipedal position. In both primates, the
main muscles that cause flexion at the hip are in the quadriceps femoris group and the sartorius. Since the quad-
ruceps also passes in front of the knee, attaching by way
of the patella to the front of the tibia, it causes extension at
the knee as well as hip flexion. The hip extensors differ between these primates. In the gorilla, it is the hamstrings muscle group (biceps femoris is shown in the figure but the
group also includes the semimembranosus and semiten-
dinosus muscles) that causes extensions when the limb is in
the position shown. The position of the limb is important because when in a more flexed position the hamstrings can also
cause extension in the human limb. Only when the limbs are
in the positions illustrated will extension cause forward motion of the pongid. The human hamstrings do not bring the
femur backward in the position shown; instead, the gluteus
maximus is the main extensor. The third important motion
at the hip is abduction (motion of the leg outward to the side
and upward). In both primates, gluteus minimus and gluteus medius act to produce this motion, and in the gorilla
this is the main function of gluteus maximus.

bottom, corresponding to its stable vertical position. The distance between the head of the femur
(the rounded top portion that fits into the acetabulum) and its vertical shaft increases in hominids as

the result of the greater lateral flare of the hips.
And because the top of the femur is far away from
the midline of the body while its bottom is close to
the midline, human femur shafts have a significant

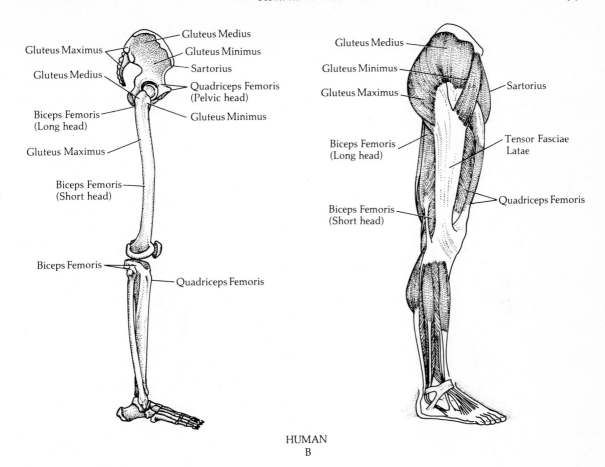

Gluteus Medius

Gluteus Maximus

Gluteus Minimus

Gluteus Medius

Sartorius

Quadriceps Femoris
(Pelvic head)

Biceps Femoris
(Long head)

Gluteus Minimus

Gluteus Maximus

Biceps Femoris
(Short head)

Biceps Femoris

Quadriceps Femoris

Gluteus Medius

Gluteus Minimus

Sartorius

Gluteus Maximus

Tensor Fasciae
Latae

Biceps Femoris
(Long head)

Quadriceps Femoris

Biceps Femoris
(Short head)

HUMAN
B

angle to the vertical as seen from the front, compared with the more vertical orientation of the femur shaft in bipedal pongids.

The remaining important changes are in the foot. The double arch of human feet is an adaptation to balance and weight support during bipedalism. However, the arch serves an additional critical function by providing leverage for the muscles that extend the foot as it leaves the ground during locomotion. The importance of this extension, called "toe-off" because it mainly involves the big toe, is realized by anyone who tries to walk on ice.

THE HUMAN PATTERN OF LOCOMOTION

Human walking allowed by the complex of changes discussed above is a unique gait in the primates. During toe-off, as the non-supporting foot leaves the ground, only the lower leg muscles are active in flexing the foot, providing the beginning of its forward swing. The hip flexors are initially active but soon stop contracting; the leg continues to swing forward as a free pendulum. Toward the end of the swing, the hamstrings begin to contract (they can act as extensors because the upper leg is flexed in this position), bringing the leg down to the ground under control. As the heel strikes the ground there is a short period of *gluteus maximus* activity. When the forward moving trunk passes over the now-supporting leg, this process begins again on the opposite side. Notice that in the striding gait the main hip extensor, *gluteus maximus*, does not act to thrust the body forward. The major muscle of the hip barely works at all! This is what makes human stride energy-efficient. It is the momentum of the forward swinging leg that brings the body forward.

a stride is energy efficient

A   B   C   D

FIGURE 4.4   *Quadrupedalism and bipedalism in a chimpanzee compared with a bipedal human, based on a figure from Kummer (1965). The spine, pelvis, and lower limb are shown, as is the position of the hip flexors: Q = quadriceps, H = hamstrings, and G = gluteus maximus. The figure shows (A) the chimpanzee in the quadrupedal position, (B) the chimpanzee in its normal bipedal position, (C) the chimpanzee in a human-like bipedal position, and (D) the bipedal human. Note that in its normal bipedal position (B) the chimpanzee maintains leverage for its hamstrings by flexing at the knee and hip. When the pongid attains the human posture, extending at these joints (C), the hamstrings have lost their leverage to bring the leg backward.*

Other gaits, of course, require *gluteus maximus* activity. Running and climbing would be impossible without the extensive use of this major muscle. While accelerating during running, the hamstrings are also used as extensors; leverage is provided for

them by leaning the trunk forward. Because these gaits require the activity of more muscles, they are more tiring. Many people utilize both the speed and distance advantages of running and the low-energy advantages of striding by alternating between these gaits.

Finally, while this discussion has concentrated on evolutionary changes in pelvis and hindlimb, the locomotor shift to hominid bipedalism must also have resulted in forelimb changes. What these involved, however, is much more obscure for two reasons. First, the locomotor pattern that characterized *prebipedal* hominids is still a subject of speculation (see Chapter 5). As a consequence, the immediate ancestral condition of the forelimb is unknown. Second, there has been little change in the forelimb during the course of hominid evolution, providing virtually no useful guidance for "backward reconstructions" of what this complex may have been like earlier. The earliest identifiably

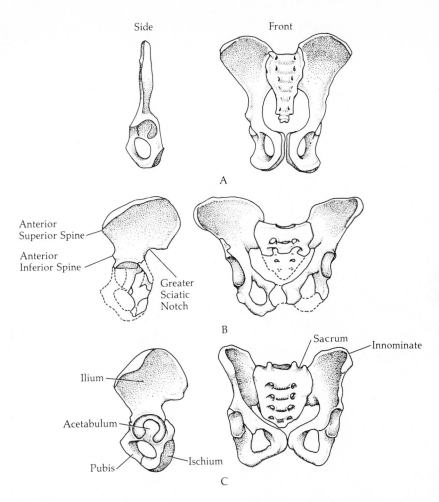

Side   Front

A

Anterior
Superior Spine
Anterior
Inferior Spine
Greater
Sciatic
Notch

B

Sacrum   Innominate

Ilium
Acetabulum
Pubis   Ischium

C

FIGURE 4.5 *Front and side views of the pelvis in a chim-panzee (A), an early hominid (B), and a modern human (C) (adapted from Campbell, 1966.) The early hominid side view is based on the reconstructed juvenile from Makapansgat; the front view is based on the Sterkfontein female pelvis. On the human pelvis, the three bones making up the hip bone (in-nominate) are named, and the position of the sacrum is shown. The sacrum and the innominates make up the pelvis. Note that there is more lateral flare in the hips of the early hominid pelvis than in the modern human one. This is because the birth canal in humans is broader and the acetabula are consequently farther apart.*

hominid forelimbs show dramatic strength adaptations (especially in flexion of the radius and ulna), and in one specimen the humerus is slightly longer (relative to the hindlimb) than in living humans.

These features could be markers of virtually any earlier form of quadrupedalism, or more likely they could correspond to unique aspects of early hominid adaptation.

Jaws and Teeth

The third important hominid distinction is found in the teeth and related portions of the upper and lower jaws. Unlike the previous two distinctions discussed, not all of these dental differences are visible in comparisons of present-day hominids and pongids (see Figure 4.6, p. 80). The living forms mainly contrast dental size and morphology at the front portion of the jaws, involving the canines and incisors, and even this comparison is somewhat misleading.

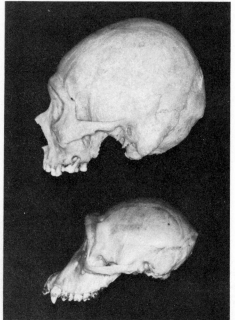

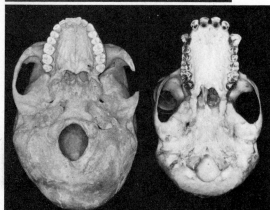

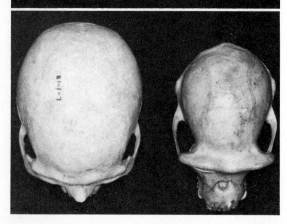

FIGURE 4.6   *Three views of a human (above or left) and a chimpanzee skull. Elements of all three hominid distinctions are apparent. The difference in brain size is seen in the larger human braincase. Locomotor differences are reflected in the balance of the head on top of the spinal cord. The view from below (middle) shows that the large opening (foramen magnum), which indicates the place where the spinal cord enters the braincase, is in a more forward position in the human cranium because the head is balanced on top of the vertebral column. The side view shows that the ridge at the back of the cranium (nuchal ridge), marking the farthest extent of neck muscle attachment, is lower in the human skull because of the more forward foramen magnum. The third distinction is in the jaws and teeth. The chimpanzee face projects forward, holding large angled incisors and projecting canines. The human face is much more vertical, leaving the nose projecting forward, and lacks the incisor angulation. In the view from below, the contrast in the size of the canines and incisors, and in the form of the canines, is clearly visible. The chimpanzee tooth row has a "U" shape because of the large incisors and the marked angle at the canines. The human tooth row shape is more parabolic, with a gentle curve at the front and divergent posterior teeth. Note the diastema between the chimpanzee canine and incisor. The posterior teeth of these primates are virtually identical. Small posterior teeth, however, are a recent hominid characteristic.*

THE ANTERIOR TEETH

The living apes are characterized by the canine-premolar cutting and slashing complex discussed in Chapter 3. Hominid canines and lower front premolars differ from their pongid counterparts in both size and form. In terms of size, hominid canines are much smaller. They have come to closely approximate the incisors in both size and form, although they are generally thicker and may be taller when they first erupt. In hominids, the canines clearly function like incisors and are mainly used to grip, hold, and tear.

The hominid lower front mandibular premolar (P_3) has also changed considerably. It no longer functions as a tooth that cuts against the upper canine. Instead, it has been incorporated into the grinding and crushing portion of the posterior dentition. The one large projecting cusp of pongid sectoral premolars became two (or more) similarly

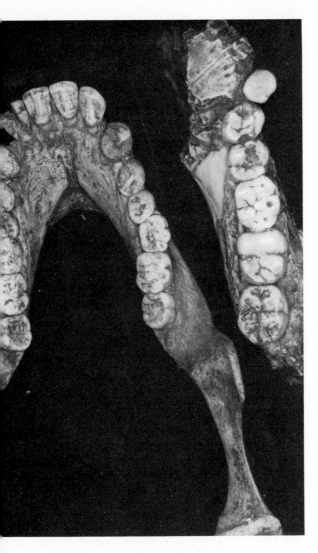

FIGURE 4.7 *Mandibles of a chimpanzee (left) and one of the early hominids (right) from Kromdraai, in South Africa. Both specimens are casts. Note the larger anterior teeth in the chimpanzee and the larger posterior teeth in the Kromdraai (TM 1517) specimen. The photo also shows the difference in canine form (incisor-like in the hominid) and in the most forward of the premolars. This tooth is pointed with a single cusp in the pongid, while in the hominid it is a large, flat grinding tooth.*

sized cusps on a more symmetrically shaped premolar in hominids. The contrast is even greater if pongids and fossil hominids are compared (see Figure 4.7).

With a change in the canine cutting complex comes a loss of gaps (diastemata) between certain teeth. In pongids there is a diastema between the upper canine and incisor, in which the projecting crown of the lower canine fits. There is also a diastema between the lower canine and premolar for the projecting upper canine to fit into. These diastemata occasionally appear in living and fossil humans, but they are rare except in the earlier human fossils.

A contrast also occurs in the incisors. Today these teeth are much larger in some pongids than in humans. Since the larger teeth take up more space in the front of the jaw, spreading the distance between the canines, this tends to make the tooth rows parallel in the pongids rather than curved as in hominids (Figures 4.6 and 4.7). In the incisors, however, it is the pongids rather than the hominids that have come to differ in their evolution. Earlier hominoids from the middle Miocene (Chapter 3) do not have chimpanzee-sized incisors, and it seems likely that hominids never passed through a large-incisor stage. In the pongids, expanded incisors seem tied to their function in food preparation. Chimpanzees use their anterior teeth for breaking open and peeling fruits with extremely tough husks, while gorillas use them for stripping and pulling leaves off stems. The common use of large front teeth in the pongids is also reflected in the size and orientation of their jaw muscles (see below).

In sum, the main differences between hominid anterior teeth and those of the living pongids lie in the loss of the anterior cutting complex involving the canines and P_3 and the subsequent functional (and partially morphological) incorporation of the canines into the incisor complex and of the P_3 into the posterior grinding complex. A secondary difference is the smaller size of hominid incisors. Although it is likely that some incisor reduction characterized hominid evolution, expansion of pongid incisors (especially in chimpanzees) appears even more dramatic.

THE HOMINID GRINDING COMPLEX

All primates grind their food into a digestible consistency between their posterior teeth, combining motions which move the teeth together (crushing) and motions which slide the teeth over each other (shearing). Hominids have come to differ from most other primates in degree, through the evolution of a grinding complex which can apply a great deal of force during chewing and stand up to the forces thus produced.

Chewing is a complex action of the lower jaw, involving motions in three directions. The basic chewing cycle common to all higher primates can be summarized as follows:

1. The lower jaw swings open and at the same time moves slightly forward.
2. The jaw begins to move back to a closed position. However, this is not the first motion in reverse. Instead, the motion is backward and toward the side with food between the teeth as the jaw closes on this food. On the other side there is a pivot at the contact of the mandibular condyle (Figure 4.2) with the cranium.
3. The food between the teeth is broken down through a combination of shearing and crushing until the food-bearing side is back in its original closed-mouth position.
4. The cycle may then be repeated on the same side or on the opposite side.

Hominids can produce more effective force during this cycle because of the size and orientation of the muscles that control the jaw (see Figure 4.8). The main muscles that produce vertical force are the anterior (front) portion of the temporalis and the masseter on the outside of the jaw, and the medial pterygoid internally. Transverse motion, occurring at the same time, is produced by the latter two muscles and the posterior portion of the temporalis. The closer these forces are applied to the food between the teeth, the more effective they are

in grinding and crushing. As Figure 4.8 illustrates, the anterior portion of the temporalis is located directly over the molars in humans, while in chimpanzees it is behind most of the molars. Similarly the human masseter is closer to the teeth than the chimpanzee masseter. The effect of these architectural differences is to make human grinding and crushing more efficient. The chimpanzee architecture emphasizes the posterior portion of the temporalis more strongly. This muscle has a horizontal orientation, and it is important in resisting forces applied to the canines and incisors when they are used for cutting, stripping, husking, and so on.

While humans appear to be more efficient in grinding and crushing than the living pongids, they are less well adapted in this direction than early hominids. Fossil hominids show evidence of much larger jaw muscles and a more anterior position for the masseter.

The ability of hominids to sustain greater chewing forces can also be better seen in fossils. On the average, fossil hominids have larger posterior teeth than living humans. Posterior tooth size seems to have been at a maximum about 2 million years ago, when hominids of modern size or smaller had premolars and molars as large as those of 400-pound gorillas, much larger than the posterior teeth of chimpanzees with body sizes similar to the fossil humans (see Figure 4.7). Larger teeth have a longer effective life when great forces are consistently applied to them. Because the teeth were large, their roots were expanded and the portions of the upper and lower jaws holding the roots were also large. Thus these early hominids were characterized by large faces and mandibles.

Only some of these earlier adaptations remain today and in fact living human and chimpanzee molars are not much different in size. One adaptation that has persisted concerns tooth enamel, the ultra-hard outer portion of teeth. The enamel is much thicker in human teeth than in African pongid teeth of similar or even larger size.

ERUPTION TIMES

A third difference between hominid and pongid dentitions concerns the eruption of the permanent teeth. In both the sequence of erupting teeth and the time of their eruptions modern humans differ

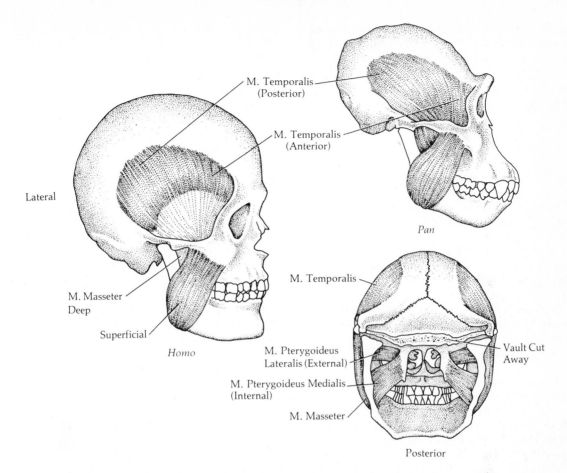

M. Temporalis
(Posterior)

M. Temporalis
(Anterior)

Pan

Lateral

M. Masseter
Deep

Superficial

Homo

M. Temporalis

Vault Cut
Away

M. Pterygoideus
Lateralis (External)

M. Pterygoideus Medialis
(Internal)

M. Masseter

Posterior

FIGURE 4.8   Position of the main muscles used in chewing, comparing a chimpanzee and a human, from Swindler and Wood (1973). In the human, the masseter overlaps more of the molar teeth, and the anterior and posterior parts of the temporalis muscle are close to equal in size. In the chimpanzee, the more projecting face places the masseter behind most of the teeth, and the posterior part of the temporalis muscle is larger and more horizontally oriented. The human complex is better adapted for bringing force through the back teeth, while the chimpanzee complex is better adapted for using the canines and incisors in cutting, gripping, and holding.

from the living pongids and almost certainly also from the ancestral condition.

In living species the main sequential difference is found in the canine. In humans, the canine (C), P4, and M2 erupt at approximately the same time; individual differences in sequence are greater than populational differences, and although the usual sequence is C-P4-M2, other sequences are common. There is a consistent sex difference for the time of canine eruption. On the average, male canines erupt nine months later than female canines within the same population. Consequently, the P4-C-M2 sequence is more common in males. In chimpanzees (best known of the living pongids), the canine erupts much later relative to the other teeth, about midway between the second and third molar (M2-C-M3). Interestingly, the sex difference in timing is similar to that in humans. Humans, then, differ from pongids in the earlier eruption of the canine relative to the other teeth.

Overall, however, permanent teeth erupt much later in humans than in pongids because of delayed human maturation, although the rate of individual tooth development is the same (see Table 4.2, p. 84). This is important in interpreting early hominoid remains. The ability to determine eruption times from the relative development of the molars

TABLE 4.2 Chronology of hominoid molar development and comparison of relative developmental stages of the molars at eruption times for living humans and chimpanzees. The length of time it takes molars to develop from the first stages of crown development through the final completion of the roots is the same in living chimpanzees and humans. However, chimpanzees begin molar eruption earlier and the successive eruptions are only three and a half years apart; in humans the molars erupt five years apart. Therefore, the *relative* development of the unerupted teeth is different at the time of corresponding molar eruption. For instance, when M_1 erupts in a chimpanzee, the unerupted M_2 has a complete crown and may have begun to develop roots and the M_3 has a partially formed crown. In contrast, when M_1 erupts in a human, the unerupted M_2 crown is not yet complete and the M_3 has not begun to develop.

CHRONOLOGY OF A MOLAR

Stage of Development	Time after the Beginning of Tooth Formation
Crown begins to develop	—
Crown is complete, none of the root has begun to form	5–6 years
Tooth erupts into occlusion	8–9 years
Root is completely formed	10–12 years

COMPARISON OF RELATIVE DEVELOPMENT AT ERUPTION

Molar	Time of Molar Eruption to Occlusion (years)	Development of Unerupted Molars at the Time of Eruption	
		M_2	M_3
Human			
M_1	6.5	crown almost complete	no visible development
M_2	11.5	eruption	crown partly complete
M_3	16.5	root complete	eruption
Chimpanzee			
M_1	3.5	crown complete, roots may have begun to form	crown partly formed
M_2	7.0	eruption	crown complete, roots may have begun to form
M_3	10.5	root complete	eruption

in immature fossil hominoids makes it possible to infer the length of maturation. The implications of these data will be explored in Chapter 7.

Characteristics and Trends

Earlier it was pointed out that most primate characteristics actually reflect trends that developed within the order. Similarly, of the three distinctly human complexes discussed here, two represent trends within the hominids themselves that resulted in dramatic change. Only bipedalism, and the osteological features associated with it, seems to have equally characterized all known hominids. Even in this case, there may come a time in the future when an early hominid will be discovered with a less than fully bipedal morphological complex.

The trend associated with increasing intelligence has been a persistent aspect of human evolution. The trends in the anterior teeth seem to have resulted in an essentially human configuration by about 2.5 million years ago; earlier hominid fossils are distinctly more primitive in this respect. The evolution of the chewing complex involving the posterior teeth, jaw muscles, and supporting bony architecture was not a linear trend; instead, it was a case of "evolutionary reversal." The chewing complex can be traced to Miocene forms with an essentially pongid-like morphology. A long period of posterior expansion reached its extreme about 2 million years ago and was followed by dental and facial reduction up to the present. That living humans are more "primitive" in these features than earlier hominids should not confuse hominid phylogeny, or mask the degree of importance of this evolutionary trend.

SUMMARY

The relation of form to function is complex, whether in living or fossil organisms, especially since most morphological features are multifunctional. In dealing with fossils, function can best be inferred from particular morphological features when there are clear analogues in living organisms and when the mechanics or physiology of the relationship is understood. Fortunately, the developmental capacity of bone to respond to the forces that act on it both during and after the period of growth and development makes it a particularly useful medium for determining the activities of extinct organisms. The same capacity, however, raises the question of whether changes in bone size or form over time are due to evolution or to developmental responses to changing functions.

Three morphological complexes have come to distinguish the hominid line: (1) changes in brain form and size that are associated with the appearance and evolution of human culture; (2) the evolution of pelvic, lower back, and lower limb changes allowing bipedal locomotion; and (3) dental evolution involving change in the anterior teeth from canine/premolar cutting to gripping with the canines and incisors, an early trend for expansion followed by differential reduction in the posterior teeth, and a general delay in the times of permanent tooth eruption combined with a relatively earlier eruption of the canine. Each of these complexes is associated with a series of behavioral changes. Moreover, each is an evolutionary trend in the lineage involving different rates of change. Whether these trends are independent of each other is a complex issue to be discussed in Chapter 5.

STATE OF THE ART

Of the various issues raised in this chapter, it is quite possible that the relation of brain size and intelligence is the most problematic. Within a related group of taxa, such as the Anthropoidea, brain size and intelligence seem related between species. Holding body size constant at about 100 pounds, a chimpanzee has a much larger brain than a large baboon and a small human has a much larger brain than the chimpanzee. Virtually any measure of intelligence ranks these three in the same order. Yet within one of the species (humans are the best known in this instance) there is absolutely no demonstrable relation between brain size and intelligence. Reconciling these two facts in an evolutionary context poses a problem: if brain size and intelligence are unrelated in humans, how could selection for increased average intelligence result in an increase in average brain size?

The basic question of what different brain sizes mean runs through all evolutionary studies. One approach, taken by H. Jerison and others, has been to estimate how much brain volume it takes to operate basic body functions and survival activities for taxa of various sizes, and from this to estimate the amount of "left over" volume presumably associated with higher-level activities. Jerison's procedure is to determine the general relation of brain size to body size for large taxonomic groups over a wide size range. Once this is accomplished, taxonomic groups with an exceptionally large relation stand out. The procedure works well within the primates: the Anthropoidea have more excess volume than the Prosimii. Surprisingly, some groups of sharks are also characterized by excess volume. Their general brain-to-body-size relation falls within the range of mammals.

Other workers, such as R. Holloway, have disagreed with this procedure, arguing in effect that it compares apples and oranges. Holloway and others suggest that the organization of the brain is of primary importance. Within similar magnitudes of size, the organization has far more to do with behavioral complexity than the amount of "extra" volume. Neural organization in animal species, however, is understood in only the most general way. Actual neural circuits are extraordinarily difficult to trace; it can take a decade to determine and compare the left-to-right visual tracking systems of experimental animals such as frogs and turtles. Similar experiments cannot be performed on humans. Thus the prospects of tracing the neural circuitry for complex human behaviors in the near future are dim, at best.

This explains why most studies of human brain organization are of the "black box" type. Models of how the brain *should* function to account for its capabilities can be delimited by studies of behavioral changes associated with accidental damage or tumor removal. "Black box" analysis can be extremely valuable. After all, the structure of the DNA molecule was determined this way. Without having viewed the structure of the molecule, Watson and Crick were able to determine how it had to be formed to account for its capabilities. However, brain function in humans is much more complex than DNA function. As yet, there is no way to test any of the "black box" models proposed.

In sum, while it seems clear that there must be some relation between brain size and intelligence, what this relation is and how it might be expressed in terms of the mechanics of brain operation remain unknown. The relation seems to work between some groups of closely related species, but it may not work between others. The contention that brain size expansion in human evolution is associated with increasing intelligence is almost certainly valid, but scientists are a long way from being able to state explicitly why.

FURTHER READINGS

CAMPBELL, B. G. 1966. *Human Evolution*. Aldine, Chicago.
  A simplified introduction to many of the biomechanical relations discussed both in this chapter and others. The book suffers mainly from oversimplification of some of the more complex functional systems.

CROMPTON, A. W., and K. HIIEMAE. 1969. How Mammalian Molar Teeth Work. *Discovery* 5(1):23-34.
  A short paper discussing the main properties of jaw and tooth functioning in mammals.

ECCLES, J. C. 1973. *The Understanding of the Brain*. McGraw-Hill, New York.
  A good discussion of models for brain function in a historical context.

ENLOW, D. H. 1963. *Principles of Bone Remodeling*. Thomas, Springfield.
  One of the basic texts on bone growth and response to the forces acting on it.

GESCHWIND, N. 1979. Specializations of the Human Brain. *Scientific American* 241(3):180-199
  The most up-to-date account of brain features that seem uniquely human.

HOLLOWAY, R. L. 1966. Cranial Capacity, Neural Reorganization, and Hominid Evolution: A Search for More Suitable Parameters. *American Anthropologist* 68:103-121.
  One of the better discussions concerning why brain size alone may not be the best measure of intelligence.

————. 1969. Culture: A Human Domain. *Current Anthropology* 10:395-407.
  Places cultural evolution in an evolutionary perspective, emphasizing the interrelations of cultural and neural evolution.

JERISON, H. J. 1973. *Evolution of the Brain and Intelligence*. Academic, New York.

The most recent detailed discussion of relative and absolute brain size in vertebrates, with special attention paid to how these sizes might be used to measure or infer behavioral complexity.

Laughlin, C. D., and E. G. D'Aquili. 1974. *Biogenetic Structuralism*. Columbia University Press, New York.
Perhaps the best current model for human brain function in an explicitly evolutionary context.

Lovejoy, C. D., K. G. Heiple, and A. H. Burstein. 1973. The Gait of *Australopithecus*. *American Journal of Physical Anthropology* 38:757-780.
A detailed but extremely important paper because of the insight it presents into how form and function can be related in both fossil and living humans.

Molnar, S., and S. C. Ward. 1977. On the Hominid Masticatory Complex: Biomechanical and Evolutionary Perspectives. *Journal of Human Evolution* 6:557-568.
An excellent review and discussion of the hominid masticatory system, comparing it to other mammals' and outlining the unique aspects.

Napier, J. R. 1967. The Antiquity of Human Walking. *Scientific American* 216(4):56-66.
A more general discussion of some problems involved in analyzing the locomotion of early hominids.

Pribram, K. H. 1971. *Languages of the Brain: Experimental Paradoxes and Principles in Neuropsychology*. Prentice-Hall, Englewood Cliffs.
A behavioral approach to human brain function modeling.

Scott, J. H. 1967. *Dento-Facial Development and Growth*. Pergamon, Oxford.
One of the fundamental introductions to growth and remodeling as they apply to the masticatory system and related facial structures.

Stent, G. S. 1972. Prematurity and Uniqueness in Scientific Discovery. *Scientific American* 227(6):84-94.
A particularly useful paper suggesting models for how preexisting neural structures can be altered and modified by experience.

Wallace, A. F. C. 1961. *Culture and Personality*. Random House, New York.
The introductory sections provide an explicit discussion of equivalence structures and how these may underlie more complex forms of human cultural behavior.

Wolpoff, M. H. 1975. Some Aspects of Human Mandibular Evolution. In *Determinants of Mandibular Form and Growth*, ed. J. A. McNamara, Jr. Center for Human Growth and Development, University of Michigan, Ann Arbor, pp. 1-64.
A discussion of evolutionary trends in hominid mandibles and teeth over the Pleistocene.

CHAPTER FIVE

Why Are There Hominids?

*T*he question of why hominids arose as a distinct lineage and the problem of how to recognize the earliest members of the lineage are connected. Without preconceived notions of what early hominids were like, we could never recognize in their fossils a line distinct from their contemporary relatives. On the other hand, preconceptions could play the role of prejudgments. Theories about why hominids originated must ultimately be tested against the facts, in this case the fossils themselves. Thus the answers to the two questions could become circular. To some degree, it is this potential circularity that has helped keep the whole topic a hotly debated issue for at least a hundred years, and will probably always prevent fully definitive answers.

This chapter examines various theories of hominid origins with reference to what can be inferred from present-day humans and other primates; the next chapter will present the fossil evidence. Following a discussion of two broad theoretical frameworks—Darwin's model and its several modern derivatives, and Jolly's model—is my own attempt to synthesize what I believe are the best aspects of the models into a possible reconstruction of why our lineage became distinct.

Limiting the Question

Having examined the complex of features that are unique in the hominids, one may reasonably ask "Why?" Why was there a lineage split in the hominoids? What factors led to the different evolutionary direction taken by the hominids? Actually, it is convenient to break the question apart this way because it is possible that two different answers are involved.

Assuming for the moment that there is an adaptive difference between early prehominids and prepongids that can be determined and that accounts for the difference in evolutionary directions, is it necessarily true that the adaptive differentiation occured at the same time as the lineage division? For instance, suppose the adaptive difference lies in savanna (African open grasslands) versus forest adaptation. Did the lineage split take place *because* some populations became savanna adapted, resulting in their genetic isolation and eventual speciation? This is only one possibility; the lineage split may have occurred *before* adaptive differentiation, and for entirely different reasons. Hominids and pongids may have been separate species long before recognizable adaptive differences accumulated between them. If the second possibility describes what actually took place, it will be very difficult either to recognize early hominids or to understand why they originated (unless we are extraordinarily lucky). They would become recognizable and distinctive only after adaptive differences evolved.

What we can hope to learn from the fossil record is the nature of the adaptive difference. If we can never be sure why hominids and pongids *diverged*, there is at least some hope of discovering why they became *divergent*. In this chapter, we will discuss and compare various theories concerning both the initial divergence and the adaptive difference. In the next chapter, specimens that might represent the earliest known hominids (i.e., the first recognizable members of the lineage) will be described with the intent of determining which theory or combination of theories best describes what seems to have happened.

Darwin's Model

The earliest important theory of hominid origins was formulated by Charles Darwin, and in one form or another his ideas have influenced the thinking of scholars up to the present time.

Darwin maintained that humans are most closely related to the African apes, with the corollary that humans originated in Africa. Given how little was then known of these pongids, this idea was more than insightful; a much better case could be made today.

In addition, he suggested an adaptive model to account for hominid origins. He was struck by the dramatic differences between pongids and humans in locomotion, canines, and intelligence and tool use, and related these to a shift from tree life to life on the ground supported mainly by hunting. A ground-dwelling primate, he argued, would benefit from bipedal locomotion since this would free the hands for carrying the weapons useful in hunting.

With these weapons as a means of adaptation, and with increasing intelligence guiding their use, large projecting canines would come to be of little importance and therefore reduce in size.

THE CASE FOR A PONGID ANCESTRY

While various authors have advanced primates as diverse as gibbons and tarsiers for the position of our closest relatives, the case for the African apes is overwhelming. Our detailed anatomical and behavioral similarities with these pongids allow no other interpretation in an evolutionary context. While specific features of some other primates also closely resemble our own, no other living creatures so closely resemble ourselves in the complex of details ranging from obvious anatomy to behavior and biochemistry. In fact, many would claim that the African apes are more closely related to humans than they are to the other living apes. Modern comparative studies of chimpanzees, gorillas, and humans show that they form a closely related group. In this regard, Darwin was clearly correct.

THE CASE FOR AN ARBOREAL ANCESTRY

The closeness of our relation to the African apes should not obscure the fact that we are *not* descended *from* them. A common ancestor of apes and humans, even if recent, is expected to be dramatically different from living humans. However, the same logic dictates that this common ancestor would be expected to markedly differ from the living apes. Where these differences might lie is of critical importance in reconstructing the hominid divergence.

The first question is one of an arboreal heritage. Did humans and apes share an adaptation to living in trees before the lineages diverged? On one level, the answer to this question is certainly yes. Most primate characteristics are the result of arboreal adaptation. Moreover, if the Oligocene hominoids from the Fayum are ancestral to the living hominids, and if the middle Miocene African proconsuls are the later representatives of this lineage, the circumstantial evidence in both cases argues for an arboreal adaptation. The (unlikely) alternative would be a pre-Oligocene origin for the hominids, since the Oligocene dryopithecine genus *Aegypto-pithecus* was arboreal.

Comparative anatomy presents evidence for much the same conclusion, if one assumes that the many detailed resemblances of humans and apes are not the result of parallel evolution. These resemblances are intertwined with a complex of features bearing on a more specific question: was the common ancestor of humans and apes a brachiator?

THE CASE FOR A BRACHIATING ANCESTRY

Brachiation as a means of arboreal locomotion is now restricted to the apes of Africa and Asia and a few genera of New World monkeys. Brachiation is a form of locomotion which uses the forearms for support and power and the pendulum-like characteristics of the swinging body to maintain forward momentum. The center of gravity of the body and most of its mass are below the support points on the hands. In considering whether hominids passed through a brachiating stage, we need to separate brachiation-associated characteristics from the more generalized shared features resulting from the common primate arboreal adaptation. This is not as easy as it may seem; one cannot simply assume that the derived features of gorillas and chimpanzees are associated with brachiation, since as adults these apes rarely brachiate. Moreover, brachiation is only one of many behaviors that require forearm support or specialized forearm activity in these apes. Many, if not all, of the morphological features associated with brachiation must be considered in the context of other activities ranging from hanging and reaching to climbing and quadrupedal locomotion.

Brachiation-associated characteristics that might be expected to appear in modern humans are in the arms and trunk. (While brachiators have short legs relative to trunk length, a long-legged adaptation is associated with striding bipedalism in humans.) In brachiators, the trunk tends to be short and the bony chest is flattened in the anterior-posterior (front-to-back) direction. The shortness of the trunk (and legs) quickens the speed of the free-swinging (pendulum-like) portion of brachiation; brachiators emphasize the fact that a shorter pendulum swings more quickly by tucking up their

legs during the later part of the swing. The chest flatness serves several functions. A long collar bone (clavicle) positions the shoulder joint far to the outside of the body, and the flat back positions the scapula transversely (Figure 4.2). Combined, these result in an outward-facing shoulder joint, contrasting with the more downward-facing joint in quadrupeds. The joint itself is shallow (allowing wider motions), and the muscles that move the arm have improved leverage because of the flat trunk. This anatomy makes possible a series of powerful arm motions to the side and above the body that are impossible in quadrupedal primates.

Brachiators are characterized by long arms relative to their trunks, specifically by long forearms and hands. The wrist characteristically is capable of extreme rotation (about 180 degrees), and the muscles are arranged so that powerful bending at the elbow can take place in almost any wrist position.

Every arm and trunk adaptation discussed above is shared by humans and the African apes, and separates them from the quadrupedal cercopithecoids. This argues most strongly that forelimb suspension and at least some aspects of the brachiation adaptation had evolved before the separation of hominid and pongid lineages.

Some features of the chimpanzee and gorilla are not shared by humans or any known hominid fossils. Besides the dental features discussed previously, there are certain peculiarities of the wrist and fingers that appear to be the result of the knuckle-walking quadrupedal adaptation in the African pongids. On the other hand, there are a number of shared derived features characteristic of humans and these pongids that are independent of the brachiation adaptation, and therefore serve to emphasize the close relationship between the species. These include expanded cranial capacities, delayed maturation, and thumb rotation and the potential for opposability (when the fingers are shortened). The shared behavioral features are far more extensive than anyone would have guessed a decade ago; they include tool making, a significant degree of language ability, and the ability to understand and use symbols. *similarities V apes +*

A REASSESSMENT

Darwin's assumptions, and the conclusions he drew from them, are now known to be only partially correct. Yet current knowledge largely supports his model. He was correct in his contention that humans are most closely related to the African apes and his supposition that humans evolved from an arboreal ape-like creature in Africa. While it is now realized that humans are not unique in their ability to make and use tools, as well as in certain other elements of culture such as language and symboling, these abilities serve to emphasize the continuity between humans and the African apes. They support the contention of relationship and make the evolutionary hypothesis of a gradual appearance of characteristically human features more understandable.

At the same time, however, new knowledge of the African apes raises new questions about human origins. If tool use, language, and so on are not unique to humans, what was the role of these abilities in human origins and why did they evolve a new magnitude of importance and complexity in humans?

Dart and the Killer-Ape Hypothesis

Raymond Dart clearly had Darwin's hypothesis in mind when he correctly interpreted the hominid affinities of the first australopithecine cranium to be discovered, in 1924. At that time, no truly early hominids were known, although the Piltdown remains from England, now recognized to be fraudulent, suggested that human ancestors were characterized by large brains and ape-like teeth.

The Taung fossil child from South Africa was the exact opposite of Piltdown; the teeth were remarkably human-like, while the brain was small and the face large. Most scholars at the time interpreted the Taung fossil as an early pongid, pointing out that it shared many similarities with pongids and only a few with hominids. Dart, however, understood the importance of the few features shared with hominids. The most outstanding of these were the small, flat-wearing canine; the position of the foramen magnum underneath the cranium, indicating a vertical spine and therefore erect posture; and certain elements of the natural cast of the inside of the cranium which suggested that the brain was slightly larger and structurally different from a pongid's. These were the three elements predicted

by Darwin—reduced canines, bipedalism, and changes in the brain.

And what of the remaining elements in the hypothesis? Dart simply assumed they were there, claiming from the outset that Taung represented a form of tool-using, hunting hominid that employed a combination of intelligence, brute strength, and weapons to become what others have called "the most vicious carnivore on the savanna." Dart made these claims on the basis of a single six-year-old specimen and in the absence of postcranial skeleton, tools, or any evidence of hunting behavior. The amazing thing is that although he may have overemphasized the importance of hunting, he was eventually proven correct in every one of his claims.

Later excavations at a South African cave called Makapansgat revealed more australopithecine specimens and a large quantity of broken and crushed animal bone. Dart believed that the animal bones were brought into the cave by the hominids living there, who broke up the bones and used them as tools and weapons. He argued that the use of animal parts preceded the use of stone tools, and created a name for the culture based on bones, teeth, and horns: Osteodontokeratic. Many scholars have since disputed the claim that these bones were broken up and used by the australopithecines, but the discovery of stone tools with australopithecines at other sites has settled the issue of whether or not these early hominids were tool makers.

More recently, renditions of human evolution based on Dart's writings have been presented by R. Ardrey and D. Morris. Using selected naturalistic studies of living primates, these authors have even further emphasized the importance of hunting among the early hominids. They both claim, in effect, that humans originated when a group of pongids became savanna-dwelling carnivores (i.e., "killer-apes"). To varying degrees, they hold this unique hominid heritage to be responsible for what they see as the "aggressive instincts" in modern humans. Their writings have led to the idea that many undesirable elements of human behavior, ranging from mob behavior to crime and ultimately warfare, are the result of this heritage and are somehow coded in our genes. A similar claim is made by some sociobiologists, although for different reasons.

The killer-ape model, then, has come to be more

than a hypothesis about hominid origins. Its implications extend to claims about the basis of behaviors in living humans. The model of how cultural behaviors may have inherited aspects (see Chapter 4) suggests it is unlikely that any *specific* behaviors (aggressiveness, war making, etc.) could be inherited. However, the question remains of how important carnivorous behavior was in hominid origins, and what if any effects this might still have on human behaviors.

A Savanna Chimpanzee

Also stemming from Darwin's model is a series of hypotheses largely the result of work by S. L. Washburn and his students (as well as others). These hypotheses make two assumptions: first, the common ancestors of hominids and pongids were much like living chimpanzees; second, hominids originated when some of these primates adapted to the savanna in a manner analogous to that of living baboons but with important differences because the anatomical and behavioral potentials of chimpanzees differ from those of baboons. Simply stated, the model asks, "What would happen if a chimpanzee-like hominoid began to adapt to grasslands?" The answer, "Hominids!" One proponent of this model, A. Kortlandt, believes that chimpanzees were much more like hominids in the past, and that their presently restricted distribution and behaviors are a result of competition with the more successful hominids.

The baboon adaptation (or more properly adaptations, since these vary by population and by season) to open grasslands is based on a complex of socially defined behaviors. The roles expected of individuals are governed by far more than their age and sex; a variety of different factors combine to define an individual's status. In a sense, baboon troops resemble a multi-celled organism, but unlike a real organism or similarly analogous colonies of social insects, individual "specializations" are adaptable and differ from situation to situation.

While the killer-ape model focuses on hunting ability, the savanna chimpanzee model of hominid origins looks at a much wider range of behaviors. What differences would a chimpanzee-like creature bring to a baboon-like adaptation? C. L. Brace and others have emphasized the importance of a dependence on tool use for survival, reflected in canine reduction. Brace views tool use as the most important hominizing factor in the Darwinian complex. G. A. Bartholomew and J. B. Birdsell focused on considerations of body size, bipedalism, and tool use, and the wider range of resources that this adaptive complex would make available to the early hominids. Others, such as A. Mann, have emphasized the social implications of tool use. For instance, Mann points out that once tools take the place of teeth in aggressive displays and behavior, a previously important mechanism of social control, the late eruption of canines, becomes useless. In male baboons, the canines are the last teeth to erupt. This serves the important social function of preventing young males from serious competition with older males until they are both physically and behaviorally mature. Tool use destroys the effectiveness of this biological control mechanism, and Mann hypothesizes that a much more complex mechanism of *social* control must have taken its place in early hominid societies.

Drawing even further on the behavioral implications of comparative primate studies, workers such as J. B. Lancaster outline sex-based role behaviors that might have characterized the "savanna chimpanzee." Lancaster's expectations for male behavior envision a wide-ranging role both socially and geographically. She argues that the males might have been adventurous, formed bonds easily both within and beyond the troop, and participated actively in the defense of females and the young, although at the same time making no direct contribution to their access to food or providing it for them. In contrast, kinship recognition and kin-defined behaviors might have been characteristic of the females. In the living social primates, the mother-infant bond tends to be maintained through life, expressed later as differential behavior of offspring toward mothers and vice versa. Lancaster suggests that such a matrifocal unit is probably the main stabilizing factor in primate groups. Moreover, females tend not to change groups, and if one does, the group itself is drastically altered since usually the entire matrifocal unit accompanies her. Lancaster argues that with more stable social units, and the likelihood of an entire lifetime spent in the same home range, the early hominid females may have carried the greater knowledge of environmental resources. Females, then, may have been more important than males in the formation of proto-cultural behavior during the early stages of its evolution.

C. O. Lovejoy has recently focused on the demographic consequences of adaptive trends in chimpanzees to provide insight into hominid origins. Lovejoy argues that the behavioral complexity of chimpanzees has led to a demographic dead end because of the long period between births required by delayed maturation. He suggests that hominids might have originated when a hominoid group developed behaviors, such as kinship recognition, to help shorten the time between births and thus allow population expansion. One facet of this argument is that bipedalism may have evolved to allow the increased number of young to be carried.

Finally, the studies by A. Kortlandt, G. Teleki, and others showing that chimpanzees can walk and run bipedally support the savanna chimpanzee hypothesis, as does the demonstration of tool making and language abilities in these primates. If we hypothesize that the common ancestor of chimpanzees and humans also shared these features that link the living species, it is no longer necessary to suppose that tool making, bipedal locomotion, and rudimentary cultural behavior originated *with* the hominids. The question instead becomes one of changes in frequency and complexity, in the hominids, of capabilities that were already present.

In sum, these authors have focused on the complex interrelationship of tool use, bipedalism, canine reduction, and intelligence and social behavior in applying a more sophisticated version of Darwin's model to the question of hominid origins. They, along with others, have attempted to demonstrate a *necessary adaptive relationship* between these four characteristics. The contention is that the adaptive potentials resulting from this relationship account for the evolutionary direction taken by the hominids.

The Seed-Eater Hypothesis

Another hypothesis concerning hominid origins has been advanced by C. Jolly. He emphasizes the features of early hominids that are not shared by living humans or African apes, and draws an analogy with adaptations in baboons. Jolly turns to the gelada (*Theropithecus*) as an analogy to the early hominids, claiming that the gelada differs from the more widely distributed baboons of the genus *Papio* in many of the same ways that early hominids differ from pongids. The parallel similarities are attributed to the same cause, a particular adaptive and dietary specialization in semi-arid open country involving collecting and eating seeds. While grasses form a large component of the gelada's diet, Jolly draws attention to those characteristics that are part of the seed-eating adaptation.

PARALLELISMS IN FORM

The gelada cranium differs from *Papio* (see Figure 5.1, p. 94) in many of the same ways that early hominid and pongid crania differ (Figure 5.2, p. 95). These differences are reflected to a lesser degree in living humans and pongids (Figure 4.6). In Figure 5.1, note that the gelada's jaws and teeth lie more directly below the cranium, while the mandible is taller and more perpendicular. The vertical part of the mandible (the ramus) begins at the position of the third molar in the gelada, while in the *Papio* the ramus begins well behind the third molar. Another contrast is in the position of the cheek. In the gelada the cheek begins over the second molar, while in the *Papio* specimen it begins over the third.

These differences reflect differences in the muscles of mastication (Figure 4.8). In the gelada the masseter attachment is in a more forward position relative to the teeth. The tooth row is in a more posterior position, and consequently a large portion of it lies directly under the anterior temporalis. Moreover, other evidence shows that the anterior temporalis is relatively larger in the gelada. These features in geladas combine to increase the force passing through the molars and premolars.

In the teeth themselves, few differences separate the living geladas from baboons. However, turning to fossil forms of *Theropithecus*, which show a more extreme version of the same adaptation, the molars and premolars tend to be relatively large, while the incisors (and sometimes the canines) may be small. This difference is also somewhat paralleled in early hominids and pongids (Figure 4.7).

The gelada postcranial bones are adapted for prolonged seed collecting from a sitting position. The head is set somewhat more vertically atop the spine than is usual in baboons, and the index finger is short, facilitating opposition with the short thumb. There are accessory sitting pads, or fat deposits, on the buttocks.

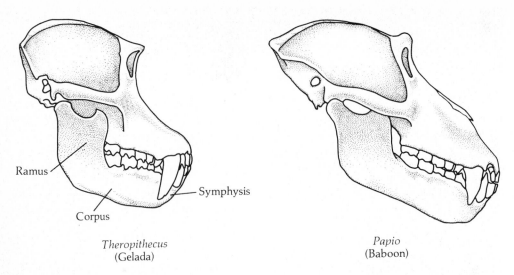

Theropithecus
(Gelada)

Papio
(Baboon)

FIGURE 5.1   *Comparison of a* Papio *and a* Theropithecus *male cranium. The position of the braincase relative to the face, and a backward shift of the teeth, allows the* Theropithecus *to produce more powerful forces through the tooth row. Parts of the mandible are labeled.*

male breeding unit might be the forerunner of the nuclear family. Even seed chewing might be a preadaptation, since when these small objects slip from between the teeth, a mobile tongue is useful in repositioning them. The same tongue mobility is used in producing many of the distinguishable sounds necessary for language.

PARALLELISMS IN BEHAVIOR

From the parallelisms in form, Jolly hypothesizes parallelisms in behavior, suggesting that the dietary specializations may be part of a more general adaptive similarity. To support this, he points to additional behavioral parallelisms. The similar habitats of both geladas and early hominids include open grasslands ranging to the semi-arid, and there are a number of behavioral similarities that are probably habitat specific. For instance, the living representatives of both primates form single male breeding units, comprising one male and one or more females.

Jolly's contention is that a seed-eating adaptation in early hominids would account for their observed morphology, given the habitat in which they are found. Moreover, the effects of seed eating could be seen as preadaptations to some of the uniquely hominid developments. Trunk verticality during sitting results in some of the anatomical changes necessary for bipedalism. Changes in the thumb/ finger proportions, useful in seed collecting, might precede the hominid precision grip. The single

A BROADER PERSPECTIVE

The seed-eater hypothesis, like the killer-ape model, focuses on a particular food in explaining hominid origins. The savanna chimpanzee model, on the other hand, emphasizes the adaptability of early hominids, and uses non-dietary aspects of their adaptation to account for the direction of their evolution. There is much to be gained from the latter approach, especially in view of two additional factors.

First, powerful chewing is characteristic of mammals that are not seed-eaters (Figure 5.3, p. 96), and seeds are not the only savanna food source requiring powerful chewing. Roots and tubers might have been a critical food source in early hominid adaptation. During the dry season, many of the savanna plants expand beneath the ground, storing nutrients, while their tops wither away. It is difficult for geladas to dig up roots and tubers with only their nails, but early hominids using chimpanzee-type digging sticks could readily obtain them. The point

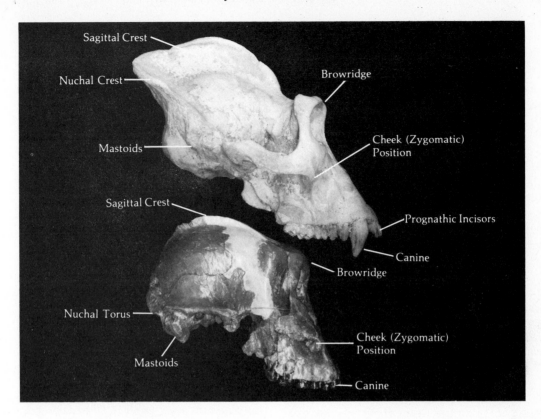

FIGURE 5.2   *The crania of a male gorilla (above) and the most robust of the male australopithecines (below, Olduvai hominid 5). Both specimens are casts. The contrasts between these parallel the* Theropithecus/Papio *contrasts shown in Figure 5.1, except for the canine reduction and low nuchal ridge position in the hominid. Some of the revelant features are labeled.*

Tuttle's Small Ape

No single hypothesis discussed above provides all of the answers to the problem of hominid origins. Indeed, they do not always ask the same questions. However, there are few important contradictions between them. A single theory of hominid origins *could* combine the best elements of all. Based on present knowledge, how would such a theory look?

MORPHOLOGY AND LOCOMOTION

is that hominid adaptability argues against a single dietary specialization in the early hominids.

Second, the seed-eater hypothesis alone does not account for the adaptive complex of tool use, bipedalism, canine reduction, and intelligence. While an adaptation to a diet requiring powerful chewing makes excellent sense in explaining the form of early hominid crania and posterior teeth, attempts to explain these other hominid features through the same dietary adaptation have only detracted from the insights provided by the hypothesis.

The evidence of comparative anatomy available to us strongly suggests that our ancestors passed through an arboreal stage characterized by forelimb suspension and at least some elements of brachiation. Whether brachiation was as well developed in early hominids as in modern African apes is somewhat obscured by the terrestrial adaptation of these apes, knuckle-walking. But homi-

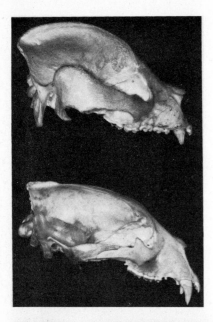

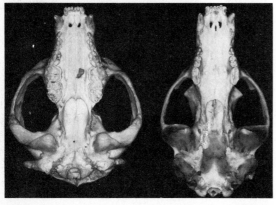

FIGURE 5.3 *Similar dietary distinctions result in the same morphological contrasts between omnivorous bears and the bamboo-eating giant pandas. The panda is above in the side view and to the left in the view from below. Note the addition and size expansion of the panda premolars and the marked buccolingual (transverse) expansion of the molars.*

the ground. This does not mean that they are more closely related to hominids than the larger African apes, but it does suggest that a small African ape may have evolved a similar form of locomotion. The idea (proposed by some earlier scholars) that hominids may have evolved from a "third" African ape which was much smaller than the present two, and whose small body size allowed it to evolve an arboreal bipedalism (like the gibbon), has recently been advocated by R. Tuttle.

While accepting many of the elements of Washburn's version of the savanna chimpanzee model, Tuttle questions whether hominids ever passed through a knuckle-walking stage (as Washburn proposes) since no clear adaptations to this form of locomotion have ever been found in the hands or forelimbs of living or fossil hominids. Instead, he suggests that small body size would allow the same form of arboreal bipedalism to evolve that characterizes the gibbon. A variety of behaviors might have combined to make an arboreal form of bipedalism advantageous in this hypothesized small ape. Besides the trunk verticality associated with arm hanging, these would include vertical climbing and standing on branches to reach food. In small forms the arms can be used in balance while trunk is vertical, while in larger forms the increased body mass makes this adaptation more difficult.

Thus Tuttle argues for a pre-grasslands adaptation divergence between hominids and pongids. Tuttle's small ape was already bipedal when it became terrestrial. Selection refined the bipedal capability into a more-or-less modern form when this small ape became less arboreal, just as knuckle-walking was refined in its larger relatives. This hypothesis could account for some of the morphological resemblances of humans and gibbons without requiring a close phylogenetic relationship between them.

WHY THE GROUND?

We may never know the exact reasons for a terrestrial adaptation in the "third" African ape. The model I would suggest is a two-stage one, based on the fact that the other two African apes *also* evolved terrestrial adaptations (they spend most of their waking hours on the ground). A common response in at least two different lineages suggests a common cause.

nids may have once been brachiators without having passed through a knuckle-walking stage, since knuckle-walking is not the only terrestrial adaptation found in brachiators.

The small apes of Southeast Asia often stand when in the trees and are almost always bipedal on

The middle and later Miocene African proconsuls lived in a habitat which appears to have been virtually unbroken forest, even in East Africa, which represented the outer fringes of their range. While the lineages leading to hominids and pongids were probably among these arboreal forms, these lineages had almost surely not yet diverged since many of the specific brachiation-associated characteristics shared by humans and apes do not appear in the proconsuls. I propose that one of the proconsul species evolved an arm-swinging adaptation much like that of New World spider monkeys at some point after about 18 million years ago. Besides the differences in locomotion, this adaptation allowed feeding at tree branch edges and may also have been associated with increased fruit eating. It was successful, leading to an adaptive radiation with at least two and possibly three or more species emerging. These almost surely included a larger (perhaps chimpanzee-sized) and a smaller (perhaps gibbon-sized) form, somewhat similar to the living orangs and gibbons of Southeast Asia.

The smaller species combined its brachiation abilities with an arboreal bipedalism, walking erectly on branches and either holding on to other branches for support or using its (presumably) elongated forelimbs for balance just as human tightrope walkers use a long pole. The larger species had too much weight in its trunk and forelimbs for this adaptation, but changes in the wrist and forearm resulting from brachiation (especially the free mobility and flexion capabilities at the wrist) made a "palms down" form of quadrupedalism impossible. Instead, knuckle-walking appeared, taking advantage of the brachiation-associated changes; weight support was on the backs of the middle finger bones with the wrist held in a fairly straight position. This is the first part of the two-stage model I suggest.

The second part involves a change to greater use of the ground in both lineages. This was *not* a change that evolved terrestrial forms from arboreal ones; instead, it was an expansion of the niche to include living on the ground.

Beginning about 16 million years ago, after some 7 million years of relative stability, a series of geological and associated faunal changes occurred in East Africa. The primary cause of these changes was the earth movements leading eventually to the creation of the rift valley that spans all of East Africa today. Formerly high areas began to lower, and

there was a great deal of associated volcanic activity. The resultant habitat changes were twofold. First, portions of the landscape that lowered also collected less rain, and many areas became too dry to support rain forests, which were replaced by parklands (scattered trees in grass) and open (dry to semi-arid) grasslands. Second, environmental mosaics (local alterations from forest to parklands to grasslands) developed over broad areas that were formerly continuous forest. Many new habitats appeared, and the mosaic nature of the environment allowed the division of these habitats into more niches than were possible in a continuous tropical rain forest environment.

These habitat changes, of course, had a dramatic effect on the local faunas. Many species became extinct, while other new ones appeared. An apparent connection between Europe and Africa allowed the introduction of new European species. I suggest that during this time the two brachiating hominoids described above began to use more terrestrial resources.

Whether this adaptive shift was "forced" by the changing ecology or was an opportunistic response to the new niches that became available will probably never be known (although I favor the second explanation). Whatever the case, the end result was the evolution of two (or more) hominoid species utilizing both terrestrial and arboreal resources in a pattern that differed substantially from that of the large and small living apes of the Southeast Asia forests. This set the stage for a further adaptive shift in the smaller of these African hominoids.

A HYPOTHETICAL RECONSTRUCTION

What were these two lineages like? The larger form might have been much like living chimpanzees. An even larger species probably evolved either from it or parallel to it, giving rise to gorillas. (A very gorilla-like upper jaw and partial face, perhaps 15 million years old, was found at the Ugandan site of Moroto.) Surviving remnants of the earlier arboreal but non-brachiating proconsuls filled niches inhabited today by monkeys.

It is the smaller hominoid that would seem to be without living analogues. It probably looked like a gibbon with an expanded braincase (more chimpanzee-like) and without the extreme arm lengthening, although the forelimbs were almost surely longer than the hindlimbs; and it probably had a more robust body than the lightly built gibbon. Males may have had double the body weight of females. The creature's behavior on the ground is of most interest to us, although it may have utilized the arboreal aspects of its niche more extensively when in competition with larger hominoids.

When terrestrial, the small hominoid was probably more often bipedal than living apes, making use of an adaptation it evolved in a purely arboreal context. A gibbon-like terrestrial adaptation is not particularly efficient, and I suspect that as the terrestrial aspects of its adaptation became more important, balancing functions in this small hominoid shifted from the arms to the pelvis, and the other changes in the pelvis and lower limbs discussed in Chapter 4 came as a necessary consequence. These changes would tend to reduce (although not eliminate) the arboreal capabilities of the creature, while making it more capable of utilizing terrestrial resources.

In its behavior, one might expect capabilities similar to the living chimpanzees', although competition with the larger hominoids as well as with smaller proconsuls would insure some differences in adaptation. Like its larger relative, the small hominoid probably made and used tools to help gather and prepare foods. It may not have been as effective a hunter as the larger hominoid, or at best it hunted much smaller game. As a primate omnivore, it probably utilized a wide range of food resources, sharing rare or particularly desirable foods with all the members of the social group. Body size differences may have resulted in the beginnings of a sex-based division of labor, at least in food gathering. The small hominoid social groups may have followed the gibbon (or gelada) model of single male breeding units; whether these combined to form larger troops is impossible to guess. A more chimpanzee-like social structure is also possible. Whatever the case, a long period of social learning for the young and a fairly complex system of communication are suggested by studies of the living African apes, and it is possible that long periods between births also characterized the females of this species.

Of special interest are the adaptive differences between the small hominoid and its larger knuckle-walking contemporary. I suggest that the small hominoid, originally the more effectively arboreal, became the more effectively terrestrial, and that this change was associated with a habitat shift.

The Savanna Shift

I believe that four factors underlay the changing adaptation of the small hominoid: (1) the availability of the grasslands habitat and the common interfaces between grasslands and forest, (2) the development of an increasingly efficient form of terrestrial locomotion (bipedal striding) at the expense of whatever knuckle-walking capabilities may have been present, (3) the potential for food collection and defense allowed by tool use, and (4) competition with the larger hominoids with their effective adaptation to mixed forest/grasslands ecotones. In other words, the small hominoids had the *capability*, the *opportunity*, and the *motive* (in the evolutionary sense) to occupy a grasslands niche (see Figure 5.4).

THE PROBLEM OF PREDATION

A primate that might have escaped predators by climbing a tree would have to evolve new ways of defending itself on an open savanna. We know that in the much later appearing terrestrial baboons, the canine complex was greatly expanded in the males. In conjunction with the evolution of an elaborately differentiated social organization, this led to an adequate defense mechanism. On the other hand, behavioral modifications must come before morphological modifications, and the small hominoid already had a series of unique behaviors which could be easily elaborated, leading to modification in a completely different direction.

In this context, an experiment reported by Kortlandt is revealing. He placed a stuffed leopard skin in the path of a forest-dwelling chimpanzee group. Their reaction was to bypass it, staying close to the trees. However, a similar stuffed leopard skin placed in the path of a parklands-adapted chimpanzee group produced a very different result. Members of the troop "attacked" the leopard, often picking up pieces of wood to use as clubs. The attackers were well coordinated and were encouraged vocally by the onlookers. This difference in behavior is likely due to the decreased availability

FIGURE 5.4   *An open savanna in modern East Africa during the dry season.*

of trees as a means of escaping predators in the parklands environment.

In a truly open savanna, trees are not available as a means of escaping predation for most of the day, although they might have provided nighttime sleeping refuges. In a primate already using tools, selection for savanna survival could readily lead to dependence on tools for defense. Tools, even as simple as clubs, make better weapons than canines for at least two reasons. First, they allow fighting at less than extremely close quarters. Second, if clubs are broken, they can be replaced, unlike canines. However, for a club to be useful as a means of defense, it must be immediately available when needed. On an open savanna, this means carrying. Carrying clubs would involve little modification in a hominoid which was already a terrestrial biped, although the behavior might help select for a more efficient pelvic balance mechanism (if it was not already present) because of the weight added to the upper torso. This would result in the loss of any remaining quadrupedal capabilities.

With the more frequent use of grasslands, and the decreasing competition with the larger hominoids, an associated change might have been an increase in body size. This would reduce the number of important predators and also increase the power available for wielding clubs and throwing rocks.

CHANGES IN DIET

Only part of this adaptive shift responds to selection resulting from problems of defense. While the issue of how the small hominoids may have avoided predation in open grasslands is important, it may have been overemphasized as the *only* selective agency involved. The importance of Jolly's work is in his demonstration that this shift involved far more than escaping predation.

The seed-eater model suggests dietary advantages in utilizing a savanna niche, once a primate species is able to take advantage of the opportunity. Jolly believes that the crucial dietary shift comes with the exploitation of a habitat where the resources are largely grasses and seeds, without many trees. In reconstructing this habitat, he argues that most contemporary grasslands are likely the artifacts of human agriculture, resulting in the clearing of large areas. Grasslands which might be expected to occur before human intervention are found today under extremely dry conditions, or where poor drainage causes periodic flooding, inhibiting the growth of trees and shrubs. In such areas there is a rich food supply in grasses and broad-leafed plants, as well as in roots and tubers. These habitats provide a concentration of high-energy yielding food resources for a primate able to take advantage of them through adaptations to the specific requirements of food collection and preparation, as well as defense in treeless conditions.

Jolly and Mann have addressed themselves to the adaptations necessary for food collection and preparation under these circumstances. The cereal grains, roots, tubers, and bean pods must be collected, and then prepared for digestion by being ground down into digestible particles. In modern people, this preparation takes place outside of the mouth through technology, resulting in corn flakes, puffed wheat, bread, doughnuts, and Kentucky Fried Chicken. Such technology was unavailable to early hominids, and the preparation of cereal grains and other savanna foods was undoubtedly oral. What these food sources require in common is the ability to apply powerful forces in chewing, and the ability to resist or slow down rapid tooth wear—in other words big jaws and teeth.

Although the gelada provides a useful analogy, I believe that there are important differences between the living geladas and our small hominoid, lying mainly in the hominoid's adaptability. While hominoids did not evolve the grass-eating potential of *Theropithecus*, there is every reason to believe that they were otherwise able to utilize a maximum number of different environmental resources. Large jaws and teeth did not make them more specialized, but instead more adaptable.

Food availability varies seasonally on the savannas of Africa. Beginning with the heavy rains of the wet season, insects and grasses are abundant. Later in the wet season, the plants flower and produce seeds. The seeds remain available through the earlier parts of the dry season, but as the dry season proceeds, the grasses wither above the ground, storing nutrients in their roots or underground stems (rhizomes). On the wetter floodplains, some green foliage remains throughout the dry season.

The situation is different in open woodlands, the hypothesized habitat of the larger hominoid that was probably ancestral to living African apes. The main fruiting season for the trees occurs in the span from the early dry season through the early wet season, just when food is most difficult to obtain on the savanna. Food resource competition would be at its extreme on the savanna during the major portion of the dry season, even if hunting were an important behavior, since this is when the savanna herbivores are the most widely dispersed. In contrast, in a woodlands ecology the major dietary competition takes place during the wet season, when the fruit-eating (frugivorous) primates must shift to a diet of far less nutritious leaves.

The adaptation of a hominoid primate to savanna conditions would involve utilizing a wide range of different and often difficult-to-obtain food sources, possibly combined with seasonal migrations. When comparing the (hypothesized) adaptive patterns of the small hominoid and *Theropithecus*, it is easy to understand why selection in the larger-brained hominoids might result in optimizing dietary adaptability.

The dietary regimes of both savanna-adapted hominoids and *Theropithecus* include several foods which require powerful chewing, such as seeds and tough bean pods. Differences between these two taxa include the grass-eating capabilities of *Theropithecus* and certain advantageous hominoid adaptations. For instance, even the simplest tool uses would be of decided advantage during the dry season when competition was most severe, and at the same time would allow the hominoids to collect roots and rhizomes, adding to the selection for large teeth and thick tooth enamel. That Pliocene hominoids used these rich food resources is suggested by the marked tooth chipping that characterizes many of the early australopithecines. It is thought that soil particles clinging to roots and rhizomes caused the chipping. Baboons and geladas, on the other hand, rarely eat roots and tubers, even during the dry season when other foods are scarce.

In sum, the small hominoid's adaptation to savanna food resources was based on an expanding adaptability. Tool use, in combination with enlarged jaws and teeth, gave the small hominoid a wide dietary range and an effective adaptation to the open grasslands during all seasons.

To what extent other behavioral capabilities hypothesized for the small hominoid were present remains unknown. The *potential* importance of these capabilities in the grasslands habitat cannot be overstated, and whatever the degree of sharing and sex-based division of labor that was present, these activities could only have increased in importance.

CANINE REDUCTION

Canine reduction is a complex issue, although it is likely tied to bipedalism and tool use. Simple tools that could be picked up and used came to replace canines in their various uses for displays and defense. In addition, breaking a pebble would produce a cutting edge for food preparation, animal skinning and dismemberment, and fighting, and the pebble (unlike canines) could be replaced. Minimal modification of pebbles surely preceded even the simplest recognizable stone tools.

As dependence on tools increased, the canines changed in their function and reduced in their size. For a primate that uses tools, there are advantages in having a small incisor-like canine. If canines are no longer needed for cutting and slashing, they are in an excellent position for gripping, holding, and pulling. Human canines are used for these purposes today, as are the large incisors of apes. Reduction of hominid canines to the approximate level of the other teeth, and their modification to a more blunted, spade-like shape, is analogous to the expansion of pongid incisors, with the added advantage of a larger root. (The size of the incisor root is limited by the space available between the palate and the nose, whereas the canine roots can continue along the side of the nose.) Furthermore, a curved root makes canines less likely to be lost during life than incisors, which have straight tapering roots.

Interestingly, the fossil record indicates that changes in hominid canines were not an early consequence of the grasslands adaptation. The canine/premolar cutting complex seems to have been an important aspect of this adaptation for a long period of time. Changes apparently came only with the increasing importance *and* sophistication of tools.

INTELLIGENCE

The fourth element of Darwin's complex is the increase in intelligence, and associated changes in the size and structure of the brain. It seems likely that expanding intellectual capacities were not one of the more important aspects of the small hominoid's grasslands adaptation. The changes that took place during this period were more in reorganization than in size. Natural casts of the insides of later Pliocene hominid crania show marked structural differences from living pongids' crania with little increase in size.

The key to what took place during the earlier stages of the grasslands adaptation probably lies in the increasing importance of behavioral adaptability and the amount of information that must be learned by the young. With more to be learned during childhood and adolescence, the advantage would lie in speeding up the rate of learning. Thus brain changes in these hominoids were probably in the development of more complex neural models and increased connectivity between association and ordering areas in the brain. Behavioral complexity became an increasingly important aspect of social structure, as well as of food gathering and defense. As discussed above, canine reduction placed emphasis on the social control of behavior, and the importance of sharing and a division of labor almost certainly led to an increasingly complex range of social behaviors. What ultimately emerged were social groups with structured role differences based on far more than age, sex, and body size.

Another effect of the developing behavioral complexity might have been the formalization of relations that allowed a shortening of the time between successive births by ensuring care for dependent infants. The subsequent increase in fertility allowed population expansion in the small species and provided an important competitive advantage over the more arboreal hominoids and perhaps also over the emerging cercopithecoids.

IT'S ONLY A MODEL

The small hominoid was, of course, a hominid. At what point it became a hominid depends on whether a phylogenetic or an adaptive difference is used as a means of definition. Phylogenetically it became a hominid when the initial smaller-larger dichotomy appeared in the still arboreal brachiating form. Adaptively, it became a recognizable hominid with the shift to an open grasslands habitat.

How much of this model is correct will ultimately be shown by the fossil record. At present, there is simply not enough evidence to be certain. There *might* have been a third small ape—at least there is a contender for the honor. However, nothing is yet known of its locomotion. In the Pliocene hominids (see Chapter 7) a polished form of bipedalism was present by about 3 million years ago. This was before full canine reduction had taken place and not long after the existence of hominids which retained some cutting functions in the canine/premolar complex. No evidence at present traces any form of bipedalism back to an arboreal ancestry. In all, the locomotor history of our lineage is unclear, and until more evidence is discovered, a number of alternatives will remain viable.

The problems surrounding the appearance of tool use and tool making are equally cloudy; how long a period intervened between the earliest tools and the earliest *recognizable* tools is unknown, and perhaps unknowable.

At best, then, the model developed here may be useful in interpreting the fossil record, or at least in providing one series of interpretations. Only subsequent discoveries will determine whether it is the best model of hominid origins.

SUMMARY

Two broad hypotheses for the origin of hominids have been presented. Darwin's model suggests a functional interrelationship between bipedalism, canine reduction, tool use, and intelligence through his contention that these form a terrestrial hunting adaptation. In an elaboration of Darwin's model, Dart emphasized the importance of carnivorous behavior in the early hominids; others, such as Ardrey and Morris, took this emphasis on agression and violence to an extreme that is unacceptable to most workers. Washburn and Lancaster, among others, have stressed the social activity aspect of Darwin's model, arguing that early hominids are the result of a chimpanzee-like primate occupying a baboon-type niche. Brace has focused on the importance of tool use for survival, while Mann explored the social implications of tool use and Lovejoy studied the demographic consequences of behaviors that allow reduced birth spacing.

A different model, essentially dietary, has been suggested by Jolly. He draws an analogy with fossil and living baboons of the genus *Theropithecus*, arguing that an adaptation to a savanna diet consisting (in part) of small difficult-to-masticate food objects could account for many of the morphological and behavioral aspects of early hominid evolution. Other workers, including this author, have broadened this concept to include a wider dietary regime while retaining the emphasis on powerful mastication as a critical factor.

Morphological comparisons of humans and the African apes suggest that human ancestors passed through an arboreal stage which very likely involved some degree of brachiation and arm hanging. Tuttle has argued that the hominid lineage is derived from a small brachiating Miocene ape which paralleled the gibbon in its emphasis on vertical climbing and arboreal bipedalism.

I suggest a possible synthesis of these models, based on the following contentions. Middle Miocene hominoids included a small brachiating species that emphasized arboreal bipedalism and at least one larger, more quadrupedal species. The massive geological changes in East Africa associated with the creation of the East African rift provided an impetus for terrestrial adaptations in these hominoids through the creation of new environmental habitats and mosaics. The hominoids began to utilize terrestrial aspects of their habitats, the larger ones relying on knuckle-walking, the smaller ones improving their bipedal capabilities.

Four factors, I believe, underlay an adaptation to the savanna by the smaller hominoid species: (1) the availability of the grasslands habitat and frequent interfaces between grasslands and forest, (2) the development of increasingly effective bipedalism, (3) the potential for collecting new foods and for defense provided by an incipient form of tool use, and (4) competition with the larger hominoid (perhaps proto-ape) species, whose adaptation may have more effectively utilized the areas where forest and grasslands met (resembling living chimpanzees). The changes in selection would, by this model, result in a recognizable hominid.

STATE OF THE ART

One of the nagging problems raised in this chapter is that of canine reduction. With few exceptions, virtually all workers from Darwin's time on have believed that large conical canines honing against a tooth in the opposite jaw is the ancestral condition for hominids. Darwin's explanation for canine reduction in size and change in form, still accepted by many today, was that tools and weapons took over their function in combat. Elaborations on this argument have offered defense, food preparation, and object manipulation as the canine functions that were taken over by tools.

Only two other general explanatory arguments have been offered. The first of these relates canine reduction to changing aspects of intertroop aggression. One possibility is that with decreasing aggressive displays and interactions in the hominids, changes in hormonal levels might account for canine reduction; another is that tools replaced the canines in aggressive interactions. In either case, canine reduction is tied to the development of a body of rules and expectations governing and displacing primary aggressive interactions between individuals. The second explanatory argument relates canine reduction to changes in the posterior dental complex associated with powerful mastication. Whether through allometry (relative growth) or because canine interlock restricted grinding, canine reduction is tied to an expansion of the posterior teeth.

Each of these arguments has its weak points. Any suggestion of tool replacement raises the problem of mechanism. Did the canines reduce because of accumulating mutations in a structure under relaxed selection, or was there selection for the reduction and change in form? If selection is the explanation, what is the advantage of reduced canines? Some workers have suggested that there is a "biological budget effect" resulting in an advantage to channeling the "wasted" energy used in developing unnecessary structures into more useful features. Another potential mechanism was proposed by W. Jungers, who ties canine reduction to the reduced space available in jaws with expanded posterior teeth. (This could also account for the earlier canine eruption in hominids.) Others, however, have looked for more directly functional advantages to the canine changes. One of these might be the elimination of canine interlock (see below). Another is the use of the canines for gripping and holding; this is best accomplished with a short blunt canine, which is better suited than the incisors because its root is much longer. In sum, while hypothetical mechanisms for reduction due to replacement by tools are not lacking, there is no way at present to choose among them. This is partly a general problem: how does one distinguish between reduction due to the lack of selection and reduction due to low levels of selection? Another contributing factor, however, is the lack of hominid fossils from the period when canines were reducing.

The aggressive display argument has the same weakness of mechanism. Moreover, the likelihood that early hominids maintained a marked degree of sexual dimorphism in canine size and form after a reduced incisiform tooth had appeared suggests that males may have continued to utilize the canines in some intertroop displays.

The suggestion that canine reduction may be tied to posterior tooth expansion can also be questioned. Jolly, who proposed this as part of his *Theropithecus* analogy, argues that the larger-toothed forms have reduced canines. Washburn and Ciochon dispute the basic data. Moreover, even if true, the argument does not explain the change in canine *form* that has characterized hominid evolution. The allometric argument suffers from the same problem. Even if it is true that the exponent of the allometric equation is smaller for the canine than for the posterior teeth, resulting in *relatively* smaller canines in forms undergoing posterior tooth expansion, neither the change in canine form nor the reduction in *absolute* size can be explained. Finally, the "data" supporting the canine interlock argument have been questioned for pongids. The traditional view that the interlocking canines prevent rotary motion during chewing has been countered in part by both studies of tooth wear and examinations of jaw motions during chewing.

To further complicate the issue, recognizable early hominids from the middle to late Pliocene sites of Laetolil (in Tanzania) and the Afar (in Ethiopia) have canines that are comparatively smaller than the earlier dryopithecines' but which were used for cutting in at least some of the specimens. While the exact anatomy of the canine honing is somewhat different from that in dryopithecines (or pongids), some size reduction clearly preceded the appearance of an incisiform tooth. Moreover, recognizable stone tools have not yet been associated with these hominids. To some extent this may argue against Darwin's hypothesis of a functional relationship between changes in the canines, tool use, and intelligence. On the other hand, it may be that the functional changes occurred as Darwin sug-

gested but the morphological results took longer to appear in the canines.

In sum, while there seems no question that hominid canines have changed in both size and form, why this happened is far from settled and exactly when is also somewhat hazy.

FURTHER READINGS

ANDREWS, P., and J. A. H. VAN COUVERING. 1975. Palaeoenvironments in the East African Miocene. In Approaches to Primate Paleobiology, ed. F. Szalay. Contributions to Primatology 5:62–103.
A fairly technical paper discussing the environmental background in East Africa at the time hominids may have emerged.

ARDREY, R. 1961. African Genesis. Dell, New York.
Popularization of the "killer-ape" hypothesis.

BARTHOLOMEW, G. A., and J. B. BIRDSELL. 1953. Ecology and the Protohominids. American Anthropologist 55:481–498.
The classic paper concerning early hominid adaptation and ecology, and how they may have influenced their morphology. Basically this is an elaboration of the Darwinian framework.

BRACE, C. L. 1970. The Origins of Man. Natural History 79:46–49.
Emphasis is placed on the importance of culture and technology.

DART, R. A., with D. CRAIG. 1959. Adventures with the Missing Link. Viking, New York.
A personal but very elaborate statement of Dart's views in a historical context.

EISELEY, L. 1961. Darwin's Century. Doubleday Anchor, Garden City.
The historic background for Darwin's ideas presented in a very readable account.

GOODALL, J. 1976. Continuities Between Chimpanzee and Human Behavior. In Human Origins, eds. G. L. Isaac and E. R. McCown. Staples Press, Menlo Park, pp. 81–95.
An introductory presentation of the "humanized" chimpanzee.

JOLLY, C. J. 1970. The Seed Eaters: A New Model of Hominid Differentiation Based on a Baboon Analogy. Man 5:5–26.
The original statement of the "seed-eater" hypothesis.

———. 1973. Changing Views of Hominid Origins. Yearbook of Physical Anthropology 16:1–17.
Probably the most comprehensive historical presentation of theories concerning hominid origins.

KORTLANDT, A. 1972. New Perspectives on Ape and Human Evolution. Department of Animal Psychology and Ethology, University of Amsterdam.
A rather different view of the ape-human divergence suggesting among other things that chimpanzees may have been far more hominid-like in the past.

KURTÉN, B. 1972. Not from the Apes. Pantheon, New York.
The best statement of a prebrachiationist viewpoint.

LANCASTER, J. B. 1976. Sex Roles in Primate Societies. In Sex Differences: Social and Biological Perspectives, ed. M. S. Teitelbaum. Anchor, Garden City, pp. 22–61.
A survey of sex roles in primate societies and a discussion of division of economic labor as a critical factor in hominid origins.

MANN, A. 1972. Hominid and Cultural Origins. Man 7:379–386.
An elaboration of the possible interconnection of human and cultural origins, followed by a discussion of direct evidence for cultural behavior in early hominids.

MORRIS, D. 1967. The Naked Ape. Dell, New York.
Popularization of the view emphasizing the possible importance of aggression in hominid origins and early evolution.

PILBEAM, D. 1972. An Idea We Could Do Without—The Naked Ape. Discovery 7(2):63–70.
A well-written reply to Morris' book.

SHAFTON, A. 1976. Conditions of Awareness. Riverside, Portland.
An attempt to draw continuities between the origin and evolution of human cognition and behavior and what can be inferred of these in the higher primates.

TANNER, N., and A. ZIHLMAN. 1976. Women in Evolution. Part 1: Innovation and Selection in Human Origins. *Signs: Journal Of Women in Culture and Society* 1:585-608.

A provocative discussion of the often neglected role of women in the adaptive changes surrounding hominid origins.

TELEKI, G. 1974. Chimpanzee Subsistence Technology: Materials and Skills. *Journal of Human Evolution* 3:575-594.

Probably the most comprehensive discussion of chimpanzee technology and an important parallel to discussions of early hominid tool use.

TUTTLE, R. H. 1975. Parallelism, Brachiation, and Hominid Phylogeny. In *Phylogeny of the Primates*, eds. W. P. Luckett and F. S. Szalay. Plenum, New York, pp. 447-480.

An introduction to Tuttle's small ape model of hominid origins.

WASHBURN, S. L. 1968. *The Study of Human Evolution.* Condon Lecture, Oregon State System of Higher Education, Eugene.

An anatomically oriented presentation of the knuckle-walking hypothesis.

CHAPTER SIX

The First Hominids

*T*heories of hominid origins must ultimately be judged against the fossil record. This chapter discusses the adaptive radiation of a certain primate group that existed between about 15 and 8 million years ago. For the group itself I will use the term "ramapithecine" to emphasize the broad similarities within it and the fact that it represents an equivalent taxonomic unit to the adaptive radiation represented by the dryopithecines. I do not mean to define the term in a formal taxonomic sense. In my view, whether or not these specimens form a valid family cannot be decided on the present evidence.

The group consists of a number of closely related forms, including the genus *Ramapithecus* as well as other genera once thought to be much more distinct from *Ramapithecus* than current evidence now suggests. There may be as many as four size forms in this radiation, and the geographic range is from the tropics to southern temperate areas of the Old World. Whether one of the lineages is ancestral to hominids is the main topic of this chapter.

The hominid-like features of the ramapithecines were first recognized in the genus *Ramapithecus*. The initial part of this chapter reviews the history of *Ramapithecus* discoveries. This is followed by a discussion of the Fort Ternan site in East Africa, where the earliest securely dated *Ramapithecus* remains and the only clearly identifiable ones from anywhere in Africa have been found. The ramapithecine diffusion into Europe is discussed with descriptions of specimens from Turkey, Hungary, and Greece. Finally, the Asiatic sample is considered; this is the area with the greatest variability. The concluding section discusses the adaptive radiation as a whole with special attention to the specific question of hominid ancestry.

When Did Hominids Originate?

The fact that our closest primate relatives live in Africa today and the presence of Pliocene hominids exclusively in Africa support Darwin's contention of an African origin. But when did this occur? The earlier middle Miocene is too early. *Proconsul* postcrania dated to about 18 million years ago lack many of the brachiation adaptations that are shared by modern humans and apes; the lineages had not diverged yet. The middle Pliocene is too late. Clearly distinguishable hominids are known from East African deposits almost 4 million years old, and slightly older specimens may also be hominids. The maximum time range for hominid origins, then, is between 4 and 18 million years ago. The minimum range, based on evidence available at this time, is from 6 to 16 million years ago, and this is the period over which the search for the earliest hominids is focused.

Discovery of the Ramapithecines

Within this time range, one hominoid primate has been presented as the earliest hominid. This is the taxon commonly referred to as *Ramapithecus*. The primate was originally identified in Asia, as the result of fossil collection on the Indian subcontinent early in this century. At that time, many scholars thought that humans originated somewhere in Asia, and early expeditions bringing back the remains of fossil apes with what were then thought to be hominid-like features stimulated the attempt to find early hominids in the tropical and subtropical regions of Asia. These Asian fossil apes are now generally classified in the genus *Sivapithecus* (sometimes used as a synonym for the European fossil ape genus *Dryopithecus*). In the first quarter of the century, various *Sivapithecus* species were proposed as being especially closely related to hominids.

A Yale University expedition to India in 1932 resulted in a great expansion of the *Sivapithecus* sample. G. E. Lewis, who described the specimens that were found, was the first to suggest that a different genus ancestral to hominids was also present: *Ramapithecus*. The best preserved specimen was part of an upper jaw (maxilla) with postcanine teeth and sockets for the canine and incisors. Lewis felt that this fragment showed hominid-like features, including a parabolic-shaped tooth row, a small canine, lack of a diastema, and reduced prognathism of the anterior teeth. These are some of the features of upper jaws that distinguish *modern* humans from apes; they are visible in Figure 4.6. Attempts to find this particular set of features in fossil jaws fit the savanna chimpanzee model, which suggested

that early hominids were descended from a primate with chimpanzee-like jaws that underwent anterior tooth reduction. However, how many of these features were actually present in *Ramapithecus* was not clear because of the fragmentary condition of the specimen. A contemporary scholar, A. Hrdlička, rejected Lewis' claims and argued that *Ramapithecus* had best be regarded as a small female ape.

The issue remained unresolved until the early 1960s when the Yale paleontologist E. L. Simons reopened the case for *Ramapithecus* as a hominid ancestor. He added more specimens to the genus by associating mandibles formerly placed in the genus "*Bramapithecus*" with *Ramapithecus*. At that time, no *Ramapithecus* mandibles and no "*Bramapithecus*" maxillas had been identified. Simons noted that the upper and lower jaws were the same size and probably represented the same taxon. The remaining Asiatic hominoids, equally fragmentary, were mainly placed in two species of the genus *Dryopithecus*, *D. sivalensis* (a medium-sized form) and *D. indicus* (a larger form), in an important revision of fossil hominoids published by E. L. Simons and D. Pilbeam. Many scholars now place these species in the genus *Sivapithecus* because of their distinctions from the dryopithecines of Europe and from the earlier proconsuls of Africa. (See Table 6.1, p.108, for a comparison of various ramapithecine forms.)

At about this time, L. S. B. Leakey recovered the upper jaw of a closely related hominoid at the Fort Ternan site in Kenya; he placed this in the genus *Kenyapithecus*. Most workers regarded *Kenyapithecus* as an early form of *Ramapithecus*. Discoveries of jaws and teeth continued through the 1960s, although none was complete enough for an accurate reconstruction of the face or tooth row shape.

In 1971, P. Andrews of the National Museums of Kenya discovered that a lower jaw from Fort Ternan belonged to the same specimen as the *Kenyapithecus* maxilla. The lower jaw extended past the midline of symmetry, and for the first time a reconstruction of jaw shape and the lower face could be attempted. Subsequent work by A. Walker provided this reconstruction, which, as it turned out, was indeed hominid-like in some respects but not in the ways suggested by Lewis.

Also in the late 1960s and early 1970s, the vertebrate paleontologist M. Kretzoi recovered a large sample of Hungarian primates also closely related to *Ramapithecus*, plus a similar larger form. He placed these in *Rudapithecus* and *Bodvapithecus*, re-

TABLE 6.1   The ramapithecine adaptive radiation of the Miocene is represented by four distinct size forms spread over the Old World. This table presents the various names that have been given these forms in the different areas where they have been recovered. Many of these taxonomic names are probably invalid. While samples of the same size differ somewhat from area to area, it is likely that these differences are due to no more than normal geographic variation, differences in dates, and the small sample sizes. Whether all of these four forms are different on the species level is unclear. *Ouranopithecus* males and females fall into two different size groups, and it is possible that at other sites, such as Pasalar and Rudabánya, the two taxa are also actually two sexes of the same taxon. The smallest is probably even smaller than a pygmy chimpanzee, the medium species seems the size of a small chimpanzee, and the large species the size of a large chimpanzee or small gorilla. The size of the very large species is uncertain, but it is probably at least as large as a gorilla.

	Africa	Near East (Turkey)	Southern Central Europe	Asia
Small	*Kenyapithecus wickeri* (Fort Ternan)	*Sivapithecus Alpani* (Çandir)	*Rudapithecus hungaricus* (Rudabánya)	*Ramapithecus punjabicus*
Medium	(?) *Sivapithecus africanus*	*Ramapithecus wickeri* (Pasalar)	*Bodvapithecus altpalatus* (Rudabánya)	*Sivapithecus sivalensis* *Ramapithecus lufengensis*
Large		*Sivapithecus darwini* (Pasalar) *Ankarapithecus meteai*	*Ouranopithecus macedoniensis* ♀ (Ravin de la Pluie) *Graecopithecus freybergi* (Pyrgos)	*Sivapithecus indicus* *Sivapithecus yannanensis*
Very Large			*Ouranopithecus macedoniensis* ♂ (Ravin de la Pluie)	*Gigantopithecus bilaspurensis* (? ♀)

spectively. Fragments of crania and postcrania were discovered for the first time. An even larger but otherwise similar hominoid, *Ouranopithecus*, was discovered in northern Greek deposits by L. de Bonis and J. Melentis, paleontologists from France and Greece. While again only jaws and teeth were found, the specimens seem to have been deposited in a single catastrophic event and may belong to the same population. This Greek hominoid provides continuity in size with an even larger Asiatic form, also closely related to the smaller species, called *Gigantopithecus*. *Ouranopithecus* bridged what was a size gap between the largest and smallest species when these were the only known.

The largest of this closely related group, *Gigantopithecus*, was first discovered in Hong Kong drug stores by G. H. R. von Koenigswald. The Chinese used fossils in many of their pharmaceutical preparations, and von Koenigswald made a habit of searching through the fossils for particularly interesting specimens. The remains of *Gigantopithecus*

were represented by a few extraordinarily large molar teeth which he found in the early 1940s.

F. Weidenreich recognized the hominid-like characteristics of these teeth, and in 1945 he published a work suggesting that *Gigantopithecus* was ancestral to hominids, and that later hominids underwent dramatic size reduction during their evolution. Subsequent work in the People's Republic of China (PRC) resulted in the identification of where the *Gigantopithecus* teeth came from (mostly South China) and the recovery of over a thousand additional teeth and three lower jaws.

In the middle 1960s, E. L. Simons discovered an earlier representative of *Gigantopithecus* in India, possibly contemporary with *Ramapithecus* and *Sivapithecus*. Finally, the last few years have seen a multiplication of the ramapithecine sample. A well-preserved mandible of *Ramapithecus* and a more fragmentary lower jaw of a larger hominoid (*Ankarapithecus*, reclassified as *Sivapithecus*), as well as numerous isolated teeth have been discovered in

Turkey. An expedition to Pakistan under the direction of D. Pilbeam has recovered essentially contemporary remains of the four Asiatic ramapithecines, as well as postcrania. On the basis of these new discoveries, Pilbeam has reevaluated his earlier view of all Asiatic hominoids, now suggesting that they are probably much more similar and closely related than once thought. Moreover, Pilbeam has now recognized the possibility that the earliest hominid may not be a *Ramapithecus* species. New specimens including a face, isolated teeth, and two mandibles have also been reported from the PRC. In sum, the twentieth century has provided a bewildering array of various-sized taxa (Table 6.1 should be a helpful guide) resembling one another and showing some resemblances to Pliocene hominids. Recognizing this relationship, I propose to call these "ramapithecines" and will devote this chapter to the problem of how they are related and the question of whether one or more of the ramapithecine species is a hominid ancestor.

Fort Ternan

The problem of relationships is probably best considered in a time sequence. Therefore, it will be useful to turn first to the earliest securely dated ramapithecine remains, from Fort Ternan in Kenya. When the primates found there died and became fossilized, between 13 and 14 million years ago on the basis of Potassium-Argon dates, the Fort Ternan site was the base of what was then a forested volcano. It was the activity of the volcano that provided volcanic deposits that could be radiometrically dated.

The volcano was one of those formed during the East African rifting process. Almost completely surrounding it was a drainage river; the fossil deposits are in what were then shallow gulleys just on the other side of the river, where the country became open grasslands. In fact, Fort Ternan has the earliest distinct savanna fauna (from the Miocene) in East Africa; here, giraffe-like and ostrich-like forms are found for the first time. In the deposits are also forest forms, including snails, rodents, some proconsuls, and the small hominoid *Limnopithecus*. The reconstruction of the prehistoric ecology and the forms present in the deposits are important because they bear on the question of whether the

ramapithecine discovered there was savanna adapted, forest adapted, or forest fringe adapted.

In this case the picture is not clear. One might expect the ramapithecine to be a forest fringe or savanna form if it is an early hominid, and some coincidental evidence suggests that it might be. The earliest ramapithecine is found at a site with the earliest appearance of savanna fauna. However, the fact that animals adapted to wet evergreen forests are also present (washed down from the volcano's slopes) raises the possibility that this ramapithecine may have lived on the forested higher mountain slopes. In the end, no firm habitat association is possible.

THE AFRICAN RAMAPITHECINE REMAINS

Kenyapithecus wickeri is the name that was given by L. S. B. Leakey to the ramapithecines found at Fort Ternan. Whether or not this is a valid taxon, it is clear that *Kenyapithecus* is remarkably similar to *Ramapithecus*. I will refer to it as the African *Ramapithecus* variant. The Fort Ternan remains are elusively incomplete. The associated upper and lower jaw give just enough information to reconstruct the lower face, and a few isolated additional teeth help complete this reconstruction. However, nothing remains of this primate above the nose or below the jaw, so that most of the information that is potentially important is denied to us.

The reconstructed specimen (see Figure 6.1, p. 110) provides evidence of the incisors, canines, and posterior teeth that gives insight into its canine functions and chewing adaptations. The shape of the reconstructed tooth row does not meet earlier expectations of the parabolic arcade. Instead, the teeth form a straight line backward from the canine, and the two tooth rows diverge from each other posteriorly. At the front, the canines are not far apart; there is little room left for the incisors, which, by inference, were probably quite small. While this pattern is quite unlike the expanded anterior teeth of living pongids, there is nothing unusual about it in the Miocene. This tooth row shape is much the same in the earlier proconsuls; it appears to be the ancestral condition in hominoids.

The Fort Ternan *Ramapithecus* differs from similar-sized proconsuls in the size of its canine relative to the molars. The canine is relatively small compared to these grinding teeth. Details of canine

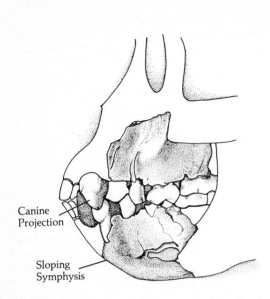

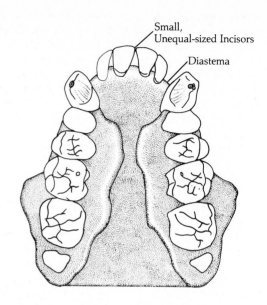

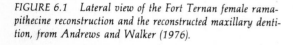

FIGURE 6.1   Lateral view of the Fort Ternan female ramapithecine reconstruction and the reconstructed maxillary dentition, from Andrews and Walker (1976).

form suggest that this specimen was a female. It is probable that males had larger canines. Nonetheless, the specimen suggests that some canine size reduction may have taken place, although *relative* canine size is still like that in some of the living pongids (matching the proportion found in female gorillas). Moreover, the *function* of the canine was clearly *Proconsul-* (pongid-) like. The tooth is pointed and its back edge is sharp. The crown projected well below the remaining teeth, and the sharp back edge cut against the front edge of the first lower premolar (see Figure 3.4). This premolar has the single cusp common in pongid and *Proconsul* teeth. In sum, the Fort Ternan primate shows no modification from the *Proconsul* canine/premolar cutting complex.

It is in the more posterior teeth and the functionally related portions of the jaws that the main differences with the earlier *Proconsul* species lie. Compared to the size of the palate, these teeth appear to be expanded in size, and their enamel is much thicker than in the proconsuls or living pongids. The portions of the jaws holding the tooth roots are also thick, and there is a pronounced buttress across the back surface of the symphysis (the

front of the mandible) which occurs in primates that produce powerful forces between their molars when chewing. Powerful chewing is also suggested by the morphology of the cheeks. The zygomatic process (Figure 5.2) swings widely to the sides of the face. Since the temporalis muscle passes to the inside of this process, occupying the space (temporal fossa) between the zygomatic and the side of the cranial vault, the wide outward swing suggests that a large space was enclosed. This, in turn, indicates that the temporalis muscle was large. An additional effect of the zygomatic form results in a more horizontal orientation for the masseter muscle (Figure 4.8), since the muscle must have a greater angle to the vertical in order to reach the widely positioned zygomatics. This acts to provide more transverse force during the jaw motions of chewing. The latter suggestion is supported by a study of the direction of the scratches on the Fort Ternan primate's molars. These were made by food particles as they passed across the teeth, and are almost always in the side-to-side direction.

Taken together, these features indicate that powerful chewing played an important part in this ramapithecine's adaptation. The large posterior teeth and thick enamel can better hold up to forces that cause tooth wear, and the thickened jaws help support the teeth when these forces are applied. The internal buttress across the front of the mandible also gives evidence of powerful chewing. When there is food between the molars, the mandible tends to be twisted, as one twists a wishbone by pushing one end up and the other down. In the mandible, twisting is caused by a combination of the force of the food and the forces of the muscles. In addition, muscular forces pull the sides of the mandible together. Similar to the wishbone, the mandible is weakest at its front; natural selection leads to the appearance of extra bone to strengthen this area when powerful chewing is an important means of adaptation.

PHYLOGENY

Considered in the simplest sense, the Fort Ternan *Ramapithecus* remains are similar to the earlier *Proconsul* species in many features. The best-preserved specimen may differ from the earlier hominoids in relative canine size, although a sample of one is too small to be sure of this. It clearly *does* differ from the earlier hominoids in the development of muscular, bony, and dental adaptations to a diet requiring powerful and/or prolonged chewing. Moreover, this adaptation is similar to that found in Pliocene hominids. Thus, there is a *prima facie* case for considering *Ramapithecus* an early member of the hominid lineage, according to Jolly's hypothesis that dietary specialization was an early distinction of hominids. Of course, a clear ecological association, knowledge of the rest of the skull and postcranial skeleton, and the discovery of modified natural objects would be most helpful in establishing this case, but at present this information is denied to us.

If *Ramapithecus* is an early member of the hominid lineage, the most critical piece of information it provides about hominid origins is the early importance of the dietary shift discussed in the previous chapter.

The Spread to Europe

The Miocene faunal exchanges which brought European species into East Africa also allowed African species to spread into Eurasia. Included in these interchanges were the various hominoids from East Africa. *Limnopithecus* might have given rise to the European gibbon-like form *Pliopithecus*, and ultimately to gibbons and siamangs. One (or more) of the *Proconsul* species was ancestral to the European fossil ape genus *Dryopithecus*. The ramapithecines were also part of this faunal exchange, giving rise

to a variety of related Eurasian forms in what was apparently a fairly successful adaptive radiation.

Ramapithecine forms as small as those known from the earlier Fort Ternan deposits are distributed from Hungary to China; dryopithecine species seem to have a more western distribution in Europe, although there is an overlap of ranges. The completeness of this Eurasian material has provided important insights into the morphology and adaptations of the ramapithecines.

SPECIMENS FROM TURKEY

A virtually complete mandible was discovered by I. Tekkaya at a site near Ankara called Çandir (see Figure 6.2). This specimen was first called *Sivapithecus*, but it has become clear that it represents *Ramapithecus*. The environment seems to have been a mixture of forest and grasslands, and the date may be as much as several million years later than Fort Ternan. The shape of the tooth row and the size and morphology of the postcanine teeth closely duplicate the less complete Fort Ternan specimen (the anterior teeth were not preserved). Also like it, the snout is extremely short; toward the front, the sides of the mandible curve sharply inward at the premolar. The symphysis differs from the earlier African specimen and even more so from the

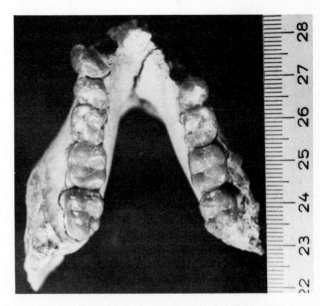

FIGURE 6.2 *Occlusal view of the Çandir mandible, one of the most complete smaller ramapithecines (only the anterior teeth are lost). (Photograph courtesy of I. Tekkaya.)*

proconsuls in two respects: it is shorter but more vertical, and the two internal buttresses are higher and more evenly developed. In both of these features, it more closely resembles the Pliocene australopithecines. The third molar is the largest of the three and is extraordinarily elongated in a triangle-like shape, pointed toward the rear. This feature was once thought to be a unique distinction of the largest ramapithecine taxon.

Another larger but more fragmentary mandible from a nearby site was classified in a new genus, *Ankarapithecus*, when it was discovered in the mid-1960s. The specimen differs from proconsuls of similar size in the relative size of its canine (which is somewhat reduced), the thickness of its molar enamel, and the robustness of the mandibular body. These distinctions are similar to those of *Ramapithecus*, although the details are not the same.

Finally, recent work by P. Andrews and H. Tobien has led to the discovery of numerous teeth indicating what may be medium and larger ramapithecine forms at the site of Pasalar in Turkey. However, this dental set raises a fundamental problem in interpreting the Turkish as well as other European samples. The large and smaller teeth are virtually identical in everything but size, and may therefore represent males and females of a single species with marked (i.e., *Proconsul*-like) sexual dimorphism.

Some of the Turkish material may have a fairly early date, although whether or not any of these specimens are earlier than the Fort Ternan remains is obscured by the fact that the dates for the Turkish material are based on faunal comparisons and therefore are relative. Whatever the case, the presence of distinctive ramapithecine forms near Africa early in time suggests that the adaptive radiation may have begun in Africa itself.

THE SMALLER HUNGARIAN FORMS

In his excavations at the Hungarian site of Ruda-bánya, M. Kretzoi has recovered the remains of four different higher primates. One of these is a macaque-sized monkey, very rare at the estimated 11–12 million year date for the site. *Pliopithecus* is also present. Kretzoi believes that ramapithecines are represented by two species; the smaller of these is of the Çandir size. Rudabánya represents the remains of a lake sheltered in a valley with oak forest

on the slopes and grasslands in the immediate vicinity.

Rudapithecus, the smaller of the Rudabányan ramapithecines, is represented by a fairly large sample of jaws and teeth. Some of the smaller postcrania found at the site might also belong to the species. Where comparisons are possible, the features of the *Rudapithecus* lower jaws and teeth are so similar to the specimens described above that the taxon is clearly the same, *Ramapithecus*. The larger sample size, however, provides evidence of variation in many of the features previously considered distinctive for the ramapithecines. For instance, while the taxon was thought to have shallow, thick mandibles, one Rudabányan mandible (RUD-1) is particularly thin and deep, although a second (RUD-17) is shallower. RUD-2, a broken and distorted specimen, provides the first evidence of the vertical portion of the mandible, the ramus. Figure 6.3 shows the RUD-2 and RUD-17 mandibles.

The RUD-2 ramus begins in an anterior position (as in the gelada, see Figure 5.1), showing that the jaw was short and by inference that the face was not projecting. Moreover, the ramus is tall and vertical, again paralleling the gelada and indicating marked facial depth. These remains provide further evidence of a ramapithecine adaptation to powerful or prolonged chewing.

The canines show little if any size reduction. For instance, in the RUD-17 male mandible, a break exposing the root of this tooth shows that it extends almost to the base of the mandible. Wear on all of the canines demonstrates that they were used in cutting and slashing; a sharpened back edge was inevitably formed by wear against the opposing tooth, aided by the thinness of the enamel (the more rapidly wearing underlying dentin leaves a thin, sharp enamel edge exposed). The unworn canines are high-crowned and project well beyond the level of the other teeth. In the process of sharpening, these seem to quickly wear down to the level of the remaining teeth, and one must assume that the cutting function was frequently used in their adaptation. The remaining dental features of the mandibles resemble the above described specimens; a sectorial anterior premolar used in cutting is combined with expanded posterior teeth with thick enamel. Interestingly, in spite of the upper canine projection, none of the mandibles shows a distinct diastema between the lower canine and premolar.

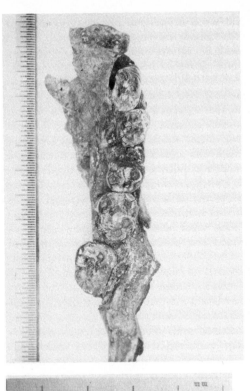

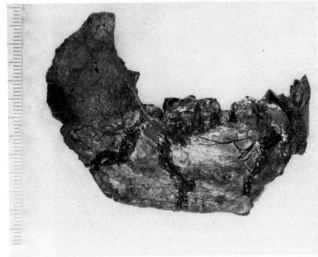

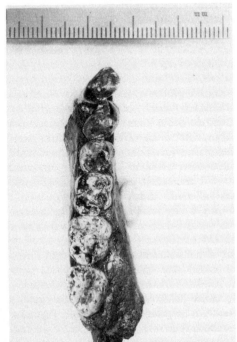

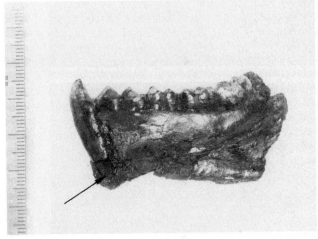

FIGURE 6.3 Two of the best preserved **Rudapithecus** mandibles. Above is RUD-2, a crushed and distorted specimen that is probably female. Note the sectoral anterior premolar and the forward position of the vertical ramus (the back portion and some of the top is missing). Below, RUD-17, a male, has an extremely long canine root that can be seen in the internal view of the mandibular body. The base is marked. Even worn, the canine projects above the tooth row.

The amount of sex difference between the apparent male (#17) and female (#2) is extraordinarily great. Excepting the canines, the percentage difference in tooth size is similar to the male-female difference in living orangs, the modern hominoid with the greatest amount of dimorphism. An equal if not greater amount of dimorphism occurred in the proconsuls, so the presence of a marked dimorphism in the Hungarian ramapithecine may be a retention of a primitive character.

The two most complete upper jaws, RUD-12 and RUD-15, may belong to a female and a male, respectively (see Figure 6.4). Although the male is older and its canine more worn, it was clearly much larger than the female's. Both specimens show a diastema between the canine and the very small lateral incisor. The central incisor of the female (one of the few known for a ramapithecine) combines a thin crown edge with a thickened crown base and strong ridges running up the sides of the internal (lingual) surface. This thickening is unlike the uniformly thin crowns and bases of the middle Miocene proconsul incisors except in the Moroto gorilla-like form. The very front of the jaw is only slightly prognathic and the incisors are vertical. The zygomatic process position is not particularly anterior (in RUD-12 it is approximately over the first molar) and the lower face was quite deep.

In sum, the small Rudabányan specimens confirm and extend the implications made from the less complete African material. Ramapithecines differ from the ancestral condition mainly in those dietary adaptations which could be predicted from Jolly's hypothesis. Darwin would not consider these forms hominids, while Jolly would!

THE LARGER RAMAPITHECINE

The larger Rudabányan ramapithecine, *Bodvapithecus*, is less well represented. The best preserved mandible, RUD-14, is somewhat larger than the *Rudapithecus* mandibles (see Figure 6.5, p. 116). The postcanine teeth equal the smaller of the Pasalar hominoids' in size. They differ from the postcanines of the smaller Rudabányan form about as much as the larger and smaller of the Pasalar forms differ. Similarly, the (unerupted) canine of this specimen is much larger than the *Rudapithecus* canines. The lateral incisor, however, is slightly smaller than its homologue in RUD-17. The postca-

nines are structurally similar, with thick enamel and low cusps. However, the P_3 is higher cusped and thus more *Proconsul*-like. At the same time, it is more compressed in the anterior-posterior direction, resembling the larger ramapithecine species as well as early hominids. *Bodvapithecus* has a higher frequency of molar cingula. Because of uncertainties in the exact age relations, it is unclear whether *Bodvapithecus* is a separate taxon or a larger male of the smaller form. Many if not all of the differences could be due to variation in time or sexual dimorphism.

A newly discovered maxilla and some bones from the upper face (RUD-44) help fill out the picture of this larger form. The shallow palate has a "U"-shaped dental arcade; the corners are marked by projecting canines (of somewhat reduced size compared with those of proconsul males of similar size). The facial bones represent parts of the region above the orbits. The supraorbital torus is thin and rather orang-like. Other similarities to orangs include orbit shape and extraordinarily prominent ridges left by the attachment for the anterior portion of temporalis (Figure 4.8). A large anterior temporalis is also part of the complex described by Jolly.

POSTCRANIA

One further aspect of the importance of Rudabánya is the discovery of postcranial bones. While some of these do not belong to primates, others are almost surely associated with the ramapithecines. The problem is which bones are associated with which ramapithecine! The simple assumption would be that the larger postcrania go with the larger ramapithecine, and the smaller bones with the smaller form. One problem with this is that two other primates are known from the site. Another is that it assumes the same jaw size–body size relations for the two ramapithecines when there has yet to be a discovery of *clearly* associated jaws (or teeth) and postcrania for any ramapithecine.

Three primate postcranial bones are particularly interesting. A moderate-sized humerus fragment from the elbow region (about the size of a small human's) is surprisingly *Proconsul*-like in form, resembling that of the largest of the *Proconsul* species. It shows none of the elbow locking mechanism associated with knuckle-walking in the African apes.

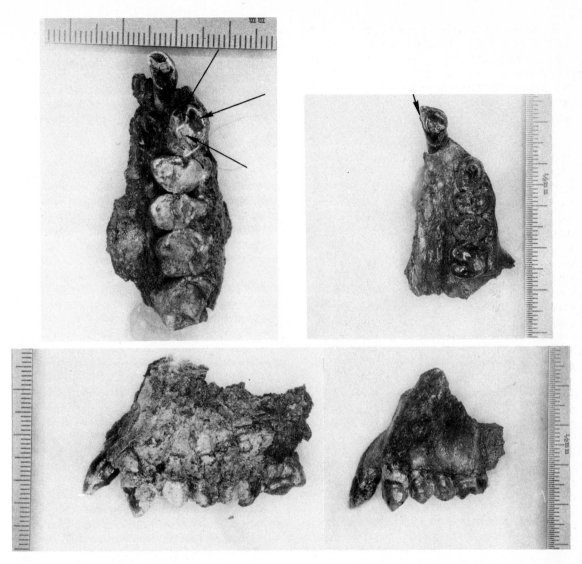

FIGURE 6.4 *Male and female* Rudapithecus *maxillas,*
RUD-15 (left) and RUD-12 (right). The older male is some-
what more prognathic. Note the three distinct wear facets on
the blunted canine (marked), two on the front face and a
third on the rear. The female canine is less worn, and has a
single shear facet on its rear face. Wear on the female incisor
(marked) reveals its strong internal ridge; the tooth is worn
to an almost chisel-like edge.

A smaller tibia fragment from the knee region resembles the tibia of quadrupedal monkeys, although it is at least double the size of any living
macaque's. Finally, the finger bones of a yet

smaller individual are slightly curved, with ridges
on the outer borders of the palm side. This adaptation to powerful flexion (closing) of the hand occurs
in primates which hang by their arms, a behavior
practiced by, but not exclusive to, brachiators.

SOME JAWS FROM GREECE

During World War II, a fragmentary primate
mandible from the Greek site of Pyrgos was discovered by a German soldier and brought to Germany,
where it was thought to represent a fossil monkey.
A recent analysis by G. H. R. von Koenigswald re-

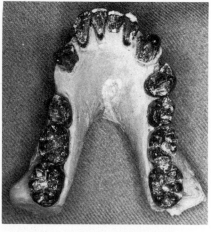

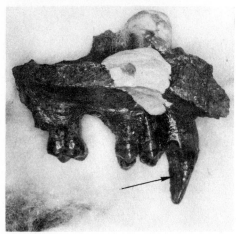

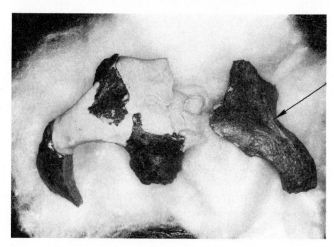

FIGURE 6.5   The larger Rudabányan ramapithecine, Bodvapithecus. *Above are two views of the juvenile mandible RUD-14 as reconstructed by E. L. Simons. The canine was not fully erupted and the (missing) third molars were not erupted. Below are views of the RUD-44 adult. A view of the maxilla (internally from the midline position) shows the canine projection and the honing wear facet on its back face (marked). The upper facial bones include a weak browridge and a very prominent ridge for the temporalis attachment (marked).*

vealed that instead it was a ramapithecine form, similar to the larger Pasalar specimens in size. Fortunately, a number of more complete similar specimens have been recovered from the Macedonian site of Ravin de la Pluie. These have been placed in a new genus, *Ouranopithecus*.

The Ravin site appears to be somewhat younger than the Turkish and Hungarian sites. It also differs in two other important respects. First, it is the only ramapithecine site in which grasslands fauna is clearly predominant, providing circumstantial evidence that this ramapithecine form was grasslands adapted. Second, the site is believed to represent a single catastrophic event; it appears that a flood deposited the remains of a large number of animals at one place, where they subsequently became fossilized. It is possible that the ramapithecine forms discovered at Ravin represent the remains of a single living population.

A number of mandibles have been recovered (see Figure 6.6, pp. 118–119), as well as a maxilla and portions of a face. Two sexes are clearly represented; the size difference between the male and female mandibles is as great as in any living primate. In the posterior teeth, the percentage difference between male and female is almost exactly the same as in the *Ramapithecus* male and female mandibles RUD-17 and RUD-2 (Figure 6.3). The Ravin specimens are much larger, however, the females exceed *Bodvapithecus* to about the same degree that *Bodvapithecus* exceeds *Ramapithecus* (Table 6.1). They are the size of the large (male) Turkish ramapithecine. Dimorphism in the Ravin mandibles is even greater for the canines than for the posterior teeth, approaching the average value for gorillas and orangs.

The long, divergent parallel tooth rows and the small incisors reflect the hominoid ancestral condition. The symphysis shape is gently curved and posteriorly elongated and thickened, unlike the more vertical form in the other European ramapithecines, but similar to the Fort Ternan specimen and the even larger *Gigantopithecus* (described below).

The Ravin specimens are dentally similar to the ramapithecines described above in most respects. However, the anterior cutting complex differs in two important ways. First, there is the matter of canine reduction. Although the Ravin canines are proconsul-like in form, they are small relative to the posterior teeth or to the size of the mandible. The unworn female canine (RPL-54) barely projects beyond the tooth row, and its relative size fits well within the range of the much later australopithecines (in fact, many of these have relatively larger canines). The male canine (RPL-55 and 75) is larger and more projecting, but even its size is much smaller than in male proconsuls. This reduction (in comparison to the ancestral condition) *may* be the result of a change in function. Evidence suggesting this comes from the form of canine wear in an old male from the site (RPL-56). His lower canines are heavily worn against the projecting upper canines. However, the *direction* of this wear is *not* front-to-back, which would maintain a sharp back edge for cutting. Instead, the direction is side-to-side, the result of lateral jaw movement. Lateral motion takes place during grinding, but the effect in this older male is to produce a canine that cannot be used for cutting. Unfortunately, this single individual can only provide a suggestion of a functional difference. Older gorilla males occasionally have the same canine wear. Only a larger sample of somewhat younger individuals will help resolve the question of whether a functional difference in canine use actually appeared in this form.

The specimens provide important information about the time of canine eruption. Males of living pongids and some the more social cercopithecoids erupt their canines at the latest possible time. As discussed above (p. 51), late male canine eruption seems to be a physiological control mechanism in primates with complex social behavior, keeping males out of competition for dominance until they are morphologically and behaviorally mature. In the Ravin specimens, the female canine (RPL-54) has erupted much earlier than the male. The female's canine seems to have come into occlusion at about the same time as the premolars and second molar. These teeth had not been in occlusion for very long before the female's death. In contrast, while the young male has about the same amount of canine wear, it is his *third* molar that had just erupted. One might hypothesize a fairly complex system of social behavior from this. In modern social primates (not including humans), males' and females' canines erupt far apart in time. Of course, there is no way to test these speculations.

The Ravin male maxilla (RPL-128) represents a tall but only moderately prognathic face. Its size is about that of a female gorilla or Orang but more specifically resembles the latter in the superior convergence of the canine roots, the position of these roots, and the transverse expansion of the postcanine teeth. Relative to an Orang (or gorilla) male, the canines are reduced.

In sum, the Ravin hominoids establish the ramapithecine pattern in a larger-sized form, one with the best circumstantial evidence of a grasslands adaptation. They confirm the appearance of marked sexual dimorphism in both canine size and form, and in the size of the postcanine teeth and jaws, for what might have been an actual biological population. The Ravin hominoids, along with the mandible from Pyrgos and the larger ramapithecines from Turkey, are clearly related to the smaller ramapithecines because of the derived features that they share. *Bodvapithecus* and the smaller Pasalar specimens lie between them in size. While the three forms may represent three species, it is possible that fewer species are involved. The influences of geography and differing habitats on the sizes of these samples are unknown, and their temporal relations are unclear. At each site, only two different-sized forms appear (Table 6.1), and at the other extreme, it is possible that only a single lineage of sexually dimorphic hominoids is represented. Whatever the case, the ramapithecine samples resemble each other and differ from proconsuls mainly in features associated with a diet (or diets)

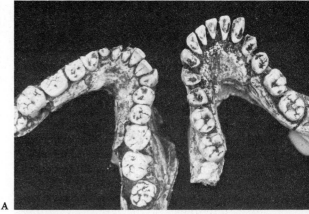

FIGURE 6.6   Larger ramapithecines from Ravin. (A) A comparison of the female RPL-54 and the Sterkfontein female australopithecine STS-52 (both are casts), (B) side and occlusal views of the female, (C) the young males RPL-75, (D) RPL-55, and (E) the old male RPL-56. The base of the RPL-55 mandible is broken away and none of the specimens have retained the ramus.

A

B

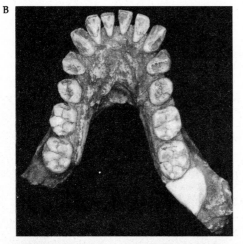

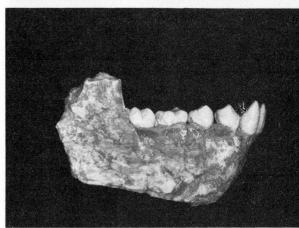

C

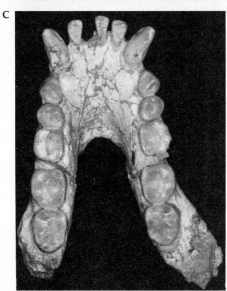

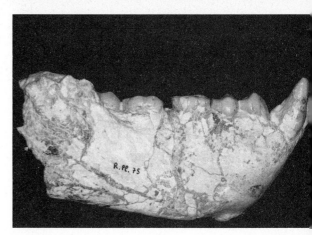

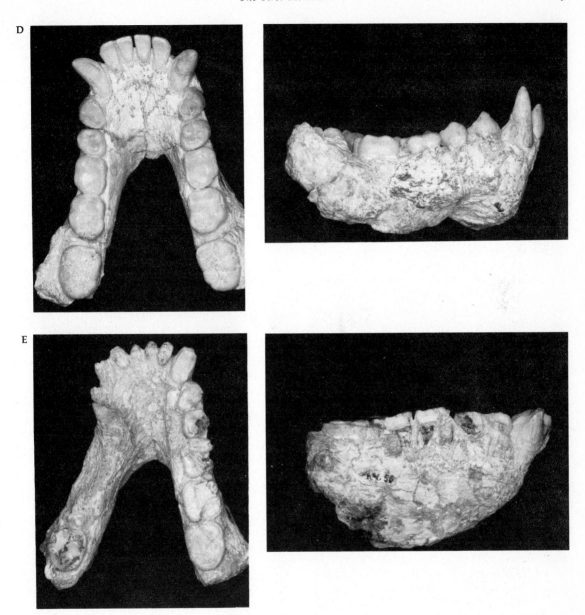

requiring powerful chewing forces. The important features conform to a Jolly-like model. Only in the evidence for some canine reduction do the forms fit Darwin's model for an early hominid, and the evidence for larger, thicker maxillary incisors fits neither of these models.

Asiatic Forms

The ramapithecines recovered from Asia span the area from India and Pakistan to south China. This is the region where ramapithecines were first identified and named, although these were probably fairly late forms, possibly not much older than 9 million years. Unfortunately, the early discovered specimens were fragmentary and many were incorrectly interpreted. As a result, an understanding of the Asiatic forms is hampered by a combination of misconception and taxonomic overkill.

THE SMALL FORM

The taxonomic name *Ramapithecus* was first applied to the smallest of the Asiatic species. Some of the small specimens were later transferred to a different taxon on the argument that they were too ape-like for a hominid ancestor. For instance, the only early specimen with an anterior mandibular premolar did not fit the predictions of Darwin's model because the tooth was sectorial. The parabolic dental arcade reconstruction of the fragmentary maxilla (YPM-13799) was also guided by the expectations of this model. Hindsight, and the recovery of more complete specimens from this region as well as others, has changed the interpretation. Almost all of the small specimens are now included in *Ramapithecus*. The recent recovery of more complete material from Pakistan as the result of D. Pilbeam's work has further confirmed this similarity.

The Asiatic small form is characterized by the same dental arcade shape, canine/premolar cutting complex, and expanded thick-enameled posterior teeth of the other ramapithecines. Interestingly, the more recent of the *Ramapithecus* sample is the most hominid-like in the cutting complex. An anterior lower premolar (P_3) from Pakistan has a small but distinct second internal cusp and a specimen from south China has two virtually equal-sized cusps. In both individuals, the P_3 has a shape that is generally less elongated than some of the earlier smaller specimens. While the tooth was still used in cutting, its form is remarkably similar to Pliocene hominids'. A diastema occurs between the upper incisor and canine, while none has been found in the mandible, and the face appears to have been short and deep with moderate prognathism in the otherwise vertical incisors. The palate is also fairly deep and very narrow. As in the areas already discussed, only teeth and jaw fragments remain; while

there are some possibly associated postcrania, no association is direct.

LARGER SPECIES

There are larger Asiatic hominid species. Two of these were placed in the genus *Dryopithecus* during the taxonomic revision proposed by E. L. Simons and D. Pilbeam. Many workers now prefer to retain these in *Sivapithecus*, a genus with notable similarities to *Ramapithecus*. I believe that these two species, *S. sivalensis* and *S. indicus*, are actually larger ramapithecines because of the derived features they share with the smaller ramapithecine forms. The molars and premolars have thick enamel, the faces were apparently short and deep, and the mandibular ramus is in an anterior position. Other features once thought to ally them with living apes are now recognized as primitive features that are shared with the smaller ramapithecine forms. These similarities are mainly in the pongid-like morphology of the canine cutting complex, once thought not to be characteristic of *Ramapithecus* in India. Much of the now confusing taxonomy was done at a time before canines and lower anterior premolars of smaller forms were known.

Moreover, there may not be two distinct species of the larger form present. Sexual dimorphism in the similarly sized Ravin hominoids almost encompasses the combined range of both "species." Some of the smaller *S. sivalensis* specimens are probably males of *Ramapithecus*, if the degree of sexual dimorphism in the Asiatic smaller form is the same as at Rudabánya or Ravin. Larger members of *S. sivalensis* could be females of *S. indicus*. The two recently reported mandibles from the PRC fit this description quite well, closely paralleling the sexual dimorphism at Ravin in their size and form contrasts. Interestingly, the molars of the larger specimen (*S. yunnanensis*) closely resemble isolated molars from south China that had been attributed to fossil Orangs.

The Asiatic samples are fragmentary and incomplete and the situation is far from clear. Whatever the case, the range of variation of these Asiatic larger forms includes features of all the large ramapithecine forms from Europe. While there are differences between the larger ramapithecines of these regions, I do not believe they are sufficient to support the many different taxa that have been proposed. Most of the differences are probably due to time and the distance between the small samples. Since the Asiatic forms were named first, this would imply that the various European taxa that have been named (Table 6.1) might best be considered variants of *Sivapithecus*. Asia, like Europe, was occupied by at least two, if not three, different-sized ramapithecines during the beginning of the latter Miocene.

GIGANTOPITHECUS

An even larger related form existed in Asia: *Gigantopithecus*. Originally, this primate was known from much later (Pliocene–lower Pleistocene) specimens recovered in China. In his publication on the mandibles and isolated teeth, the Chinese paleontologist Ju-Kang Woo described a taxon ranging from large to massive. The incisors were small and the canines were small relative to the posterior teeth (although absolutely large). While pongid-like in form (especially resembling the orang), the projecting canines were worn transversely (like the Ravin male specimen RPL-55) to a blunted posterior edge that could not be used for cutting. The anterior lower premolars were bicuspid, resembling hominids more than any Miocene hominoid, and the posterior teeth had thick enamel. Sexual dimorphism in the canines, mandibles, and remaining teeth was marked. One unusual aspect of the molars was their elongation, a feature shared with the Fort Ternan ramapithecine. If this description sounds familiar, it is because the pattern is the same as described for the Miocene ramapithecines, although expressed at a larger size.

Gigantopithecus has also been identified in deposits of equal age to the small ramapithecines, according to D. Pilbeam. This earlier *Gigantopithecus* is best known from a mandible (see Figure 6.7, p. 122) recovered from the wall of a house in the Indian state of Bilaspur. Later discoveries have been mainly of isolated teeth, and some earlier discovered teeth once called *Dryopithecus giganteus* might also represent the same taxon, although they might also belong to larger members of the large ramapithecine form (one third molar is identical to the Ravin male third molar).

Compared with the Chinese *Gigantopithecus* sample, the tooth row shape, anterior premolar form, and details of the symphysis in the Bilaspur *Gigantopithecus* mandible are more like those in the Fort Ternan and Ravin ramapithecines, which is not surprising given the fact that it is probably at least 7 million years old. Wear on the canine is transverse; rather than sharpening, and the angle of wear is low relative to the surfaces of the other teeth. The latter fact indicates that the upper canine was not strongly projecting and confirms other features which suggest that the Bilaspur *Gigantopithecus* was a female.

A decade ago, when only the largest (*Gigantopithecus*) and smallest (*Ramapithecus*) of the ramapithecines were known, endless suggestions of the relation, or lack of relation, between these were proposed. Now that one or more intermediate-sized ramapithecines are recognized, it has become clear that *Gigantopithecus* represents the largest species in what is very probably a single adaptive radiation. The Bilaspur female is only slightly larger than the biggest Ravin male.

ECOLOGY

Recent analysis of the sites in Pakistan known to have preserved ramapithecine remains suggests that they lived in an environment consisting mainly of open woodland and low brush. Grasslands occurred only in small patches, and there were no true forests. With the exception of the Ravin sample, most of the ramapithecines have been found in a similar mixture of grasslands and woodlands. This makes it impossible to determine whether they preferred one habitat to the other or the opportunities presented by the boundary between them.

An Adaptive Radiation

The Eurasian ramapithecines underwent an adaptive radiation, resulting in at least several distinct lineages. No evidence of a similar radiation has been found in Africa, although it should be admitted that there are virtually no hominoid fossils known from the time of Fort Ternan to the earliest

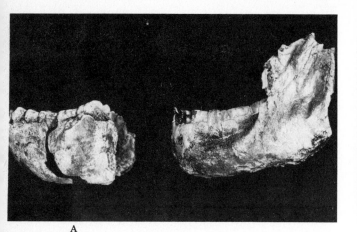

A

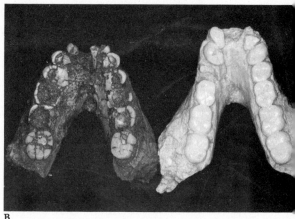

B

FIGURE 6.7   The Bilaspur Gigantopithecus *female man-dible compared with mandibles of the larger australopithe-cines from East Africa. In A, a side-view comparison with the Lake Turkana male ER-729 (to the right). In B, it is compared with a male (left) from Omo (L7–125) in a view of the dentitions. All of the specimens shown are casts.*

australopithecines, a span of some 9 million years. The jaws and teeth indicate that the Eurasian adaptive radiation involved size distinctions. The smallest of the lineages was probably in the 25-pound range, while the largest was at least as large as living gorillas.

ADAPTIVE DIFFERENCES

Size by itself might account for the ecological separation of the ramapithecine lineages; species that vary over this size range can utilize very different dietary items and are affected by different groups of carnivores. The shared similarities of the dental mechanisms combine small incisors, a canine/premolar complex used for cutting in most of the forms, and adaptations to exerting powerful forces in chewing. These similarities might suggest that, other than for size differences, the lineages were adaptively similar. However, this need not be the case. Jolly believes that the ramapithecine dental mechanisms evolved in an adaptation parallel to the geladas, mainly a savanna adaptation involving seeds and other hard objects. The same complex,

however, appears in giant pandas which eat bamboo (Figure 5.3), and in some of the New World leaf-eating monkeys. The point is that once a morphology providing for powerful chewing forces evolved in the ramapithecines, subsequent adaptations using vastly different resources may have followed.

The adaptive radiation might be represented by different-sized species living in the same or similar habitats, but it might also have resulted in very different habitat utilization, locomotion, and so on. One lineage, perhaps the smallest in Eurasia if the Rudabányan finger bones are associated with it, may have been an arboreal arm-hanging form that ate leaves. At the other extreme, primates the size of *Gigantopithecus* probably only rarely utilized trees. A terrestrial adaptation involving powerful mastication does not *necessarily* mean either a savanna habitat or a diet of seeds. For all we know, *Gigantopithecus* may have been a forest-dwelling bamboo-eater, subsequently replaced by the giant panda. My guess is that with the eventual discovery of more complete remains, and associated postcrania, a much wider range of adaptations will be recognized in the ramapithecines than is presently conceived.

FATE OF THE RAMAPITHECINES

The ramapithecines were a fairly successful radiation. Compared to the relic population of the living pongids, they occupied an extraordinarily wide range, matched among living primates only by the macaque/baboon radiation and by humans. Yet the fact remains that it *is* the macaque/baboon radiation that occupies most of this range today and not ramapithecines. The living apes, although restricted in range, nonetheless represent descendants of the other major radiation arising from the proconsuls. What happened to the ramapithecines?

If the ramapithecines are ancestral to hominids of the Plio-Pleistocene, we are then the living representative species. However, this does not fully answer the question *because all ramapithecines cannot be ancestral to living humans.* Leaving aside, for the moment, the question of which might have been, what happened to the others?

No dramatic climatic or faunal change has taken place in all of the areas where ramapithecines lived, so the answer must lie in competition and replacement. At least some of the ramapithecines were out competed by better adapted animals. I believe it is possible that the baboons and macaques themselves provided part of this competition, and the possibility that giant pandas replaced *Gigantopithecus* has already been discussed, although the late date of the Chinese forms raises the possibility that hominids may also have played a role in their extinction.

Finally, accumulating evidence suggests that one of the larger ramapithecine species may be ancestral to living Orangs. The first substantive hint of this special relationship came from a microscopic study of the tooth enamel in the living and fossil forms. Following this, a new *Sivapithecus* species from Yunnan province in south China was announced. *Sivapithecus yunnanensis* combines the tooth size and proportions found in other larger ramapithecine species (especially the Greek form) with a very Orang-like dental morphology. Indeed, similar isolated teeth from south China had been previously attributed to an extinct giant fossil Orang species.

In sum, the fate of some ramapithecine species is no longer a complete mystery. There is reason to postulate that one species is ancestral to *Gigantopithecus*, which in turn only recently became extinct, while another may be ancestral to living Orangs. Other ramapithecine species, however, became extinct, and if one ramapithecine is ancestral to hominids, there is still the question of what factors led to the success of one species in the context of the others' failure.

Hominid Ancestors?

The ramapithecines are at the right place and in the right timespan to be hominid ancestors. Moreover, their morphological distinctions from the earlier proconsuls either parallel the later hominids if they are not ancestral, or foreshadow them if they are. This provides circumstantial evidence that hominids originated among the ramapithecines, although it does not prove the case since hominids could have originated at a more recent time than the latest known ramapithecines. Once it is established that *some* of the ramapithecines parallel the later hominids, there remains the possibility that *all* of them did. Nonetheless, there is much to be said for the idea that we should spend more time dealing with the fossils at hand than wondering about fossils that haven't been found yet. The fact is that if hominids did not originate among the ramapithecines, no other potential ancestral form is known after the middle Miocene.

Which Ramapithecine?

Which ramapithecine makes the most likely hominid ancestor? On the basis of morphology, a good case could be made for each of the known forms. *Gigantopithecus* is probably the most hominid-like in its canine/premolar complex. That its jaws and teeth are extraordinarily large need not exclude it from hominid ancestry since hominids with similar posterior tooth and jaw sizes are found later in time (Figure 6.7). That the Chinese forms are too late to be ancestral (in the Dragonbone cave of Jianshi district, Hupei province, both hominid and *Gigantopithecus* teeth are found) should not obscure the question of whether the *earlier* portion of the lineage could be ancestral.

The "large" species makes an equally credible ancestor. Canines in the Greek and south Chinese female specimens are the most reduced of any ramapithecine canines and were early erupting. It is not clear whether a change in function had also occurred. Excepting the canines and lower anterior premolar, the remaining teeth are indistinguishable from early hominids' (Figure 6.6). In *Gigantopithecus* the corresponding teeth are relatively narrow, and in the small ramapithecine species they are markedly smaller than in the early hominids.

The small species is the one generally accepted as the hominid ancestor. However, the best case for the small species is not based on morphology at all.

A CASE FOR AFRICA

There are two lines of evidence that suggest that if any ramapithecine is ancestral to hominids, it is the small African form. First, there is the seemingly close (if not ancestral) relation between one of the Asiatic species and living Orangs. Biochemical and genetic studies indicate that Orangs are not as closely related to hominids as are the living African pongids. This suggests an earlier split between the lineage leading to Orangs and the lineage leading to hominids, and by implication the argument for an earlier split must also involve the Asiatic ramapithecines. Second, there is circumstantial evidence. The fact is that to date, the earliest recognizable hominids and the earliest distinguishable stone tools are found in Africa. In other words, current evidence suggests an African origin. The only African ramapithecine is the small form from Fort Ternan. Interestingly, if the above arguments are correct and if the Fort Ternan ramapithecine is ancestral to hominids, it may also be ancestral to the living African pongids (a point raised by L. O. Greenfield in a review of this problem).

Moreover, while only three fragmentary African specimens span the time between Fort Ternan and the middle Pliocene, these could support the hypothesis of an African *Ramapithecus* ancestry for hominids. The three specimens come from the northern Rift Valley of Kenya. One of these, an upper molar from Ngorogoro, is a *Ramapithecus*-sized tooth. However, it may be early enough to represent *Ramapithecus* itself. A lower first molar is from Lukeino; it is dated to slightly over 6 million years ago and is intermediate in size between *Ramapithecus* and the Pliocene hominids. Finally, there is a mandibular fragment from Lothagam Hill, approximately 5.5 million years old. The single remaining molar is only slightly larger than the Lukeino molar, and the preserved portion of the mandibular body retains some features shared by *Proconsul* and ramapithecines.

In sum, the African ramapithecine is probably the best candidate available for a Miocene hominid ancestor. While it differs from some of the morphologically better ramapithecine candidates, these differences are mainly in the more primitive canine/premolar complex and might be the simple result of its earlier date. If no ramapithecine is a hominid ancestor, the appropriate species has not yet been found.

THE IMPLICATIONS OF PARALLELISM

If *Ramapithecus* (the small form) is ancestral to Pliocene hominids, all of the other ramapithecines evolved in different directions or became extinct in spite of the features shared with the line that was successful. In fact, the same conclusion applies if one of the other ramapithecine lineages turns out to be the ancestral one. Clearly, the ramapithecine characteristics were successful at one time, but did not insure continued survival. The hominid line must have developed additional features that led to its *continued* success. While we can never be sure what these developments involved, the Pliocene hominids show the morphological changes associated with tools, complex behavior, and bipedalism, and the odds are that the key to their eventual predominance lay within this complex.

The potential importance of bipedalism is questionable and in any event unknown. Tuttle's model suggests that all of the ramapithecines may have been bipedal to one degree or another. Conversely, none of them may have been, and the bipedal adaptation may be a fairly recent development. At present, we have no means of judging because of the absence of clearly associated postcrania and the lack of any remains from the Miocene that suggest bipedality.

In my view, the success of the lineage leading to Pliocene hominids most likely lay in a growing dependence on tool use and cultural behavior in its adaptation, and the consequences that this dependence had on the direction of its evolution. The results of this dependence range from an increasingly complex system of socially defined roles and expectations to changes in birth spacing, adaptability, and habitat utilization.

The evolution of more complex social behavior may have begun with the increased need for social controls that came with the substitution of tools for canines and the loss of a physiological social control mechanism (late eruption of large canines). The structural aspects of social behavior came to extend far beyond this and ultimately were incorporated in the structure of the developing brain. Australopithecines show evidence of the resulting neural reorganization. Combined with a rudimentary technology, the compartmentalization of behavior through the appearance of more roles resulted in the ability of hominid societies to make better use of existing resources and to utilize more varied habitats.

Another effect of increasing social complexity led to a radical change in hominid demography with obvious advantages: the decrease in birth spacing. Compared to cercopithecoids, chimpanzees must learn a great amount of information as children; this delays their maturation and leads to a prolonged period of child dependency and intensive learning. Since chimpanzee females do not reproduce while they have a dependent offspring, the period of time between successive births is five to six years. The even greater amount of information that hominid children needed to learn resulted in a further slowdown in their maturation. However, this would not have resulted in even more widely spaced births if extended kinship relations were recognized as part of the increasing social complexity discussed above. Once child rearing can be shared with other related females, it is possible for females to reproduce while they still have dependent children. The result was the monthly estrus cycle of human females, and the decrease of birth spacing to as little as two years. During the same reproduction span, hominid females could give birth to three or more times as many offspring as their chimpanzee counterparts, with profound demographic consequences. C. O. Lovejoy suggests that a decrease in birth spacing was a critical factor in hominid origins, arguing that it allowed rapid population expansion in a species combining a short lifespan and maturational delay. For reasons that will be discussed in the next chapter, I believe that the australopithecines had already made this change, and that it was one of the important consequences of the behavioral innovations that might have taken place in one of the ramapithecine lineages.

Whether these behavioral changes related to tool use were indeed the factors responsible for the success of any ramapithecine species is a conjecture. However, it need not remain so, since many of these changes have morphological and behavioral consequences that could be discovered. The final test of these ideas will come with the eventual discovery of crania with preserved internal details and of actual living sites from the later Miocene.

MODELS OF HOMINID ORIGINS

What implications does a ramapithecine ancestry have for the models of hominid origins? As discussed above, no direct evidence of either ramapithecine bipedalism (or any other form of locomotion) or tool use has been found. However, the absence of evidence does not eliminate the possibility that one or more of the ramapithecines made tools and/or walked bipedally.

Most ramapithecines combined a pongid-like canine/premolar cutting complex with changes in the jaws and posterior teeth that allowed powerful chewing forces. This would suggest that the hominid dietary shift came before substantial canine reduction and change in function, and supports many aspects of Jolly's hypothesis. It surely emphasizes the adaptive importance of dietary changes early in hominid evolution. However, the evidence is insufficient to show that these changes led to an early exclusive grasslands adaptation; most of the ramapithecines are found in environmental mosaics, mixing elements of grasslands and woodlands. This is where the ramapithecines died and were buried. It may not be where they lived. For instance, if these primates were water-dependent, their death near water would far more likely result in burial and preservation than their death on an open savanna, and sources of water almost inevitably are surrounded by trees. However, this is another case of the absence of evidence. The presence of ramapithecine fossils in environmental mosaics may not prove that they lived there, but at the same time it cannot be used to prove anything else.

Little direct support is provided for Tuttle's model, although it is also true that no evidence argues against it. Tuttle predicted that the earliest hominids would be small, and the earliest ramapithecine fits this prediction.

The one clear implication of a ramapithecine ancestry for hominids is that the hominid adaptive shift would seem to have involved two steps. The first is a dietary change which may or may not be associated with bipedalism or tool use. This change occurred at the base of the ramapithecine adaptive radiation. The second, I believe, is unique to the single surviving lineage and involved Darwin's complex of interrelated bipedalism (perhaps already present), tool dependence, and intelligence. This second shift was probably associated with an improved grasslands adaptation. If it took place in Africa, as most evidence suggests, its details await the filling in of the last substantial gap in the hominid fossil record—the span between Fort Ternan and the earliest australopithecines.

SUMMARY

Most of the available evidence suggests that hominids originated no earlier than 16 million years ago and no later than 6 million. Within this timespan, only one primate taxon has sufficient resemblances to later hominids to be a possible ancestor. This taxon is represented by a series of species forming an adaptive radiation which I refer to as the ramapithecines.

While numerous taxonomic names have been proposed for ramapithecine samples, most of the variation could probably be encompassed by only a few distinct species varying over space and time and exhibiting marked differences in canine size that suggest a large amount of sexual dimorphism in each. Other differences among ramapithecine samples include relative canine reduction, P_3 form and molarization (cusp addition), the frequency of cingula, and palate depth. The least taxonomic diversity has been found in Africa, possibly the earliest home of the ramapithecines, while the greatest diversity is in Europe and Asia. It would appear that as the ramapithecines spread, they diversified.

What the radiation holds in common are largely aspects of dietary adaptation, conforming to Jolly's hypothesis that hominids arose as forms adapted to diets requiring powerful, prolonged chewing. The shared derived features (compared to proconsuls) include posterior teeth with thick enamel, emphasis on rotary grinding, evidence for expanded masticatory muscles, short snouts and deep faces, thick mandibular bodies and internally strengthened symphyses, and in some forms the addition of a second cusp on the P_3. There also may be some degree of relative canine size reduction. Shared primitive features include anterior shearing between the upper canine and P_3, marked sexual dimorphism, and straight tooth rows converging toward a narrow incisor region. The ramapithecines differ from all living hominoids in the extraordinary development of the muscles and structures associated with mastication, and differ from all except the hominids in their geographic range.

Postcrania show a marked size range, and suggest locomotor adaptations varying from arm hanging to some form of forelimb weight support, possibly involving elbow locking in the larger Indian form. The problem is that, at present, associations between the postcrania and the numerous jaws and teeth cannot be determined. Furthermore, remains that would indicate whether any of the forms was bipedal are lacking.

Only one of the ramapithecines, if any, could be an ancestor to later hominids. The two other Pleistocene survivals would seem to be *Pongo* and *Gigantopithecus*. Regarding hominid ancestry, a good "morphological case" could be made for each of the species, but only *Ramapithecus* itself is found in Africa, and no hominids are known from outside of Africa significantly earlier than the Pleistocene.

If one of the ramapithecines is ancestral to hominids, support is provided for many aspects of Jolly's hypothesis, but as applied to prehominid adaptation. While the tool-using causality of Darwin's model cannot be excluded because the evidence one way or another is simply not present, canine reduction and change in form would seem to be a late-developing hominid characteristic. However, the dramatic success of only one ramapithecine species (if any) places additional importance on the Darwinian complex of tool use, bipedalism, and intelligence for this surviving portion of the adaptive radiation. It also emphasizes the demographic and behavioral consequences of reduced birth spacing. If none of the ramapithecines is ancestral to hominids, no other potential ancestor can be recognized at the present time.

STATE OF THE ART

One example of a "typical" ongoing argument in hominid origins studies is over the status of the largest ramapithecine, *Gigantopithecus*. Suggestions of possible hominid ancestry for at least some *Gigantopithecus* remains come from F. Weidenreich, J. K. Woo, F. B. Livingstone, R. Eckhardt, J. T. Robinson, and D. W. Frayer. Weidenreich hypothesized that the earliest hominids were gigantic, and that subsequent hominid evolution passed through a series of size reductions from *Gigantopithecus* through smaller forms such as "Meganthropus" (an early hominid from Indonesia) and finally to *Homo erectus* as represented in Java and later in China. His main argument rested on the size comparison of "Meganthropus" and *Homo erectus* mandibles and the even larger dimensions of the *Gigantopithecus* material, then known only from dental remains in China. He felt that the australopithecines, with "Meganthropus"-sized jaws, were aberrant hominids and that the mainstream of human evolution occurred in Asia.

Livingstone suggested that this size reduction may have been the result of a savanna adaptation, involving a switch from a more pongid-type diet to hunting. He argued for the "killer-ape" model of human origins. A dietary shift could have resulted in dental and mandibular reduction from a more *Gigantopithecus*-like condition. Although massive teeth and mandibles could be selectively advantageous in bone crunching (a point also supported by F. Szalay), they presumably reduced when pebble choppers came to be used for the same purpose. Eckhardt further elaborated this model, showing that only a small shift in selection over a rather short period of time need have occurred to derive an australopithecine-like dentition from *Gigantopithecus*. However, Eckhardt dealt only with the dentition. In the absence of both cranial and postcranial remains, it is impossible to tell how long a time the necessary changes might have required since we don't know *what* features had to change. And, the demonstration that such evolution *could have* occurred is not the same as proof that it actually *did* occur.

Both Robinson and Frayer accept the possibility of a *Gigantopithecus* ancestry for hominids on the contention that the *Gigantopithecus* adaptation is a logical extension, backward in time, of the australopithecine adaptation. Here, the similarity with the hypothesis proposed by Livingstone and Eckhardt ends, since Robinson and Frayer interpret the adaptation as one of specialized plant eating, rather than hunting. They both suggest that the seed-eating hypothesis of hominid origins predicts the evolution of a *Gigantopithecus*-like form prior to dependence on tool use. Frayer (although not Woo or Eckhardt) accepts the contention that the Chinese sample is too late in time to be ancestral to hominids, and suggests a lineage split in which one branch evolved into hominids while the other evolved into a later *Gigantopithecus* species, as represented in China. The Chinese specimens presumably continued an evolutionary trend in which large size, instead of tools, was an important defensive adaptation. Elsewhere tool use, suggests Frayer, might have transformed populations similar to the Bilaspur *Gigantopithecus* into true hominids through reductions in body and canine size. This was the view maintained by Woo in his monograph on the Chinese sample.

Other interpretations of the early *Gigantopithecus*, notably those of Simons and his co-workers, have typically argued more from the date than from morphology that it represents an "aberrant pongid" with some parallelisms to hominids resulting from dietary similarity. The date has become an increasingly difficult problem, however, with the discovery of *Gigantopithecus*-sized teeth contemporary with similar ramapithecines in the Siwaliks of Pakistan. One form can hardly be too recent to be a hominid ancestor if a contemporary form is not.

In my view, the most convincing argument against an early *Gigantopithecus* form as a hominid ancestor is its absence from late Miocene deposits in Africa. Yet few other hominoids are known from African deposits representing this timespan, so that morphology, dating, and geographic range still leave the issue unresolved.

FURTHER READINGS

ANDREWS, P., and H. TOBIEN. 1977. New Miocene Locality in Turkey with Evidence on the Origin of *Ramapithecus* and *Sivapithecus*. *Nature* 268:699–701.

A brief discussion of the recently discovered dental sample from Turkey.

ANDREWS, P., and A. C. WALKER. 1976. The Primate and Other Fauna from Fort Ternan, Kenya. In *Human Origins: Louis Leakey and the East African Evidence*, eds. G. L. Isaac and E. R. McCown. Benjamin, Menlo Park.

The most complete description of the Fort Ternan *Ramapithecus* remains and their ecological setting.

ANDREWS, P., and I. TEKKAYA. 1976. *Ramapithecus* in Kenya and Turkey. In *Les Plus Anciens Hominides*, eds. P. V. Tobias and Y. Coppens. Paris: CNRS, pp. 7–25.

Discussion of the Çandir mandible and its relation to the Fort Ternan specimens.

GREENFIELD, L. O. 1979. On the Adaptive Pattern of "*Ramapithecus*." *American Journal of Physical Anthropology* 50:527–548.

A wide-ranging discussion of features shared by the various ramapithecine forms, their relation to the proconsuls, and the problem of hominid ancestry.

KRETZOI, M. 1975. New Ramapithecines and *Pliopithecus* from Lower Pliocene of Rudabánya in North-eastern Hungary. *Nature* 257:578–581.

A brief report of the Hungarian ramapithecines and their significance.

LEAKEY, L. S. B. 1962. A New Lower Pliocene Fossil Primate from Kenya. *Annals and Magazine of Natural History*. Series 13, 4:689–696.

Leakey's original and in many ways far-sighted report on the Fort Ternan ramapithecine.

MOLNAR, S., and D. G. GANTT. 1977. Functional Implications of Primate Enamel Thickness. *American Journal of Physical Anthropology* 46:447–454.

The only comprehensive study of hominoid molar enamel thickness and its implications.

PILBEAM, D. 1978. Rearranging Our Family Tree. *Human Nature* 1:38–45.

A well-written illustrated account of the new fossil hominoids from Pakistan and their role in changing interpretations of the ramapithecines.

————, et al. 1978. New Hominoid Primates from the Siwaliks of Pakistan and Their Bearing on Hominoid Evolution. *Nature* 270:689–695.

A description of the New Pakistan ramapithecines and a discussion of their significance in interpreting the ramapithecines as a distinct taxonomic group and as possible hominid ancestors.

SIMONS, E. L. 1964. The Early Relatives of Man. *Scientific American* 211(1):50–65.

The best introductory statement of Simons' earlier views regarding *Ramapithecus*, written when only a few very fragmentary remains were known.

————. 1976. *Ramapithecus*. *Scientific American* 236(5):28–35.

Probably the most comprehensive statement of Simons' current interpretation of *Ramapithecus*, including a discussion of most of the new material as of 1975.

————, and P. C. ETTEL. 1970. *Gigantopithecus*. *Scientific American* 222(1):77–85.

A review of the Bilaspur *Gigantopithecus* mandible and the circumstances surrounding its discovery.

TATTERSALL, I. 1975. *The Evolutionary Significance of Ramapithecus*. Burgess, Minneapolis.

A simple introduction to the "classic" argument for *Ramapithecus* as a hominid.

TELEKI, G., E. E. HUNT, JR., and J. H. PFIFFERING. 1976. Demographic Observations (1963–1973) on the Chimpanzees of Gombe National Park, Tanzania. *Journal of Human Evolution* 5:559–598.

Chimpanzee demography in a context comparing it with humans, including a discussion of how early hominids may have differed from both.

WATERFALL, W. 1979. Form and Function: the Anatomists' View. *Mosaic* 10(2):23–29.

A very up to date discussion of recent theories and speculations concerning hominid origins and early adaptatons, including comments provided by A. Walker, C. O. Lovejoy, and A. Mann on their current research.

WOO, JU-KANG. 1962. The Mandibles and Dentition of *Gigantopithecus*. *Palaeontologia Sinica*. New Series D, No. 11.

The most complete analysis of the Chinese *Gigantopithecus* remains and their possible significance in human origins and evolution.

XU, QUING-HUA, and LU QING-WU. 1979. The Mandibles of *Ramapithecus* and *Sivapithecus* from Lufeng, Yunnan. *Vertebrata Palasiatica* 17:1–13.

Presentation of new ramapithecine specimens which resemble the Greek remains.

PART THREE

DEVELOPMENT OF THE HOMINID PATTERN

CHAPTER SEVEN

The Earliest People

The australopithecines of Africa are the earliest hominids that are definitively human in their attributes and in what can be inferred of their behavior. "Australopithecine" is a term that once had taxonomic meaning. Now it is used instead to refer to a grade of organization that characterizes hominids from the Pliocene and earliest Pleistocene. The first australopithecine fossil to be found (recognized by R. Dart, see Chapter 5) was a juvenile cranium from the later portion of the australopithecine timespan. It was discovered in 1924 in South Africa. Later findings were first mainly confined to the Transvaal region of South Africa, until the discovery of an East African form at Olduvai Gorge in Tanzania in the late 1950s. Olduvai was an important source of hominid remains, and further exploration in East Africa led to the discovery of extremely rich deposits to the north and east of Lake Turkana (formerly Lake Rudolf) in Kenya and southern Ethiopia, and more recently in central Ethiopia and south of Olduvai Gorge in Tanzania.

Australopithecine sites extend into the Pliocene (approximately 5.5 to 2 million years ago, as used in this text) and span most of the earlier portion of the Pleistocene, the so-called basal Pleistocene. The dates for these sites range from being firm radiometric determinations to being pure guesswork, but no australopithecine forms appear to be younger than approximately 1.3 million years. Moreover, while jaws and teeth that fit into the australopithecine range appear outside of Africa in the later part of the basal Pleistocene, it is not clear that these actually represent australopithecines; no definite australopithecine fossil is known from outside of Africa.

This chapter is concerned with the pre-Pleistocene early hominids of East and South Africa, which I believe are all australopithecines of the genus *Australopithecus*. The various main sites (see Map 1, p. 132) are discussed in a temporal sequence so that evolutionary trends can be demonstrated. The earliest of these are in East Africa. Laetolil provides evidence of jaws and teeth as well as some footprints, and the somewhat later Hadar material adds details of the postcranial skeleton and cranial vault. The earlier of the South African sites overlap the later Hadar sequence in time. These have

131

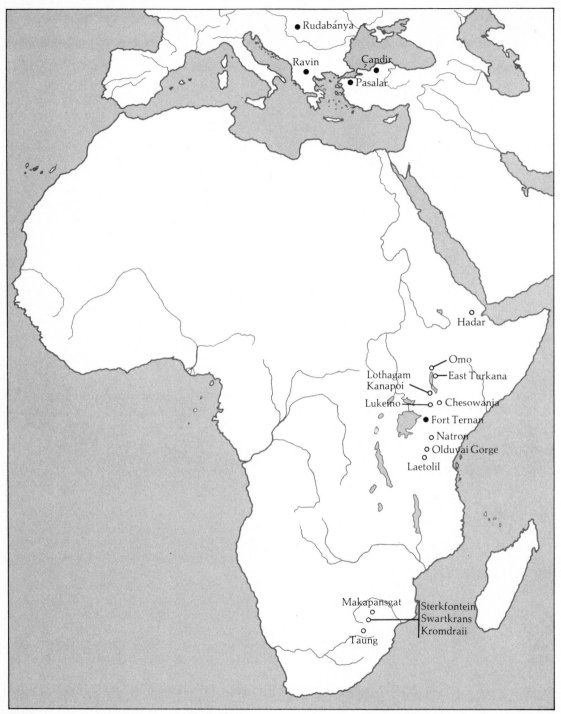

MAP 1   Early hominid and ramapithecine distribution in   early Homo erectus specimens have been found. (From
Europe and Africa. Dots indicate the ramapithecine sites,   Nystrom Series of Desk Maps.)
and open circles indicate sites where australopithecines and

yielded the best samples of the crania of Pliocene australopithecines. The later South African sites also have crania, but materials of equivalent age in East Africa are almost entirely dental.

The structure of the chapter is to discuss the earlier East African sites, the earlier South African sites, the later South African sites, and then the later East African sites. Each section deals first with the new information provided by the sites, then the inferences that can be drawn from this information, and finally the comparisons that are possible with earlier material. The concluding section attempts to suggest what living australopithecine groups of this timespan might have been like.

Pliocene Australopithecines

The earliest hominid sample clearly recognizable as australopithecine comes from the Tanzanian site of Laetolil, south of Olduvai Gorge. An upper jaw fragment was discovered there by the German paleontologist Kohl-Larsen several decades ago, but the bulk of the discoveries are the result of recent work by M. Leakey. A sample of over twenty individuals is dated to about 3.8 million years ago. Much farther north, in the Hadar region of Ethiopia, an international expedition under the direction of D. C. Johanson and M. Taieb has collected a large sample dating from about 3.5 to about 2.6 million years ago. Slightly younger, although still in the Pliocene, are a series of fragments (mostly dental) from the Brown and White sands of the Usno formation and Member B of the Shungura formation in the lower Omo basin of southern Ethiopia, just north of Lake Turkana, recovered by expeditions directed by Y. Coppens and F. C. Howell. Finally, the earlier of the South African sites— first excavated by Dart (Makapansgat) and R. Broom (Sterkfontein)—also appear to date to the later Pliocene. Each of these sites provides important knowledge concerning the earlier australopithecines. Moreover, comparing the earlier and later Pliocene sites reveals some of the evolutionary trends that were taking place in what this author believes to be a single lineage. Interestingly, *recognizable* stone tools appear only toward the end of this span.

The East African sites have a number of features in common. They are all in the immediate vicinity

of water, either a lake or a slow river. This is probably because hominids have the best chance of being buried and fossilized on a lakeshore or near a river that periodically overflows its banks. The terrain near the water almost always has a narrow band of trees, which in turn border open grasslands that range from dry to semi-arid. Thus, which environment or environments the hominids lived in cannot be determined from the East African evidence alone; where they usually lived may not be the same as where the few specimens that became fossils died.

However, evidence from South Africa helps resolve this problem of habitat. At Makapansgat and Sterkfontein, the hominid fossils were buried and fossilized in caves. The hominids did not *live* in the caves, which were mostly shallow rock shelters or just holes with a large shaft opening into an underground chamber. Furthermore, the interment was not intentional. Hominids and other animals were washed into these caves or fell in. C. K. Brain, the Director of the Transvaal Museum in Pretoria, recently wondered whether a similar process was taking place today. He climbed to the bottom of a modern shaft similar to the australopithecine-bearing caves of the Pliocene, and discovered that the same process continues by finding the remains of a cow that had fallen in about a week before.

The discovery of australopithecines in these caves removes the possible bias due to water burial by showing where australopithecines who were not buried by water lived. These areas were not much different in the Pliocene than they are today. Open grasslands which tend toward the drier side at Sterkfontein and slightly toward the moister at Makapansgat predominate, with patches of parkland and woods in the immediate vicinity. The elevation of the region provides a winter habitat that is extremely dry and can become quite cold.

Finding early australopithecines in this region clearly indicates two things. First, they must have been grasslands adapted. If they were restricted to regions near bodies of water, forest, or boundaries between forest and grassland, they would never have found their way into the South African caves. Second, the Pliocene hominids were much more adaptable than many scholars give them credit for. The Transvaal was by no means the hospitable environment that the East African lakeshores must have been. Seasonal extremes in rainfall and temperature created a habitat that must have been un-

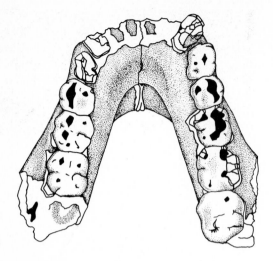
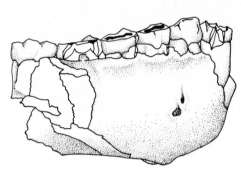

FIGURE 7.1   The Laetolil 4 mandible, courtesy of T. White. Note the asymmetric shape of the anterior premolar, with the dominant outer cusp and small inner one. The diastema between it and the (broken) canine contrasts with the crowding between the two premolars.

comfortable during some portions of the year. In contrast to the hominids, no living or fossil apes were able to adapt to this region.

By implication, the East African australopithecines must also have been able to utilize habitats strikingly different from the environments they were fossilized in, but not necessarily very far away.

Laetolil: Jaws and Teeth

The large hominid sample from the Tanzanian site of Laetolil is thus far mainly made up of jaws and teeth. Nonetheless, these have provided important information because they are the most primitive known, more closely resembling those of the proconsuls than any other Plio-Pleistocene hominid sample.

ANTERIOR CUTTING

Probably the most important dental information comes from the anterior teeth, mainly in the canine/premolar morphology. Fortunately, these teeth are known in specimens showing several degrees of wear, ranging from the unworn LH-3 to the more moderately worn LH-14 and finally to the very worn LH-4 mandible, shown in Figure 7.1. Both upper and lower canines tend to be fairly squat and more rounded at the base than their ramapithecine counterparts. In their unworn form, these teeth are triangular in shape with a pointed tip and sharp edges on both leading and trailing surfaces (see Figure 7.2). As the lower canines began to wear, the tip became blunted (or broken) to the level of the other teeth and no honing maintained the sharp back edge. Thus there appears to have been no cutting between the *front* of the *upper* canine and the *back* of the *lower* one. It is not surprising that the small wear facet on the leading edge of the upper canine of LH-5 (Figure 7.2) is flattened, dulling the edge.

The trailing surface of the upper canine occludes against the P_3, and a small diastema separates this tooth from the lower canine. In the LH-5 maxilla the trailing edge is sharpened. T. D. White, who described these specimens, points out that sharpening of this edge is maintained through a combination of thin (outer hard) enamel and expanded (inner softer) dentin. Once the dentin is exposed, it wears faster than the enamel, leaving a sharp enamel edge on the back of the tooth. This edge must cut against the lower premolar, but it is in the morphology of the cutting complex that the Laetolil hominids differ from ramapithecines (and proconsuls). In the latter, the back edge of the upper canine cuts against the sharpened leading edge of the

FIGURE 7.2 *Some Pliocene maxillas from East Africa. Above and middle are views of the Laetolil 5 female maxilla, courtesy of T. White, and below is a view of the Afar male maxilla AL-200. (Courtesy of D. C. Johanson.) In the top view, the Laetolil female maxilla is compared with two unworn male canines from the site. In the occlusal views (center and lower), note the thinness of the enamel and the sharp angle of the posterior wear facets on the maxillary canines (marked). Below, the right (reader's left) canine of the Afar maxilla is out of its socket, making it appear unusually projecting. The wear on the incisors is uneven; the heavier wear on the lateral incisors may have been due to their function in stripping. In both maxillas there is a diastema between the canine and incisor.*

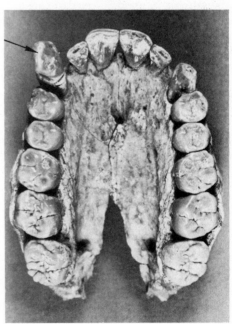

P_3 (see Figure 3.4). In the Laetolil hominids, the cutting action could probably better be described as chiseling. The P_3 resembles the ramapithecine homologue. When unworn, it has sharp leading and trailing edges. In the ramapithecine tooth, a third sharp edge extends inward and downward from the pointed single cusp (Figures 6.3, 6.5, and 6.6 show this rather well). In the Laetolil premolars, a second smaller cusp is raised to the inside along this ridge (the tooth is *bicuspid* although its cross-section is still *sectorial*). This acts to raise the angle of the third premolar's transverse ridge until it is almost in the occlusal plane, angled at close to 90 degrees to a line formed by the postcanine teeth. In the Laetolil hominids, the back edge of the upper canine (oriented more or less vertically) occludes against this roughly horizontal transverse ridge on the P_3. As the vertical edge of the upper tooth moves down and to the side of the horizontal edge of the lower tooth, a chiseling-like motion, cutting takes place.

Why the detail about this morphological complex? First, it would be too simple and somewhat misleading to state that the Laetolil hominids *retain* a canine/premolar cutting complex, although cutting does take place. Moreover, the details of the complex only vaguely point in the direction of the ramapithecines. While bicuspid P_3s characterize *Gigantopithecus*, the tooth had been completely incorporated into the grinding complex. This incorporation characterizes only the oldest of the Laetolil hominids (LH-4, for instance). The closest analogue is a newly discovered *Ramapithecus* P_3 from Pakistan which shows a small second cusp and a somewhat raised ridge between the cusps. In general, however, the ramapithecines do not retain the diastema between the canine and P_3.

A POSSIBLE MODEL OF THE C/P_3 COMPLEX

These data suggest a two-stage hypothesis for the change in the C/P_3 complex in hominids. In the first stage, canine reduction (but not change in form) resulted from selection to decrease the amount of canine interlock. This would allow freer transverse motion of the jaw during chewing, and would be advantageous in a primate evolving an efficient grinding system. The reduced canine would be shorter and overlap the adjacent tooth in the opposite jaw only slightly. While providing for more effective grinding, these changes would have an adverse effect on the anterior cutting system, especially between the upper canine and P_3 since the canine must overlap with the entire anterior face of the P_3 during the cutting motion. The hominid response was to retain the cutting function by changing the position of the occluding sharp surfaces to the top of the P_3. This was accomplished by raising the second internal cusp on the P_3 and shifting the cutting surface from the anterior face of the tooth to the ridge between the cusps. With the occlusion taking place at the top of the tooth, a much shorter canine could still effectively cut. The result was the sectorial bicuspid P_3 found at Laetolil; sectorial because the tooth was used to cut and bicuspid because there were two cusps.

The second stage to the model apparently took place later. This involved the change in function that likely came with the development of sharp-edged stone tools, shifting the cutting function out of the mouth completely. The canine subsequently was incorporated into the incisor functional complex, and the P_3 (already bicuspid) into the grinding complex, with accompanying morphological changes discussed below.

OTHER FEATURES OF THE JAWS AND TEETH

Another primitive feature retained by the Laetolil hominids is a marked sex difference in the size and form of the canines. Male canines are easy to distinguish by their larger size and higher, more tapered crowns.

The postcanine teeth are fairly large, falling within the range of the larger-sized ramapithecine sample (such as the specimens from Ravin). However, unlike the trend for elongation in the largest of the ramapithecines (*Gigantopithecus*), size expansion in the Laetolil postcanine teeth was accomplished through broadening, resulting in teeth that are relatively broad compared with their length.

The mandibles themselves are characterized by moderately thick bodies. The symphysis is rounded and evenly curved; two buttresses extend across its internal face, and as in most ramapithecines the lower buttress extends much farther backward than the upper one.

The maxillary dentitions reflect the conditions in the lower teeth. Plus we have additional knowledge gained from a complete series of incisors. The single unworn central incisor closely conforms to the ancestral condition in its length relative to the posterior teeth; it does not differ from the relative length in *Proconsul africanus* or the Rudabányan male RUD-15. However, the transverse breadth is considerably less than in the earlier ramapithecines. The tooth is more *Proconsul*-like in its proportions and its lack of internal marginal ridges. Both dimensions are relatively small compared with those in living chimpanzees. The lateral incisors are markedly smaller than the centrals, and are reduced compared with the ancestral condition (for this tooth) in both dimensions.

In sum, the Laetolil dentitions only somewhat approach the ramapithecines' in their combination of features. They maintained an ability to cut between their upper canine and P_3, although the exact morphology differs from both proconsuls and living pongids. The canines show no reduction compared with the ramapithecines'; while some reductions appear in the incisors, the Laetolil teeth are actually more *Proconsul*-like. Breadth expansion of the posterior teeth and the buttressing behind the symphysis provide the main evidence of an adaptation to powerful grinding and crushing.

FOOTPRINTS AND LOCOMOTION

Also found at Laetolil was a sequence of several overlapping ancient ground surfaces. Each of these preserves the remains of a fairly wet, sandy region near what must have been a water hole. The ground surfaces were covered with footprints, ranging in size from those of small birds to elephants. Ash falls or other debris covered these surfaces, preserving the prints.

In 1977 and again in 1978, M. Leakey announced the discovery of several sets of human-appearing footprints crossing these floors. While the preservation ranged from poor to excellent, the total body of evidence shows that a small, bipedal striding primate lived in the area and frequented the water hole locality. It is likely that it was the same species whose skeletal remains were discovered nearby, although almost certainly not the same individuals. Even more firmly than any skeletal remains that could be found, this establishes the mode of locomotion for the earliest australopithecine sample. It gives hominid bipedalism a greater antiquity than either hominid canine form or significant brain size expansion (see below).

A NEW SPECIES?

Many features of the Laetolil sample are truly primitive compared with those of later hominids. Recognizing this, D. C. Johanson and T. D. White have recently suggested that the Laetolil sample along with the largely similar Afar hominids (see below) be designated as a new species of the genus *Australopithecus: A. afarensis.*

Afar: Postcrania

Far to the north, an even larger sample of early hominids has been recovered from the Afar, in the Hadar region of Ethiopia. The sample includes the usual jaws and teeth, as well as a fairly complete face and cranial base, some cranial vault fragments, portions of a child's skull, and most importantly postcranial remains, including much of a single associated skeleton. The stratigraphic sequence at the site seems to date from about 3.5 to approximately 2.6 million years ago. Hominids have been found from virtually all time levels.

THE DENTITIONS

In many respects the Afar dentitions are similar to those from Laetolil, although the larger sample size results in more variation. One collection from the Afar consists of the remains of a number of individuals who may have died either at the same time or close together in time. This collection (from the 333 locality) has virtually the full range of variation found at the Afar excavations, which suggests that marked variation was a normal populational characteristic of the early hominids, just as it seems to have been in the ramapithecines.

Differences from the Laetolil anterior teeth are virtually non-existent. Their size, relative to the posteriors, is almost identical. The main Afar distinctions appear to be a somewhat less projecting canine and the lack of a diastema in any of the mandibles. Some of the lower anterior premolars resemble the Laetolil form and some completely lack the secondary cusp. Others are more symmetric, with almost equal-sized cusps. However, while the morphology often resembles that found at Laetolil, the functional evidence is somewhat different. None of the Afar specimens shows the chiseling-like wear facets on the upper canine and P_3. The wear on these dentitions reflects the end of a series of behavioral changes in the hominids. The Afar P_3 is fully incorporated in the grinding complex, and the canine was not used in cutting. However, some of the canines still projected beyond the occlusal plane of the other teeth and show multiple flat wear facets as the result. The remaining teeth also resemble the Laetolil sample, although they show more variation in size.

Much of this variation appears to be the result of dramatic sexual dimorphism. For instance, a female and a male maxilla (AL-199 and AL-200) show as much percentage dimorphism in their posterior teeth as living orangs, and some of the male and female mandibles differ even more. However, dimorphism in the canines, while greater than in the other teeth, is much less than in the living pongids or in the proconsuls.

In sum, the few differences between the Afar and Laetolil dental samples may be the result of a later date for Afar. Within the Afar specimens, the variation in size and morphology is marked, and much of it is probably the result of sexual dimorphism.

CRANIA AND MANDIBLES

No complete crania are known from the Afar, and the fragmentary specimens have only been described in the most preliminary way. These seem to combine very small cranial vaults with large prognathic faces characterized by widely flaring, well-developed cheeks. The thin vault is small relative to the cranial base, which retains an extraordinary number of many pongid-like details. The lines marking the muscle attachment areas for the nuchal and posterior temporalis muscles (see Figures

4.8 and 5.2) meet at the back of one skull (AL-333-45), forming a compound crest. The fairly complete juvenile face seems to resemble the Taung australopithecine child.

The mandibles vary widely, ranging from specimens similar to Laetolil 4 to others, generally smaller, which have a narrower anterior region and more closely resemble the ramapithecine (proconsul) condition of straight, posteriorly divergent tooth rows. These variants may reflect differences in size, sex, or both. An even greater range is suggested by the less complete fragments. Generally, the differences parallel those already discussed for tooth size, and it is likely that a major component in the variation is a size-related one resulting from a significant average difference between males and females.

The ramus is vertical and very large relative to the mandibular body. Once again there is a marked size difference between the male and female rami.

Probably the greatest distinction from the Laetolil mandibles is at the symphysis. The Afar specimens tend to be more vertical on the external face. Internally, the two buttresses are more equal in size, and the lower buttress is more rounded and less shelf-like.

POSTCRANIA

The greatest importance of the Afar material is found in the postcranial sample. Afar provides the first early hominid postcranial material that is fairly complete, including much of the skeleton of an extraordinarily small female (Figure 7.3). The pelvis and lower limbs of this skeleton show a complete adaptation to the striding bipedalism of later hominids, while the arms appear to have been slightly longer (relative to the legs) than in living humans.

The innominate is fully hominid in features and proportions, corresponding to its functions in locomotion. There are distinct anterior spines (superior and inferior) and a greater sciatic notch (see Figure 4.5). The ilium is short relative to its breadth, and it flares outward at the hip. Similarly, the ischium is short. These features, and others, are the result of an adaptation to bipedal striding, providing for the same muscle positions that are found in living humans. A large birth canal is maintained by a broad sacrum at the back of the pelvic inlet. The anterior-posterior dimension of the birth canal is large

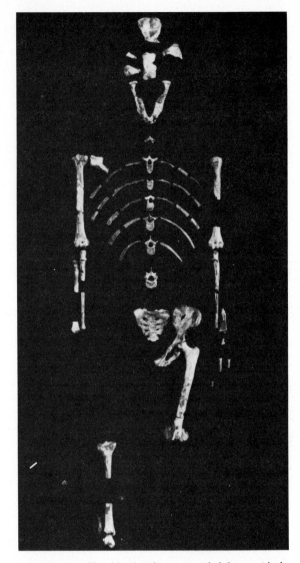

FIGURE 7.3   The Afar female postcranial skeleton, with the associated jaw and cranial fragments. (Courtesy of D. C. Johanson.)

enough to give birth to australopithecine-shaped heads (at birth) with ease. The inlet is unusually broad. C. O. Lovejoy, who reconstructed the specimen, suggests that this breadth reflects the broadening of the pelvic basin that is required to support the lower viscera during upright stance.

The lower limb shows the corresponding adaptation to striding. For instance, the femur is angled strongly outward from the base, showing that while the tops of the legs are far apart (broad birth canal), the knees meet at the midline of the body. Lovejoy's analysis of motions that are possible at the knee indicates that the adaptation to bipedalism included the finer points that might be expected to have evolved after the major more basic changes. The available evidence provides a real contrast with the canine/premolar cutting complex, which seems to have only recently changed from proconsul-like functions.

While the locomotion was fully human, the postcranial skeleton reveals some differences between the Afar hominids and living people. One of these is size; this small female was only between 3½ and 4 feet in height. Other more fragmentary postcranial remains represent larger individuals, and judging from the evidence of sexual dimorphism in the teeth, males may have averaged as much as double the weight of females. This would suggest males about the size of pygmy males, and females smaller than those in any living human group.

A second difference is in the bony features reflecting muscularity. It is clear from the size of the joint articulations, the morphology and buttressing of many of the bones (ranging from the fingers to the long bones), and the thickness of the limbs that the Afar hominids were muscularly powerful. Their strength was probably far more like that of a chimpanzee of similar size than that of much larger modern humans. Bony adaptations to strength come as the result of powerful and prolonged muscle use.

A third difference is in the relative length of the forelimbs. The Afar female has relatively longer arms than are usually found within human populations. However, the arms are much shorter than are ever found in a primate quadruped or any of the living pongids. They are too short to have been used in locomotion, and in any event the pelvic and lower limb adaptations to bipedalism would make quadrupedal locomotion as difficult for the Afar hominids as it is for us. While some authors have suggested that the longer arms may reflect an arm-hanging adaptation, they are not different enough from living humans' to make this much more effective than our own (not insubstantial) ability to hang by the arms. The longer arms may instead reflect a recent change in locomotion. Alternatively (or additionally), the explanation could lie in the use of clubs and other tools which are most effective when applied as far from the body as possible. A combination of muscular strength and arm elongation would maximize the distance between an Afar hominid and an animal being clubbed. This could be quite important both for defense and in hunting.

Additional postcranial remains from the area represent most skeletal elements. While these are as yet largely unstudied, preliminary work on the remains of several hands and feet reveal a combination of strength-related, modern human, and chimpanzee-like features. Yet both the foot and the hand appear to have been fully human in form and function.

Earlier South African Sites: Crania

The cave sites of Sterkfontein and Makapansgat (and probably Taung) seem to date to the later Pliocene, approximately 2.5 million years ago. These sites thus provide a later sample of the lineage, allowing one to determine the evolutionary trends within it. Moreover, they include the earliest sample of well-preserved early hominid crania, besides numerous teeth, mandibles, and some additional postcrania. Although the two sites are several hundred miles apart, they may be considered together because of the similarity of the fauna and the hominids found in them. The specimens are generally regarded as *Australopithecus africanus*.

DENTITIONS

There are a large number of teeth in the earlier South African sample, although fewer complete or fairly complete dentitions compared to the Afar sample because of the fragmentation that takes place during events surrounding deposition in the caves where they are found. The Afar and South African samples are large enough to show some clear evolutionary trends. One of these is an average size increase in the postcanine teeth of about 10 percent for the linear dimensions (slightly greater for the anterior mandibular premolar). The estimated body size ranges overlap almost completely. This dental expansion may indicate an average body size increase, or it could be the result of selection favoring more powerful mastication in individuals of the same size.

The incisors stay the same approximate size; there might be some reduction in the upper centrals, but the sample of incisors is too small for us to be sure of this. Thus the South African incisors are *relatively* smaller compared with the postcanine teeth. The canines in the South African sample, in contrast, are clearly reduced in size to about 75 percent of the earlier Afar sample average. Morphologically, the male canines are similar to the earlier specimens; although lower crowned, some of the male canines projected beyond the tooth row. Female canines, on the other hand, are greatly reduced in crown height and are level with the incisors. Except in a few of the large males, all of the canines wear flatly. The consequences of the canine function change are more evident in the form of the anterior lower premolars (see Figure 6.6); these are almost invariably symmetric and bicuspid with equal-sized cusps.

The same marked sexual dimorphism characterizes tooth size differences. The larger South African sample allows comparison of averages for males and females. The percentage difference in the postcanine teeth is on the order of that in living orangs. While the canine size dimorphism is less than in the pongids, it is greater than the dimorphism in the remaining teeth. No evidence shows a decrease in dimorphism compared with the earlier East African hominids, and there is little if any decrease compared with the ramapithecines.

Not all of the individual differences can be due to sex. Some must be due to the normal variation within populations, while others reflect the fact that, with few exceptions, numerous different populations are represented within the sample.

POSTCRANIA

Sterkfontein and Makapansgat provide four innominates; two are juvenile, a third is a fragmentary adult, and the fourth belongs to a partially complete female postcranial skeleton from Sterkfontein. In addition, there are several femoral fragments. These confirm the implications of the Afar skeleton, demonstrating a complete skeletal adaptation to bipedalism. In fact, this later material is even more modern appearing with its shorter ilium and deeper acetabulum (hip socket). Like the ear-

lier Afar female, the Sterkfontein female (STS-14) was very short (about 4 feet). A larger postcranial sample, however, gives an idea of how height was distributed. Six individuals have an estimated average height of 53 inches, ranging from about 44 inches to 63 inches. Two of the individuals are much larger than the other four, and one of the former is associated with a mandible that can be classified as male because of the size of the canine. Hypothesizing that the two larger individuals are male and the four smaller ones female results in male and female average heights of 60 inches and 49 inches (STS-14 is the pelvis of an "average" female). A female average height that is 82 percent of the male average contrasts with the 89 to 95 percent range in our species.

The robustness of the limbs and the size of features that relate to muscular power (muscle attachments, relative joint areas) indicate that these hominids were heavier than modern people of the same height, the greater weight largely reflecting the added musculature. I estimate an average weight of about 110 pounds for this sample, ranging from 58 to 180 pounds for the individuals. Average male and female weights are about 150 pounds and 85 pounds, resulting in an average dimorphism of 57 percent. (Females today average 80–85 percent the weight of males.)

CRANIA

The earlier South African sites provide the first good sample of complete or fairly complete early hominid crania. These include a complete (but toothless) Sterkfontein female cranium, a fairly complete male cranium also from Sterkfontein, and numerous more fragmentary faces and braincases (see Figure 7.4). The specimens combine three categories of features: some are remarkably primitive, others are the result of bipedalism and some brain-

FIGURE 7.4 *Some views of the most complete Sterkfontein crania. A and B show STS-5, the best-preserved female. The arrow in B indicates the low position of the nuchal torus, marking the most posterior extent of the neck muscles (contrast with the pongid in Figure 4.6). C and D show the STS-71 male. E and F show the STS-17 male. Note the high position of the temporal lines (marked by arrows) in these males.*

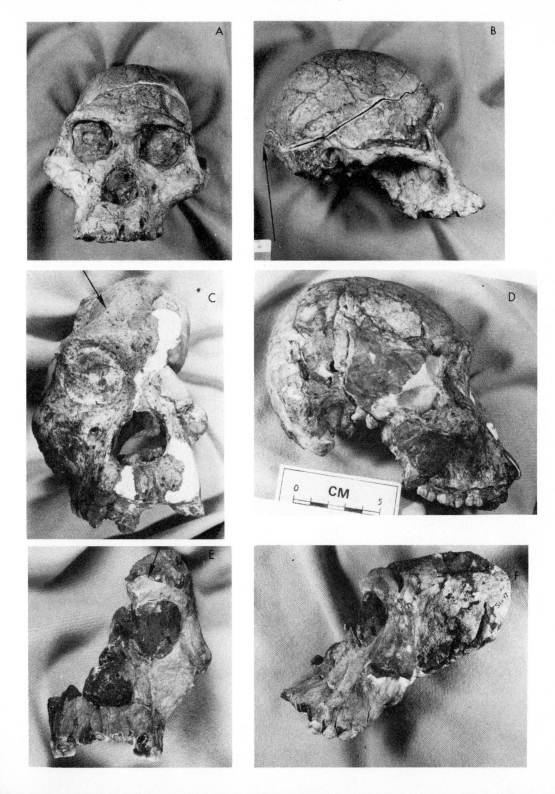

case expansion, and still others are adaptations to a diet requiring powerful chewing.

The first set of primitive features is seen in the combination of a large prognathic face and a small braincase, which creates a rather chimpanzee-like appearance. The average cranial capacity at the two sites is just over 450 cc. This is slightly less than a half-quart. Chimpanzees of approximately similar size have an average cranial capacity of about 385 cc, while the average for gorillas is over 490 cc. As in modern pongids, the braincase is narrow in the frontal area, and the receding forehead begins behind the brows rather than above them. Although the canines are reduced compared with the earlier Pliocene samples, their roots are still long and robust. A buttress for the canine root can be seen passing upward from the tooth row along the sides of the nose.

Another pongid-like feature is the occasional (inferred) appearance of sagittal crests. This crest is a bony prominence that runs along the top of the cranium as the temporal lines, marking the edge of the temporal muscles, migrate upward during growth, meeting at the midline of the vault. A crest will form along the top where these muscles meet. While none of these specimens actually has a sagittal crest preserved, the morphology of two male crania shows that the missing top portions probably had a crest.

Finally, turning to the cranial base, the foramen magnum (see Figure 4.6) is in a more posterior position and at an angle slightly less horizontal than in living hominids. The configuration of the foramen magnum is intermediate between modern humans and chimpanzees. However, the independent pelvic evidence for bipedalism shows that the position and angle of the foramen magnum could not correspond to a significant locomotor difference. The subsequent changes in the area were probably related to something other than locomotion.

Superimposed on these features is a second set, resulting from some of the distinctive hominid adaptations. As discussed above, the average cranial capacity is somewhat larger than in chimpanzees of similar size. The most forward part of the braincase is better developed than in chimpanzees so that the forehead is somewhat more filled out. Other changes in the brain (discussed below) also affect cranial shape. At the back of the cranium, the neck (nuchal) muscles are in a lower position than in

pongids. This results from the slightly more forward position and the downward orientation of the neck-head articulation. In bipeds, the head is better balanced on the vertically oriented neck, while in the pongids, the balance is tipped toward the face because of the more rearward position and orientation of the spine and its articulation with the head. Therefore, the pongids require more musculature behind this articulation.

The third set of features characterizing these crania results from the dietary adaptation. To begin with, the posterior teeth are large compared with the size of the hominids. Tooth size falls within the range of variation of gorillas, although body weight is only a quarter of the gorilla average. Corresponding to the large teeth, the areas of both jaws holding the tooth roots are thick and deep. The face itself tends to be deep, and the ramus of the mandible is high and vertical (especially in the males; females have shorter faces and consequently a lower ramus). Buttresses appear across the inner face of the symphysis, responding to the powerful forces acting on the mandible during chewing. The position of the zygomatics is variable, but they tend to be forward (again especially in the males).

In sum, the crania could be thought of as chimpanzee-like with larger brains, better cranial balance atop the spine, facial and dental adaptations to powerful mastication, and smaller canines and incisors. Yet, these crania are somewhat less chimpanzee-like than the Afar sample. Most of the changes are on the cranial base and posterior region. The South African crania have a more expanded occiput, a lower nuchal muscle position, and a more modern configuration of the mastoids and the mandibular articulation. It is possible that there is some cranial capacity expansion.

NEURAL REORGANIZATION

Recent studies by R. L. Holloway have involved the internal casts of the braincases. These endocasts reflect the external morphology of the brain, and from them Holloway has been able to show three important ways in which these australopithecine brains differ from pongid brains. These are:

1. Expansion of the posterior parietal association areas

2. Greater complexity of the frontal lobes, especially in some of the speech areas
3. Expansion of the temporal lobes

These areas (see Figure 3.5) correspond to some of the unique developments of the human brain. The areas showing evidence of dramatic expansion in the australopithecine endocasts are just those frontal and posterior parietal portions which seem to underly the complex neural models whose behavioral manifestations are regarded as culture. Holloway believes that the earlier South African australopithecines had already undergone such an encephalization of behavioral structure, and that their brains appear to differ from ours in size more than in organization. Specifically, the expansion of the frontal and the posterior parietal areas provides evidence for cognition, categorization, symbolization, cross-modal transfer, ordering, discrimination of relevant from irrelevant elements in numerous contexts, and a connected verbal-auditory association area and motor-speech area. Moreover, there are indications that motor areas for speech production were fairly well developed.

Thus Holloway's inference from the endocasts is that the earlier South African australopithecines were capable of a wide range of human behaviors, and that the underlying neural models for many of these had already become encephalized. Moreover, some of the evidence hints at the presence of both the neurological and motor requirements for a human form of language. The fairly well advanced representation of these capabilities in the late Pliocene suggests a considerable evolutionary history for them. The evolutionary basis for these changes seems to extend fairly far into the past and might be a reflection of changes associated with early hominid origins.

Later South African Sites

South African sites dating somewhat later in time are represented by three cave sites, all within a mile of each other in the Transvaal. These are Swartkrans, Kromdraai, and the upper levels at Sterkfontein. The exact time relation of these sites to one another is not clear, except that Kromdraai is probably the youngest. Moreover, determining the time

that elapsed between the earlier and later South African samples has also proved to be difficult, mainly because of the lack of radiometric dates from this volcanoless region. Estimates of the time difference range from 500,000 years to as much as 1.5 million years. The later sites could be latest Pliocene or early Pleistocene. Finally, some evidence suggests a slight climatic difference between the earlier and later sites. Whatever difference there was, it did not produce any significant changes in the habitat. At the most, grasslands might have become slightly better represented in the area immediately surrounding the caves.

The largest of these sites is Swartkrans; only a few individuals have been found in the other two, although each has yielded a fairly complete cranium. The Swartkrans sample is probably the largest from any hominid site that predates the appearance of modern people.

A CONTINUED DENTAL TREND

The large later South African dental sample differs from the earlier sample in much the same way that the latter differs from the yet earlier East African australopithecine samples. Essentially, the anterior teeth remain the same size while the posterior teeth expand further. However, the pattern of expansion is different in an interesting way; it mainly involves the middle of the posterior tooth row, P^3-M^1 in the maxilla and P_4-M_1 in the mandible. These increase by about 10 percent, while the remaining posterior teeth are virtually unchanged. Sexual dimorphism also remains unchanged in the dental remains.

RATE OF MATURATION

Included in the large dental sample are numerous juveniles in various stages of incomplete tooth eruption. This fact allowed A. Mann to make two important determinations. Mann was first interested in how long it took australopithecine children to mature. He reasoned that if these early hominids were adapted to using complex behavior, if not actually culture, their period of learning would have to be comparatively longer than the living pongids' (just as the pongids' period of learning is comparatively longer than monkeys'). The most intensive learning occurs in the very young, followed by an adolescent period when the adult behaviors are practiced in play. Thus Mann hypothesized that the whole period of skeletal maturation would be expected to be longer in early hominids than in pongids. Since tooth eruption is part of the skeletal maturation process, he reasoned that eruption times should be relatively far apart if australopithecines were slow to mature.

Mann used a comparative model of tooth eruption and development based on living humans and chimpanzees (see Table 4.2 and accompanying text discussion). The molars of both take the same time to develop. However, chimpanzees mature more rapidly, so their first permanent molar erupts at a younger age, and the successive molar eruptions are closer together (about three and a half years apart). In humans the first permanent molar erupts later, and the successive eruptions are separated by about five years (except in people who make little use of their teeth—these have an even further delay in the eruption of the last molar, if it erupts at all). Combining these two facts means that when the first molar erupts, the *relative* development of the second and third (unerupted) molars is very different in humans and chimpanzees. The chimpanzee unerupted teeth must be further developed since they will be erupting much sooner.

With these models based on the living species for comparison, Mann then took X-ray photographs of the juvenile Swartkrans mandibles with first or second molars just erupted, to determine the development of the unerupted molars. In every case, he discovered that the Swartkrans australopithecines fit the human pattern; they did not have rapid successive eruptions as in chimpanzees, and they were not "half-way" between the two contrasting models.

Like bipedalism, then, it appears that maturation delay was the same in these early hominids as in modern humans. Additional analysis of the earlier South African juveniles showed that they fit the same pattern. Mann concluded that the early appearance of maturation delay corresponded to the necessity for learning complex behaviors. It is unlikely that it required delayed maturation to learn how to make simple stone tools properly. Instead, it would seem to reflect a behavioral aspect of australopithecine adaptation that otherwise could not be directly observed.

DEMOGRAPHY AND ITS IMPLICATIONS

Mann further reasoned that learning cultural information that required this maturation delay must have resulted in important adaptive advantages because of certain related disadvantages that he noted from a second part of his analysis. One obvious disadvantage to maturation delay is the increased susceptibility of the young to disease, starvation, and injury. This would place a special strain on australopithecine societies.

A second problem was realized from an attempt to determine the age at death for individuals. Once the period between successive tooth eruptions is known, the *rate* of tooth wear can be determined the following way. In australopithecines (and humans), when the second molar erupts the first molar has five years of occlusal wear. When the third molar erupts, there is ten years of wear on the first molar. From these known degrees of wear (and others), it is possible to form a fairly accurate picture of how long any tooth has been wearing. Adding this to the time of eruption provides an approximate age at death.

This technique has been used to estimate the age at death of 168 of the Swartkrans specimens, and some of their demographic characteristics can be determined if one makes two assumptions. First, although Swartkrans is a random sample of many populations, we must assume that the ages in the sample are like the ages in an "average" real population and there was no long-term change in population size over the relevant timespan. Second, we must assume that approximately one-fourth of those born died before the age of three but were not all fossilized because of the fragility of the bone in the very young.

The average age at death at Swartkrans is between eleven and twelve years. Assuming that reproduction began at the age of twelve (a figure that is high for chimpanzees and low for humans) and calculating that birth spacing averaged three to four years (which is significantly less than in chimpanzees), we encounter the following situation at Swartkrans. If a mother gives birth to her first offspring at the age of twelve, the odds are better than 50–50 that both parents will *not* survive until this offspring is old enough to reproduce. If her second offspring is born when she is fifteen, the parents have a 75 percent chance of not living until this second offspring is of reproductive age. They almost certainly would not live to see a third off-spring reproduce. Delayed maturation combined with a short life expectancy creates the problem of raising numerous orphaned offspring. This is the second disadvantage.

How the australopithecines met this problem cannot be directly known. I believe their solution lay in the development of extended kinship relations and the recognition of kin not in the direct line of descent, such as siblings and their mates (and offspring). Extended kinship systems would provide a means of insuring that orphaned children would be cared for and enculturated to australopithecine expectations and traditions. One indirect indication that selection would favor such an arrangement is the high mortality rate observed in chimpanzee orphans.

THE LATER SKULLS

Crania are known from the three later South African sites. While many fragmentary specimens were recovered, their condition is generally not as good as that of the earlier crania. Cranial capacity is known for only one specimen, a natural endocast from Swartkrans with a capacity of 530 cc. Crania that appear to have been larger and smaller than this (but too incomplete for an estimate of cranial capacity) are also known from that cave, so the single known capacity is probably not an extreme. This suggests that there was a trend for some cranial capacity increase; none of the earlier South African crania are this large. In his studies of the Swartkrans endocast, Holloway concluded that the distinctively hominid features were better developed than in the earlier specimens.

The Swartkrans crania show a remarkable amount of variation in form (see Figure 7.5) yet a number of features characterize many of them. In terms of range, smaller crania resemble those from the earlier levels at Sterkfontein, while larger ones tend to be more robust, with better developed muscle markings, more anterior cheeks, and thicker buttressing structures. Thus, while the range overlaps with the earlier sample, the *average* tends toward larger size and greater robustness. Some of this range is due to sexual dimorphism (see Figure 7.6, p. 146). For instance, males have larger faces and larger canines, and sagittal cresting is more common. However, other elements of variation are

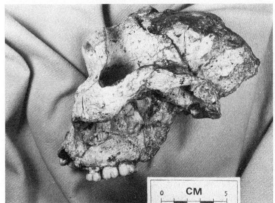

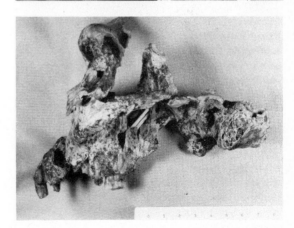

FIGURE 7.5   *Side views of three adult Swartkrans crania: SK-46 (above), SK-48 (middle), and SK-80 (below). None of these is complete. Damage has removed the entire rear of the male cranium SK-46 and crushed the top downward and the face forward. In SK-48 the back half of the braincase is telescoped into the front half. In the female SK-80, the whole top of the braincase is missing.*

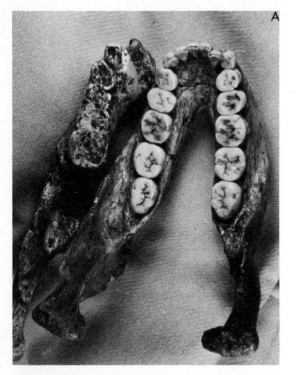

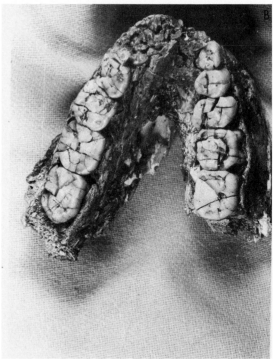

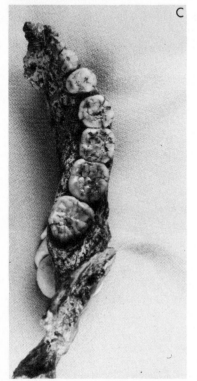

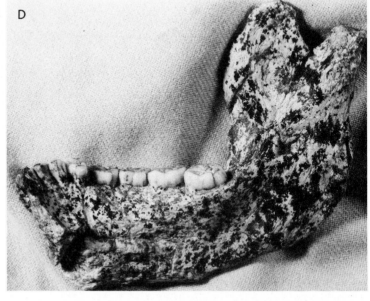

FIGURE 7.6   *Variation in South African australopithecine mandibles. A shows occlusal views of an earlier Sterkfontein male (STS-36, left) and a later Swartkrans female (SK-23). B shows the Swartkrans male SK-876, and C and D present the SK-34 female. The main difference between the males and females is in the size of the canine. Note the thinness of the anterior of the SK-34 mandible where it is broken and the very tall ramus.*

also displayed. There are larger and smaller females and larger and smaller males, suggesting that like the earlier sites, Swartkrans represents samples from many different populations that inhabited the area over the centuries that the cave deposits were formed. These populations were probably not identical in their adaptations to the region.

The crania from Kromdraai and the later Sterkfontein deposits are similar but not identical to those found at Swartkrans. The Sterkfontein specimen (STW-53) resembles one of the smaller Swartkrans females and some earlier Sterkfontein females in its (her?) marked prognathism, small thin vault, and distinct nasal spine (holding the cartilage of the mid-nose). The Kromdraai skull (TM-1517) appears to be similar to some of the larger Swartkrans females. While incomplete, the Kromdraai cranium may have had a capacity markedly larger than the Swartkrans specimen with a known capacity, the SK-1585 endocast.

These crania reveal one other interesting facet of the early hominids. Relative to dental age, the cranial sutures (contacts between the separate cranial bones) close quite early. This indicates that the growth of the brain stopped earlier in the maturation process than occurs in living people. Several decades ago, Weidenreich suggested this was the case for *Homo erectus*. In living populations, brain growth is approximately complete by the age of eighteen, although most of the growth takes place much earlier in life. After growth is complete, the cranial sutures begin to close and eventually fuse with each other at an advanced age (35-70+). In the australopithecine crania, suture fusion is already underway at the time of the third molar eruption. This suggests that brain growth ceased much earlier than in living humans. It is possible that australopithecine children were born relatively more mature, and that there was thus less brain growth to take place after birth.

POSTCRANIA

Swartkrans and Kromdraai have yielded a number of additional postcranial remains. Additional portions of the pelvis are known from both sites. The more complete specimens, from Swartkrans, show all of the features associated with bipedalism and a small birth canal (or pelvic inlet).

The best-preserved specimen (SK-3155) is the most undistorted from South Africa (Figure 7.7, p. 148). It shows the dramatic flare at the hips that characterizes the australopithecines because of their combination of broad hips and narrow birth canals (or pelvic inlets in the males, see Figure 4.5). The several femurs known combine thick shafts and rather elongated necks, again because of the combination of broad hips and narrow inlets—the neck must be longer to reach from the shaft to the hip socket. Of the additional fragments, some hand bones are unusual for their robustness and the prominence of their muscle attachments. A very fragmentary associated skeleton from Kromdraai seems to have closer-to-human proportions of forelimb and hindlimb than the much earlier Afar female.

Pliocene Trends

The South African hominid sequence is the best represented region for the later Pliocene (and perhaps earliest Pleistocene), while the earlier East African sites of Laetolil and the Afar provide a good sample for the middle and earlier Pliocene. As far as can be determined, there is a series of features that appear to be common in all of these Pliocene specimens, while others change systematically over time.

COMMON FEATURES

The Pliocene australopithecines are surprisingly human-like in some features. These include a bipedal striding locomotion, a trend for short birth spacing, and some elements of structural reorganization of the brain. They resemble the earlier proconsuls in their relatively small incisors, large faces relative to the braincase, molar size progression (the first is smaller than the second, which is gener-

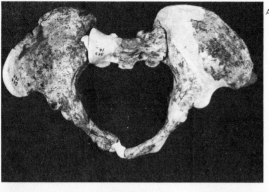
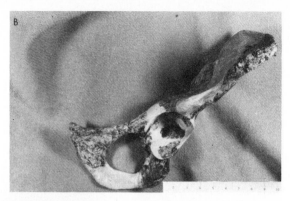
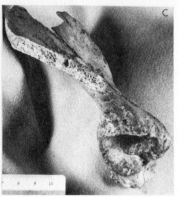
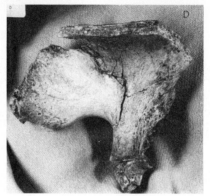

FIGURE 7.7   The best preserved of the South African hip-bones (see also Figure 4.5). STS-14 is shown in A and B. The reconstructed pelvis is viewed from above in A, while B gives an anterior view of the left side. C and D show anterior and side views of the SK-3155 innominate, and E gives a side view of the very crushed SK-50 innominate. The Swartkrans specimens are later in time.

ally smaller than the third), canine cutting in the earlier forms, and marked sexual dimorphism. More specific resemblances to the ramapithecines lie mainly in the development of the ability to produce powerful forces in chewing, and the morphological features that are associated with it. These same features distinguish them from living pongids, and are only partially reflected in living humans. The Pliocene australopithecines differ from all of the living hominoids in their relative posterior tooth size (compared to body size), the extraordinary development and angulation of the anterior temporalis and masseter muscles, the thickness of the mandibular bodies, the pronounced double buttressing across the back of the symphysis, and other details resulting from the adaptation to powerful chewing.

CHANGING FEATURES

Changes that can be observed in the Pliocene australopithecines involve many of the features discussed above. Comparisons with the earliest Pliocene forms are limited to jaws and teeth. Canines change in function and reduce markedly in size over the Pliocene. Their form changes from the irregular pointed teeth with sharp posterior edges in the earlier sample to the more blunted, lower-crowned teeth with rounded edges common later. The corresponding changes in the lower anterior premolar (P_3) result in the bicuspid sectorial tooth of the earlier sample becoming symmetric, with two cusps of virtually equal size. Functionally, a canine/premolar cutting complex changes into a blunter lower canine used in gripping and a bicuspid premolar incorporated into the grinding complex.

Posterior tooth size increases throughout the

Pliocene. The earlier changes involve all of the postcanine teeth, while later changes are mainly in the middle of the tooth row. The molars simply expand in size, but the premolars tend to add additional cusps and become more molar-like in appearance. Because the dental sample is so large, it is possible to demonstrate that these changes are *average* changes, reflecting frequency differences in the underlying gene pools. In the *ranges* of variation, size and form overlap almost completely among these samples. The process of size expansion involves the more frequent appearance of larger teeth and the less frequent appearance of smaller ones.

To some extent, the changes in posterior tooth size and perhaps cranial capacity might be the result of increasing body size. While the samples are too small for certainty, it appears that average body size in the early South African sample might be slightly larger than in the Afar sample, and there is a better established size increase in the later South African sample. However, as with the teeth, variation in body size is very large, and the ranges of the samples overlap almost completely. Some evidence suggests that more than body size increase is involved in the dental changes. The specific expansion in the later South African sample is restricted to the middle portion of the posterior tooth row. Combined with some of the facial changes described below, this suggests an adaptation to an even more powerful and efficient chewing complex in this sample.

Cranial changes involve an apparent expansion in cranial capacity between the earlier and later South African samples; my estimate is about a 20 percent increase in volume. Holloway believes there are some additional organizational changes in the brain, especially in an expanding posterior parietal area. Moreover, faces of the later specimens tend to be larger, with thicker and more anterior cheeks and deeper lower faces (holding the posterior tooth roots). Again, these are average changes, with largely overlapping ranges in both size and morphology between the earlier and later samples. Other changes involve the size of the temporal fossa (the area between the side of the cheek and the cranium that allows the temporal muscle to pass through) and the frequency of sagittal cresting.

In sum, these directional changes seem to combine three factors. The canine/premolar complex responds to the earlier change in function. There is probably some increase in average body size and

cranial capacity. The tendency is to improve the adaptation to powerful chewing.

East African Later Pliocene

The later Pliocene fossil record from East Africa is better dated than the South African sample, but unfortunately much more fragmentary and smaller. The Pliocene remains are almost completely limited to the sites in the Omo River basin in southern Ethiopia, just north of where the river flows into Lake Turkana in Kenya. Only a few remains dated this early are known from the Turkana region to the southeast. The fossilization of the Omo specimens was not particularly good. As they became exposed through erosion, the poorly fossilized bone quickly weathered away, leaving mainly teeth and a few jaws to be found by the French and American expeditions that have been working there for the past ten years. Only a few incomplete cranial or postcranial remains have been discovered.

DENTAL REMAINS

The dental remains from members C-J of the Shungura formation at Omo span the entire middle and later Pliocene (and extend into the Pleistocene). There are large enough samples of some of the teeth to allow comparisons over time. These comparisons provide an evolutionary picture that is almost identical to that from South Africa (see Figure 8.1, p. 161). The earliest samples resemble the teeth from the Afar in their small size, although none of the anterior lower premolars that have been recovered is as sectorial in appearance as those from the earlier sites. Later samples show size expansion for the posterior teeth, and by about 2.5 million years ago average tooth size was about the same as in the earlier South African sample.

In the last half million years of the Pliocene, average tooth size continued to expand, as in the South African sample. However, something else happened in this latest Pliocene span which was of critical importance in the evolution of our lineage. This will be discussed in the next chapter.

OTHER OMO MATERIAL

A few mandibles and other fossilized materials are known from the Omo region. The earlier mandibles are not especially distinct from their South African counterparts, and the best preserved cranium, a braincase from a juvenile that is about 2.1 million years old, is extraordinarily small (about 400 cc) with muscle markings that are very pronounced for a young individual. This cranium (Omo-338) has an elongated braincase shape and small capacity that resemble the earlier South African sample. However, a number of features more closely resemble the later, more robust sample. These derive from a well-developed masticatory apparatus and include temporal lines that meet at the middle in an anterior position (there would have been a sagittal crest had the youth lived longer), marked development of the nuchal line, and a large overlap of the temporal onto the parietal bone.

Of greater importance is the dating of recognizable human artifacts from Omo. No artifacts are known from the earlier South African sequence (or from Afar and Laetolil). Crude stones that were clearly modified by humans first appear at Omo between 2.5 and 2 million years ago. These are pebbles which have been struck one or two times on each side to produce sharp-edged flakes and a jagged edge on the pebble. To date, these are the earliest recognized artifacts. How long a period of even simpler modification might have preceded this is unknown. "Recognizable" is the key word, since any simpler form of human modification cannot be distinguished from breaks that occur naturally.

Some Ideas About Australopithecine Lifeways

In almost any sense of the word, the Pliocene australopithecines are the first people we can recognize, and are almost certainly our ancestors. They lived in a variety of environments, spread at least from East Africa to South Africa. The ecological interpretation of sites where they are found almost inevitably shows different ecozones in the immediate area. Both forest or parkland and open brush or grassland are always present. They are found in the same areas where baboons are found today. When relative counts are possible, it seems they occurred in about the same density as the baboons that were contemporary with them in these areas. Lest we

think of this as a purely tropical adaptation, the high veld in the Transvaal is well south of the equator and is 5,000 to 6,000 feet above sea level. In the winter, the vegetation withers, and the temperature often falls well below freezing at night.

AN AUSTRALOPITHECINE GROUP

Australopithecines were generally small but very powerful people. The average size was only slightly greater than living pygmies, although some individuals were as much as 5½ feet tall. If we could observe an australopithecine in its normal activities, it seems probable that its locomotor gaits would not appear different from those of a powerful modern human, although its ability to climb may have been a bit more skillful than our own. The differences in physical appearance would contrast with the similarities in locomotion. The australopithecine's head would look very unusual. These were creatures with crania about the size of a chimpanzee's, but with jaws and teeth that fit into the gorilla range. We would be struck by the long arms, huge face, and small braincase atop a small but very muscular body. The larger specimens may well have looked like a combination of a gorilla-like head (without the projecting canines) atop a very muscular but humanformed body.

It is likely that australopithecines lived in fairly large groups. An anthropologist would be much more inclined to call these groups "bands" than "troops." Such a band would have a large number of children and subadults. There would also be a smaller number of older individuals (up to 35 years). A few members of the band might be recovering from injuries. One femur from East Africa was broken during life, but the individual lived long enough for the break to heal and the leg to become fully functional again. A broken leg is much more serious for a biped than it is for a quadruped, and the fact that the break *healed* indicates that the individual was taken care of by others.

It would be easy to tell males and females apart because the males would be significantly larger and stronger. This is probably the result of different activities by males and females, with the male activities requiring considerably more strength. In particular there was almost certainly a division of labor in food gathering activities. Given the tendency of males to range widely and cooperate with one another, they were probably responsible for providing animal protein (by hunting or scavenging). Females, with their more intimate knowledge of the resources over the home range and the limitations imposed by the care of young children, more likely gathered plant foods. Together with the development of a formalized system of food sharing, these behavioral patterns combined to produce a remarkable new adaptability through the multiplication of resources that a group could use.

A YEARLY CYCLE

The diet of the band probably varied greatly from season to season and from area to area. Most of the animal remains found at australopithecine living sites are either those of small or very young animals, or appear to be the result of scavenging larger animals. When bones from larger animals are found, they are almost always only those skeletal parts that are left by carnivores. The few findings of whole large animal skeletons could well reflect fortunate instances of animals stuck in mud, or otherwise immobilized. so that they could be butchered. I do not believe that the organized hunting of large mammals was a usual australopithecine activity. Since scavenging and small-game hunting would not provide a sufficient or consistent enough food supply to support a group all year round, the australopithecine diet required a large amount of plant foods.

The seasonal effect on both the group composition and activities was probably far greater than in any subsequent human population. At the beginning of the wet season, large groups (perhaps a hundred or more individuals) consisting of many smaller extended family units may have congregated along lakeshores, or at other particularly desirable localities, to harvest the succulent new grass growth and the dense insect populations. It is possible that a mating peak occurred at this time, which might have resulted from the increased nutritional intake compared with the dry season conditions. If so, it would provide the opportunity for gene flow between numerous different australopithecine groups. As the wet season proceeded, and the various grasses flowered and seeded, this large group may have broken up into smaller foraging units. Competition between these units, and with *Theropithecus*-type baboons, probably led different groups to depend on different grasses. The absence of large numbers of these cercopithecoid seed-eaters allowed some groups (perhaps the smaller hominids) to harvest the shorter grasses, while in other regions significant competition with *Theropithecus* may have resulted in a larger-sized hominid adaptation to harvesting particularly tall grasses, or to bipedal foraging in wet or slightly flooded areas.

With the onset of the dry season and the eventual depletion of most seeds, the hominid groupings may have divided even further into the basic extended family units. The narrow-ranging but dense populational accumulations of the wet season would disperse in a wide-ranging search for scarce food resources. During this season of scarcity, different group adaptive patterns would have the greatest importance. Some groups living near woodlands may have migrated to these, taking advantage of the dry season fruiting period. It is possible that these were groups of larger individuals, since they would be in competition with *Papio*-type baboons, which might result in an advantage for larger-sized tool users. In addition, large size is more easily maintained on a diet of fruits than one of seeds. (It has been estimated that it takes from 1/3 to 1/10 the feeding time to maintain a large hominid on a fruit diet than on a diet of seeds.)

Other groups of australopithecines, possibly the smaller forms, would remain on the grasslands during the dry season, perhaps as a result of competition with the larger forms or because of the absence of nearby woodlands. In these groups, roots, seed pods of Leguminosae, and animal protein formed the main dietary staples, and there would not be significant competition with the *Theropithecus*-type baboons. Scavenging and hunting small game were probably important throughout the year, but these activities would be particularly critical during the dry season.

Some indirect evidence suggests that food may have been a seasonally limiting resource for australopithecines. Many specimens show evidence of interrupted enamel development on their teeth, which is typically the result of periods of sickness or starvation, and lack of certain minerals. Dry season food shortages might have been especially critical since a nine-month gestation would result in dry season births (assuming mating at the beginning of the wet season). The relative helplessness of hominid infants and the necessary dry season population movements would emphasize the importance of bipedal carrying and the effectiveness of the hominid stride in allowing long-distance, low-energy locomotion.

DAILY ACTIVITIES

Australopithecine food gathering would appear to have combined scavenging, some small-scale hunting, and the intensive collection of plant foods. If there were differences in the food gathering activities of males and females (as we assume there were), this would imply two important hominid developments—sharing and the use of a home base which was occupied for a significant length of time. Infants, juveniles, and some adults would remain at the home base while others were collecting (by gathering, hunting, or scavenging) the food resources that would be brought back and shared. Tools of various sorts were made and used at these bases; other tools used for butchering and dismembering animal carcasses were probably made on the spot of an animal kill (whether hunted or scavenged) and left there.

At the home base, adult activities were probably intensely watched and practiced by the juveniles. They learned how to make tools and when and how to use them. This, however, was probably only a small part of what they had to learn and practice. I believe it likely that a complex of social behaviors was transmitted from generation to generation, and that a large part of growing up for an australopithecine child involved learning these behaviors, and practicing them in play.

It is unlikely that we are ever going to find direct anatomical evidence showing whether or not early hominids could speak. In addition, the capability for language in chimpanzees is now known to be based largely on gestures instead of sounds, opening up a new set of problems in the explanation of human language origins. The gestural basis for chimpanzee communication might be expected from the general primate trend to emphasize vision and touch at the expense of hearing. A species with a long evolutionary history of exploring its environment through vision and touch might, not surprisingly, evolve a system of communication involving these senses. This casts the origin and evolution of human language in a new light, since the hominid *innovation* seems not to be language capability or the ability to symbol, but rather *the vocalization* of these behaviors. Assuming that the ancestors of australopithecines had the same capabilities as chimpanzees, the question of human language origins revolves about the ability to vocalize. When and why would the vocalization of complex information have become adaptively important?

Jolly suggests that the adaptation to intensive collection of savanna plant foods would lead to many members of early hominid groups being out of sight of one another, and consequently select for vocalization. Moreover, in his view, the broad and mobile tongue which is so useful in eating small objects, acting to continually replace the food between the teeth, would be a preadaptation for the production of the many distinguishable sounds required in articulate speech. These changes in selection precede the known australopithecines. By the Pliocene there would be additional selection for complexity in the transmitted information. The prolonged maturation of australopithecines involved far more than learning to make tools, and the selection to speed up this learning process, and to make it more accurate through an effective open verbal communication system, was intense.

Consider, for instance, the implications of using a home base as a focus for food gathering activities. Planning and executing different activities requires foresight. Communication about such activities, in turn, requires the development of displacement in the communication system. (Displacement is the ability to communicate about objects or events removed in time or space.) It is difficult to imagine how communication in a band would not soon come to include displacement when males go out to seek animal protein (a chancy food source) while females gather the highly predictable plant foods, and they all return to the home base.

Of course, learning a complex communication system requires practice. C. F. Hockett suggests that verbal play should be added to the other categories of play involving experimentation and the practice of behaviors that australopithecine children probably engaged in. The interesting point is that verbal play could be one of the important factors leading to the development of displacement.

In sum, the period when we would expect an open vocal communication system to become advantageous precedes the australopithecines. Then there is the additional evidence of development of the speech-related Broca's area in the brain where the motor control of speech occurs, and the morphological suggestions of neural reorganization. Thus there are ample reasons to expect a form of human speech in the australopithecines, and there is no morphological basis for claiming they were incapable of it. While the contention cannot be proven, I suggest that if we could hear an australopithecine band, they would be chattering away.

SOCIAL ORGANIZATION

The organization of a large band of australopithecines with a complex communication system, sexual differences in food gathering roles, periods of separation from and return to a home base, food sharing, and a large number of children and juveniles in the process of growing up suggests to me that many other elements of human social behavior were .probably present. Learned role differences, with their complexity of behavioral expectations, is the human adaptation to exactly these types of circumstances. There is good reason to believe that role differences had a multitude of origins—in sexual behavior, food gathering activities, and the complex of social control mechanisms that evolved as tools took over the earlier functions of canines. It is reasonable to conjecture that selection acted to change the frequency and complexity of social behaviors to a more human-like condition in the australopithecines, where they would be of obvious adaptive importance.

Consider, for instance, the evolution of human kinship. Kinship behavior in nonhuman primates is restricted to the occasional appearance of lifelong male-female bonding and to differential behavior of adult offspring toward mother or siblings (matrifocal units). In the australopithecines, economic necessity, delayed maturation, and a short lifespan combined to select for the development of extended kinship relations and a much more complex system of kinship behaviors. There is every reason to expect the presence of systematic role differences based on sex, age, and relationship in the australopithecine adaptive system. These are learned behaviors which had already been subjected to encephalization of their underlying structures, making the learning process easier and faster, and leading to the development of consistent behavioral patterns.

The early emergence of complex kinship behavior was likely a consequence of (if not an actual participating factor in) the development of economic division of labor. To work, this division requires a formal system of food sharing. Indeed, social anthropologists such as Lévi-Strauss have argued that the basic structure of the human family arose through the economic interdependence of the sexes that results from the division of labor. While it has been further suggested that the family is strengthened by economic necessity, it may be more reasonable to suppose that both the family

and economic division of labor are aspects of a single emerging adaptive system, each depending on the other to function. Formalized kinship relations, then, provide the structure for food sharing.

Moreover, the demographic consequences of australopithecine adaptation (discussed earlier) seem to require that the families be extended units, forced to spread horizontally rather than vertically through related kin because of the hominids' short lifespan and delayed reproduction. In other words, by the time of the australopithecines, the extended family could well have been a fairly complex social unit.

One final consequence of this adaptive social unit might have been the suppression of estrus. J. B. Lancaster argues that the physiological and behavioral changes that accompany ovulation in most female primates, acting to attract potential mates, would disrupt the family structure, if not the pattern of resource utilization. If the intense cyclic sexual activity associated with estrus were replaced by continuous sexual interest under behavioral control and amenable to structuralization, sexual activity could become a major bonding factor within the family. It is quite possible that this was reinforced through the appearance of the incest taboo.

CULTURE

We have been conjecturing what a single australopithecine band might have been like. With all the concern as to whether the australopithecines possessed culture, the concept has been used in the sense of "culture with a capital C." Among living peoples, there are a variety of different cultures, which we might think of as culture "with a small c." There is some reason to believe that cultural differences were also characteristic of australopithecines.

The common elements of australopithecine diets probably involved a large number of different food sources available in grasslands and thorn-bush savannas. Continued selection for the adaptation to powerful chewing resulted from a combination of the hardness of available foods (and the grit clinging to many of them) and the need to prepare these foods orally. Yet the differences in body size and (to a lesser extent) tooth wear that can be observed suggest differences in adaptation and environmental utilization within this context. Similar adaptive differences in living groups do not lead to as extensive differences. To find the same amount of morphological variation between living groups, the adaptive differences must be much greater. However, culture was probably a far less effective means of adaptation among australopithecines than it is among people today. This would account for the evidence of muscularity and power in australopithecine skeletons. It would also account for the more extreme morphological responses to dietary and adaptive differences between australopithecine populations, as well as the great amount of sexual dimorphism within them. Differences in the environment would lead to a greater morphological adaptive response if morphology was a more important part of adaptation.

These morphological differences suggest that there were various adaptive patterns among the australopithecines and, thus, a variety of different cultures. Because of these cultural differences, it is possible that within the general limitations of australopithecine adaptation, different populations may have exploited the same environments in different ways, reflecting habit and preference rather than the necessity of utilizing different resources.

SUMMARY

While the Pliocene australopithecines are recognizably hominid, the earlier samples retain a surprising number of *Proconsul*-like features. The Laetolil dental sample is characterized by rather large (for a hominid) incisors and the retention of large projecting canines and a canine/premolar cutting complex that made use of a sharp transverse ridge across the P_3, raised to the occlusal level by the addition of a second P_3 cusp. Some of the Afar dentitions are similar, although others have a more symmetric P_3 with equal-sized cusps and little canine projection. The Afar P_3s were incorporated into the grinding complex. Postcanine tooth size at these sites is generally smaller than in later hominids but falls closest to the large ramapithecine. Marked sexual dimorphism in canine size and form, and in postcanine tooth size, is also retained by these samples. Footprints at Laetolil reveal the early presence of bipedal locomotion. The Afar postcrania show a complete morphological adaptation to bipedal striding locomotion less than a million years later. The postcranial bones differ from those of modern humans mainly in the much smaller size of the birth canal, the adaptations of the bone to extraordinary power and prolonged muscle use, and relatively long arms. The Afar crania reveal a surprising number of chimpanzee-like features.

The earlier South African crania are recognizably hominid in detail but surprisingly pongid-like in general proportions. They reveal three main features: a large face combined with a small braincase, vertical orientation atop the spinal column, and adaptations to powerful mastication. The dental sample has smaller anterior and larger posterior teeth than the earlier ones from East Africa. No specimens show canine cutting or asymmetric P_3 form, but the marked sexual dimorphism is maintained. Study of the endocasts indicates that the main elements of human brain-form are discernable.

The later South African sample continues these trends further. Moreover, the large sample size allows determination of the average lifespan (11–12 years) and a good estimate of birth spacing (3–4 years). The combination of extended periods of maturation and short lifespans probably made orphaning common and suggests the early importance of the extended family. The relatively short birth spacing (compared with pongids) was a distinct hominid advantage, made possible by sociality.

Finally, the later Pliocene remains from East Africa are dentally and cranially similar to the later South African sample in mean size, range, and morphology.

In spite of the marked changes that occurred over the timespan of these samples, I believe that no evidence contradicts the proposal that they represent a single evolving hominid lineage. The observed variability is no more than one would expect from the differences in time and location and the presence of marked sexual dimorphism. Moreover, the samples seem to follow a single complex of evolutionary trends. Bearing in mind the presence of temporal variation over a roughly 2-million-year span, there is something to be said for the contention that the earlier portion of the lineage be regarded as a separate species (*Australopithecus afarensis*), directly ancestral to *Australopithecus africanus*. Ultimately, whether such a division is made is arbitrary. The important point is that a single evolving lineage seems to be represented. In a direct sense, this lineage is ancestral to the lineage leading to *Homo sapiens*.

The total pattern of the australopithecine morphology and behavior was human in any reasonable sense. Of course, they were not people of the same intelligence and adaptive potential as living groups. The unique features of their morphology attest to the limitations on their adaptability and on their ability to make use of all available resources. Nonetheless, in them we can find evidence for almost every element of the unique behavior that distinguishes us from our closest relatives.

STATE OF THE ART

Probably the most controversial position taken by the author in this chapter is the contention that the *Pliocene* australopithecines represent a single lineage, ancestral to later hominids. This single-species hypothesis was once applied to the entire australopithecine sample, although it is now known to be invalid in the early Pleistocene. The question is whether it remains a valid interpretation of the Pliocene remains.

From the time of the earliest discoveries in South Africa, workers such as R. Broom and later J. T. Robinson maintained that more than one australopithecine species was present. Robinson formalized this contention in his dietary hypothesis, arguing that the earlier South African specimens represented a generalized, omnivorous culture-bearing australopithecine form, while the later sites mainly yielded a robust vegetarian-specialized form contemporary with a few fragmentary remains of a "more advanced hominid." These were classified respectively as *Australopithecus* (later *Homo*) and *Paranthropus*; the common usage came to be "gracile" and "robust" australopithecine.

E. Mayr, C. L. Brace, and later this author argued that competition between similar hominid forms should invoke the competitive exclusion principle. Since neither extinction nor geographic separation occurred in South Africa in the later Pliocene, the expected result was marked character divergence to reduce competition. It was argued that the similarities and degree of overlap between the South African samples was so great, when the total samples were considered, that no character divergence could be demonstrated. The alternative explanation was that there was no character divergence because

a single lineage was represented, with the earlier samples ancestral to the later ones.

The main dispute between these hypotheses has come to focus on whether there was a "more advanced hominid" in South Africa contemporary with the later (robust australopithecine) forms. Robinson argued that two jaws and (what was later discovered to be) a fairly complete cranium from the Swartkrans cave represented a more advanced form, first naming it "Telanthropus" and later sinking the genus into *Homo erectus*. A number of workers (W. L. Straus, A. Mann, this author) disputed the claim. The main mandible (SK-15) fell in the range of morphological overlap between australopithecines and later hominids, and over a decade ago this author pointed out that therefore its taxonomic affinities must be decided by its date. (To illustrate the point, the recently reported discovery of australopithecine-sized teeth among U.S. Navy recruits does not demonstrate that there are australopithecines in the Navy.) In fact, it was subsequently discovered that the mandible *did* date to a much later time, so that while it probably does represent *Homo erectus*, it is not contemporary with the australopithecines. The cranium, SK-847 (see Figure 7.5), was reconstructed by R. J. Clarke, who (in a paper with F. C. Howell) argued that the composite represented a more advanced hominid. In turn, this author maintained that the combination of prognathic large face, very small thin vault, and moderate browridges, along with other features, indicated australopithecine affinities, and consequently suggested it would be better interpreted as a small female robust australopithecine. More recently, A. R. Hughes and P. V. Tobias reported a similar specimen (STW-53) from the upper levels of the Sterkfontein cave (perhaps roughly contemporary with Swartkrans). While these authors place it in yet another taxon (*Homo habilis*), the same combination of large prognathic face and small thin vault suggests australopithecine affinities, in this case perhaps even more like the earlier Sterkfontein sample. The issue of a more advanced contemporary hominid remains unresolved.

While this is pretty much where the argument stands in South Africa, it is not the end of the discussion. As we will see in the next chapter, subsequent discoveries in East Africa from the early Pleistocene indicated the presence of an australopithecine form with a far more robust masticatory apparatus than the so-called "robust" australopithecines of South Africa and another form which was more gracile but showed evidence of expanded cranial capacity compared to the "gracile" South African forms. These are generally interpreted as separate hominid lineages. It is one of the great curiosities of the field that these new data have been used to support both arguments in the South African controversy.

Those who support Robinson's dietary hypothesis can point to the new East African material as a vindication of their views. The differences they were seeing were there all along, as their more marked expression in East Africa clearly shows. The South African material is viewed as an earlier, but less well expressed, representation of the same two lineages.

Those who support the hypothesis of a single species in South Africa draw the opposite conclusions from these same data. They argue that if there were two genetically separate lineages, they would be as morphologically distinct as the later East African forms because of competitive exclusion. They contrast the similarities between gracile and robust samples in South Africa with the marked divergence in East Africa, and conclude that only a single lineage was represented. The "more advanced hominids" contemporary with the robust australopithecines are seen as small female members of the same species. The brain size of both disputed specimens appears to have been extraordinarily small, greatly contrasting with the second lineage in East Africa.

Moreover, there is a third interpretation that can be applied to the South African hominids. Recognizing the similarities between the gracile and robust samples, and the presence of an evolutionary trend to develop a more robust masticatory apparatus, it can be argued that neither is ancestral to *Homo erectus* in East Africa. Both could be ancestral to the more robust East African early Pleistocene australopithecine, or perhaps simply represent a separate extinct lineage. This position would suggest that Robinson's dietary hypothesis was correct, but that it represented the results of an evolutionary trend rather than the results of character divergence between contemporary species.

My position is set out in this chapter and the next. I believe that for most of the Pliocene the development of robustness in the masticatory structures was selectively advantageous in a single hominid lineage, represented in both East and South Africa, but this situation changed about the beginning of the Pleistocene. But this is only one of several possible interpretations of the material.

FURTHER READINGS

Bishop, W. W. 1976. Pliocene Problems Relating to Human Evolution. In *Human Origins: Louis Leakey and the East African Evidence*, eds. G. L. Isaac and E. R. McCown. Benjamin, Menlo Park, pp. 139–53.

An insightful discussion of the relation of environment, adaptation, and evolution in the early hominids, and problems that underlie environmental and ecological interpretations.

Broom, R. 1950. *Finding the Missing Link*. Watts, London.

Broom's own story of the South African discoveries and his interpretations of them.

Butzer, K. W. 1974. Paleoecology of South African Australopithecines: Taung Revisited. *Current Anthropology* 15:376–382.

A thorough discussion of the paleogeography of the South African australopithecine-bearing caves.

Holloway, R. L. 1974. The Casts of Fossil Hominid Brains. *Scientific American* 231(1):106–116.

A simplified introduction to Holloway's work on the fossil endocasts.

————. 1975. The Role of Human Social Behavior in the Evolution of the Brain. Forty-third James Arthur Lecture on the Evolution of the Human Brain. American Museum of Natural History, New York.

A more detailed discussion of the above, with implications concerning cultural behavior.

Howell, F. C., and Y. Coppens. 1976. An Overview of Hominidae from the Omo Succession, Ethiopia. In *Earliest Man and Environments in the Lake Rudolf Basin*, eds. Y. Coppens, F. C. Howell, G. L. Isaac, and R. E. F. Leakey. University of Chicago Press, Chicago, pp. 522-532.

A brief review of the Omo remains with references to the more detailed reports.

Isaac, G. 1976. The Activities of Early African Hominids: A Review of the Archaeological Evidence from the Timespan Two and One-half to One Million Years Ago. In *Human Origins: Louis Leakey and the East African Evidence*, eds. G. L. Isaac and E. R. McCown. Benjamin, Menlo Park, pp. 483-514.

A discussion of the East African archaeological remains, marred only by the assumption of a KBS tuff date of 2.6 million years.

Johanson, D. C., and T. D. White. 1979. A Systematic Assessment of Early African Hominids. *Science* 203:321-330.

The authors' statement of arguments supporting *Australopithecus afarensis*, a brief description of some of the Afar cranial remains, and the rationale behind the idea that most African australopithecines became extinct.

Le Gros Clark, W. E. 1967. *Man-Apes or Ape-Men? The Story of Discoveries in Africa*. Holt, Rinehart, and Winston, New York.

Probably the best single account of the South African australopithecines.

Lovejoy, C. O. 1974. The Gait of Australopithecines. *Yearbook of Physical Anthropology* 17:147-161.

A discussion of australopithecine locomotor capacities.

Mann, A. 1975. *Paleodemographic Aspects of the South African Australopithecines*. University of Pennsylvania Publications in Anthropology, Number 1, Philadelphia.

The basic study of australopithecine aging and demography, with implications concerning cultural behavior.

Robinson, J. T. 1963. Adaptive Radiation in the Australopithecines and the Origin of Man. In African Ecology and Human Evolution, eds. F. C. Howell and F. Bourliere. *Viking Fund Publication in Anthropology* 36:385-416.

One fairly explicit statement of Robinson's dietary hypothesis and its taxonomic implications.

————. 1972. *Early Hominid Posture and Locomotion*. University of Chicago Press, Chicago.

The classic descriptive work on the australopithecine postcranial skeleton, and a statement of Robinson's most recent views on australopithecine adaptation and phylogeny. The discussion of gait contrasts with Lovejoy's work (above).

Schaller, G. G. 1972. Are You Running with Me,, Hominid? *Natural History* 81(3):61-68.

An ecological interpretation of australopithecine adaptation based on modern studies in similar habitats.

Tobias, P. V. 1975. Brain Evolution in the Hominoidea. In *Primate Functional Morphology and Evolution*, ed. R. E. Tuttle. Mouton, The Hague, pp. 353-392.

An excellent review of ideas concerning brain evolution prior to the discovery of the large brain early Pleistocene East African specimens.

————. 1976. African Hominids: Dating and Phylogeny. In *Human Origins: Louis Leakey and the East African Evidence*, eds. G. L. Isaac and E. R. McCown. Benjamin, Menlo Park, pp. 377-422.

An up-to-date account of the more recent developments in South Africa and the relations of these sites to East Africa.

White, T. D. 1977. New Fossil Hominids from Laetolil, Tanzania. *American Journal of Physical Anthropology* 46:197-230.

A technical report on the earliest large hominid dental sample from Laetolil.

Wolpoff, M. H. 1974. The Evidence of Two Australopithecine Lineages in South Africa. *Yearbook of Physical Anthropology* 17:113-139.

A technical discussion of the South African material and the question of whether more than one lineage is indicated by the data.

————. 1976. Some Aspects of the Evolution of Early Hominid Sexual Dimorphism. *Current Anthropology* 17(4):579-606.

A basic presentation of the evidence for marked sexual dimorphism in the australopithecines.

CHAPTER EIGHT

The Evolution of Hunting

T he earlier portion of the Pleistocene, called the basal or the Lower Pleistocene, is widely regarded as representing the span from about 2 million to 0.7 million (700,000) years ago. At the beginning of this period, our lineage was represented by australopithecines restricted to the African continent. By its end a new species, *Homo erectus,* had spread throughout the tropics and semitropics of the entire Old World. Underlying both the new species and its extended range was an important hominid adaptive change, with consequences extending to the present day.

Because the changes that took place in the basal Pleistocene are complex, involving the evolution of two contemporary lineages and their subsequent interaction with each other as well as with the environment, this chapter (following a brief outline of the African sites) is divided into two sections covering consecutive timespans. Within these, cranial and dental trends in each lineage are examined, followed by a discussion of the adaptive differences that progressively accumulated between the hominid forms. Involved in the adaptive complexes were the appearance of recognizable stone tools and a shift to hunting as a means of gaining predictable food sources in one of the lineages.

After defining the timespans and sites involved, the next section, dealing with the earliest timespan, concentrates on the appearance of the two hominid lineages. It presents arguments for the nature of the adaptive differences that came to separate these lineages, and suggests a series of behavioral and physiological changes that accompanied the evolution of hunting. The following section is concerned with the appearance of *Homo erectus* and the evolutionary trends reflected by this development. Subsequent evolutionary change in the second lineage is also discussed, especially in regard to the possible interactions between the lineages. The chapter concludes with a model of the origin of the *Homo erectus* morphological complex. The morphological features are tied to the requirements of an evolving adaptive system.

Earliest Lower Pleistocene Australopithecine Sites

Australopithecines of the Lower Pleistocene are known only from the East African rift valley sites, unless the latest of the South African sites discussed in the last chapter range into this period. The three main areas with hominids from this span (see Map 1, p. 132) are the two Lake Turkana sites (Omo and the region east of the lake) and Olduvai Gorge in Tanzania. Geographically between these are some additional sites dated to about 1.5 million years ago at which single specimens have been found: Chesowanja and Natron. Like the earlier East African hominid habitats all these sites are in the immediate vicinity of lakes (if not actually on the lakeshores) with regions ranging to the semi-arid nearby. Besides the hominid fossils themselves, the three main sites have yielded the remains of "living floors"—archaeological remains resulting from the habitation of a home base.

TEMPORAL RELATIONS

Three main sites span the time period of the earliest Lower Pleistocene (see Table 8.1, p. 160). Beginning with the northernmost of these, the portion of the Omo sequence we are concerned with begins with the volcanic ash deposit (tuff) F, which is latest Pliocene, and extends through the deposits above it marked by tuff G, to no more than 1.8 million years ago. Only a few Omo specimens are more recent than this. The relevant East Turkana deposits extend from those that are below the several ash deposits that have been called the KBS tuffs to considerably later deposits. KBS dates at Turkana probably range from 1.6 to 1.8 million years BP, and it is unlikely that most of the specimens considered here that are older than the tuffs (or below them) extend much into the Pliocene, if at all. The later Turkana specimens span the period from 1.6 to 1.3 million years ago. Finally, at Olduvai Gorge the Lower Pleistocene is represented by three spans. The earliest comprises Bed I (the lowest deposits) and the lower portion of Bed II; an average date is about 1.8 million years ago. The second span consists of the remainder of Bed II, and the third is Bed III. Bed IV at the gorge marks the beginning of the Middle Pleistocene.

THREE PERIODS

Some critical events in hominid evolution take place at the very beginning of the Pleistocene. To focus on these, the discussion will be divided into three periods that are represented at these three main sites. The earliest of these is the latest Pliocene/earliest Pleistocene, approximately 2.0-1.7 million years ago. This period is marked by Members F and G at Omo, Bed I and lower Bed II at Olduvai Gorge, and the deposits below the KBS tuffs at Turkana. Most of the specimens in this period are no younger than 1.7 million years.

The second period ranges approximately from 1.7 to 1.3 million years ago. In it are the few more recent Omo specimens, the remainder of Bed II at Olduvai Gorge, deposits above the KBS tuffs at Turkana, and the single-specimen sites of Chesowanja and Natron. Most of the specimens are between 1.5 and 1.6 million years old.

The third period (roughly 1.3 to 0.7 million years ago) is poorly represented in Africa; there is one specimen from Turkana and a few from Olduvai Bed III. However, during this span hominids appear in other parts of the world. This spread, and its consequences, will be examined in the next chapter, which is concerned with the third period.

The Earliest Pleistocene

The first period marks what many have considered the earliest Pleistocene. The hominids known from this period are all australopithecines, in the opinion of this author. These differ from Pliocene australopithecines in some respects, and the evidence suggests that a lineage division took place in the australopithecines resulting in two contemporary species. These two species continued their evolution, existing as separate lineages through the first two periods. The evolutionary tendencies in each came to differ substantially; one became extinct, while the other continued its evolution into more recent hominids and eventually ourselves.

DENTAL TRENDS

The dentitions tell an important part of the story during the first period. This is because tooth size

TABLE 8.1 Tentative approximate positions of the African Pliocene and Lower Pleistocene sites, keyed to the best current radiometric date estimates and the known paleomagnetic stratigraphy. Faunal correlations for the South African sites are suggested; no absolute dates are known for these important hominid occurrences, although their relative stratigraphy appears to be accurate. See Map 1, p. 132, for the geographic positions.

Date (in millions of years)	Paleomagnetic		Olduvai (Beds)	Omo (Tuffs)	East Turkana (Tuffs)	Other East African Sites	South Africa (Fauna)
	Epoch	Event					
.5	Brunhes Normal						
		Jaramillo	Bed IV				
1.0							
	Matuyama Reversal		Bed III ? ↑ ↓ ?	L	Chari		
1.5			Bed II		Okote KBS(12)	Chesowanja Natron	
		Olduvai		I_2 G F E D	KBS(130/131)		? ↑
2.0		Reunion	Bed I				Kromdraai Swartkrans Sterkfontein (Upper)
2.5	Gauss Normal	Kaena				Chemeron	Sterkfontein (Main) ? ↑ Makapansgat
3.0		Mammoth		A, B, Sands ↑	Tulu Bor	Afar	
3.5							
	Gilbert Reversal	Cochiti				Laetolil ? ↑ Kanapoi	
4.0		Nunivak					
4.5							
5.0							
5.5						Lothagam	

FIGURE 8.1 *Temporal distribution of second lower molar breadth during the Pliocene and Lower Pleistocene in Africa. The second lower molar has the largest sample of any tooth, and breadth is used because this dimension does not change with age and wear. The frequency distribution and average (represented by a dot) are given for each period, and the average date and sample composition are indicated. Three modern human groups are presented for comparison of range and variation of means within a species.*

played an adaptive role in the ecological distinctions that accumulated between the lineages. The Pliocene trend in East Africa was for an increase in average posterior tooth size. The teeth from the Pliocene form single-peaked distributions not unlike living populations in their range. The mean for each more recent sample is larger than the last (see Figure 8.1), showing that as in the South African sequence, posterior dental expansion was occur-

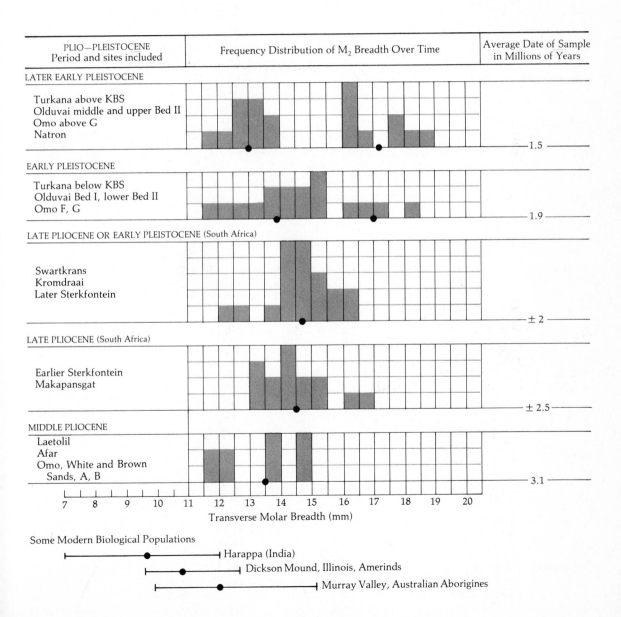

ring. However, in the earliest Pleistocene, the total range of variation for the posterior teeth becomes larger than ever before, and seems to form two separate distributions with a gap between them. The smaller-sized distribution is only slightly smaller than the later Pliocene australopithecines and almost completely within their range. The larger-sized distribution, however, is much larger than the later Pliocene australopithecines and largely above their maximum range. It is in this larger-sized sample that the australopithecine specimens approaching *Gigantopithecus* in tooth size (Figure 6.7) can be found. Compared with the later Pliocene sample, posterior expansion is mostly in the mid-row, where power is most efficiently applied. The premolars expand by 15 percent, about twice as much as the molars, and add extra cusps (see Figure 8.2).

In contrast to these trends in the postcanine teeth, the canines and incisors do not appear to change at all from their absolute size in the later Pliocene. Moreover, in the earliest Pleistocene, the anterior teeth of the two contemporary distributions do not differ in *absolute* size. However, because of the posterior tooth difference, the *relative* size differs substantially. Finally, the differences in size and form between male and female canines remain distinct in both distributions.

The appearance of this non-overlapping distinction between two contemporary samples in posterior tooth size seems to reflect an adaptive difference in diet or food preparation, or both. The lack of overlap is probably the result of a lack of gene flow, allowing the adaptive differences to accumulate. The dental differences could be a marker of character divergence. In other words, the likelihood is that the distinct distributions represent distinct species, and the differences in tooth size reflect differing adaptations affected in part by the competition between them. Further insight into the differences between these species is gained from examining the crania and jaws from this period.

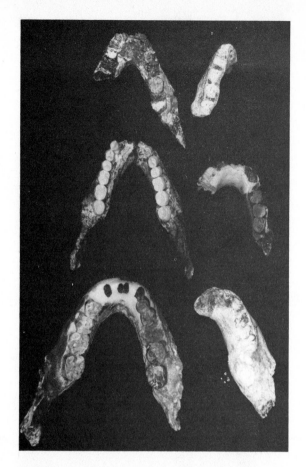

FIGURE 8.2   *Variations in Lower Pleistocene mandibles from east of Lake Turkana in East Africa; all specimens shown are casts. Above are two earlier specimens from below the KBS tuffs (1.6–1.8 million years BP), ER-1482 (left) and ER-1501. The middle two specimens represent early Homo erectus (ER-992 to the left, with the two halves in approximate position, and ER-730). Below, hyper-robust specimens ER-729 (left) and ER-1469 are compared. The top two could be ancestral to both lineages represented below.*

EARLY PLEISTOCENE CRANIA

Fairly complete cranial remains are known from th Turkana region and Olduvai Gorge. The Olduvai material was discovered first, setting the stage for the subsequent interpretation of East African hominids discovered later.

When Louis and Mary Leakey first reported on the discovery of a massive cranium from Olduvai Gorge in 1959 (Olduvai hominid 5, or "the nutcracker man"), emphasis was placed on its humanlike features (Figure 5.2). The later discovery of much smaller jaws and teeth, and ultimately of a cranium, provided a contrast between a large and small form of australopithecine that was without equal in South Africa. These were soon placed in separate taxonomic categories: the larger was *Zinjanthropis boisei* and the smaller *Homo habilis*.

Later discoveries in the Turkana region were made by the Leakeys' son, Richard. The remains of three crania from the deposits below the KBS level and a fourth from just above these tuffs seemed to represent the smaller-toothed Olduvai form, while two specimens from above the tuff represented the larger form. The interpretation of these specimens and their relation to the Olduvai ones was confused for some years by claims that the KBS tuff, and therefore the specimens under it, was much older than the Olduvai deposits. These deposits are now widely recognized as being the same age.

Both of these forms are recognizably australopithecine (see Figure 8.3, p. 164). They share a number of features that characterized the Pliocene hominids, including a large prognathic face relative to the braincase, marked sexual dimorphism, thin cranial bone, moderate development of the brow-ridges, and a short low-positioned attachment area for the neck muscles. The specific adaptations to powerful mastication are also present in both forms. These include an anterior position for the robustly developed, widely flaring zygomatics, marked development of the anterior temporalis muscle, and large posterior teeth.

THE HYPER-ROBUST LINEAGE

Although these features are held in common, their expression and direction of change differ in the two forms. The larger-toothed form seems to represent a continuation of the Pliocene trend for posterior dental expansion and more efficient positioning of the muscles used in chewing, without a further substantial increase in brain size. Posterior teeth and the associated cranial and mandibular structures quickly became more massive in this form than in any previous hominid (Figures 4.7 and 6.7).

The crania of this form, which might be called "hyper-robust," differ from the later South African sample in the same direction and manner as the later South African sample differs from the earlier one. However, the extent of the differences is much greater for the East African hyper-robusts. For instance, the height of the face increases by 9 percent between the earlier and later South African samples; between the later South African sample and

the hyper-robusts, this increase is 30 percent. The lower portion of the face expands more than the upper, probably a result of the larger posterior tooth roots and the greater forces exerted on them. Areas of the cranium and face where muscles attach are particularly well developed and buttressed in the hyper-robusts. In his analysis of the large Olduvai male, OH-5, P. V. Tobias recognized these relations and concluded that while the hyper-robusts represented an extreme version of the evolutionary trends in South Africa, the South African forms were more closely related to each other than either was to the more extreme East African forms.

Recognizing the morphological distinctions of this hyper-robust form, it is probably best to consider it a distinct taxon, *Australopithecus boisei*, following Tobias, in spite of the fact that the evolutionary trends represented by the lineage are a continuation of many of the earlier trends. It is the degree of expression of the trends and the presence of a contemporary hominid lineage undergoing evolutionary change in a rather different direction that argue for this taxonomic distinction. Using dental criteria, this lineage did not become distinct much before 2 million years ago.

THE *HOMO* LINEAGE

The smaller-toothed form still retains a massive posterior dentition compared with later hominids. On the average, posterior tooth size is only slightly less than in the later Pliocene australopithecines (Figure 8.1), and all of the facial and mandibular adaptations to powerful chewing are present (Figures 8.2 and 8.3). However the *direction* of change is opposite to that in the larger-toothed form, which had expanded so much dentally that the two no longer overlapped in posterior tooth size. A second, equally important, trend in the smaller-toothed form is the continued expansion of cranial capacity. The known male cranial capacities range between 700 and 800 cc, while female capacities range from 500 to 600 cc. Compared with the latest Pliocene hominids, this is an expansion of some 15 percent or more.

Thus, while the hyper-robust specimens present a much larger chewing apparatus superimposed on crania of similar capacity to the South African forms, the other lineage at first shows little change

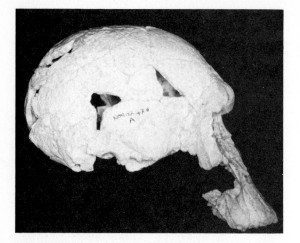

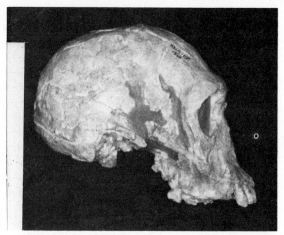

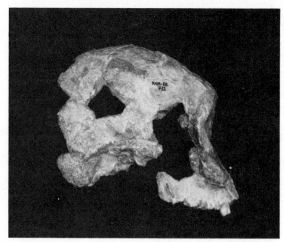

FIGURE 8.3   *Male (left) and female (right) specimens of the two australopithecine lineages*: Homo habilis *(above) and* Australopithecus boisei *(below). All four are from Lake Turkana, and the specimens shown are casts. Above are ER-1470 (left) and ER-1813 (right), while below, ER-406 is to the left, and ER-732 is right.*

(slight reduction) in the chewing apparatus combined with larger cranial vaults. Males such as ER-1470 (Figure 8.3) have faces as large as any from Swartkrans, with massive forward-positioned cheeks, evidence of large postcanine teeth, and so on. However, cranial capacity is over 750 cc, and with the added room for temporalis attachment,

there is no sagittal crest. Similarly, females such as the Olduvai specimen OH-24 or ER-1813 from east of Lake Turkana (Figure 8.3) have much smaller faces but still retain the features associated with powerful chewing. The clearest distinction between this lineage and the hyper-robust one can be seen in the relation of tooth size and cranial capacity, since the evolutionary trends in these go in opposite directions.

The first-discovered specimens representing this lineage were placed in the species "*Homo habilis.*" Because of the very fragmentary nature of these early discoveries, and the then unresolved problem of the South African dates, there was continuous argument as to whether the East African specimens were anything more than a variant of *Australopithe-*

cus africanus. With the much larger and more complete sample now available, coupled with the likelihood that the South African australopithecines were earlier in time, the argument that these late australopithecines should retain the species name "habilis" is enhanced. Whether this species should be in *Australopithecus* or *Homo* is probably arbitrary. However, given the fact that the lineage split in the latest Pliocene represents a split between *Australopithecus* and the immediate ancestors of *Homo erectus*, I believe that using the designation *Homo habilis* may be the more appropriate way of classifying this taxon, following the arguments proposed over a decade ago by L. S. B. Leakey and P. V. Tobias, and recognizing that most of the specimens are already known under this name. This would make it the earliest member of the genus *Homo*, an affinity reflected in the *direction of change* expressed by its characteristics rather than in the characteristics themselves. In terms of its morphological and behavioral affinities, *Homo habilis* is a taxon with the australopithecine grade of organization.

EARLY PLEISTOCENE POSTCRANIA

A large number of postcranial remains are known from the Lower Pleistocene in East Africa, mainly from the Lake Turkana deposits but a few also from Olduvai and Omo. Unfortunately, only a single specimen is associated with cranial or dental material which would allow one to determine which lineage it represented. The OH-7 hand, associated with the *Homo habilis* juvenile parietals and jaw, suggests a powerful but extremely small individual. While the postcrania are similar to the South African ones in showing a complete adaptation to bipedal locomotion, additional information is provided regarding size variation. Limb sizes correspond to body heights ranging from 4 to 6 feet. The forms of various bones, ranging from the OH-7 fingers (those which are actually hominid) to the numerous Lake Turkana femurs and the extraordinarily robust male innominate ER-3228, show numerous skeletal adaptations to the normal exertion of great strength. The strength adaptation is clearly common to both lineages. What is interesting, and as yet undeterminable, is whether there was a body size difference between them.

SOURCE OF THE ADAPTIVE DIFFERENCE

The presence of adaptively different contemporary hominids in the earliest Pleistocene is the result of a two-step process: a lineage division, followed by the accumulation of adaptive distinctions between the lineages. The exact cause of the first step is unknown, and may remain so. Speciation requires geographic isolation, but where and why this took place cannot be determined. How widespread either lineage was is also unknown since specimens from this critical period are known only from East Africa. Evidently, geographic isolation of some late Pliocene populations resulted in the development of genetic isolation, leaving each lineage free to establish its own evolutionary tendencies. The rapid accumulation of differences between the lineages leads one to suspect that the isolated populations may have fortuitously represented the smaller or larger part of the size range. It is also possible that a punctuated equilibrium model may best explain the process, with the isolated populations at the extreme end of the adaptive range and thus under selection to change quickly once genetic isolation was established. However, dramatic replacement is not a necessary alternative to a more gradual evolutionary interpretation in this case. More than enough time is involved to account for the accumulating differences between the lineages.

Whatever the circumstances of the lineage division, the different directions taken by the contemporary lineages clearly reflect differing adaptive patterns. Selection to increase the differences in adaptation almost certainly was in part the result of competition between the forms, a consequence of competitive exclusion. The two are consistently found at the same levels, and no attempt to demonstrate a difference in habitat based on their places of death has been successful. Competition for at least some limiting resources between culture-bearing, tool-using, intelligent hominids could be expected to have been intense.

The comparisons discussed above show that at least two demonstrable differences were involved in the distinct adaptive patterns. One of these was associated with diet and food preparation. Changes in the larger-toothed lineage involved an adaptation to dietary items requiring even more powerful or prolonged chewing. A body size increase in this lineage may account for part of this change, with much larger hominids requiring more food. Unfortunately, while numerous postcrania have been found at the East African sites, there are virtually no associations of skull and body parts. According to work by C. O. Lovejoy, the known postcranial remains cannot be separated into two functionally different groups. This is not surprising given the complete adaptation to striding bipedalism in the Pliocene australopithecines, but it does not help the problem of determining which postcranial remains belong with which lineage. Really large postcrania appear for the first time during this period. Some individuals were probably 6 feet tall or taller. Like the earlier postcranial remains, the limbs are thick and massive. One large male innominate from below the KBS tuffs (ER-3228) has an extraordinarily narrow pelvic inlet, suggesting it might represent the smaller-brained form.

Apart from a possible increase in body size, a dietary explanation for the dental expansion might lie in an improved adaptation to semi-arid conditions. Such an adaptation could have become possible with the technological innovations of the late Pliocene, which produced recognizable artifacts. Sharper digging tools and better cutting edges might have allowed the more effective collection of difficult-to-chew foods, resulting in expansion into a more arid habitat and selection for jaws and teeth with increased chewing capacity. Unfortunately, here too the necessary data are lacking.

Changes in the smaller-toothed lineage may not have been as intense at first. However, they laid the basis for a continuing adaptive trend that ultimately proved to be the more successful. This trend involved reduction of the chewing complex and expansion of cranial capacity. It is tempting to suggest that these were associated with each other, the implication being that the evolving adaptive pattern included broad adaptive changes, not simply a switch to foods that were less difficult to chew. Some insight into what a Lower Pleistocene adaptive shift may have involved is provided by the archaeological sites from Olduvai.

SOME HELP FROM ARCHAEOLOGY

The oldest recognizable stone tools are termed "Oldowan." Crude Oldowan tool complexes appear as early as the late Pliocene and continue up to the present time. Living people have been observed making tools which could be called "Oldowan" for specific purposes. At one time, an earlier industry called "Kafuan" was thought to precede the Oldowan. However, it was found that the so-called Kafuan tools could not be distinguished from the results of natural fracturing.

Oldowan tools generally are modified pebbles, or flakes struck from pebbles, with relatively simple fracturing. Two things distinguish them from rocks with natural fracturing. First, the flaking occurs on both sides of an edge; naturally fractured rocks are usually flaked on only one side. Second, the tools are often manufactured in types of stone not normally found at the site or even in the nearby area. Rocks brought in from other areas are called "manuports." Oldowan tools are often called "pebble tools" because one of the most common Oldowan artifacts is the fractured pebble, or cobble, with a single bifacially (both sides, or faces) flaked edge. However, there are many tool types in Oldowan assemblages. It is apparent that pebbles were flaked to more than one shape, and that the flakes themselves were often used and resharpened when they became dull.

Stone tools represent only a small part of the tool-making activity of early hominids. However, stone tools need no preservation to remain at a site, whereas organic material must first be preserved, and often is not. Consequently, we know much more about stone tools than any made of wood or bone. Yet, in the Lower Pleistocene, there is some evidence of the vastly richer complex of nonstone tools that were made and used. Even if the evidence for Dart's proposed prelithic (Osteodontokeratic) industry of tools made from bones, teeth, and horns is discounted, there are preserved bones at Olduvai and Sterkfontein which are sharpened and scratched in a manner that suggests the broken bone was used for digging.

The main characteristics of Oldowan tools are their crudeness and their opportunistic forms. While the edges are sharp, they are far from straight. In addition, the so-called functional "types" may be more in the eyes of the beholders than in the intent of the australopithecines. Various tool types which are recognizable in later industries can be noted in Oldowan assemblages. However, there is little evidence that these "types," including specialized woodworking tools like burins, were intentionally shaped. Instead, the production of Oldowan implements seems to have been a more haphazard activity. A number of attempts at production were likely made, and the most useful results utilized. One can picture an australopithecine picking through a pile of flakes (perhaps the result of making a pebble chopper) for one or two that would be useful for a specific purpose—perhaps some long, thin flakes that could be used to cut the cartilage and tendons in a joint in order to dismember an animal. This is a very important behavior because it marks the beginning of associating form with function. However, it is quite another state of affairs to be able to *manufacture* a tool with the required shape in mind.

The earliest recognizable tools from Omo can best be described as broken pebbles with little standardization of form, perhaps a consequence of the poor material available for flaking. The earliest Turkana tools occur within the KBS tuffs and are slightly later. Only a few tool categories are represented, and the workmanship is extremely crude. Yet the early Lower Pleistocene was not a period of technological stagnation. Only several hundred thousand years after the earliest appearance of tools at Turkana, a better-made tool assemblage found in the region, called the Karari industry, is characterized by much more diverse collections and a great increase in the number of tool types. Similarly, Bed I and lower Bed II at Olduvai represent a period of not more than 200,000 years, and a comprehensive study by M. D. Leakey shows that considerable change took place during this span.

One of the most important aspects of Oldowan tools is that they have been found on living floors (excavated camp sites) at a number of localities in East Africa. The excavated surface represents the place where hominids once lived, and the debris on the surface is the result of hominid activities. Living floors give us some information about australopithecine behavior. For instance, at some of the Olduvai sites, a pattern can be found in the distribution of animal bones. There is a central circle in which all of the bones are smashed into very small pieces. Surrounding this circle there are also animal bones. These, however, are whole. The types of bones inside the circle have marrow, while the unsmashed bones outside have little or no marrow. It appears that there were area-specific functional activities. In one area, bones containing

marrow were smashed and the marrow extracted, while outside of this area other bones were discarded. The hominids were making maximum use of marrow bones in a habitual place and manner.

The bones themselves are of some interest. At the Bed I Oldowan sites at Olduvai Gorge, there are generally only *portions* of the skeletons of large animals. *Complete* animal skeletons represent either small species or very young members of larger species. I believe that this evidence, along with the very large size of the australopithecine posterior teeth, supports the hypothesis that most of the meat in australopithecine diets was scavenged. The limb portions most frequently found are those left by the hunting carnivores after they have eaten part of their prey.

Of course, some hunting must have occurred. However, hunted game seems restricted to very small, young, or slow animals. Earlier australopithecine hunting may not have been significantly different from chimpanzee hunting. Hunting in modern human groups differs from chimpanzee hunting in three important respects:

1. When it occurs, it is a consistent and role-specific behavior.
2. Opportunism is reduced because hunting patterns are learned and planned.
3. Game larger than the predator (people) is regularly hunted.

I do not believe that the latter two characteristics regularly apply to the meat gathering activities of earlier Bed I australopithecines.

By lower Bed II times, only a few hundred thousand years later, the evidence provided by living floors differs in three important respects. First, as already mentioned, a greater variety of tool types can be distinguished, and the tools generally appear to be better made (more symmetric forms, straighter edges, etc.). Second, there is a wider variety of different types of sites. This suggests that hominids were beginning to conceive of making different sets of tools for different functional activities, perhaps such as killing, butchering, collecting, and so on. Third, at the living sites, remains representing all the body parts of large animals are found in higher frequency, and the bones are more fragmented. These are not the result of carnivore kills, but instead probably represent the hunting activities of the hominids themselves and their improved ability to utilize both meat and marrow.

THE EVOLUTION OF HUNTING AND ITS CONSEQUENCES

Combining the archaeological evidence with the evolutionary direction taken by the smaller-toothed hominids strongly implies that it was the evolution of hunting (and associated behavioral changes) that accounted for their successful adaptation. This change in adaptation probably originated with the niche expansion made possible by the late Pliocene technological innovations. Earlier australopithecines were not effective hunters and only part-time scavengers. This may have been because a scavenging and hunting pattern requires more calories than a more sedentary pattern based on collecting. According to C. Peters, the difference in calorie requirements is substantial regardless of body size, approximately 33 percent. Thus it is unlikely that hunting could have become a very important activity until hunting techniques became relatively efficient, as measured by the calories obtained compared with the energy expended.

The archaeological sites showing scavenging in lower Bed I at Olduvai also suggest intensive gathering by implication. (Studies of African scavengers conducted by G. Schaller show that scavengers must rely on other food sources for their survival.) These sites could be associated with either or both of the australopithecines. However, in the smaller-toothed form, hunting gradually came to replace scavenging as a means of obtaining animal protein. This replacement occurred during the period between lower Bed I and lower Bed II.

There are numerous implications involved in this adaptive shift. The obvious dietary one is the increase in the amount of meat in the diet. The increase in amount, however, may not have been as important as the greater predictability of obtaining meat that would result from organized hunting. As meat became a more predictable part of the diet, it could replace some of the more difficult-to-chew plant foods that had been dietary staples. This would be especially critical during the dry season.

An associated series of changes could be expected in the development of technology for food preparation and in the improvement of manufac-

turing skills. These were probably an important factor in the increasing number of tool types within the Olduvai sequence. The later (Developed) Oldowan sites coexist in areas with sites with a toolkit little different from the earlier Oldowan. Whether this reflects different cultural adaptations or function-specific toolkits made by the same group is unclear. Whatever the case, Developed Oldowan toolkits include some new tool types, such as a crudely pointed chopper-like tool and small scraping tools. A roughly circular tool usually showing evidence of battering greatly increases in frequency. The battering on these spheroids is thought to result from pounding foods to make them easier to chew. If so, there was a marked improvement in food preparation. Every increase in the amount of cutting, chopping, or smashing that took place before food was chewed would have decreased the need to maintain a chewing complex that produced powerful forces. A combination of the changes in diet and food preparation probably accounts for the direction of change in the postcanine teeth.

Some Physiological Changes

There are other implications of the shift to hunting that can be explored. Hunting has only rarely been observed in primates. When the adaptation appears in a primate species, the particular characteristics shared by primates are used to develop a pattern of both behavior and morphology unlike that of most other hunting animals. Since primates rely heavily on vision, early hominid hunting was probably diurnal (daytime). This would be advantageous because most carnivores hunt at dawn or dusk and therefore would provide little direct competition (if not danger). In addition, there is every reason to believe that the early hominids were extraordinarily social, even for primates. Thus the inference is that hominid hunting was a social activity. In Africa today, the only diurnal social carnivore besides ourselves is the wild dog. These carnivores prefer game weighing approximately 125 pounds or less. Therefore, it is possible that a niche for a social diurnal carnivore was open in the earliest Pleistocene, and that it was occupied by the first hominid hunters.

There are certain physiological requisites for diurnal hunting in the tropics. It is of great advantage for a tropical diurnal hunter to be heat-adapted so as to allow intense activity during the hottest part of the day. In other words, the adaptation must be for getting rid of excess heat. Modern people are adapted for this, and it is likely that these adaptations originated when tropical hominids became consistent diurnal hunters.

If Pliocene hominids followed the pattern of most primates, they were probably covered with body hair. Body hair itself can be a heat adaptation if metobolic heat is not particularly high. Hair creates a dead-air space between the skin and the outside of the hair, and air is an excellent insulator. Thus in an animal that is relatively inactive during the day, solar radiation heats up the outside of the hair while the skin is insulated from the heat. Many modern desert-dwelling people use a similar adaptation, substituting loose robes for body hair. However, in a primate that is active during the day, as a diurnal hunter would have to be, a very different problem arises—getting rid of excess metabolic heat. In this case, an insulator surrounding the skin is not helpful.

Basically, there are two ways of getting rid of heat, radiation and conduction. Radiation is a process in which heat is emitted from a warm object in the form of infrared waves. Conduction occurs when a warm object is directly connected to a cooler medium that can transmit heat away from it. The efficiency of radiation depends on the *difference* in temperature between the object radiating (a hot person) and the surrounding medium (air). In hot areas, where air temperature is as high as body temperature, if not higher, radiation is not effective. Modern people get rid of excess heat through the process of conduction by the mechanism of sweating. When sweat drips off a body, each drop carries away a certain amount of heat. However, if a drop of sweat *evaporates*, raising its temperature by 1 degree when it changes its physical state from liquid to gas uses over 250 times as much heat as it takes to raise the temperature of the same drop 1 degree without evaporation. In other words, evaporation of sweat is an extremely effective way of getting rid of metabolic heat.

Extensive body hair both acts as an insulator and makes drop formation and therefore dripping easy, thus reducing the amount of sweat that evaporates. For these reasons, the hominid adaptation to the tropics involved reduction in the number and size of hair follicles and the development of sweat glands all over the body. These characteristics allow the effective heat-loss mechanism of sweat evaporation to operate efficiently. Even today, some tropical hunters can kill their prey by literally walking them to death. Most (but not all) mammals can be exhausted by being kept active during the heat of the day; since they lack as effective a heat-loss mechanism, they overheat sooner than the human chasing them. In this regard, the human stride mechanism is particularly effective, since it allows fairly rapid locomotion over long periods with only minimal use of the largest hip muscle—*gluteus maximus*. Human stride keeps the metabolism operating at a low level, while sweating provides an effective heat-loss mechanism. They combine in a unique hominid adaptation to tropical diurnal activity.

There are two important results that stem from this adaptation. First, it makes hominids water dependent. A sweating hominid is a thirsty hominid. Most major hominid sites are found adjacent to or near water. Of course, this is partly due to the fact that preservation is more likely. However, the generalization is also true for archaeological sites without preserved bone. By indicating that a water supply was important, this suggests an early beginning for selection leading to the effective hominid diurnal adaptation. However, hunting cannot always take place in the vicinity of water, especially when it becomes increasingly less opportunistic. Carrying water depends on one of the most basic human inventions, and one unfortunately not commonly subject to preservation—the container. The innovation of containers was one of the most important human cultural adaptations, and probably one of the critical factors that led to the development of effective organized hunting.

Coincidently, the innovation of containers may have been one of the factors resulting in the average body size increases that characterized the latest australopithecines and/or the earliest *Homo erectus* populations. (It is not clear with which of these taxa the limbs showing larger body sizes are associated.) In the absence of sufficient water in arid areas, it is necessary to maximize the ratio of body surface area to body weight to improve heat loss through radiation. This ratio is maximized when body size is reduced. It is possible that by providing sufficient water during daily activities, containers helped remove the earlier small-size limitation on hominids adapted to arid or semi-arid regions. If so, this is one of the many cases in which a cultural adaptation affects behavioral adaptations and ultimately leads to morphological change.

The second important result of the heat adaptation involves skin color. A variety of skin colors occur in chimpanzees and probably also occurred in earlier hominids. This is because no particular selection acts on skin color in a primate covered with body hair. However, the loss of body hair led to specific skin color selection in humans as the result of two independent selective pressures: vitamin D synthesis (see Chapter 9) and skin cancer.

The substance giving pigmentation to the skin, melanin, is produced by melanocytes. These pigment-producing cells occur in the bottom portion of the epidermis (the outer layer of skin). There are no population differences in numbers of melanocytes, although their activity in producing melanin, and consequently average populational pigmentation, can vary considerably. Melanin acts to limit the amount of ultraviolet radiation that can penetrate the skin. Extensive ultraviolet penetration has two effects that are disadvantageous in the tropical adaptation discussed. First, even mild sunburn resulting from ultraviolet penetration significantly reduces the rate of sweating, and of course severe sunburn is extremely painful. Second, sufficient penetration leads to skin cancer. Together, these result in selection favoring dark skin as part of the hominid adaptation to tropical diurnal activity.

We will never know with certainty when this adaptation began. The main behavioral change is the shift to activity during portions of the day when most primates rest to reduce metabolic heat. *If* this behavioral change is connected with an ecological shift from a scavenging/gathering adaptation with some small-scale hunting to a hunting/gathering adaptation, then it is likely that these early hunters were dark-skinned and had little body hair. I believe this is the most probable reconstruction. However, it is possible that there was sufficient diurnal activity by the Pliocene australopithecines for these changes to have occurred earlier.

Possible Social Changes

We may also consider the question of what changes a shift to hunting might have caused in the structure of hominid society. Increased reliance on

hunting affected both the geographic and the ecological range of hominid populations. The hunting adaptation also resulted in more free time because fewer people-hours were necessary to provide food. There were two reasons for this. First, meat is a more compact food source than plant foods. Less has to be eaten to obtain the same amount of food value. Second, hunting behavior became increasingly less opportunistic; hunts were planned and cooperatively executed. This situation contrasts with one in which most animal protein is obtained by scavenging, which depends on the success and appetite of local carnivores, or the fortuitous butchering of animals caught in natural traps. This change in adaptation provided the opportunity for more complex social interactions within and between populations.

Although hunting is often thought to characterize the more "bestial" aspects of humanity, it may actually represent one of the most important humanizing influences in our evolution. Behaviorally, the human pattern of hunting depends on technology (weapons and tools for dismemberment), cooperation in both hunting and the associated differential food gathering activities, sharing, and communication. Food gathering activities almost surely involved both hunting game and collecting plant foods. The latter, probably responsible for the bulk of the diet of early Pleistocene hominids, was almost certainly a female activity given the large size difference between males and females. Moreover, technology played a more critical role in the evolution of this and related activities than in the evolution of hunting *per se*; implements are extremely important in both obtaining and preparing plant foods, while containers are critical for carrying them back to the home base once the pattern of eating all foods at their source is left behind.

Socially, one might expect greater formalization of role-specific behavior to accompany the shift to a hunting/gathering adaptation. Sex-based division of food procuring activities and the beginning of male responsibility for females and offspring, probably behaviors that were already present, became more important and were likely formalized in the developing role structure to a much greater extent. Ritualization of sharing, development of strategies requiring cooperation between males, and attempts at long-range planning are additional associated cultural behaviors that might be expected to become increasingly important. The emphasis on formalization and ritualization is not misplaced. I believe it is these aspects of behavioral structuralization that account for the marked increase in brain size. The simple idea that "hunting requires more intelligence" ignores the likelihood that the Pliocene australopithecines were already the most intelligent creatures on the planet.

The pattern of differential food gathering activities depends on the earlier appearance of certain behaviors: using a home base, developing sharing as an expected behavior, and evolving language capacities at least complex enough to allow displacement. As these increased in importance, they became incorporated into the human behavioral system as structured, learned behaviors, expressed in contexts reflecting stratification based on sex, age, and differential access to resources ranging from foods themselves to knowledge about them. In a word, these activities can probably best be described as human culture.

Finally, the development of organized hunting resulted in a distinct shift in human ecology. Hunting, of course, provided an additional (and more efficient) means of obtaining animal protein, which ultimately became a consistent and predictable part of the diet. This helped extend the geographic and ecological range of the species by adding to the resources that could be utilized by each population.

At the same time, however, organized hunting moved the human populations to a higher position on the local ecological pyramids. With increased dependence on the biomass of other animals, human population densities fell in many areas. Another factor leading to the decrease in population density is the water dependence that comes with the hominid heat adaptation, making available water a much more important population limiting factor. Population size and density in hunting hominids was limited by the scattered water supplies in many areas. What this means is that, for a variety of reasons, fewer hominid hunters could be supported per square mile than hominid scavenger-gatherers. Thus, while evidence at both East and South African sites suggests about the same density of australopithecines and baboons, the population density of modern hunter-gatherers in the same areas is much lower than that of baboons, in spite of the fact that the baboons are hunted. The total number of hunting/gathering hominids went up as their range increased, but population densities in most areas went down.

Put another away, particular bands occupied wider ranges and were constantly moving throughout these ranges, depending on the distribution of both game and water sources at any particular time. It is likely that under these conditions more contact between populations occurred, and therefore there was more gene flow. Increased contact between populations probably also led to the development of more complex social relations. The range of role relations and other formalized behaviors depending on individual expectations would have to expand greatly with increased contact between populations. It is likely that regular mechanisms to formalize relations between such groups evolved. In the ethnographic present, such mechanisms can be as diverse as extended kinship, complex trade systems (including trading potential mates), and warfare.

The implication I wish to draw is that the adaptive shift involved is much wider reaching than a simple dietary change. I believe that this shift led to the development of far more complex, socially defined interactions both within and between groups of these late australopithecines. Such interactions involve the development of more detailed behavioral expectations and their associated neurological models. While the only direct evidence underlying these suppositions comes from the increased complexity of stone tools and consequently of the rules governing their manufacture, I believe that the totality of these changes led to the changes in selection that resulted in the appearance of the species which is immediately ancestral to our own—*Homo erectus*.

Middle Lower Pleistocene Developments

The next Lower Pleistocene sample, approximately spanning 1.7 to 1.3 million years ago, provides evidence for the continued evolution of both hominid lineages in East Africa. While clear resemblances are seen with the earlier ancestral forms, the result of divergent evolutionary trends is a more dramatic adaptive and morphological distinction.

THE LARGER-TOOTHED FORMS

While no complete crania of the hyper-robust forms are known from this period, dental and mandibular evidence shows an even further increase in posterior tooth size (Figure 8.1) and the size of the associated mandibular structures (Figure 8.2). Posterior teeth of the females (Figure 9.1, p. 190) are larger than those of the males of the Pliocene forms, and expansion of the P_4 is so great that this tooth is larger than the first molar in some specimens (Figure 6.7).

Interestingly, the few fragmentary crania from this timespan have suggested enigmatic developments in the *Australopithecus boisei* lineage. The partial cranium from Chesowanja appears to have had an expanded cranial capacity, and the even more fragmentary Turkana specimen ER-733 may have been similar. Moreover, ER-733 also has thickened cranial bone and somewhat expanded browridges (the significance of these will be discussed below). A full understanding of the later changes in this lineage must await the recovery of more complete specimens.

While the lineage divergence may be the result of a niche expansion allowed by an increasingly efficient adaptation for powerful chewing in *Australopithecus boisei*, my guess is that competition with the second lineage had come progressively to restrict other food sources by this time. This competition, rather than a prey-predator relation (as some have suggested), probably accounts for the hyper-robusts' eventual extinction. The successful lineage expanded into their niche, reducing the same foods to edibility through technology rather than with powerful teeth and jaws.

THE SECOND LINEAGE

The second lineage also underwent considerable change. Only some of this is reflected in the continued decrease in posterior tooth size (Figure 8.1). A suite of rather different features appears in the crania known from this lineage. In spite of the dental similarities and overlap in range with the earlier australopithecines, most scholars recognize the later members of this lineage as a separate species— *Homo erectus*.

Early *Homo Erectus* Crania

The earliest recognizable crania of *Homo erectus* appear in the Lake Turkana deposits between

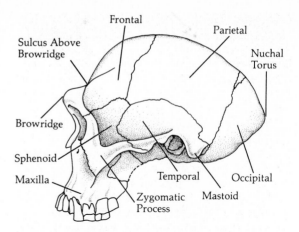

FIGURE 8.4   *Early African* Homo erectus. *Above is a drawing of ER-3733 showing the main cranial bones and some other features common in* Homo erectus *crania. On page 173 are three views of ER-3833 (left) and ER-3733 (right), contrasting what I believe are male and female features. The male is more robust, and has better developed cranial buttresses. Both specimens are casts.*

about 1.5 and 1.6 million years ago. Within this timespan, a number of fragments as well as two virtually complete crania have been recovered. Another cranium and additional fragments date to just younger than 1.5 million years; the specimens are so similar that it is probably best to consider them together. One of the most interesting aspects of early *Homo erectus* is that the specimens are distinct and recognizably not australopithecine in their grade of organization. While most features of the sample overlap with australopithecine features, the combinations are different. This probably indicates dramatic changes in the direction of selection. The possibility also exists that *Homo erectus* evolved in a different area and replaced the Turkana australopithecine populations during this timespan.

The best preserved of the early crania is the ER-3733 female, dated to between 1.5 and 1.6 million years ago. This cranium (see Figure 8.4) gives evidence of numerous features contrasting with the australopithecines'; although varying in frequency and development, the same complex still characterizes this lineage over a million years later.

The virtually complete skull has a capacity close to 900 cc, combined with a posterior dentition of moderate size and anterior tooth sockets suggesting teeth close to the Pleistocene australopithecine (i.e.,

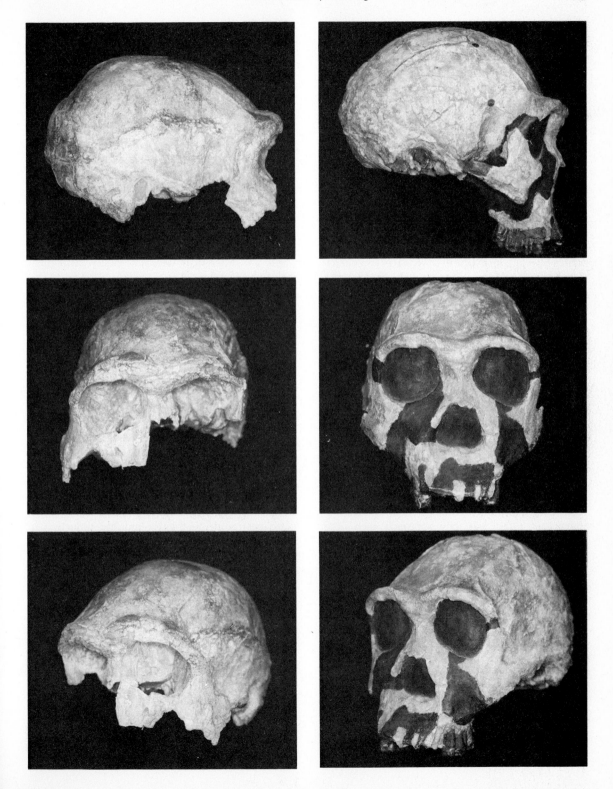

Homo habilis) average. This combination, however, is quite different from that found in Homo habilis specimens, in which a posterior dentition of the ER-3733 size is normally associated with a cranial vault with two-thirds the capacity or less. For instance, an earlier female of this lineage (ER-1813, Figure 8.3) has a posterior dentition of about the same size but a cranial capacity of only 505 cc. An earlier male (ER-1590) with a cranial capacity 100-200 cc less than ER-3733 has a posterior tooth area 32 percent larger.

ER-3733 is most like late australopithecine females in her facial features, including posterior tooth size, development of the zygomatic bones (which are large and robustly developed, shelving evenly into the lower face just above the teeth), reduced prognathism of the lower face, the narrow distance between the orbits, and the thin vertical dimension of the browridge. Moreover, the face is narrow relative to its (not insubstantial) height. The thickness of the cranial bones falls within the australopithecine range.

On the other hand, grade differences from the late australopithecines are substantial. Besides the larger cranial capacity, there are proportional differences in the vault dimensions. These are mainly greater length (front to rear), greater breadth of the frontal bone just behind the orbits (i.e., less postorbital constriction), and greater backward extension of the cranial rear behind the foramen magnum. The forward projection of the browridges is marked, and there is a deep groove separating them from the forehead. The temporal lines (marking the edge of the temporalis muscle) rise high on the cranial sides, but they approach each other most closely toward the top of the cranium rather than in the more forward position common in australopithecines. Finally, there is a thick nuchal torus (ridge) and significant expansion in the area available for the attachment of the neck (nuchal) muscles. Facial differences include a broad nasal opening with a distinct lower border (rare in australopithecines) and projecting nasal bones. The facial breadth is small relative to the frontal breadth, and the resulting small size of the temporal fossa suggests a reduced temporalis muscle.

Initial descriptions of the ER-3733 vault suggest a marked resemblance to the late female Homo erectus specimen from Choukoutien (see pp. 194-198) reconstructed by F. Weidenreich. This similarity is more apparent than real and is seen mainly in the side view. Even in this view, one can see the much smaller vault, less bulging forehead, and larger face of the earlier African female. There are other differences in robustness, vault thickness, and some details of the occipital bone which point to grade and possibly clade distinctions between these two specimens, the earliest and latest representatives of Homo erectus.

Slightly later than ER-3733 is an extremely similar specimen (ER-3833) with a virtually identical vault size and a detailed replication of morphological features. However, the browridges, nuchal torus, mastoids, and cranial base are far more massive, and the vault is somewhat thicker. Although the lower face is missing, the zygomatics appear to have been very thick and widely flared. These are differences which normally distinguish males and females.

A third Turkana cranium from this date range, ER-1805, was found at a roughly equivalent stratigraphic position. The face was broken away from the cranium and the browridge area lost. Otherwise the cranium is fairly complete and there is an associated mandible. The specimen shows some closer resemblances to the australopithecines than does ER-3733, and yet I believe the functional pattern indicates that it is best interpreted as an early Homo erectus. Australopithecine-like features include the small cranial capacity (582 cc) and low vault, the size of the face relative to the braincase, and the presence of a sagittal crest (Figure 9.8, p. 207). However, there are some significant contrasts with the normal australopithecine condition. The broad frontal suggests a narrow temporal fossa; the moderate postcanine teeth also indicate reduction in masticatory power. The relatively great length of the cranium and the fact that the sagittal crest is in a posterior position both show that it was the posterior rather than the anterior aspect of the temporalis muscle that was emphasized. The whole cranial base is expanded due to an extraordinary development of spongy bone (pneumatization) forming a shelf over and behind the ears. Moreover, at the rear of the vault, the temporal lines meet the nuchal torus, helping even further extend the shelf at the back of the cranium and over the mastoids and ear openings.

The importance of this cranium is that it is transitional between the australopithecines and early Homo erectus. In my view, a cranial capacity of this size is not unexpected in early Homo erectus. By itself, it is not sufficient to exclude the cranium from the taxon. However, whether ER-1805 is considered an erectus-like australopithecine or an australopithecine-like erectus, its very existence argues for the local evolution of the former into the latter.

A more recent male specimen was found in upper Bed II, Olduvai Gorge. OH-9 is a massive faceless cranium (see Figure 8.5, p. 176) with the largest capacity of all the early specimens. The browridge is the largest known for *any* hominid in both its thickness and its projection in front of the moderately sloping forehead. The cranial base is broad, with heavy buttressing where muscles attach. The spongy structures above the mastoids assume massive proportions so that the more perpendicular parietals of the australopithecine condition become an evenly sloping cranial wall. Yet the vault bones are fairly thin.

Besides these crania, there are bits and pieces of fragmentary cranial vault scattered over this time range that show the same distinct features. An attempt to account for these cranial distinctions will follow a brief discussion of the teeth, mandibles, and postcrania of early *Homo erectus*.

Mandibles and Teeth

The early *Homo erectus* mandibles include a number of moderate- to small-toothed specimens, mostly from east of Lake Turkana. I believe that most of these represent females (Figure 8.2). There are some larger, more robust specimens, much smaller than the contemporary hyper-robust mandibles, that probably represent the corresponding males. Combined, these mandibles reflect a degree of sexual dimorphism that is similar to that found in earlier hominids. Marked dimorphism in the mandibles is equivalent to that in the crania.

The size of the posterior teeth in these specimens is reduced compared with the late australopithecine average (Figure 8.1), although falling within the australopithecine range. Reduction is greatest in the middle posterior teeth, where earlier the most expansion took place. Relatively, the second and third molars are less reduced than the first, and the fourth premolar is generally equal to or smaller than the third. However, similar to the earlier hominid condition, the premolars are broad relative to the molars. Canines and incisors are also within the australopithecine range and below the mean

(probably because more females are represented than males). Morphologically, the postcanine teeth show the same multiple cusps that were found in the australopithecines, although in contrast the P_4 is not especially molarized and more closely resembles P_3. Another difference is the lack of significant hyper-molarization (cusp addition) in the posterior aspect of the Turkana juvenile ER-820 dm_1.

While the mandibular bodies in this sample show some features reminiscent of the australopithecines, on the average the bodies are smaller and thinner. On the back face of the symphysis, a more weakly developed torusing system and horizontal bone surface behind the incisors are present, and appear in specimens as young as ER-820 (about eight years old). Corpus dimensions and proportions are well within the australopithecine range, and the ramus seems to have been broad and tall.

Postcrania

Among the numerous isolated postcrania from Turkana are specimens found at the ER-3733 level and above it. In my view, it is not possible to distinguish individual australopithecine from early *Homo erectus* specimens on the basis of any consistent morphological difference (see papers by M. H. Day for a contrary view), although the remains show variation in many characteristics. Analysis of the few relatively complete later *Homo erectus* postcrania indicates that on the average *Homo erectus* differs little, if at all, from the australopithecines in a series of features that result from powerful muscular activity and a narrower-than-modern pelvic inlet. These include thick cortical external bone in the limb shafts, marked midshaft anteroposterior flattening in the femur, relatively long femoral neck length, and femoral necks which are vertically tall relative to their breadth (to resist bending).

An Adaptive Model of the Origin of Homo erectus

From the present evidence, it seems likely that populations recognizable as *Homo erectus* appeared in Africa by no later than 1.5 million years ago. For some time prior to that, numerous australopithe-

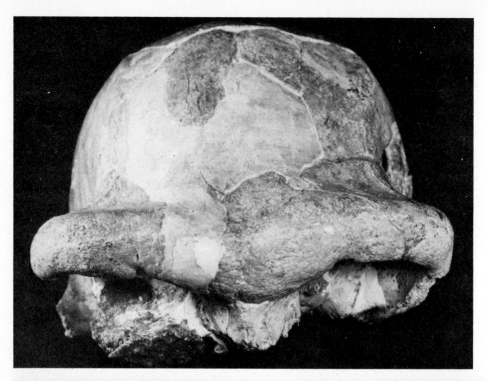

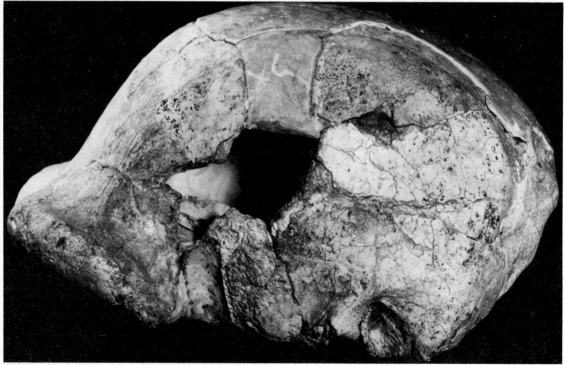

FIGURE 8.5   Side and frontal views of Olduvai hominid 9,
a male early Homo erectus from upper Bed II. (Courtesy
of C. L. Brace.)

cine populations had been changing in a direction which ultimately led to the great increase in the frequency of features described in the discussions of early *Homo erectus* morphology. I believe that the behavioral changes underlying this pattern of morphological evolution were a consequence of the development of new gathering and food preparation techniques and of consistent and successful diurnal hunting.

There are average differences between the early *Homo erectus* sample and the australopithecines that are both size-related and morphological. However, most features that occur in the erectus sample can be found, at lower frequency, in the australopithecines. The main changes can best be discussed in broad causal categories.

CHANGES RELATED TO BRAIN SIZE

One important cause of cranial differences lies in the expanding cranial capacity. The extent of actual expansion, however, remains unclear since some of the brain size increase is probably due to larger average body height. Whatever the case, *Homo erectus* has a larger average cranial capacity than the later australopithecines, although there is a great deal of overlap between the samples.

Early erectus crania are not simply "blown up" australopithecine crania; the proportions also differ. Disproportionate changes are due to both the expansion of specific areas within the brain and the changing balance of forces acting on the skull (to be discussed below). For instance, the height and breadth of the braincase increased by about the same percentage, while the increase in cranial length is much greater. In this case, the disproportionate change may be due to both an expansion of the posterior parietal lobes of the brain and selection to increase the horizontal angle of the posterior temporalis muscle. A similar example is found in the expansion in cranial breadth. The skull as a whole increases in breadth much more than the braincase alone does (Figure 9.8, p. 207). The effect of this disproportionate change is mainly to expand the basal region of the cranium where the neck muscles attach. Indeed, changes associated with better-developed neck muscles are one of the most dramatic aspects of early *Homo erectus* crania. The occipital bone (Figure 8.4) becomes much larger, while the parietals barely change at all. Besides the

increase in breadth, most specimens have a prominent torus across the back of the skull (nuchal torus), which, with the posterior extension of the occipital bone, makes both the foramen magnum and the outer ear openings appear to be more anterior (although their positions actually remain about the same). Finally, the expansion of the frontal bone is mainly in breadth. While this probably reflects an expansion of the frontal lobes, it also makes the temporal fossa smaller, which could not happen if the temporalis muscle was not decreasing in size.

DIET-RELATED CHANGES

Superimposed on the expanding brain size and changes in cranial proportions are differences due to dietary change. The posterior dentition is subjected to less vertical force during chewing, and consequently there is reduction in the structures enclosing or supporting the vertical anterior part of the temporalis and the facial structures supporting the masseter muscle.

The posterior teeth undergo some degree of reduction. Associated with this reduction is a decrease in molarization, especially in dm_1 and P_4. Similarly, the mandibular corpus reduces in robustness, and a different relationship of height and breadth develops. The height of the mandibular corpus does not decrease; in fact, it actually increases. Since mandibular corpus height has a high correlation with body height, I believe this provides some evidence of an average body height increase in early *Homo erectus*. In the absence of clearly associated limbs, this cannot be verified, but later *Homo erectus* samples indicate that an average height increase over the australopithecines of close to 6 inches eventually characterizes this species.

CHANGES IN THE CRANIAL BUTTRESSING SYSTEM

The remaining changes occur in the thickness of the cranial bones and the system of buttresses—the browridge and nuchal torus (Figure 5.2). The average parietal thickness is greater in early erectus, while the thickness of the browridge virtually doubles. Changes in the cranial buttressing system (discussed below) come as a result of two factors, cranial strengthening and the evolution of increased vertical and horizontal *anterior* tooth use.

Strengthening

F. Weidenreich regarded the thickened cranial bone and marked torus system of *Homo erectus* as means to strengthen the cranial vault. Such an adaptation might result from blows to the head received while hunting large mammals with weapons effective only at close range. Reports of healed scars on many *Homo erectus* crania support this idea. Some of the strengthening features are also affected by increased muscle use. Along the cranial base, from the ear openings on back, the *Homo erectus* crania develop thick spongy bone, forming a pronounced nuchal torus (as distinguished from a *crest*, which is directly caused by muscle pull). This spongy bone development provides a lightweight means of strengthening across the area of neck muscle attachment, indicating that the neck muscles have increased in size and strength (an idea supported by the expansion of their attachment area on the occipital bone).

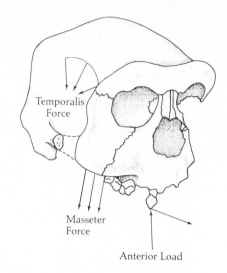

FIGURE 8.6　*Drawing of the later Indonesian* Homo erectus *cranium Sangiran 17 showing the positions of the main jaw-associated muscles that resist a force on the front teeth (see also Figure 4.8) and the combined horizontal and vertical components that such a force must have (unless the force is completely vertical).*

Anterior Tooth Loading

Increased use of the anterior teeth in environmental manipulation provides a second, equally important, explanation for this buttressing system, without conflicting with the first. Holding something between the front teeth and using the neck muscles to pull it creates both vertical and horizontal forces between the teeth, the former from holding the object in place and the latter as the result of the pull (see Figure 8.6). The front of the mouth is a convenient position for powerful gripping, pulling, and twisting. Observed uses of this "third hand" include holding bone drills, straightening wood spear shafts, stripping hides, and loosening rusted gasoline drum covers. The much larger front teeth and related muscles in *Homo erectus* suggest a much wider range of activities.

The *horizontal* forces, when great enough, are associated with expanded neck muscles, nuchal torus development, cranial lengthening to increase the horizontal component of the posterior temporalis, and an expansion of this muscle in size (see Figure 8.7). One of the most dramatic changes resulting

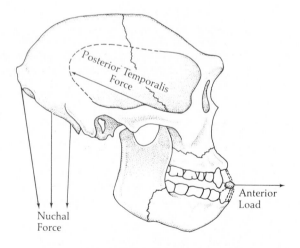

FIGURE 8.7　*Side view of F. Weidenreich's reconstruction of the Indonesian late Lower Pleistocene cranium Sangiran 4 and the Sangiran 1 mandible. The drawing shows a load between the anterior teeth exerting force in the horizontal direction, and indicates the positions of the two main muscles that can resist it. The nuchal (neck) muscles bring the cranium backward, and the posterior temporalis brings the mandible backward. Both of these muscles are well developed in* Homo erectus.

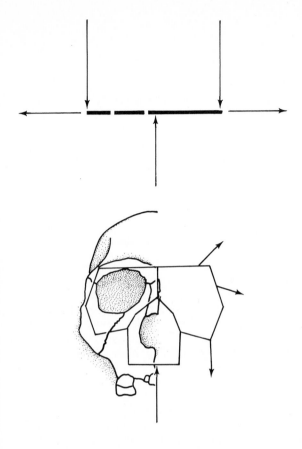

from increased horizontal loading is the expansion of the neck muscles' attachment area. This area is 2.6 times greater in early erectus, and there is no overlap with the australopithecines (including those hyper-robusts with the largest faces). The development of spongy bone across the back of the cranial base provides support for the increased forces of the expanded neck muscles.

The effect of *vertical* anterior forces (see Figure 8.8) was analyzed by the experimental work of B. Endo. He showed that these forces result in bending in the area above the eyes (supraorbital region). The bending can be resisted by either a high forehead or a buttress; in modern humans the high forehead is effective, while the smaller-brained early hominids developed browridges. The supraorbital region might be thought of as a beam, with the tooth load exerting an upward force in the center and the anterior temporalis and masseter exerting downward and outward forces on the edges. Expansion of the buttress (browridge) corresponds to the increase in forces applied to it.

SEXUAL DIMORPHISM

Unfortunately, the sample size is far too small to determine whether early *Homo erectus* maintained an australopithecine-like degree of *canine* sexual dimorphism. However, the size differences between large and small mandibles from Africa suggest that an australopithecine-like degree of body size dimorphism was characteristic.

FACIAL CHANGES

Early *Homo erectus* faces are known from only a few of the African specimens. It is probably unwise to generalize from these. However, it would appear that there is little change from the earlier australopithecines in facial height, although the upper face expands at the expense of the lower. Moreover, the early erectus faces seem to maintain robustly developed zygomatics, which originate just above the molar row in a moderately posterior position. Two differences which seem significant are the broadening of the nose and the decreased prognathism. The nasal bones appear to have been prominent, but the frequency of this feature in the australopithecines is unknown because damage in this region is common.

FIGURE 8.8   A simplified model of the reaction of the face to vertical *anterior loads, based on a drawing of the ER-3733 face. The model is derived from B. Endo's facial stress analysis. In the face below, the upward-pointing arrow represents the force of an object between the teeth. This force is provided by the force of the mandible on the object. Therefore, the muscles closing the mandible also produce forces on the face. These are represented by the arrows on the right, and the main lines of facial resistance to these forces are represented by a simple beam model. The lower (downward-pointing) arrow represents the masseter force, and the upper ones the anterior temporalis force. The actions of these forces meet in the area above the eyes. Their effects in this area can be reduced to a simpler model by representing the region above the eyes by a beam (shown above). On this beam, a central force acts upward, and the forces to the sides act to bend the beam downward and pull it outward. It is the concentration of bending and tensile (producing tension) forces in the beam (supraorbital region) that creates the necessity of strengthening. In early hominids with low foreheads, the strengthening takes the form of a buttress, or torus, called the supraorbital torus or the browridge.*

SUMMARY

The lineage division in the late Pliocene or earliest Pleistocene resulted in contemporary species of australopithecine grade. The extent to which the presence of each influenced the evolution of the other is unknown, but the rapid marked divergence of these species suggests that competitive exclusion played an important role. The hyper-robust lineage could be thought of as an unsuccessful attempt at a pattern of hominization based on only some of the australopithecine characteristics. Yet its continued evolution over what might have been as much as a million years in the face of competition with the other australopithecines and ultimately with *Homo erectus* (by 1.5–1.6 million years BP) puts this lack of success in a different light.

Moreover, the hyper-robust lineage may have played a critical role in human evolution. Competitive exclusion resulted in adaptive differences in *both* lineages. We may wonder what the direction of evolution in our lineage might have been if it had never been in competition with the hyper-robust one. Would the critical adaptive shift to hunting have taken place without this competition, or would the descendants of the Pliocene australopithecines still remain as a little-changed savanna-adapted form?

Whatever the case, the adaptive shift did take place in one lineage, and its consequences can hardly be overemphasized. At the base of this lineage, the late australopithecine form, *Homo habilis*, is characterized by most of the facial and dental adaptations to a diet requiring powerful mastication that evolved in its ancestor, *Australopithecus africanus*. The trend for decreasing robustness in this complex is barely expressed, if at all. At the same time, however, there is clear evidence of expanding cranial capacity and other evidence that makes a marked increase in cultural complexity appear likely. Direct evidence suggesting behavioral changes includes an increase in the types of tools that are found and improvements in their manufacture. The East African camp sites reveal a gradual improvement in the procuring of animal protein (more fairly complete skeletons of large animals are found) and in the ability to utilize both meat and marrow. The adaptive shift to diurnal hunting in tropical regions may have been accompanied by certain physiological changes: loss of body hair, development of sweat glands all over the body, and the appearance of dark skin pigmentation. The first two changes make hominids water dependent, and thus the hunting adaptation may have relied on the innovation of containers.

Social developments in the *Homo* lineage during this time will always remain inferential. It is proposed that these involved the formalization and ritualization of role behaviors, including sharing and exchange, cooperation between males, planning and coordination of food gathering activities, and regularization of contacts between different groups. Thus it is argued that the consequences of the adaptive shift to hunting were primarily humanizing.

Homo erectus appears after the evidence for these developments. The new morphological combinations and developments are viewed as the result of the behavioral changes discussed above. The erectus sample shows cranial expansion (especially in the frontal and the posterior portions of the skull), thickening of the vault bone and torusing system, and reduction in posterior tooth size (plus reduced molarization in some teeth). These changes are tied to increasing cranial capacity (a response to the structural aspects of behavior), increased anterior tooth use, decreased posterior tooth use, and the more common occurrence of injuries during hunting. These represent evolutionary trends which continue through the later evolution of the lineage.

STATE OF THE ART

As in the preceding chapter, one of the main problems raised here is taxonomic and phylogenetic. This can probably best be viewed in a historical context. When the East African discoveries first began to accumulate in large numbers in the early 1960s, attempts were made to interpret them within the framework of J. T. Robinson's dietary hypothesis. It was generally felt that the very robust specimens represented *Paranthropus* and the gracile specimens *Australopithecus*, although not always consistently or by the same authors.

L. S. B. Leakey, who with his wife, Mary, made the first East African discoveries (at Olduvai Gorge), created separate taxa for the two forms: *Zinjanthropus boisei* for the robust form and *Homo habilis* for the gracile one. This contention of taxonomic distinction for both East African forms has been consistently supported by P. V. Tobias, the South African anthropologist-anatomist who wrote the descriptive monograph on the OH-5 remains. Robinson disagreed with both placements, suggesting that the robust specimens represented *Paranthropus* and the gracile ones *Australopithecus africanus*. (He later proposed that *A. africanus* be renamed *Homo africanus*.) With a few prominent exceptions, most workers seemed to agree with Robinson's judgment, except for those who had never supported the distinction between *Paranthropus* and *Australopithecus* in South Africa. These prominent exceptions regarded *Homo habilis* as a separate, unique taxon showing more advanced features than the *Australopithecus africanus* sample from South Africa. Questions about the validity of this taxon, and the general difficulties in classifying a recognizably transitional form, provided the meat for what was the major anthropological debate concerning early hominids during the 1960s. In retrospect, what seems to have kept this debate going was the lack of really well preserved remains and the general disregard of the time difference between *Homo habilis* in East Africa and *Australopithecus* to the south.

The next specimens to be discovered were found at Omo. These were placed in three taxa: *Australopithecus africanus, Homo habilis,* and *Paranthropus*. The subsequent discoveries at East Turkana were, at first, placed in none of these taxa to avoid further confusion. Later, generic placement into *Australopithecus* and *Homo* (without species designation) was attempted. By the mid-1970s, it was clear that the various taxonomic names were being used differently by different workers and that there were at least three distinct views of how the samples were related phylogenetically.

The simplest view was that all the specimens represented geographic, temporal, or sex-based variants of a single variable lineage. A second view argued for two distinct lineages; however, the composition of these varied depending on the worker

concerned. The two lineages corresponded to the omnivore and vegetarian of the dietary hypothesis. The third view argued for three (or more) distinct lineages. Again, their composition varied with the author concerned. Some saw *Australopithecus africanus–Homo habilis* as one lineage, with *Paranthropus* and *Zinjanthropus* representing the other two. Others saw the gracile species as separate lineages and combined *Paranthropus* and *Zinjanthropus* in one.

In the mid-1970s, two things happened that substantially altered the entire interpretive picture. First, some dating problems were resolved with the accumulating evidence for the 1.6–1.8 million year KBS dates at Turkana and for early dates for at least some of the South African sites. Second, the clear association of *Homo erectus* crania with hyper-robust australopithecines by 1.5–1.6 million years ago was demonstrated at Lake Turkana.

Did this resolve the above contentions? The answer here is yes, in part, but at the same time a new series of problems was raised. The clear temporal placement of *Australopithecus africanus* in South Africa approximately three-quarters of a million years before *Homo habilis* in East Africa made the hypothesis that these represented an ancestral-descendant sequence acceptable to most workers (see Chapter 7 State of the Art for one contrary view). The demonstration of adaptively distinct lineages showing different evolutionary directions in the early Pleistocene in East Africa disproved the single-species hypothesis for this time range, thus eliminating one of the alternatives debated in the early part of the 1970s.

Some of the issues now being debated are the same ones debated earlier, while others are new. For instance, the exact relationship between the so-called robust australopithecines in South and East Africa is coming under increased scrutiny. One reason for this is the uncertainty regarding the Swartkrans date. Absolute dates are not possible, and faunal dates have ranged from about 2.1 to 1.6 million years BP. The former would enhance the possibility that the Swartkrans hominids are ancestral to the hyper-robust australopithecines of East Africa, a view held by many. At the same time, however, it could also support the interpretation that these hominids are ancestral to all later hominids; that is, they existed before the lineage division (a viewpoint I favor). The late date would force one of two interpretations. The Swartkrans hominids could be later representatives of the hyper-robust lineage. In this case, either the lineage was extraordinarily variable (the criticism that was leveled against the single-species hypothesis when it was applied in East Africa) or it was evolving in the same direction as *Homo*, markedly reducing the robustness of the masticatory structures. The second interpretation would be that the Swartkrans sample represents a third, late-surviving lineage restricted to South Africa. This question is far from resolved.

Another problem concerns the number of lineages present in East Africa. *Homo habilis* has become a "taxon whose time has come"; there is nothing else available to call the segment of the lineage after the speciation of the hyper-robust form and later than *Australopithecus africanus* but earlier than *Homo erectus*. Some of the controversy surrounding this taxon can be resolved through an understanding of the distinction between its *taxonomy* (*Homo habilis*) and its *grade* (australopothecine). However, is this the only gracile australopithecine present in East Africa in the early Pleistocene? Some workers argue that *Australopithecus africanus* is also present. The rationale for this argument is again as dependent on dating problems as on actual morphology. The question is whether there are any non-hyper-robust australopithecines contemporary with or later than the earliest appearance of *Homo erectus*. If so, these would constitute a third lineage. None is later than the 1.5-million-year-old tuff at Turkana; the problem exists between 1.5 and 1.6 million years BP in this area. Specimens such as ER-1813 (Figure 8.3), which I have suggested are females of *Homo habilis*, occur within the same broad timespan as *Homo erectus*. The problems of cross-correlation over the 700 square miles of the

Lake Turkana site do not allow finer resolution than this. In other words, ER-1813 may be older than the *Homo erectus* specimen ER-3733 (Figure 8.4), or it may be the same age or even younger. The temporal relation cannot be proven at present.

The data allow several possible interpretations, each of which is supported by at least one worker. The interpretation I favor is that specimens such as ER-1813 represent *Homo habilis* and therefore will be found consistently older than *Homo erectus*. A second interpretation is that ER-1813 (and similar specimens) is not a female of *Homo habilis* but rather represents a gracile form of *Australopithecus africanus* that survives past the origin of *Homo erectus* just as the hyper-robust lineage does. This contention, supported by R. E. F. Leakey and others, would imply that only the larger-brained specimens (which I have been calling the males) belong to the ancestral taxon. A third interpretation agrees with the second in suggesting that some of the smaller gracile specimens are not females of *Homo habilis*. This interpretation, held by workers such as C. L. Brace, would make them females of early *Homo erectus* (implying that ER-3733 was male). If there is a bright side, it is that at least no worker has suggested that these "problem" specimens are females of the hyper-robust lineage!

Despite such problems, the discoveries of the past several years have probably created more agreement than disagreement concerning hominid evolution. While debates and disagreements continue, they concern finer and finer points as accumulating discoveries provide a firmer basis for understanding which interpretations cannot be correct, and what evidence is needed to decide between those that might be.

FURTHER READINGS

DANIELS, F., P. W. POST, and B. E. JOHNSON. 1972. Theories of the Role of Pigment in the Evolution of Human Races. In *Pigmentation: Its Genesis and Biologic Control*, ed. V. Riley. Appleton-Century-Crofts, New York, pp. 13–22.

An excellent review of the state of the art for hypotheses concerning the function and distribution of skin color.

DAY, M. H. 1976a. Hominid Postcranial Remains from the East Rudolf Succession. In *Earliest Man and Environments in the Lake Rudolf Basin*, eds. Y. Coppens, F. C. Howell, G. L. Isaac, and R. E. F. Leakey. University of Chicago Press, Chicago, pp. 507–521.

———. 1976b. Hominid Postcranial Material from Bed I, Olduvai Gorge. In *Human Origins: Louis Leakey and the East African Evidence*, eds. G. L. Isaac and E. R. McCown. Benjamin, Menlo Park, pp. 363–374.

These two papers provide the best overview of the East African postcranial remains.

ENDO, B. 1970. Analysis of Stresses Around the Orbits due to Masseter and Temporalis Muscles Respectively. *Journal of the Anthropological Society of Nippon* 78:569–573.

One presentation of Endo's biomechanical model for browridge function.

Isaac, G. L. 1971. The Diet of Early Man: Aspects of Archaeological Evidence from Lower and Middle Pleistocene Sites in Africa. *World Archaeology* 2:278–299.

A discussion of earlier Pleistocene dietary changes reflected in the archaeological record.

Laughlin, W. S. 1968. Hunting: An Integrating Biobehavioral System and Its Evolutionary Importance. In *Man the Hunter*, eds. R. B. Lee and I. DeVore. Aldine, Chicago, pp. 304–320.

An excellent presentation of the consequences of a hunting adaptation in hominids.

Leakey, L. S. B. 1966. *Homo habilis, Homo erectus*, and the Australopithecines. *Nature* 209:1279–1281.

One view of the relations between these taxa as represented in East Africa.

———, P. V. Tobias, and J. R. Napier. 1964. A New Species of the Genus *Homo* from Olduvai Gorge. *Nature* 202:7–9.

The original definition of the taxon *Homo habilis*.

Leakey, R. E. F. 1972. New Fossil Evidence for the Evolution of Man. *Social Biology* 19:99–114.

A discussion of the earlier Lake Turkana (Rudolf) remains with emphasis on sexual dimorphism in the hyper-robust forms.

———. 1976. An Overview of the Hominidae from East Rudolf, Kenya. In: *Earliest Man and Environments in the Lake Rudolf Basin*, eds. Y. Coppens, F. C. Howell, G. L. Isaac, and R. E. F. Leakey. University of Chicago Press, Chicago. pp. 476–483.

A brief review of the Turkana discoveries as of 1976 with a complete bibliography for the *American Journal of Physical Anthropology* descriptions.

———, and A. C. Walker. 1976. *Australopithecus, Homo erectus* and the Single Species Hypothesis. *Nature* 261:572–574.

The first announcement of ER-3733 and its implications for the single-species hypothesis applied to East Africa.

Lovejoy, C. O. 1975. Biomechanical Perspectives on the Lower Limb of Early Hominids. In *Primate Functional Morphology and Evolution*, ed. R. H. Tuttle. Mouton, The Hague, pp. 291–326, 560–561.

Probably the most complete functional analysis of the lower limb remains.

Newman, R. W. 1970. Why Man Is Such a Sweaty and Thirsty Animal: A Speculative Review. *Human Biology* 42:12–27.

A thorough discussion of the hominid heat adaptation.

Peters, C. R. 1979. Toward an Ecological Model of African Plio-Pleistocene Hominid Adaptations. *American Anthropologist.* 81:261–278.

A useful discussion of ecology, adaptation, and hominid speciation.

Schaller, G. B., and G. Lowther. 1969. The Relevance of Carnivore Behavior to the Study of Early Hominids. *Southwestern Journal of Anthropology* 25:307–341.

One presentation of the carnivore model of early hominid evolution and the origin of complex social behavior.

Tobias, P. V. 1965. New Discoveries in Tanganyika: Their Bearing on Hominid Evolution. *Current Anthropology* 6:391–411.

The argument for the existence of *Homo habilis* as a distinct taxon as presented before the discovery of fairly complete material.

———. 1967. *The Cranium and Maxillary Dentition of Zinjanthropus (Australopithecus) boisei.* Olduvai Gorge, Vol. II. Cambridge, London.

The best account of the morphology and phylogeny of a hyper-robust australopithecine.

———. 1978. The Earliest Transvaal Members of the Genus *Homo* with Another Look at Some Problems of Hominid Taxonomy and Systematics. *Zeitschrift für Morphologie und Anthropologie* 69:225–265.

A thoughtful account of the current status of *Homo habilis* in terms of its grade and clade, and the position of the Sterkfontein and Swartkrans fossils (STW-53 and SK-847) proposed as members contemporary with australopithecines.

———, and G. H. R. von Koenigswald. 1964. A Comparison Between the Olduvai Hominines and Those of Java, and Some Implications for Hominid Phylogeny. *Nature* 204:515–518.

An explicit model for the position of *Homo habilis* in early hominid evolution.

Walker, A. 1976. Remains Attributable to *Australopithecus* in the East Rudolf Succession. In *Earliest Man and Environment in the Lake Rudolf Basin*, eds. Y. Coppens, F. C. Howell, G. L. Isaac, and R. E. F. Leakey. University of Chicago, pp. 484–489.

A thoughtful discussion of the East African hyper-robust forms in an adaptive context, and their relations to *Homo habilis*.

———, and R. E. F. Leakey. 1978. The Hominids of East Turkana. *Scientific American* 239(2):54–66.

An illustrated review and analysis of the late australopithecine and early *Homo erectus* material, considering the various possible interpretations of their relationships.

CHAPTER NINE

The Spread of Humanity

O ne of the most important consequences of the adaptive shift involved in *Homo erectus* origins was habitat expansion. With the additional food resources available through organized hunting, groups were able to make use of new habitats. Also, as discussed in the preceding chapter, the hunting groups required a wider geographic range. Combined, these resulted in the spread of *Homo erectus* outside of Africa. By a date which may be as early as 1.4 million years ago, the human populations inhabited most of the tropical and subtropical regions of the Old World (see Map 2).

Once established in new geographic areas, human populations began a process of adaptation which ultimately led to accumulating adaptive differences. However, this did not happen at once. For some period of time, evolutionary changes in various parts of the world paralleled each other. While gene flow among populations was undoubtedly a contributing factor, I believe that the parallel evolutionary changes were mainly the result of the level of adaptive sophistication. The technology and

social organization of these early hunters simply did not allow marked differences in adaptation, even when habitats, and the opportunities they presented, varied from place to place.

The populations involved in this initial spread of humanity represent that portion of the hominid lineage commonly regarded as *Homo erectus*. The chapter begins with a discussion of the Acheulean industrial complex, which appeared about 1½ million years ago and lasted at least as long as the Oldowan complex. The development of the Acheulean complex relates to the adaptive grade characterizing the early *Homo erectus* populations, and its evolution parallels and intertwines with the morphological changes in the lineage. Following this is an examination of the earliest *Homo erectus* populations outside of Africa, comparing them with the earlier or contemporary Africans. A third section deals with subsequent evolutionary changes in four geographic areas with well-represented hominid samples: Indonesia, China, Africa, and Europe. The chapter concludes with a summary of the main morphological trends in *Homo erectus*, presenting an adaptive model to account for the changes.

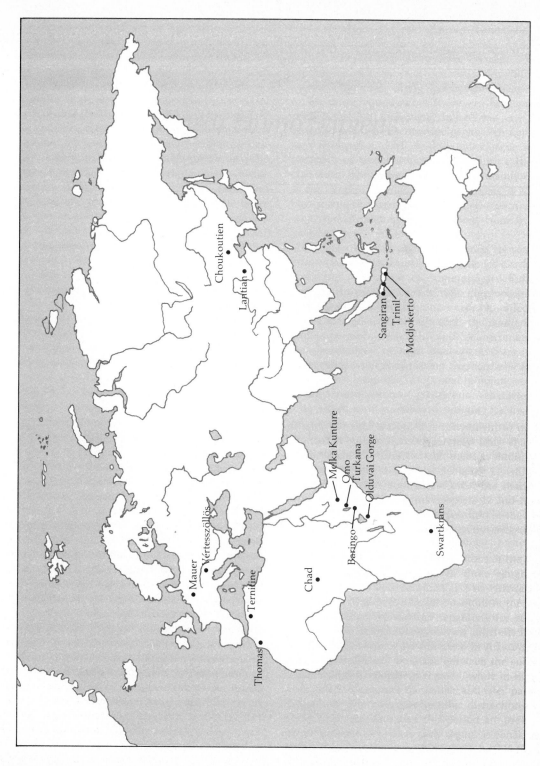

MAP 2 *Geographic positions of the main* Homo erectus *sites.*

Choukoutien

Lantian

Sangiran
Trinil
Modjokerto

Melka Kunture
Omo
Turkana
Olduvai Gorge
Baringo
Swartkrans

Vértesszöllös
Mauer
Ternifine
Chad
Thomas

Appearance and Importance of the Acheulean Industrial Complex

A recognizable change in hominid stone tool industries was concurrent with the initial geographic spread. It is not clear whether there was a causal relation or whether the expansion in range and the technological changes were both aspects of the same developing adaptive pattern. Whatever the case, the changes in technology had clear adaptive consequences and, more indirectly, helped orient the direction of morphological evolution. These technological changes can be best documented in East Africa, where the archaeological record has enough time depth for us to trace their origin and subsequent development.

By the time of middle Bed II at Olduvai, a more complex, better-made tool set was being manufactured (Figure 10.9, pp. 242-243). Many of these tools were made from large flakes that were first struck from cores. Some workers have suggested that it was this innovation of producing large flakes to be worked into tools that underlay or stimulated the developments that followed. Stone tool industries of this sort, called Acheulean, are characterized by the common appearance of a pear-shaped, pointed general-purpose tool called the hand axe or *biface* (since the two edges that meet at the point are the modified ones). It is probable that the Acheulean industries developed from the Oldowan industry. Later Oldowan (called "Developed" Oldowan) is also characterized by bifaces, although cruder in manufacture (i.e., skill in producing the final form) and lower in frequency. The evolution of technology, like that of morphology, seems to have been continuous.

The hand axe is an interesting and important tool. Once it appears, like the earlier Oldowan pebble chopper, it continues to occur right up to the present time. Its shape and the few observations of living people who use similar tools suggest that the hand axe was essentially a paleolithic boy scout knife: an all-purpose tool used for cutting, digging, chopping, woodworking, drilling, and so on. The tool underwent considerable change and refinement over its long history. This refinement is probably tied to the evolution of hand-and-eye coordination in hominids. G. L. Isaac suggests that the complexity of design and the precision with which it is executed can help indicate both the level of technological capability and the complexity of rule systems. If this idea is valid, these underwent considerable change during the Oldowan timespan and continued significant change during the Acheulean, extending into the Middle Pleistocene.

The Acheulean complex is characterized by far more than the development and increasing frequency of the hand axe. Numerous new types of tools appear, almost doubling the number of tool types. Many of the tools indicate more concentrated periods of workmanship during their manufacture, and some were resharpened after being used. Large cutting implements form the largest single category of tools, although chopping tools and spheriods are also common. In the earlier assemblages, the vast majority of the tools are unmodified flakes; retouch (or reworking) becomes much more common later.

More important than the expanded range of tool types is the appearance of standardization and consistent refinement of form. The Acheulean tools differ from the haphazardly shaped Oldowan tools in the development of clearly established intent, greater skill, and a more complex set of rules. In this regard, it is interesting that differences between the material cultures of different geographic regions become established during the Acheulean.

The direct adaptive importance of these Acheulean developments is that they make functional specialization possible. Better-made tools, reflecting a more precise superimposing of a preconceived form, can be more usefully applied. The tools themselves show only the broadest functional differences. However, these differences were distinctly reflected in fairly well made forms. This expansion of technology probably helped broaden the resource base and allowed the hominids to make better use of resources in any single habitat.

Finally, it would appear that Acheulean industries were developed by *Homo erectus*. However, there is not a one-to-one relationship between the species and the industry. *Homo erectus* has been found in areas where only Oldowan (or Oldowan-like) industries have been recovered. It would probably be a mistake simply to attribute Oldowan industries to the australopithecines and Acheulean industries to *Homo erectus* in a predictive sense.

Lower Pleistocene Humans Outside of Africa

The evidence showing that humans spread to other continents during the Lower Pleistocene is both paleontological and archaeological, being based on discoveries of fossil hominids and/or their tools.

LOWER PLEISTOCENE EVIDENCE FROM EUROPE

Although to date no hominid remains have been found in Lower Pleistocene deposits in Europe, there are numerous archaeological sites which seem to date from this timespan. Estimated dates in France range from the Lower Pleistocene at Chilhac to the most recent Lower Pleistocene at Vallonet. Other European hominid sites are dated only by the appearance of reversed paleomagnetism (Badger's Hole in France, Stránská Skála in Czechoslovakia) or Lower Pleistocene fauna (Šandalja in Croatia). What the early European sites have in common is the association of Oldowan tools with Lower Pleistocene fauna, often in a context which suggests that the presence of the fauna is the result of hominid hunting or scavenging activities. (At Badger's Hole the remains of sea mammals, including whales, are found in the cave.)

At the French cave site of Escale, which appears to be somewhat younger than Vallonet, there is some evidence suggesting the use of fire. There are traces of ash and charcoal as well as fire-cracked rocks and circles of reddened earth up to a yard in diameter that suggest hearth areas. This may be the earliest evidence of fire use by hominids, although we cannot be certain because the date is unclear.

The question is who was making the fire, manufacturing the Oldowan tools, and hunting? Associations of a human species and tool types on an *a priori* basis are impossible. One cannot say definitely that australopithecines made Oldowan tools, erectus made Acheulean tools, and so on. The association of humans with specific behaviors, on the other hand, may be possible since it is changes in behavior that change the selection acting on human morphology. In this case, the combination of hunting and the use of fire suggests that it is an early population of *Homo erectus*, rather than of australopithecines, that is responsible for the earliest known European habitation.

EARLY HOMINID SPECIMENS FROM THE PEOPLE'S REPUBLIC OF CHINA (PRC)

Hominid remains of Lower Pleistocene age have been reported from three regions: a lower first molar discovered in a drugstore in the Badong District, Hupei Province; three lower molars from Dragonbone cave in the Jianshi District, Hupei Province; and a pair of upper central incisors from the Yuanmou site in Yunnan Province.

Initial analysis of the molars led to the conclusion that their closest affinities were to *Australopithecus africanus*. However, some workers now dispute that conclusion. The molars are quite large. In grinding area, they are above the average for the East African Pleistocene australopithecines. Two of the teeth are a pair (from opposite sides of the jaw) with what appears to be an anomalous morphology. The other two differ from the normal australopithecine condition in that they are relatively elongated in contrast to the relative broadening found in the African samples.

The Yuanmou incisors are also somewhat anomalous in that they lack contact facets for the lateral (adjacent) incisors. Morphologically, these teeth resemble australopithecine incisors and are distinct from many *Homo erectus* specimens because the Yuanmou teeth lack internal marginal ridges. These ridges are especially characteristic of the later Chinese *Homo erectus* sample from Choukoutien (see below).

I doubt that the question of possible australopithecine affinities for these specimens can be decided on the basis of teeth alone (and even if it could, the evidence presented is mixed). Determining affinities is difficult enough with relatively complete mandibles. However, although the dates are not completely clear, at present there appears to be good evidence for a megadont (large-toothed) early hominid on the Asian mainland. While I do not believe that it is an australopithecine, only the future discovery of cranial remains can resolve this issue.

However, if it is true that only early *Homo erectus* is found outside of Africa in the Lower Pleistocene, the tooth size range of the early Asian hominids provides an expected range for early *Homo erectus* in Africa, where problems of taxonomic association are confused by the presence of two taxa. The early PRC specimens have a molar size range which extends beyond the presently accepted upper limit of the early African *Homo erectus* range. In fact, the largest teeth match some *Australopithecus boisei* specimens in size, although none of the teeth from Asia shows an equivalent degree of multiple cusp addition. This suggests that larger-toothed early *Homo erectus* specimens may yet be found (or identified) in Africa.

There is every reason to believe that considerably more material from this timespan will be discovered in China. An important artifact site (Hsihoutu Village) has been found in Lower Pleistocene deposits in Shansi Province. These sites verify the early occupation of China by hominids which are probably best regarded as members of the genus *Homo*.

EARLY INDONESIAN HOMINIDS

The earliest fairly complete hominid material from outside of Africa has been found in Indonesia, where, interestingly, human fossils were first systematically sought. E. Haeckel, a German evolutionist of the last century, actually named the fossil that he presumed would be found there "Pithecanthropus"—the ape (Pithec) man (anthropus). His student, E. Dubois, went to Indonesia to find this fossil, and in 1891 he did! This was only the first of many specimens, ranging from the early Pleistocene to modern times, to be discovered on the island of Java, which was once connected to mainland Asia.

The stratigraphic sequence on Java is broken into three broad horizons, mainly on the basis of faunal differences. Each horizon represents a great time range. The earliest of these, the Djetis, is Lower Pleistocene in age. One series of radiometric dates suggests that it may extend into the Pliocene, but this is far from certain. Whatever the case, hominid remains have been found in the upper (latest) one-third of the Djetis horizon. In a very general sense, these probably correspond in age to the Lower Pleistocene *Homo erectus* specimens found in Africa. Above the Djetis lies the Trinil horizon of the Middle Pleistocene. *Homo erectus* is also found in these

strata. Finally, atop the Trinil lies the Ngandong horizon, which is also hominid-bearing (see Chapter 10).

At present, the remains of at least ten hominids have been reported from the Djetis formation at the Sangiran site. Only a few of these were actually discovered in their natural stratigraphic position; most of the others were purchased from local villagers, and consequently only an approximate stratigraphic position is known for them. Two of the specimens with known positions are crania (one early and the other late in the sequence), and the others are mandibles.

Of these Djetis-level crania, the earliest is a skullcap of a child approximately eight-to-ten years of age. This cranium from Perning (formerly called the "Modjokerto skull") may have a fairly early date within the sequence and may even be as old as the early African *Homo erectus* specimens. Like some of these crania, it has a small capacity, about 650 cc, which would have been only slightly larger had the child survived to adulthood. Even at its young age, *Homo erectus* characteristics such as a browridge, nuchal torus, and spongy bone development at the cranial base (Figure 8.4) had begun to appear.

The second partial cranium is that of an adult male; it is from the very top of the Djetis and is probably less than a million years old. This specimen, consisting of the back of a cranium and a palate, represents the fourth hominid recovered from the Sangiran area. (A tooth once thought to be an associated incisor is actually a canine from another individual.) Sangiran 4 shows a more dramatic expression of *Homo erectus* features (including vault thickening, spongy bone development at the cranial base, and a thick backward-projecting nuchal torus) than any of the males from Africa. Additional thickening of the vault occurs at the midline, where a keel runs lengthwise along the top of the skull, and also along the line marking the uppermost attachment of the temporalis muscle (Figures 8.7 and 9.3). These buttresses almost certainly are present to provide additional strength to the vault.

The associated palate is primitive in some respects. For instance, the large canines projected below the level of the adjacent teeth, and there was a diastema (gap) between them and the lateral incisors. The latter is not an unusual feature since, of the six isolated canines from the Djetis, two did not actually touch the adjacent incisors. A large Middle

Pleistocene male, Sangiran 17, also has this feature. Yet other features of the palate contrast with the australopithecine condition. Although the anterior teeth were prognathic, the prognathism is much reduced compared with that in the earlier hominids. The lower face is shortened, but both the palate and the nasal opening are greatly broadened. The palate is very large relative to the size of the teeth. Also, the base of the cheeks is in a posterior position.

Djetis Mandibles

The sample of mandibles from the Djetis is only approximately dated, with one exception. This is the fairly early specimen from Kedungbrubus, which may be as old as the Perning cranium. In a recent examination of the fragmentary specimen, P. V. Tobias established that it belonged to a juvenile, with the P_3 in the process of erupting. Its other characteristics are extreme robustness (relative thickness of the body) and the presence of two well-defined internal buttresses on the inside of the symphyseal area. Positions of the other mandibles are less clear, although most of them can be related to the horizon. Although many of the remaining mandibles may be outside the australopithecine time range, it is interesting that both large and small teeth and mandibles have been found in the Djetis (see Figure 9.1, p. 190). The robust specimens were once placed in the genus "Meganthropus." F. Weidenreich saw this genus as a link between *Homo erectus* and its presumed giant "ancestor" *Gigantopithecus*. J. T. Robinson, on the other hand, claimed that "Meganthropus" was a robust australopithecine, which evoked a negative reply from G. H. R. von Koenigswald and began a debate that has continued to the present. It has become evident that teeth and mandibles alone cannot be used to distinguish australopithecines and *Homo erectus* without associated cranial material, except at the extremes of the ranges.

Two aspects of the mandibular sample are of interest. First, the marked size differences may correspond to a degree of sexual dimorphism as great as in the australopithecines. The fact that both the smaller and larger forms seem to reduce over time helps support this interpretaton. Second, the sample as a whole overlaps with the australopithecines in both size and morphology. On the average, these

are the largest specimens attributed to *Homo erectus* outside of Africa. That they are also among the earliest is probably not a coincidence.

Djetis Dental Remains

A large number of isolated teeth have been collected by G. H. R. von Koenigswald. He believes that it is possible to distinguish the earlier specimens associated with Djetis fauna from the later specimens associated with Trinil fauna on the basis of their color and fossilization. The dental sample attributed to the Djetis, including the teeth in the jaws discussed above, features very large posterior tooth size. The average size is large, about the same as that for *Homo habilis*. However, like the early Chinese specimens, the molar teeth are relatively elongated. The anterior teeth are also large, especially in breadth. Because of the shape difference in the molars and the fact that none of the jaws shows definitive australopithecine characteristics, it is my opinion that these teeth indicate large tooth size in early *Homo erectus* rather than the presence of an australopithecine group outside of Africa.

WHO WAS THERE?

From the dated tool- and hominid-bearing sites, it seems evident that a hominid that was most likely *Homo erectus* spread throughout the Old World tropics and subtropics soon after it evolved as a recognizably distinct species on the lineage. Morphologically, many of the early specimens are robust in their jaws and teeth, with features associated with powerful chewing that are only moderately different from those of the australopithecines in some cases, and with ranges of variation that overlap with the earlier hominids. The brain size expansion in the known sample is anything but dramatic, and marked sexual dimorphism appears to have been maintained. Yet the morphological complex that distinguishes the early African *Homo erectus* sample from the australopithecines is present, and the trends in the lineage are recognizable if not better expressed. Whether these trends form a unique evolutionary direction as a consequence of hunting remains unproven, but it is the best explanation of the evolutionary trends and the expanding hominid range that has been suggested.

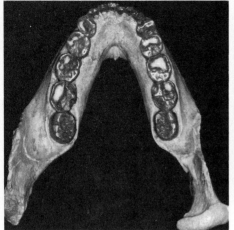

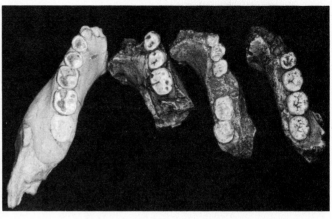

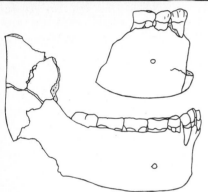

FIGURE 9.1   Comparison of some of the Homo erectus mandibles from Indonesia and an Australopithecus from Makapansgat and Lake Natron. Above (left to right) are occlusal views of the Natron mandible, MLD–40, and Sangiran 6, 9, and 1. All specimens are casts. Sangiran 1 is female, and the other two Sangiran mandibles are male. The largest male, Sangiran 6 (formerly attributed to "Meganthropus"), has a mandibular body as thick (above view) and as tall (drawing below) as the Natron australopithecine female, although the posterior teeth are much smaller and the P₄ is not molariform. Australopithecine-like features are also seen in Sangiran 9; the shape of the tooth row forms a "V" similar to that found in much earlier hominid specimens from the Afar and Lake Turkana (ER-1482).

What the few specimens show is that the earliest hominids outside of Africa were not much different from their African contemporaries and presumed ancestors. These specimens are australopithecine-like in their combination of small cranial capacity and expanded posterior teeth, but those features that are diagnostic are clearly not australopithecine. Both their projected dating and their complex of morphological features identifies them as early populations of *Homo erectus*.

Homo erectus *of the Middle Pleistocene: Continued Change*

The Pleistocene is divided into lower, middle, and upper stages. The division between the first two is now generally agreed to conform to the last major reversal of the magnetic poles, resulting in the "normal" polarity existing today. Radiometrically, a date of about 700,000 years BP probably best marks the end of the Lower Pleistocene (Table 8.1).

By that time, *Homo erectus* populations had spread throughout the tropics and semitropics of the Old World. These populations underwent considerable further evolution in a variety of different habitats and continued their geographic spread into temperate climates during the Middle Pleistocene. To some degree, genetic continuity appears to have been localized, at least over broad geographic areas; however, the occurrence of both cultural and genetic communication throughout the species is indicated by the fact that similar technological and morphological changes characterize populations as much as 10,000 miles apart.

Because of this combination of localized continuity and species-wide changes, it is convenient to discuss the main evolutionary trends in later *Homo erectus* by geographic area. The best sample spanning this period is from Asia. The African sample consists mainly of jaws, and *Homo erectus* remains appear in Europe only at the very end of the time range for the species, approximately 400,000 years ago.

The Sequence in Asia: Cranial Evolution

Asia provides the best evidence of continued cranial changes in *Homo erectus* during the Middle Pleistocene. The earliest specimen is Sangiran 4 (discussed above) from the very top of the Djetis horizon on Java. Stratigraphically above it is a series of crania associated with Trinil fauna; a date from near the top of the Trinil series is 500,000 years BP, while crania from the middle portions are dated to 830,000 years BP. In south China, a single cranium from Lantian is approximately the same age as the Trinil age specimens, and the Choukoutien cave site is later still (perhaps only 450,000 years old). Thus from Asia one can piece together about a half-million years of evolutionary change for *Homo erectus*.

INDONESIAN CRANIA

The earlier Middle Pleistocene crania from Java come from three sites, all associated with Trinil fauna. These sites are Sangiran, Trinil, and Sambungmachen. The last may be somewhat younger, and although the skullcap from Sambungmachen is clearly related to the Trinil and Sangiran specimens, it will be discussed in Chapter 10. Trinil is the site where the first *Homo erectus* cranium was discovered (Trinil 2), as well as six femurs of less certain associations. The majority of the specimens come from the Sangiran site—five fairly complete crania (Sangiran 2, 3, 10, 12, and 17) plus a number of cranial fragments. Stratigraphically, Sangiran 3 is the oldest and Sangiran 10 the youngest.

Sangiran 17 is virtually complete, while the other specimens consist of skullcaps and occasional facial fragments. The specimens fall into two size groups, larger and smaller, which almost certainly correspond to males and females. All of the specimens

exhibit expanded cranial vaults (especially in length and breadth of the braincase and of frontal constriction), thickened cranial bone, a distinct angulation of the cranial sides at the temporal line, basal spongy bone development, thick projecting browridges separated from the forehead by a broad groove (sulcus), and greatly expanded nuchal muscle attachments (see Figure 9.2, p. 192).

The females (Trinil 2, Sangiran 2, 3, and 10) are smaller and thinner than the males and have much weaker muscle-attachment-related features (temporal line, nuchal plane) and cranial buttresses (sagittal keel, browridge, nuchal torus). The zygomatic bone associated with Sangiran 10 is quite small, and an isolated lower face, Sangiran 15b, has a shallow palate and short facial height.

The males (Sangiran 12 and 17) are much larger and more robustly developed. Two important sex-related features are the larger mastoids and the marked projection of the central portion of the nuchal torus. Sangiran 17 (see Figure 9.3, p. 193) is the only known complete *Homo erectus* male cranium. As I have reconstructed it, the face combines moderate height with marked flaring cheek development and very pronounced facial prognathism. Where comparable, there is more sexual dimorphism in the facial dimensions than in the vault. It is likely that the marked prognathism is a regional clade feature since prognathism in living populations is greatest in the Australasian area.

Indeed, other systematic differences distinguish the Indonesian *Homo erectus* sample from both the African remains and the Choukoutien sample (see below). Figure 9.4, p. 194, compares crania from Indonesia and Choukoutien. Compared with the African sample, holding sex constant, the Indonesian specimens have much thicker vaults, less projecting browridges, greater nuchal muscle area and nuchal torus development, and more marked development of the sagittal keel and the thickening and angulation at the temporal line. Although the same sex cannot be compared, the Sangiran 17 face is much more prognathic than the ER-3733 face.

A CONTEMPORARY FROM CHINA

The early cranium from Lantian, in south China, is similar to the Indonesian specimens. The 780 cc cranial capacity is smaller than that of any cranium yet reported from Indonesia except the early Pern-

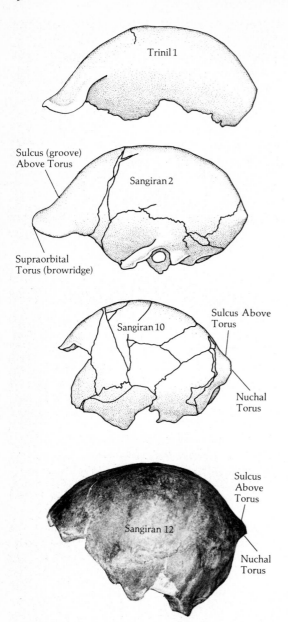

FIGURE 9.3   On page 193, comparison of the author's Sangiran 17 reconstruction (right) with a cast of the Lantian reconstruction. The specimens are not shown at the same scale, and the mandible used in the Lantian reconstruction is from a different individual. The back of the Lantian vault is missing.

ing specimen and a new undescribed natural endocast. Notable features include a very low cranial height and a marked narrowing of the frontal behind the orbits. The forehead is very low and appears to have a sagittal keel, although this is somewhat distorted due to crushing. Both the cranial bones and the supraorbital torus (browridge) are extraordinarily thick; the parietal thickness exceeds that of all other *Homo erectus* specimens. While the browridges project markedly, they differ from those of the Indonesian specimens in that they are not continuous over the nose. The central portions arch downward and do not actually meet at the middle of the face. A large portion of the left temporal bone is heavily buttressed and shows the beginning of what was probably a very broad temporal fossa. In sum, the vault shows a combination of small brain size, lack of frontal expansion, thickening of the vault bone and buttressing, and bony evidence of powerful chewing that aligns it with early *Homo erectus*. Other features may reflect individual variation or a difference in clade.

The reconstructed face is broad but neither tall nor robust, contrasting with the vault in a manner which is parallel but not identical to Sangiran 17. The palate is broad and deep, with widely spaced incisor sockets for the (missing) anterior teeth. The base of the cheek begins in a more anterior position than is the case in the Indonesian palates, but the distinct canine fossa (groove between the side of the nose and the cheek) resembles that in the Sangiran 17 face. The lower face is only moderately prognathic, and the lower margin of the nose shows the remnants of a projecting nasal spine. Below this margin, the lower portion of the face is extremely flat, resembling Sangiran 4. It is unfortunate that almost completely opposite portions of the vault are preserved in Sangiran 4 and the Lantian cranium, since it is my impression that these specimens are very similar.

FIGURE 9.2   The first Trinil cranium (top) and the three earlier Sangiran crania from the Trinil horizon are shown in this view, and the main characteristics of the cranial buttressing system are labeled. In most cases, the torus (nuchal or supraorbital) is separated from the bone above it by a broad groove, or sulcus. The nuchal torus is especially variable. Its extreme development in Sangiran 12 suggests the individual may be a male. All four of the vaults lack both the face and the cranial base.

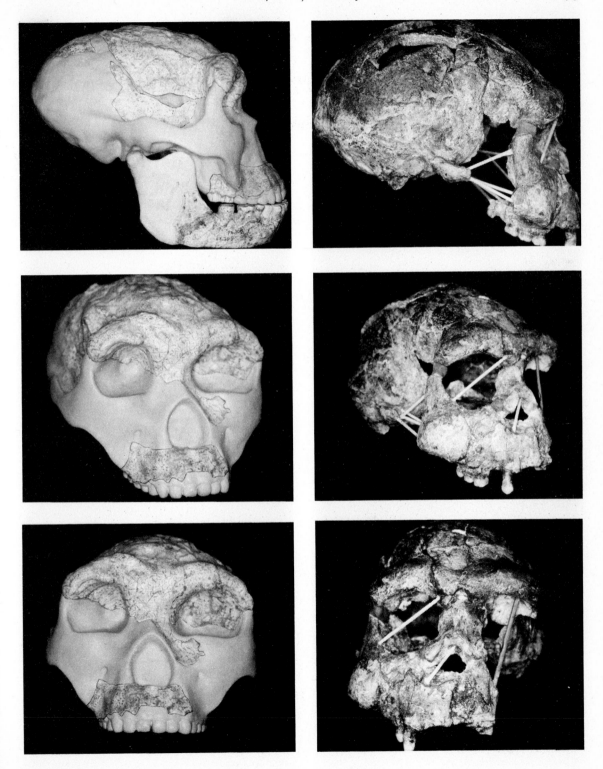

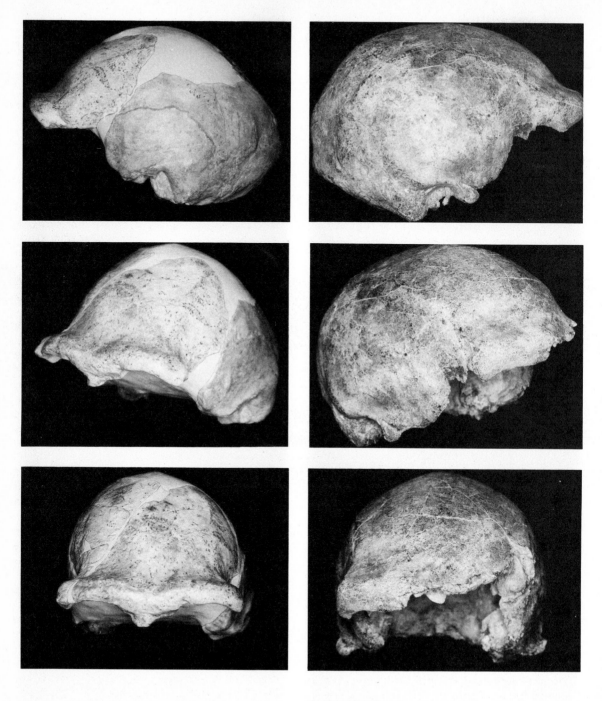

FIGURE 9.4   Comparison of the Sambungmachen cranium (right) and the Choukoutien cranium 5 reconstruction. Both specimens are late in the Homo erectus sequence in their respective areas. Note differences in the sulcus above the browridge, the frontal bulge, and the nuchal torus.

CHOUKOUTIEN

The Choukoutien sample is a large and diverse collection. Specimens were discovered in both excavations prior to World War II as well as in those initiated after the war and continuing to the present. The excavations have resulted in one of the largest hominid collections from a single site. Moreover, a series of papers and monographs on the prewar specimens by F. Weidenreich provides what are probably the most detailed descriptions and analyses of any fossil hominid collection. This is fortunate because all of the earlier material disappeared during World War II under circumstances that have never been clarified to anyone's satisfaction.

The Choukoutien site consists of a cave that is part of a cave complex located not far from the modern city of Peking. Some 400,000 to 500,000 years ago, humans lived in the rock shelter portion of the cave at or near its opening. Choukoutien represents the most northern temperate extension of *Homo erectus*; the climate then was not much different from today's, which is similar to that in the northern United States in seasonal extremes and temperature averages. During the span of the human occupation, the climate oscillated between colder and warmer several times. The cave lay on an ecotone border between evergreen forest and lower, more open grasslands.

The Choukoutien hominids were evidently big-game hunters, bringing kills back into the cave from both the forested areas and the open grasslands. Most of the animal remains belong to two species of red deer; the hunters concentrated on these prey and utilized them intensively for long periods of time. Yet none of the artifacts from the cave is clearly associated with hunting; cave activities included tool making (modification of wood and bone) and the preparation of vegetable foods. One whole layer in the deposit contains dense concentrations of hackberry seeds, and these are also scattered within other layers. In addition, there are broken ostrich egg shells (which might also have served as containers) and some pointed bones and antlers that were probably used for digging.

One final important aspect of this temperate occupation is the evidence of the use of fire. The cave deposits include at least four thick layers of ash. The latest represents an open occupation after the cave roof had collapsed. In this case, the ashes are concentrated in two spots, suggesting that the fire was confined to a specific area. In the other layers, human fossil remains are found near the ash deposits. These layers also contain scorched stones and bones. Most workers feel that while the Chou-koutien inhabitants could contain and use fire, the ash layers are not persistent enough to show that they could make it at will. The importance of fire in the winter adaptation and for cooking could hardly be overstated.

At first glance, the cranial sample that has been recovered to date appears surprisingly homogeneous (see Figure 9.5, p. 196). F. Weidenreich argued that there was no systematic difference between specimens from the top to the bottom of the cave, but in a more recent discussion P. Chia and others have claimed that systematic changes can be seen. There are a number of morphological features which, although differing in expression, characterize the sample. While larger than the earlier specimens from China and Indonesia, the Choukoutien crania are still basically long and low, with the greatest breadth at the cranial base and the greatest braincase breadth just above it and far to the rear of the skull (Figure 9.8). A distinct cranial buttressing system includes basal spongy bone continuous with the nuchal torus, a sagittal keel extending over both the frontal and parietals, and a continuous browridge (supraorbital torus). The low vault and large nuchal torus result in a very angled occiput, but in contrast to earlier specimens, there is a distinct bulge in the center of the frontal bone. This feature results in a higher forehead and accentuates the sulcus between the browridge and the forehead.

In spite of their similarities, the Choukoutien crania should not be thought of as a uniform sample. Superimposed on the "grade" features held in common, there is considerable variation at the site, as there is at all human fossil sites where there are more than a very few specimens. For instance, the Choukoutien crania vary greatly in length, and cranial capacities range from 915 cc to 1,225 cc.

The cranial variation that occurs is not regular enough to all be considered simply sexual dimorphism. Weidenreich noted that if muscle markings are used to suggest sexes for the specimens, there are both large and small males and females. He concluded that sexual dimorphism could not account for all the size variation and instead suggested the presence of a small and a large "type."

All of the crania Weidenreich examined were broken open at the base, and the faces were detached. In one specimen, he attempted to reconstruct the face using an associated maxillary fragment. Now that other *Homo erectus* faces are

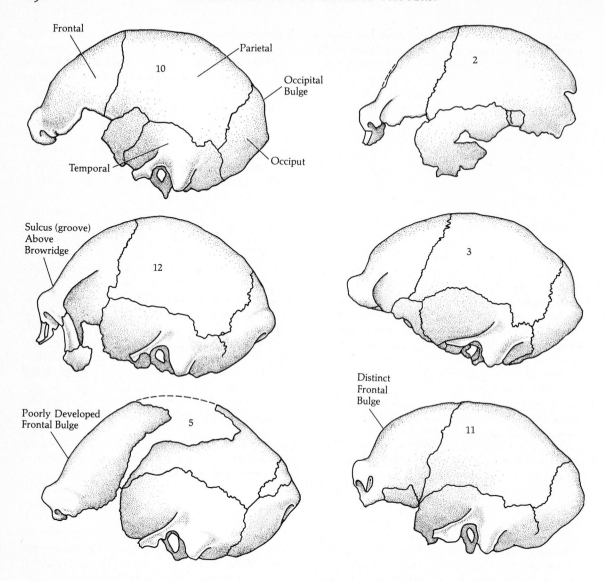

FIGURE 9.5   *The six most complete of the Choukoutien crania, drawn to the same scale.*

known, it is apparent that this reconstruction was fairly accurate, although the face was probably broader and taller. The reconstructed face of the female cranium combines a high cheek region and large orbits with a very reduced tooth-bearing portion of the maxilla. The nasal bones are broad and relatively curved, and (as in the later-discovered faces) the nose opening is broad. However, contrasting with Indonesian specimens, the lower face (as reconstructed) is not especially prognathic except just at the level of the alveolar margin (the region of the jaw holding the teeth) in the area holding large incisor roots with their vertically oriented crowns. The base of the small zygomatic is rather high above the palate, and there is a very distinct angle between the cheek and the external palate wall. In these latter features, the maxilla used in the reconstruction resembles two additional partial maxillas from the site.

The face reconstructed by Weidenreich was the

first known for *Homo erectus*, and thus has usually been considered representative of the taxon. However, the specimen is very late in the lineage and moreover is a female; the gracility and small size have been misleading. Comparison of the reconstruction with the earlier male face from Sangiran and the much earlier East African specimens provides a number of significant contrasts. On the average, *Homo erectus* faces are larger and more robust than supposed when the reconstructed face was the only one known.

Dental Trends

Two important developments mark the Choukoutien dental sample. First, there is significant posterior reduction when compared with the earlier *Homo erectus* samples from Indonesia or Africa. The reduction is not uniform; it affects the posterior molars more than the other teeth. The Indonesian sample is about midway between the australopithecine and Choukoutien averages. When the samples are arranged in temporal order, there is a clear and consistent trend to reduce posterior tooth size (and in some cases cusp number). However, while there is a significant average difference between the Choukoutien sample and earlier hominids, the range of variation for individuals still overlaps with the smaller australopithecine dentitions.

The second development is in the anterior dentition. While there is no average difference between later australopithecines and early *Homo erectus* in any anterior teeth, some expansion occurs in the later-dated Choukoutien maxillary anteriors. There is marked expansion in the I^2, represented by transverse breadth, although little change occurs in the I^1. As a result, the central and lateral maxillary incisors are close to equal in size.

In his discussion of the Choukoutien dental sample, F. Weidenreich argued that most of the teeth clearly fit a large and a small form that correspond to a distinct sex difference. Morphological differences between male and female dentitions are mainly restricted to the canines. If his attributions are correct, the degree of sexual dimorphism in the Choukoutien dental sample is little different from that in the australopithecine dental sample. This contrasts with the seemingly reduced dimorphism in the Choukoutien crania.

Choukoutien Mandibles

There is a fairly large mandibular sample from Choukoutien, including materials discovered after World War II. These mandibles show a considerable amount of variation, more in fact than the crania. Weidenreich also considered this variation to be the result of sexual dimorphism, The two most complete mandibles, labeled H1 and G1, have been interpreted as female and male. If this attribution is correct, it is interesting that the female mandible is too small to fit any of the complete crania, while the male mandible is too large!

The Choukoutien mandibles are characterized by large size and robustness, although both of these features are quite variable. Taken as a whole, the sample is intermediate between the earlier Indonesian specimens and later hominids. The symphysis is large and well angled, although with no trace of a chin. Part of its size seems to be the result of the large anterior tooth roots. The vertical ramus is high, even in the smaller specimens, but not particularly broad. It begins at a position within the posterior tooth row, as in the Indonesian and African erectus mandibles.

A contemporary mandible from Lantian is generally similar to the Choukoutien mandibles. One interesting distinction is the congenital absence of the third molars. This is the earliest known case of missing third molars, a probable consequence of posterior tooth size reduction.

Choukoutien Limbs

A number of postcranial remains are known from Choukoutien. While these can be compared with the first Indonesian femur from Trinil, a pronounced pathology on the bone and some uncertainty in its date limit the value of the comparisons. The Choukoutien postcrania from the original excavations include seven femur fragments, two humerus fragments, a clavicle shaft, and a hand bone. Later excavations have recovered an additional humerus shaft and a tibia shaft.

Basically, the limbs are characterized by adaptations that lend great strength to the bone. An example of these adaptations can be seen in the femurs, which show three modifications to increase the strength of the bone and its ability to withstand compressive and bending forces: relative shaft thickness, anteroposterior flattening of the shaft, and thick cortical bone of the shaft walls. None of these features differs significantly from the australopithecine condition. The Trinil femur is somewhat larger than any from Choukoutien, and its shaft does not show the same degree of anteroposterior flattening.

Relations to the Earlier Specimens

It is evident that the Chinese *Homo erectus* specimens are very closely related to the Indonesian sample. The morphological features that tie these samples together include most of the basic aspects of cranial shape. Although there are differences in average cranial capacity and forehead shape, the Choukoutien and Indonesian specimens share the same long, low, thick vault morphology with its greatest breadth at the cranial base. The cranial buttresses (browridge, nuchal torus, spongy bone development over the mastoids) are equally well developed in both samples, and in both the vaults thicken and angle at the temporal lines. These features suggest a similar grade in the development of the cranial strengthening system, as well as a general equivalence of brain shape.

The features that distinguish the Choukoutien sample from the Indonesian one may reflect differences in clade, although there are also some grade differences. Regional clade may account for the facial distinctions, although sex must also be taken into account since the reconstructed Choukoutien face is female and the best-preserved Sangiran face is male. Other clade differences may be reflected in the forehead form, the difference in frontal sinus development (the sinus is small or absent at Choukoutien but expanded in Indonesia), and some distinctions at the back of the cranial vault. Distinguishing grade and clade differences is still an unsettled issue. However, some obvious grade differences are seen in the brain size expansion and the reduction of sexual dimorphism in the Choukoutien crania. The Choukoutien crania also differ in the "filling out" of certain regions, such as the frontal (mentioned above), the occiput above the nuchal torus, and the sides of the vault. Interestingly, the recently completed cranium 5, which is from much higher in the cave (i.e., later) than the other Choukoutien specimens, continues many of these grade trends (see Figure 9.4). The vault is higher, larger, and thinner than in the other specimens. The browridge is reduced, and the occiput above the nuchal torus is expanded. To the extent that morphological dating is useful, the Choukoutien specimens would seem to be more recent than the bulk of the Indonesian sample.

The African Sequence

DIRECT EVIDENCE OF ADAPTATIONS

Middle Pleistocene *Homo erectus* sites are found all over the African continent, in a variety of different habitats. Our knowledge of occupation sites is no longer dependent on the preservation of bone; most sites are characterized by archaeological materials, while only a few preserve any hominid remains. *Homo erectus* sites are generally found near water—along rivers or streams and on the shores of the ocean or lakes. Most of these sites are in regions characterized by dry grasslands not far from the water; there is no evidence for a true forest habitation. Thus *Homo erectus* populations lived in areas where the greatest concentration of game can be found, and the dependence on water is not unexpected given the hominid pattern of diurnal hunting.

The African sites provide evidence of several different aspects of *Homo erectus* adaptation. Sites can be divided into three main types: family or multifamily camps, kill sites, and gathering sites. The larger camp sites, covering an area of about 150 square feet, may have supported as many as 50 people at a time, while many of the small sites were probably occupied by no more than a family group. Later in the Middle Pleistocene, some sites show evidence of simple structures, perhaps windbreaks or shelters. Another aspect of adaptation is the appearance of special-purpose tool kits. The apparent living sites contain a wide variety of different tools. Tool concentrations at other sites seem to mark the place where an animal was butchered. These tool kits usually comprise many sharpened flakes and a few large cutting implements. The third functional type of site characteristically has a large number of crude bifaces, often attaining a pick-like form. These sites are found near forests or areas of heavy vegetation and are probably associated with gathering activities—digging, chopping and shredding, and perhaps some initial crushing of edible plants.

The archaeological sites indicate that *Homo erectus* hunted medium- and large-sized mammals, including giant baboons. This strongly suggests that hunting was cooperative and organized, perhaps involving several different groups for particularly large animals. The main hunting weapons were likely clubs, modified rocks, and in the later portions of the timespan we find crudely sharpened wooden spears.

Finally, while the various African sites show functional specializations, there is a correspondence with European and Asian sites in the types of tools made, the manufacturing skill, and the activities they seem to represent. The lack of regional differences suggests that in spite of the wide geographic range of *Homo erectus* populations and the differing ecological conditions they encountered, the level of efficiency in exploiting the environment was not high enough to allow particular specializations within the niche.

HOMINIDS FROM OLDUVAI GORGE

Except for a single female mandible found in the later deposits of the Swartkrans australopithecine cave (SK-15), *Homo erectus* specimens are known only from central and northern Africa. The most southern of these hominid-bearing sites is Olduvai Gorge, where the Bed IV deposits begin the Middle Pleistocene sequence. Bed IV is dated to about 600,000–700,000 years ago and is roughly contemporary with the later Trinil horizon deposits in Indonesia. Although the Bed IV sample is small, it includes crania, mandibles, and postcrania.

The mandibles are similar to those from Choukoutien, combining small bodies and reduced posterior teeth. However, body thickness tends to be greater, especially at the symphysis, where one of the specimens (OH-22) has two internal tori and an elongated extension of bone behind the incisors.

There are three fragmentary crania: OH-25 (the parietal of a juvenile with marked spongy bone development), OH-11 (a small palate similar to the Sangiran 4 palate but shallower and with a smoothed nasal margin), and a fragmentary cranium, OH-12. The last is probably from a small female; the capacity is only 738 cc. The walls of the

cranial vault and the browridge are both thin, but otherwise OH-12 resembles OH-9 (from upper Bed II) in its lack of a sharp parietal angle, lack of a distinct sagittal or parietal thickening, and its expanded nuchal torus, which is set off from the occipital above it by a broad groove. The persistence of this combination of features over three-quarters of a million years suggests that they may reflect a regional clade.

The postcrania from Bed IV belong to a single individual, OH-28, represented by most of a large innominate and a femoral shaft. The lever arm for the hamstrings is small (as in australopithecines and living people). The ilium has marked flare, and a thickened pillar extending from the acetabulum to the top of the bone attests to powerful abductor forces.

OTHER SUB-SAHARAN SPECIMENS

To the north, in Kenya, a hominid mandible and four postcrania (a metacarpal, two phalanges, and a virtually complete ulna) have been found in the Kapthurian formation west of Lake Baringo. The site is somewhat more recent than 650,000 years BP (the date of a volcanic tuff below it) and contains a fairly advanced Acheulean industry. The mandible has a thinner body than the Olduvai specimens, and the teeth are smaller. However, the ramus is very broad and high (suggesting that the face was large). The associated ulna is shorter, more curved, and relatively thicker than the complete australopithecine ulna from Omo. It allows a determination of tooth size relative to body size for the Baringo specimen. This relation is very reduced compared to the australopithecine condition.

Four other erectus specimens have been found in this northern area of East Africa. A virtually complete femur (ER-999) comes from the Guomde formation east of Lake Turkana. The walls of the shaft are thicker than in any other erectus femur. This may partly account for the lack of shaft bending (bowing), since a thick shaft can resist forces that cause bending without altering its shape. In shaft shape ER-999 is surprisingly like the Trinil 1 femur and contrasts with the other East African specimen (OH-28) and the Choukoutien femurs: there is little or no flattening of the shaft at its top and midsection. M. H. Day and his co-workers hypothesize that all *Homo erectus* femurs can be distinguished by

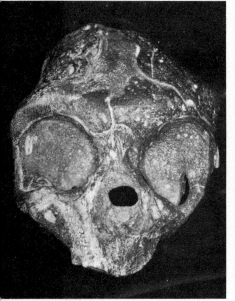
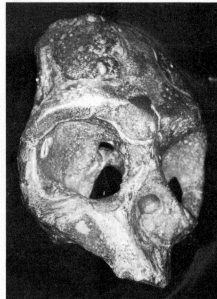
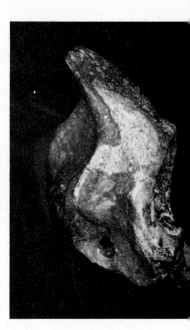

FIGURE 9.6   Three views of the Chad facial fragment.
Note the extreme weathering of the specimen: the supraorbitals have been eroded away, and the lower face below the
nose is not completely preserved to the position of the tooth
roots.

the complex of three strengthening features found
in the Choukoutien sample (thick shafts, thick
shaft walls, and anteroposterior shaft flattening)
and use these criteria to determine which of the
Turkana limbs with ambiguous associations may
represent Homo erectus. However, the morphology
of ER-999 and the Trinil femur contrast with this
model and indicate that other variants are possible
for the taxon.

At a third site in Ethiopia, Gomboré in Melka
Kunture, an extraordinarily thick cranial vault fragment and part of a robust but modern-formed humerus attest to the presence of Homo erectus. Finally,
to the west, a very eroded and weathered frontal-
facial fragment (see Figure 9.6) was discovered in
the vicinity of Lake Chad. The characteristic erectus features of the face include its marked breadth
combined with reduced facial height, relatively
large orbits, and a frontal bulge above the (eroded)
browridge. However, what remains of the lower
face suggests an australopithecine-like prognathism. The region below the nose is actually concave in profile.

THE NORTH AFRICAN SAMPLE

The final African Homo erectus sample comes
from two sites, the Thomas quarry in Morocco and
Ternifine in Algeria. On the basis of faunal remains, a date of about 700,000 years BP has been
suggested for Ternifine. This puts it at the approximate age of Olduvai Bed IV. The material from the
Thomas quarry is somewhat younger, perhaps the
age of the Baringo remains. Three fairly complete
mandibles (see Figure 9.7), a parietal, and some isolated teeth have been found at Ternifine; at the
nearby Thomas quarry, a frontal-facial fragment
with an upper dentition and a mandible of a second
individual have been recovered. Together these

FIGURE 9.7   (A) Four fairly complete **Homo erectus**
mandibles. Above in occlusal view are Ternifine 1 and 2 (upper left and right) and Mauer and Ternifine 3 (lower left
and right). (B) The mandibles in side view. Positions are the
same. Some of the features that can be seen to vary are the
shape of the tooth row, the thickness of the body relative to
the teeth, the divergence and angle of the condyles, the height,
breadth, and angle of the ramus, the curve of the symphysis,
the depth of the notch at the top of the ramus, and the degree
of curvature at the base of the corpus. While various authors
have considered each of these to have great taxonomic importance, they appear to be normal variants for the taxon.

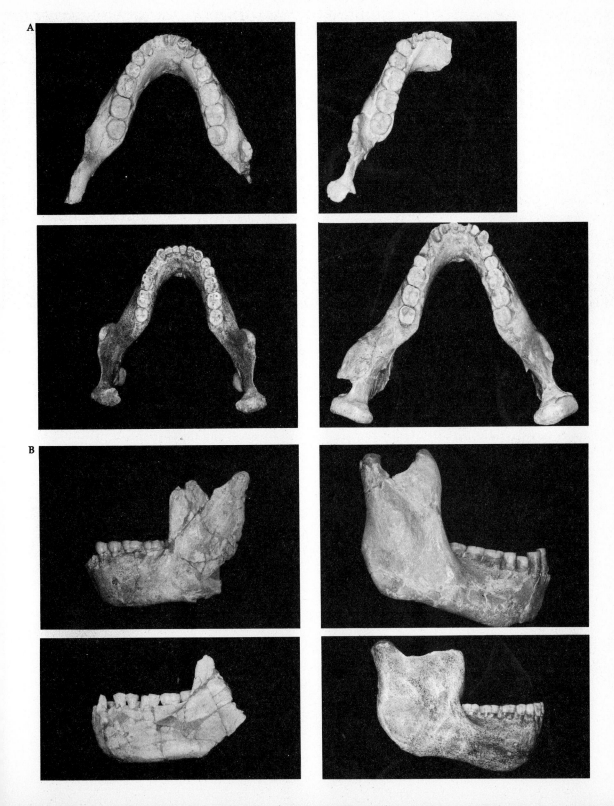

constitute a North African Acheulean-associated erectus sample that shows characteristics of both the sub-Saharan African sample and the earlier sample from Indonesia.

The dental sample includes virtually complete mandibular dentitions (lacking representation of only the central incisor) plus a number of isolated teeth. While posterior tooth size falls within the Choukoutien range, it is consistently above the mean. The anterior teeth are very large; the canines and lateral incisors of two specimens fall above the Choukoutien range. The sample shows clear evidence of canine and incisor expansion compared with earlier Homo erectus. At the same time, relative posterior tooth reduction is marked (although not to the degree at Choukoutien); the third molar is consistently smaller than the second, and at the extreme (in the Thomas mandible) it is even smaller than the first molar. There appears to be no relation between the size of the mandibles and the size of the teeth. In fact, the mandible with the largest body (Ternifine 3) has one of the smaller dentitions, while the considerably smaller Thomas mandible has the largest posterior teeth.

Considered together, the four mandibles have very high, although not particularly broad, corpus dimensions. While they are neither as tall nor as robust as the earliest Indonesian mandibles, their height exceeds that of the sub-Saharan sample and the specimens from Choukoutien. The symphyses have a marked posterior angulation and no trace of a chin, and only Ternifine 3 has any indication of a double buttressing system on the internal surface. The ramus is complete, or virtually complete, in Ternifine 2 and 3. In the former the ramus is broad and low, while in the latter it is even broader and markedly higher (Figure 9.7).

Unfortunately, there are only a few portions of erectus crania from North Africa. The single parietal from Ternifine is probably a different specimen from any of the three represented by the mandibles since it appears to be juvenile. It is quite large, and while it is fairly thin, this may be a result of the individual's youth. Reconstruction suggests that the parietal represents a large cranial vault. A cranial capacity of about 1,300 cc has been estimated.

In contrast to the earlier Ternifine parietal, the frontal-facial fragment from the Thomas quarry (Thomas III) seems to be rather small (perhaps female). However, the browridge is prominent and projects well in front of the orbits. The frontal an-

gle is low. The maxillary dentition (complete from the lateral incisor) is quite large. The incisor and the first two molars fall above the Choukoutien range reflecting the same anterior tooth expansion seen in the mandibles. The third molar is smaller than the second, as is the case in all known erectus palates.

THE AFRICAN SAMPLE AS A WHOLE

The Homo erectus sample from Africa is diverse in time, space, and body parts represented. Yet, with the possible exception of the mandibles, no single skeletal element is present in large enough number to allow really detailed comparisons with other areas, or between the earlier and later portions of the African sample itself.

The two late crania (Thomas III and OH-12) are small compared with earlier African specimens. Some area-specific continuity might be suggested by features including the thin vault bones and rounded contours of OH-12; while the contrast in browridge with the earlier OH-9 could hardly be greater, the structure is similar in the ER-3733 female. The Thomas and Chad faces show basic Homo erectus proportions but provide little new information. In Africa the earlier specimens are mostly males and the later ones females—the opposite of the situation in Indonesia.

Turning to the postcrania, the Olduvai innominate is the only known for the taxon. It resembles the larger australopithecine innominate from Lake Turkana except for some proportional differences due to a larger pelvic inlet. The associated femur is similar to the Choukoutien femurs, while the Turkana femur differs from these but closely resembles the Trinil specimen. Yet the fact that there are equivalent variants in two widely separated areas may be important.

The African mandibles are characterized by marked variability as well as some similarities. For instance, the difference in size between SK-15 from South Africa and Ternifine 3 marks the maximum extent of the known Homo erectus range. Morphological variation also characterizes the sample (see Figure 9.7). At the same time, average characteristics resemble Homo erectus from other regions. Considered in an evolutionary context, the most australopithecine-like aspects are centered about the symphysis. The marked thickening and double torusing seen in some of the specimens are matched in the Kedungbrubus mandible and Sangiran mandibles 6 and 9. These are the three early extra-African specimens with the region preserved. While on the average the African mandibles are larger and more robust than the Choukoutien sample, it is tempting to suggest that all of these features reflect no more than their earlier date.

Finally, like the mandibles, the dental sample is intermediate in size (and date) between the Indonesian and Choukoutien averages, although the greatest similarities lie with the latter. Posterior tooth size reduction is particularly marked in the third molar, while the latest specimens show expansion of the anterior teeth.

Late Homo erectus *in Europe*

The *Homo erectus* skeletal sample from Europe is very late compared with the long sequences in Asia and Africa. The specimens seem roughly contemporary with Choukoutien. Within the European glacial sequence, they are generally regarded as earlier than or contemporary with the Mindel glaciation (see Chapter 1). Including these specimens in *Homo erectus* is more a matter of tradition than the result of any distinct morphological complex. Since they are among the very latest in the *Homo erectus* time range, they closely resemble early *Homo sapiens,* which follows. Conversely, slightly later European *Homo sapiens* specimens such as Petralona, Steinheim, and Bilzingsleben, retain so many *Homo erectus* features that a good case can be made for including them in the earlier taxon. Europe provides a particularly good example of how arbitrary the division of a lineage becomes when the sample is large.

The German site of Mauer is probably the earliest, although least securely dated, of the European sites. When the Mauer mandible was discovered in 1907, in a quarry near Heidelberg, it was recognized as being very large and robust (the sloping symphysis retains two internal tori) and was noted for its especially broad ramus (Figure 9.7). Later comparisons revealed that it could be matched by the extreme in living humans. With the large *Homo erectus* sample now available for comparisons, Mauer is seen as a fairly gracile specimen with reduction in ramus height and posterior dentition. In contrast, the anterior teeth are large.

The Hungarian site of Vértesszöllös is more securely dated; a study of the microfauna places it in the same time range as Choukoutien. Remains of two individuals have been found. One is a juvenile, represented by the fragments of a milk canine and a molar. An analysis of these teeth shows that they are particularly similar to teeth from Choukoutien. The second individual is an adult, represented by most of an occiput. The bone is thick and has a well-developed nuchal torus across its back. The great breadth of the bone leads to a very large nuchal muscle attachment area, exceeding the erectus average. The upper part of the occiput is flattened, as in other erectus specimens, and a groove separates the nuchal torus from the portion of the occiput above it (occipital plane). The size of the occiput suggests a cranial capacity of over 1,300 cc, matching that estimated for the Ternifine parietal. The total picture is of a large-brained, heavily muscled erectus specimen.

The few teeth from the European Mindel glaciation show characteristics that are predictable from the evolutionary trends found in Asia and Africa. Specifically, there appears to be a combination of posterior dental reduction and anterior expansion compared with earlier specimens. The Mauer posterior teeth are among the smallest of the entire erectus sample. Milk canines have been found at Vértesszöllös and Vergranne. The Vergranne specimen is one of the largest upper milk canines known, larger than any australopithecine dc^1.

Adaptive Trends in Homo erectus

Homo erectus is the first hominid taxon known to have migrated from Africa. It seems clear that common evolutionary trends characterized the most widespread populations. At the same time, there is a long history of attempts to show specific continuity between *Homo erectus* samples in various areas of the world and living populations of *Homo sapiens,* beginning with F. Weidenreich and continuing with C. Coon, N. W. G. Macintosh, and others. The weak point of this thesis has always been in its use of a static model for "race" formation (depending on longlasting barriers to gene flow) and the resulting contradiction with the presence of worldwide evolutionary trends. Moreover, the fossil evidence has never been sufficient to either completely confirm or refute it.

There does seem to be some evidence of regional differences in later *Homo erectus*, especially at the periphery of its range (Indonesia and Europe). Distinct gene pools would seem to imply geographic isolation, and yet the worldwide participation of *Homo erectus* populations in evolutionary changes requires the presence of significant gene flow. One model which avoids this contradiction provides for a dynamic maintenance of continuous variation through the interaction of gene flow and selection. The former would act to reduce variation between populations, while the latter would act to increase it over wide geographic areas where selective pressures differ. When these two opposing forces reach a balance, continuous variation can be maintained for long periods of time. In contrast to the static model, this dynamic one emphasizes the long-term importance of gene flow connecting the most widespread populations, and accounts for both the maintenance of distinctions and the spread of evolutionary changes. It is my opinion that it accurately describes the appearance of geographic differences in later *Homo erectus*, which in some regions may be continuous with the regional differences that occur today.

Yet, one should not overlook the common aspects of selection acting on *Homo erectus* populations. The most widespread source of these is the hunting adaptation. The common evolutionary trends reflect the occurrence of similar adaptations in different areas. The most important human adaptation is primarily cultural. Pleistocene human populations were adapted for effectively bearing and transmitting cultural behavior, and this adaptation was common to all geographic variants of *Homo erectus*. Advantageous cultural changes and technological innovations can spread much more rapidly than genes. Thus common changes in natural selection acting on human populations could produce the same genetic changes in widely separated areas *without* a great amount of gene flow occurring. Another factor was probably the relatively low efficiency of resource use. This would reduce the amount of adaptive specialization that was possible in varying habitats. For instance, a lack of specialized weapons would preclude many of the prey-specific specializations that can be observed in big-game hunting today.

Paradoxically, one of the most important effects of this adaptation was probably to increase the frequency of contacts between groups. Almost certainly, with this came the development of structured expectations governing such contacts, which inevitably involve the exchange of mates. Mate exchanges have critically important social consequences, and biologically have the effect of sustaining a slow, but constant, exchange of genetic material throughout the range of the species. Thus, the same factors that helped establish worldwide differences in grade may have helped retain regional differences in clade.

TECHNOLOGY

The evolution of Acheulean industries in *Homo erectus* populations involved two main factors: a marked improvement in skill, which almost surely resulted from a more accurate preconception of tool form, and an expanded ability to translate the preconception accurately into a better-made product through a series of rules (hand-and-eye coordination). The second factor is an increase in the number of different distinguishable tools, and the appearance of fire use and eventually of fire-hardened spears. Specific tool types became better defined, and more work seems to have been involved in their manufacture.

Several new flaking techniques supplemented the earlier "stone-on-stone" process that characterized the Oldowan and earlier Acheulean assemblages (see Figure 10.9, pp. 242–243). The most important of these was the discovery that softer objects (such as wood or antler) could be used to strike off flakes. An indirect percussion technique may also have come into use. This involves using wood, bone, or antler as an intermediary between the hammerstone and the object being flaked. These new techniques resulted in much greater control over the size and form of the flake being struck, and consequently over the form of the completed tool. Hand axes and cleavers from this time appear aesthetically pleasing because of their regular form, symmetry, and straight edges. That aesthetics may have begun to play a role in their conception and manufacture is suggested by evidence of red coloring material, seemingly collected by hominids, at Olduvai upper Bed II.

ADAPTIVE PATTERNS

With these changes comes more meager evidence suggesting the beginning of differing adaptive patterns beyond what might be immediately expected from variations in environment and habitat. For instance, at the late erectus site of Ternifine, virtually every animal in the surrounding region (representing a number of different habitats) was used for food, while in contrast at Choukoutien some 85 percent of the fauna is made up of two species of red deer. These observations suggest the late development of new and more effective means of obtaining animal protein, one of the most important single factors influencing the evolution of the lineage.

However, animal protein is only part of the dietary picture, and possibly not even the most important part if studies of living hunter-gatherer groups are relevant. With few exceptions, protein makes up less than 50 percent of the diet of almost all modern hunter-gatherers. Thus the evolution of *Homo erectus* probably involved the utilization of new animal *and* plant resources, which increased food predictability during each season. Other important developments include improvements in the means of gathering these food resources, and the development of food preparation techniques to supplement and/or replace the preparatory functions of the jaws and teeth. With these developments broadening the fundamental niche, there may have been an increasing tendency in the latest erectus populations to utilize more distinct and less overlapping realized niches (resources actually used, in contrast to those that potentially could be used).

Morphological Trends

Remains of *Homo erectus* are numerous (as a reader of this chapter must appreciate) but widely scattered. Moreover, unfortunate accidental sex distributions (the majority of early Indonesian but late African crania are female and vice versa) make it difficult to sort out the actions of the three main causes of variation: time, geography, and sexual dimorphism. Nonetheless, whether the different geographic areas are considered separately or the sample is combined across space, the same broad evolutionary trends can be shown to characterize *Homo erectus*. These trends are reflected in increasing cranial capacity, decreased forces acting on the posterior teeth, and increased anterior tooth loading, and they can be related to the adaptive complex discussed above.

When comparing the evolutionary changes associated with the origin of *Homo erectus* (Chapter 8) and the changes that took place as populations spread throughout the Old World, these later changes could be characterized to some extent as "more of the same." Indeed, many of the evolutionary trends continue through the timespan of the lineage, including the expansion of cranial capacity, the reduction in posterior tooth use and the size of the teeth and related structures, and the increasing importance of anterior tooth use as evidenced by size increase and expansion of the nuchal muscles and basal spongy bone. Other features that originated with *Homo erectus* remain fairly stable through the existence of the lineage, indicating that they represent persistently effective adaptations. This is particularly true of the cranial vault strengthening system (bone thickness, sagittal keel, supraorbital and nuchal torus development) and the indications of body strength expressed in limb form and outer bone thickness. It may also be the case for body height.

CRANIAL CAPACITY

The cranial capacity increase observed between early *Homo erectus* and the australopithecines is continued, although at a slower rate, within the lineage. Using the Lower and Middle Pleistocene boundary (ca. 700,000 years BP) to separate the specimens into earlier and later *Homo erectus* samples, average capacity increases from 843 cc to 1,067 cc. The latest crania (from Choukoutien and Vértesszöllös) have the largest capacities.

How much of this increase might be related to body size is unknown because we have too few postcrania to determine whether there is a body size increase within *Homo erectus*. Considering the erectus sample as a whole, a substantial amount of the total cranial capacity increase over the australopithecines appears to be the result of body size increase. Height changes from an australopithecine average of 55 inches to an average of 64 inches in the late erectus sample. Average australopithecine weight has been estimated at about 115 pounds, and if erectus was slightly less robust, the weight average for the later sample would be about 170 pounds. Thus, if body size in the earlier erectus sample is approximately the same as in the later, as I believe, the actual (i.e., relative to body size) cranial capacity increase between early and late erectus is about as great as that between early erectus and the australopithecines.

In the expansion of the braincase, all parts of the brain do not change equally. This can be demonstrated by considering changes in the braincase as a whole and changes in the frontal and occipital bones separately. The most marked braincase increase is in height and length. The breadth of the braincase barely changes at all. However, the *difference between* braincase breadth and total cranial breadth (measuring basal spongy bone development) increases as the result of improved strengthening of the cranial base (see Figure 9.8).

The differential expansion of the frontal bone can best be seen in the development of frontal bulging (Figure 9.5) in later crania, such as those from Choukoutien and Chad, and accommodates the expansion of the frontal lobes. Expansion of the occiput involves both brain size increase and expansion of the nuchal muscle attachment area. Brain size increase affects the occipital plane (the occiput above the nuchal torus). Among other things, this portion of the bone encloses the posterior parietal association areas of the brain, where cross-modal transfer takes place. Between early and late *Homo erectus*, this occipital plane expansion is one of the greatest proportional changes that can be demonstrated.

While increasing body size may be a factor in the expansion of *Homo erectus* brain size (see above), the most important cause is the continued process of neurological structural reorganization. Judging from the differential expansion of the frontal and occipital bones, the likelihood is that the main expanding elements are in the two corresponding regions of the brain, the frontal lobes and the posterior parietal region, and that expansion involves (1) increased connections between the sensory and motor association areas and some frontal areas (affecting monitoring, ordering, and sorting), and (2) development of an even more complex network of direct connections in the posterior parietal association area. Finally, the importance of the bulk increase in brain size should not be overlooked. The increase may do no more than expand the number of connections within an australopithecine (=human) structure, but this results in a new magnitude of possible neural pathways. The implication in terms of complex cultural behaviors cannot be overstated, especially when the bulk increase is combined with evidence that it is particularly the

frontal and posterior parietal areas that are differentially expanding (the very areas where many of the circuits "come together"). *Homo erectus* probably evolved all of the complex neural models underlying human cultural behavior from a far smaller brain with the basic human organization.

SPEECH

Human speech capacity is an extremely complicated behavior, involving the development of tracts between the motor and associated speech areas and between the frontal and posterior parietal portions of the brain. The basis for speech ability would seem to lie more in neurological structures than in morphological ones. The importance of the frontal–posterior parietal tract is that it allows the frontal area to "make sense" out of the cross-modal associations of the posterior parietal area, while the motor–associational speech area tract provides a pathway for this information to reach the motor-speech area.

The evolution of language ability seems tied to the appearance of hemispheric dominance and asymmetry. The marked bilateral asymmetry in size and morphology in the newly discovered Choukoutien cranium 5 provides one of the few direct morphological correlates with the ability to speak in humans. Thus, there is every reason to believe that *Homo erectus* was capable of human vocal language.

DECREASING POSTERIOR TOOTH USE

Direct evidence for decreasing posterior tooth use is found in dental reduction and the reduction of the supporting bony structures of the face and mandible. These changes result directly from the progressive replacement of some vegetal foods by meat as a consistent and predictable dietary item and from the development of more effective food preparation techniques, including cooking in the later populations.

Posterior tooth size reduction is one of the most dramatic changes that occurs between the australopithecines and early *Homo erectus*, and an equally great reduction takes place over the timespan of the lineage. The pattern of reduction affects the later-erupting teeth of each type more than the ante-

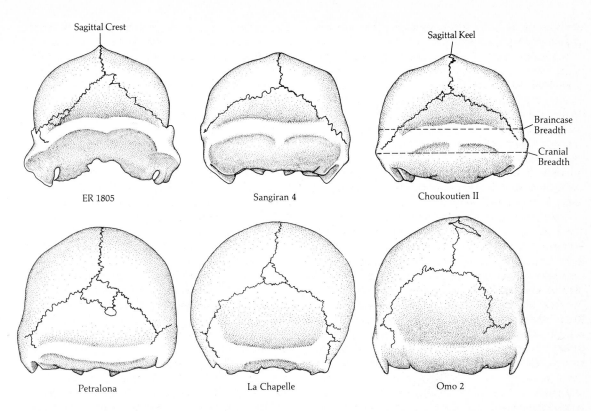

Sagittal Crest

ER 1805

Sangiran 4

Sagittal Keel

Braincase Breadth

Cranial Breadth

Choukoutien II

Petralona

La Chapelle

Omo 2

FIGURE 9.8 *Posterior cranial views for an evolutionary sequence in* Homo. *Only the later* Homo sapiens *specimens La Chapelle (European Neandertal) and Omo 2 are approximately synchronic (Chapter 11). ER-1805 is a very early* Homo erectus *or a transitional specimen, Sangiran 4 and Choukoutien 11 are earlier and later* Homo erectus *from Asia, and Petralona is an early* Homo sapiens *from Europe (Chapter 10). In the later specimens, note the decrease in basal expansion due to spongy bone development and the increase in the breadth of the braincase. This results in the eventual change in the position of greatest cranial breadth from the base (where it measures the cranium but not the braincase) to a higher point on the parietals (where total cranial and braincase breadth become the same). Also note the eventual loss of the sagittal keel. Differences between La Chapelle and Omo 2 reflect geographic variation.*

late *Homo erectus*. Selection seems to maximize grinding area in the young while reducing the occlusal area in adults (since the later-erupting teeth reduce most). The importance of maximum grinding area in the young is also suggested by the contrasting fact that the deciduous (milk) teeth expand in size over this timespan (and in fact well into the Upper Pleistocene). The increased importance of grinding area in the young may correspond to earlier weaning, which might help promote shortened birth spacing (one means of allowing population expansion).

The structures supporting the posterior teeth also reduce. In the mandible, the main effect is to dramatically decrease the breadth of the corpus; corpus height changes less and the total mandibular dimensions barely change at all. On the average, breadth at the symphysis and internal buttressing also reduce substantially. More mandibular reduction takes place along the *Homo erectus* lineage than between early *Homo erectus* and the later australopithecines. The later *Homo erectus* sample shows an average reduction of corpus height and breadth to about 75 percent of the earlier erectus

rior earlier-erupting teeth. Thus P4 decreases more than P3, and M3 decreases more than M2, which in turn decreases more than M1. In fact, while the third molar is larger than the first and second in the australopithecines, it is smaller than both molars in average. At the symphysis, breadth reduction is the same while height reduction is some 10 percent less. Thus the symphysis becomes relatively taller, although this is obscured by its even curvature and backward angulation.

In the maxilla, reduction of the posterior teeth and their roots markedly decreases the size of the lower face, especially below the level of the nose. Most of this change occurs between the australopithecines and early *Homo erectus*, but the three fragmentary maxillas from Choukoutien, Sangiran 15b and 17, and the Chad lower face suggest that the progression continues through the lineage.

With the decrease in posterior tooth use comes a further reduction in the size of the anterior temporalis. The temporal lines tend to merge toward each other in a more posterior position, and the temporal fossa decreases in size. A decrease in the power of the masseter muscle is indicated by the great reduction in the size of the zygoma. This can be seen when comparing earlier (ER-3733 and Sangiran 17) and later (Choukoutien and Chad) specimens.

OTHER FACIAL CHANGES

Interestingly, while the lower portion of the erectus face reduces compared with the australopithecine condition, the upper portion expands. One change compensates for the other and there is little net change in average facial height (measured from the top of the nose to the teeth). For a variety of reasons, facial breadth increases in *Homo erectus* and continues increasing through the evolution of the lineage. One contributing factor is the expansion of the frontal, which pushes the position of the temporal fossa outward and requires broader faces in spite of the fossa's decreasing size. A second factor is the probable increase in anterior tooth size (discussed below). As a result, broad nasal openings and large, widely spaced orbits characterize all but the earliest *Homo erectus* faces. A third factor is the expansion of orbit size. It is possible that an increase in the size of the eyes, and more importantly in the number of rods and cones, is related to an expansion of visual information processing capacity (and consequently to the continued posterior expansion of the brain).

INCREASING ANTERIOR TOOTH USE

A general trend to increase maxillary anterior tooth breadth can be clearly demonstrated. All three anterior teeth expand in later erectus, but the greatest change is in I^2, which becomes equal to I^1 in size. The changing pattern of anterior tooth use is not directly associated with chewing food. Instead, it appears to result from using the mouth to grip and hold objects. Another factor may be new patterns of food preparation associated with animal protein, such as gripping meat while cutting off pieces, preshredding for the young, and so on. Greater use of the anterior teeth as part of the tool kit seems to accompany the elaboration of more traditional tools and an improved ability to exploit the habitat—in other words, the evolution of more skillful means of environmental manipulation.

We have seen that vertical loading of the anterior teeth is functionally related to the size of the browridge when the forehead slope is left constant (Figure 8.8). Since the height of the forehead increases in later *Homo erectus*, the size of the browridge should decrease. However, there is no reduction. Therefore, one may suspect a corresponding increase in vertical anterior loading.

Finally, an increase in horizontal loading is indicated directly by the fact that the nuchal muscle attachment area expands by 31 percent in later *Homo erectus* compared to the earlier erectus sample. Since there is no evidence of a change in cranial balance, the increasing nuchal musculature most likely corresponds to more powerful horizontal loading of the anterior teeth (Figure 8.7). Another aspect of this change is the expansion of basal spongy bone.

FEATURES THAT DO NOT CHANGE

A number of morphological features show little or no change over the timespan of the *Homo erectus* lineage. Many of these, although not all, contrast with the australopithecine condition.

The browridge, sagittal keel, and nuchal torus show no evidence of significant change within the lineage. While these structures vary, the size and projection of supraorbital and nuchal tori and the sagittal thickening remain important characteristics in erectus that clearly distinguish the taxon from the australopithecines. Similarly, there is no average change in vault thickness.

While the dimensions of the mandibular corpus undergo differential reduction, the overall total length/breadth/height dimensions of the *Homo erectus* mandibles remain the same, and do not differ substantially from those of australopithecine mandibles, except for the greater breadth across the condyles, which corresponds to a broader cranial base.

There is little difference between the known elements of the *Homo erectus* postcranial skeleton and that of the australopithecines, except for features which correspond to the average body size increase and a larger birth canal (or pelvic inlet in males). The main distinctions of australopithecine postcrania, compared to our own, lie in the narrower birth canal and the evidence of greater muscularity and muscle power. There is reason to believe that a similar interpretation can be applied to the morphology of the erectus postcrania.

The only known erectus ilium (OH-28) does not appear different from the largest of the australopithecine ilia in most important respects. It is relatively large, with a marked lateral flare and a strong anteriorly positioned buttress. While the specimen is not complete enough to ascertain birth canal (or pelvic inlet) dimensions, these observed features are the result of a narrower birth canal than normally occurs today. More indirect evidence from the femurs also indicates a narrower-than-modern pelvic inlet in *Homo erectus*, only slightly larger than in the australopithecines. Specifically, with a narrower inlet, the femur neck must be longer to reach the acetabulum. Moreover, the longer neck develops stronger bending forces in the vertical plane and consequently tends to be relatively tall. *Homo erectus* femur necks are both relatively long and tall. In sum, these features suggest that the erectus pelvic inlet was broader than the australopithecine average but narrower than the average in modern humans.

The other aspect in which *Homo erectus* limbs are similar to the australopithecines', and unlike ours, is in the evidence of muscularity and powerful muscle use. Again using the femur for an example, since it is the best-represented bone, the relative thickness of the shafts, the thickness of the shaft

walls, and the anteroposterior flattening of the mid-shafts are all very australopithecine-like and contrast with the morphology of modern human femurs. What this suggests is that great strength and prolonged muscular activity were used in normal behavior on a day-to-day basis.

VARIABILITY

One final characteristic of *Homo erectus* which does not seem to change substantially over the timespan of the lineage, or for that matter between the australopithecines and early erectus, is the presence of marked variation in virtually all features. While some of the variation is geographic and temporal, in the samples with numerous specimens the level of variability is high. In large samples, such as those for the mandible or the dentition, variation is fully as great as in the australopithecines.

One important factor that accounts for some of the variation is sexual dimorphism. While the bimodal canine distribution of the australopithecines is lost in *Homo erectus*, determination of sex at even the latest sites (such as Choukoutien) results in a degree of dimorphism in many features that is almost as great as that found in the earlier hominids. It is likely that there were substantial sex-based role differences in *Homo erectus* society, perhaps partly as the result of different food gathering activities, with the male activities requiring size and power. While sex is not known for many of the erectus remains, in the dentitions and mandibles the evidence suggests that sex-based size differences, although perhaps reduced from the australopithecine level, are still marked.

Nonetheless, the importance of individual variability should not be overlooked. In many of the specimens discussed, extraordinary robustness or gracility in one body region is not matched in another. Every individual has a unique combination of features. Individual variations in these combinations is a characteristic shared by most hominoid species and is probably at its extreme in Pleistocene fossil and living hominids. *Homo erectus*, no less than other hominoid species, seems to have been characterized by marked individual variation.

SUMMARY

The sample we refer to as *Homo erectus* represents a segment of an evolving lineage. There are distinct trends in the evolution of this species, which spans the time period from over 1.5 million years ago to less than 500,000. These trends, where they can be documented, lead to so much change that, in general, the early erectus sample is midway between the australopithecines and the late erectus sample in most changing features. Rather than thinking of erectus as a stage in human evolution, it is probably more accurate to think of this sample as a series of links between the australopithecines and our own species, *Homo sapiens*.

Homo erectus populations spread through the tropics and subtropics of the Old World soon after the earliest specimens appear in Africa. Population increase and expansion into new habitats provides the best evidence of a dramatically new and more effective adaptation in the lineage. Nonetheless, the full adaptive potential of hominids was far from realized, despite evidence suggesting speech and fairly complex structured relations between populations and a brain size which, although small by modern standards, fits within the functionally normal range. The similarity in adaptive patterns and skeletal morphology over the species' entire range indicates a lack of ability to exploit varying habitats in specific and efficient ways.

While evidence of European habitation during the Lower Pleistocene is restricted to archaeological remains, hominid fossils are found in both Indonesia and south China. These early hominids are characterized by small cranial capacity (two specimens) and posterior teeth and mandibles which, although reduced on the average, still extend far into the australopithecine range. Sexual dimorphism is dramatic enough to have been interpreted as taxonomic difference by some.

Subsequent trends in cranial evolution are best known from Asia, where the Indonesian sequence continues into the Middle Pleistocene (beginning about 700,000 years ago) and is followed by the late (perhaps 350,000 years old) large sample from Choukoutien. The crania show evidence of continued expansion, expecially in the frontal and posterior parietal areas of the brain. The nuchal muscle attachment area also continues to expand. Interestingly, sexual dimorphism appears somewhat reduced at Choukoutien. The cranial vault strengthening system does not appear to change. There is no significant variation in vault bone thickness or the development of the supraorbital torus, sagittal keel, or nuchal torus over time. There is some evidence of average facial reduction in some features. No later cranium shows the zygomatic or lower facial development of earlier African specimens or Sangiran 17.

The other known crania are more fragmentary and add little to what can be determined in Asia. A late Olduvai specimen, OH-12, is very small and has diminutive browridges. Frontal-facial fragments from Chad and the Thomas quarry have the normal *Homo erectus* facial proportions, combining a short lower face, expansion in the upper face, and relatively great facial breadth. They differ greatly in forehead slope and development of the frontal bulge, and Chad shows a prognathism that is reminiscent of the australopithecine condition. The latest specimens, from Ternifine, Choukoutien, and Vértesszöllös, have the largest cranial capacities.

Mandibular changes neatly fit a pattern of reducing mandibular robustness and muscularity. The earliest specimens (from the Djetis and Trinil horizons on Java) are the largest and relatively thickest. The later African sample is somewhat reduced in comparison, although it maintains equal, if not greater, variability. The latest specimens (from Choukoutien and Mauer) are the most reduced. They have the thinnest bodies, and their ascending rami are the smallest known for the taxon.

Similarly, tooth size shows consistent change over time, with the permanent posterior teeth reducing and, toward the end of the timespan, the anterior teeth expanding. Posterior tooth reduction affects the rear molars and premolar more than the front teeth of each class. Interestingly, at the same time, the deciduous teeth show a size increase.

Evolutionary changes in the postcrania cannot be analyzed because of the lack of distinguishable (from late australopithecine) specimens from the Lower Pleistocene. The known (later) postcrania suggest an average height of about 64 inches and corresponding weight average of approximately 170 pounds. The limbs are extraordinarily robust. Their shape and the thickness of the outer bone indicate a normal level of muscular strength unknown today. Brute force and prolonged physical exertion must have been primary means of dealing with everyday circumstances. The single known innominate reflects the same muscularity, superimposed on other distinctions resulting from a smaller-than-modern pelvic inlet.

In all, while some aspects of the *Homo erectus* adaptive complex remained stable, others were subject to improvement and change over the time-span of the lineage. Although the process was gradual and continuous, the accumulating changes ultimately resulted in populations so recognizably different that by analogy with living forms a new species name is required, *Homo sapiens*.

The evolutionary trends visible in the erectus sample are largely the result of the evolution of planned and coordinated daytime hunting, efficient and predictable gathering, and new food preparation techniques. Directly and indirectly, these major adaptive shifts were the result of both cultural and morphological innovations which led to behavioral changes that in turn altered the nature and direction of selection acting on hominid popula-

tions. If *Homo erectus* was a hunter, the important point is that erectus was a *hominid* hunter, adapting to the new exploitive pattern both culturally and morphologically. The broadening of the fundamental niche greatly increased the ecological and geographic range of the species. The commitment to culture as the major hominid adaptive mechanism was complete, and the effects of this commitment played the single most critical role in the evolution of *Homo erectus* morphology.

Selection acting on all erectus populations vastly increased behavioral complexity and adaptability. Moreover, perfection of the hunting adaptation was an important guiding factor. At the same time, some evidence suggests that regional population differences appeared, especially at the periphery of the hominid range. These may have been maintained for long periods of time through the interaction of local differences in selection and the opposing effects of gene flow. It has been argued that some of these population differences are continuous with regional differences that occur at the present time.

STATE OF THE ART

One important issue considered in this chapter was originally raised by F. Weidenreich. This concerns the specific relation of the Choukoutien (and ultimately other Chinese fossil) material to modern Chinese. Weidenreich argued that these *Homo erectus* fossils shared an unusually large number of features with the living populations of China, concluding that the Choukoutien sample represented a "direct ancestor of *Homo sapiens* with closer relation to certain Mongolian groups than to any other races." The common features he pointed to were the sagittal keel; extra bones at the rear of the cranium where the occiput and parietals meet (cranium 5 in Figure 9.5 shows such an extra-sutural bone); shovel-shaped lateral maxillary incisors (the internal perpendicular edges have marginal ridges, making this suface resemble a coal shovel); widely flared, flat zygoma; the low profile of the upper nose; and anteroposterior flattening of the femurs.

Subsequent workers such as C. Coon, A. Thoma, and J. Aigner have supported this contention. In its broadest interpretation, Weidenreich meant that while *Homo erectus* was broadly ancestral to *Homo*

sapiens, the Chinese populations of the earlier species probably contributed more genes to living Chinese than were contributed by *Homo erectus* populations anywhere else in the world. This is an important statement because it argues against the contention of a replacement model that modern *Homo sapiens* populations originated in a single small area and spread throughout the world, replacing indigenous groups (i.e., a punctuated equilibrium model).

In his book *The Origin of Races*, C. Coon developed a more specific interpretation of Weidenreich's contention, suggesting that the Mongoloids (and in fact each of what he termed the "five major races" of humanity) each originated as a distinct race during the time of *Homo erectus*. Coon suggested that each race evolved more or less independently, crossing what he called the "sapiens threshold" at different times. The biological difficulties in his argument (races having continued existence over time and evolving from one species into another at different rates), as well as the potential racist interpretation of the contention that some races have been in the species *Homo sapiens* longer than others, have resulted in the widespread rejection of Coon's ideas.

Many also dismissed Weidenreich's more general contention at the same time. The question is whether this latter decision was justified. To be sure, many, if not all, of the specific features Weidenreich pointed to as showing a special relationship between the Middle Pleistocene and living populations of China are now recognized as more widespread than he had reason to believe. A sagittal keel appears in later (than Choukoutien) European crania. Extra-sutural bones are common in *Homo erectus* and later crania wherever they are found, as are shovel-shaped incisors. The shape of the upper nasal profile varies markedly at Choukoutien (compare crania in Figure 9.5), and flat, widely flared zygoma and femoral flattening are general early hominid characteristics whose origin is found in the African australopithecines.

On the other hand, there are observable elements of local continuity that are difficult to dismiss. Even in *Homo erectus*, evidence for a special relationship between the Indonesian and Chinese samples is substantial, and many feel that one can continue to trace southern populations of this line through the later Ngandong sample (Chapter 11) and perhaps even to living Australian aborigines. Similarly, a series of later fossils may show continuity between Choukoutien and recent Chinese populations.

A. Thorne has suggested a model which might account for the appearance of these accumulating geographic distinctions. He argues that during the spread of *Homo erectus* outside of Africa, the action of drift might have limited the genetic variability in the more outlying populations. This would result in less genetic variation within these populations but marked frequency differences between them. At the same time, within-population variation would be higher in the area where the species originated. Consequently, in European and Asian *Homo erectus* samples, there is limited variation and noticeable continuity between the earlier and later *Homo* specimens, while the varia-

bility of the African *Homo erectus* samples is more marked (although there is also some evidence for continuity and geographic distinction).

Since evolutionary change depends on both the direction of selection and the genetic variation already present, one might expect differences to accumulate between outlying hominid populations even if the action of selection was exactly the same (an unlikely assumption) because of the initial genetic differences. Thus populations in Europe and Asia (for example) might become increasingly divergent, while maintaining local continuity in the observable morphological changes. Of course, this process could not continue indefinitely without speciation; gene flow between populations would place a limit on how much difference could accumulate and how independent the evolutionary trends in each peripheral area could become. In fact, the presence of some gene flow is a necessary assumption for the model, since clinal (gradual) differences in a wide-ranging species can be maintained for long periods of time only when the actions of gene flow and local differences in selection balance each other.

Thorne's ideas have important implications for interpreting later changes associated with the appearance of modern *Homo sapiens* populations. A replacement model of this appearance, arguing that modern populations evolved in one area and rapidly spread throughout the inhabited world, would have to require that new populations entering an area had the numerous locally distinctive features that were already present. The suite of features would have to be different for each peripheral area. Thorne's model is important for understanding the origins of modern geographic differences.

In sum, while Coon's interpretation is unacceptable, there remains as much evidence to support Weidenreich's original contention as there is to support an Upper Pleistocene replacement model. While neither interpretation can be proven, data presented in Chapters 10 and 11 are relevant to the discussion and in my view provide more weight for Weidenreich's argument than for the replacement model.

FURTHER READINGS

BORDES, F. 1968. *The Old Stone Age.* McGraw-Hill, New York.
Probably the best introduction to the specifics of paleolithic archaeology.

CHIA, LAN-PO. 1975. *The Cave Home of Peking Man.* Foreign Languages Press, Peking.
An excellent summary of the Choukoutien remains with emphasis on the results of work over the past three decades.

CLARK, J. D. 1976. African Origins of Man the Toolmaker. In *Human Origins: Louis Leakey and the East African Evidence,* eds. G. L. Isaac and E. R. McCown. Benjamin, Menlo Park, pp. 1-53.
A good introduction to cultural origins and evolution in Africa, but especially useful for its discussion of Acheulean cultural and associated *Homo erectus* behavioral evolution.

DAY, M. H. 1971. Postcranial Remains of *Homo erectus* from Bed IV, Olduvai Gorge, Tanzania. *Nature* 232:383-387.
A brief report on the only known *Homo erectus* innominate and the associated femur.

ENNOUCHI, E. 1975. New Discovery of an Archanthropian in Morocco. *Journal of Human Evolution* 4:441-444.
A brief description of the Thomas quarry frontal-facial fragment.

HOWELL, F. C. 1977. The Hominization Process. In *Horizons of Anthropology,* 2nd ed., eds. S. Tax and L. G. Freeman. Aldine, Chicago, pp. 59-74.
An excellent review of the behavioral aspects of earlier hominid evolution.

HOWELLS, W. W. 1965. *Homo erectus. Scientific American* 215(5):46-53.
Howells' view of the taxon over time and space, emphasizing the replacement model.

JACOB, T. 1973. Paleoanthropological Discoveries in Indonesia with Special Reference to the Finds of the Last Two Decades. *Journal of Human Evolution* 2:473-486.
Review of the recent Indonesian discoveries.

KLEINDIENST, M. R., and C. M. KELLER. 1976. Towards a Functional Analysis of Handaxes and Cleavers: The Evidence from Eastern Africa. *Man* 11:176-187.
Functional interpretations for the marker tool of the Acheulean.

VON KOENIGSWALD, G. H. R. 1956. *Meeting Prehistoric Man.* Thames and Hudson, London.
A personal account of the earlier Indonesian *Homo erectus* and *Gigantopithecus* discoveries.

————, and F. WEIDENREICH. 1939. The Relationship Between *Pithecanthropus* and *Sinanthropus. Nature* 144:926:929.
Discussion of the close relation of Indonesian and Chinese *Homo erectus.*

LE GROS CLARK, W. E. 1964. *The Fossil Evidence for Human Evolution,* rev. ed. University of Chicago Press, Chicago.
Although out of date, this is probably the best introduction to the morphology of fossil hominids.

MANN, A. 1971. *Homo erectus.* In *Background for Man,* eds. P. Dolhinow and V. M. Sarich. Little Brown, Boston, pp. 166-177.
A well-written introduction to the *Homo erectus* remains.

PFEIFFER, J. E. 1972. *The Emergence of Man,* rev. ed. Harper & Row, New York.
An introduction to the archaeological and behavioral aspects of earlier hominid evolution, especially strong in its discussion of the Middle and earlier Upper Pleistocene.

RIGHTMIRE, P. 1979. Cranial Remains of *Homo erectus* from Beds II and IV, Olduvai Gorge, Tanzania. *American Journal of Physical Anthropology* 51:99-116.
A comparison of the Olduvai and Lake Turkana erectus remains and a discussion of their place in the African evolutionary sequence.

SARTONO, S. 1972. Discovery of Another Hominid Skull at Sangiran, Central Java. *Current Anthropology* 13:124-126.
Description of one male Indonesian cranium, Sangiran 12, and the most complete of the mandibles, Sangiran 9.

————. 1975. Implications Arising from *Pithecanthropus* VIII. In *Paleoanthropology: Morphology and Paleoecology,* ed. R. H. Tuttle. Mouton, The Hague, pp. 327-360.
Analysis of the most complete Indonesian cranium, Sangiran 17.

SHAPIRO, H. L. 1974. *Peking Man.* Simon and Schuster, New York.
The story of the Choukoutien remains and the mystery of their disappearance.

THORNE, A. G., and M. H. WOLPOFF. 1980. Regional Continuity in Australasian Hominid Evolution. *American Journal of Physical Anthropology* (in press).
A discussion of the center and edge hypothesis and the dynamic model of long-term regional distinctions maintained by the opposing actions of gene flow and selection.

WEIDENREICH, F. 1940. Man or Ape? *Natural History* 45:32–37.
Presentation of Weidenreich's reconstructed female cranium and a discussion of its significance.

———. 1945. Giant Early Man from Java and South China. *Anthropological Papers of the American Museum of Natural History* 40:1–134.
Weidenreich's description of the Sangiran crania (2, 3, 4), the Djetis mandibles, and the (then) known *Gigantopithecus* teeth, in which he presents his hypothesis of an evolutionary sequence of reducing gigantism in hominid evolution.

———. 1949. Interpretations of the Fossil Material. In *Early Man in the Far East*, ed. W. W. Howells. Wistar, Philadelphia, pp. 149–157.
One of his final statements of the Asian material and its significance in human evolution. Reference to the more detailed monographs on the Choukoutien remains is found at the end of the book.

WOLPOFF, M. H. 1971. Vértesszöllös and the Presapiens Theory. *American Journal of Physical Anthropology* 35:209–216.
A technical discussion of the problems involved in interpreting the Vértesszöllös remains.

WOO, JU-KANG. 1966. The Skull of Lantian Man. *Current Anthropology* 7:83–86.
A brief account of the Lantian cranium.

———, and LAN-PO CHIA. 1954. New Discoveries About *Sinanthropus pekinensis* in Choukoutien. *Scientia Sinica* 3:335–358.
A review of the earlier post-liberation excavations at Choukoutien.

PART FOUR

THE EVOLUTION OF MODERN PEOPLE

CHAPTER 10

Early Homo Sapiens

T he first populations of our species, *Homo sapiens*, appear in the later portion of the Middle Pleistocene. Where they can be compared with late *Homo erectus* populations, there is continuity in both adaptive patterns and morphological features. Early *Homo sapiens* in Indonesia closely resembles the latest Asian *Homo erectus* sample in many respects, and the same can be said for populations in Africa and Europe, although with less certainty because the samples are smaller.

To some extent, the distinction between these two species in the genus *Homo* is an arbitrary one, based more on a temporal division than on a suite of morphological features or adaptive tendencies (see Figure 2.2). However, morphological distinctions are present in even the earliest *Homo sapiens* samples. Some of these represent a continuation of the trends which were recognized in *Homo erectus*, while others involve changes in selection that result in the appearance of new features.

Beginning about 100,000–150,000 years ago, toward the end of the Middle Pleistocene, the evolution of our species is marked by a change in se-

lection. For this reason, it is convenient to discuss the earlier populations separately (this chapter), emphasizing the direction of their evolution and the reasons why it changed. Chapter 11 will consider *Homo sapiens* populations after the change in evolutionary direction, and Chapters 12 and 13 will examine the appearance and evolution of the more modern populations that are directly ancestral to living people.

This chapter begins with discussions of the earliest members of our species in three geographic areas: Indonesia and continental Asia, Africa, and Europe (see Map 3, p. 218, for positions of the main sites). These are considered separately for several reasons. One is that the problems inherent in the limited fossil samples are different. In Africa a convenient division can be made between the sub-Saharan and more northern regions, while in Europe it is useful to separate the earlier and later parts of the sample. Moreover, geographic distinctions that begin to accumulate over this period are probably better understood when each region is considered alone. The next section summarizes the differences between early *Homo sapiens* and *Homo erectus*. This is

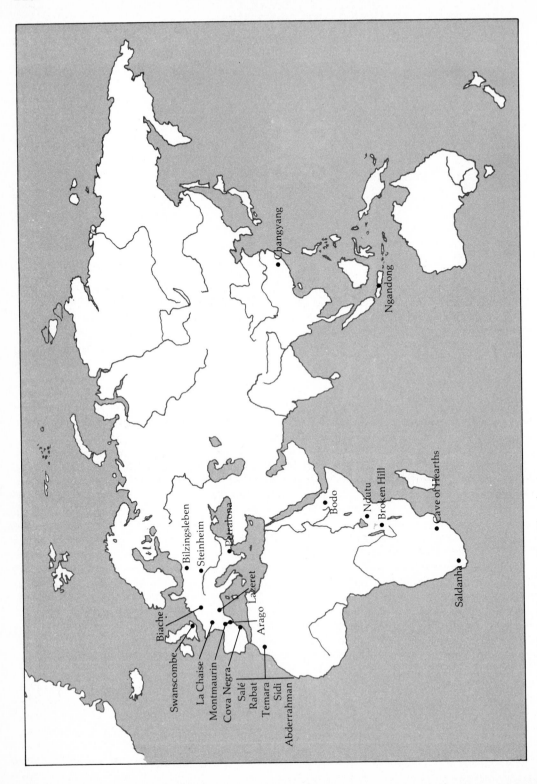

MAP 3   *Geographic positions of the major sites with early*
Homo sapiens remains.

followed by a discussion of the behavioral and technological changes that orient the direction taken by evolution over this period, and a reconstruction of some aspects of adaptation that are suggested by the archaeological and morphological remains. Finally, the appearance of geographic distinctions is related to differences in adaptation allowed by an increasing adaptive sophistication.

Cranial and Dental Evolution in Asia

The most marked changes in early *Homo sapiens* are known from the crania. A large sample from Indonesia and specimens from China and Japan reveal a set of features common throughout the entire hominid range. However, there is also some evidence of geographic distinctions which are retained through the subsequent evolution of the lineage. Probably no area conforms to the expectations of A. Thorne's model (see Chapter 9, State of the Art) better than Asia.

THE INDONESIAN SAMPLE

Indonesia is an excellent place to begin the discussion of cranial evolution since the largest single collection of later Middle Pleistocene crania comes from the island of Java. The collection includes a single cranium from Sambungmachen and fifteen specimens (two tibias and thirteen vaults or vault fragments) from the banks of the Solo River near Ngandong. The Ngandong sample (sometimes called the Solo sample) was discovered in the 1930s (except for a few recent fragments) and its dating has been a persistent problem. It was once relegated to the Upper Pleistocene on the contention that the crania were associated with some bone harpoon points. This association has proven to be incorrect, and because of the faunal relations and stratigraphic position of the site, most workers now believe it is considerably earlier. A single known potassium-argon date of 250,000 years BP is not unreasonable, but must be confirmed.

The Sambungmachen cranium has also not been precisely dated. it is probably older than the Ngandong sample and may approach or even exceed the age of Choukoutien. Clearly, a good deal of research remains to be done on both dates and the suggestions made here must be considered tentative.

The Sambungmachen site is in central Java not far from Sangiran. The date of the skullcap found there is uncertain because it was discovered in an area where it is possible to confuse river terrace deposits with the underlying older deposits. As mentioned above, it may be approximately the same age as Choukoutien. The importance of the specimen is that it provides a morphological link between the (probably) earlier Sangiran *Homo erectus* sample and the Ngandong specimens to be discussed below. Sambungmachen (Figure 9.4) is a male with the same vault size as a Ngandong female. The features which are similar to those of Sangiran *Homo erectus* crania include the broad depression over the browridge (especially over the nose), small mastoids, and the lack of backward projection for the nuchal torus. Yet other characteristics foreshadow the features that are common at Ngandong. The general shape of the occipital and temporal bones and the thickening of the browridge at the outer corners help suggest an ancestral relation. Moreover, they indicate that some local clade features in the region have considerable antiquity. This is especially visible in the forehead, where there is an absence of the centrally located frontal bulge (boss) common at Choukoutien and also found in the later specimens from the Chinese sites of Mapa and Da-Li (see Chapter 11).

The Ngandong crania were recovered over a span of several hundred feet along the Solo River (not all together as has sometimes been stated). Considering them together as a sample may be justified, but they do not represent a single biological population. All of the crania (see Figure 10.1, p. 220) lack faces, and the cranial base is preserved in only two (6 and 11). It is likely that the cranial bases and faces were broken away to remove the brains. Thus our knowledge is limited to details of the cranial vault. There are a number of clade similarities that point to a specific relation between this sample and the Indonesian *Homo erectus* sample, a contention supported by the intermediate position of Sambungmachen. Nonetheless, I believe there are significant differences between the two samples, and I disagree with those who regard the Solo hominids as a late-surviving variant of *Homo erectus*.

The Solo crania are larger than the later *Homo erectus* crania from Asia (the Choukoutien and later Indonesian specimens); average cranial capacity in-

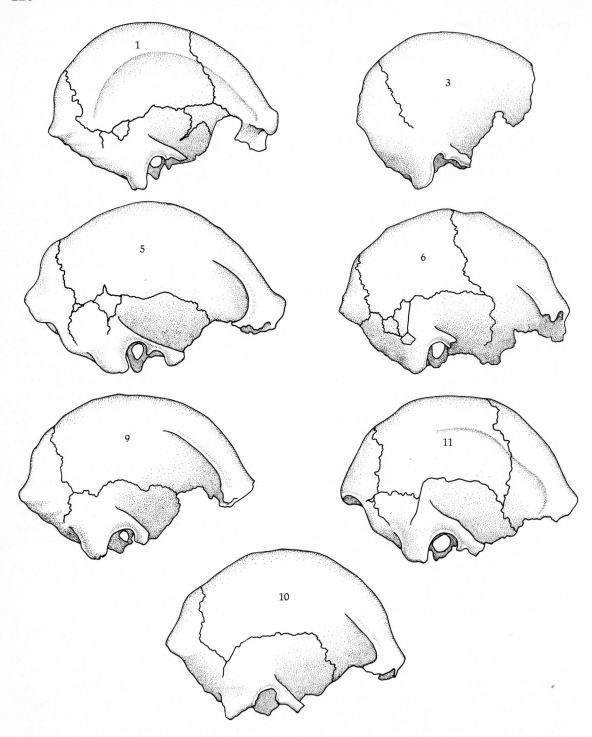

FIGURE 10.1   *The seven best-preserved crania from Solo.*

creases by 10 percent to 1,154 cc. Moreover, they are not simply expanded versions of the earlier crania, and some of the differential changes do not continue the trends observed in *Homo erectus*. For instance, in *Homo erectus* cranial breadth increased much more than braincase breadth as the basal spongy bone expanded. Comparing the Solo sample to the later *Homo erectus* sample reveals a very different pattern: braincase breadth increases while the total cranial breadth remains much the same. The other marked expansions are in cranial height and in the breadth of the frontal bone where it borders the temporal fossa. Thus these crania are taller than those in the earlier sample and show less frontal narrowing and much less difference between cranial and braincase breadth.

Two other changes reveal differential expansion of certain parts of the brain. Continuing a trend seen in *Homo erectus*, both frontal and occipital areas seem more filled out. Expansion of the frontal lobes brings the forehead above the supraorbitals from its earlier position behind them. Posterior parietal expansion is seen in the marked bulging of the occiput above the nuchal torus. A distinct regional feature is the backward extension of the torus at the outer corner of the orbit, along the temporal line. This forms a backward-facing triangle that can be found in Late Pleistocene Australian crania.

A consequence of the changing forehead morphology is expressed in the browridge. With a higher forehead to help resist stress (see Figure 8.8), browridge thickness reduces. In the Solo sample the main reduction is in the central portion of the torus. The browridge more closely approximates the contours of the orbits, and a depression over the nose results in its distinct separation into right and left sides.

Another aspect of changing selection is seen in the occiput. While the upper portion of the bone expands, the attachment area for the nuchal muscles decreases by some 30 percent. In most earlier hominids this attachment area makes up the major part of the bone, but in the Solo sample the proportions are reversed. At the same time, there is an expansion in the size of the nuchal torus. This structure is more prominent than in the earlier Indonesian crania, especially in its backward projection.

The general impression of the Solo sample suggests very powerful and muscular people. This is expressed in the bony evidences of muscle attachments, as well as in the form and thickness of the bones themselves. While they may not have been as powerful as earlier humans, the development of the nuchal region (although reduced) suggests that large faces and front teeth were probably still an important part of hominid adaptation. The evolutionary trend was toward reduction, but direct evidence indicates that there was still selection for maintaining strengthened crania. As an example of such selection, four of the crania show healed scars where the scalp was penetrated during life.

Of the thirteen crania or cranial fragments, nine are adult or at least fully grown and one is clearly a young juvenile or child (in this assessment I differ from Weidenreich). I believe that adult crania 5, 9, 10, and 11 are male and that 1, 4, 6, and 8 are female. The young specimen, cranium 2, is probably male. Sex determination is based on cranial size, projection and size of the nuchal torus, and the development of a prominence at the middle of this torus in the males. These features show no overlap between males and females. Other characteristics that do overlap but show an average difference include vault thickness and development of the lines and crests marking muscle attachments. While Weidenreich regarded the degree of sexual dimorphism as less than at Choukoutien, I believe that the opposite is the case and that in general the Ngandong crania are more variable.

Finally, there are some broad similarities between this sample and the Choukoutien hominid sample, especially Choukoutien 5, which was found much higher in the cave than the other specimens. At the same time, features of the forehead and occiput suggest a continuing Indonesian clade.

AN UPPER JAW FROM CHINA

North of Indonesia, only a few scattered remains have been discovered in the later Middle Pleistocene deposits of Southeast Asia and China. The most important is a maxillary fragment from Changyang, a region considerably south of Choukoutien. Because of its forward-positioned cheeks, the specimen has been reported as a distinct Asian variant. The evidence for cheek position is far from clear, however. The nose reveals an interesting combination of features, including narrow lower breadth and a sharp, upward-curving lower nasal border lacking a projecting nasal spine. Below it, the maxilla is moderately prognathic and convex in sagittal view. The size of the canine socket and the development of a bony buttress around it suggest that the tooth was probably quite large.

African Remains

Later Middle Pleistocene hominids are found throughout the African continent. Except for Broken Hill, each site is generally represented by only a single specimen. Dating remains a problem; not one absolute date is known for the period. Interpretation of the finds has been confused by both the dating problem and the fact that the African remains are rarely considered by themselves but instead are usually lumped together with specimens on other continents, often with widely disparate dates. Although the samples are small, considered together these remains suggest a combination of grade features shared with the Solo hominids and the appearance of other characteristics which may indicate a geographically distinct variant.

BROKEN HILL

A cranium, maxilla, frontal bone, and postcranial bones were discovered in a cave pocket exposed by lead mining near Broken Hill in Zambia. A geochemical analysis comparing the hominid remains with animal bones from the pocket suggests that they may have been contemporaneous. The fauna is broadly similar to other Middle Pleistocene fauna. In addition, the artifacts found in the cave pocket, which were once thought to be First Intermediate (between the Early and Middle Stone Ages), are now considered late Early Stone Age, or Sangoan. Thus both fauna and artifacts indicate a Middle Pleistocene age.

The Broken Hill cranium, with its complete face, presents a contrast of ruggedness and gracility (see Figure 10.2). The cranium is marked by a very large browridge, a low forehead, and a well developed occipital area. These features combine to give it the superficial appearance of a *Homo erectus* skull, but in

fact the specimen is considerably more modern looking.

It resembles the Solo crania in its expanded capacity (about 1,300 cc), cranial height, frontal breadth expansion and encroachment of the frontal over the supraorbitals, change in occipital proportions due to expansion of the upper part of the bone and reduction of the nuchal muscle attachment area, and close correspondence of cranial and braincase breadth. In some ways, the cranium is unlike any from Solo. While the browridge is better developed (especially in the central portion), the nuchal torus is greatly reduced. The vault bones are generally thinner, but the sagittal keel is better expressed and extends over the frontal bone; the combination probably provides the same strength as thicker bones and a less developed keel.

The face of this male is quite large in overall dimensions. Yet the reduction in the nuchal area is reflected in the gracility seen in structures that support facial muscle attachments. For instance, the zygoma are thin and delicate, resembling those of *Homo erectus* females, and markedly reduced compared with those of erectus males. They enclose a small temporal fossa. The lower face is somewhat expanded compared with earlier specimens. This is almost certainly the result of large incisor roots.

The incisors (and canines) are larger than those of male *Homo erectus* specimens, while the posterior teeth are about the same size except for the reduced third molar. The virtually complete maxillary dentition is heavily worn. Many of the teeth have very deep caries (cavities), and some have completely rotted away. Thus chewing, if not breathing through the mouth, must have been very painful.

A special feature first noted in this specimen is found in the cheek region, to the sides of the nose and below the orbits. The bone in this region holds the roots of the teeth. Above these is an area of bone which encloses a large hollow space called the maxillary sinus. In the Broken Hill face, the maxillary sinus is expanded. As a consequence, the outer bone surface to the sides of the nose has an inflated or "puffed out" appearance. When there is a deep groove to the sides of the nose, the feature is called a "canine fossa." Broken Hill lacks this fossa. One hypothesis relates this sinus expansion to the increased use of the incisors. Many later specimens also have expanded maxillary sinuses.

The nose in the Broken Hill face is quite large

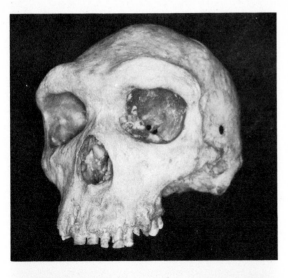
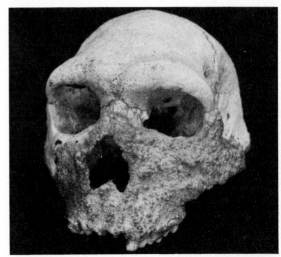
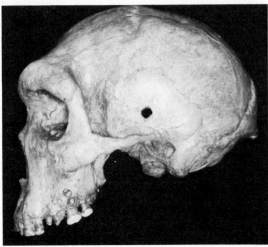
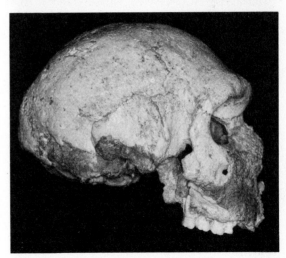

FIGURE 10.2 *Comparison of the crania from Broken Hill (left) and Petralona. The darker rough surfaces on the Petralona face are areas of yet-uncleaned matrix.*

and has a sharp lower margin. The upper jaw is only moderately prognathic; the incisor portion at the front projects forward slightly more than the top of the nose. However, the prognathism is much less than occurs in the australopithecines, and in general the tooth-bearing portion of the face is much smaller in all dimensions except breadth.

The second maxilla discovered in the cave is frequently overlooked. Although fragmentary, the palate appears quite similar in size and shape to the palate of the cranium. Both specimens have long tooth rows, deep palates with steep walls in the molar region, and a very great distance between the molar rows. The greatest difference is in the much smaller canines and lower face of the second (possibly female) maxilla. The presence of a third individual is suggested by a thin frontal fragment, although this may be associated with the maxillary fragment.

The Broken Hill postcranial sample (two innominates plus various limb bones) represents three or possibly more individuals. The bones are robust but surprisingly modern in form and proportion. Of all the bones, only a tibia can possibly be associated with the male cranium (because of its close physical proximity). The body height suggested by this complete bone is approximately 68 inches. Other aspects of the postcrania are discussed on pp. 236-237.

OTHER SUB-SAHARAN REMAINS

A cranium from Saldanha in the Orange Free State, South Africa, is like the Broken Hill cranium in most respects, although the face and cranial base were not preserved. The size and contours of the vault, the strong posterior angle of the browridge as seen from above, and the reduced nuchal torus combined with an expanded and bulging occipital plane align these crania with each other.

The recently discovered Ndutu cranium from Tanzania, reconstructed by R. Clarke, helps confirm that these features represent an evolutionary trend in early *Homo sapiens* populations in Africa. As with the above crania, there is more contrast with earlier specimens in the occiput than in the frontal region. What remains of the broken frontal suggests expanded breadth and a rather high angle for the forehead. Although the nuchal torus is as thick as in some of the more robust Solo specimens, the occiput above it is high, and the occipital plane bulges outward. The development of spongy bone at the cranial base is reduced, and the parietal walls are fairly vertical, as in the Broken Hill cranium. Unfortunately, not enough of the browridge remains to determine its size or shape. Interestingly, the vault lacks a sagittal keel although the vault bones are thick. There are marked outward bulges at the center of the parietals—a characteristic particularly common in Upper Pleistocene African populations. The face is about 80 percent the size of the Broken Hill face. It shows little alveolar prognathism, and the nose was prominent. The Ndutu cranium is probably female.

Another sub-Saharan specimen is a mandible from the Cave of Hearths at Makapansgat in South Africa. Along with a radius fragment that is roughly contemporary, the mandible come from Early Stone Age deposits equivalent to Broken Hill in age. The posterior teeth are reduced in size, and the second molar is much smaller than the first. As in the earlier Lantian mandible, there is congenital absence of the last molar.

Finally, a new Ethiopian find from the site of Bodo is superficially similar to the more southern specimens, although the cranium is larger and the face is broader and more massive. The specimen was reconstructed by its discoverers, G. Conroy, C. Jolly, and D. Cramer. The nose is extraordinarily broad, and the thick, robust zygomatics angle strongly backward from it, separated from the nose by a very shallow canine fossa. A long, sloping frontal begins above the thick browridge, and the temporal fossa appears to have been large. If anything, the features associated with robustness are more pronounced than in the Broken Hill cranium, although the face is somewhat shorter.

SOME COMPARISONS

The South and East African specimens are similar to the Solo crania in grade but not detail. In general, they can be seen to differ from the Asian sample in cases where different morphological combinations accomplish the same purpose (thinner vault bones but stronger sagittal keel, for instance). The browridges tend to be more posteriorly angled toward the sides and are better developed centrally. In most specimens the nuchal torus is reduced, whereas it is expanded at Solo. Nonetheless, virtually every feature of this sample can be found in the Solo crania. Differences are mainly in the frequency and combination of features. Thus, if a geographic variant is truly present, it is distinguished by the frequency of common grade features to a greater degree than by the appearance of unique ones.

The sub-Saharan sample provides evidence of early *Homo sapiens* faces, which are unknown from Indonesia. All the faces are large, but they vary from the robust features of Bodo to the gracile structures of Broken Hill and Ndutu. While some of the variation probably reflects sexual dimorphism, both Bodo and Broken Hill appear to be male, and the contrast between them should be attributed to other factors.

NORTH AFRICA

North African specimens come from a number of sites along the Atlantic coast of Morocco. They are dated to the later Middle Pleistocene through faunal and geological correlations.

The Rabat juvenile specimen (13–14 years old) was probably complete when fossilized. However, it was blasted to pieces during a mining operation. What remains is part of a mandible (Figure 10.5), maxillary pieces, an almost complete dentition, and a large number of cranial fragments (few bigger than a quarter). Taking age into account, the moderately thickened vault appears to combine both erectus-like and more modern features. Impressions of the internal blood vessels that supplied the brain and proportions of the occipital lobes are reminiscent of earlier hominids, while the high occiput with reduced nuchal torus more closely resembles the (perhaps) contemporary sub-Saharan sample. Posterior tooth size is somewhat reduced compared with the late *Homo erectus* average. The main reduction is in the mandibular molars. The premolars of the mandible and the maxillary posterior teeth more closely resemble those of earlier hominids. In contrast, the incisors (as measured by transverse breadth) are larger than those of late *Homo erectus*, and the canines are about the same size, or larger.

The other two mandibles in the North African sample are from Témara and Casablanca. Casablanca is about the same age as Rabat, while Témara may be somewhat younger. Both have larger postcanine teeth than Rabat. Taken together, the three jaws differ from the earlier North African *Homo erectus* sample mainly in expanded anterior tooth size, while the molar size progression shows relative reduction toward the back of the jaw.

A recently reported cranium from Salé combines a small vault with features reminiscent of the sub-Saharan early *Homo sapiens* sample (see Figure 10.3, p. 226). The cranial capacity is estimated to be 930–960 cc, and the greatest cranial breadth is at the base. The cranium exhibits marked postorbital constriction and a sagittal keel. It further resembles other crania of early African *Homo sapiens* in the shortened nuchal plane (and expanded occipital plane above it); very reduced nuchal torus; high, rounded occiput; lack of a marked forehead slope (like Broken Hill); and marked parietal bulging (as in the Ndutu cranium). As is the case with the other African crania, the most dramatic changes are in the occiput. While this bone is extraordinarily broad (by modern standards), its lack of a prominent nuchal torus and the general rounding of the contour represent the most marked expression of trends seen in the other African specimens. Unfor-

tunately, the face and part of the frontal are broken away. Nonetheless, the small size and gracility of the specimen suggest that it is female.

ADAPTATION AND CHANGE IN AFRICA

Unlike the situation in Asia, the archaeological associations of the African specimens are well known. All are from sites with late versions of the Acheulean industrial complex. If *Homo sapiens* evolved within the Acheulean, the origin of at least some of the changes (or continuations) in selection might be sought in the adaptations this lithic industry reflects.

The Acheulean complex supported what J. D. Clark calls "unspecialized hunting societies" at its onset, although later developments included the appearance of regional and even local variants. These argue for the evolution of new adaptations and cultural specializations. The lithic technology itself is characterized by more trimming and retouch. Clark suggests that this might be the result of more persistent use of the same tool, which then needs to be resharpened as it becomes blunted. This, in turn, could mean that camping places were occupied for longer continuous periods (more effective habitat utilization).

In some areas, a new method for the preparation of flakes, called the "Levallois technique," appeared (see pp. 242–243). Sets of roughly circular stones may have formed projectile weapons. When the stones in a set are tied together with strings of different length, the resulting bola, thrown with a twirling motion, can be used to trip or injure game. Evidence from other areas suggests that wooden spears with fire-hardened points were probably in use. These weapons had the important effect of increasing the distance between the hunters and their prey. Another innovation, spread from earlier times, was the use of fire (reported from the Makapansgat early *Homo sapiens* levels). This probably had an important effect on the continued posterior dental reduction if it indicates (as most workers believe) that many foods were cooked.

While we have little direct evidence of the vegetal foods consumed, the continued development of hand axes and (later) even more pick-like forms used in digging attests to the importance of plant resources. The range of fauna that was hunted reflects an increasingly effective resource utilization.

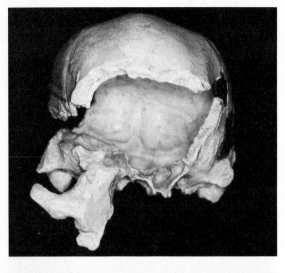
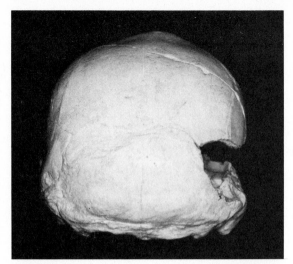
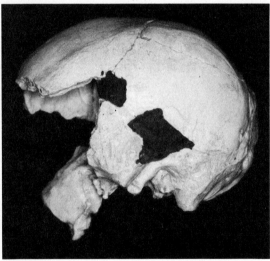
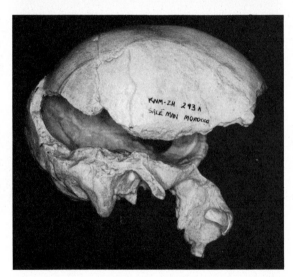

FIGURE 10.3   *Some views of the Salé cranium (cast). Although smaller, it closely resembles the European female cranium from Swanscombe, especially in the rounded, broad occiput and reduced nuchal torus. Part of the frontal and the face are broken away.*

As a whole, the earliest African *Homo sapiens* sample shows a combination of braincase expansion, reduction in the cranial superstructure, and posterior tooth reduction. The latter changes could probably best be subsumed under the concept of gracilization. Less positively, there seems to be some evidence suggesting an increase in anterior tooth size (and use). The sample differs from the Solo specimens more in the more gracile occipitals than in changes affecting the frontal. Yet the same grade features are present in both areas.

Perhaps changing attitudes about the African sample can best be exemplified through the history of the Broken Hill fossils. The cranium, which seemed so robust and primitive when first reported fifty years ago, is now considered gracile, large-brained, and reduced when compared with earlier specimens. Taken to be a recent African Neandertal by some, and a late-surviving *Homo erectus* by others, Broken Hill can now be viewed as a male temporally and morphologically between these, in a population with marked sexual dimorphism. What some regarded as perhaps even a "freak" or a "throwback" has become a legitimate member of a sample that represents an early variety of our own species.

The Evolutionary Sequence in Europe

Hominid remains are well represented in the Middle Pleistocene deposits of Europe. They are found over a span roughly defined by the beginning of the Mindel glaciation and the end of the Riss (400 to 120,000 years ago). In some respects, however, Europe is the most difficult area to deal with. While there are many sites, virtually every one has only one specimen and so there is a tendency to compare individuals rather than samples. This is further complicated by uncertainties in dating, a problem affecting all but the latest specimens. Since the sample as a whole retains many *Homo erectus* features, the lack of accurate dating confounds the other problems which surround a sample that spans both sides of an arbitrary line dividing two species on a lineage. In many cases, it is simply impossible to determine whether specimens should be regarded as late *Homo erectus* or early *Homo sapiens*.

Since the division between these is arbitrary, the problem may not be serious. However, dating uncertainties also make it difficult to establish clearly the trends for evolutionary change. What I have done is to break the sample into three broad time spans, while recognizing that some of the specimens may be inaccurately placed. The earliest of these is the Mindel and pre-Mindel span, already covered in the discussion of *Homo erectus* in Chapter 9. Specimens included in this span are Vértesszöllös, Mauer, and Vergranne. The second span is roughly equivalent to the interglacial between the Mindel and the Riss. This is the so-called "great interglacial," which is now known to include small glaciations in at least some areas of Europe. The third span corresponds to the Riss glaciation.

THE INTERGLACIAL SAMPLE

Until recently, most of this sample was thought to be well dated. However, recent work has questioned the application of the European glacial stages over all but very limited areas. Moreover, specimens once "securely" dated to this interglacial have been re-analysed. For instance, Swanscombe may actually come from the Riss/Würm interglacial, while Steinheim may derive from a Riss deposit. These suggestions are supported by the discovery of a new cranium from northern France (Biache) dated to the Riss, which closely resembles Swanscombe and Steinheim. Conversely, the Petralona cranium from Greece, which was first reported as Würm in age, is now said to be older (perhaps considerably) than 350,000 years.

The fact is that none of the presumed pre-Riss specimens is securely dated; their position is best regarded as probably lying between the latest *Homo erectus* occurrences and the better-dated Riss hominids. For this reason, the pre-Riss specimens will be considered together. No sample more clearly shows the complex relationship between morphology, date, and phylogeny. A morphological definition of speciation (morphospecies, Figure 2.2) would regard the dating problem as irrelevent. But in view of the fact that the sample is transitional (whatever its taxonomy), could the morphology be expected to show clear taxonomic affinities? A chronological definition of speciation (chronospecies) cannot be accurately applied because of uncertainties in the dating. Moreover, it is not clear what to compare the sample with. In the absence of earlier *Homo erectus* known from Europe, might comparisons not confuse grade distinctions with geographic ones? In all, there is an ambiguity underlying the treatment of the European specimens that simply cannot be resolved at present.

THE FEMALES

The Swanscombe skull fragments (Figure 10.8) are the oldest known human remains from Britain. They were also the first of this European sample to be discovered. Originally a parietal and an occiput were found, in the mid-1930s, and the other parietal was recovered in 1957. The first interpretation of this specimen was that it was "virtually indistinguishable" from modern crania, although even then it was recognized as unusually low and broad. The occipital contour is evenly rounded, and there is no substantial development of a projecting nuchal torus. Consequently, the contour of the specimen, in side view, is modern appearing, though small.

Unfortunately, many of the features that might be useful in determining the relationships of the Swanscombe cranium are missing. However, there are hints of what these might have been like from the remaining vault bones. To begin with, although the first impression of the skull form is modern, the combination of features is not. The probability of finding a modern cranium with the Swanscombe dimensions is extremely small. The cranial height falls at the low end of the modern human range of variation, while the breadth of the occiput falls at the very high end. Only a very large modern skull would be expected to have the great occipital breadth, while only a very small one would have the cranial height.

Other archaic features lie at the rear and base of the cranium, where the development of spongy bone is marked and the nuchal muscle attachment area is large. In the lack of a pronounced nuchal torus, Swanscombe differs dramatically from the more robust specimens discussed above, but it still falls within the sample range, resembling the most gracile of the Solo females. More specifically, the features of the Swanscombe vault are virtually identical to those of the Salé cranium (Figure 10.3). Unfortunately, both specimens lack the face and the portion of the frontal just above and behind it, so that proposals of what the browridges may have been like are without resolution. What the vault features *show* is powerful development of the neck muscles, and what they *imply* is a female-sized Middle Pleistocene face.

The form of the missing portions of the Swanscombe cranium can be estimated with reasonable accuracy using a cranium from the German site of Steinheim. This specimen consists of an almost complete skullcap and face (see Figure 10.4). The base of the cranium is broken open in a manner similar to the crania from Choukoutien. Unfortunately, the skull must be analyzed with great caution since it is badly damaged and warped. The whole left side has been twisted toward the midline, so that the single (fourth) premolar is almost at the middle of the cranium. Moreover, the back of the cranium is warped underneath and to the side, making the nuchal region appear more rounded than it actually was. Finally, the incisor-bearing portion of the upper jaw is broken away, which makes the face look much smaller and less prognathic than it probably appeared in life.

As preserved, the dimensions and features are very inaccurate and should not be taken "literally." However, they are sufficient to show that the braincase and face were small. The face is delicate in appearance. It is approximately the size of the Choukoutien female face reconstructed by Weidenreich and resembles it in the marked projection and substantial thickness of the browridges and the position of the forehead behind rather than above them. But there are numerous specific contrasts with the late *Homo erectus* female. For instance, the browridge in Steinheim forms a double arch, conforming to the contour of the orbits, and thins toward the sides. Steinheim also exhibits more midfacial prognathism (forward projection of the nasal region and above). Expanded maxillary sinuses extend the entire face forward, but the midface is not expanded enough to obscure the canine fossa.

Where the two can be compared, compensating for distortion, Steinheim and Swanscombe are quite similar. Both have a small cranial capacity (the estimate for Swanscombe is 1250 cc and the smaller Steinheim vault was probably under 1000 cc). Other shared features include marked reduction of the nuchal torus and rounding of the occiput, and narrowing of the frontal (inferred from the angle of the parietals in Swanscombe). Both have fairly vertical parietals; cranial and braincase breadths are about the same. Finally, both contrast with two other European crania that are roughly equivalent in date.

THE MALES

The first of these is the cranium from Petralona, a Greek site near Thessalonika. It was discovered by some shepherds when they fell into a cavern that is part of a complex cave system. Some reports state that they found a whole fossilized skeleton laid out on a limestone slab. However, other reports are contradictory, and the fate of the postcranial skeleton which was presumably found with the cranium is unknown. In many respects, the Petralona cranium is a European version of the Bodo and Broken Hill crania. The specimen combines an extremely large face with a low and robust braincase (Figure 10.2). There are great similarities between it and Broken Hill, and yet there are important differences.

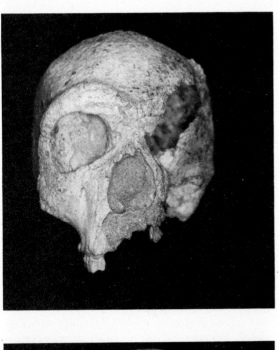
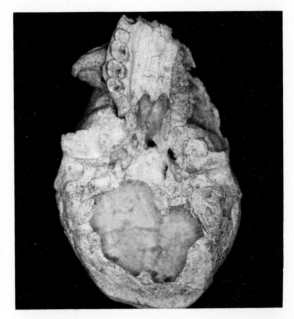
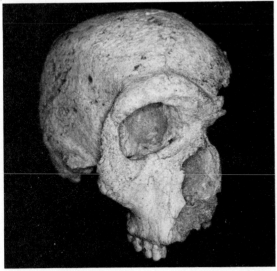
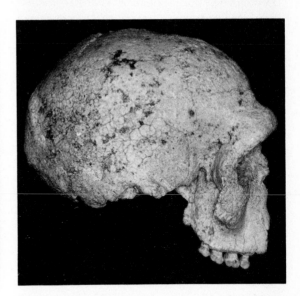

FIGURE 10.4   *Four views of the distorted Steinheim cranium. Note the damage to the left side and cranial base. The face in front of the premolars is broken away, and the base is so twisted that the teeth lie almost on the midline of the cranium.*

The basic dimensions of the braincase are similar to those of Broken Hill. However, the Petralona cranium is lower, broader, and more robust. It has more spongy bone at the cranial base than any other Middle Pleistocene specimen. The maximum cranial breadth is considerably greater than the braincase breadth (Figure 9.8). Some of this contrast is due to the extreme asymmetry of the Petralona cranium. As seen from the rear, the right cranial wall slopes outward, while the left wall is vertical (more like other early *Homo sapiens* specimens) and this side has less spongy bone. The asymmetric development affects the entire braincase; for instance, the right parietal is considerably more bulging than the left. The back border of the right temporal is flanged outward, possibly as the result of powerful horizontal fibers of the posterior temporalis muscle on this side.

The system of cranial buttresses is well developed in Petralona, but in almost the opposite manner from in the Solo crania. The nasal and midorbital portions of the browridge are extremely thick, and (as in Steinheim) there is marked thinning to the sides. Also, the browridge follows the superior orbital border (as in both Steinheim and Broken Hill), rather than forming a straight line. At the center, a slight furrow separates the two sides. There is a small sagittal keel involving only the parietals, and a low but thick nuchal torus extends across the back of the cranium.

The occiput is very broad; the estimated nuchal muscle attachment area is much greater than in Broken Hill. Because of the low, thick nuchal torus that does not project strongly, this whole region resembles the possibly earlier Vértesszöllös occiput. Also like Vértesszöllös, Petralona has a large extra-sutural bone at the top of the occiput. Such bones usually form when the lambdoidal suture (between the occiput and the parietals) is under stress, as might result from powerful nuchal action drawing the occiput downward.

The tall Petralona face is undistorted and is one of the best preserved from the Middle Pleistocene. The large rectangular orbits are widely separated and overlie robustly developed zygoma, which are much deeper and more robust than those in Broken Hill, more closely resembling the Bodo face in development and ruggedness. The lower border of the zygoma angles gradually downward until it merges with the outer wall of the maxilla in a rather low position; the lack of a distinct angle to this border is called the "flying buttress." While the cheeks begin in a fairly forward position, they angle strongly backward so that the fronts of the cheeks are at an angle of more than 45° to a plane from one side of the skull to the other. The maxillary sinuses are very large and are expanded outward, giving the face a puffy appearance, completely lacking a canine fossa (the region to the sides of the nose is convex). This morphology is associated with a forward projection of the entire face. What remains of the nose is prominent in profile and broad.

Finally, the very large dentition is set in a broad palate, marked by straight but diverging posterior tooth rows and a very straight line of anterior teeth, with the canine marking the corner. Both the size and proportions of the dentition and the form of the palate closely resemble Broken Hill.

Another robust hominid from this period is represented by bones from the DDR (German Democratic Republic) site of Bilzingsleben. Several cranial fragments and a molar have been reported from this north German site, dated to the Mindel/Riss interglacial. It is possible that different specimens are represented, although D. Mania, who discovered the remains, believes they are all from a single individual. The frontal fragment, comprising mainly the central areas of the browridge (Figure 10.8), is characterized by an extremely thick supraorbital torus, thick cranial bone, and a wide distance between the orbits. As in *Homo erectus* crania, there is little curvature of the torus over the orbits, but in contrast the flat forehead is not separated from it by a marked groove.

A second fragment (perhaps from the same individual) consists of two portions of the occiput, making up most of the bone. The occiput above the nuchal torus is wide and high, merging evenly with the low, broad torus. This region appears to resemble both Petralona and Vértesszöllös, although it was smaller than in either and has a thicker nuchal torus.

SOME PROBLEMS

Bilzingsleben and Petralona would make good "males" in a population containing females like Steinheim and Swanscombe, if that population had more sexual dimorphism than living people. Of course, they were not in the same population, but the point is that sexual dimorphism on a scale not unlike that found in earlier hominids *could* account for the variation in these crania. The pattern of features that differ fits a dimorphism model; the main contrasts are less in overall cranial size and capacity than in the functionally related features of facial size and robustness and the cranial buttressing system. Interestingly, these Europeans seem more closely to resemble *Homo erectus* in some features than early *Homo sapiens* males from Africa and Asia. However, the differences are more of frequency than of type. Bodo has a face as robust as Petralona's, and the Ndutu occiput retains erectus-like

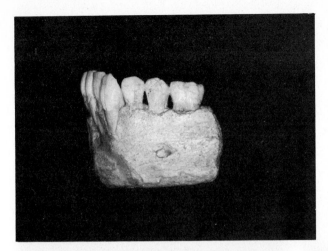
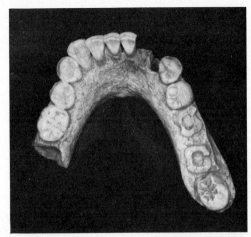
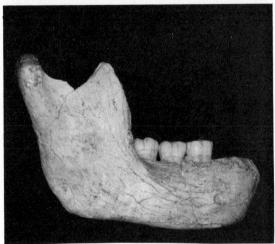
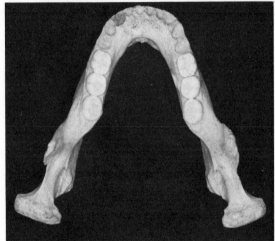

FIGURE 10.5 Two mandibles of early **Homo sapiens.** *Above is the Rabat jaw and below the Montmaurin specimen. Note the missing teeth on the left side of Rabat and the unerupted third molar.*

features and proportions. Similarly, the features contrasting with *Homo erectus* found in Swanscombe and Steinheim are also seen in Salé, as well as in some of the Solo specimens.

Should the sample be regarded as late *Homo erectus*? The males (especially Bilzingsleben) show few features that differ substantially from *Homo erectus* in Asia, and it is not clear whether these are due to differences in grade or geographic differences. Steinheim shows marked similarities to the Chou-koutien (reconstructed) female in the facial and frontal regions. The important contrasts with *Homo erectus* lie in the forward extension of the midface (seen in both sexes) and the reduction of occipital breadth and nuchal torus development. However, the earlier Vértesszöllös occiput does not differ from these male occiputs in any important way except size, and in this respect it is actually "more modern." Finally, the single European mandible reported from this timespan, Montmaurin from France (see Figure 10.5), resembles the Mauer mandible in its robustness but is about the right size to fit Steinheim. It also differs from Mauer in having less broad rami, but in general morphology, lack of a chin, outward angulation of the condyles, and other features, it closely resembles the earlier European mandible attributed to *Homo erectus*. It is difficult to make a completely convincing case that this sample should not be regarded as late *Homo erectus*.

On the other hand, should the earlier European sample and this one be lumped together and all the specimens considered early *Homo sapiens*? This position was argued by F. C. Howell before the discovery of Bilzingsleben and Vértesszöllös. Much of his argument, however, rested on distinctions that are probably geographic. Yet it is difficult to separate these samples in any convincing way, and if the occipital differences between Mindel/Riss crania and *Homo erectus* crania provide their greatest distinction, these differences also characterize Vértesszöllös. Moreover, there are strong parallels between the European sample and the African specimens attributed to early *Homo sapiens*.

My taxonomic usage in these chapters is a compromise between the above opinions. However, since my interpretation depends on the (uncertain) dates of the specimens, to the extent that there is an issue, it cannot be clearly resolved at present.

THE RISS SAMPLE

In the past few decades, a number of hominid sites dating to the Riss glaciation have been reported. All are in western Europe. To date, these sites have yielded a good number of cranial fragments, teeth, and mandibles, as well as a few postcranial remains. The large number of recent European finds, however, should not be taken as an indication of an unusual population density for these hominids, but rather of an unusual population density for the archaeologists and others seeking early human remains.

The French sites include Arago, Lazeret, the La Chaise cave of Suard, and Biache-Saint-Vaast (see Table 11.1, pp. 258-259). The Spanish site of Cova Negra is said to be of equivalent age, although I do not believe the faunal correlations are completely clear (the specimen may be younger).

The Arago cave, in southeastern France, is the earliest of these sites and has the largest hominid sample. At least twenty-three individuals have been reported, dating from the earliest portions of the Riss and possibly as old as 275,000 years. Of these, at least eight are children. Some adult specimens are represented by single teeth and cranial fragments, but Arago 2 and 13 are fairly complete mandibles, and Arago 21 is the front portion of a cranium with a complete face and crushed frontal bone.

The Arago cranium (see Figure 10.6) mainly provides information about the face. The small vault is too crushed to indicate much more than that the frontal begins over the browridge and does not narrow much behind it. Like Broken Hill, Arago 21 combines elements of robustness and gracility. The browridges are fairly large and prominent, lying between those of Steinheim and Petralona in size. Below them, the broad but fairly small face is dominated by expanded zygomatics, which shelve evenly onto the maxilla in a low position (as in Petralona). Maxillary puffiness replaces the canine fossa and the alveolar region is markedly prognathic. M. A. de Lumley, who has described and analyzed many of the French and Spanish specimens discussed in this chapter and the next, suggests that Arago 21 is probably male. In my view, comparison of the face with earlier (and later) specimens and the teeth with other Arago individuals indicates that it could be female.

Sex determination for the two well-preserved mandibles (see Figure 10.7, p. 234) is less ambiguous. Differences in size and robustness are consistent with the idea that Arago 2 is female and Arago 13 is male. (The Arago 21 teeth lie between these in size.) The much larger male has a very high, narrow ramus and sloping symphysis, while the ramus in the female is lower but much broader and the symphysis has one of the earliest discovered traces of a chin. At the base of the symphysis there is a moderate bulge, which, in specimens with a more prominent development, is called a "mental eminence" (or more commonly, a chin).

The Arago teeth are remarkable for both their size and their variation. The largest mandibular dentition, Arago 13, has a posterior dental set bigger than any known for *Homo erectus*! A second large dentition, Arago 1, has 90 percent of the area, and the posterior teeth of the female mandible (Arago 2) are 65 percent the size of Arago 13's. In comparison, the posterior dentition of the smallest *Homo erectus* mandible is 75 percent the area of the largest. Yet all of the Arago variation is restricted to a single site and a limited timespan. The teeth of Arago 1 and 13 fall well within the late australopithecine size range, as well as in the range of morphological variation. Yet when all of the Arago teeth are combined, which is a better estimate of the populational characteristics, the average poste-

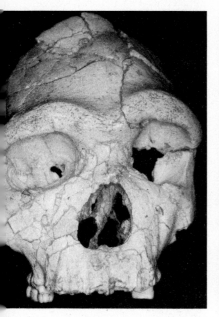
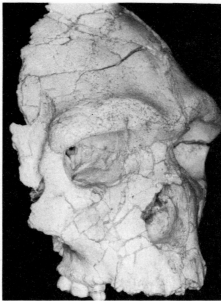

FIGURE 10.6 The Arago 21 cranium. The frontal bone of this specimen has been pushed upward and is broken in a number of places. Note the asymmetry of the face, which results from crushing. The right orbit and left zygomatic bone are more accurately preserved. In the side view, the cranium is shown articulated with the Arago 13 male mandible.

rior tooth size at Arago is reduced compared with *Homo erectus.*

Finally, there are a number of fragmentary postcranial remains from the Arago cave. In 1978 a virtually complete innominate was discovered. The specimen is so new that it has not yet been published (that is, described in print). It is said to be large and robust, but virtually modern in its morphological features.

The relations between the Arago sample and the earlier European specimens are clear, especially in facial and mandibular morphology. The marked variability at Arago, a probable consequence of sexual dimorphism, shows how misleading other sites with only single specimens might be (especially when sex determination is unclear) and helps emphasize the idea that it is samples and not individuals that should be compared.

All of the remaining Riss-dated specimens are later in time (Table 11.1). The most complete cranium is from Biache. This specimen is virtually identical to Swanscombe; even the same parts are preserved, although Biache also includes the back of the temporals and a palate with posterior teeth. It differs from Swanscombe mainly in having a flattened area at the back of the skull in the region where the occiput and parietals meet. The vault is small and fairly low, the nuchal muscle attachment area is weakly developed, the occiput is rounded, and the mastoids are small. The specimen is probably female. Its posterior teeth are 95 percent the area of Arago 21's, but otherwise the two cannot be compared since different portions of the cranium are preserved.

Crania are represented at the La Chaise cave of Suard by part of a vault, an occiput, and additional fragments. A child's mandible and a number of teeth have also been found at the site. The vault, Suard 1, includes the frontal (without forehead) and the parietals. The specimen is long, low, and thick-boned. The estimated maximum cranial breadth is very great, and the point of maximum breadth does not fall at the cranial base, as it does in earlier specimens. Instead, it is partway up the parietals. This is a consequence of two evolutionary trends which characterize the Riss adult sample. One is the reduction in spongy bone development at the cranial base, which decreases its breadth. The second is the continued expansion of the parietal association areas of the brain, which increases

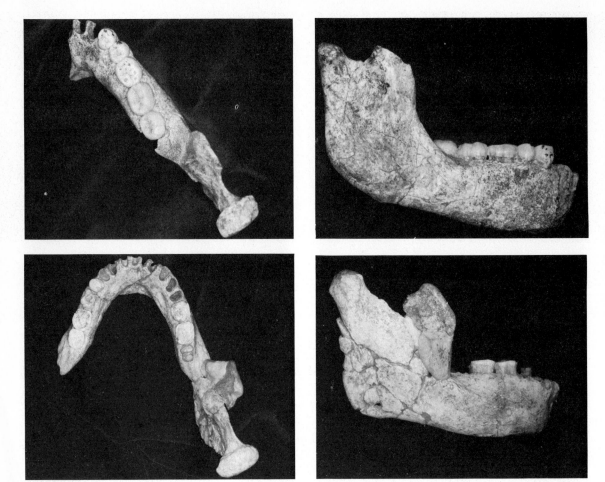

FIGURE 10.7   Comparison of the Arago male and female mandibles (male above).

the breadth across the parietals. As a result, the shape of the vault as seen from the rear is circular, with the maximum diameter about one-third the distance from the base to the top (see Figure 9.8). The Suard occiput (La Chaise 2) is similar to the female occiputs in the earlier sample (see Figure 10.8), as well as the Biache occiput. Viewed from the side, the contour is fairly circular, and there is minimal nuchal torus development. The position of the torus is low; the occipital plane above it is expanded, while the nuchal plane below is shortened.

Although more fragmentary, the Cova Negra pa-

rietal (Figure 10.8) is similar to the Suard 1 parietals in the circular contour of the outline as seen from the rear and in the (estimated) great cranial breadth. However, it differs in the shape of the bone. The Cova Negra shape is roughly square: all four borders are about the same length. The Suard 1 parietals, on the other hand, are relatively elongated.

The Lazaret cave, near Nice, has yielded remains of three hominids from the later part of the Riss. Two are represented by single teeth, and the third by a parietal. The associated industry is described as "evolved" Acheulean. The two teeth are a milk molar and a small, worn lower canine. The parietal (Figure 10.8), belonging to a juvenile about nine years old, has been studied in some detail. Although some of the characteristics may be due to

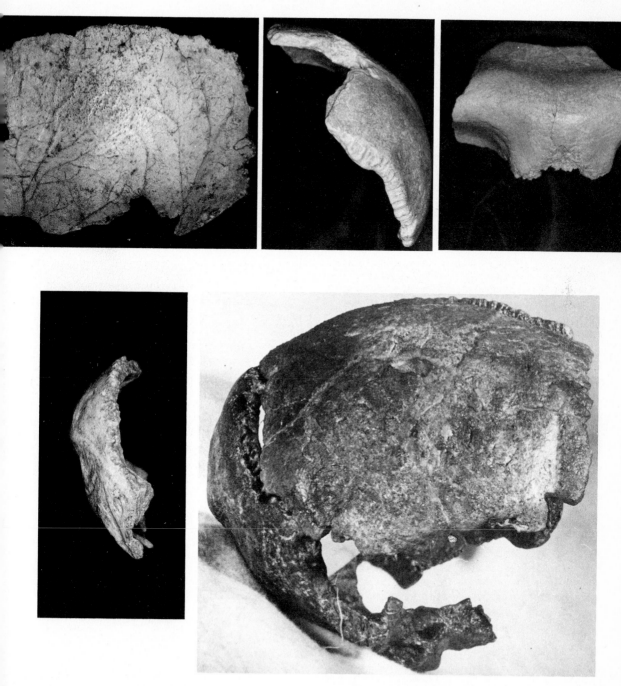

FIGURE 10.8 *Some of the European cranial fragments. Above, from left to right, are the Lazeret parietal shown in internal view (the pathology leading to death is seen in the upper center portion of the bone), a posterior view of the* Cova Negra parietal (cast) showing the semicircular contour, and a frontal view of the Bilzingsleben supraorbital fragment. Below are side views of the La Chaise 2 occiput (left) and Swanscombe (courtesy of C. L. Brace).

its youth, the shape of the bone is elongated (like the Suard parietals), and the top (sagittal suture) does not have as much curvature as occurs in modern crania. The youth apparently died as the result of a bone infection.

CONTINUITY AND CHANGE IN EUROPE

Some important continuities characterize the early *Homo sapiens* samples from Europe. The pre-Riss and Riss segments of the lineage share a high frequency for a number of facial features, including fairly marked browridge development in both sexes (especially if Arago 21 is female, as I suspect), maxillary puffing to the extent of canine fossa loss, strong development of the zygomatics (usually accompanied by a strong backward angle), and a great degree of sexual dimorphism in size and robustness. Moreover, there is little change in average cranial capacity, vault bone thickness, or the size of the posterior dentition.

On the other hand, some changes do occur over this timespan. There may be some expansion of anterior tooth size (the samples are too small for certainty). In addition, the females are characterized by an occipital region that is reduced in robustness from the *Homo erectus* condition to the point where the nuchal torus is either weak or virtually absent. Whether a more robustly developed region is common to the males is uncertain since no male occiputs can be clearly identified in the Riss sample. However, the most significant contrasts between the interglacial and Riss samples are in proportions and robustness. In the later sample, features reflecting muscular activity are not as robustly developed. Basal spongy bone is not as extensive, and the portion of the occiput above the nuchal torus expands at the expense of the portion below it. The nuchal muscle attachment area is not extremely affected by this change, however, because there is a commensurate expansion in occipital breadth (part of a general expansion in cranial breadth). These changing relations result in a more horizontal orientation of the nuchal muscle attachment area. They also cause the point of maximum cranial breadth to shift from the base of the cranium in earlier specimens to a position partway up the parietals in the later ones. Finally, the few comparable mandibles differ mainly in the appearance of a rudimentary external projection at the base of

the symphysis in some of the later specimens. This is the first trace of a mental eminence, or chin.

The amount of variation at sites such as Suard and Arago is also an important characteristic of the Riss sample, although, as we have seen, great variation is a feature of almost all Pleistocene hominid sites with two or more specimens. In some instances, the Riss hominid variation has been interpreted as the result of great sexual dimorphism, while in others as the result of different coexisting lineages. The second interpretation will be discussed in the State of the Art section.

Postcrania

The postcranial remains for this Middle Pleistocene sample are so few and so widely scattered that it makes more sense to discuss them together than by geographic area. The bones that have been discovered include a fragmentary humerus shaft from Japan, two tibias from Solo, a fragmentary radius from the Cave of Hearths, innominates from Monaco and the Arago cave, and a variety of unassociated remains from Broken Hill, including two innominates, femurs, a tibia, and some upper limb portions. While the latter cannot be directly associated with the Broken Hill cranial remains, it is tempting to suggest that the large male innominate, the largest of the femurs, and the tibia might belong with the male cranium. This would leave the smaller female innominate and possibly a femur to represent a second individual, as well as the remains of at least one additional (even smaller) individual. One of these could be associated with the second maxilla and the other with the frontal fragment.

In general, these remains conform to the *Homo erectus* pattern of bony adaptation to muscularity and strength, although the expression of this pattern is not as pronounced. For instance, while the shaft walls of the limbs remain thick, there is less of a tendency for the antero posterior flattening that responds to bending. Instead, the limb shafts are more evenly circular.

The innominates (two from Broken Hill, a third from Arago, and a fourth from the Prince cave at Grimaldi, in Monaco) show less flare of the hip than earlier hominid innominates. With the reduced muscular leverage, the buttressing features of the bones are more pronounced, since more force is necessary for the same functions. The reduction in iliac flare corresponds to an increase in the breadth of the pelvic inlet, moving the hip joints farther apart. An additional feature associated with pelvic inlet size is seen in the Prince female innominate; the inlet is also expanded in the anterior-posterior direction. The tendency for larger inlets is the result of bigger head size at birth, a consequence of the trend for cranial capacity increase.

Five of the bones (the Japanese humerus, the smaller Solo tibia, the radius from Cave of Hearths and the two larger limbs from Broken Hill) are preserved well enough to allow an estimate of bone length, which in turn can be used to estimate body height. The average height of the five individuals represented is 63.3 inches. This is 1 inch shorter than the erectus average, and on the basis of these limbs, we must conclude that there is no significant change in body size.

Early Homo sapiens *and* Homo erectus

To review, the main morphological differences between the Middle Pleistocene early *Homo sapiens* sample and the late *Homo erectus* sample are found in the differential changes in cranial size and morphology, and to a lesser extent in the face. Dental differences conform to the continued trends for posterior reduction and anterior expansion. There is obvious continuity between the earliest members of our own species and the latest *Homo erectus* representatives in each area where large samples can be found.

THE POSTERIOR DENTITION

On the average, the posterior teeth of early *Homo sapiens* are reduced compared to those of late *Homo erectus*. Reduction is greater in the molars than in the premolars. In spite of the average reduction, several early sapiens specimens have immense posterior dentitions, and generally the males of this sample (Broken Hill, Petralona, Rabat, Arago 13) are well above the *Homo erectus* average. However, the female dentitions are markedly smaller, producing an average reduction. Why the degree of sexual dimorphism in these teeth should exceed that of late *Homo erectus* as represented at Choukou-

tien is unknown. It should be remembered, however, that other skeletal elements, such as the mandibles, suggest that the dentitions may underrepresent the extent of Choukoutien dimorphism.

THE ANTERIOR TEETH

The direction of size change in the anterior teeth is quite different. Although the sample is small, it is apparent that the canines and incisors are in the process of continued size increase, as measured by transverse breadth. The central incisor expands by 9 percent, the lateral incisor by 7 percent, and the canine is slightly, but not significantly, broader when compared with the late *Homo erectus* sample.

There are also some morphological changes in the anterior teeth. One of these is an increased frequency of marginal ridges on the internal sides of the incisors (lingual shoveling). Another is an increased tendency for the canine to be incisiform, even more closely approximating the incisors in morphology. (This is shown by the decreased frequency of asymmetry and pointed crowns in the unworn specimens.)

The increase in incisor breadth suggests a greater use in environmental manipulation. Both the breadth dimension and shoveling add strength when the incisors are used for gripping, holding, and pulling, or for other functions that involve a loading pattern resisted by the nuchal and posterior temporalis muscles. This suggests that there was a continued increase in the use of the front teeth for purposes other than chewing food. Even in living humans, the jaw muscles can exert more force than the hands, and the nuchal muscles provide a powerful force for pulling an object held in the mouth. Increasing use of the anterior teeth is a trend observed through the evolution of *Homo erectus*, and the evidence suggests that this trend continued in the earliest members of our own species. Indeed, we shall see that a whole new pattern of detail, control, and foresight in the production of tools and manipulation of objects evolves during this period.

THE FACE

The faces of early *Homo sapiens* are represented by six complete or almost complete specimens and a number of additional fragments. On the average, overall facial size appears to be about the same in the early *Homo sapiens* and late *Homo erectus* samples (holding sex constant). However, there are some proportional changes. These reflect a continuation of trends in *Homo erectus*—decreasing use of the premolars and molars and increasing use of the anterior teeth.

The height of the lower face (below the nasal margin) increases slightly in relation to total facial height, but the zygomatics are generally smaller in early sapiens (both relative to facial height and in absolute terms). This change is probably mostly in response to decreasing use of the masseter muscle and the effect of this decrease on the growth of the cheek region.

Another indication of decreasing masticatory muscularity can be seen in the lack of facial breadth change considered in conjunction with the fact that the minimum frontal breadth increases by 14 percent. Together, a shrinking breadth at the outside of the face and an expanding frontal result in a smaller temporal fossa and, by inference, a smaller temporalis muscle. In all, the early sapiens faces are *relatively* narrower, with smaller and less flaring cheeks.

Other facial changes are associated with the increasing use of the anterior teeth discussed above. These changes result from the pattern and magnitude of the forces that affect the area of the face holding the tooth roots. Holding an object between the anterior teeth and pulling or twisting it through the use of the nuchal and posterior temporalis muscles (Figure 8.7) creates forces that pull the crowns of these teeth outward. One consequence of this is that the roots, and the lower portion of the face holding them, are expanded in the early *Homo sapiens* sample. While this serves to anchor the front teeth better and reinforce them, it also means that during pulling while gripping (i.e., anterior tooth loading), the whole front part of the lower face (the teeth, their roots, and the bone holding them) is pulled outward, producing a strain in the facial bones. This strain is greatest in the bone just above the anterior tooth roots. Of course, immediately above it is the nasal aperture, where there is no bone. Thus the strain is concentrated in the bone just to the sides of the nose, where the canine roots help transmit it to the midfacial region. At the same time, forces in a quite different direction are generated by the simultaneous downward pull of the masseter muscle on the lower border of the zygomatics (Figure 8.6). The result is a combination of bending and tension, producing strain patterns that unreinforced bone would be unable to resist. Therefore, it is advantageous for the bone in this area to be strengthened.

MECHANISMS OF REINFORCEMENT

Strengthening could occur a number of ways, but what seems to have happened in this case is the simple addition of more bone in the area where the strain is greatest, along the sides of the nose. The bone added is, in effect, an expanded maxillary sinus. The internal cavities of the maxillary sinus provide great strength without the massive bulk that would be added if "solid" bone were used. (The same principle is applied to the manufacture of steel girders: hollowing the inside maximizes strength while minimizing weight.) Because of this expansion of the maxillary sinus, the canine fossa disappears; the area to either side of the nose becomes flat or convex as the maxillary sinus expands into what was earlier a concave region.

The other consequence of increased forces between the front teeth is found in the browridge. This structural buttress does not change in size (see below) in spite of the generally higher and more anterior foreheads, which provide an improved ability to resist strain.

THE MANDIBLES

Mandibles are only moderately represented in the early *Homo sapiens* sample. The known specimens vary markedly in size (for instance, the Arago male and female specimens). A systematic difference appears in three areas of the mandible and continues as a trend through the lineage.

One change is in the relative thickness of the body. The breadth of the corpus (mandibular body) decreases relative to corpus height. This is probably a direct result of the decreasing size of the posterior teeth and their roots. The second change is in the position of the vertical ramus. Especially in the later mandibles, the ramus appears to be in a more posterior position relative to the teeth. Since the ramus represents the attachment of the mandible to the cranium, the effect of this change is to place the teeth in a more forward position. This corresponds to the increasing facial prognathism in the sample.

The third change occurs at the symphysis. In the earlier *Homo sapiens* sample, the symphysis is narrower than in *Homo erectus*; when internal buttresses are present at all, they are reduced in size. In the later sapiens sample, some specimens (such as the Arago female) show a partial reversal in the position of the buttress. It is on the external face of the symphysis instead of the internal face, and in this position it is called a mental eminence, weakly developed in this instance.

A biomechanical explanation for the appearance of the mental eminence during the latest Middle Pleistocene has been developed by T. D. White. In small-brained hominids (and all pongids), the temporalis muscle (see Figure 4.8) has an inward orientation from the mandible because it attaches on a small braincase. When the breadth of the braincase is less than the breadth of the cranial base, it is also less than the breadth of the mandible, accounting for the inward direction of the muscle. This inward orientation acts to pull the sides of the mandible inward when the muscle is used, creating the need for an *internal* buttress where the sides meet (the mandibular tori in australopithecines and some *Homo erectus* specimens).

Over time, as the temporalis decreased in size, these buttresses became poorly expressed, if they were present at all, since there was less force pulling the sides of the mandible together. If the reduction in posterior tooth use had been the only change taking place in human evolution, the eventual result would have been a thin symphysis with no buttress. However, a second relevant change was the expansion of the brain through the Pleistocene. As the brain became larger, the braincase expanded until eventually the breadth of the braincase was greater than the breadth of the cranial base and therefore greater than the breadth of the mandible. We have noted that this change in proportion first appears in the latest Middle Pleistocene hominids (see discussion of Cova Negra and Suard). As a result, the fibers of the temporalis muscle angle outward from the mandible as they extend toward their cranial attachment. In this case, the temporalis muscles draw the sides of the mandible apart, so buttressing is necessary on the *external* surface of the symphysis rather than on the internal one. The external buttress first appears as a slight bulge (in the Arago female); and in later

mandibles a mental eminence, or true chin, appears.

THE BRAINCASE

Cranial capacity in the early *Homo sapiens* averages 1,166 cc, and ranges from 945 cc to 1,325 cc. This represents an 11 percent expansion in volume from the later *Homo erectus* sample. The vault dimensions, however, expand differentially. Maximum length and breadth do not change at all. In contrast, cranial height, the breadth of the parietals, and the minimum breadth of the frontal all increase by about 14 percent. This differential expansion is surely due to the changing proportions of the brain itself, with increases in its height and breadth relative to length, and reflecting the expansion of the frontal lobes.

A combination of increasing parietal breadth and decreasing spongy bone development at the cranial base brings the braincase breadth close to the total cranial breadth in the earlier part of the sample. By the time of the Riss glaciation, the braincase is broader than the cranial base in some specimens.

Expansion of the frontal lobes not only affects minimum frontal breadth, but also results in the general encroachment of the frontal forward and above the browridge. In all of the crania except Steinheim, which is similar to *Homo erectus* in this region, the frontal begins its upward slope directly over the browridge, rather than behind it. This expansion of the frontal to a position over the browridge, as well as the increase in its slope, might be expected to lead to a reduction in the size of the browridge (but it doesn't!).

Some of the most dramatic changes are in the occipital region. The attachment area for the nuchal muscles decreases by about 30 percent between late *Homo erectus* and early *Homo sapiens*. Both the development of spongy bone and the size and prominence of the nuchal torus decrease at this time. This is interesting in view of the other evidence suggesting an increase in anterior tooth use (larger anterior teeth, maxillary puffing, and lack of expected reduction in the supraorbital torus). Are these data contradictory? Three possibilities suggest themselves. First, the series of biomechanical models and inferences which I advocate may be wrong. Second, assuming the biomechanical models are correct, the pattern of anterior tooth loading may be changing to require *more vertical* forces but *fewer horizontal* ones in the direction that would require powerful nuchal muscle use (see Figure 8.6). There is no independent means of testing for this possibility. Third, there may be little actual loss of muscle power because of the more horizontal orientation of the reduced nuchal muscle attachment area. If one considers the direction of the nuchal muscle fibers to be roughly vertical, they would require more room for attachment on a sloping surface than on a horizontal one. Think of a cut made across a pencil. It will expose more surface area if it is angled than if it is exactly perpendicular to the shaft. Consequently, the reduced surface area for nuchal muscles may hold approximately the same total muscle cross-section as the larger but more angled surface in earlier hominids.

An equally important change occurs in the occipital plane, the portion of the occiput above the nuchal area. There is a 13 percent increase in the length of this plane, measured from the highest point of nuchal muscle attachment to the top of the bone. This is a direct consequence of increase in the size of the upper occipital and posterior parietal lobes. In late *Homo erectus*, the length of the occipital plane is only 86 percent the length of the nuchal plane, while in the early *Homo sapiens* sample, this percentage has increased to almost 109 percent. The occiput has expanded in breadth and height to enclose much larger posterior parietal lobes. As a result, the occipital plane is more rounded and has a greater angle with the horizontal.

In sum, most of the cranial changes are the result of the relative as well as absolute expansion of the brain and the reduction in the cranial strengthening system (see below). Since this expansion is not due to larger average body size, it reflects real evolutionary changes in the brain, and results in both general cranial expansion and the differential development of specific areas. As F. Weidenreich pointed out, in the evolution of *Homo sapiens* the role of the jaw muscles has decreased and the role of the brain shape has increased in determining the final form of the skull.

THE CRANIAL STRENGTHENING SYSTEM

The remaining changes that appear in early *Homo sapiens* are in the gradual reduction of the cranial

features thought to be associated with strengthening—torusing and bone thickness. In part, the reduction of these features is probably due to the increased capacity of the expanded braincase to perform the same functions. The structures that reduce are the torus above the ear and mastoids, the sagittal keel, and the nuchal torus.

However, taking sex differences into account, the browridge does not reduce despite the higher forehead. Moreover, little if any reduction characterizes the later (Riss) portion of the sample. On the average for the entire sample, the middle portion of the browridge is about the same as in later erectus, and the outer portions (from about the center of the orbits) are slightly larger. In this regard, however, rather different trends characterize early *Homo sapiens* in Indonesia. In the Indonesian sample, the central portion reduces, while in the Euro-African sample, it is about the same as in later erectus. That this torus maintains its thickness in spite of the higher forehead is a direct consequence of increased vertical forces in the anterior dentition (Figure 8.8).

With regard to the thickness of the vault bone, the trend toward average decrease seems to reflect two things. First, the greatest thicknesses in the earlier vaults are found in regions where muscle attachments are supported (as along the temporal line) and thinning here reflects reduction in muscle use. Second, the appearance of weapons that can be used at a distance reduced selection to maintain thickened bone as a protection against hunting injuries.

CULTURE AND MORPHOLOGY

The main changes observed in the crania and teeth of early *Homo sapiens* result from the combination of differential brain size expansion, continued powerful use of the anterior teeth, and decreased use of the posterior teeth. These morphological changes form a positive feedback cycle with the behavioral and technological changes taking place at the same time.

The increasing ability of technology to replace morphology in human adaptation would seem to be responsible for many of the changes discussed. New food preparation techniques, including the use of fire for cooking, probably had much to do with the reduction of the posterior teeth and associated structures. The earliest known spears appear at this time, along with more effective projectiles. These weapons helped put a distance between the hunters and their large prey, which eventually led to reduction in the features associated with skeletal strengthening. The expansion of cranial capacity and the continued differential expansion of certain parts of the brain can be attributed to the requirements of evolving social-cultural systems.

At the same time, however, the increasing technological complexity resulted in more extensive use of some morphological features as part of the tool kit. The effect on the anterior teeth and associated structures influenced a number of aspects of facial evolution, including retention of a large browridge (in spite of the more vertical forehead), expansion of the maxillary sinus, and the related appearance of midfacial prognathism. The interrelationship of human morphological and cultural evolution had become complex by the end of the Middle Pleistocene.

Adaptive Patterns in Early Sapiens

As we have seen, the evolutionary changes in the morphology of early *Homo sapiens* suggest some recognizable behavioral tendencies. The archaeological record elaborates and expands our knowledge of these important behavioral changes.

CONTINUED ACHEULEAN EVOLUTION

The archaeological record for this period is complex because of the development of new techniques and tools and the appearance of extensive geographic variation. Unfortunately, no tools can be directly associated with the largest sample, from Solo. Generally, when there are associated industries, these are geographic variants of the later phases of the Acheulean complex. In Africa this is the terminal portion of the Early Stone Age, while in Europe the Swanscombe industry is what F. Bordes calls "middle" Acheulean. Since many of the morphological developments seen in the early sapiens samples are a continuation of trends that began in the erectus sample, it should not be sur-

prising that the industries they are associated with represent continued development of the earlier Acheulean industries.

The main distinguishing characteristics of the later industries are found in the refinement of pre-existing tools, although some new types of tools were also developed. It appears that people had a clearer mental image of the tool to be made before manufacture began, and the degree of standardization for the various tool types was greatly increased compared with the earlier (erectus-associated) industries. Forms such as the oval and the triangle were accurately reproduced with a great number of standardized variations. These developments largely depended on the evolution of both the ability to preconceive form and skill in producing that form. There are no "hand axe genes" in the human genotype; it was the structural aspects of the neural models underlying tool-making behavior that were inherited and thus subject to evolutionary change. The observable industries are important because they reflect the degree of motor skill and the complexity of the rule systems underlying the imposition of increasingly arbitrary form on the environment.

A wide variety of tools have been found at the later Acheulean sites, including hand axes of so many different sizes and forms that they were probably made for a variety of purposes. In addition, there are sharp-edged cleavers (a chopping and cutting tool the size of a hand axe) and, in the later stages, backed blades (one side is blunted for handling). Tools for working wood, such as burins, have been found, and there are numerous flakes made into scrapers and notched "denticulate" tools. Worked bone and wood are rare because they are less likely to be preserved than stone, but a sharpened wooden spear was recovered from the English site of Clacton. However, there is little evidence of hafting stone onto wood, making composite tools.

Tool kits varied from place to place, and the combination of refinement and standardization of older tool types and the development of new tool types greatly increased the adaptability of human populations. Early *Homo sapiens* populations occupied new niches because they were able to make use of more resources. Moreover, finer habitat divisions within a given region appeared, suggesting more effective exploitive patterns for micro-environments.

PREPARED CORES AND THEIR IMPLICATIONS

During this period, two significant developments in tool-making technology occurred which laid the foundation for the subsequent evolution of *Homo sapiens* populations. An early discovery, already mentioned, was that stone can be shaped by softer materials, such as bone or wood, as well as by stone itself. The use of softer striking materials allowed finer work to be done, producing straighter and sharper edges (see Figure 10.9).

The second development was truly revolutionary. This was the invention of the prepared core, or "Levallois" technique. Prior to this, stone was shaped by striking flakes with another stone and later with bone or wood. The implement was shaped as flakes were struck off. In Oldowan and early Acheulean industries there is great variation in the finished tools and often the appearance that tool "types" were more the result of accident than of design. That is, many tools may have been struck, and the ones that looked most like cleavers used as cleavers, the ones most like hand axes used as hand axes, and so on. Throughout the Acheulean, the evolution of skill and foresight is shown by the increasing standardization of tools. It is apparent that forms were preconceived and that greater and greater effort was made to flake the implement into the desired shape. Retouch work on the flakes shows that they too were fashioned into specific shapes. With increasing skill, and the ability to preconceive form and translate the mental image accurately into performance, the raw material itself began to impose fewer limitations on the final product. As far as we can tell, these behavioral changes were related to the evolution of certain parts of the brain. And it was not until these changes occurred that a complex manufacturing technique such as the Levallois could arise.

What makes the Levallois technique revolutionary is that it introduced a second step into the manufacture of tools, further removing the form and initial preparation of the raw material from the form of the finished product. The technique (Figure 10.9) consists of preparing a piece of stone, or core, to a specific shape (something like a turtle shell) so that when a single flake is struck from it, it will immediately have the shape required. The struck flake is the finished tool and usually needs no addi-

Levallois

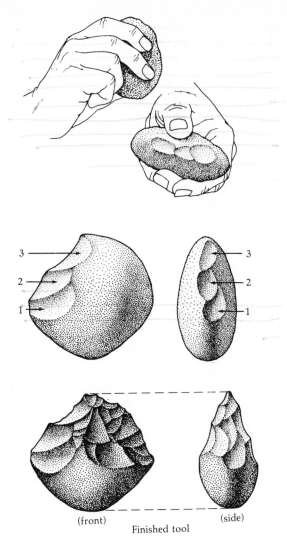

(front)   (side)

Finished tool

FIGURE 10.9 *The three early Paleolithic tool-making techniques (from Jolly and Plog, 1979). To the left is the direct percussion technique (stone-on-stone) responsible for the Oldowan and many Acheulean tools. The use of a softer striking material (center) that appeared in the Acheulean period allowed much finer control over the end product. A variant of this technique is indirect percussion, in which a stone is used to strike a shaft of bone or wood that is positioned on the developing tool. To the right are the basic stages of the Levallois technique. Development of the prepared core was one of the last basic technological innovations to have worldwide distribution before modern times. Stages 1–3 show the production of the core, and in stage 4 the tool is struck from it.*

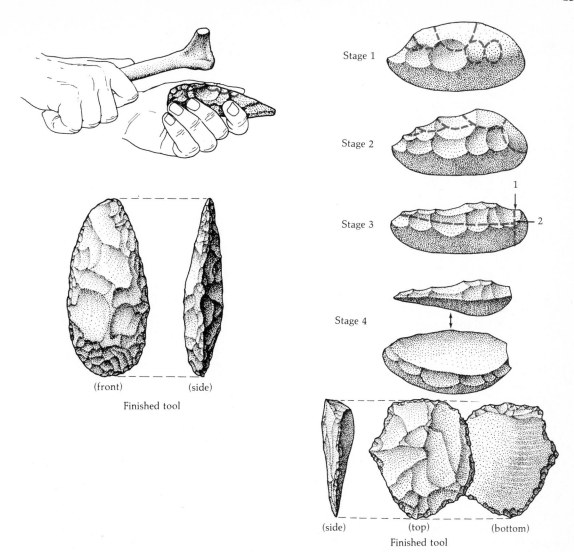

(front)   (side)

Finished tool

Stage 1

Stage 2

Stage 3

Stage 4

(side)   (top)   (bottom)

Finished tool

tional retouch on its extremely sharp edges. This was not simply a more skillful way of fashioning stone. It required a certain degree of neurological complexity and the ability to formulate (or learn) and follow a complex set of rules. When tools are made by direct (or indirect) percussion, there is an immediate feedback as the stone is being worked, since each step makes it look more like the desired form. The Levallois technique does not have this feedback potential because the core does not look like the Levallois flake that will be struck from it.

The prepared-core technique appeared in Africa, Europe, and Asia within the middle-to-later stages of the Acheulean industrial complex in the Middle Pleistocene. The technique was first used to further refine the manufacture of tool types already present, but by the beginning of the Upper Pleistocene, its potential to produce a whole new range of tool types had begun to be exploited. The neurological evolution that allowed the discovery of this technique came as a result of selection occurring during the timespan of the Acheulean complex. Once present, the technique opened up a new adaptive potential, leading to changes in selection that ultimately resulted in the evolution of morphologically modern populations.

LIFEWAYS

What were the ways of life of the Middle Pleistocene sapiens populations like? In Europe, some insight has been gained from a recently excavated living site in the French city of Nice, Terra Amata. The site, discovered during the course of digging a foundation, probably dates from the end of the Mindel glaciation. The climate was apparently "brisker" and more humid than that of today, although on the French Riviera these could hardly be called "hardship" conditions. A number of hut floors were discovered, the remains of perhaps the earliest human habitation structures known. These were oval in shape, ranging from 26 to 49 feet in length and 13 to 20 feet in width. A series of stakes, about 3 inches in diameter, were driven into the sandy ground to hold the walls, which were braced by rocks around the outside. A number of much larger posts, about a foot in diameter, supported the roof along the long axis of the hut. At the center of each hut, there is a fireplace (or hearth). A small wall of cobbles (which served as a wind screen) to the northwest side of each hearth shows that the huts were far from draft free. Distinct work areas where tools were made can also be identified within the huts.

The inhabitants were big-game hunters. The faunal remains, representing mostly young animals, include (in order of abundance) the stag, elephant, boar, ibex, rhinoceros, and wild ox. However, it is important to note that the bones of a large number of small animals, such as birds, rodents, and turtles, were also found, as were oyster, mussel, and limpet shells and a few fishbones. The pattern of exploitation was extensive, utilizing a very wide range of resources. Tools discovered include hand axes, cleavers, and scrapers. In addition, some tools appear to be projectile points and were possibly hafted onto wooden spears. Thus the extremely close-quarters hunting pattern of erectus was no longer necessary.

Some of the other artifacts recovered have great importance in understanding the adaptation of early sapiens. There are several bone tools, including the arm bone of an elephant with a point hammered on one end and another bone with a fire-hardened point. Finally, on a nearby dune a spherical imprint in the sand filled with a whitish substance was found. H. de Lumley, who excavated the site, believes that this may have been the impression left by a wooden bowl. In addition, some pieces of red ocher (a red mineral with the consistency of soft chalk) were discovered. Their ends were smooth from wear. De Lumley suggests that the red pigment was used for body decoration.

With all the evidence of extensive habitat exploitation, the camp at (what is now) Nice represents only a small part of the total adaptive pattern. Analysis of the plant remains in some human feces that were discovered shows that the habitation was short term, occurring in late spring or early summer. The huts quickly collapsed after the people left, as evidenced by the fact that some of the freshly chipped stones were not exposed to weathering (which indicates that they were soon covered up). The presence of numerous overlapping hut floors indicates periodic seasonal occupation. How far the group ranged during the year is unknown, but one relevant fact is that some of the tools are made of material that is available only in an area at least 30 miles from the site.

Almost nothing is known of the people themselves. A single footprint measures 9½ inches in length, which indicates a height of about 5 feet. We cannot determine whether this is typical or atypical for the population. Although there is no other direct knowledge of this population, there are human fossils from Europe dating roughly to this period. The Vértesszöllös and Mauer specimens are probably earlier, while Petralona, Bilzingsleben, Swanscombe, and Steinheim are later.

There are eleven distinct living floors at Terra Amata. These are so precisely superimposed over one another that de Lumley believes they almost certainly represent eleven consecutive years of occupation. The similarities in the structures, tools, and floor patterns suggest that many of the same individuals may have been involved in these consecutive occupations. In other words, a group (perhaps tribe) came to the same area at the same time each year, systematically exploiting its resources. Their occupation was brief, and Terra Amata was probably one of many habitation spots the group utilized during its seasonal movements. This gives evidence of stable, and rather complex, social institutions.

Other examples can be drawn from Africa, where the archaeological record reveals a wide range of different adaptive patterns over this period. Acheulean sites seem to be concentrated in savanna and parkland areas and are inevitably close to water. In the earlier stages of the Acheulean, the distribution of sites is rather limited, but the situation changes by the end of the Middle Pleistocene. F. C. Howell and J. D. Clark suggest that the increase in the number of sites, the wider distribution of sites, and the greater artifact densities at particular sites indicate an expansion of range and a higher population density. This suggests an increasingly effective cultural adaptation. Later sites appear in new habitats, forest and semiarid areas that were formerly unoccupied. The effectiveness of the Acheulean hunting adaptation had evolved to allow a wider range of resources to be utilized.

No structures have been discovered in Africa. However, sites range from caves to open-air occupations. At the Cave of Hearths, one of the Makapansgat caves in South Africa, there is evidence of hearths in the Acheulean layers. Open-air sites are more numerous. Two of the larger excavated sites dating to this time period are Isimila in Tanzania and Olorgesailie in Kenya.

At Olorgesailie, there are numerous occupation levels on what was the shoreline of a lake. Based on the size of the living floor at one of the later Acheulean levels, J. D. Clark suggests that as few as nine individuals at a time may have inhabited the site if a modern Bushman-type pattern was followed. However, the density of artifacts is very great, as is the density of preserved fauna. For instance, at one of the levels the remains of 65 giant baboons were preserved, with the long bones broken open for marrow. These data suggest that the site was visited regularly for a long period of time, with each successive occupation adding to the debris.

Different tool kits suggest different activities, sometimes on the same living floor and at other times differentiating habitations from each other. At one of the Olorgesailie living surfaces, there are the remains of a number of large dismembered hippos. The tool kit found among them contains many large heavy-duty cutting tools and a small number of utilized but unretouched flakes. These are probably butchering tools. Another tool kit includes numerous small light-duty tools plus few large cutting tools. These may have been used in preparing small fauna and also flora. There are also workshop areas where tools were manufactured and often discarded.

SOCIAL COMPLEXITY

In all, the adaptive patterns revealed by the early sapiens sites shows that humanity had advanced well beyond the successful opportunism that seems to have characterized the australopithecines and the earlier *Homo erectus* sample. Instead, we find an adaptive pattern that takes advantage of a maximum number of environmental resources. In one case, animals were stampeded into a swamp at Torralba, Spain, which shows that direct control of the environment had begun.

There is good reason to suspect the presence of a complex social hierarchy, with highly structured behavior occurring both within and between groups. With the almost certain presence of language, the use of body decoration, and the building of structures, the way of life of early *Homo sapiens* tribes may not have been vastly different from that of some living peoples.

Of course, if we were able to observe such a tribe, differences would be noticeable. Technology, for instance, would be limited, although not crude. What would be striking would be the absence of things, not the absence of skill in making what was used. Many social institutions would probably be well developed, especially those governing and regulating individual interactions and defining roles. Others, such as mythology and religion, are generally considered very recent additions to cultural behavior and might have been poorly expressed, although E. G. d'Aquili and C. Laughlin have presented strong arguments to the contrary. These authors draw on research concerning the structural aspects of brain functions in the two asymmetric cerebral hemispheres. They argue that the simultaneous functioning of both hemispheres may provide a neurological basis for the human ability to deal with the polar opposites that underlie all myth and religious structures. In effect, they suggest that the division of models for conceptualizing external data into polar opposites is a *necessary consequence* of a functional asymmetry in the brain and thus that generating a myth structure is a basic aspect of human cognition. Given the evidence for neural reorganization found in the australopithecines and the marked asymmetry of *Homo erectus* endocasts, these authors believe that myth and religion became established in human culture long before the appearance of *Homo sapiens.*

I believe that the most striking differences in the behavior of early *Homo sapiens* populations when compared with living people would be in what their technology couldn't do and in the noticeable amount of brute force used where modern groups substitute technological solutions. It is for this reason that technological changes seem to have dramatic consequences for the subsequent evolution of human morphology.

ART AND ITS IMPLICATIONS

The red ocher found at Terra Amata is not the only evidence from this period for the forms of decoration and graphic representation we term "art," and it is not even the most direct. The earliest direct evidence is the intentional engraving on an ox rib recovered from the Riss layers at Pech de l'Aze, France. The associated industry is Acheulean. The basic engraving consists of a series of connected double arcs running from left to right. The various marks were made with different tools, and therefore possibly at different times. Later, other simple figures were added, including a series of angles and sets of double marks. The result is a rather complex set of engravings. Were these notations or representations? A. Marshack believes that while the markings cannot be completely interpreted, the result is clearly "intentional, cumulative, and sequential." Furthermore, similar patternings can be found as recently as 8500 B.C. The evidence suggests that with early sapiens comes the beginning of decoration. Graphic art did not "suddenly emerge" with the appearance of modern *Homo sapiens* populations in Europe. Instead, it has considerable antiquity.

One important implication of the appearance of graphic art is the direct evidence it provides for cross-modal transfer and language capability. Marshack argues that decoration results in symbolic artifacts that can only be interpretable in a cultural context. Moreover, he contends that their design and manufacture provide direct evidence of cross-modal transfer, an ability we have previously inferred from the evidence of cerebral asymmetry and the expansion of the relevant brain areas suggested by the endocasts. According to Marshack, the early art objects provide evidence for "motivation, planning, cognitive modelling, symbolic sequencing, and an exceedingly fine acuity in the kinesthetic, somesthetic, and visual inputs." These are the same capabilities that underlie human language behavior and must be associated with the evolution of vocalized language. It is surely not accidental that the earliest evidence of graphic art and

the appearance of the prepared core technique date to the same timespan.

OTHER EVIDENCE OF SYMBOLIC BEHAVIOR

Finally, there is the tantalizing evidence from the Riss deposits of the Lazeret cave, where the remains of a series of tents were found, extending outward from the cave mouth. Just inside the door flap of each tent was the skull of a wolf. The obvious interpretation is a symbolic one.

In all, the activities of the later populations of early *Homo sapiens* may have involved the origins of art and religion. We will see that these important behaviors undergo a great florescence of breadth and complexity in the descendants of these people—the so-called Neandertals of Europe and people of the same time period in Africa.

The Appearance of Geographic Differences

The evidence of successful human adaptation to a wide range of climates and environments suggests other physical adaptations not readily visible on the skeleton. One of these involves skin color. I believe it is likely that early *Homo sapiens*, if not late *Homo erectus*, populations had roughly the same pattern of skin color distribution that occurred at the close of the Pleistocene (that is, today's pattern without the influence of post-Pleistocene cultural adaptations and migrations).

We have already discussed the evolution of dark pigmentation in the tropics (Chapter 8). This seems closely tied to the evolution of diurnal (daytime) hunting and may be a million and a half years old, if not older. Lighter pigmentation occurs in areas away from the tropics. What is the adaptive advantage of lighter pigmentation in more temperate areas?

A key to the answer was discovered when it was noted that black children in the United States were more prone to rickets than white children. It was determined that without milk or bony fish in the diet, vitamin D can be produced only by the action of ultraviolet radiation (a component of sunlight) on substances in the lower layers of the skin. Since vitamin D is essential to normal phosphate and calcium metabolism, an insufficiency of this vitamin results in the development of rickets. The amount of ultraviolet (UV) radiation that reaches the ground depends upon latitude. The farther away from the equator, the less UV radiation. In addition, local conditions can be influential: cloud cover screens out some UV radiation, but more of it can reach the ground at high altitudes. Finally, it was verified that heavily pigmented skin absorbs ultraviolet radiation, rather than transmitting it to the lower layers where vitamin D is produced.

Putting these facts together, in temperate areas (especially those subject to cloud cover, such as northern Europe) there is selection against heavy pigmentation in populations without a significant amount of milk or bony fish in their diet because there is not much ultraviolet radiation present. Heavy pigmentation would act to prevent the little radiation available from penetrating the outer layers of the skin and stimulating vitamin D production. The likely adaptation of wearing clothing during the winter, thereby covering much of the skin when the least amount of radiation is available, would compound the problem.

There is no evidence of significant consistent consumption of bony fish before the Upper Paleolithic (at least 25,000 years ago) and milk consumption by adults came even later, with the domestication of animals. Consequently, it is likely that temperate-adapted populations of the Middle Pleistocene were under selection resulting from rickets, which would lead to skin depigmentation. Selection for depigmentation would have begun only when winter habitation of temperate areas be-

came common. In Asia the first populations inhabiting temperate areas were late *Homo erectus*, whereas in Europe the earliest good evidence for persistent winter habitation is later and involves early *Homo sapiens* populations. As a result, it is likely that early sapiens populations had a skin color distribution similar to the distribution at the end of the Pleistocene, although depigmentation in areas with minimal ultraviolet radiation, such as northern Europe, may not have been as extreme as it is today, as suggested by the evidence of rickets in some Upper Pleistocene specimens from the area.

In any event, there seems to be some evidence that characteristics which we associate with modern geographic variants of our species began to sort themselves out toward the end of the Middle Pleistocene. Geographic differentiation also appears in skeletal morphology. For instance, the cranial morphology of the Solo sample is clearly continuous with that of early Australian aborigines. The sample from the PRC shows a resemblance to modern Chinese. In Africa the later specimens reveal features, such as pronounced parietal bulging and reduction of occipital robustness, which become common in the Upper Pleistocene. Finally, in Europe the retention of prominent browridges and the appearance of maxillary puffing and midfacial prognathism in this early sample foreshadow features which become characteristic later.

In most aspects of skeletal morphology, differences corresponding to recent or modern geographic variants become even more obvious in the Upper Pleistocene. Skeletal remains in Africa, Asia, and Europe from the Middle Pleistocene show more apparent similarity than Upper Pleistocene samples.

SUMMARY

The division between late *Homo erectus* and early *Homo sapiens* is an arbitrary one, based more on convention than on the appearance of dramatic change or unique features at the point in time (about 400,000 years ago) when samples the author identifies as early *Homo sapiens* first appear. Once the division is made, however, morphological distinctions can be determined. Early *Homo sapiens* samples combine changes that are a continuation

of evolutionary trends within *Homo erectus* with changes that suggest new or differently directed selection acting on human populations. One of the continued trends is in brain size expansion. Skeletally, there are increases in cranial size and changes in cranial proportions (expansion of the upper occiput and expansion of the frontal positioning the forehead over the browridge), decreases in posterior tooth size (especially for the later-erupting premolar and molars), and some expansion in anterior tooth size. One important reversal in a trend is the decrease in the size of the attachment area for the nuchal muscles and in the development of the supportive spongy bone at the cranial base.

Consequences of these trends are seen in the cranium, face, and mandible. Braincase breadth approaches cranial breadth in the earlier portion of the sample as the brain expands and the spongy bone development reduces. In some of the later crania from Europe (Riss glaciation equivalent), the braincase is broader than the cranial base. The resulting change in orientation of the temporalis muscle causes an external buttress (mental eminence) to appear on the symphysis of some mandibles. To an extent, reduction in the attachment area for the nuchal muscles is compensated by a more horizontally oriented nuchal plane. Evidence for anterior tooth use, including the size of the teeth and the size and projection of browridges, indicates an equal if not increased importance for this anatomical addition to the tool kit. An additional effect of horizontal forces acting on the anterior teeth appears in the expanded maxillary sinus, providing increased structural strength to the midface. As a result, the midface projects more (midfacial prognathism), the maxilla appears "puffed out" in some specimens, and the canine fossa is either absent or only slightly expressed. These latter developments reach their extreme in Europe.

Superimposed on these changes is a gradual decrease in the skeletal indicators of muscularity and strength. Both cranial and postcranial features associated with powerful muscular activity are reduced, although they remain far more developed than in any living population. It seems clear that however modern the social aspects of early *Homo sapiens* behavior may have been, there was a lack of corresponding technological sophistication. Strength and endurance were used in activities that later came to rely more effectively on technology.

In spite of the limited technology there are numerous indications that the adaptive patterns of early sapiens populations were becoming increasingly efficient and their structured behaviors recognizably modern. The later Middle Pleistocene archaeological record shows a habitat expansion and the appearance of specific habitat-related differences in adaptation, some of which are reflected in physiology and skeletal morphology. Both arguments based on comparative neurology and direct evidence of rudimentary decoration and other forms of symbol use suggest that all aspects of modern human social behavior were present from the earliest appearance of *Homo sapiens*.

The end of the Middle Pleistocene saw the appearance of a new technological process, the Levallois technique for manufacturing tools. Whether by diffusion or independent invention, the technique appeared through the range of the species and began a series of technological and adaptive changes which had dramatic effects on the direction and rate of evolutionary change.

STATE OF THE ART

The interpretation of phylogenetic relationships in this chapter has been unilinear. The author accepts the proposition that *Homo erectus* populations are both broadly and specifically ancestral to the early *Homo sapiens* populations that follow them. While a case can be made for some special local continuities in certain features, especially in Indonesia and Europe, no evidence seems to indicate the presence of contemporary lineages in either late *Homo erectus* or early *Homo sapiens* populations of the Middle Pleistocene.

However, there have been alternative phylogenies proposed for these samples. Some of them date to a time when samples were much smaller, but others are quite recent. Probably the most widely accepted alternative interpretation is the "presapiens hypothesis," best presented by the French paleontologist H. Vallois in a 1954 British publication. The hypothesis, mainly applied to Europe, proposes that two separate lineages can be found as early as the Mindel/Riss interglacial. One lineage (presapiens) evolved directly into modern *Homo sapiens* populations and closely resembled these modern forms at an early date. The second lineage (preneandertal) evolved into the European Neandertal populations of the earlier Würm glaciation (see Chapter 11) and subsequently became extinct. In 1954 Vallois accepted only one Middle

Pleistocene European fossil as representing presapiens, the Swanscombe partial cranium (Figure 10.8).

According to Vallois, presapiens specimens are characterized by a thick, low-vaulted cranium with great occipital breadth, roughly square parietal borders, and lacking a prominent nuchal torus. The frontal is described as "upright and completely lacking any [supraorbital] torus." His description of the frontal is particularly curious since neither Swanscombe nor the only other European fossil he considered presapiens (Fontéchevade, a French cranium from the Riss/Würm interglacial) preserved the supraorbital region. Vallois regarded the other early European fossils known in 1954—Mauer, Steinheim, and Montmaurin—as preneandertal.

That the presapiens hypothesis received wide acceptance is probably more a reflection of the general belief that the Würm Neandertals were something apart from the mainstream of human evolution (a problem discussed in the next chapter) than a result of convincing European fossil evidence for an early lineage division. Yet, with the discovery of more fossil material predating the Upper Pleistocene, there have been continued attempts to show that two separate forms were present.

Outside of Europe, L. S. B. Leakey suggested that the fragmentary remains from Kanjera in Tanzania represented a Middle Pleistocene presapiens. These have more recently been redated to the Upper Pleistocene. The late date of 29,000 years BP formerly suggested for the Broken Hill site also provided support for contemporary lineages. More recently, L. C. Briggs proposed that the Ternifine (*Homo erectus*) mandibles represented two different hominid types. In a landmark publication on Middle Pleistocene hominids, F. C. Howell also argued for contemporary lineages, although in his view these were separated on a continental basis, with "pithecanthropine" populations in Asia and northwest Africa contemporary with more modern European populations. D. Collins suggested a different approach. He attempted to demonstrate contemporary hominid lineages associated with what he

interpreted as different culture traditions.

Initial interpretations by A. Thoma argued for early contemporary lineages in Europe. Thoma contended that the Vértesszöllös occipital represented a member of the presapiens lineage even earlier than Swanscombe. However, the main supporters of the presapiens hypothesis are found among French paleoanthropologists. Workers such as J. Piveteau and M. A. de Lumley argue for the presence of two European forms during the Riss glaciation. Their reasoning depends mainly on the shape of the parietal bone. Presapiens is said to have a square parietal shape, while the preneandertal shape is rectangular, elongated from front to back.

I believe that all of this "evidence" is weak, or even nonexistent, and that no evidence *clearly* supports the contention of contemporary European lineages during the later Middle Pleistocene while broader geographic differences seem to reflect *clade* rather than *grade*. Within Europe, the marked similarities between Steinheim and Swanscombe have been recognized by most workers, and arguments concerning what the missing Swanscombe frontal might have been like are probably pointless. Most of the Swanscombe "presapiens" characteristics (low, thick vault and broad occiput, for instance) are shared with all early *Homo sapiens* specimens, while others (notably the lack of a prominent nuchal torus) probably relate to its sex rather than its taxon. Parietal shape discussed for the Riss specimens is notably variable in every fossil and living sample containing more than one or two of the bones (including the Neandertal sample). It is unlikely that this feature has any taxonomic importance. The discovery of what I believe to be male counterparts to the earlier-recovered females from the European Mindel/Riss, mainly Petralona and Bilzingsleben, places the problem in a different perspective by emphasizing the similarities of the females while providing new evidence of the generally archaic characteristics of the sample as a whole. In all, I believe there is adequate evidence to dismiss the presapiens hypothesis.

FURTHER READINGS

D'AQUILI, E. G., and C. LAUGHLIN. 1975. The Biopsychological Determinants of Religious Behavior. *Zygon* 10:32–58.

A theoretical work, drawing heavily from recent research on human brain function. The paper has important implications for the interpretation of behavior in earlier humans.

BILSBOROUGH, A. 1976. Patterns of Evolution in Middle Pleistocene Hominids. *Journal of Human Evolution* 5:423–440.
General discussion of Middle Pleistocene trends.

CLARKE, R. J. 1976. New Cranium of *Homo erectus* from Lake Ndutu, Tanzania. *Nature* 262:485–487.
Description of the Ndutu cranium reconstruction.

HOWELL, F. C. 1960. European and Northwest African Middle Pleistocene Hominids. *Current Anthropolgy* 1:195–232.
An excellent, detailed review paper on the Middle Pleistocene hominids and the associated archaeological remains as of 1960. The paper includes descriptions and interpretations of late *Homo erectus* specimens from Ternifine, Mauer, and Choukoutien, as well as of the European early *Homo sapiens* specimens from Steinheim, Swanscombe, and Montmaurin.

————, and J. D. CLARK. 1963. Acheulean Hunter-gatherers of Sub-Saharan Africa. In *African Ecology and Human Evolution*, eds. F. C. Howell and F. Bourliere. Aldine, Chicago, pp. 458–533.
Discussion of the archaeology and inferred adaptive patterns in the Middle Pleistocene of Africa.

HRDLIČKA, A. 1930. The Skeletal Remains of Early Man. *Smithsonian Miscellaneous Collections*, Vol. 83.
This is Hrdlička's major descriptive monograph on the human fossil record as it was known in 1930, concluding with a detailed statement of his unilinear interpretation. It is referenced in this chapter because of the excellent discussion of the Broken Hill remains, but it is an equally important reference for the European specimens discussed in Chapter 11.

JAEGER, J. J. 1975. Découverte d'un Crâne D'Hominidé dans le Pléistocène moyen du Maroc. Colloque Internationale CNRS No. 218. *Problèmes Actuels de Paléontologie—Evolution des Vertébrés*, pp. 897–902.
Description of the Salé cranium.

DE LUMLEY, H. 1969. A Paleolithic Camp at Nice. *Scientific American* 220(5):42–49.
The excavation and interpretation of Terra Amata.

————, and M. A. DE LUMLEY. 1974. Pre-Neanderthal Human Remains from Arago Cave in Southwestern France. *Yearbook of Physical Anthropology* 17:162–168.
A brief discussion of the Arago remains.

MARSHACK, A. 1976. Implications of the Paleolithic Symbolic Evidence for the Origin of Language. *American Scientist* 64:136–145.

Probably the best introduction to the origin of art and symbolic behavior, considering both the actual physical evidence and relevant theory.

PIVETEAU, J. 1970. Les Grottes de La Chaise (Charente). Paléontologie Humaine 1. L'Homme de L'Abri Suard. *Annales de Paléontologie Vertébrés* 56:175–225.
Description of the specimens from the La Chaise cave of Suard (Riss) and a discussion of parietal form as support for the presapiens hypothesis.

POULIANOS, A. N. 1967. The Place of the Petralonian Man Among Palaeoanthropoi. *Anthropos* 19:216–222.
A brief discussion of Petralona.

RIGHTMIRE, G. P. 1976. Relationships of Middle and Upper Pleistocene Hominids from Sub-Saharan Africa. *Nature* 260:238–240.
A framework of continuous morphological change in sub-Saharan Africa.

SABAN, R. 1975. Les restes humains de Rabat. *Annales de Paléontologie Vertébrés* 61:191–245.
Description of the Rabat cranial remains and their evolutionary position.

SINGER, R. 1958. The Rhodesian, Florisbad, and Saldanha Skulls. In *Hundert Jahre Neanderthaler*, ed. G. H. R. von Koenigswald. Bohlau, Koln, pp. 53–63.
Comparison of the three crania in the context of continual evolution in Africa.

VALLOIS, H. V. 1954. Neandertals and Praesapiens. *Journal of the Royal Anthropological Institute* 84(part II):1–20.
The basic presentation of the presapiens hypothesis.

VANDERMEERSCH, B. 1978. Les premeirs néandertaliens. *La Recherche* 9:694—696.
Announcement and brief discussion of the Biache cranium and its position in the European evolutionary sequence.

VLČEK, E. 1979. A New Discovery of *Homo erectus* in Central Europe. *Journal of Human Evolution* 7:239–252.
A good description of the Bilzingsleben cranium and its position, as seen by Vlček, in the European hominid sequence.

WEIDENREICH, F. 1951. Morphology of Solo Man. *Anthropological Papers of the American Museum of Natural History* 43(3):205–290.
The classic, uncompleted monograph on the Solo crania. These are also discussed in some detail in the 1943 monograph on the Choukoutien crania.

WELLS, L. H. 1947. A Note on the Broken Maxillary Fragment from the Broken Hill Cave. *Journal of the Royal Anthropological Institute* 77:11–12.

An analysis of the Broken Hill maxillary fragment.

WOLPOFF, M. H. 1980. Cranial Remains of Middle Pleistocene European Hominids. *Journal of Human Evolution* (in press).

A discussion of the importance of sexual dimorphism in understanding the evolutionary sequence in Europe.

CHAPTER ELEVEN

Neandertals and Their Relatives

The end of the Riss glaciation in Europe marks the beginning of the Upper Pleistocene. While it has proven difficult to extend this definition to other geographic areas, radiometric dating techniques have helped show which specimens are probably contemporary with this European event and which are earlier or later. When these dates are available, the Upper Pleistocene is generally understood to begin about 130,000 years ago.

Hominids of the Upper Pleistocene belong to our own species, *Homo sapiens*. Where evolutionary sequences are best established, it can be shown that the Upper Pleistocene hominids are first characterized by a continuation of the Middle Pleistocene evolutionary trends (seen in *Homo erectus* and earliest archaic *Homo sapiens*), followed by a reversal in the direction of some of these trends in subsequent archaic *Homo sapiens* populations, which eventually leads to the appearance of modern *Homo sapiens* populations almost everywhere in the (then) inhabited world by between 30,000 and 40,000 years ago. This chapter is concerned with the earlier portion of the Upper Pleistocene and the evolutionary

changes in archaic *Homo sapiens* which resulted in modern *Homo sapiens*. Chapter 12 will examine the earliest modern *Homo sapiens* populations, and Chapter 13 will trace their subsequent evolution.

In Europe, the earliest Upper Pleistocene *Homo sapiens* populations (i.e., archaic *Homo sapiens*) have been traditionally called "Neandertal." This term has been used to refer to both a clade and a grade, resulting in a certain amount of confusion when it is not made clear which usage is meant. Its traditional use as a grade term by authors such as Hrdlička, von Koenigswald, and Tobias (as well as myself) has resulted in references to non-European contemporary populations as regional Neandertals (e.g., "Asian Neandertals," "African Neandertal"), "Neandertaloids," or "Neandertal peoples." However, since Neandertal is also a clade term, other authors have argued that these uses are equivalent to calling living Indonesians "tropical Europeans." To avoid any possible confusion, I will restrict the use of the term here to its clade meaning, referring to Europe and the earlier population of the Near East.

If Neandertal is not to be used to refer to a grade,

what becomes of concepts such as A. Hrdlička's "Neandertal phase of man"? Contrary to recent expressions by some authors, redefining the term does not make the grade concept disappear. There are still two important questions. Do the European Neandertals represent the regional variant of a worldwide evolutionary grade? Do they become extinct without issue or are they ancestral to the more modern populations that follow them?

I believe that there was such a worldwide grade, equivalent to the worldwide grade represented by living populations. Perhaps "archaic *Homo sapiens*" is the most appropriate term for it. This grade, in my view, is morphologically intermediate between the earliest *Homo sapiens* populations discussed in Chapter 10 and the earliest modern *Homo sapiens* populations discussed in Chapter 12. However, the argument that this early Upper Pleistocene sample represents a more or less worldwide evolutionary grade, broadly ancestral to more modern populations, is not meant to prejudge the question of whether a specific ancestral-descendent relation can be demonstrated in each area of the world. This must be decided on the basis of local evidence.

Analysis of hominid evolution in the earlier Upper Pleistocene is complex for two reasons. First, the samples are large. More recent populations are bound to be better represented by fossils; in addition, the practice of burial becomes widespread during this period, which increases the number of remains. Second, clear elements of continuity appear in the evolutionary sequences of various areas. This makes it necessary to distinguish common or grade features (and their evolution) from those which are area-specific.

The available samples allow five separate geographic areas to be considered: mainland Asia, sub-Saharan Africa, North Africa, the Near East, and Europe (see Map 4, p. 254). These will be discussed in the order given, which corresponds to the order of increasing sample size. Europe is discussed last even though the evolutionary sequence covering the full timespan is probably best represented there. I feel that this sequence can be more accurately understood after the grade characteristics of the non-European hominids are reviewed, since the European (so-called "classic") Neandertals show evidence of a specific climatic adaptation superimposed on the more common grade features.

Following this is a review of the "Neandertal problem." This "problem" really pertains only to Europe and involves the specific question of whether the European Neandertals were ancestral to the European populations of early modern *Homo sapiens*. Yet evidence from other areas must be considered, since if more modern populations did not evolve in Europe, their origins must be sought elsewhere. The chapter concludes with a discussion of Neandertal lifeways and adaptation, presenting an argument that these people were modern in all behavioral details.

Specimens from Asia

Only a very few specimens from this timespan—the equivalent of the late Middle or early Upper Pleistocene—have been found on the Asian mainland, all in China. Isolated teeth have been reported from Lipu and Tung-tzu, and there is a new undescribed cranium from Da-li. However, the best-known specimen is the Mapa skullcap from south China (Kwangtung Province, not far from Hong Kong).

The specimen consists of the braincase, missing only the occiput, and retaining only the upper portion of the face (see Figure 11.1, p. 255). While it is larger than any of the Choukoutien crania, there are many points of resemblance to those earlier inhabitants of north China. The similarities are found mainly in the face and frontal. The fairly thick browridges are arched over the orbits (less strongly expressed arching occurs in the Choukoutien specimens). There is a groove between the browridges and the forehead, which bulges centrally very much like the Choukoutien foreheads. A sagittal keel (another Choukoutien characteristic) begins at about the center of the forehead. Another similarity is found in the rounded shape of the orbits.

The important distinctions from the Choukoutien specimens involve grade differences. The vault is broader (especially toward the rear) and much thinner. The profile is more evenly curved in both the sagittal and transverse planes. The browridges dip downward over the nose, and there is a high nasal angle and deep depression of the nasal root, suggesting a much more prominent nasal profile. The cheeks seem to angle markedly backward toward their outer edges. In life, this would have accentuated the nasal angle.

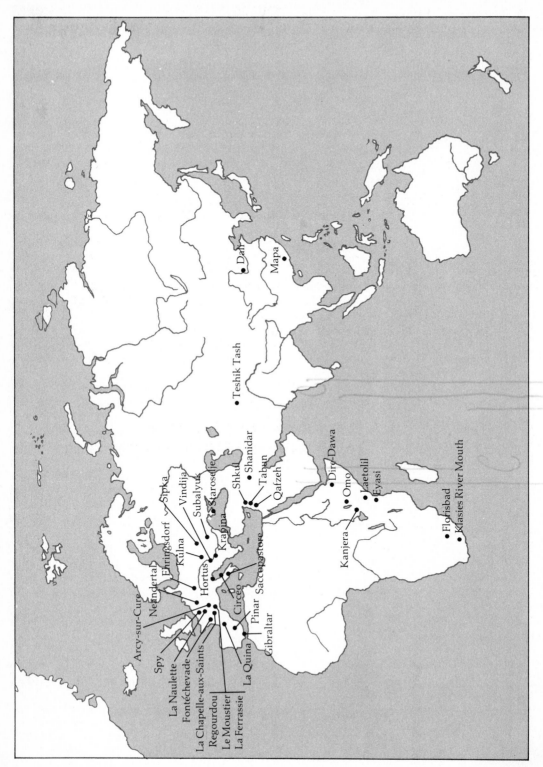

MAP 4   *Geographic positions of the main Neandertal sites and other sites with roughly contemporary hominid remains.*

Generally, the features that resemble the Chou-koutien sample also contrast with the (closer in time) Ngandong sample to the south. It would be reasonable to claim that Mapa is more like living Chinese than the Choukoutien people are. At the same time, there are many similarities with the Würm-dated Europeans, and some workers, such as W. W. Howells, have regarded Mapa as a Nean-dertal specimen.

The Da-li cranium appears to be a virtually complete version of Mapa, sharing practically all of the clade features discussed above, and providing additional information about the face (it is relatively short) and the back of the vault (it lacks the occipital flattening common in the European Neandertals).

In sum, these specimens represent the same grade as the archaic *Homo sapiens* populations in Europe. At the same time, there are enough resemblances to the earlier inhabitants of north China (and contrasts with populations to the west and south) to hint at a clade relationship of some antiquity on the Asian mainland. Only the recovery of additional specimens will eventually clarify the balance between gene flow and local continuity in this region.

Early Upper Pleistocene Africa

Over this period the fossil and archaeological record is far more complete in Africa than in Asia, and the emerging picture of hominid evolution has become fairly well understood. Because few African fossils were known and Africa was often regarded as the "dark continent," earlier workers generally attempted to fit African fossils into the European framework. However, this has changed over the past several decades to an understanding that the opposite approach is far more reasonable. It is Europe that lies at the periphery of early human habitation. During the Upper Pleistocene, Africa likely supported a human population many times larger than the European one. With its diversity of habitats and optimum conditions, Africa lies at the center of the evolutionary picture. Indeed, much as A. Thorne's model predicts (see Chapter 9 State of the Art), there is more morphological diversity among the African hominids than among those in Europe

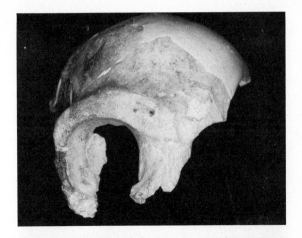

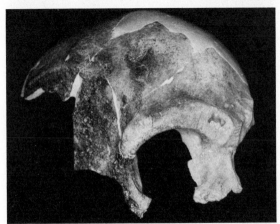

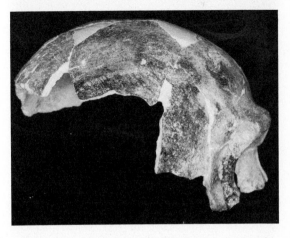

FIGURE 11.1 *Three views of the Mapa cranium. Note the position of the elevated forehead behind the browridges. The nasal angle is pronounced, although less so than in contemporary Europeans (see Figure 11.8).*

or Asia at the periphery. (Nevertheless, hominid morphology in all areas is variable, and in no case could a "type" specimen be used to characterize the whole sample.) The recent redating of many African Upper Pleistocene sites has made it clear that major technological innovations and efficient habitat-specific adaptations appear as early in Africa as anywhere else, if not earlier. Much the same can be said of the evolving hominids.

Our discussion of the continent begins in East Africa, where the earliest Upper Pleistocene remains are found, and then the later South African evidence is considered. North Africa is discussed last because by the Upper Pleistocene the human and archaeological remains from the northern and northwestern coastal regions generally resemble those from Europe and the Near East more than do remains from sub-Saharan Africa.

THE OMO SPECIMENS

Date determination is a continuing problem for the African remains. The oldest Upper Pleistocene East African specimens with any hope of fairly accurate dating come from the Kibish formation at Omo (in Ethiopia), the same broad area north of Lake Turkana that has yielded many australopithecine fossils. Radiometric dating of the later hominid remains has been beset with problems. The faunal date of 60,000 years BP appears likely, making these Omo specimens roughly contemporary with the early Würm glaciation in Europe (see Table 11.1, pp. 258–259). Numerous Levallois (prepared-core) flakes are found in the deposits, although there is no direct association with the hominids.

The Omo sapiens material represents at least three individuals. Only the cranial remains have been described, although there are numerous post-crania. The two fairly complete crania (Omo 1 and 2, see Figure 11.2) are from the same approximate level, but are not directly associated. Their particular importance lies in both the features they share and the variation that occurs between them.

Both crania are large (over 1,400 cc). Their similarities include a broad nuchal attachment area, an expanded occiput above this area, fairly thick cranial bone, and a sagittal keel. These are fairly archaic features. Other aspects of these specimens are more modern. Although in both the cranial base retains a fair amount of spongy bone, and is

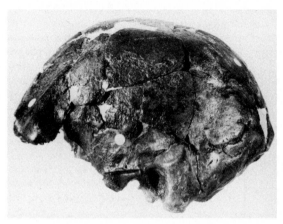

FIGURE 11.2   Comparison of the Omo crania—Cranium 1 above and 2 below. (Courtesy of M. H. Day)

the site of greatest cranial breadth, the maximum braincase breadth is high, and thus the cranial walls are vertical. Omo 1 and 2 are also similar to each other, and contrast with specimens from other areas, in the form of the browridge region. The frontal is long, broad, and downward sloping. As it approaches the orbits it thickens, so that the supra-orbital torus is actually a slight bulge on the end of an otherwise smooth bone. The upper rims of the orbits come to a thin rounded edge. There is no prominent bar over the orbits and no separation of this region from the frontal.

The contrasts between Omo 1 and 2 are in proportions and morphology. Omo 2 more closely resembles the Broken Hill cranium, although it is more filled out (Figure 9.8), while Omo 1 appears more modern in its higher vault, reduced nuchal torus, and higher, more rounded occiput.

A mandible associated with Omo 1 has a definite chin, and an isolated canine would be judged small against the anterior teeth of contemporary Europeans. Postcranial material belonging to Omo 1 is said to be robust but not outside the range of living people.

The most interesting aspect of the variation at Omo is that while one cranium appears more "modern" than the other, there is every reason to believe they represent individual variants of similar populations. There are similarities with the Middle Pleistocene African sample in both the morphology and the pattern of variation. The Omo 2 vault and occipital region represent a larger, fuller version of Broken Hill, while the rounded higher occiput of Omo 1 corresponds more closely to Salé. Interestingly, the frontal shows both the best evidence of continuity and the most marked morphological difference in this African sequence. The continuity is found in the sagittal keel and the long, broad, and fairly flat shape of the bone; these are characteristics shared with both earlier and later specimens. At the same time, the reduction and form of the supraorbitals have no corresponding variant in the Middle Pleistocene African sample, although these features are shared with other African crania that seem to date to the earlier Upper Pleistocene.

OTHER EAST AFRICAN CRANIA

Three additional East African sites have yielded crania that may belong to this time period. Two of these, Kanjera and Eyasi, are poorly dated. At both sites the crania were discovered in the 1930s in a very fragmentary condition. In addition, the reconstructions and dates were questioned because the reconstructed crania looked different from both the contemporary European sample and the only other early African cranium known at that time, Broken Hill.

The best dated and most complete of the specimens is from the Tanzanian site of Laetolil. A cranium with a virtually complete face was recently recovered during the search for the much earlier hominids that are also found in this area (see Chapter 7). In general shape the cranial vault resembles Omo 2, although the features are generally more robust and the cranial bone is extraordinarily thick. The supraorbitals are much better developed than

in the Ethiopian specimens and more closely resemble those of Broken Hill. The supraorbital torus is thick and extends prominently in front of the low forehead. While the frontal angle is low, the cranium is fairly high because the frontal bone is very long. The face contrasts with the cranial vault. It is lightly constructed, short, and has a distinct canine fossa.

The Laetolil cranium may be earlier than the Omo specimens, and it is tempting to suggest an evolutionary sequence in which it represents an intermediate between Omo and Broken Hill. However, the date and its relation to the Omo date are uncertain, and there is only one specimen of unknown sex involved. It is more reasonable to regard Laetolil as being in the same broad spacial and temporal sample as Omo and emphasize the apparent variability that results. Certainly, the Laetolil face provides the only morphological link between the earlier Broken Hill and Ndutu specimens and Florisbad, a somewhat later specimen from South Africa (discussed below).

The Kanjera remains were discovered by L. S. B. Leakey in an area near the shore of Lake Victoria in Kenya. There were 42 cranial fragments belonging to four individuals. Of these, 37 were discovered on the surface, and five were excavated from undisturbed deposits. The crania were so badly broken up that accurate reconstructions of their detailed shape can probably never be made.

Both excavated and surface specimens agree in the virtual lack of any supraorbital development and in the high, rounded form of the occiput. The single facial fragment is lightly built. When this site was considered Middle Pleistocene in age, it could be used to support the presapiens hypothesis. However, recent dating suggests that the human remains are much younger, perhaps Late Pleistocene, and thus the modern features can be explained by the later date.

The third East African site that should be considered is Eyasi, near Lake Tanganyika in Tanzania. Fragments of three fossil crania were discovered, and a complete cranium was reconstructed by H. Weinert. Based on the published pictures, F. Weidenreich questioned the reconstruction's accuracy and the conclusions Weinert drew from it. (Weinert thought the skull was similar to *Homo erectus*.) I have examined Weinert's reconstruction and can only comment that it is even worse than Weidenreich imagined.

TABLE 11.1 Dated *Homo sapiens* specimens from the past 200,000 years. The table shows the stages of the last two European glaciations and the corresponding temperature curve for southeastern France, abstracted from works by Miskovsky. These temperature fluctuations seem to have been common throughout northwestern Europe, but were only partially reflected to the east and south. Following this column are the positions of the European Neandertals with radiometric dates (see footnote) and then the positions of sites which have been dated only to glacial stage (mostly due to the work of Heim and de Lumley). The next pair of columns shows the positions of radiometrically dated Near Eastern specimens (from Stewart), then the positions of those that can be geologically correlated or dated by amino acid (from works by A. Jelinek, and Bada and Masters-Helfman). Finally, the last column positions the dated specimens from Africa (reviewed by Tobias).

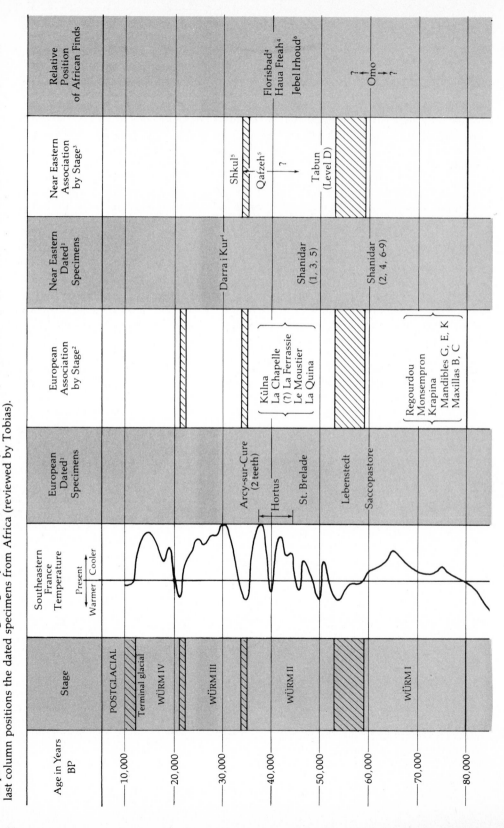

258

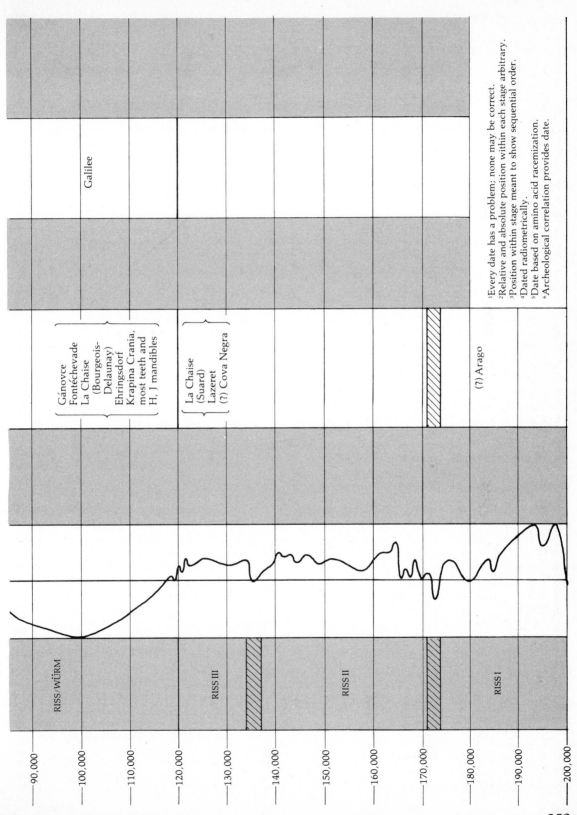

Galilee

Gánovce
Fontéchevade
La Chaise
(Bourgeois-
Delaunay)
Ehringsdorf
Krapina Crania,
most teeth and
H, J mandibles

La Chaise
(Suard)
Lazeret
(?) Cova Negra

(?) Arago

[1]Every date has a problem; none may be correct.
[2]Relative and absolute position within each stage arbitrary.
[3]Position within stage meant to show sequential order.
[4]Dated radiometrically.
[5]Date based on amino acid racemization.
[6]Archeological correlation provides date.

RISS/WÜRM

RISS III

RISS II

RISS I

90,000
100,000
110,000
120,000
130,000
140,000
150,000
160,000
170,000
180,000
190,000
200,000

259

Fortunately, the occiputs of both Eyasi 1 and 2 are fairly complete, and some information may be gained from them. Both are broad and have a reduced nuchal torus (more so in Eyasi 1). The difference in torus development is reminiscent of the difference between Omo 1 and 2.

Only a small portion of the right supraorbital region of Eyasi 1 remains. There is no separation between the frontal bone and the browridge, and the torus is projecting but not particularly thick. (The impression of a large torus actually comes from the reconstructed portion.) Weidenreich described this browridge as "the thickened end of an otherwise continuous frontal slope," a description which holds equally well for the Omo crania, and probably for the Kanjera material as well if the thickening of this "thickened end" is reduced.

While varying in detail, as a whole these East African crania share a number of traits. Some of these, such as the form of the frontal bone and of the browridges, may be regionally distinct. Compared with the Middle Pleistocene remains, vault expansion and reduction of the cranial buttresses are the main evolutionary trends. Yet, the individuals are not identical, and problems in dates as well as uncertainty in sex determination make it difficult to resolve the sources of variation.

SOUTH AFRICAN REMAINS

Beginning with Broken Hill and Saldanha, the southern part of Africa has produced a long series of important archaic and modern sapiens specimens. The most recent of the archaic specimens is the fragmentary cranium from Florisbad. Various radiocarbon dates from the peat layer in which the fossil was discovered have resulted in a date range of from 35,000 to over 47,000 years BP; the most recent attempt found the specimen older than 42,600 years. This is a later date than the estimates for most other crania in this archaic sapiens group. The specimen consists of the sides and part of the face of an adult cranium (see Figure 11.3). Most of the back and base are missing. The frontal and the face are the most diagnostic of the preserved features.

The face is rather interesting, although there is almost nothing to compare it with in the other African Upper Pleistocene specimens except for Laetolil and Jebel Irhoud 1 (see p. 262). Most of the maxillary portion is broken away. From what remains, it is apparent that the face is large and broad, but gracile. It has been reconstructed as moderately prognathic, and there is a definite canine fossa. Although somewhat broader, both the face and the leading edge of the frontal above it resemble the Laetolil specimen. In all, if it is compared with the Broken Hill face, there is significant breadth expansion, gracilization, and height reduction (proportionally more in the alveolar region than in the area above). Judging from the size of the tooth sockets and the preserved third molar, the dentition is modern in size.

As in the East African specimens, the frontal bone is very broad, flat, and fairly high. There is even less postorbital narrowing than in the Omo crania. Once again, the browridge can be described as a thickening at the forward edge of the sloping frontal bone. However, this thickening is much greater than in the East African specimens, exceeding even Broken Hill in the region over the nose, although thinning considerably toward the sides.

Florisbad has long been considered a phylogenetic "link" between the Broken Hill/Saldanha complex of features and living African populations. It is not a modern skull, nor is it simply an "African Neandertal." Combined with the other archaic Upper Pleistocene remains, it not only provides such a link but also confirms the existence of a widespread geographic variant with its own evolutionary tendencies. Just how widespread this variant might have been is suggested by the numerous features Florisbad shares with the Omo crania (especially Omo 2) and with the Jebel Irhoud 1 cranium from North Africa (discussed below).

Moreover, the distinctness of this African variant would seem to extend back at least into the Middle Pleistocene. Workers such as P. Rightmire suggest that there is an evolutionary continuity between Middle and Upper Pleistocene specimens. Features generally characteristic of this variant include a long, broad, flattened frontal (with variable supra-

FIGURE 11.3   Comparison of some African specimens. Jebel Irhoud 1 is shown to the right (three views), and Jebel Irhoud 2 is to the upper left. Below it to the left are views of a cast of the Florisbad reconstruction. Where comparable, Florisbad and Jebel Irhoud 1 are remarkably similar, while the two Jebel Irhoud crania show a number of contrasts.

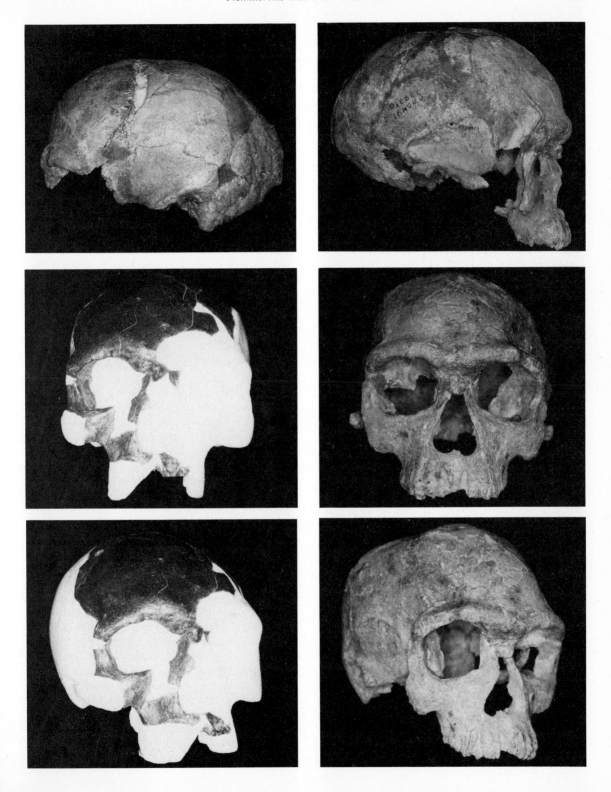

orbital development), an anterior position for the highest point on the cranium, and nearly vertical parietal walls above a broad, massive cranial base. According to Rightmire, evolution of this braincase form over the Middle and early Upper Pleistocene was largely a matter of cranial capacity expansion, "filling out" various areas, which gradually resulted in a steeper occiput and a broader frontal bone.

The only other South African human remains that might date to this timespan are from the Klasies River cave (see Chapter 13 for a discussion of the Border Cave remains, which some workers believe are equally old). Although yet unpublished, there are apparently a number of cranial fragments and two fairly complete mandibles. The frontal and zygomatic fragments are described as gracile; although generally similar to Florisbad, the frontal is more lightly built. The mandibles show a very marked difference in robustness and chin development. The smaller is very robust, megadont (large tooth size), and lacks a chin, while the larger has a chin and is relatively thinner and more gracile.

NORTH AFRICAN SPECIMENS

North African remains from the earlier Upper Pleistocene are limited to the coastal areas of Morocco. Two crania and a juvenile mandible from Jebel Irhoud are archaeologically correlated with the nearby radiometrically dated site of Haua Fteah. These are about 40,000–45,000 years old. An undated cranium from Dar-es-Soltan is probably more recent (see Chapter 13), and an upper jaw from Tangier appears to be the same age or more recent. Thus this sample is contemporary with the latest of the sub-Saharan specimens discussed above.

Crania

The two Jebel Irhoud crania (Figure 11.3) are broadly similar in size; in general, their similarities and differences parallel those of the Omo crania. They have numerous features that to a varying degree are found in sub-Saharan Africa, and yet others, especially in the forehead and occipital region, are unique. The vaults are fairly high and very broad. The browridges are continuous and prominent (but not especially large), and the bulging

forehead begins above them, although separated from them by a groove. The occiputs are well rounded and the position of the prominent nuchal line is low. The differences between the crania could be due to sex; if so, not much dimorphism is expressed. Cranium 2 has stronger temporal lines, a more angled occiput, a larger nuchal area, more prominent mastoids, and more robust spongy bone development at the cranial base. These features suggest it might be male. Cranium 1, possibly female, is generally less robust, although the differences are not great. With the cranial base reduction, the parietals are more evenly curved as seen from the rear, and their shape is almost circular. There is a moderate parietal bulge.

The face of Jebel Irhoud 1 is complete except for the teeth. It is fairly tall and quite broad, almost equalling the Broken Hill face in breadth. However, like the roughly contemporary Florisbad face, it is much more delicately built. The zygomatics are very thin, although there is a robust masseter attachment. At their base, they form a sharp angle with the face, and there is a distinct canine fossa. There is none of the midfacial prognathism of the Middle Pleistocene European or earlier African specimens. Instead, there is considerable alveolar prognathism; the incisor-bearing portion of the face projects beyond the rest of the face. In these features, the face closely resembles both Florisbad and Laetolil, while contrasting with the contemporary Europeans.

While in its face and the general contour of the cranium, Jebel Irhoud 1 resembles the less complete Florisbad cranium, the points of resemblance are not shared by cranium 2. It is possible that the differences at Jebel Irhoud are due to sex, and that the resemblances of Jebel Irhoud 1 and Florisbad reflect the fact that both are females of a widespread African variant. If so, the flatter, broader frontal of Florisbad more closely aligns it with the succeeding sub-Saharan African populations, whereas it has been argued (see pp. 338–339) that the Jebel Irhoud specimens are probable ancestors of the much more recent Mesolithic (pre-agricultural or early agricultural) North Africans.

It is easy to see continuity with earlier samples. A population with the features of Broken Hill or Rabat could develop into one with the Jebel Irhoud features through facial reduction (especially in the maxillary area), frontal expansion, and some expansion of the upper portion of the occipital bone.

However, to do so would require a set of cranial changes somewhat different from those taking place to the south.

Jaws

A maxillary fragment and some teeth were recovered from the northern end of the Moroccan coast, southwest of Tangier. Although dated to the equivalent of Würm, their actual provenience is not clear since they had apparently fallen from a higher (later) horizon. There are two individuals represented, one by the maxilla and the second by a single large, very worn M^2. The canine and P^3 are extremely large. Although juvenile (the second molar was unerupted), the maxilla is massive and thick. The lower border of the nose is rounded rather than sharply bordered and most important there is no canine fossa. In these features it resembles the Rabat maxilla and contrasts with the face of Jebel Irhoud 1 (except for the similar rounded nasal margin).

There is a small mandibular sample from the Upper Pleistocene, consisting of specimens from Jebel Irhoud, Haua Fteah, and possibly Témara (although this unpublished specimen may date to the Middle Pleistocene). The sample is just large enough to hint at a few shared features. The Jebel Irhoud mandible, belonging to a child of slightly more than seven years, has a definite chin. Its anterior teeth are quite small. The 40,000-year-old Haua Fteah mandibles consist of only the posterior portions. In both mandibles, the ramus is rather short and squat; its anterior edge begins at the position of the third molar. The latter feature is significant because it reflects the lack of marked midfacial prognathism. When this prognathism is expressed in its extreme, the maxillary teeth are so far forward that the mandibular teeth must shift forward to meet them. Since the ramus (articulating with the cranium) might be thought of as remaining in the same position, the forward shift of the teeth places it behind the tooth row. Thus these mandibles "fit" the morphology of the Jebel Irhoud 1 face with its distinct canine fossa and lack of midfacial prognathism. However, the fact that the Tangier maxilla has a more "puffed" appearance and lacks a canine fossa shows that this more European-like morphological complex was not completely absent from the area.

THE AFRICAN SEQUENCE

Considered as a whole, this African sample is roughly equivalent in time to the Würm glaciation in Europe (Table 11.1). It may be as much as 200,000 years younger than the Middle Pleistocene sample from Africa, and at present no specimens are known to fill this gap. Thus we may glimpse the beginning and the end points of the archaic *Homo sapiens* sequence in Africa but have no knowledge of what happened in between except by extrapolation.

The beginning point (Chapter 10) saw the widespread appearance of an erectus-like sample with expansion of cranial capacity, anterior tooth size expansion, reduction of the nuchal muscle attachment area (and associated cranial buttressing), and some facial gracilization. Cranial variation was marked, probably as a result of sexual dimorphism. It was suggested that the sample reflected the consequences of increased social and technological complexity and the possible beginnings of habitat-specific exploitive patterns among people who were fairly effective, robust big-game hunters.

To some extent, the end point of the archaic sequence is characterized by a continuation of the above. Crania are larger (especially in height and breadth) and more filled out; nuchal attachment areas and basal buttressing are further reduced. Faces are reduced and their features far more gracile. Reflecting the same technological developments that underlie these cranial and facial changes, habitat-specific adaptive differences are more pronounced, although they do not reach a high degree of efficiency in utilizing available resources until the end of this period.

Other changes, however, suggest a different evolutionary direction. Reduction, rather than continued expansion, characterizes the small anterior tooth sample, and most (although not all) of the faces reflect a reduction in anterior tooth use through the more common appearance of reduced maxillary sinuses (less expanded maxillas) and more gracile zygomatics. Clearly, something happened to replace the continued powerful use of the anterior dentition. Another new factor may be the reduction in skeletal variability, perhaps reflecting a decrease in sexual dimorphism. The two Omo crania, and the two crania from Jebel Irhoud, each share a number of similarities. Even when considering these four specimens together, the range of variation is considerably less than in the well pre-served Middle Pleistocene Africans (Broken Hill, Bodo, Ndutu, and Salé). It is much more difficult to find sexually diagnostic features in the early Upper Pleistocene sample, and one possible interpretation is that there is a decrease in the differences be-tween the demands of male and female roles.

Whatever happened between them in terms of morphological evolution, the later African sample is more like modern *Homo sapiens* in every feature that distinguishes it from the archaic one. Further, many workers suggest that the later African sample of archaic *Homo sapiens* is specifically more like modern *African* populations than is the contempo-rary early sapiens sample to the north. This bears on the eventual fate of the earlier Würm Europeans and will be considered after a discussion of the sample widely termed "Neandertal."

The Near East

In the area of Eurasia loosely termed the Near East, the archaic *Homo sapiens* sample is now generally recognized to span the period of time from the Riss/Würm interglacial to the Würm II/III inter-stadial (Table 11.1). However, prior date estimates have been the major problem barring the interpre-tation of this important sample. At one time, most or all of the Near Eastern archaic sapiens specimens were thought to come from the latest portion of this timespan (western European Würm II equiv-alent). Even earlier it was thought that the bulk of the (then known) sample was dated to before the Würm glaciation.

THE EARLIEST ARCHAIC SPECIMENS

Specimens from three Israeli sites are currently claimed to predate the Würm, and two of these perhaps even the Upper Pleistocene. However, the case for the two presumed older sites' antiquity is far from convincing.

The earlier portions of the Ubeidya site seem to extend well into the Middle Pleistocene. However, the three cranial fragments and two teeth reported from Ubeidya are not heavily fossilized, and the almost vertical strata at the site make it difficult to determine exactly where the material comes from.

Moreover, chemical dating shows that the human bones are younger than the associated faunal re-mains.

The situation at Hazorea does not inspire great confidence in the antiquity of the bones, since the five human skull fragments and the hand axe in-dustry reported were all recovered from a plowed field. Combined with the lack of clear provenience, the morphological attributes of the fragments do not suggest great antiquity.

This leaves the frontal-facial fragment from Mugharet-el-Zuttiyeh, or the Galilee skull. Al-though once thought to be younger, geological and archaeological comparisons have made it increas-ingly clear that the specimen dates to between 105,000 and 120,000 years ago. The specimen, which is probably female, combines thick, promi-nent supraorbitals with thin and rather delicate zygomatics, much like the Steinheim female cra-nium. The supraorbitals project well in front of the frontal and are separated from it by a groove. Be-low them, the upper portions of the nasal bones show a low nasal angle. Other archaic morphologi-cal features include a marked postorbital narrow-ing, a narrow maximum frontal breadth relative to the upper facial breadth, and a thick orbital mar-gin. In sum, this pre-Würm female differs little from pre-Würm *Homo sapiens* females in Europe (see below), which suggests that the genetic ties of the archaic Near Eastern populations may be to Eu-rope.

SHANIDAR

The Shanidar cave, in the Zagros mountains of Iraq, provides the earliest large datable Near East-ern hominid sample. The fossils represent at least nine individuals, two children and seven adults, and every specimen includes postcranial remains. Some of the Shanidar hominids were killed by rockfalls. In one case, the bodies were recovered and buried in one spot, with a male (4) placed above two females (6 and 8), who were placed above a baby (9). The grave was then covered with flowers.

Although the specimens are spread through sev-eral strata in the cave they cluster into two groups. The earlier group consists of specimens 2, 4, 6–9, and the estimated date is approximately 60,000 years BP. According to R. Solecki's interpretation of the complex burial, 4, 6, 8, and 9 may have been closely related. The later group—specimens 1, 3, and 5—has been directly dated by radiocarbon to an age of 46,000 years.

The Earlier Shanidar Group

In the earlier group, specimen 2 is the best preserved. According to work by T. D. Stewart and E. Trinkaus, this fairly complete postcranial skeleton and crushed cranium belonged to a rather short young person. The height was about 62 inches if male (as generally thought) or 60 inches if female. (The formulas for estimating height from long bone lengths are different for males and females.) Unfortunately, no feature allowing positive sex determination was preserved for Shanidar 2. While it has generally been considered male, recent work shows that there has been a tendency for scientists to classify more human fossils as male than is probably correct because of their generally greater-than-modern robustness. Two other skeletons with limbs from this level provide little additional guidance. Assuming Shanidar 4 is male, he was about 64 inches tall. The much smaller (probably female) Shanidar 6 was 57 inches tall.

The Shanidar 2 cranium appears to have been very large, although it is too fragmentary for an accurate brain size estimate. The vault is characterized by a rounded occiput, robustly developed basal area, and large mastoids. The better-preserved facial area indicates a large face with a continuous browridge of moderate thickness and an inflated maxillary sinus with the corresponding lack of a canine fossa. The even more fragmentary Shanidar 4 cranium appears generally similar where comparable. The browridge is reported to be thick centrally, with little thinning toward the sides.

Shanidar 2, 4, and 6 have fairly complete dentitions. While the samples are small, the average canine size and posterior tooth size appear to be reduced compared with the Middle Pleistocene European sample. The amount of reduction is about the same as that discussed for Africa. The mandibles of specimens 2 and 4 are fairly stout. The ramus of Shanidar 2 is low compared with those of Riss and Mindel/Riss Europeans (shorter face?). The most significant aspect of the two mandibles is the forward shift of the tooth row relative to the ramus and body. This feature, associated with the forward shift of the maxillary teeth, is an indirect result of midfacial prognathism. As a consequence, the ramus begins behind the last molar, and the mental foramen (the hole allowing the nerve, artery, and vein supplying the lower face to pass from inside the mandible, see Figure 11.1) is positioned under the first molar. In specimens without this forward shift of the teeth, the mental foramen is positioned under the premolars. (The postcrania are discussed below.)

The Later Group

Shanidar 1, 3, and 5 are from the upper levels of the sequence of Mousterian (prepared core) bearing deposits, dated to 46,000 years ago. All three specimens are probably male.

The sex of Shanidar 1 can be determined from features of the pelvis. His height, however, presents a more difficult problem in spite of the fact that some of the limbs are almost complete. This is because of a major pathology and possibly associated amputation performed on his right arm. When the specimen was discovered, the uppermost portion of the right humerus was found to be extremely thin, and the lower portion as well as all of the remaining bones of the right forearm were missing. Since almost all of the left forearm was found, it would appear that the right arm was not functional, resulting in its atrophy, and possibly as a result of this the arm was amputated during life. The bones of the left arm indicate a height of 64–66 inches, but these may have been hyper-developed as a result of the amputation. Lower limb lengths suggest that a smaller height (about 62 inches) may be more accurate.

The amputation and the fact that Shanidar 1 survived it and lived to a fairly old age for his time (over 30) provide some insight into several aspects of life in the Shanidar cave. Shanidar 1 supplemented his working left hand with his mouth; the wear on his front teeth reflects their distinctive use for purposes other than chewing. The amputation indicates that some form of preventive medicine was practiced. That Shanidar 1 survived the trauma implies a period of intensive care following it. He probably was an important contributing member in his society, and his contributions were certainly not in hunting!

Indeed, Shanidar 1's pathological disorders were

not limited to the right arm. The left ankle was abnormally developed in a way that suggests an injury to the lower leg early in life. The right ankle was arthritic, possibly from bearing most of the body weight. The results of other injuries were found on the cranium. The most severe of these flattened the lateral border of the left orbit. Yet these were the same people who buried their dead and covered the graves with flowers.

The Shanidar 1 cranium, reconstructed and partially described by T. D. Stewart, is very large compared with the earlier and contemporary specimens already discussed (see Figure 11.4). The cranial capacity is 1,600 cc, and the braincase is broader and higher than in the Middle Pleistocene European males. Brain size expansion and reduction in the basal spongy bone contribute to the more filled-out appearance of the skull. The frontal and posterior parietal areas are expanded; in Figure 11.4 note the posterior position of the maximum cranial height, the bulging frontal above the supraorbitals, and the bulging occiput above the low, weakly developed nuchal torus. There is virtually no postorbital narrowing.

The face is large but gracile in the development of the zygomatics. The nose was prominent, although its angle to the face was not particularly high. An expanded maxillary sinus results in a convex surface to the side of the nose, and there is a corresponding gap between the last mandibular molar and the front of the ramus. The mandible has an incipient mental eminence. Finally, there is no substantial tooth size difference from the earlier specimens.

E. Trinkaus has reconstructed the Shanidar 5 cranium and face (Figure 11.4). The specimen combines a number of features which result in a more archaic appearance than is usual in the Upper Pleistocene hominids. The frontal portion of the cranium is long and low, and it is separated from the thick browridges by a shallow groove. The supraorbitals follow the orbital contour, attaining their maximum thickness in the central region. Below them is the largest of all Neandertal noses; the nasal bones show a very high angle in lateral profile and follow an "S"-shaped curve so that they begin to angle downward at their most anterior point. The nose is bordered by expanded maxillary sinuses, leading to a flat canine fossa region (as in Shanidar 2). The robustly developed zygomatics

merge evenly onto the maxilla, as in the western European Neandertals. Trinkaus observes that the I¹ shows the same occlusal rounding as the I¹ in Shanidar 1. The few preserved teeth are large.

Comparisons of this cranium with Shanidar 1 are of great interest. Since the specimens are found in the same cave, at the same approximate time, and because they are both males, their differences can only be attributed to individual variation.

AMUD

The Amud site, near Lake Tiberias in Israel, may be approximately the same age as the later Shanidar remains or perhaps younger. The remains of four individuals have been recovered. Of the more fragmentary material, Amud 2 is a piece of an adult upper jaw, and Amud 3 consists of cranial and facial fragments from a child about four years old. Amud 4, a portion of an infant's temporal bone, comes from the earliest layer. Amud 1, a complete cranium, can be skeletally sexed as male. He has the largest cranial capacity of any of the Near Eastern specimens (1,740 cc) and analysis of the associated skeleton suggests that he is probably also one of the tallest individuals (about 68 inches).

Amud 1 (Figure 11.4) differs from Middle Pleistocene hominids in other features besides height. The skull is more strongly curved and the occipital is higher. The attachment area for the nuchal muscles is low, and there is neither a nuchal torus nor a significant flattening above it. The browridges are somewhat reduced and tend to separate into central and lateral portions (especially on the right side). The reconstructed face has a Shanidar-like magnitude of midfacial prognathism, and the last mandibular molar is in front of the ramus. Indeed, the Amud 1 cranium is particularly similar to the Shanidar male crania, and his postcrania also show similarities to that sample, although they are markedly larger. H. Suzuki and F. Takai, who described the specimens from Amud, argue that Amud 1 differs from the Shanidar males mainly in the division of the supraorbital torus into separate elements and the prominence of the mental eminence. While the importance of the site would be enhanced with a clarification of its date, the Amud male appears to be morphologically similar to the early Würm-equivalent Near Eastern specimens.

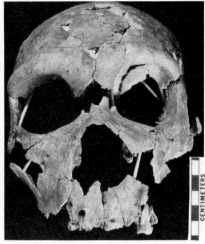

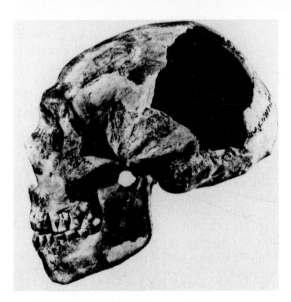
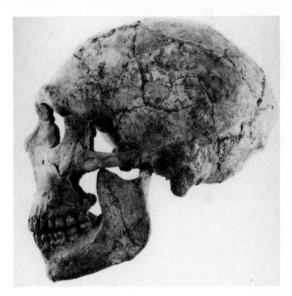

FIGURE 11.4   Earlier Near Eastern crania. At top are two views of Shanidar 5 as reconstructed by E. Trinkaus and printed with his permission. Below are views of Shanidar 1 (left) and Amud 1. (Shanidar 1, courtesy of T. D. Stewart; Amud 1, courtesy of H. Suzuki)

THE TABUN CRANIUM

The Tabun female cranium (Figure 11.7) and associated postcranial skeleton, from the Wadi-el-

Mughara of Mount Carmel in Israel, is now recognized to be from the same approximate time as the later Shanidar remains, if not in fact earlier. In the original description by T. McCown and Sir Arthur Keith, Tabun was compared with the sample from the nearby site of Skhul (Chapter 12), then thought to be roughly contemporary. The earlier date now recognized suggests that comparison with Shanidar is more appropriate. The Tabun female bears a resemblance to the Shanidar material that may not be apparent if sex differences are not taken into account (contemporary Shanidar specimens are male).

This female cranium is the smallest of the Near Eastern sample, although body height was 61 inches. It contrasts with the Shanidar male crania (although not with Amud) in the smooth, rounded, high contour of the occiput, the virtual lack of a nuchal torus, and the marked reduction of basal spongy bone. The Tabun face is short. While the nose was not especially prominent, the entire face projects anteriorly, responding to midfacial prognathism. (Much of the maxilla is broken away, making it impossible to determine how expanded the maxillary sinus was.) The mandible reflects this condition through a forward shift of the tooth row, leaving a gap between the last molar and the ramus. Interestingly, the symphysis lacks any external buttress. The supraorbitals follow the contours of the orbits but are heavy and prominent, a characteristic of earlier European females. If the main contrasts between this female cranium and the Shanidar crania are due to sex, there appears to have been a large degree of size dimorphism (for instance, compared with the African sample discussed above). Yet the morphological features do not contrast as greatly, and in many areas Tabun is surprisingly robust for a female of her time. Although an earlier maxillary dentition from the site shows marked incisor shoveling, the teeth in the Tabun dental sample are generally smaller than the Shanidar dentitions.

THE COMBINED DENTAL SAMPLE

Average tooth size for the later Near Eastern dental sample does not differ substantially from the earlier one. (Shanidar 1 and the two Tabun maxillas have slightly smaller dentitions, Amud is about the same, and Shanidar 5 is larger.) Combined, they provide a more adequate sample for comparison with the Middle Pleistocene Europeans. In a word, the comparison shows reduction. The premolars reduce most, by about 15 percent, while canine reduction is 8 percent and the molars reduce 5 percent. Too few incisors are known from the earlier Europeans for comparison. However, the Near Eastern incisors are larger than the average for late *Homo erectus.*

POSTCRANIAL REMAINS

Fairly complete postcranial remains are known from Shanidar, Amud, and Tabun. This is a fortunate consequence of the fact that these people buried their dead. The limbs show reduction or loss of many of the features associated with strength and muscle use found in earlier hominids. For instance, anteroposterior shaft flattening in the femurs is less pronounced, and the shaft walls for all the limbs are thinner. Muscle markings tend to be less prominent.

One rather different feature appears in the pelvis of the Tabun female where the pubis is unusually elongated. This is a consequence of the fact that while the average cranial capacity of this sample has expanded considerably compared with earlier hominids, there is no change in *average* body height. In the Shanidar 1 male and Tabun female, cranial capacity can be directly compared with body size. The expanding vault (at birth) eventually reached the limits of the unchanged pelvic dimensions. The relation is much larger than ever occurred in earlier specimens. For instance, the ratio in this Shanidar male is 30 percent greater than that in the Broken Hill male. In fact, the Shanidar and Tabun ratios even exceed those of living people; modern populations are generally taller but do not have larger cranial capacities, or looking at the ratio another way, living populations with the same average body height as this Near Eastern sample have smaller average cranial capacities. The main consequences of the relative expansion in cranial capacity are found in the pelvis.

Larger crania in adults almost certainly meant larger crania at birth. This would require anterior–posterior expansion of the birth canal in the females. A commensurate expansion of the pelvic inlet in males would also be expected. In the early *Homo sapiens* sample from the Near East, this expansion was accomplished through a marked elongation of the pubis (Figure 4.5). The elongation acts to swing the wings of the pelvis outward and backward, resulting in a very australopithecine-like configuration. In the australopithecines, the configuration resulted from a small birth canal and a narrow sacrum—narrowing at the back rather than broadening at the front. However, the biomechanical requirements are the same, and the archaic *Homo sapiens* pelves resemble the australopithecines' in their very anterior positioning of the iliac buttress and the marked distance between the ischium and the acetabular rim. However, because the elongation which made the birth canal larger involved the pubis, it is here that the most distinctive aspect of the pelvis is found. The upper portion of the pubis is longer and thinner than in any earlier hominid sample. However, this part of the pubis is very broad, presumably to resist bending during childbirth.

Finally, the Near Eastern postcrania provide some indications of the magnitude of sexual dimorphism in body size. The males average 64 inches in height and the females 59 inches. The percentage difference in body height falls within the range for living people. In contrast to living populations, however, few differences in *robustness* or features reflecting strength and muscularity distinguish males from females in this archaic *Homo sapiens* sample.

COMPARISONS WITH AFRICAN CONTEMPORARIES

The early Würm-equivalent Near Eastern hominids, like their African contemporaries, represent the end point of archaic *Homo sapiens* evolution. Similarly, in this area very little bridges the gap between Middle Pleistocene *Homo sapiens* and this much later sample. While the crania, mandibles, and teeth evidence the same sort of tendencies that were discussed for Africa, many of the specifics differ between these regions. Similarities involve the expansion of cranial capacity and the differential expansion of frontal and occipital areas, shrinking of the basal structures associated with strengthening, and reduction and gracilization of the face. On the other hand, no Near Eastern hominids show the browridge reduction expressed in many of the sub-Saharan Africans, and similarly anterior tooth size reduction is not as great in the Near East. Lack of substantial reduction in the anterior teeth may be causally related to the maintenance of large supraorbitals, as well as to the marked expression of expanded maxillary sinuses and the related morphological complex of midfacial prognathism, lack of canine fossae, and anterior positioning of the mandibular teeth relative to the mental foramen and ramus.

Superficially, the North African crania resemble the contemporary Near Eastern crania, especially in cranial and upper facial form. However, there are detailed specific differences in the faces, including alveolar prognathism, the reduction of midfacial prognathism and appearance of canine fossae, and dental reduction in North Africa. As we will discuss, the Near Eastern sample most closely resembles the contemporary Europeans.

Postcranial comparisons with the contemporary African sample cannot be made; there are only a few postcrania from Omo and these have not been described in print. The Near Eastern postcrania show no significant difference in body size compared with earlier hominids, but strongly suggest a reduction in muscularity and strength. The extent of sexual dimorphism in body size also diminishes, reaching the magnitude found in living populations. A unique morphological complex in the pelvis results from the relative cranial capacity expansion and involves anterior–posterior lengthening of the birth canal through elongation of the pubis.

Now that we have discussed the end points of archaic *Homo sapiens* evolution in two areas, we turn to the one region where there is an intervening sample. Europe provides these missing data, but the fact that regional distinctions can be shown within Africa and between Africa and the Near East makes it necessary to be cautious in generalizing from the European sequence, since it too may be unique.

The European Riss/Würm

Europe provides the best sample of archaic *Homo sapiens* specimens that can be dated to the period between the Riss and Würm glaciations (Table 11.1). The European evidence spanning this period is regionally distinct and is clearly foreshadowed by the slightly earlier Riss sample (Chapter 10). In spite of some uncertainties resulting from insecure dating for many of the specimens, the sample that can probably be dated to this period is large.

The greatest single dating problem is the relation of what is recognized as the beginning of the Würm in eastern, southern, and western Europe. The Würm climatic oscillations are thought to have begun in western Europe between 70,000 and

80,000 years ago; there were two less severe cold oscillations preceding the two main glacial events in early Würm. (Early Würm ends some 35,000 years ago.) Both the number of oscillations and their timing in central and southeastern Europe are less clear. Do these correspond to all of early Würm in western Europe? Or only to the main two glacial advances distinguished in the west? Or perhaps to only one of these, or conversely to an even longer period? What is recognized as the Riss/Würm interglacial may extend later in time in southern Europe, and it is possible that some sites called "interglacial" in these areas are actually contemporary with more northern sites called "glacial." Conversely, some eastern European glacial sites may be earlier than any to the west.

WESTERN EUROPE

The western European sample is all from France and Spain. Two crania from the Italian site of Saccopastore that are usually considered in this interglacial have been radiometrically dated to about 60,000 years ago, which makes them equivalent to Würm I in time.

Mandibles in this sample include four virtually complete specimens, one each from the French sites of Abri Bourgeois-Delaunay at La Chaise and Malarnaud, and two others from the Spanish sites of Bañolas and Atapuerca. The mandibles present a remarkable size range, while the morphological variation is not as great. For instance, the largest (Bañolas) and smallest (Malarnaud, from an individual about fourteen years old) differ by more than the Arago mandibles. Malarnaud was virtually adult and not likely to grow more; the fact that both ramus and corpus are extraordinarily small suggests it is a female. In contrast ramus height in Bañolas is even greater than in the Arago male. However, as a whole, all the mandibles are more gracile than the earlier European specimens. Both the corpus and the ramus are thinner on the average, and not surprisingly posterior tooth size is reduced. In Bañolas the ramus begins at the last molar, while the La Chaise ramus begins behind it. Finally, all these mandibles have fairly thin symphyses with neither internal nor external buttresses. The Atapuerca sample includes several additional mandibles, more fragmentary than the specimens discussed above. These recently discovered specimens are extraordinarily similar to the smaller of the Krapina mandibles (see below) in symphysis form, body proportions, and dental features such as anterior tooth size and the high-cusped form of the P_3. This suggests the presence of gene flow and morphological continuity between western and central Europe.

The crania are all fragmentary. Specimens are from the French sites of La Chaise and Fontéchevade. The parietals, occipital, and temporal from La Chaise suggest a long, low cranium with marked posterior breadth. The impressions left by the brain on the inside of the occiput are markedly asymmetric; the larger left side indicates right-handedness.

The two cranial fragments from Fontéchevade have been interpreted as "more modern" than later Neandertal specimens. The main feature thought to show that these specimens represent "pre-sapiens" is the supposed lack of a browridge in both. This interpretation is used to support arguments for the presence of two lineages in Europe before the Würm: "presapiens," ancestral to living people, and "preneandertal," ancestral only to the European Neandertals (see discussion in Chapter 10 State of the Art). Fontéchevade 2 consists of a skullcap with parietals and most of the frontal, missing only the supraorbital-bearing portion (see Figure 11.5). Fontéchevade 1 is a frontal fragment from a possibly juvenile individual consisting of the portion just over the nose and some surrounding bone from behind it.

Fontéchevade 1 has two characteristics which are said to distinguish it from earlier specimens and also from some of the later European Neandertals—thin cranial bone and the virtual absence of any bulging corresponding to the central portion of a browridge. However, interpretation of the fragment is confused by the possibility that it is a juvenile, since these features could reflect no more than a young age at death (thicker cranial bone and a torus might possibly have developed later in life).

The Fontéchevade 2 situation is more complex because the entire face and browridge region are broken away. The French paleontologist H. Vallois argues that no browridge was present because of the form of the remaining frontal and the position of its sinus. However, C. L. Brace has noted a Krapina specimen with a similar frontal form but with a large torus, and others have disputed the interpretation of frontal form. It seems to me that argu-

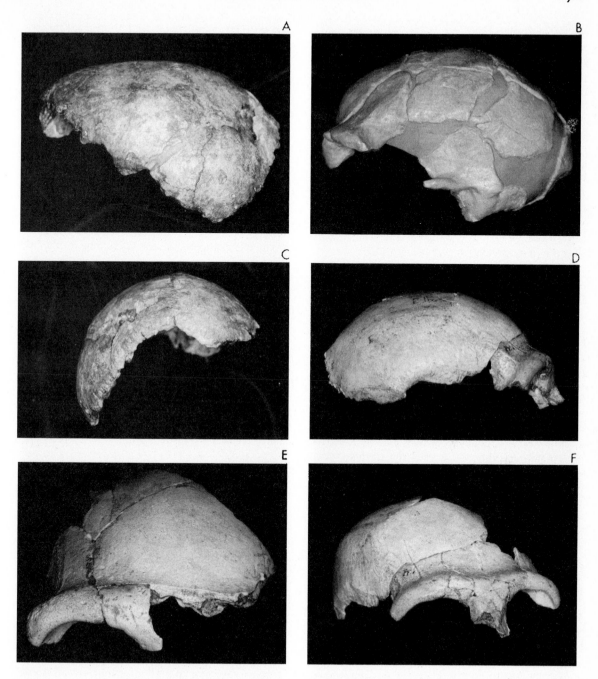

FIGURE 11.5 *Some European crania from the Riss/Würm. A and C are side and rear views of the Fontéchevade 2 cranium; B is a cast of the Kleinschmidt reconstruction of Ehringsdorf H; D and F are side and angled views of Krapina E; and E is the reconstructed Krapina D frontal (central supraorbital fragment added by the author).*

ments about the morphology of missing cranial portions can come to no good end.

Apart from the question of browridge morphology, the Fontéchevade crania show a cluster of features similar to contemporary and earlier specimens. Fontéchevade 2 is very broad and low.

While cranium capacity is moderate (about 1,350 cc), contemporary crania from eastern Europe have similar capacities. The parietal breadth of the cranium is very large, and the location of the maximum breadth at the far rear of the cranium results in a cranial contour, as seen from the top, which is very similar to that of the Würm Neandertals. The occipital breadth must also have been rather great. As seen from the rear, the contour of the parietals is circular, with the greatest breadth about midway up the bone. In fact, this contour resembles Riss specimens such as the La Chaise (Suard) skullcap. Instead of being "more modern" than the later European Neandertals, Fontéchevade 2 is similar to them or more archaic.

CENTRAL AND EASTERN EUROPE

Using the Rhine and the German high plains as the eastern border of western Europe, the Riss/Würm sample from regions farther to the east and south is much larger than its western counterpart. Specimens from Ehringsdorf in East Germany and Krapina in Croatia have been subject to an especially diverse range of interpretatons, which may have been more the result of faulty or incomplete reconstructions than divergent morphological characteristics. Actually, I believe that a basic similarity exists between this sample and the contemporary western European sample, which suggests similar adaptations and gene flow between the regions.

A complete endocast (natural cast of a cranial cavity) with some adhering cranial bone, and natural casts of parts of a radius and fibula were discovered in a Riss/Würm context at the Czechoslovakian site of Gánovce. The cranium is long, broad, and rather low, similar in these respects to Fontéchevade 2; cranial capacity is 1,320 cc.

A large hominid sample has been recovered from the site of Ehringsdorf, near Weimar (DDR). A cranium (H), adult and adolescent mandibles (F and G), four parietals (A through D), and a femur shaft (E) have been reported.

Ehringsdorf H is rather archaic in appearance. The frontal begins behind the moderate browridge, and a frontal bulge is retained. The cranium is reminiscent of Steinheim in these features. Another archaic feature is the lack of expansion of the occipital plane. As seen from the side, there is considerable expansion of the parietal lobes, and the

mastoids are large. As viewed from the rear, the reconstructed outline of the braincase is circular. The greatest breadth is about midway up the parietals, and the basal breadth is greatly reduced. However, this aspect of cranial shape is variable at Ehringsdorf. The isolated parietals are much thicker than the vault bones of Ehringsdorf H. The contrast suggests that in spite of the supraorbital development, the H skull is a female. Like Arago 21, which I believe is also female, Ehringsdorf H retains fairly robust features in the upper face. Parietal C is also rounded in posterior contour, while B and D (probably males) are more sharply angled between horizontal and vertical surfaces, as in the Solo specimens and many *Homo erectus* crania.

The two mandibles (F and G) belonged to an old adult (Figure 11.11) and a juvenile. They share the combination of large (particularly broad) anterior teeth and reduced or modern-sized posterior teeth. In both mandibles, the third molar (unerupted in the juvenile) is considerably smaller than the other two. In the adult, the forward border of the vertical ramus begins distinctly behind the third molar. Moreover, the mental eminence is rather well developed in both specimens. However, the prognathism and forward angle of the incisors overshadows this external buttress and makes the mandibles appear receding and chinless.

KRAPINA

The final Riss/Würm site to be considered is farther to the south, the Krapina cave in Yugoslavia. Krapina has yielded one of the largest fossil hominid samples from a single site (Figure 2.3). Based on the dentitions about eighty individuals are represented. The material was originally described in a series of papers and a rather complete monograph by the Croatian excavator D. Gorjanović-Kramberger in the first decade of this century. His excavation techniques were far in advance of contemporary practices. For instance, Gorjanović used the fluorine method of relative dating to show that the hominid and Pleistocene faunal remains at Krapina were contemporary some fifty years before the same technique was used in England to discredit the antiquity of the Piltdown material. Although specimens were scattered through the timespan of the site, most were recovered from a Riss/Würm layer called the "*Homo* zone" (Table 11.1).

Krapina Teeth

Because of its large size, the Krapina dental sample is particularly informative. There are 191 isolated teeth and 90 additional teeth in or associated with jaws. This extensive sample allows analysis of tooth size, variation, morphology and wear characteristics.

Taken as a whole, the Krapina teeth are larger than their Riss/Würm counterparts elsewhere. Only earlier hominids have larger posterior teeth, and no Pleistocene hominid sample has anterior teeth which average as large as those from Krapina. The major factor contributing to the anterior tooth size expansion is the development of two structures on the inner (lingual) surfaces of the teeth: strong tubercles (bulges of enamel) at the base of the teeth and marked marginal ridges (shoveling) on the incisors (see Figure 11.6, p. 274). Both of these serve to strengthen the teeth when they are subject to horizontal loading without greatly increasing the amount of dental material. Other evidence of anterior tooth use can be found in the pattern of wear. In some of the more complete specimens, incisor wear exceeds the wear on the surrounding teeth, and the wearplane sometimes slopes toward the outer face of the tooth in a manner which suggests that these teeth were used in a very different way from the remainder of the dentition.

While it is likely that normal individual variation accounts for many of the dental differences at Krapina (Figure 11.6), comparison of size in complete adult mandibles suggests that sexual dimorphism to the extent seen in *Homo erectus* may also be a contributing factor. As in the Choukoutien sample, the mandibles show more dimorphism than the teeth or crania.

A different facet of these dental remains provides an insight into the people's lifeways. The individual ages indicate that an overabundance of young people died in the cave (or an underabundance of older adults). Many of the teeth show developmental deformities that are associated with periods of sickness and/or starvation during the time of tooth development. It is possible that the cave was used as a shelter for the sick (most of whom would be children) while the remainder of the tribe inhabited open-air sites as they followed game. This would account for the relative scarcity of adult remains at the cave, since many of the adults would have died elsewhere.

Krapina Mandibles and Crania

Of the sixteen or more mandibles or mandibular fragments, only a few are adult and only mandible J is complete. According to F. H. Smith, all of the adults represented were prognathic, with the ramus beginning behind the last molar. The symphyses are straight but angled posteriorly, and only the adolescent mandible D shows evidence of a chin. Variation in the adult corpus size is extreme, and it is likely that small specimens, such as G, are female, while H and J are male (Figure 11.6).

The sample of upper jaws is smaller than the mandibular sample, and unfortunately no maxilla can be associated with a cranium. The faces do not appear to have been large, and no specimen has a canine fossa.

Analysis of the cranial sample presents many problems because of the extreme fragmentation of the bones. There is a literally uncounted number of largely unidentified cranial fragments. The best-preserved specimen is the C skull (Figure 11.7, p. 275), which lacks most of the base and posterior region and the lower face. Although widely regarded as a female, its browridges are among the thickest at the site. The widely separated orbits angle considerably toward the rear, resulting in a pronounced "beaking" at the facial midline, reflected in the backward angulation of the zygomatics. The face is delicate and lightly built compared with earlier specimens. The frontal, discovered among the fragments and reconstructed by the author, shows a moderate bulge of the forehead. However, archaic features include a low cranial height, thick vault, and marked spongy bone development at the cranial base, where the greatest cranial breadth is retained. The mastoids are small, a feature sometimes found in the Würm Neandertals. Many of these features seem to have been common in European females (Arago 21 and Ehringsdorf H, for example). Moreover, while there are similarities with the northern specimens from other areas (for instance, the angled face of Mapa), the combination of facial beaking and a high nasal angle (prominent nose) is characteristically European.

The less complete crania and cranial fragments, where comparable, provide a series of contrasts and consistencies. For instance, cranium E (Figure 11.5) is smaller and more delicately built than the C skull but has an even higher nasal angle and in life probably had a more prominent nose. While the brow-

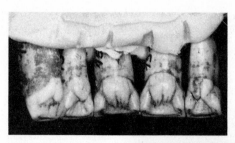

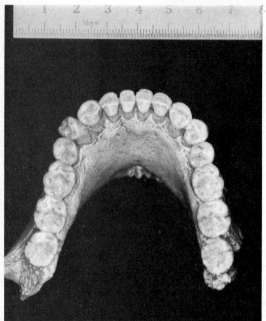

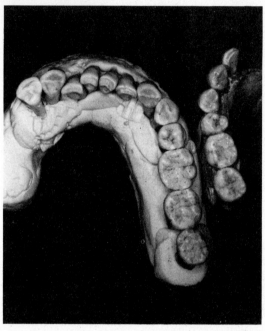

FIGURE 11.6   Elements of dental variation at Krapina. At top is the associated maxillary anterior tooth set K, showing the extraordinary tubercle development at the base of the teeth and the incisor shoveling (the view is from the inside). In the middle, mandible H is to the left, and in the right photo dental set L (the largest at the site) is shown beside mandible D (far right). Below are the male and female adult mandibles H and G.

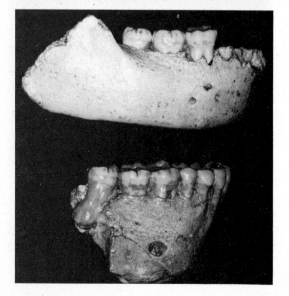

FIGURE 11.7   On opposite page, the best preserved of the female Neandertal crania. Beginning with the uppermost specimen, the figure shows a geographic gradation from the Near East to southwestern Europe (no northern females are clearly distinguishable). Above is Tabun (reconstructed by the author) from Israel, below it is Krapina C (reconstructed by the author) from Yugoslavia, below this is Saccopastore 1 from Italy, and finally the Gibraltar cranium.

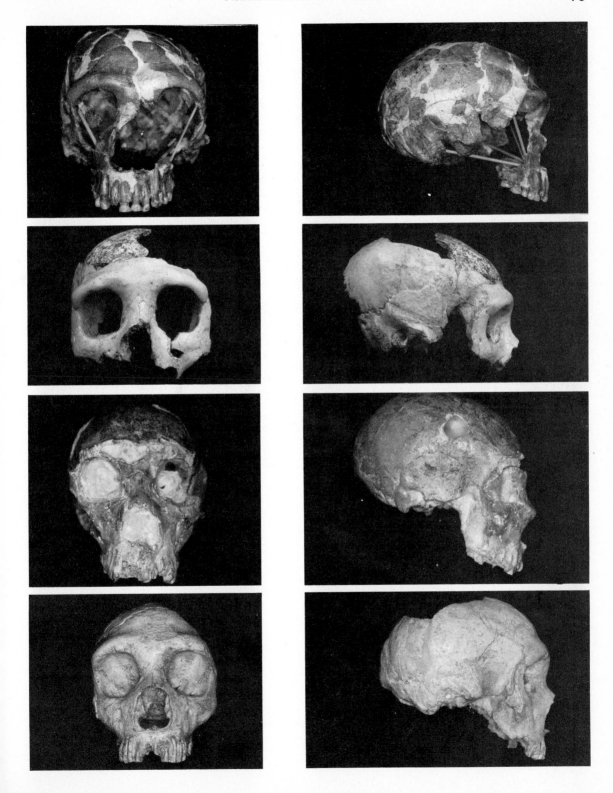

ridges are smaller than the C skull torus, unlike the latter they are clearly divided from the low frontal by a groove. The third fairly complete specimen, the so-called D cranium, consists of the frontal and parietal associated by Gorjanović and the occipital added by C. L. Brace. The robustness of the temporal markings on the frontal (Figure 11.5) and the presence of a sagittal torus suggest that the specimen may be male, although the browridges are only moderate in thickness and projection. The juvenile B cranium preserves much the same areas as Biache and is similar to it in size and in the presence of flattening at the rear of the cranium.

The numerous more fragmentary pieces are important to an assessment of the variability at Krapina. Temporal fragments, for instance, reveal variation in the mastoid process that ranges from mastoids even smaller than in the C skull to a large projecting structure. The large sample of supraorbital fragments gives evidence of an average reduction in browridge thickness compared with the earliest European *Homo sapiens* sample. It also reveals variation in both the size and morphology of the region; some specimens have virtually no torus at all.

In sum, while the best-preserved Krapina crania show some degree of variation, the isolated fragments suggest that the actual cranial variation at the site was far greater than these few specimens indicate. Appreciation of this variability has been hindered by the fact that the two most nearly complete specimens (C and E) are probably female.

Krapina Postcrania

An enormous number of fragmentary postcranial remains were recovered from Krapina (Figure 2.3). For instance, there are 130 specimens catalogued from the lower trunk and limbs alone, which could represent as many as ninety different individuals. Data from these remains provide evidence for a moderate-sized robustly built physique. As to height, the sample average of about 61 inches is not much different from the *Homo erectus* average. The range for the sample estimated from five limbs with reconstructable lengths is 57 to 66 inches; the tallest specimen is about 16 percent taller than the shortest.

Krapina provides the earliest fairly complete

postcranial set for *Homo* that has been found. While these postcrania are fully modern in function, there are a number of characteristics which diverge from the modern condition. Foremost among these is the marked thickening of the shaft walls in all the long bones. However, the specimens are reduced in this respect when compared with *Homo erectus* limbs, and the shaft shapes are less flattened. Most other distinctive features of these postcrania appear to be the result of two broad adaptive complexes. The first of these was already discussed in regard to the Near Eastern specimens. It is the unusual elongation of the front of the pelvis and the associated thinning of the upper portion of the pubis, anterior shift of the buttress running up the ilium, and so on. This complex appears as the result of large head size at birth and therefore reflects the expansion of cranial capacity. A second set of characteristics, including the curvature of the ribs, the angle of the scapular-humeral joint, and other features of the scapula and clavicle, provides evidence supporting A. Hrdlička's contention that the trunk was more rounded, or "barrel-shaped," than in living humans. The significance of this trunk form is discussed below.

Krapina's Place in European Evolution

The importance of Krapina results from the size of the sample and the fact that nearly all body parts are represented. While an excellent description of the material was available early in the development of European paleoanthropology, it was never given the full consideration it deserved. Perhaps this was the result of the typological thinking prevalent earlier in this century. One or two specimens (especially the C skull and J mandible) came to represent the entire sample. However, workers were aware of the variability. In fact, there was an attempt to show that both modern-type people and Neandertals were present. It was thought that the former population exterminated the Neandertals and butchered them, thereby accounting for the fragmentary condition of the bones. Such an interpretation cannot be supported. The "modern type" is actually represented by the remains of very young individuals and bone fragmentaton is the common condition at most sites.

In today's context, Krapina presents a gracilized

development based on earlier European morphology. Its most unusual aspect is the magnitude of anterior tooth size expansion. The size of the sample provides insight into the extent of genetic variation present at one location in pre-Würm Europe. This genetic variation provided the basis for subsequent evolutionary change.

EVOLUTIONARY TRENDS IN THE EUROPEAN SAMPLE

Although the sites involved are widely separated and not all skeletal elements are represented in large number, some clear and consistent evolutionary trends can be seen to characterize the Riss/Würm sample in both eastern and western Europe. It seems best to begin a discussion of trends with the mandibles and teeth, where the samples are largest.

The single most significant change in the mandibles is the posterior positioning of the ramus, which in most specimens is separated from the back of the third molar by a gap. Associated with the ramus position is a posterior placement of the mental foramen. This reflects the fact that the entire face from the top of the nose to the teeth was in a more anterior position, as if pulled forward, a trend first visible in the Mindel/Riss European sample. The morphology is associated with the structural adaptations to greater forces applied between the upper and lower front teeth.

Another distinction is the first fairly frequent appearance of an external buttress at the symphysis, or a chin. Studies by T. D. White indicate that this development was an indirect consequence of the expansion of cranial capacity and shrinking of the cranial base.

The dental sample is characterized by average posterior tooth size reduction and anterior tooth expansion (see Figure 11.9), especially in transverse breadth. In both cases, the changes continue evolutionary trends apparent in the archaic *Homo sapiens* sample when compared with *Homo erectus*.

The few fairly complete Riss/Würm crania are larger than those in the earlier European sample. Average cranial capacity for four specimens (Krapina C, Ehringsdorf H, Fontéchevade 2, and Gánovce) is 1,355 cc, although this should be regarded with some caution since it is based on estimates. This exceeds the 1,190 cc average for the four earlier European *Homo sapiens* crania by 14 percent. The Riss/Würm crania are higher and markedly broader than the earlier skulls, although cranial length is somewhat shorter. In almost all cases, the greatest breadth is above the cranial base, positioned low or midway on the parietals at the very rear of the skull. This is the result of parietal expansion combined with reduction in basal spongy bone development. The spongy bone above the mastoids is reduced, and the mastoids themselves tend to be relatively small (although markedly variable). The occipitals show a continued expansion of the upper portion at the expense of the nuchal muscle attachment area. There appears to have been average reduction in the browridge, with the range extending to specimens in which its development is minimal. Yet many specimens (including the known females) retain moderate supraorbitals. Again, most of these changes continue earlier evolutionary trends.

The few postcranial remains that are fairly complete suggest no significant height change for the sample. Three developments characterize the specimens. First, the limb bone adaptations to strength and muscle use are reduced (especially the flattening of the limb shafts and the outer shaft bone thickness). Second, the pelvic remains reflect the relatively large brain size at birth through the morphological complex resulting from pubic elongation. Finally, the shape of the clavicles and ribs and the angle of the joint between the humerus and scapula suggest that the trunks of these people were relatively "barrel-shaped."

The European Würm Neandertals

The European Würm Neandertals are probably the single most intensively studied group of fossil humans, with numerous general works reviewing their morphology, adaptation, ecology, and behavior. The main point of these studies has generally been to call attention to and explain what appears to be a number of "unusual" features in their anatomy, with special reference to the question of whether or not the latest European Neandertal populations were ancestral to the "modern" *Homo sapiens* populations that succeeded them.

The vast majority of the sample was excavated some time ago under less-than-perfect conditions, and thus the exact stratigraphic position of some of the important finds is unknown. Recent reviews of the older sites and the careful excavation techniques used with more recent discoveries allow many specimens to be placed within the context of the four main European Würm advances (see Table 11.1). Specimens now thought to be dated to Würm I and the Würm I/II interstadial (approximately 55,000–75,000 B.C.) include Krapina mandibles G, E, and K and maxillas B and C, Monsempron, Saccopastore 1 and 2, and Regourdou. The major specimens from Würm II (approximately 40,000–55,000 B.C.) are the six La Ferrassie specimens, the full La Quina sequence, La Chapelle, the Hortus sample, Jersey (St. Brelade), Kůlna, Mt. Circeo cranium and mandibles, Vindija cave, and Staroselje. Some of the important undated specimens are Gibraltar, the Spy skeletons, and most of the eastern European specimens, such as Šala, Subalyuk, and some of the isolated teeth from Krapina. These cannot be dated more accurately than to the "earlier" Würm.

While "early Würm" may be sufficient for discussing the relation of this sample to earlier or later ones, it is important to subdivide the specimens as much as possible in order to look for evolutionary trends and geographic variation within the Würm. The best temporal division is between the Würm I/II interstadial and Würm II; the best geographic divisions are between the northern, eastern, and southern European samples. However, since all specimens cannot be accurately dated, the discussion of evolutionary trends within the sample involves somewhat fewer specimens than the discussion of differences between the total sample and earlier or later ones.

CRANIAL FORM

Considering the sample as a whole (see Figures 11.7 and 11.8) and for the moment ignoring the geographic, temporal, and sex differences within it, there are a number of average differences that distinguish these Europeans from the earlier (almost certainly ancestral) European populations. Since the Riss/Würm cranial sample is rather small, comparisons may not be fully accurate. Yet virtually every feature of the Würm Neandertal sample is found in lower frequency. Compared with this earlier sample, the Würm Neandertal cranial capacity averages 6 percent larger, and the crania tend to be slightly longer and narrower. Compared with Middle Pleistocene archaic *Homo sapiens* specimens, the Neandertal average capacity is 33 percent larger. Changes in the Neandertal crania leading to the increased capacity are more morphological than metric, involving the development of bulges in the forehead, occipital plane, and posterior parietals.

Spongy bone development at the cranial base is markedly decreased. Combined with the parietal expansion this results in the consistent pattern of braincase breadth exceeding basal breadth. The position of maximum breadth is far to the rear of the cranium, about midway up the parietals. Thus as seen from the rear, Neandertal crania take on a circular appearance (Figure 9.8), and viewed from the top, they are teardrop-shaped.

Changes in the occiput are significant. Most specimens do not have a nuchal torus. Instead, the farthest extent of nuchal muscle attachment is generally marked by a line (called the nuchal line). This line is lower than the nuchal line (or torus) in earlier Europeans. Thus the length of the nuchal muscle attachment area decreases, while the height of the occiput above it increases. Even though there is an increase in occipital breadth, and therefore in the breadth of the nuchal muscle attachment area, the total effect is to further reduce the attachment area for these muscles. This area is only 85 percent as large as in the Middle Pleistocene archaic *Homo sapiens* sample, and 56 percent the size of the area in *Homo erectus*. The decreasing attachment area and reduction (or loss) of the torus provide evidence for reduction in the strength of the nuchal muscles.

Another change in the occiput is the flattening of the occipital plane, called "bunning," seen in many of the specimens. This flattening occurs on the upper part of the bone and includes the back portion of the parietal bones. Its purpose seems to be the elongation of the very back of the skull without a great increase in cranial capacity. This is particu-

FIGURE 11.8   *The best preserved of the European Neandertal males. The upper two crania are from northern Europe and the lower two from the south. Beginning with the top cranium, the specimens are La Ferrassie and La Chapelle (both from France) and Mt. Circeo and Saccopastore 2 (both from Italy).*

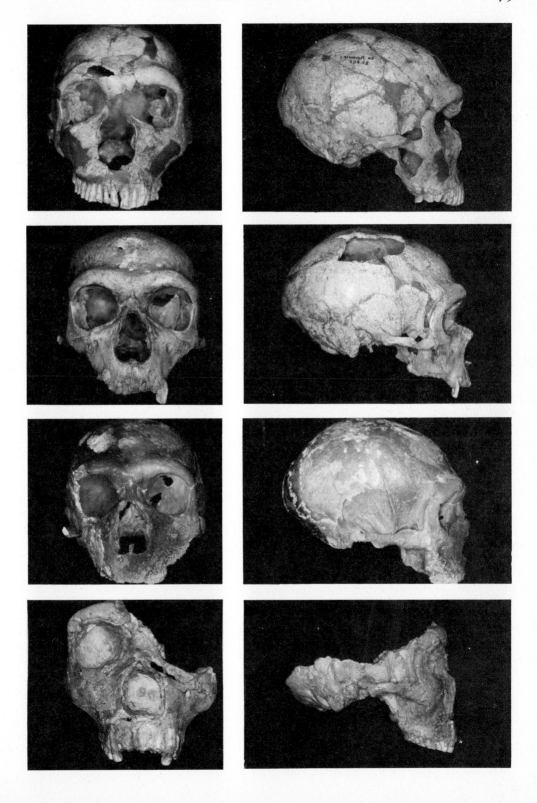

larly important for maintaining a relatively horizontal nuchal plane. The first appearance of "bunning" is in the Riss (Biache), so the change is one of frequency. To some extent, the more horizontal orientation of the nuchal plane is a compensation for its decreased area. While the total area of nuchal muscle attachment decreases, and the lever arm for the musculature is shorter, the more horizontal plane maintains a larger muscle cross-section than its size suggests.

Other characteristic features of the posterior region, including the decrease in spongy bone and moderate (but variable) size of the mastoids, are probably consequences of reduced muscularity. The small mastoids may also result from the more posterior placement of the mastoid process due to the backward elongation of the temporal/occipital area of the cranial base. In this sample, the rear of the cranium is both larger and more backward-projecting than was the case for *Homo erectus*.

THE BROWRIDGE

While adult browridge size in this sample is remarkably variable, average characteristics combine reduced projection and decreased thickening compared with the Riss/Würm sample. Compared with the Middle Pleistocene specimens from Europe, all aspects of the browridges are markedly reduced or, to use Weidenreich's term, "degenerated." The torus is continuous over the orbits and ranges from virtual absence to large size. It arches over the eye sockets rather than forming a straight bar. The torus is not only thinner but generally appears much less prominent, mainly because the frontal begins above it. Moreover, the frontal is characteristically bulging, providing a distinct raised forehead. There are no cases of sagittal keeling on the frontal.

THE FACES

In some dimensional respects, the Neandertal faces are remarkably similar to the Middle Pleistocene archaic sapiens sample, while in others they are unique. Many of their features result from a continuation of earlier evolutionary trends. While only slight average reduction occurs in measures of facial height, breadths of the upper and middle

faces reduce by close to 10 percent. At the same time average nasal height and breadth increase, breadth about twice as much as height. The maximum cranial breadth exceeds the (reduced) breadth across the cheeks, which would probably accentuate the narrowness of the face in life through the contrast of a face narrower than the head.

Many of the unique features of Neandertal facial morphology center about the nose. A fully fleshed Neandertal nose must have been a phenomenal object. Almost every specimen is characterized by a nasal aperture of very large dimensions. The few remaining nasal bones, those not destroyed by the Neandertal habit of breaking open the midface to remove the brain, indicate that north of the circum-Mediterranean area the nasal profile was highly angled (see La Chapelle, Figure 11.8) so that the fleshy nose was extremely prominent. (Few fleshy reconstructions accurately show this.)

Directly to the sides of the nose, the maxillary sinuses are expanded outward, giving the mid-maxilla a puffy appearance and a convex surface. To the sides of this region, the zygomatics angle strongly backward. Combined with the great cranial breadth, the total effect of these features is a strongly projecting midfacial profile to the sides of a larger projecting nose, which could only have accentuated its appearance.

The prominence of the nose and maxillary sinus expansion are part of the Würm Neandertal adaptive complex expressed in the prognathism of the total face. From the top of the nose to the tooth row, the entire face projected strongly in front of the cranium, although its profile was fairly vertical. The degree of alveolar projection was actually reduced compared with earlier hominids, but above the lower face the projection was markedly greater. This projection, the strong posterior angulation of the cheeks, and the high nasal profile resulted in a combination, in exaggerated form, of facial features now characteristic of many Europeans.

However, in the Neandertal sample the degree of facial projection varies both by sex and by geography (see Table 12.1, p. 313). Projection of the middle and upper face is greater in the northern males than in the southern ones, but greater in the southern males than in the females. The southern males and females also differ from the northerners in their reduced backward extension of the skull, although not in cranial height or browridge projection.

COLD ADAPTATION

The nasal morphology, and features associated with it, is the single most distinctive feature of Neandertal faces. There is an adaptive explanation for this morphological complex. One of the primary functions of the nose is to warm and moisten the inspired air. The size and shape of the nose are related to the efficiency of this function. Nasal breadth is also affected by the breadth between the canines, since the roots of these teeth run along the sides of the nose. The breadth across the canines is large in the Neandertals because the anterior teeth are large; this probably accounts for the large nasal breadths in all of the early *Homo sapiens* samples. Thus, before the emergence of cold-adapted Neandertals, there was a background of broad nasal openings in early *Homo sapiens*. Selection to improve the efficiency of the nose in warming and moistening air built on what was already present. Expansion in length, breadth, and projection increase the functional capacity of the nose by providing for more internal volume in the nasal cavity, where the warming and moistening occur. Thus the large size of the Neandertal nose is an adaptation to very cold and dry conditions—conditions characteristic of the Arctic tundra today, but which prevailed over much of northern and central Europe during the last glaciation.

Nasal size is not the only cold adaptation of Neandertal facial morphology. As C. Coon points out, in living people the nasal passages lie close to the arteries that supply blood to the brain. Breathing in cold air would act to cool the blood in these arteries, and this could be disadvantageous because the brain is sensitive to temperature changes and must be kept fairly warm. Neandertals descended from European early sapiens populations which, as we have seen, already had expanded maxillary sinuses and midfacial prognathism resulting from stress on the anterior teeth. This whole morphological complex appeared at the same time that the incisors increased in size. Selection to maintain arterial blood temperature acted on this already present complex in the cold-adapting Neandertals. Further increases in midfacial prognathism expanded the distance between the nasal passages and the arteries supplying the brain, which reduced cooling of these arteries by inspired cold air.

The actual morphological alterations involved an increased facial projection without any substantial change in the size of the maxillary sinus (which, in any event, is unrelated to cold adaptation). This is why Coon could describe Neandertal faces as "appearing" to be the result of taking a Middle Pleistocene face by the nose and pulling it forward. The angle of the cheeks to a transverse (ear-to-ear) plane is marked, as this imaginary pulling of the nose brings along the structures to its sides.

Another consequence of the increased total facial projection is a real expansion of the cranial base (measured from the top of the nose to the back of the cranium). The foramen magnum "appears" to be in a more posterior position; this has been interpreted as a peculiar "overspecialization" of the Würm Neandertals. However, the foramen magnum is *not* farther back. Instead, the face is farther forward. Facial projection is greater in the northern sample than in the southern one, as one might expect if it corresponds to a cold adaptation.

There are some other indications of cold adaptation in the European Neandertals. These occur in the cranium and in the postcranial skeleton (discussed below). For instance, on the front of the face, under the orbits and to the sides of the nose, there is a foramen (hole) through which one of the arteries supplying blood to the face passes. In a cold adaptation, one might expect the blood supply to be greater since the face would be exposed to cold air, even with rather sophisticated clothing. This foramen is much larger in Neandertals than in earlier Europeans, allowing more blood to flow to the face.

In sum, the development of total facial prognathism, expansion of all nasal dimensions, and the enlargement of the opening for the facial artery are all part of a general Neandertal cold adaptation, one which could evolve because of features that were already present in the ancestral hominid populations of Europe.

THE PERMANENT DENTITIONS

As mentioned above, some aspects of Neandertal cranio-facial morphology are related to the dentition. In the Riss/Würm sample, the anterior teeth expanded while the posteriors reduced; however, reduction characterizes most of the subsequent evolution of both the posterior and the anterior

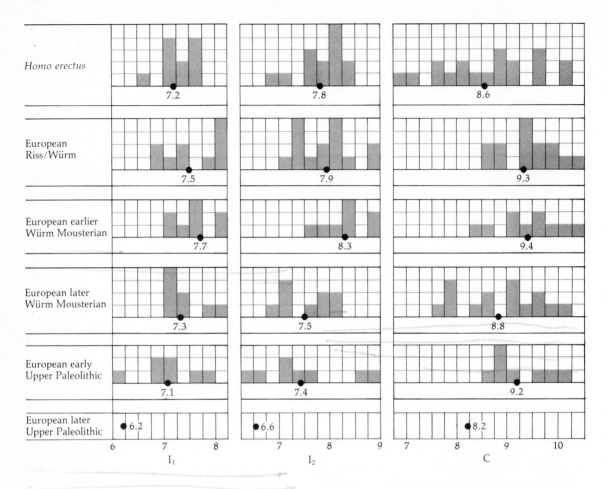

FIGURE 11.9   This comparison of frequency distributions for the transverse breadihs of the mandibular anterior teeth illustrates the reversal in direction for anterior tooth size. The actual breadths in millimeters are given on the bottom scale, and the averages are indicated. Compared with Homo erectus (top), the Riss/Würm European sample shows expansion in all three anteriors. The later Würm European Neandertals show varying degrees of reduction compared with both the Riss/Würm sample (except for the I_2) and Homo erectus. The distribution for the earliest European Upper Paleolithic sample is also shown, and finally the means for the later Upper Paleolithic sample (Gravettian, Magdalenian) are indicated (to be discussed in Chapters 12 and 13). The frequency changes show both a shift of range and a loss of specimens at one end or the other, when comparing samples.

teeth. This represents a change in the direction of selection acting on the anterior teeth (Figure 11.9).

Dividing the sample into Würm 1 and 2 sets, a continued reduction of posterior tooth areas through the earlier Würm can be shown. While in their average posterior tooth size the Würm Neandertals fall within the worldwide modern human range, they reflect part of a general trend for posterior tooth reduction in Europe. On the average, this sample is smaller-toothed than the Riss/Würm sample but larger-toothed than living Europeans.

The anterior teeth continue their expansion during the earlier Würm. However, the later Würm sample shows substantial reductions in the size of the canine and incisors. These decrease even beyond the size of the Riss/Würm sample and generally approach Homo erectus. While one might take the view that Homo erectus gave rise directly to these later Neandertal populations (including well-known "classic" specimens such as La Ferrassie), it is more likely that the smaller teeth reflect a change in the direction of selection acting on these populations. The important point is that this change can be seen *within* the European Neandertal sequence; anterior reduction is not something that first appears with recognizably modern *Homo sapiens* populations. This evolutionary progression is responsive to a changing pattern in these hominids' use of the anterior teeth as part of the tool kit.

T. D. Stewart first proposed the idea that the anterior teeth of some Neandertals were worn in a peculiar manner as the result of functions other than chewing; this was based on his study of the Shanidar 1 remains. C. L. Brace later demonstrated that this "peculiar" wear was not restricted to Neandertals with amputated arms, but also appeared in perfectly healthy specimens. He suggested that the Neandertals quite regularly used their anterior teeth for purposes other than chewing. We have come to regard this as a complex that evolved through the entire Pleistocene. What is interesting about the Neandertals is that they present the first evidence of reduction in anterior tooth use. While large by modern standards, the Würm Neandertals' anterior teeth are smaller than those of their ancestors.

The fact that the reduction eventually leading to the very small incisors in living populations began in Würm and continued through the late Neandertals indicates that the trend for incisor reduction did not originate in a more "modern" population migrating into Europe, nor in a change in selection resulting from the appearance of Upper Paleolithic industries that are found with the more modern populations that eventually evolved (see Chapter 12). Rather, this reversal in the direction of a major evolutionary trend was the result of a change in selection acting on *Neandertal* populations, which in all likelihood was initiated by technological developments within their Levallois-technique industries. These evolving techniques allowed a fine control over the final form of a tool regardless of the material used. Once they were present, a proliferation of tool types was inevitable, and eventually technologies based on many special-purpose tools appeared. Hand axes and choppers, the "boy scout knives" of their time, were replaced by special-purpose tools, and stone tools for working bone and wood proliferated. The development of efficient special-purpose tools made of stone, wood, and bone reduced the need for using the incisors as part of the tool kit, both directly as tools and more in-

directly as a vise while using other tools. As one would expect, the change in behavior (i.e., the development of special-purpose tools) preceded the change in morphology (incisor reduction).

The beginning of size reduction in the anterior teeth also helps explain the observed trend of decreasing attachment area for the nuchal muscles and the reduction in browridge size, although the latter was also aided by the ability of the higher Neandertal foreheads to resist strain without a supraorbital buttress. These skeletal changes began before the dental one, perhaps because the form of the structures concerned was more sensitive to changing behavior patterns.

Although change in the direction of evolution for the size of anterior teeth appears in the Neandertals, they still have some of the largest anterior teeth of any fossil hominid sample. This has a definite effect on their total morphological pattern. The large incisor roots help maintain the large lower face and keep the front of the palate broad, accounting in part for the large Neandertal nasal breadth. The strain in the maxillary bone (especially to the sides of the nose) from consistent loading of the front teeth helps account for the expanded maxillary sinus.

EVOLUTION OF DECIDUOUS TOOTH SIZE

One final aspect of the Neandertal dental changes bears on the life histories of these populations and earlier ones. The deciduous teeth have been mentioned only briefly in the discussions of dental evolution. This is because the samples are small, and the pattern of dental changes can best be understood when the full Pleistocene evolutionary trend is reviewed. Four distinct deciduous samples are large enough to be compared: *Homo erectus*, Middle Pleistocene archaic *Homo sapiens* from Europe, the Riss/Würm sample from Europe (almost entirely from Krapina), and the European Neandertals (see Figure 11.10, p. 284).

Some changes in the deciduous anterior teeth reflect changes in the permanent anterior dentition. The incisors and to a lesser extent the canines expand in size. However, the trend in the deciduous molars is the exact opposite of the trend in the permanent posterior teeth. While the permanent posterior dentition shows continuous size *decrease* between these samples, the deciduous molars con-

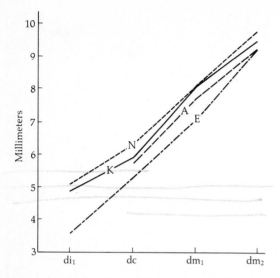

FIGURE 11.10   *Evolutionary changes in the deciduous mandibular dentition of* Homo. *Averages for transverse breadth in millimeters (vertical scale) are given for four samples. In temporal order, these are* Homo erectus *(E), Middle Pleistocene (or archaic)* Homo sapiens *from Europe (A), the Krapina Riss/Würm sample (K), and the Würm European Neandertals (N). Note that size increase characterizes all of these teeth, including the deciduous molars.*

tinuously *increase* in size. The European Neandertals have the largest deciduous molars of any fossil *Homo* sample.

The changes in diet, food preparation, and cooking might be expected to result in a parallel reduction for the deciduous and permanent posterior teeth. Moreover, improvement in child care should act in the same direction. Thus the appearance of the opposite trend may seem surprising. I believe that this trend can be explained by the contention that hominids were under selection to increase population size through earlier weaning and shorter birth spacing. Australopithecine birth spacing was estimated to average between three and four years; in contrast, some living human populations space births by an average of only two years. This short spacing does not represent the average time between *live* births. Pregnancy is rarely initiated before the previous offspring is weaned, and weaning rarely occurs before the full deciduous dentition is erupted (about two and a half years). However, if there is a stillbirth or the newborn quickly dies, a new pregnancy can be initiated al-

most immediately. The resulting birth will be spaced less than two years after the previous birth. When high infant mortality is common and live births are spaced less than three and a half years apart, an overall average of two years for all births can result.

Shortened birth spacing is the only effective alternative to lowered mortality rates for increasing population size. The spread of early *Homo sapiens* into new habitats and the more effective exploitation of specific niches show that population sizes and densities did increase over the Pleistocene. If these increases reflect the effects of shorter birth spacing, as I believe, the increase in deciduous molar size could be explained by the earlier weaning of the young, which would cause children to begin wearing out their deciduous teeth at an earlier age. There would be more wear since each tooth would be used for a longer span, and selection might be expected to result in size increase to prolong the effective life of the teeth.

This combination of short birth spacing and high mortality rates is not common among living hunter-gatherers. They are probably not a good model for the Upper Pleistocene hunter-gatherers, who lived in more optimal environments but exploited them with less technological efficiency. I suspect the demographic balance for living hunter-gatherer populations, generally inhabiting marginal environments, results from the marked improvement in both infant and adult survivorship that came with the extraordinarily effective late Pleistocene and Holocene adaptive changes. Consequently, these living populations have lower mortality but wider birth spacing, which acts to prevent further population increase. The situation is somewhat different in modern societies with both further improved survivorship *and* short birth spacing. Recent population increases in these have been dramatic, and in the long run not necessarily advantageous.

MANDIBLES

Two important evolutionary trends are apparent in Würm Neandertal mandibles, involving the forward positioning of the tooth row with respect to the ramus and the appearance of a true chin, or mental eminence. Since both of these features first appear in the Riss/Würm European sample, the Würm morphology represents a shift in frequencies rather than the sudden appearance of new features (see Figure 11.11).

The anterior positioning of the tooth row is one of the consequences of total facial prognathism, since the more forward positioned maxillary dentition must be met by the mandibular dentition. This morphology is common in the earlier Würm Neandertal sample, although not universal (La Naulette, for instance, lacks it). The gap between the last molar and the ramus reduces in the later sample, and again some specimens (such as La Quina 9) lack it completely.

The appearance of a chin corresponds to a different, independent evolutionary trend—the expansion of the braincase and resulting medial angulation in the temporalis muscle (discussed earlier). Chins become common in many Würm II Neandertals.

POSTCRANIA

Neandertal postcrania are characterized by a number of features once thought to be distinctive or unusual but now known to be characteristic of even more ancient hominid postcranial remains. Moreover, adequate understanding of this material has been plagued by early reconstructions of the La Chapelle skeleton. These remains are from an old male who suffered from severe arthritis, which deformed many of his skeletal elements. Along with other misconceptions, this led to a 1913 reconstruction of Neandertal posture as bent-kneed, with head thrust forward and a divergent big toe, which "may have played the part of a prehensile organ," according to M. Boule. While it is true that later work has shown this to be incorrect, the image of "Alley-Oop" is still with us.

To begin with, how large were the European Neandertals? They are often described as "short and stocky," but this description is actually the result of a backward perspective, comparing them with living people rather than with their contemporaries and ancestors. Based on the known postcranial remains, the average height for seven Neandertal male specimens is about 64 inches, while the two female specimens average 60 inches. This is virtually identical to the average height for *Homo erectus* and for the Near Eastern sample, and it is the same as the average height of the French population at the turn of the century. Therefore, instead of being

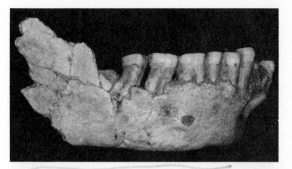

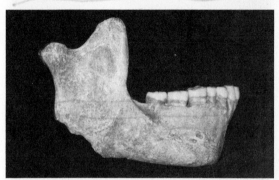

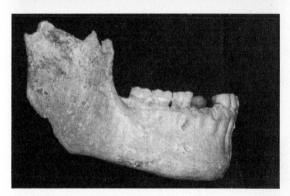

FIGURE 11.11 *Three mandibles showing trends in the evolution of mandibular form. At top is the Ehringsdorf adult from the Riss/Würm, middle is Regourdou from the early Würm, and below is Mt. Circeo 2, probably from Würm II. Note the progressive development of the mental eminence and the more forward position of the mental foramen relative to the teeth (under and toward the rear of the M_1 in Ehringsdorf but under the P_4 in Mt. Circeo). All three have a gap between the last molar and the front of the ramus.*

particularly short, the European Neandertals were actually the same height as earlier and contemporary hominids. It would be more accurate to characterize some later populations as "tall."

To some extent, body proportions within this sample suggest a cold adaptation through trunk thickening and limb shortening. Several lines of evidence indicate a large, rounded trunk relative to body size. For instance, the clavicles (collar bones) are long relative to body height; their pronounced "S" shape, the reduced rib curvature, and shoulder morphology all indicate a "barrel-shaped" trunk. Similarly, the vertebrae tend to be vertically short compared with the horizontal dimensions of their bodies. A deep, rounded trunk maximizes heat retention in the body core.

In the limbs, the bones farther from the trunk are short relative to those closer: radius compared to humerus, and tibia compared to femur (see Figure 11.12). While these proportions are within the modern human range, they are at the lower end. Shortening the limb lengths farthest from the body also helps retain heat, since heat loss is greatest away from the trunk. It is not unexpected that this relative limb shortening does not characterize the Tabun female, who lived in a considerably more hospitable environment (what is now Israel). Finally, all of the limbs were short relative to body weight (or, conversely, one might think of the body as heavy relative to its height). I prefer to think of it as limb shortening for two reasons. First, the length dimensions of the limbs are small relative to the shaft thickness and articular surface size. The ratio of limb thickness to limb length exceeds that in *Homo erectus*, although other indications of body strength and muscularity seem reduced. This ratio also exceeds that of contemporary skeletal material from the Near East. Consequently, I do not view it as an additional strength-related adaptation but rather as a climatic one. Second, the limbs are short relative to the size of the hands and feet, although hand and foot lengths are "normal" in relation to estimated weight.

Other morphological features seem clearly related to skeletal robustness and muscular strength and activity. Many of these adaptive features are reminiscent of the *Homo erectus* and australopithecine condition, although their expression is generally reduced. A result of strength adaptation combined with limb shortening in this sample can be seen in the femur shaft curvature in the anterior-posterior plane (or shaft bowing). Shaft bowing is a direct response to muscle force—in this case, a combination of marked muscularity and body weight relative to the shortened limbs.

OTHER SKELETAL FEATURES

Early studies of Neandertal feet (Figure 1.1) suggested that they were unusual in many respects. This conclusion was the result of comparisons with modern western Europeans, who normally wear shoes. More recent studies have shown that Neandertal-like feet are characteristic of most preindustrial modern populations; thus the supposed Neandertal distinctions turn out to be more an artifact of not wearing shoes than of a particular Neandertal adaptation.

Recent work by J. Musgrave demonstrates that while Neandertal hands were "squat and powerful," the thumb was not short, as previously believed, although the muscularity of the index finger was marked. These features indicate an especially powerful precision grip.

Relatively complete pelves (Figure 11.12) and more fragmentary innominates indicate a series of features which result from a combination of skeletal robustness and an extraordinarily deep birth canal (or pelvic inlet in the males). General robustness of the pelvis is indicated by a thick, prominent iliac pillar, a large acetabulum relative to other dimensions, and a dominant anterior inferior iliac spine. These features also characterize earlier innominates from Krapina, Arago, Prince, and Broken Hill.

Superimposed on this complex is an additional set of features which can be related to the fact that in the European Neandertals cranial size was large relative to body size, a relation similar to that found in the Near Eastern specimens. Using the brain size–body height relation of modern people for comparison, we find that European Neandertal brains were close to 330 cc larger than those of living people of the same height. Birth canal lengthening was important in these hominids, given the likelihood that head size at birth was also large. Consequently, the innominates are very large

FIGURE 11.12 Some Neandertal postcrania. At top are two views of the Neandertal innominate. To the lower left are a femur, humerus, and radius from this specimen, and to the lower right, the male (larger) and female radii from La Ferrassie.

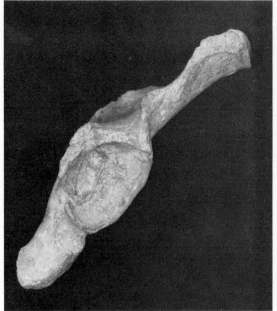

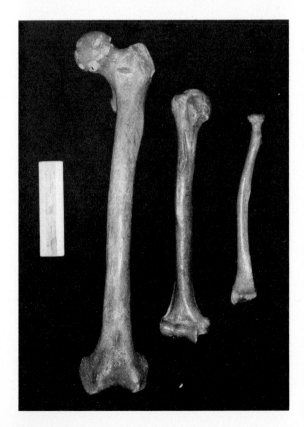

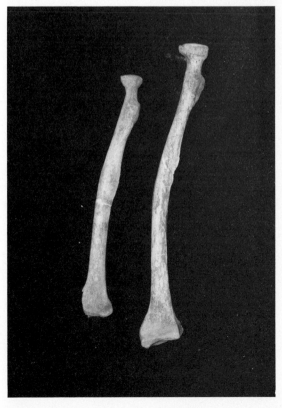

in both height and breadth relative to measures of body size, such as femur length. In the Neandertals, there is the same pubic elongation and anterior-posterior broadening that was found to characterize the contemporary Near Eastern sample. The associated outward and backward change in the position of the pelvic blades results in what appears to be a more anterior position for the iliac pillar and the acetabulum, again paralleling the morphology of the Near Eastern forms.

The few earlier *Homo sapiens* innominates known, from Broken Hill, Arago, and Prince, contrast with this complex related to pelvic inlet expansion and appear more modern (especially in their more posterior placement of the iliac pillar). These earlier people were not significantly different from Neandertals in height. However, they lack the skeletal evidence of trunk thickening and relative limb shaft thickening which suggests that they may not have been as heavy.

In contrast, the Neandertals (of the same approximate height) are both heavier and have larger cranial capacities. This indicates that their large capacities may be better analyzed relative to weight than to height. While Neandertals have been characterized as being unusually large brained relative to their height, their brain size is of modern proportion relative to their estimated weight. This supports other arguments suggesting that Neandertal limbs reflect cold adaptation through shortening.

VARIABILITY IN THE NEANDERTALS

Following the above discussion of Neandertal characteristics, it is especially important to emphasize the variability in the European sample and attempt to understand its causes and evolutionary importance. The European Neandertals are anything but the "homogeneous and invariant" sample that they are often considered to be. More than is the case for any other group of fossil hominids, the interpretation of the European Neandertals has been plagued by the "type" concept and the idea that the sample has little variability. In the words of C. Coon, "They are in fact so homogeneous that a strong selective agency must have been pruning off deviant individuals."

As a result of the lengthy and prestigious publi-

cation by M. Boule in 1913, the "old man of La Chapelle" came to represent the total Neandertal sample. The fact that a similarly detailed publication has recently appeared on the equally complete and likely more "typical" skeletal remains from La Ferrassie (discovered at about the same time) has not significantly detracted from this impression. However, the history of this problem is not simple, since other Neandertals have been described in some detail, including Gibraltar, Le Moustier, the two Saccopastore crania, Mt. Circeo, the Spy material, and La Quina 5. As early as 1930, a detailed review of all the then-known Neandertals by A. Hrdlička suitably emphasized their variability.

The choice, whether or not purposeful, of La Chapelle as the "typical" Würm Neandertal was particularly unfortunate for two reasons. First, the Würm sample is extremely variable and thus no single specimen could adequately represent it. Second, within the range of Würm Neandertal variation, many features of the La Chapelle skeleton lie at the extreme. In no other specimen are the distinctive Neandertal characteristics so pronounced.

The often unrecognized point is that other Würm Neandertals differ from La Chapelle (Figure 11.8), and in some cases the contrast is considerable. Le Moustier and Gibraltar (Figure 11.7), for instance, have much smaller browridges. Le Moustier also lacks occipital flattening, or "bunning." That this thirteen-year-old juvenile was old enough to have developed both features is indicated by their presence in younger specimens, such as the Pinar fronted from Spain or the Teshik Tash youth (aged eight or nine) from Russia (Figure 12.9). Almost every feature shows equivalent variation. In the Neandertal skullcap from Dusseldorf, the forehead is considerably lower than in La Chapelle. In Spy 2, it is higher. The usual rounded cranial contour, as seen from the rear, finds its exception in the parallel-sided Spy 2. In the mandibles, the contour of the symphysis varies from completely chinless in La Chapelle, Regourdou (Figure 11.11), and Le Moustier to a definite chin development in La Ferrassie, Mt. Circeo 2 (Figure 11.11), and La Quina 9.

Although much of this variation is temporal, some of it follows no particular pattern over time. Nor do the archaic or modern variants all appear on the same specimens. For instance, Le Moustier combines browridge reduction and lack of bunning but has a chinless mandible, while La Chapelle, which is "hyperneanderthal" in most features, has one of the highest foreheads. Mixed into the Neandertal range of variation is a set of less common but clearly present features which, when in higher frequency, characterize early populations of modern *Homo sapiens*.

One major factor contributing to systematic variation in the Neandertals is sexual dimorphism. A measure of the amount of dimorphism can be ascertained by comparing the reconstructed heights of specimens with sexable postcrania. Average female height is 94 percent of the male average; in living human populations, the female percentage usually averages 92–95 percent, and the contemporary Near Eastern sample also falls within this range. Thus the degree of dimorphism in body size is within the living human range and reduced from earlier samples.

Reduced size dimorphism makes sex determination of the skeletons more difficult. Another contributing factor can be seen in the comparison of the largely complete La Ferrassie male and female postcranial skeletons. While there is a 6-inch difference in reconstructed body heights (the 66-inch male is the tallest European Neandertal specimen), there is a lack of corresponding sex difference in skeletal features that result from strength and the level of muscular activity. In fact, the female femur shaft is relatively thicker and shows more anteroposterior flattening, although the relative head size of the femur and relative head and shaft size of the humerus are smaller. In contrast, living humans, who have the same *size* dimorphism, display much more dimorphism in *skeletal robustness*.

Sex determination from skeletal remains provides a small series of male and female crania (Figures 11.7 and 11.8). From these, a different and contrasting picture of sexual dimorphism in the vault and face emerges. As in modern humans, sex differences are greater in vault length and height than in the various vault breadth measures. However, average dimorphism in the Neandertals is *three times* as great. Dimorphism in Neandertal facial heights is greater than in breadths (especially of the lower face). The former greatly exceeds the living average. While some female specimens, such as Gibraltar, have markedly reduced browridges, the large size of this structure in the Spy female suggests that this may not be a consistent sex differ-

ence. Large browridges were a persistent feature of earlier *Homo sapiens* European females.

Fate of the Neandertals

The fate of these "classic" Neandertals of Europe has remained one of the most vexing problems in the history of modern human paleontology. Whether the Würm cold-adapted European Neandertal populations were directly ancestral to the more modern populations that follow them, or were replaced or extinguished by these populations, is the crux of the disagreement between the *unilinear* theory and the *preneandertal* theory.

UNILINEAR AND PRENEANDERTAL THEORIES

According to the unilinear theory, the European Neandertal populations were directly ancestral to later populations. The preneandertal theory suggests that the Würm Neandertals were derived from an ancestral population in the Riss/Würm that gave rise to both this group *and* modern sapiens forms. The Würm Neandertal populations became "overspecialized" and were replaced by the modern sapiens populations (the presapiens theory differs in placing the latest common ancestor even earlier, possibly during or before the Mindel glaciation).

While the preneandertal and unilinear theories appear to be distinct statements of widely divergent views, a closer examination suggests that they are not mutually exclusive. Since at the present time no worker believes that the Würm-adapted Neandertals were a separate human species, incapable of producing fertile offspring with the (presumed) contemporary ancestors of living populations, perhaps the question should be restated: Do any paleoanthropologists believe that *no* European Neandertal populations contributed genetically to the later populations living in the same area? Do any suggest that *all* Neandertal populations gave rise to later populations? When the positions are stated in this extreme way, the answer to both questions is really "no." The disagreement, then, is about the relative contribution of the Neandertal gene pool to later populations. However, the question then becomes: How much Neandertal contribution is necessary for the unilinear theory to be correct? How little for the preneandertal theory? There is no satisfactory answer.

There are three morphological bases for the preneandertal theory: the "overspecialization" of the European Neandertals, the inability of evolutionary forces to change the "overspecialized" Neandertals into (so-called) modern Upper Paleolithic populations in a short timespan, and the coexistence in other parts of the world of populations that appear more modern.

Overspecialization

In so far as the morphological evidence is concerned, the concept of overspecialization in the European Neandertals is largely attributable to F. C. Howell. He lists as overspecialized characteristics those features which were found to be most common in the northern Neandertal sample. However, as we have discussed, every one of these is subject to variation, and many are the result of cold adaptation based on a morphology otherwise like the earlier Europeans'. These various cold adaptations do not preclude the possibility of further change under changed selection. Because of their variability, if a change in selection made the combination of morphological features which we think of as characterizing modern sapiens advantageous and the combination of the more common Neandertal features disadvantageous, there is every reason to believe that the northern Neandertal populations could have responded successfully, since *every modern sapiens feature was already present*, although at low frequency. Moreover, the fact that the most critical aspects of Neandertal adaptation were cultural raises the possibility of rapid, extensive adaptive change without any genetic involvement.

Insufficient Time

The second morphological argument proffered to support the preneandertal theory is that there was insufficient time for the Neandertals to evolve into more modern populations. There are several problems with this argument. First, we do not actually know how much time is involved. None of the northern sample known to be Neandertal is dated later than about 40,000 years BP (Table 11.1). Second, the actual changes that would have to have occurred are probably not as great as usually supposed. The general assumption that Upper Paleolithic Europeans were identical to living Europeans is simply incorrect (see Chapter 13). In fact, there is a greater difference in most metric and many morphological features between early Upper Paleolithic Europeans and many living European populations than there is between the early Upper Paleolithic Europeans and the preceding Neandertals. Third, the latest Neandertal specimens differ from the Riss/Würm European sample in a direction which makes them more like the early Upper Paleolithic populations of Europe (see Chapter 12). Late Neandertals are characterized by the fairly common appearance of a chin, anterior tooth reduction, and the beginnings of reduced midfacial prognathism.

Late specimens from central and eastern Europe are particularly interesting. The Šala frontal has remarkably thin browridges, especially in the lateral portions. The Kůlna adult maxilla shows evidence of a canine fossa as well as some dental reduction, although a parietal from the cave maintains a Neandertal-like curvature. A marked case of anterior dental reduction is found in the Šipka juvenile mandible, which also evidences chin development and other "modern" features. However, the best case comes from the Croatian site of Vindija, where a sample of at least twenty fragmentary specimens associated with very late Mousterian shows marked anterior tooth size and browridge reduction (see Figures 12.1–12.3). Farther to the east, the infant cranium from the Russian site of Staroselje (Figure 12.4) has been offered as an example of evolutionary continuity. The specimen seems to show essentially modern features but was found in a Mousterian context. However, the young age and possibility of pathology have obscured the interpretation.

A similar analysis in western Europe is hampered by lack of precise dating for many of the remains discovered earlier in this century. To some extent, dating is less critical in the west than the lack of good dates in the east, since population movements to western Europe would necessarily pass through central or eastern Europe and ultimately be reflected by transitional samples there. Of the directly datable western material, anterior dental reduction is shown by the few late Mousterian teeth from Arcy-Sur-Cure, but the latest well-dated western European Neandertal site is l'Hortus (both are in France). The bulk of the Hortus hominid remains come from the latest and coldest portions of Würm II. The best-preserved specimens are mandibles, and these show modern sapiens features to an even greater degree than the eastern European material, although combined with them are features more characteristic of Neandertals. The most dramatic of the more modern features is the degree of anterior tooth reduction (Figure 11.9).

In sum, the argument of insufficient time is a weak one for three reasons. First, how much time actually separates the latest distinguishable Neandertal sample and the earliest recognizably modern one in any specific European area is unknown. Second, the earliest modern *Homo sapiens* populations are not as modern-appearing as most people imagine. Most features overlap those of Neandertals (difficulty in precise identification relates to the first point), and the amount of change that would have to have taken place is completely misrepresented by comparing a Neandertal to a living person. Third, among the Neandertals themselves, evolutionary trends result in demonstrable changes in the direction of the earliest modern European *Homo sapiens* samples which follow them temporally.

Contemporaries Outside of Europe

The third morphological basis of the preneandertal theory—the appearance of "more modern-looking" contemporary populations in other areas of the world—is probably essentially correct, although often difficult to verify since most of the European Neandertal sample cannot be precisely dated. Yet it is likely that the Omo skeletal remains in Ethiopia and part of the North African sample overlap with the Neandertal sample in time. It is possible that the Near Eastern Qafzeh remains (Chapter 12) also overlap with the latest Neandertals.

When the European and African samples are compared, it is interesting that the same features that make the Omo crania (especially Omo 1) look "more modern" (that is, a higher forehead, smaller supraorbitals, a larger mastoid, and so on) are exactly those features which best describe average differences between Europeans and Africans today.

Within Europe itself, a geographic distinction is possible between the southern specimens and cold-adapted forms from France, Germany, and eastern-central Europe. Comparisons are hampered by the absence of a fairly complete female cranium from the north and must therefore be limited to males. The two southern European male crania are Saccopastore 2 and Mt. Circeo. It is my contention that these represent the grade morphology without the cold adaptation superimposed and consequently appear more "modern" because the expression of some features is less extreme. The same could be said of the contemporary Near Eastern sample, which shows greater similarities to the southern European specimens than to the northern ones. For instance, comparing both of these southern samples with the one from northern Europe, while the marked similarity of the specimens indicates that there was continuous gene flow (arguing against models suggesting that the "classic" Neandertals were isolated), the southern European and Near Eastern specimens show less total facial projection (a cold adaptation in the northern sample).

In other words, the differences between these contemporary Würm humans do not seem due to one group's being "more advanced" than another. Instead, they seem to be the result of the same sorts of evolutionary forces that lead to differences between *living* populations. The evolutionary forces acting to cause regional differences between Würm populations were a combination of climate-related differences in selection, local differentiation, and local genetic continuity. (People are more closely related to their immediate ancestors than to other members of the same species living far away.)

LOCAL CONTINUITY

The presence of local morphological continuity extending into the timespan of Neandertals and characterizing different parts of the world provides one of the strongest arguments for a "Neandertal phase" for human evolution in Europe.

On the basis of direct paleontological and paleoanthropological evidence, there is much to be said for the idea that the major human geographic differences extend at least into the Neandertal time range, if not to the period immediately before the Würm (see Weiss and Maruyama reference). Somewhere between 30,000 and 45,000 years ago, more or less modern-looking populations of *Homo sapiens* appeared throughout the inhabited world. In Europe, these more modern populations resemble no archaic sample more than they do the Würm Neandertals.

The model that would explain the combination of local continuity and worldwide evolutionary changes involves similar responses to new selective pressures resulting from the spread of *ideas*, as well as the spread of *genes*. Such a model regards the appearance of modern sapiens as the result of changes in selection acting on archaic *Homo sapiens* populations due to prepared core based industries and the cultural, adaptive, and ecological changes that developed along with them. There are good reasons to believe that this model, which seems to apply so well in other parts of the world, can also be used to account for the morphological continuity between the Neandertal populations of both central and western Europe and the early modern populations that follow them.

Changing Lifeways

At least some, if not most, Upper Pleistocene populations of archaic *Homo sapiens* were the immediate ancestors of modern *Homo sapiens*. The evidence suggests that the evolution of modern sapiens populations occurred locally and was probably not the result of a quantum jump and the eventual replacement of earlier *Homo sapiens* by a small group of "superior" people. We have every reason to believe that the earlier sapiens populations were extremely adaptable, articulate, and intelligent. As the result of the local cultural specializations which evolved in the Middle Paleolithic, they occupied almost all of the habitats of the Old World.

Habitat expansion included three main types of adaptation: an open-area cold adaptation, which allowed populations to utilize arctic areas without dependence on caves; a high-altitude adaptation, which led to the crossing of western Asia's northern mountain barriers; and the first effective adaptation to tropical rain forests.

In Europe, there were adaptive differences between populations that continued to utilize highland caves and rock shelters (most of the western European skeletal material is from these groups) and populations that adapted to the open plains. Yet only a few archaeological distinctions separate

these adaptive patterns. Instead, we find a wide variety of different traditions. At the sites of plains-adapted groups, a few new artifacts appear. These include some bone points (also known from the cave site of Krapina), a pick-like axe made of an antler, and bifacially flaked projectile points.

In Africa, the developing forest adaptation was best expressed in a culture called the Sangoan. Very heavy tools were stressed, including a large pick that may have been a digging tool and some axes specialized for woodworking.

These cultural specializations helped select for physical differences which form the basis of modern human geographic variation. We have seen that many of the features which distinguish Upper Pleistocene archaic samples in Africa, Europe, and Asia are the same features which distinguish peoples in these areas today. In other words, the subsequent pattern of human evolution involved local continuity as well as common aspects of widespread change. This local continuity reflects both already established genetic differences and increasing degrees of differences in selection.

These Upper Pleistocene people were extremely successful, hunting the largest land mammals (often to the point of extinction), while varying in their adaptive patterns from place to place so completely that several tribes may have been able to live in the same area without serious competition. That is, the fundamental niche was so broad that the niches actually used by different groups in the same region no longer had to overlap. These people built complex shelters, harnessed the use of fire, predetermined the form of their tools, undoubtedly made clothing with pieces put together with lacing, cared for their handicapped, and in general probably exhibited all of the behaviors that can be observed in living people.

Recent publications by P. Lieberman and his coworkers have suggested that the European Würm Neandertals were incapable of making many of the modern human vowel sounds and thus were incapable of rapid modern speech. The argument supporting this is based on a reconstruction of the La Chapelle vocal tract, which (it is claimed) is similar to that of a human infant, and on a computer simulation of the sounds this tract could produce. This is the latest of many attempts to relate speech ability to a skeletal feature (speech was once claimed to be correlated with the chin), and judging by the reaction it evoked, it is probably no more successful that the earlier ones. Criticisms have focused on the effect that the distortion in the La Chapelle cranium has on the reconstruction, the possibility that the reconstructed throat couldn't be used to swallow, and the inappropriateness of using the anatomy of an infant to reconstruct the anatomy of an adult. Moreover, indirect evidence provided by art forms, burials, and other expressions of symbolic behavior suggest the presence of the neurological correlates of speech.

The archaic *Homo sapiens* provide the first clear evidence of religious belief. They systematically buried their dead, often in an east-west orientation. They laid flowers on one of the graves at Shanidar, placed the head of the young man from Le Moustier on a pillow of flints, and generally treated their dead in such a way as to show that they were considered more than spoiled meat.

Animals played an important part in the symbology of their world. The direct evidence extends well before the Würm glaciation, for instance the placement of wolf skulls at the Riss-dated Lazeret site, discussed in the preceding chapter. At the Teshik Tash cave in southern USSR a Neandertal adolescent was buried surrounded by six goat skulls with their horns pushed into the ground. In the Swiss Alps, similar rings of cave bear skulls have been found. At Regourdou, there may have been cave bear burials. Cave bears, it would appear, were given the same ritual treatment as humans, and this so-called "cave bear cult" provides insight into the importance of ritual and symbolic behavior in the Neandertals.

Symbolism and ritualism extended beyond these behaviors and included the further development of art forms. Of course, many art forms that cannot be preserved may well predate archaic *Homo sapiens*. In fact, given the evidence for supernatural or abstract belief, it would be curious if this were not so. They may have danced, sung, painted and decorated their bodies, and transmitted a rich tradition of folklore from generation to generation. However, their use of graphic art was rudimentary.

Body decoration was probably practiced much earlier, as indicated by red coloring material at Olduvai Bed II and later at Terra Amata. Red and yellow ocher and black manganese are found at many archaic sapiens sites, both in powder form and as short sticks that appear to have been rubbed on a soft surface (human skin? animal hides?). Evidence of other forms of body decoration is rare. An animal bone with a hole bored in it was found at Pech de l'Aze in France; it may have been worn around the neck. A reindeer phalanx and a fox canine were made into pendants at La Quina.

Decorated objects occur regularly over this timespan, although they are not common. This corroborates the observation that the European Mousterian burials have far fewer grave goods than Upper Paleolithic burials. However, it is far from clear whether this suggests a less complex social stratification. In a review of the decorated objects which have been discovered, A. Marshack argues for widespread consistencies in patterning. Objects exhibiting a series of parallel scratches have been found as far apart as La Quina, France, and the Hungarian site of Tata. At the latter site, there are also implements which appear to have been used for grinding pigments used for coloration and a section of mammoth tooth carved into an ovoid shape. While these decorated objects seem rudimentary compared with the well-known Upper Paleolithic cave paintings, these paintings do not "suddenly appear" with modern sapiens populations in Europe. Instead, the paintings postdate this appearance by about 10,000 years and therefore could represent the result of continuous evolution from the earlier, more rudimentary efforts of archaic Homo sapiens.

These *Homo sapiens* populations entered what K. Butzer calls the "last frontier." This includes the first stable adaptations to both tropical forests (archaic African sapiens) and the Arctic tundra and steppe (European Neandertals). The critical factors allowing this expansion of the fundamental niche were tied to adaptations allowed by a proliferation of both stone and bone tools, the invention of composite tools, the development of structures adequate for an open-area habitation in frigid regions, and the further evolution of efficient hunting and food gathering techniques.

SUMMARY

Archaic *Homo sapiens* populations were scattered throughout the Old World; their range extended into the arctic regions surrounding the continental glaciers and into tropical rain forests. The sequence of evolutionary development before the time of the Würm glaciation is best understood from remains in Europe. These specimens show a continuation of many evolutionary trends discussed for Middle Pleistocene *Homo sapiens* samples. Cranial capacity expands, while all of the structures associated with buttressing or strengthening the cranial vault reduce or disappear. Faces appear more gracile, although the stress-related features associated with anterior tooth loading (expanded maxillary sinus, forward position of the tooth row) are even better expressed, and the anterior teeth increase in size. The postcranial skeletons show reduced robustness, but there is no change in average body height. During the last 100,000 years, humans spread into previously unoccupied habitats (especially forests and more northern areas), and their artifacts show the consequences of the Levallois technique as new and/or more efficient tools proliferated.

By about 100,000 years ago, some changes in selection become evident. These changes are probably a direct consequence of the improved efficiency in technology evolving through the earlier Upper Pleistocene since they involve the further substitution of technology for muscular strength. Skeletally these changes are seen in further reductions in robustness, thinner shaft walls in the limbs, and a more circular shaft shape. One unique development in the postcranial skeleton is the appearance of pubic elongation in the European and Near Eastern samples. This resulted in a deepening of the birth canal (or pelvic inlet in males) and was a consequence of continued cranial expansion without significant increase in body size.

Perhaps the most dramatic effect of technological changes, or at least the effect with the most far-reaching morphological consequences, is the reduction of the anterior dentition and the facial structures associated with its use. The anterior teeth show the beginning of a trend for size reduction which has continued to the present day. Supporting structures for these teeth also begin to reduce, so that by the end of the early Würm in Europe and the Near East, and earlier in Africa, midfacial prognathism and the anterior positioning of the tooth row decrease in expression and frequency. At the same time, other trends, such as cranial capacity expansion, posterior tooth reduction, facial gracilization and so on, continue. The magnitude of sexual dimorphism approaches that of present-day populations in some features (body size, tooth size), although it remains marked in cranial and mandibular size.

Area-specific adaptive differences became evident. In east and sub-Saharan Africa, these involve marked reduction or loss of the supraorbital torus in many specimens, reduction in the anterior teeth, and the common appearance of broad, flat, high frontals. A distinct canine fossa appears early in time. In Europe, geographic distinctions are mainly centered on the cold-adapted features that are superimposed over a "grade" morphology such as is represented in the Near Eastern sample or earlier Riss/Würm European specimens. Cold adaptation is expressed cranially by the expansion of the nasal aperture, the further projection of the total face (separating the nasal passages from their usual close proximity to arteries supplying the brain), and a corresponding posterior extension of the occiput (bunning). Postcranially, the skeletons seem to have short limbs in proportion to body weight.

While the question of whether the European Neandertals are ancestral to modern European populations is still debated, most workers accept a comparable relation for archaic and modern sapiens populations in other parts of the world. Evidence for this contention was specifically discussed for China, eastern and sub-Saharan Africa, and North Africa. In Europe itself, both the preneandertal theory and the unilinear theory may be considered extremes. What if *some* of the European Neandertals are ancestral to later populations? The author tends to support the unilinear interpretation, viewing the European Neandertals as a geographic variant of a worldwide grade in human evolution. Moreover, indirect evidence concerning their lifeways and adaptations, ranging from art and burial to their efficiency in niche exploitation, suggests that their behavioral potentials and capabilities were the same as living humans'.

STATE OF THE ART

The fate of the "classic" Neandertals is probably still the most widely debated topic in paleoanthropology. I emphasized the unilinear view, following the tradition of Schwalbe, Hrdlička, Weidenreich,

Coon, and Brace. It is argued that continuity in skeletal morphology, as well as the lack of clearly refutatory evidence, best supports the contention that the earliest modern Europeans were mainly the descendants of the European Neandertals. A similar case has been made for the archaeological sequence in Europe, although, as with the skeletal evidence, other interpetations have been offered.

Contrary arguments take the form of the pre-sapiens and preneandertal hypotheses, both concluding that the European Neandertals had no progeny. The former, discussed in Chapter 10, is the less widely accepted. The preneandertal hypothesis, on the other hand, has gained wide acceptance, although it is unclear whether a majority of workers hold this view. The position that the European Neandertals represent a local divergence with little antiquity before the Würm has been supported with both European and non-European evidence.

The European evidence cited is almost exclusively Fontéchevade. With the more recent reconstructions, no worker in the past few decades has proposed the Ehringsdorf cranium as a presapiens (although it was once regarded as such), and not one early (i.e., phases I and II) Würm specimen from anywhere in Europe has been regarded as anything but Neandertal. In the case of Fontéchevade, both S. Sergi and H. V. Vallois have shown that cranium 2 is like Neandertal crania metrically and morphologically in all features except the form of the forehead, *and this area was not preserved.*

A better case can be made using evidence from outside of Europe, if one wishes to make the assumption that the appearance of modern *Homo sapiens* in other areas before the latest Neandertals disappeared from Europe is evidence that the former replaced the latter *within* Europe. Even if this assumption is made, the problem is not simple, since the date (or date range) beyond which distinguishable Neandertals can no longer be found remains unclear. Only a few of the specimens thought to be late have been dated radiometrically and most of these are jaws and teeth. While the changes in the jaws and teeth are significant, they involve changes in frequency, and therefore individual specimens cannot easily be classified as Neandertal or modern *Homo sapiens*. Moreover, since anatomically modern *Homo sapiens* is known to be associated with Middle Paleolithic industries in some areas, dates on archeological sites without skeletal material are of no use. The fact is that in

western Europe not one recognizably Neandertal cranium is dated later than 50,000 years ago.

If 50,000 years BP is taken as the time of the latest morphological Neandertals in western Europe, no modern *Homo sapiens* remains anywhere are convincingly dated earlier. If 40,000 years BP is used for this date, a few sites may provide evidence for overlap. One such specimen from Southeast Asia is the recognizably modern cranium from the Niah cave in Borneo (Chapter 13), reported as a burial in one publication and as the result of secondary deposition in another. The date of 40,000 years BP proposed for it has been variously described as deriving from charcoal "in direct association" with the skeleton and "from an equivalent level." There are serious problems with the dating of this specimen.

Near Eastern sites may provide evidence of overlap. The best case would be Qafzeh in Israel, where modern (although very robust) specimens are associated with a Levalloisian industry. Again, the problem is in the date. Both radiocarbon and amino acid procedures have resulted in widely disparate dates sometimes lacking consistency and ranging between 33,000 and 55,000 years ago. The Skhul sample, also from Israel, is probably too late to be contemporary with the western European Neandertals although here too precise dates are unknown. (These sites are discussed in Chapter 12.) Border Cave in South Africa (Chapter 13) is another example that has been cited. It is claimed that amino acid dating places an essentially modern adult cranium at about 90,000 years BP. However, it is not clear whether amino acid procedures work for specimens of this age, and in any event the skull was excavated under less-than-perfect conditions and its position in the stratigraphic sequence is far from certain.

In sum, the evidence for modern *Homo sapiens* contemporaries outside of Europe (assuming the later date for European Neandertal disappearance) has either proved to be very illusive or simply isn't there. Those who are concerned with the problem can take their pick, which is exactly what they have done.

Finally, even if a modern *Homo sapiens* sample were found outside of Europe at a date earlier than the latest European Neandertals, the question of whether it was ancestral to modern Europeans would still remain. The fact is that these early modern specimens do not look European. Niah resembles an Australian Aborigine female, Border Cave is African in appearance, and the Near Eastern specimens have been regarded as virtually everything *but* European in their affinities. Most workers supporting the preneandertal hypothesis have relied on "couldn't have" arguments regarding the European Neandertals as much as on demonstrations of where alternative ancestors evolved and how they got to Europe. Neandertals, it is claimed, couldn't have evolved into modern Europeans because there wasn't enough time, because they were overspecialized, because they couldn't form vowels, and so on. "Couldn't have" is a phrase this author has come to regret, and there is just enough hard evidence to suggest that it may not be appropriate in interpreting Neandertal evolution.

FURTHER READINGS

BINFORD, S. R. 1972. The Significance of Variability: A Minority Report. In *The Origin of* Homo sapiens, ed. F. Bordes. UNESCO, Paris, pp. 199-210.
  A fairly balanced discussion of the two alternative archaeological models for late Neandertal evolution and the possible origin of modern *Homo sapiens*.

BOULE, M., and H. V. VALLOIS. 1957. *Fossil Man*. Dryden, New York.
  The classic French view of Neandertals, including a detailed description of La Chapelle.

BRACE, C. L. 1964. The Fate of the "Classic" Neanderthals: A Consideration of Hominid Catastrophism. *Current Anthropology* 5:3-43 and 7:204-214.
  The historical context of ideas surrounding Neandertal interpretations, and a strong statement of the unilinear view. Published comments by other workers provide an excellent insight into the state of the art in 1964.

———. 1968. Neanderthal. *Natural History* 77(5):38-45.
  An introduction to Neandertals.

BROSE, D. S., and M. H. WOLPOFF. 1971. Early Upper Paleolithic Man and Late Middle Paleolithic Tools. *American Anthropologist* 73:1156-1194.
  Archaeological and morphological arguments for the unilinear view in an adaptive framework.

DAY, M. H. 1972. The Omo Human Skeletal Remains. In *The Origin of* Homo sapiens, ed. F. Bordes. UNESCO, Paris, pp. 31-35.
  Description of the Omo crania.

HOOTON, E. A. 1947. *Up from the Ape*, rev. ed. MacMillan, New York.
  A well-written description of Neandertal and other fossil remains, and a statement of the viewpoint which underlies the interpretations held by many living American paleoanthropologists.

HOWELL, F. C. 1957. The Evolutionary Significance of Variation and Varieties of "Neanderthal" Man. *The Quarterly Review of Biology* 32:330-347.
  Probably the best statement of Howell's views, supporting the preneandertal hypothesis.

HOWELLS, W. W. 1975. Neanderthal Man: Facts and Figures. *Yearbook of Physical Anthropology* 18:7-18.
  Howells' metric assessment of European Neandertals, in part a reply to Brose and Wolpoff (above).

———. 1976. Explaining Modern Man: Evolutionists *versus* Migrationists. *Journal of Human Evolution* 5:477-496.
  The most recent statement of Howells' view of Neandertal replacement.

HRDLIČKA, A. 1927. The Neanderthal Phase of Man. *Journal of the Royal Anthropological Institute of Great Britain and Ireland* 57:249-274.
  Hrdlička's classic statement of the unilinear interpretation applied to western Europe.

JELÍNEK, J. 1969. Neanderthal Man and *Homo sapiens* in Central and Eastern Europe. *Current Anthropology* 10:475-503.
  The unilinear interpretation applied to eastern Europe, with descriptions of Šipka, Šala, Ehringsdorf, Kůlna, and many important later finds discussed in Chapter 12.

KENNEDY, K. A. R. 1975. *Neanderthal Man*. Burgess, Minneapolis.
  An introduction to Neandertals, supporting the preneandertal hypothesis.

VON KOENIGSWALD, G. H. R., ED. 1958. *Hundert Jahre Neanderthaler*. Bohlau, Koln.
  A compilation of reports on Neandertals and Neandertal adaptations marking the 100-year anniversary of the first Neandertal discovery.

LIEBERMAN, P., E. S. CRELIN, and D. H. KLATT. 1972. Phonetic Ability and Related Anatomy of the Newborn and Adult Human, Neanderthal Man, and the Chimpanzee. *American Anthropologist* 74:287–307.

The classic statement of the hypothesis that Neandertals were incapable of human speech.

MANN, A., and E. TRINKAUS. 1974. Neandertal and Neandertal-like Fossils from the Upper Pleistocene. *Yearbook of Physical Anthropology* 17:169–193.

A review of the recent European Neandertal finds and the differing interpretations that have been proposed for them.

MARSHACK, A. 1976. Some Implications of the Paleolithic Symbolic Evidence for the Origin of Language. In *Origins and Evolution of Language and Speech*, eds. S. R. Harnad, H. D. Steklis, and J. Lancaster. *Annals of the New York Academy of Sciences* 280:289–311.

One of several very important discussions of language origins and symbology included in this volume.

RIGHTMIRE, G. P. 1978. Florisbad and Human Population Succession in Southern Africa. *American Journal of Physical Anthropology* 48:475–486.

A discussion of how the cranium links with earlier and later populations and some more general evolutionary problems in the region.

SERGI, S. 1962. Morphological Position of the "Prophaneranthropi" (Swanscombe and Fontéchevade). In *Ideas on Human Evolution*, ed. W. W. Howells. Harvard University Press, Cambridge, pp. 507–520.

A complexly written analysis of the European Neandertals and earlier specimens, emphasizing the southern sample.

SMITH, F. H. 1976. The Neandertal Remains from Krapina: A Descriptive and Comparative Study. The University of Tennessee Report of Investigations, No. 15, Knoxville.

The best English description of the Krapina remains and their interpretation.

STEWART, T. D. 1977. The Neanderthal Skeletal Remains from Shanidar Cave, Iraq: A Summary of Findings to Date. *Proceedings of the American Philosophical Society* 121:121–165.

An extraordinary report of the circumstances of discovery and initial interpretation of the Shanidar hominids.

STRAUS, W. L., and A. J. E. CAVE. 1957. Pathology and the Posture of Neanderthal Man. *Quarterly Review of Biology* 32:348–63.

The classic analysis of Neandertal posture.

SUZUKI, H., and F. TAKAI, EDS. 1970. *The Amud Man and His Cave Site*. University of Tokyo Press, Tokyo.

A comprehensive report on the Amud specimens, with detailed comparisons with other Near Eastern finds and European Neandertals.

TOBIAS, P. V. 1968. Middle and Early Upper Pleistocene Members of the Genus *Homo* in Africa. In *Evolution and Hominidation*, 2nd ed. , ed. G. Kurth. Fischer, Stuttgart, pp. 176–194.

A review of the African remains, with reference to the original descriptive works.

TRINKAUS, E. 1977. The Shanidar 5 Neandertal Skeleton. *Sumer* 33:34–41.

Description of the newly reconstructed Shanidar 5 cranium and skeleton.

VALLOIS, H. V. 1949. The Fontéchevade Fossil Man. *American Journal of Physical Anthropology* 7:339–360.

A study of these important specimens and a strong statement of the presapiens hypothesis.

WEIDENREICH, F. 1943. The "Neanderthal Man" and the Ancestors of "Homo Sapiens." *American Anthropologist* 45:39–48.

Probably the best statement of Weidenreich's unilinear interpretation.

———. 1947. The Trend of Human Evolution. *Evolution* 1:221–236.

Analysis of the main trends in the evolution of *Homo* with a discussion of their causes.

WEISS, K. M., and T. MARUYAMA. 1976. Archaeology, Population Genetics and Studies of Human Racial Ancestry. *American Journal of Physical Anthropology* 44:31–50.

Essay on the data and their limitations, emphasizing the evidence for Upper Pleistocene population distinctions.

WOO, JU-KANG, and RU-CE PENG. 1959. Human Fossil Skull of Early Paleoanthropic Stage Found at Mapa, Shaoquan, Kwangtung Province. *Vertebrata Palasiatica* 3:176–182.

Report on the Mapa cranium and its position in human evolution.

CHAPTER TWELVE

The Transition

The density of the fossil record covering that period of time when the change from early to modern *Homo sapiens* occurred (about 30,000 to 40,000 years ago) is great enough to provide hints of a possible transition, but there is not quite enough evidence (and in too few places) to subdue the conflict between the varying explanatory hypotheses. Only in a few areas have sufficient specimens been recovered to demonstrate whether or not there was a morphological transition. Single, isolated remains cannot be used for this because the changes taking place were more in frequency than in "type." The best-represented areas are the Near East and central/eastern Europe.

These geographic limitations are unfortunate, since the origin of modern populations is really a worldwide phenomenon, whether due to replacement, *in situ* evolution, or a combination of these. Yet focus on Europe and the Near East brings us to the one area where genetic continuity between modern populations and their immediate, more archaic-appearing predecessors has been seriously questioned. The problem is complex because it has two components: the worldwide extent of the change and the local questions of continuity.

This chapter considers the question of the transition, beginning with a model to account for the changes that mark the origin of modern *Homo sapiens*. This is followed by a brief discussion of the latest Neandertals, an account of the transitional specimens in the Near East and Europe, and an analysis of the behavioral changes that apparently accompanied the morphological ones.

A Model of Modern Homo sapiens Origins

There is no question that modern *Homo sapiens*, as represented by populations with decreased frequencies of archaic-appearing features and increased frequencies of robustly expressed modern ones, appeared throughout the inhabited world by 30,000 years ago. It is my view that the reasons for this evolutionary development can be understood and documented in terms of worldwide changes in selection acting on already differentiated local populations of archaic *Homo sapiens*. Polar extreme positions are that this appearance was *either* the result of migration and replacement from some as-yet-unknown core area of evolution ("punctuated equilibrium") *or* the result of *in situ* evolution of genetically distinct and isolated "major races." Both are probably unacceptable. An explanatory hypothesis must take both migration and local evolution into account, and moreover be able to explain:

1. the worldwide nature of the phenomenon
2. the tendency to increase geographic differences
3. the gradualness of the changes
4. the increase in the rate of changes

I believe that an explanation for these developments relates to the consequences of the last series of cultural and technological changes that were truly worldwide (before the industrial age): the appearance of Middle Paleolithic industries and the development of the prepared-core technique.

The major behavioral changes within the Middle Paleolithic were the result of the tool specialization made possible by the prepared-core technique. This had two general effects. First, the development of special-purpose tools stimulated and accelerated the trend for replacing muscle by technology which already marked the course of human evolution. Special tools made for special purposes are more efficient in their application, and this helped reduce the need for sheer muscle power. Second, increases in the types of specialized tools allowed the development of local cultural specializations, which ultimately led to human groups' occupying a wider range of habitats while making better use of the resources in each area. The evolution of local specialization and expansion of the geographic range resulted in the differences in selection from place to place which in turn helped establish the geographic differences that we recognize today as characterizing human "races."

The improvement in technological efficiency was responsible for the trend of general body strength reduction, marked by changes in limb form and bone thickness, reduction in muscle attachment areas and robustness, and reduction or loss of the skeletal buttresses. It was probably also responsible for the decrease in the magnitude of skeletal sexual dimorphism, as improving technology lessened the differences in strength requirements between male and female roles.

One direct effect was in the use of the anterior teeth, with consequences appearing in the face and cranium. Technological developments in the Middle Paleolithic resulted in better-made and more efficient tools such as knives, burins, drills, and scrapers. Moreover, the invention of composite tools allowed a more effective application of leverage and force. The result was a decrease in the use of the jaws to hold and pull, the vise-like actions that had gained great importance. Less vise-time was required, and less vise-power was necessary. One direct consequence was reduction in the size of the anterior teeth and the supporting musculature, an evolutionary trend already observed in the later Neandertals and contemporary early *Homo sapiens* populations. However, there were other structural effects of this change.

Previously, large, functionally important front teeth required large roots. Along with the stress in the lower face resulting from the use of the teeth in pulling, these helped maintain the large faces, expanded maxillary sinuses, and midfacial prognathism of the earlier hominids. The pattern of facial stress during anterior tooth loading maintained selection for a supraorbital buttressing system and a large nuchal muscle attachment area. As the functions of these teeth changed and their size reduced, a series of related morphological changes took place:

1. The lower face reduced significantly, especially the stress-bearing areas for anterior loading. Areas that reduced in size include the maxilla below the nose, the maxillary sinus on either side of the nose, and the zygomatics above the masseter attachment.
2. Supraorbital reduction occurred, due to both decreased anterior loading and the ability of the higher forehead to resist stress without additional buttressing.
3. Midfacial prognathism subsequently decreased, appearing to place the foramen magnum in a more anterior position.
4. Mandible length decreased as the face became less prognathic. This positioned the tooth row more posteriorly, closed the gap between the last molar and the ramus, and made the chin even more prominent.
5. The nuchal musculature reduced, resulting

in a shorter and lower attachment area and a narrower occiput.

6. Ultimately, as the result of the above, came the redistribution of cranial mass into a more spherical shape; crania became shorter and higher.

The model I would propose for modern sapiens origins is based on the hypothesis that selection would change existing archaic sapiens gene pools in the direction necessary to account for the appearance of populations with more modern features. I believe the model is credible because every feature said to characterize these modern populations is present, although at lower frequency, in the earlier populations of Europe and elsewhere. New genetic material is not required to account for these changes, although the possibility of mutation or migration cannot be discounted.

The frequency changes by themselves lead to the appearance of apparently "new" morphological features as combinations that were once rare become common and once common combinations become rare. This is a simple fact of probability and a result of independent assortment of the chromosomes. If there are three *independent* features in a population, each with a frequency of 90 percent, the expected number of individuals with all three is only 72.9 percent ($.9 \times .9 \times .9$). If the frequency of each of these features reduces to 50 percent, they will be found together in only 12.5 percent of the individuals ($.5 \times .5 \times .5$). By changing the frequencies of various characteristics, the evolutionary process affects populations the same way. As the genes responsible for a polygenic structure decrease in frequency, the frequency of the structure does not decrease proportionally *but rather much more dramatically*. I believe that one of the most convincing aspects of this model is that while the general direction of change is the same everywhere, the specific changes in each area, their rate, and their timing differ in a manner which seems dependent on the genetic variation already present in earlier populations.

Because this model involves the action of selection causing frequency changes in characteristics already present, it can only be applied where there are evolutionary sequences with reasonably large samples. The areas that best fit this criterion are Europe and the Near East.

The Late European Neandertals

Large samples of fairly well dated late Neandertal remains have been recovered from two European sites, l'Hortus in France and Vindija in Croatia. In both cases, the material is fragmentary. These samples take the trends found within the European Neandertal Würm sample to their extremes, and while morphologically the specimens more closely resemble Neandertals than anything else, the samples have the highest frequencies of modern *Homo sapiens* characteristics.

HORTUS

The cave of l'Hortus, excavated by the de Lumleys, has thus far yielded about fifty hominid fragments dated to the latest portions of Würm II. While jaws and teeth are best represented, cranial fragments and postcranial remains have also been found. Hortus 4 (about fourteen years old) is the best preserved of the twenty-one jaws retaining teeth (see Figure 12.1). The specimen combines a poorly developed mental eminence with an anterior position for the ramus relative to the teeth.

Dental reduction in the l'Hortus sample occurs in all the teeth, but especially characterizes the anteriors. These are smaller than in the rest of the late Neandertal sample. That the incisors were still used for gripping is indicated by oblique and horizontal scratches across the exterior faces of two teeth; these scratches might have been made as meat gripped between the teeth was cut with a knife. While M. A. de Lumley concludes that this sample is not evolving in a more modern direction, I place a rather stronger emphasis on the evidence for anterior dental reduction, since I believe this change is a key to understanding many of the facial and cranial distinctions of modern *Homo sapiens* populations in Europe.

FIGURE 12.1   *Late Neandertal mandibles from l'Hortus and Vindija. At top are side views of Vindija 226 (left) and Hortus 4 (also shown in occlusal view at the bottom of the figure). The middle occlusal views are of Vindija mandibles 231 (left) and 206 (right).*

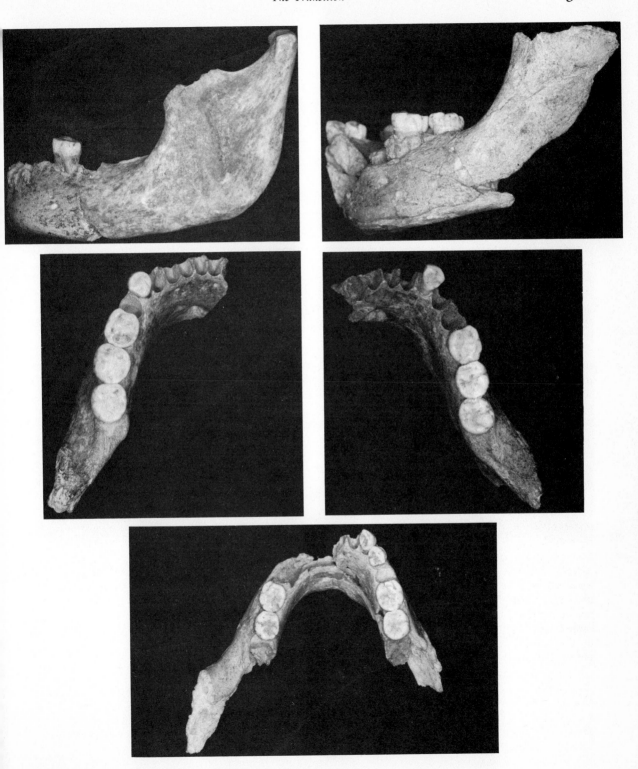

VINDIJA

The Vindija cave, excavated by M. Malez, is only some 15 miles from the Croatian site of Krapina. A large (and increasing) number of fragmentary hominid remains have been recovered from the very latest Mousterian layers (directly overlain by Aurignacian, which is an early Upper Paleolithic industry). The specimens are generally more complete than at l'Hortus, although again mainly jaws and teeth are represented.

The Vindija teeth are larger than those in the Hortus samples, although the few anterior teeth also are reduced. The mandibles vary in size (Figure 12.1); most have a distinct (although not prominent) mental eminence. While the ramus usually begins behind the last molar, the distance is much less than at nearby Krapina, and in one specimen the ramus overlaps the last molar. Generally, the mandibles are less Neandertal-like than the Hortus mandibles, but the real distinction of the Vindija sample lies in the development of the supraorbitals (see Figure 12.2). The sample includes as much variation as any site we have discussed (see Figure 12.3), but the average and range of browridge size and projection are greatly reduced compared with those measures for other Neandertal samples. Finally, two partial maxillas are completely modern in their reduced facial height, narrow nasal opening, prominent nasal spine, and other details.

I believe that it is most appropriate to regard this late Mousterian-associated sample as Neandertal in its morphology. Its importance is twofold. First, the sample allows a fairly accurate determination of the direction of evolutionary trends in these late Neandertals. Populations in central/eastern as well as western Europe were evolving in the direction of modern European *Homo sapiens*. Second, Vindija is one of the rare sites with specimens associated with the early Aurignacian.

FIGURE 12.2   *Vindija supraorbital fragments 262 (A), 261 (B), 260 (C), and 224 (D). See Figure 13.7 for Vindija 202. Note the variation in thickness.*

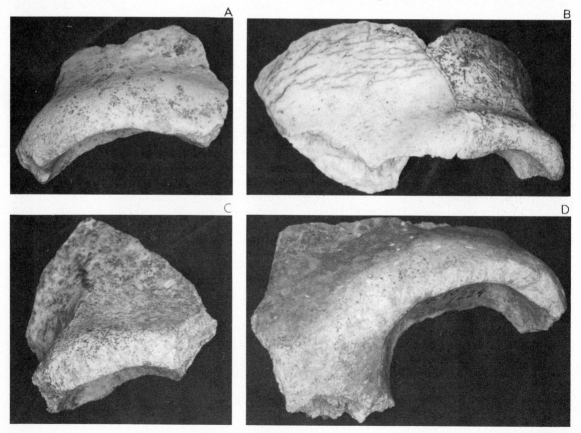

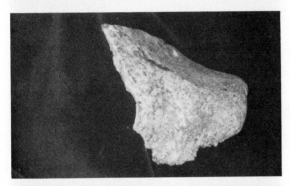

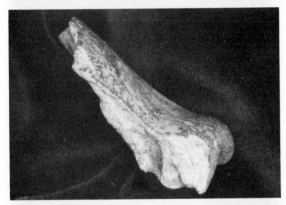

FIGURE 12.3   Lateral view of Vindija supraorbital fragments (from top) 262, 202, 260, and 261. These show the variations in the thickness and projection of the torus and in the development of the sulcus separating it from the forehead.

In this case, there are a few specimens from the Aurignacian level immediately covering the latest Mousterian with its Neandertal sample. A mandible and a parietal as well as a few anterior teeth come from this level, and these are identical to the Neandertal remains below in all details. While there is not enough material to be sure the populations represented were Neandertals, at the least one can say that there is no evidence of morphological change corresponding to the archaeological distinction between the levels.

STAROSELJE

The Russian site of Staroselje was briefly mentioned in the last chapter. The cranium of a child no more than two years old (see Figure 12.4, p. 304) was found associated with a late Mousterian industry. The cranium is generally regarded as very modern in appearance. Studies by E. Vlček and others show that Neandertal children look more modern than Neandertal juveniles or adults, largely because the superstructures associated with robustness are undeveloped and the face grows proportionately far more than the cranium. Nonetheless, in a recent study V. P. Alexeyev attempted to account for the expected growth changes and still concluded that the infant was more modern than not in its morphology and metric features. I am more concerned with the modern aspects of the cranium than with its specific taxonomy, since whatever is eventually decided, Staroselje remains a transitional Middle Paleolithic-associated specimen.

THE MISSING EVIDENCE

While the affinities of most of these late specimens seem to lie with the Neandertals, the demonstration of continued trends in the Neandertal sample leading to average changes and higher frequencies of features that resemble those of early modern European populations suggests that the former may have evolved into the latter. What is

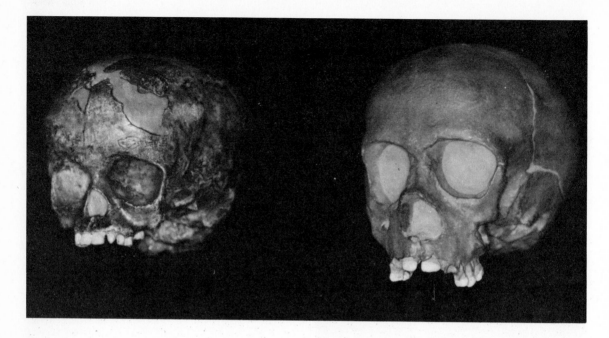

FIGURE 12.4   Cast of Staroselje (left, 2 years old) and La
Quina 18 (6.5 years old) compared.

missing is the convincing evidence of additional
specimens, especially complete adults, from this
timespan or slightly later. If continuous evolution
with minimal migration is the best model for the
European sequence, it will take larger samples of
fairly complete specimens to make this clear. Such
samples from the right timespan do exist, but unfortunately not in Europe.

The Transitional Sample from the Near East

The one area allowing focus on the critical period
between 40,000 and 30,000 years ago is the Near
East, especially the coastal region of Israel. Although plagued with dating problems, several sites
are almost certainly within this timespan.

These are the sites which seem either to postdate
the Würm II glacial span completely or to fall at its
very end. Specimens from these sites postdate the
European Neandertals, and there has been considerable discussion as to whether they should be

called Neandertal or early modern *Homo sapiens*, although they are all associated with Mousterian industries. As in the earlier Near Eastern sample,
sites range from the most northern parts of the area
(Darra-I-Kur in Afghanistan) to Israel. The most
securely dated of the remains is a temporal bone
from Afghanistan described as transitional between the European Neandertals and modern
populations.

THE LEVANT SITES

Unfortunately, dating problems have plagued
the Levant material, beginning with the initial interpretation of the Israeli site of Skhul as Riss/
Würm, "proving" that modern populations evolved
before the European Neandertals. Skhul has still
never been directly dated, although geological and
archaeological inference and a recent amino acid
date all suggest that a range of 31,000–33,000 years
BP is very likely.

Cranial and postcranial fragments representing
at least fourteen individuals have been found at
Skhul (see Figure 12.5). The sample is one of the
latest from the Near East to be discussed, and along
with the sample from the nearby site of Qafzeh, it
is probably the least archaic. However, the sample
is really not identical to living populations of *Homo*

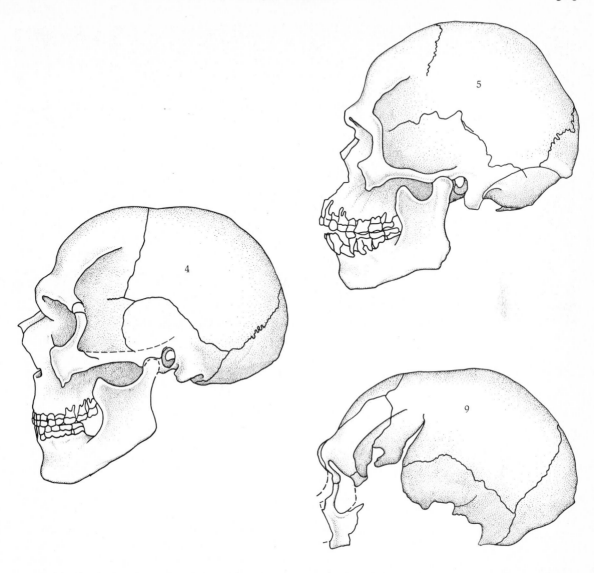

FIGURE 12.5   *The three best-preserved Skhul crania.*

sapiens, and like the other Near Eastern samples, it is characterized by a mixture of modern and archaic features. Its marked variability continued to amaze T. D. McCown and A. Keith throughout their description of the material.

The features most closely resembling the archaic *Homo sapiens* samples seem related to the anterior dentition and its use. The front teeth are the smallest in the Near Eastern sequence but still closely approximate those of the Würm II European Neandertals in size. Facial breadths are similar to the

Europeans', but facial heights are somewhat reduced. Midfacial prognathism remains marked, although it is less extensive than in the southern Europeans. Consequently, in the mandibles the gap between the last molar and the ramus is considerably reduced or absent. The chin is fairly prominent, and the known faces have a canine fossa (Figure 12.5).

Related to the above, the nuchal area of the cranium is extensive; average breadth is the same as in the archaic Europeans, and the maximum extent of muscle attachment rises high above the cranial base. Other cranial features, however, are somewhat less archaic than the earlier Europeans'.

While length and breadth of the crania are similar, in the Skhul sample the maximum breadth lies higher on the parietals, leading to loss of the circular contour of the earlier specimens. The maximum height of the Skhul crania is greater, and with the more vertical forehead, the size and projection of the supraorbitals reduce. In the Skhul supraorbitals there is a greater tendency to approximate the modern human condition, in which the ridge over each eye is divided into a lateral and medial element by a distinct groove. Occipital variation is also fairly modern. The occipital bones are high and rounded, and there is a complete absence of bunning.

Skhul was the first large archaic-appearing *Homo sapiens* sample of crania to be discovered after Krapina. As with the interpretation of that Croatian site, the great variability present at Skhul was often taken to mean that different human species, or races, were all present together and probably making war and not love. Much to their credit, the original describers, McCown and Keith, interpreted the variation in features to mean that the Skhul sample was in the process of evolutionary change and was transitional in morphology between archaic and modern *Homo sapiens*.

The Skhul postcrania provide important information regarding size, proportions, and dimorphism. The average height for the sample is 66 inches, the tallest for any fossil sample thus far discussed. The range is from 57 to 71 inches, and sexual dimorphism in estimated body height is 91 percent (males average about 69 inches and females about 63). The dimorphism is about the same as in the European Neandertal sample and within the range of living populational means.

However, in certain limb ratios, the Skhul hominids differ from the archaic Europeans and instead resemble Tabun. The important difference occurs in the ratios of radius to humerus and tibia to femur. These ratios are respectively 4 and 7 percent greater in the Skhul hominids than in the Würm-adapted Neandertals. When limb lengths are compared with available measures of trunk height, the relative differences are even more dramatic. Relative to the known vertebrae, the Skhul 5 femur is a full 30 percent longer than the La Ferrassie femur, and the humerus difference is 24 percent. This difference is accentuated by the fact that the vertebrae in the La Ferrassie Neandertal male are larger in absolute height. The cause of the difference is the relative limb shortening in the cold-adapted Europeans.

Morphologically, the Skhul postcrania are characterized by the loss of many features related to muscular strength. Shaft proportions and measures of the articular surfaces are not expanded relative to limb length. Moreover, there is a marked change in shaft form; for instance, the femurs generally lack midshaft flattening. In these features the Skhul sample is robust but essentially modern. Similarly, while the innominates are robustly developed, they lack some of the distinctive features seen in the European Neandertals and the earlier Near Eastern sample. The iliac pillar is in a more posterior position, and the pubic ramus is neither unusually elongated nor superiorly flattened. The change in pelvic morphology results from a smaller cranial capacity *relative to* body height in this Near Eastern sample (body height has increased).

The second of the Israeli sites is the cave of Qafzeh, where a series of burials were recovered from several Mousterian levels. Various radiocarbon estimates suggest an age of 44,000 to 56,000 years, while an amino acid date may indicate a younger age, equivalent to Skhul specimens. At least fifteen individuals have been reported. The specimens are robust in many respects, but of all the Near Eastern samples, Qafzeh is generally the least Neandertal-like.

The sample is quite variable (see Figure 12.6). As in the Skhul sample, individual specimens range from Neandertal-like to fully modern. The specimens are impressively robust. For instance, Qafzeh 9 (which B. Vandermeersch believes is a female) resembles the European Neandertals in the robustness of her muscle attachments, anterior tooth size, and so on. These features are even more archaic-appearing in males such as Qafzeh 6.

The Qafzeh people may have been even taller than those at Skhul. The Qafzeh sample tends to have larger anterior teeth and more prognathism in the incisor-bearing portion of the lower face. Otherwise, there are numerous similarities. The faces are moderate in size, and the female supraorbitals

FIGURE 12.6 Qafzeh adult crania (from top) 9, 6, 3, and 7. Variability exceeds that found at Skhul. Note differences in the supraorbitals, prognathism of the face, form of the occipital, and development of the mastoids.

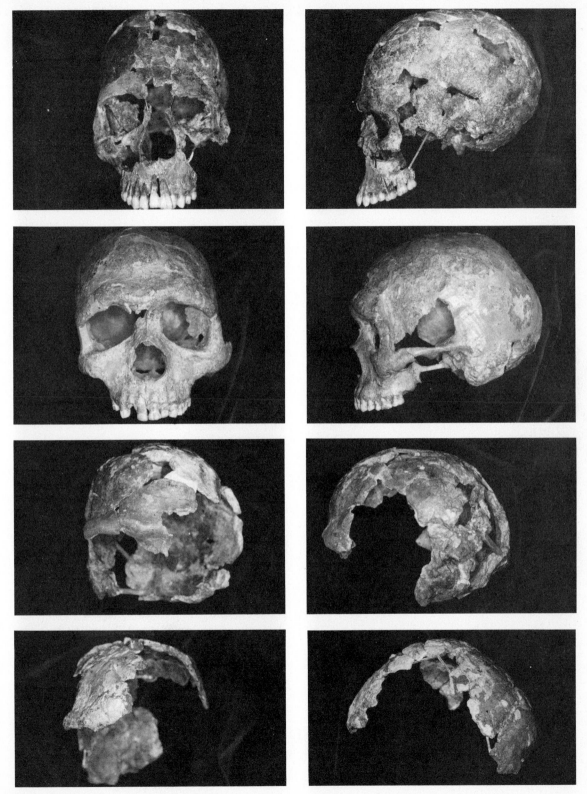

are divided into lateral and medial elements by a groove, while this division is poorly expressed in the males. Midfacial prognathism is reduced. The preserved faces have a canine fossa, and the mandibles generally do not retain the gap between the last molar and the ramus. Other features resembling the Skhul sample (see Figure 12.7) are the fairly high foreheads, rounded occiputs with a low position for the nuchal plane, and fairly prominent chin development. Limb proportions are similar to those found at Skhul, but the development of strength-related features is greater in the Qafzeh males.

H. Vallois and B. Vandermeersch consider the Qafzeh sample similar to the one from Skhul. It represents a transitional, if not fully modern, population associated with a Mousterian industry.

EVOLUTIONARY TRENDS IN THE NEAR EAST

Some significant trends characterize the Near Eastern sequence. When this sample is compared with the earlier Near Eastern sample (Chapter 11), it is clear that the direction of these trends is toward anatomically modern *Homo sapiens*, and as a result the later sample is "transitional" in every sense of the word, although still asssociated with a Mousterian industry. No clearer case could be made for the causal relation between the technological and behavioral changes arising during the Mousterian and the morphological complex common in early modern sapiens.

One key series of changes occurs in the dentition. Size and morphology of the posterior teeth do not change at all over this span except for some M^3 reduction. However, there is marked reduction in the size of the canines and incisors. This averages close to 10 percent, a large reduction for the short time involved.

The later Near Eastern specimens are considerably taller than the earlier ones; average height increases by about 6 inches. As with most features, the height average for the earlier sample closely approximates that of the European Würm Neandertals. With the increase in body size comes an average cranial capacity increase (from 1537 to 1556 cc). However, relative to body size, the cranial capacity of the later sample is smaller, accounting for the loss of pubis elongation and associated pelvic features. The increase in cranial capacity is ef-

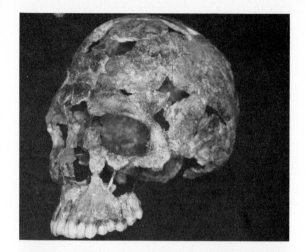

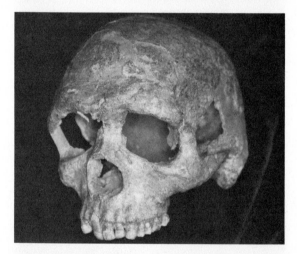

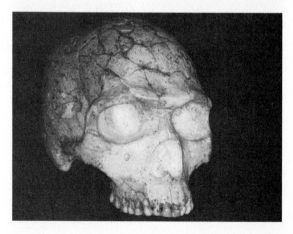

FIGURE 12.7   *Qafzeh and Skhul crania compared. From top, these are Qafzeh 9 and 6 and Skhul 5.*

fected mainly by increases in cranial length and height; cranial breadth actually decreases. Midfacial prognathism also decreases and the canine fossa becomes common. However, since the alveolar portion of the face remains prognathic, a relative increase in alveolar prognathism results. An even more dramatic change is the 12 percent reduction in facial height.

Mandibular changes are mainly a consequence of the reducing anterior dentition and decreasing midfacial prognathism. The frequency of chin occurrence changes from moderate to common, and there is a clear tendency for the gap between the last molar and the ramus to decrease, although few specimens entirely lack this gap.

In the postcrania, the main characteristics we have discussed as markers of muscular activity change greatly. Reductions occur in relative limb shaft thickness, thickness of the shaft walls, and size of the articular surfaces for all of the postcrania. While these features are very well developed in comparison with present-day populations, they are markedly reduced compared with the earlier sample. Given the strong developmental aspect of these features, it is possible that this timespan sees rapidly altering activity patterns.

Three points of particular interest arise from this discussion of the Near Eastern sequence. First, the similarities between the earlier archaic Near Eastern sample and the European Neandertals, especially the southern specimens, provide evidence of genetic continuity which speaks against the contention that the European Neandertals were genetically isolated. If the Near East and Europe can be considered a region in which common attributes are maintained through similar adaptations and gene flow, the evolutionary changes in the Near East must be considered evolutionary changes in *Neandertals.*

Second, the later Near Eastern sample provides the clearest evidence that the origin of the features associated with anatomically modern *Homo sapiens* lies in the preceding Neandertal populations, and that the cause of the changes making these features more common can be found in the activities of the Neandertals and in the technology of industries based on the Levallois technique.

Finally, the large size of the later Near Eastern sample allows comparison of rates of change in various features. While marked changes characterize many features, it seems likely that the dentition changed more slowly than the face and the postcra-

nial skeleton. The late Near Eastern dentitons have reduced only slightly and differ little in size from those of the Würm II European Neandertals. The more conservative nature of the dental changes is probably due to the fact that the skeleton is more directly responsive to changes in activity during growth and development. This in turn provides evidence for the suggestion that the skeletal changes may be partially developmental, responding to different activities. Moreover, if the observed differences are partly developmental, the amount of genetic difference between Neandertals and early modern *Homo sapiens* populations may not be as great as is suggested by metric and morphological comparisons.

The later Near Eastern specimens are truly transitional between Neandertals and living populations of *Homo sapiens.* Thus we have a picture of the Near Eastern Neandertals "caught in the act" of evolving into modern sapiens, and in every case associated with a Middle Paleolithic prepared-core industry.

The Archaeological Transition

Paralleling the morphological transition from archaic *Homo sapiens* to more modern populations is an archaeological transition between the stone tool industries of the Middle and Upper Paleolithic. While these transitions are related, the formerly accepted assumption that they represent the same phenomenon is demonstrably incorrect in the Near East, where more modern populations are associated with Middle Paleolithic industries. In Europe the earliest Upper Paleolithic sites are found directly above Middle Paleolithic (Mousterian) sites, often with no hiatus between the two. The main difference is the increased number of blade tools struck from special prismatic cores in the Upper Paleolithic. In many cases, it is not clear which tradition a site belongs to, and it is common for individual sites to be reclassified from Middle to Upper Paleolithic or vice versa.

While the morphological situation in Europe is not as clear, increasing archaeological evidence suggests that the earliest Upper Paleolithic industries evolved directly from Middle Paleolithic ones. In western Europe, the earliest Upper Paleolithic industry (called the Chatelperronian or Lower Perigordian) is characterized by large numbers of Mousterian tools (50 percent in the earliest samples) mixed with tools made on long blades struck from prismatic cores. Few woodworking tools (common in later industries) are found. However, there is an emphasis on Mousterian-like projectile points. A number of archaeologists have noted the marked similarity between this industry and the Mousterian (especially the form called "Mousterian of Acheulean tradition"), and the contention that the earlier evolved into the later is widely accepted. The earliest Upper Paleolithic sites are dated to 33,000–34,000 years ago.

In central and eastern Europe, the earliest Upper Paleolithic industry (the Szeletian) is even more Mousterian-like and is probably earlier in time than its western European counterpart (the earliest dates may exceed 35,000 years ago). Along with high frequencies of Mousterian tools, the Szeletian is characterized by a triangular projectile point that was probably mounted on a wood shaft to make a stone-tipped spear. Blade tools are rare and there are few woodworking tools. In central and eastern Europe, the earliest Aurignacian sites may be contemporary with the Szeletian, and some authors believe the two industries are functional specializations of the same tradition. The local Aurignacian also retains large numbers of Mousterian tools, but it has a higher frequency of blade tools and a distinctive projectile point with a split base made of bone.

The early Upper Paleolithic industries in both western and eastern Europe cannot be attributed simply to the appearance of new people from somewhere else. There are too many elements of local continuity. What seems to have been taking place is the appearance of a new technique for making tools (striking long blades from prismatic cores) that increased in frequency within the Upper Paleolithic sequence and a behavioral change that centered on the production of well-made projectile points of various types.

Early Modern European Specimens

Skeletal remains of early modern *Homo sapiens* in Europe are numerous and diverse. Understanding of the European sequence has been hampered more by problems of dating, reconstruction, and publication than by a lack of sufficient fossil remains. Most of the important specimens were discovered before 1925. Symptomatic of this situation, early attempts to demonstrate continuity between Neandertals and the later, more modern inhabitants of the continent were marred by misdated specimens and faulty reconstructions, while arguments supporting discontinuity for these hominids relied on Piltdown and Galley Hill (now recognized to be recent), a Riss/Würm date for Skhul, and the continued representation of La Chapelle as the "typical" Neandertal and Cro Magnon as the "typical" early modern sapiens. Even worse was the habit of comparing La Chapelle with a modern cranium (usually French) and then claiming that the time available between La Chapelle and the first appearance of anatomically modern sapiens was too short to account for the observed differences. This assumes that the earliest modern *Homo sapiens* populations to appear looked like the living French, which has been demonstrably false since the turn of the century.

There is no doubt that some early modern European crania are Neandertal-like in appearance. The question is whether the proper chronological sequence exists to demonstrate an evolutionary sequence from more Neandertal-like to less Neandertal-like populations, and whether natural selection can be posited as the cause of such a sequence.

In this regard, it is critical to pinpoint the earliest of the European modern sapiens specimens. If the selection hypothesis is correct, it is this sample which would be expected to show transitional features; specifically, it should be characterized by a higher frequency of Neandertal characteristics than the later, more modern-appearing samples. Moreover, one might expect this sample to show a continuation of the evolutionary trends visible in the European Neandertal sequence if the continued morphological changes are the result of the action of selection on *in situ* populations.

Central Europe is particularly rich in early modern sapiens remains. Moreover, it has yielded a long sequence of Szeletian and Aurignacian tool assemblages, which are usually considered transitional between the Middle and Upper Paleolithic. Unfortunately, no hominids directly associated with the Szeletian have yet been discovered.

MLADEČ

The largest, and in many respects the most informative, of the early Upper Paleolithic sites of eastern and central Europe is Mladeč. Much of the material from this central Moravian site was described in some detail as early as 1925 by J. Szombathy, and yet generally no mention is made of it in English and French summaries of the Upper Paleolithic hominids and their relation to the earlier Neandertals. The date of Mladeč (Lautsch in German) is now thought to be within the interstadial following Würm II, making it contemporary with Skhul (and possibly Qafzeh) in the Near East and possibly also with the Šipka juvenile Neandertal mandible, which comes from a nearby area deeper in the mountains. The associated Aurignacian industry is said to combine elements of the Szeletian and Aurignacian. Archaeological correlations suggest a date of 30,000–33,000 years BP.

Mladeč is extremely important because of its date and because of the morphological variability present at the site. Some of the material, including several adult crania, were destroyed at the end of World War II. Five of the adult crania (see Figure 12.8, p. 312), as well as a number of mandibles and postcrania, had been published, but unfortunately the other three, which were from the lowest levels, had not been described. One might say that Mladeč is the Skhul of Europe. In fact, the morphological variability at the site probably exceeds that at Skhul. Unlike the Skhul situation, however, sex can be determined for the crania, and the bulk of the variability results from marked sexual dimorphism.

The adult females, crania 1 and 2, are rather modern in appearance, although quite robust compared with later Upper Paleolithic Europeans (almost equaling the later males). Mladeč 1 has a moderately developed supraorbital torus, small mastoids, and marked posterior cranial flattening. Mladeč 2 has no supraorbital torus and large mastoids, and the back of the cranium (where preserved) is higher and rounder. The browridge of Mladeč 1 is of the modern European form. It is made up of a very well developed central element (over the nose) divided from the weakly developed portions to the sides by a groove at the approximate position of the middle of each orbit.

The three males, crania 4, 5, and 6, are characterized by low braincases, thick cranial bone, posterior cranial flattening, marked spongy bone development, and thick, projecting supraorbitals (although also of the modern form in that they are divided into central and lateral elements). While Mladeč 6 is the largest and in some respects the most archaic-appearing of the crania, Mladeč 5 is more complete and thus can better be compared with Neandertals. The cranial contour of this specimen is remarkably similar to La Chapelle's except for the slightly higher forehead and less projecting occiput in the Mladeč male. The two best preserved males, crania 5 and 6, have small mastoids and expanded nuchal areas with spongy bone. Their occipital breadth average is greater than the European Neandertal average. Indeed, most of the cranial metrics approximate those of the male European Neandertals except for the measures of upper facial projection (see Table 12.1, p. 313). The forward projection at the top of the nose is about the same as in the Neandertal males from southern Europe, while central browridge projection is matched only by the northern European males. In both cases, projection is greater than in the Near Eastern transitional sample. The continuity of facial prognathism in the sample from Mladeč is with the European Neandertals.

While no facial material is directly associated with the male crania, there are two isolated maxillas, several mandibles and mandibular fragments, and additional isolated teeth. One maxilla is an almost exact duplicate of the Mladeč 1 maxilla. The second is very broad and robust, with a wide nasal aperture. The canines preserved in this maxilla (as well as several other isolated ones) are above the Neandertal average, but the only remaining incisor is below the earlier average. Similarly, the best-preserved mandible retains a canine above the Neandertal average and a lateral incisor below it.

Little work has been done with the numerous postcrania from the site. The femur shafts appear fairly slender and somewhat flattened. The size of the best-preserved bone (a humerus) indicates a fairly tall individual (68 inches).

KRAPINA

The Krapina A skull fragment comes from level 8, one of the highest at the site and possibly at or

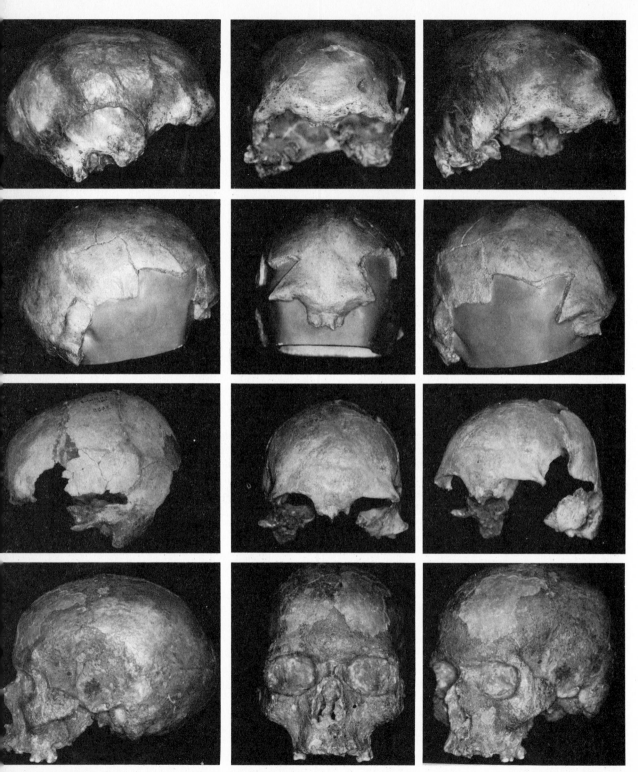

FIGURE 12.8   Maldeč male (upper two) and female (lower
two) crania. From top, these are numbers 5, 6 (cast), 2, and 1.

just below the position from which a radiocarbon date of about 31,000 years BP was determined. M. Malez regards this as a Würm II/III interstadial level. If so, Krapina A is younger than the Mousterian-associated Neandertal remains from the nearby Vindija cave, since those were buried during a cold period. What remains of this juvenile specimen shows a fairly low, but very broad, cranial vault with a high curved forehead and virtually no browridge development. The proportions suggest Neandertal affinities (a proposal supported by F. Smith in his analysis of the site). However, there is a dis-

TABLE 12.1 The table shows the distances from the top of the outer ear opening to some points on the cranium and face (all measurements in millimeters). The upper portion compares the Neandertal samples by sex and geographic position, and below are data for Mladeč and the averages for the even later site of Předmost (see Chapter 13). The measures of facial projection are to the point between the incisors and the bottom and top of the nose. The measure to the browridge expresses both upper facial projection and the size of this structure, while the measure to the top of the skull reflects cranial height. Finally, the measure to the back of the skull also combines two characteristics, the length of the cranium and the backward projection of the occiput.

Midline Distance from the Top of the Outer Ear Opening to:	Point Between the Central Upper Incisors	Bottom of the Nose	Top of the Nose	Browridge	Top of the Skull	Back of the Skull
NEANDERTALS						
Northern ♂ Neandertals						
La Chapelle	127	117	108	112	110	106
La Ferrassie	130	115	113	117	111	101
Spy 1			111	116	106	96
(Average)	(129)	(116)	(111)	(115)	(109)	(101)
Southern ♂ Neandertals						
Mt. Circeo	119	113	103	106	105	105
Saccopastore 2	127	115	107			
(Average)	(123)	(114)	(105)	(106)	(105)	(105)
SOUTHERN ♀ NEANDERTALS						
Gibraltar	113	108	104	108	110	85
Saccopastore 1	120	107	95		96	91
Krapina C			103	107	106	
(Average)	(116)	(107)	(101)	(107)	(104)	(88)
EARLY MODERN HOMO SAPIENS CENTRAL/EASTERN EUROPE						
Mladeč 5 ♂			104	115	111	99
Mladeč ♀						
1	113	104	93	99	114	102
2			99	104	106	
(Average)	(113)	(104)	(97)	(102)	(110)	(102)
PREDMOST ♂ average	(109)·	(104)	(107)	(109)	(118)	(103)
PREDMOST ♀ average	(109)	(102)	(94)	(101)	(110)	(98)
WESTERN EUROPE						
Cro Magnon 1 (♂)	119	108	108	114	123	99
Combe Capelle (♀)	112	105	94	103	112	103

proportion between browridge development and vault size when Krapina A is compared with juvenile Neandertal crania (see Figure 12.9). The browridges are no more developed than in very young Neandertals (aged 2–4 years), while the vault dimensions are larger than in any Neandertal juvenile, including Teshik Tash (8–9 years old) and Le Moustier (13 years old). The size of the vault is probably a better criterion for determining age. If Krapina A is as old as it appears, the combination of features suggests it should be regarded as a morphologically transitional specimen.

The only other late Krapina specimen is the B maxilla, from the level just below (7). No features of this juvenile allow certainty in assessing its affinities. The deciduous anterior teeth are small.

CONTINUITY

Even before the discovery of the Mladeč material, the German scholar G. Schwalbe recognized that in central and eastern Europe a rather convincing case could be made for the hypothesis that the earliest modern sapiens samples represent a morphological transition between the Neandertals and later sapiens populations. More recently, eastern European authors such as J. Jelinek have suggested that the evolutionary sequence in this area can best be interpreted as the result of frequency changes in characteristics already present in the Neandertal populations.

Changing Activities

The model proposed for the appearance of these transitional samples, and ultimately for the appearance of modern *Homo sapiens*, involves changes in human behavior during the later stages of the Middle Paleolithic. Some insight into what these changing activity patterns may have involved is provided by an analysis of Near Eastern sites conducted by S. R. Binford. Her analysis of stone tool assemblages and associated faunal remains suggests that a generalized pattern of exploiting all available food sources changed to a more efficient specialized pattern centered on a few migratory herd mammals. According to Binford, this more specialized

exploitive pattern is first found in the latest Mousterian. The more efficient exploitation of dense protein accumulations "on the hoof," the likelihood of cooperation between different local groups for the period of the hunt, and the widespread use of composite weapons (stone points mounted on shafts) might have combined to reduce the necessity for individual robustness and body strength. Moreover, intensive hunting of large herd mammals may have helped select for larger body size, since a longer stride would be an advantage.

The Upper Paleolithic has long been recognized as the period of big-game hunting in Europe, and one of the main characteristics of the early Upper Paleolithic sites is their projectile points. Later sites such as Předmost and Kostenki (Chapter 13) are known for their extraordinary accumulations of mammoth remains. Binford's contribution was to show that the adaptive change in hunting took place earlier. Like the morphological transition, the characteristic Upper Paleolithic hunting pattern was a consequence of developments in the Middle Paleolithic.

The most likely explanatory hypothesis is that the morphological transition was a direct consequence of these changing activity patterns. Moreover, many of the morphological changes, especially concerning the form and robustness of the postcranial skeleton, may have been a developmental response to reduced stress during growth. A similar explanation may be offered for reductions in facial size and projection. Thus the observed morphological changes in the transitional samples may not be an accurate reflection of the magnitude of genetic change. Interestingly, recent work by D. W. Frayer suggests that males changed much more than females during the early Upper Paleolithic. This gracilization of the males might be expected to accompany the dramatic change in hunting patterns.

FIGURE 12.9   *The Krapina A cranial fragment (middle) is compared with the much smaller cranium (a child 2½ years old) from Pech L'Aze (above) and the slightly smaller cranium (8 to 9 years old) from Teshik Tash (below). In spite of the great size and probable age difference, note the similarities between Krapina A and Pech L'Aze in lack of browridge development, forehead profile, and the suture running down the center of the frontal bone (metopic).*

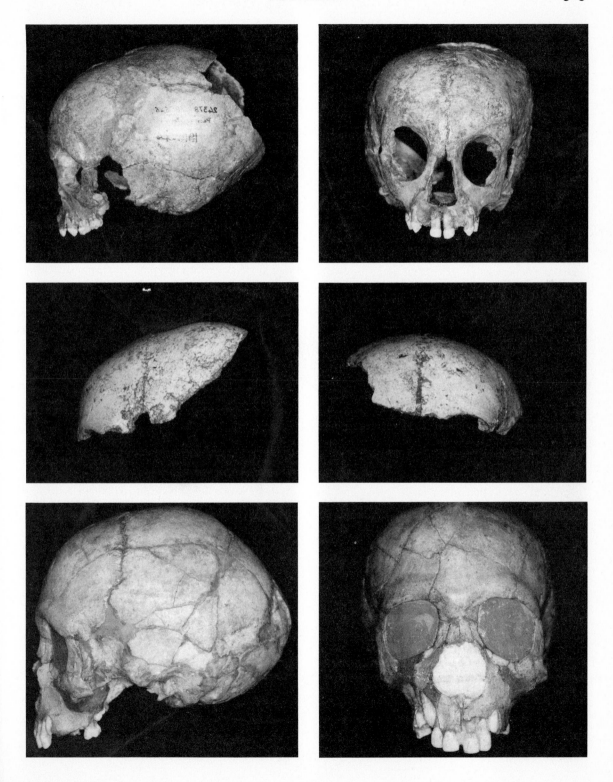

SUMMARY

Evolutionary trends expressed by the latest Neandertals of both eastern and western Europe are in the direction of more modern *Homo sapiens*, as exemplified by the populations that follow them in time. Although the materials are fragmentary, samples from l'Hortus and Vindija show reduction in the anterior teeth and in the browridge, as well as a higher frequency of mental eminence development and features of the mandible reflecting decreased midfacial prognathism. The samples are Neandertal in their affinities; it is the *direction* of the changes they show that is important.

Following these in time are the morphologically transitional samples. In many respects, the transitional sequences in the Near East and Europe are the reverse of each other. In the Near East, morphologically intermediate, if not recognizably modern, specimens are found in a Middle Paleolithic context. In central and eastern Europe, morphologically intermediate, if not recognizably Neandertal, specimens are found in an early Upper Paleolithic context. An important exception to this generalization is the Staroselje cranium, which resembles the Near Eastern situation in that a modern (or modern-like) specimen is found in a Middle Paleolithic context. The fact that the archaeological contexts are different suggests that this morphological transition may have been independent of the appearance of Upper Paleolithic industries.

In both areas, the intermediate specimens are characterized more by their combination of features than by a sudden change of one "type" into another. Many of the changing characteristics seem related to decreasing anterior tooth use. These include a reduction in incisor size, a decrease in midfacial prognathism, and the reduction and morphological "degeneration" of the supraorbitals. There is some decrease in the occipital area, probably as a consequence of continued reduction in nuchal muscle use. Indeed, there is a general narrowing of the cranial vault. The same cranial capacity is maintained through a commensurate increase in cranial height. There is a substantial increase in average body height. Robustness-associated features involving limb shaft thickness and flattening reduce. It should be noted, however, that these are average changes. These samples are transitional because some individual specimens closely resemble Neandertals in most of these features, although no complete specimen combines all of them.

The evolutionary changes resulting in recognizably modern *Homo sapiens* populations are not confined to Europe and the Near East, although the transition seems best represented in these areas. Florisbad in South Africa and the Omo (and possibly Eyasi) sample in East Africa attest to parallel changes in other parts of the world. The morphological changes seem to center about the long-term effects of the prepared-core technique, as well as the appearance of new behaviors and activity patterns. Binford's suggestion—that the behavioral changes are characterized by the appearance of specialized habitat usage emphasizing an effective exploitation of a few herd mammals—has much merit. The appearance of projectile weapons is tied to this developing exploitive pattern. The effects of these changes combined with the continued substitution of technology for strength that began much earlier are reflected in anterior dental reduction, browridge reduction and degeneration, the reduction of limb robustness, limb lengthening, and all of the associated changes in the muscular-skeletal system. Moreover, the humans of the European Upper Paleolithic would seem to be a *consequence* of the changing adaptive pattern.

By the end of the transitional period, some 30,000 years ago, populations of recognizably modern *Homo sapiens* had appeared throughout the inhabited world. While we can never completely discount the hypothesis that they arose through punctuated equilibrium, evolving in a yet-undiscovered area and rapidly replacing the indigenous populations everywhere else, I find the lack of substantial evidence supporting this hypothesis and the weight of the evidence supporting a more gradualistic localized model convincing.

STATE OF THE ART

Some idea of the problems surrounding modern *Homo sapiens* origins and the interpretation of transitional sites can be seen in the various attempts to make sense out of the Skhul remains. The dating of the site is an issue unto itself, but even leaving aside the various timespans it has been placed in (ranging from the Riss/Würm interglacial to post-Würm II), the morphological complex at the site has had the widest variety of interpretations.

In their descriptive monograph, McCown and Keith took a typological approach. They prepared a list of twenty-five descriptive characteristics for a sample comprising Skhul and Tabun. Tabun was included in the sample because, due to a faulty archaeological interpretation, Tabun was then thought to be much closer to Skhul in time than is now recognized. These twenty-five characteristics were compared with "Neandertal Man" as defined by Boule (which meant La Chapelle) and with "Cro Magnon Man." The latter referred to a western European modern *Homo sapiens* sample somewhat later and more modern than the eastern European specimens discussed in this chapter. McCown and Keith concluded that of the twenty-five characteristics, three resembled Neandertal, seven were like Cro Magnon, twelve were intermediate, and three were common to all three. Their conclusion was that the Near Eastern sample was an intermediate one in which more modern features predominated. However, the authors felt that a closer relation might be shown with eastern European Neandertals, such as Krapina, and combining this observation with the large percentage of intermediate characteristics, they placed the Near Eastern sample in what I have been calling early modern *Homo sapiens*. They further argued that the intermediate status of the sample was the result of a separate (from Europe) evolution of Neandertals into modern *Homo sapiens* in western Asia.

Other interpretations soon emerged. At one extreme, A. Thoma once argued that too many differences separated Skhul from modern *Homo sapiens* for it to be ancestral, according to the mutation model he proposed (each different trait was supposed to be the result of an independent mutation). At the other extreme, W. W. Howells (as well as this author) treated the Skhul sample as essentially modern, although preserving some elements of Neandertal morphology. The third view was that these specimens represented the results of hybridization between "classic" Neandertals as represented in Europe and an early form of modern *Homo sapiens*. In the words of E. A. Hooton, "When Cro Magnon met Neanderthal, one or the other may occasionally have bled, but I think that they surely bred (if the sexes were properly assorted)."

With the redating of Tabun and the discovery of the Qafzeh remains, which are at least as modern as Skhul, the site is surely due for a reappraisal and more relevant comparisons. Moreover, a new archaeological analysis by A. Ronen suggests the possibility that the skeletal material may not all be (more or less) synchronic, as is commonly assumed. Two groups of different ages are possible. Finally, the reconstructions of the three most complete crania, 4, 5, and 9, could probably be improved, and cranium 7 has not yet been cleaned from its matrix and reconstructed. How the resolution of these matters will affect the eventual interpretation of the Skhul remains is unknown, but the odds are that we have not heard the last word about this large and important Near Eastern site.

FURTHER READINGS

ALEXEYEV, V. P. 1976. Position of the Staroselje Find in the Hominid System. *Journal of Human Evolution* 5:413-422.
  Description of Staroselje and its affinities.

BINFORD, S. 1968. Early Upper Pleistocene Adaptations in the Levant. *American Anthropologist* 70:707-717.
  Discussion of the activity changes that seem to develop in the latest Middle Paleolithic and their implications for hominid evolution.

BORDES, F. 1972. Physical Evolution and Technological Evolution in Man: A Parallelism. *World Archaeology* 3:1-5.
  One argument for a feedback relation between cultural and physical aspects of human evolution.

————, ed. 1972. *The Origin of* Homo sapiens. UNESCO, Paris.

A particularly useful collection of papers dealing with the morphological, archaeological, and ecological aspects of the transition and clearly presenting several current models of modern *Homo sapiens* origins.

Brace, C. L. Refocusing on the Neanderthal Problem. *American Anthropologist* 64:729–741.

The relevance of Skhul as a transitional sample to the Neandertal problem.

Jelinek, J. 1976. The *Homo sapiens neanderthalensis* and *Homo sapiens sapiens* Relationship in Central Europe. *Anthropologie* 14:79–81.

The argument for continuity between Neandertals and modern *Homo sapiens* in eastern Europe.

de Lumley, M. A. 1973. Anténéandertaliens et Néandertaliens du bassin Méditerranéen Occidental Europeén. Études Quaternares (Université de Provence), Mémoire 2.

Cited here for the detailed description and analysis of Hortus, this publication is also important for Chapter 11, since it includes the best descriptions of many other specimens (Cova Negra, Lazeret, Banolas, Prince, and others).

McCown, T. D., and A. Keith. 1939. *The Stone Age of Mount Carmel*, Vol. II. Clarendon, Oxford.

The description and analysis of Tabun and Skhul, with comparisons to some of the European Neandertals.

Pradel, L. 1966. The Transition from Mousterian to Perigordian: Skeletal and Industrial. *Current Anthropology* 7:33–50.

A detailed discussion of the case for a local archaeological transition in western Europe. The comments and Pradel's response following the paper are especially useful.

Schwalbe, G. 1906. *Studien zur Vorgeschichte des Menschen.* Schweizerbartsche, Stuttgart.

The classic statement of unilinear evolution in Europe.

Szombathy, J. 1925. Die Diluvialen Menschenreste aus der Fürst-Johanns-Höhle bei Lautsch in Mähren. *Die Eiszeit* 1–34, 73–95.

The only description of the Mladeč remains.

Vallois, H. V., and B. Vandermeersch. 1975. The Mousterian Skull of Qafzeh (Homo VI): An Anthropological Study. *Journal of Human Evolution* 4:445–456.

A brief description of the male cranium with some discussion of its affinities.

Valoch, K. 1968. Evolution of the Paleolithic in Central and Eastern Europe. *Current Anthropology* 9:351–390.

A discussion of the origin and early evolution of the Upper Paleolithic industries in central and eastern Europe, arguing the case for a transition from the local Mousterian. Comments following the paper provide an introduction to the problems raised by this contention.

Vandermeersch, B. 1972. Récentes Découvertes de Squelettes Humains à Qafzeh (Israël): Essai d'interprétation. In *The Origin of* Homo sapiens, ed. F. Bordes. UNESCO, Paris, pp. 49–54.

A brief summary of the recently discovered Qafzeh remains.

Vlček, E. 1967. Die Sinus Frontales bei Eroupaischen Neanderthalern. *Anthropologischer Anzeiger* 30:166–169.

Discussion of Neandertal growth and supraorbital development.

————. 1970. Relations Morphologiques des Types Humains Fossiles de Brno et Cro-Magnon au Pleistocene Supérieur d'Europe. In *L'Homme de Cro-Magnon*, eds. G. Camps et G. Oliver. Arts et Métiers Graphiques, Paris, pp. 59–72.

Attributes and variation in the European early modern *Homo sapiens* sample.

Wolpoff, M. H., F. H. Smith, M. Malez, J. Radovcić, and D. Rukavina. 1981. Upper Pleistocene Homonid Remains from Vindija Cave, Croatia. *American Journal of Physical Anthropology* (in press).

A discussion of the Vindija remains in the context of modern European origins.

CHAPTER THIRTEEN

Modern People

Probably the most important thing to remember about the earliest modern *Homo sapiens* populations is that they did not look especially modern. Systematic studies show that the samples which are recognized as early modern *Homo sapiens* are probably as different from living populations as they are from the preceding archaic *Homo sapiens*. We recognize them as an early form of modern sapiens, rather than as archaic sapiens, because they show a higher incidence of "modern" characteristics and a lower incidence of archaic ones. However, no living population has so high a frequency of archaic characteristics.

There was substantive and important evolutionary change in the later portions of the Upper Pleistocene (Würm III and IV, beginning some 35,000 years ago). While evolutionary change took place all over the world, as a result of the cultural specializations of the Middle and Upper Paleolithic, the changes were not always in the same direction. The cultural and morphological differences which we observed in the Middle Paleolithic become more distinct and pronounced in the later Upper Pleisto-

cene while at the same time common elements of evolutionary change in both culture and technology can also be seen.

Modern *Homo sapiens* is not invariably linked to Upper Paleolithic industries. In Europe and the Near East, Neandertals gave rise to modern sapiens within the Middle Paleolithic. When authors refer to the "Mousterian Man," whom they are talking about is far from obvious. In many places, early modern populations developed industries which we call Upper Paleolithic. Here the relationship seems more direct, since the skeletal remains associated with Upper Paleolithic artifacts have thus far always been those of early modern *Homo sapiens*. However, the reverse is not true; modern *Homo sapiens* populations appeared even where Upper Paleolithic industries did not develop.

Thus it makes little sense to refer to the early modern sapiens sample as "Upper Paleolithic Man," and even less sense to refer to it as "Cro Magnon," as is so often done. This names a worldwide phenomenon after a single site in France, and not even the earliest one! No one has ever proposed calling early modern sapiens "Mladeč Man," although this would be far more appropriate since that important Czechoslovakian site is much earlier than Cro Magnon and the hominids are morphologically more archaic. The lack of recognition of the very early modern sapiens sites in eastern Europe is part of a general eclipse of eastern European physical anthropology, which has had a profound effect on the interpretations of modern human origins.

Modern *Homo sapiens* samples everywhere are distinguished from the preceding archaic sapiens by anterior tooth reduction, facial and browridge reduction, and cranial height increase. In all early modern sapiens samples, these changes are less pronounced than they are in living populations. The frequency of archaic characteristics can be seen to decrease over time, both their individual occurrence and more dramatically their combined occurrence. However, these changes occurred at different rates in various areas. In addition, the archaic populations varied from place to place; therefore, even if the rates of change were the same, there would be differences in modern morphology. For instance, the browridge in the east African sample from the earlier Upper Pleistocene was already largely reduced, whereas in the contemporary European sample, especially in the males, it was large and well developed. Even if the rates of change were the same in these areas, one would expect modern east Africans to have smaller browridges, and a lower frequency of individuals with large browridges, than modern Europeans.

In sum, the characteristics of living populations are the result of both the action of selection over the past 30,000 years and the morphological complex inherited from the preceding populations. Both of these factors have differed from place to place, and the consequence is the large amount of morphological variation that occurs in our polytypic species.

This chapter approaches the complex problems of the later Upper Pleistocene by considering the evolutionary sequences in three broad geographic areas: Asia, Africa, and Europe. The discussion of Asia includes the sequence on the mainland, the peopling of the Americas, and the developments to the south in Indonesia, Melanesia, and finally Australia. The discussion of Africa proceeds from south to north: first the South African sequence, then sites in central and east African areas, and last the North African remains. Europe is divided into east-

ern and western portions and evolutionary changes in each are discussed and compared. Map 5 shows the locations of the major sites.

In each area, special attention is given to the adaptive basis for the late Pleistocene evolutionary changes and the evidence for the appearance of distinct regional subcontinental morphological complexes. In Asian populations, morphological complexes regarded as "Mongoloid" and "Australoid" in living groups become distinguishable at the endpoints of continuously varying clinal distributions. In Africa the evolving distinction is between "Negroids" and "Bushmen." In Europe less prominent differences appear between the various so-called local "races." The chapter concludes with a summary of the late Pleistocene evolutionary process.

Modern Homo sapiens *in Asia*

CONTINENTAL ASIA

The appearance of the earliest anatomically modern *Homo sapiens* populations on the Asian mainland is undated. None of the seemingly early specimens can be dated beyond the most general timespan, such as later Upper Pleistocene, and even these generalizations are uncertain in many cases. For instance, a specimen from the north China site of Ordos has long been considered to represent early modern *Homo sapiens*, but recent work suggests it is probably very recent, perhaps post-Pleistocene. Tingsun is another enigmatic site. Two upper incisors and a lower molar from there have been regarded as early Upper Pleistocene, but their morphology and the marked size reduction of the incisors are surprisingly modern for such an early date. This is not to say that the date is incorrect because of the morphology, but rather that it must be confirmed by more accurate dating methods in order to establish the exact timing of dental reduction and the appearance of other modern features on the Asian mainland.

The combination of a modern-appearing cranium and skeletal robustness more characteristic of earlier populations is suggested by the Liukiang cranium and the postcranial material associated

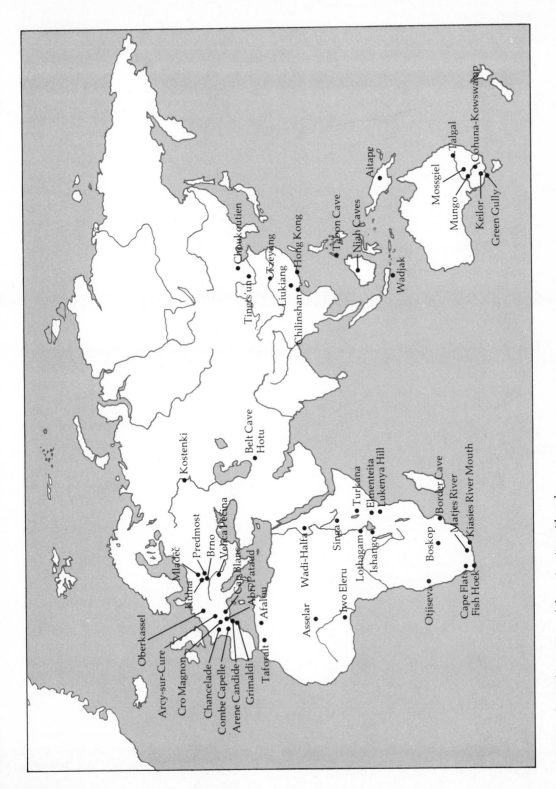

MAP 5 *Geographic positions of the major sites with early modern* Homo sapiens *remains.*

with it. Although also basically undated the specimen's association is with cold-adapted fauna (while the site is in south China), and the likelihood is that it dates to the later Würm. The estimated femur length and small vertebrae of this female suggest a very short individual (56 inches) relative to the much taller people who live in the area today. The femur is robustly developed; the shaft wall is relatively and absolutely thick. In contrast, the cranium is quite modern in appearance (see Figure 13.1), especially in the facial region, which is very reduced in size and robustness. Compared with Dali, there is a marked reduction in facial projection. The occipital region is somewhat less modern. In profile it is angled, and the nuchal region is much more robust than is normal in present-day inhabitants of the area. The cranium has an elongated frontal bone and distinct thickening along the sagittal suture. The supraorbitals are small, although larger than average for modern Chinese females, and the face is low, broad, and relatively flat, which J. K. Woo interprets as indicating an ancestral relation to living Chinese. The specimen is quite unlike the earlier Upper Paleolithic sample from Europe in its complete lack of midfacial prognathism.

A second female cranium is known from Tzuyang, which is far to the west, well into the mountainous regions of Szechuan Province. It too can be dated to a cold period, which again is probably the last glaciation. This cranium is smaller and more gracile than Liukiang, although there is a resemblance in the prominence of the supraorbitals

(compared with living Asians). Among the more archaic features are the robust development in the supramastoid area and the large occipital area.

If these two specimens show certain resemblances to the living populations of China, they also lack a clear distinction from living populations to the south. This latter resemblance is further established by an undated palate (found in a Hong Kong drugstore) which is distinctly similar to the late Pleistocene sample from Indonesia in size, robustness, alveolar prognathism, and guttered (or indistinct) lower nasal margin. A similar set of features is found in the palate of the Chilinshan cranium from south China, also undated. In this specimen, the lower nasal border is guttered and quite wide, but alveolar prognathism is only moderate. The zygomatics are rather flattened and are positioned forward, although not as markedly as in living Chinese.

In sum, the early modern sapiens specimens from south China are sufficiently different from living populations to suggest that the "Mongoloid" complex of characteristics had not yet been fully established, or at least was not common in the area. On the other hand, the specimens provide a reasonable basis for the evolution of the full expression of this complex. The required changes would be a shortening and broadening of the cranium, an increase in cranial height (both early crania are rather low), a reduction in the browridges, a forward expansion and size increase for the zygomatics, and a significant reduction in skeletal robustness and limb thickness. As things stand, it is apparent that this early sample is more archaic than living populations. Moreover, there are more similarities between it and contemporary populations farther south than exist between the peoples of these regions today.

There are some marked distinctions between this sample from south China and the early modern European specimens discussed in Chapter 12. While the regions share many evolutionary trends, in general the Asian sample has more supraorbital reduction, better-expressed facial flattening, and much less facial projection.

It is possible that the more distinctive "Mongoloid" complex of characteristics developed farther north. Early modern *Homo sapiens* sites are extremely rare in north China. The major site is the Upper Cave at Choukoutien, probably no more than 15,000 years old and perhaps even younger.

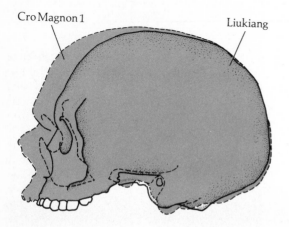

Cro Magnon 1

Liukiang

FIGURE 13.1   *A comparison of the Liukiang female and the male from Cro Magnon, emphasizing the difference in facial projection.*

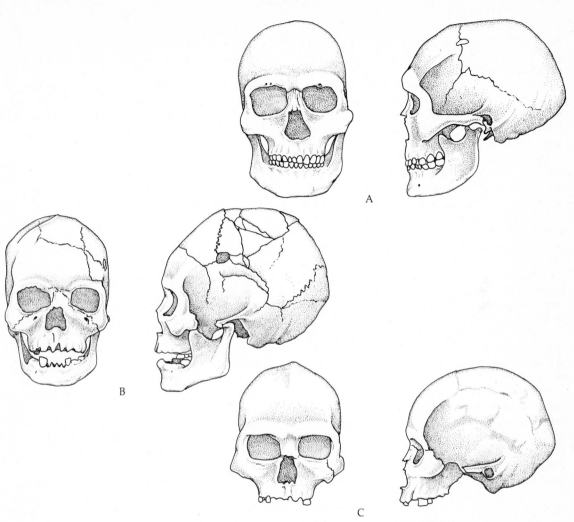

FIGURE 13.2 *The three crania from the Upper Cave at Choukoutien, after Hooton, 1947. A is the male 101, B the "Melanesoid" female 102 with artificial deformation, and C is the "Eskimoid" female 103.*

The remains of approximately eight individuals were found in the Upper Cave. The three crania, a male and two females, are the best known specimens (see Figure 13.2), but there were also mandibles and mandibular fragments, a maxilla, and some postcranial bones, including a femur. Unfortunately, all of these disappeared along with the rest of the Choukoutien material during World War II.

F. Weidenreich, who did a preliminary study of the material before it was lost, described the two female crania as "Eskimoid" and "Melanesoid" and the male as "proto-Mongoloid." The male cranium is long and rather low and has very prominent supraorbitals. The zygomatics are especially large and strongly angled, so that the face is wide and flat. The Eskimoid female cranium is quite similar to the male, and its zygomatics are even more flaring. However, this cranium is smaller and more gracile, and there is no browridge. The second female has been claimed to show evidence of artificial deformation of the frontal, perhaps the result of carrying a load on her back supported by a strap across the forehead. What contributes to the cranium's Melanesoid appearance is the forehead flattening. The vault is high compared with the Eskimoid female's. Interestingly, high flat foreheads are also characteristic of Pleistocene Australians. The evidence for artificial deformation in the frontal of this female is far from certain. The Upper Cave mandibles and postcrania are modern in appearance.

The Upper Cave specimens differ from the earlier south China specimens mainly in facial projection and development of the zygomatics. Indeed, midfacial projection seems to be fairly common in northern Asia at the end of the Pleistocene. This is one of the factors that led A. Thoma to conclude that Paleosiberians resembled eastern European Neandertals; in a recent paper he argues for genetic continuity between these Neandertals and living populations in northern Asia. The degree of facial prognathism is low compared with the Neandertals but high by living Asian standards. The development of the zygomatics is probably not directly related to climate. Recent research suggests that the extreme zygomatic development found in living Eskimos results from the importance of the masseter muscle during certain anterior tooth functions, such as softening and stripping hides.

Trying to piece all of this evidence together, it seems to me that the earliest known modern *Homo sapiens* samples from the mainland of Asia are not modern insofar as they do not resemble any specific living group in the area and have a higher frequency of some archaic characteristics. During the later portions of the last glaciation, there is a gradual reduction of the more archaic features and the beginnings of the development of the "Mongoloid" morphological complex seen in living Asians.

However, even by the time of the Upper Cave remains, the "Mongoloid" complex is far from fully developed, at least skeletally, and the morphological features which today so clearly distinguish continental Asians from populations to the south (e.g., Melanesians) do not seem to be present. This is why Weidenreich interpreted the crania as representing diverse racial variants. The known samples, from both south and north China, contain some characteristics which today are only found south of the mainland. This very likely means that these more local geographic distinctions had not yet evolved, and that what is sometimes called the "Mongoloid race" had not become a fully distinct morphological entity even by the end of the last

glacial advance. This in turn calls into question the common assertion that the so-called "Mongoloid" characteristics represent a cold adaptation, an idea that has always been rather difficult to support in view of the fact that most of the populations having this complex do not live in cold areas. If the high frequencies of the most distinctive characteristics evolved in Asia *after* the last glacial advance, the idea becomes even more difficult to sustain.

While the early modern sapiens sample from Asia is regionally distinct, showing consistent differences when compared with contemporaries in Europe and Africa, it is unlikely that evolution in this area was completely independent. The argument of local continuity in the presence of worldwide changes requires the presence of gene flow. There always seem to be both characters showing local continuity and characters suggesting the direction of regional relations. A. Thoma, for instance, presents evidence for morphological continuity between eastern European and Near Eastern archaic sapiens populations (as represented by Shanidar, Amud, and Teshik Tash) and Paleosiberians from regions even farther to the north and west. In fact, he argues that these eastern Neandertal specimens bear a closer resemblance to living northern Chinese and Siberians than do the Liukiang and Upper Cave crania.

Whatever the case, the morphological variability in the early modern *Homo sapiens* sample from continental Asia is more than sufficient to account for the later evolution of modern Asians, Amerinds, Eskimos, and even Melanesians by (different) changes in the frequency of characteristics already present. It is likely that this sample represents the populations from which living Asians, Amerinds, and Eskimos directly evolved, and which may also have contributed significantly to the ancestry of living Melanesians.

The present evidence strongly suggests that these groups became more distinct later in time. In some cases, when and why the distinctions became predominant is far from clear, but C. L. Brace has recently proposed an evolutionary model to explain the marked changes in the dentition and face. He suggests that the significant dental reduction (and associated facial reduction) that characterizes part of Australasia was the direct result of marked changes in food preparation that came with the invention of the earth oven and the development of pottery. (These innovations are associated with the beginnings of agriculture.) The new techniques allowed foods to be boiled, often reducing both meat and vegetables to the consistency of a soft mush. As a result, selection maintaining the large Pleistocene dentition was relaxed, and dental reduction followed. These techniques affected both the front end of the dental arch and the posterior teeth, since they acted to diminish the use of the anterior teeth for food preparation and the use of the posterior teeth for mastication.

South China appears to have been one of the independent centers for the food-producing revolution and the development of pottery. There seems to be a direct relation between the antiquity of agriculture and the degree of dental reduction. Brace has demonstrated that tooth size in other living Oriental groups increases in rough proportion to their distance from China. However, this pattern is not simply the result of changes in selection, since there have been substantial migrations of the Chinese to the south and east. A combination of gene flow due to these migrations and changing selection resulting from the introduction of the new food preparation techniques seems to account for the dental and facial reduction in the Aboriginal large-faced Southeast Asian populations.

AMERICAN ABORIGINES

American archaeologists such as P. Martin hypothesize that people reached the New World from Siberia as big-game hunters, perhaps following the game they hunted as the herds migrated. While this would be impossible today, studies show that during the glacial advances, enough ocean water was locked atop the continents in the form of ice to lower the sea level significantly. (Sea level lowering accounts for the much earlier hominids found on the present island of Java.) A sea level drop of 150 feet or more exposes a land connection between Siberia and Alaska, closing off the Bering straits. This has happened numerous times in the past, including as recently as 12,000 years ago, and game and hunters may have crossed over this "land bridge" between the two continents. Another possibility is that people crossed the Bering straits in boats; this technology was available at least as early as 32,000 years ago.

Whatever the case, the initial migrants seem to have been few in number. Skeletal remains of Paleoamerinds are quite rare. Moreover, they are morphologically modern and could easily have been derived from an Asian population such as that represented at the Upper Cave at Choukoutien. A. Hrdlička argued for decades that no Paleoamerind remains fall outside the range of variation found in living Amerinds. This has yet to be refuted. Descriptions of the few early remains are relatively incomplete, with several exceptions. Only three sites can be dated to older than 10,000 years using techniques not dependent on bone collagen or amino acid dating, which seem especially problematic for the North American material because of treatment (preparation, storage) after their discovery. In order of age, the best-dated older sites are Guitarrero cave in Peru (12,500 years BP), Tepexpan in Mexico (11,000 years BP), and Marmes rock shelter (11,000 years BP) in Washington State. Dating problems with the Laguna Beach and Los Angeles specimens probably should preclude them from consideration, but even if they were included, the possible generalizations remain much the same.

The Guitarrero female mandible is small but robust and shows a strong differential wear pattern on the teeth, contrasting the heavily worn anterior dentition with the only slightly worn posteriors. T. Lynch and K. Kennedy suggest that this might result from non-masticatory uses of the anterior teeth superimposed on a grit-free diet emphasizing meat. The Tepexpan cranium is robust, especially in the prominent supraorbitals and low forehead, but the great cranial breadth relative to length appears very modern. In spite of the well-developed supramastoid area and the nuchal torus, the occiput should probably not be regarded as Neandertal-like (as was once claimed). Moreover, similar if not more "archaic-appearing" crania can still be found in living Amerinds. This is the normal range of human variation. Finally, the fifty fragments of a subadult from the Marmes rock shelter were described as indicating a robust but modern-appearing individual with some "Mongoloid" features, a description which hardly separates it from living Amerinds.

The California specimens with more problematic dates provide little additional morphological information. The Laguna skeleton is described as gracile, and the frontal bone lacks a browridge. The Los Angeles cranium similarly appears modern, as do the various remains recovered in the San Diego vicinity.

As a whole, the New World Paleoamerind sample cannot be distinguished from modern Amerinds by any particular set of features. Indeed, the total variation represented easily falls within the range of skeletal collections from individual sites (see Figure 2.1). There are neither morphological nor archaeological grounds for suggesting a particularly great antiquity for this sample.

INDONESIA AND MELANESIA

In regions to the south of China, specimens with characteristics similar to those of living Australian Aborigines have been dated to the late Pleistocene. One of the earliest modern specimens from this area is claimed to be the cranium from the Niah cave in Borneo. However, there are serious problems with the date (40,000 years BP) suggested for it; the specimen was probably buried, and the actual dated human remains come from what is thought to be an "equivalent" layer in another portion of the cave. The Niah specimen is a juvenile (the third molar is unerupted) female in extremely fragmented and distorted condition. Enough of the cranium is present to show that she had no browridge development. The short, broad face, broad nose, and large palate are features that are common in living Australian and Tasmanian females.

In Indonesia, two crania stratigraphically above the Solo material come from the site of Wadjak, Java. The Wadjak specimens were discovered by E. Dubois before he discovered the first *Homo erectus* cranium. However, they were not reported for over thirty years. The fauna associated with them appears to be much younger than the Solo fauna, and the specimens may actually be quite recent. Wadjak 1 is a fairly complete cranium with a piece of mandible and Wadjak 2 is a fragmentary cranium with a complete mandible and maxilla. Dubois suggested that the specimens were, respectively, female and male. Both crania are large and robust, falling within the range of living as well as fossil Australians. In Wadjak 1 the browridge is well developed only over the nose. The browridges of the second specimen are larger and more continuous over the orbits. Other apparent differences between them are of the order one might expect between a male and female. The Wadjak 2 cranium is more robust, the occipital more angled, and the jaws and teeth large. Both Wadjak faces are large, broad, and prognathic in the tooth row portion, and

the noses are broad and guttered. These are all features that are common in the Australian Aborigines.

However, other facial features are reminiscent of samples from China. The cheeks project strongly to the sides, and the full face is flat, resembling the face of the young "Melanesoid" Upper Cave female. It has been occasionally suggested that the Wadjak specimens represent an evolutionary link between the earlier Solo sample and the later Australian Aborigines (and similar populations). This view probably overemphasizes their archaic features; the specimens are fully modern in every feature. Where they differ from living populations is in the area-wide distribution of features they reveal. They are less differentiated from their mainland contemporaries to the north.

South of Indonesia and north of Australia, there is only the fossil frontal bone from Aitape in New Guinea, which is no more than 5,000 years old. It resembles the frontal bone of a modern Australian Aboriginal female.

In sum, the fossil record for the area from Indonesia to Australia has a gap between the Solo material and specimens which, for all intents, are modern (although archaic-looking) *Homo sapiens*. The Solo sample itself provides the only link between Indonesian *Homo erectus* and modern Aboriginal populations in Australia and related areas.

As on the Asian mainland, the dentitions of the early modern sapiens specimens are extraordinarily large; apparently the bulk of the posterior dental reduction as well as significant amounts of anterior reduction did not take place until after the appearance of agriculture. The major cranial changes involved in the appearance of modern sapiens came before these dental changes. The picture is not quite as clear as in the mainland China sequence, however, because with the spread of agriculture from China came the spread of smaller-toothed people. Before this, the little evidence available suggests that the indigenous populations were morphologically similar to each other, characterized by the large teeth and faces of their earlier Pleistocene ancestors. Moreover, beginning with specimens from south China, resemblances to living Australian Aborigines are great enough to suggest that an early widespread population was ancestral to the Australians. It is at this point that the picture becomes complex, since subsequent changes north of Australia were apparently due to a combination of gene flow (migration) and changes in selection resulting from the associated spread of agriculture and cooking technology involving the earth oven. As a result, there are more population distinctions and more diversity south of China today than appear to have been present at the end of the Pleistocene.

AUSTRALIA

Due to the efforts of many workers, a long sequence with many skeletal remains is known for the Australian continent. Habitation sites in Australia extend back to at least 32,000 years BP. This not only predates the apparent earliest appearance of humans in the Americas, but also required an early appearance of rather sophisticated technology. Even at the lowest sea level of the Würm, which occurred *after* 32,000 years BP, the straits separating Australia, New Guinea, and Tasmania from the Celebes and Borneo were at least 40 miles wide. Although the Celebes, Borneo, and the rest of Indonesia were connected to the Asian continent during much of the low sea period, none of these ever had a direct connection to Australia. Therefore, a seafaring technology was needed for humans to spread to Australia, and it is apparent that this technology was available before 32,000 years ago.

The earliest Australian human remains are from Lake Mungo, where a fragmentary cremated female (Mungo 1) and a more complete articulated male burial (Mungo 3) have been dated to respectively 25,000 and more than 30,000 years BP. Both specimens are very gracile, with well-rounded foreheads, weak muscle attachments, and weak or moderate browridge development. Contrasting with these modern features is a marked expansion of the nuchal plane in both crania. This is functionally associated with very heavy anterior tooth wear. The mandibular show heavy anterior wear directly. The incisors and canines are worn much more than the posterior teeth. Australian workers have suggested that similar "gracile" crania have existed throughout the local fossil sequence, including specimens such as Keilor (about 15,000 years old) and Green Gully (about 8,000 years old). These are said to fall within the modern range of variation for Australian Aborigines, but at the gracile end.

The "gracile" sample has been contrasted with specimens that are somewhat more robust and archaic in appearance, although not earlier in time (see Figure 13.3, pp. 328–329). These include some of the Kow Swamp group (including Cohuna), dated to between 9,000 and 13,000 years BP, Maroona (only about 1,200 years old), and Talgai, Nitchie, and Mossgiel, which are all undated but probably equally ancient. Because of the suggested morphological contrasts with the more "gracile" group, it has been argued that these represent late survivals of an earlier, more archaic migration to the continent.

The "archaic-appearing" sample is characterized by robust crania with large faces and teeth. The frontals are more archaic than the occipital regions. Generally, the frontal bone is long, broad, and fairly straight as it recedes backward. Supraorbital tori range from virtually nonexistent (as in Talgai) to strongly developed and prominent. There is marked narrowing of the frontal behind the supraorbitals. Although an occipital torus commonly occurs in most modern Australian Aboriginal groups, its development in this sample is greater than normal today. Yet generally the occiputs are high, rounded, and well filled out, providing a contrast with the frontal regions. While it has been suggested that this contrast might result from an artificial deformation of the foreheads, most workers discount this possibility. Another distinction of the sample is the thickened bones of the cranial vault.

The faces, teeth, and mandibles parallel the archaic appearance of the frontal regions. The faces are large, and robustly developed zygomatics flare widely to enclose large temporal fossae. Mandibles tend to be thick especially in the symphyseal region, and the teeth are large compared with most living Australian groups, although their size is approached in recent and living populations of the Murray River Valley not far from the site of the Kow Swamp excavations.

The features of the "archaic-appearing" sample have been described as *Homo erectus*-like. Of course, the specimens are not *Homo erectus*, and many, if not most, of the resemblances to this earlier species are in archaic features generally found in other early modern *Homo sapiens* samples. Yet Australian scientists such as A. Thorne point to some specific morphological features that may reflect a regional genetic continuity with the much earlier Indonesian fossils from Solo. But it should be emphasized that these resemblances involve features found in different specimens. No single Australian specimen could be mistaken for a member of the Solo sample. Most resemblances are in the frontal. In Kow

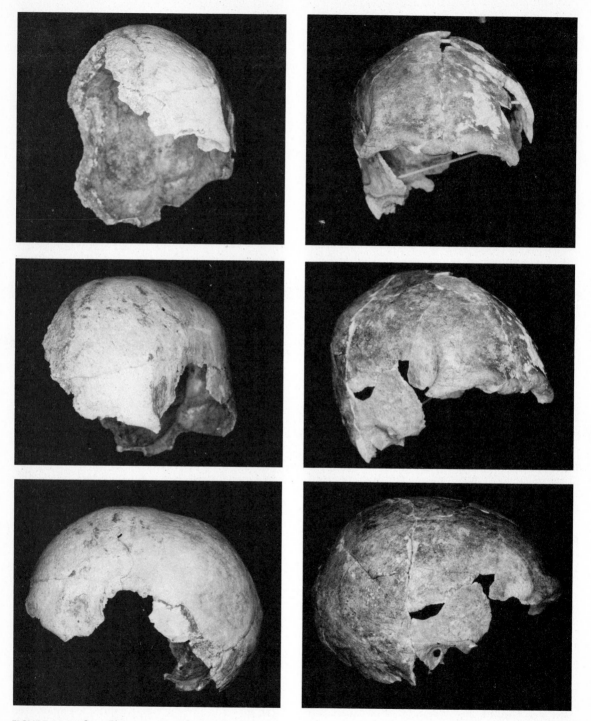

FIGURE 13.3   Some Pleistocene Australian male crania
(three views of each); from left to right, these are Mungo 3
(the oldest) and Kow Swamp crania 14, 1, and 5.

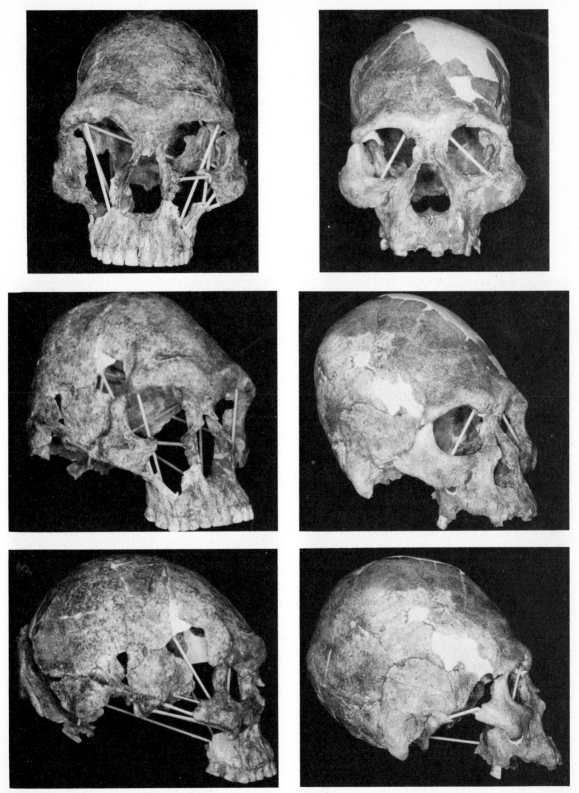

Swamp 15, the browridge is continuously developed, dipping only slightly over the nose, and its thickness is close to the Solo average. The frontal of Kow Swamp 1 retains a sagittal keel that runs almost to the browridge and eliminates the groove between the browridge and the forehead. The outer portion of the browridge in Kow Swamp 9 follows the temporal line backward, forming a backward-pointed triangle at the upper corner of the orbit. In Cohuna, the temporal line forms a ridge across much of the frontal, and the minimum breadth of the frontal is well behind the orbits. In Kow Swamp 9, the nuchal torus is thick and backward-projecting, and above it there is a distinct groove. These features argue for continuity in clade, but it should be remembered that superimposed on them are dramatic differences in grade. In the end, the Kow Swamp and other "archaic" Australian fossils are fully modern in grade.

I believe that the idea of contrasting groups has resulted from overemphasis on a few specimens and the fact that when the first Mungo specimen (the female, Mungo 1) was discovered, neither of the two fairly complete Kow Swamp females (4 and 16) had been reconstructed. Actually, Mungo 1 closely resembles Kow Swamp 4 and 16, while Mungo 3 (male) resembles Kow Swamp 14 in browridge development and Kow Swamp 14 and 15 in frontal curvature. In other words, the range at a single site encompasses most of the known fossil material. If there are not distinct morphotypes on the continent, the necessity of postulating an earlier, more archaic and a later, more modern migration falls away. Moreover, it remains unclear whether the fossil sample is more variable than the living Aborigines, as has been claimed, since no comparison of variability has ever been made between it and *several* different living populations.

In sum, the Australian fossil record shows an early appearance of modern *Homo sapiens* populations with a relatively sophisticated technology. The fossil sample is variable. While individual features fall within the range of variation for modern Australian Aborigines, a number of specimens have combinations of features which cannot be found today. Finally, the resemblance of some specific characteristics to the morphology common in the Solo sample is so marked that it is difficult to deny an evolutionary relationship in the Australasian region, a point suggested by F. Weidenreich several decades ago.

The archaeological record gives some insight into the selective pressures that might have helped maintain high frequencies of archaic features as recently as the date for Kow Swamp. The main technology was based on unprepared core tools and large flakes. Most of the preserved tools, scrapers, and knives were actually tools used to make other tools of bone and wood. Cultural adaptations were by no means "primitive," as is often suggested. By at least 30,000 years ago, humans were occupying the full range of coastal and inland river- and lake-related ecozones on the Australian continent. The continent's isolation did not cause cultural tradition to stagnate; instead, local cultural evolution was characterized by innovation. For instance, ground stone axe heads dating to over 20,000 years ago have been found, making them the oldest in the world. Hafted (attached to wood) tools ranging from axes to mounted flakes date to over 25,000 years BP. Grinding dishes and millstones are found all over the continent and have great antiquity, at least to 18,000 years BP. The continent-wide use of seeds and vegetables prepared by grinding might help account for the maintenance of a robust masticatory apparatus. Probably the greatest surprise has been the discovery of cave decorations over 20,000 years old, making them as old as most of the European cave paintings.

The late Pleistocene hunting/gathering adaptation did not continue unvarying throughout the post-Pleistocene period. The giant marsupial game animals soon became extinct. Hunting innovations such as the boomerang, which allows the possibility of killing from a distance, were widespread (although the boomerang did not reach all portions of Australia). In other parts of the world, hunting was one of the important selective pressures for maintaining large and very thick and robust bones, and with the innovation of new techniques, there is inevitably accelerated reduction in skeletal robustness. It is interesting that the Kow Swamp area in southeastern Australia is one of the regions to which the boomerang did not spread. More recently (about 6,000 years ago), a new technology and probably also new populations entered Australia from New Guinea. This influx of technology and genes affected some areas more than others. The adaptive changes that resulted from the new technology (including the earth oven) allowed a far more effective utilization of resources. Both migration and the changes in selection resulted in a decreasing frequency of the more archaic features common to the late Pleistocene big-game hunters and gatherers. The influx of new people, with their ideas and technology, occurred only a few thousand years after the date of Kow Swamp, where the large sample shows that the frequencies of archaic characteristics were still high.

The African Sequence

As recently as 1963, C. Coon was able to describe the appearance and early evolution of modern *Homo sapiens* in Africa as an "unsolved mystery." He ultimately argued that the evolutionary process there seemed to "lag behind" that on the other continents. It would now appear that neither statement could be further from the truth; south of the Sahara and in east Africa, the transition to modern *Homo sapiens* occurred early. The increasingly excellent record of dated hominid remains has resulted in a view perhaps best expressed by P. Beaumont and J. Vogel: "Possession of these preferred regions [African savannas] . . . would have been in the hands of peoples who were culturally advanced, rather than retarded."

SOUTH AFRICA: THE EARLIEST SPECIMENS

The South African evidence suggests a continuous line of hominid evolution, with early modern sapiens derived from the local archaic sapiens populations, as represented by Broken Hill, Saldanha, and the Cave of Hearths. Unfortunately, few fossil human remains span the later period of evolution.

Florisbad (Chapter 11) is the best-preserved late archaic specimen from this region. It could probably just as readily be considered early modern *Homo sapiens* in both morphology and date. Like the early modern sapiens specimens in Europe, it foreshadows local living populations without exactly matching any of them. What makes Florisbad particularly important in the local sequence is its combination of intermediate grade features with specific resemblances to earlier crania from Broken Hill and Saldanha. The other site with similar antiquity is the Klasies River cave, also discussed in Chapter 11.

Unambiguous representatives of modern *Homo sapiens* in this region are from Border Cave and Origstad rock shelter. Other remains once considered early, such as the Skildergat cave cranium (Fish Hoek), Springbok Flats, Cape Flats, and Boskop, are of dubious antiquity.

Over the period from 1941 to the present, at least four individuals have been recovered from Border Cave. Of these, specimens 1 and 2 came from an area dug up by a guano prospector and thus are without certain provenience. Border Cave 1 is a fairly complete adult cranium. Border Cave 2 is a toothless mandible. Number 3, an infant about three months old, was recovered from what appeared to be a shallow grave during early excavations by R. Dart. This is the only specimen with known provenience. The fourth individual, represented by a mandible, is a burial of uncertain associations. The archaeological associations of Border Cave 1 and 2 are said to be with the Middle Stone Age. Assuming the infant burial was not from a significantly higher level in the cave, radiocarbon determinations of the final Middle Stone Age at Border Cave may make the specimen older than 48,000 years.

It is particularly unfortunate that Border Cave 1 was collected haphazardly and without adequate stratigraphic records, since unverified estimates of its antiquity range from 15,000 years to more than 100,000 years. The cranium consists of a frontal portion, side, and part of the base. The back portion of the cranium is missing. In side view, the forehead is moderately high, although the skull itself does not have extremely great height. The parietals bulge outward in a high position. The frontal region is broad (narrower than the Florisbad cranium but broader than crania of most modern South Africans), and the browridge is well developed, although again not as much so as in Florisbad. In particular, the form of the torus is different from Florisbad's; it is completely absent over the nasal root, appearing first over the orbital rim, and thinning considerably toward the sides. This morphology, although not the torus thickness, occurs in recent populations of "Negroes" and the small living Bushmen populations of South Africa. Indeed, a general metric affinity to these groups has been demonstrated by P. Rightmire.

When compared with living populations, the Border Cave infant (Number 3) remains show a series of features which, according to H. de Villiers, align the specimen with both South African "Negro" and Bushman infants. She suggests that it might represent an early undifferentiated population, if the dating and provenience can be confirmed. Thus, both Border Cave specimens seem to show particular affinities to living South African populations.

Recent discoveries at the Origstad rock shelter support the hypothesis that a widespread late Pleistocene African population combined features of both living Bushmen and "Negroids." The mandible of an infant, dated to about 28,500 years ago and associated with a Late Stone Age industry, was systematically compared with modern South African Bantu and Bushmen infant mandibles. The specimen could not be distinguished from the Bantu sample.

It seems to me that two broad conclusions can be drawn from the South African evidence. The first is that modern *Homo sapiens* may have appeared in a Middle Stone Age context. While the Middle Stone Age is not really equivalent to the Mousterian of Europe in time or technology, it does mark the earliest appearance of numerous special-purpose tools and persistent use of the prepared-core technique in South Africa. The second conclusion is that the appearance of early modern sapiens populations was a local phenomenon. These populations seem clearly related to earlier sub-Saharan Africans and probably evolved from them. The evolutionary sequence I would propose begins with populations represented by specimens such as Broken Hill and Ndutu, continues through intermediates such as are represented at Laetolil and Florisbad, and ends with essentially modern populations in the final portion of the Middle Stone Age. Whether these latter populations are earlier than the first appearance of modern sapiens elsewhere (such as Mladeč, Qafzeh, or Mungo) cannot yet be resolved because of the uncertainties of association at Border Cave.

THE BUSHMAN/"NEGROID" DIFFERENTIATION

P. Rightmire suggests that in terms of most characteristics, the Border Cave adult cranium would not be out of place in a collection of living "Negro" crania, although it would be at the extreme end of the range in browridge size and frontal breadth. H. de Villiers argues for morphological affinities between the Origstad infant and modern Bantu ("Negroid") children. These contentions raise a difficult set of problems, since it is generally assumed that south of the Zambezi River, Africa was inhabited only by Bushmen until fairly recent (i.e., Iron Age) times. A compromise position has been suggested by several different authors, all arguing for various reasons that there were no distinct Bushmen and "Negroid" populations until not much before the end of the Upper Pleistocene.

P. V. Tobias, for instance, suggests that these modern groups have genetic differences that require no more than 15,000 years of separation to establish. H. de Villiers, who stressed the Bushmen-like characteristics of the Border Cave infant, and the Bantu-like characteristics of the Origstad infant, also points to the numerous similarities between these infant specimens. These contentions are not as contradictory as they seem because the statistical procedures used to place the fossils in various modern populations begin with the assumption that the fossils actually belong in one of the populations tested. If there were actually no distinct Bushmen or "Negroid" populations at the time (the later Upper Pleistocene), the statistical procedures may suggest affinity but they cannot show group identity if the groups were not there. I would argue that the best conclusion is that these early modern populations had not yet differentiated into the modern groups now living in South Africa.

Why would increasing populational differences have evolved toward the end of the Pleistocene? There are probably a number of reasons. Late Stone Age culture and technology resulted in a much more efficient use of environmental resources. The earlier adaptations of the Middle Stone Age were broad but not efficient. For instance, at the Die Keiders cave and Kiasies River mouth at the southern tip of Africa, evidence for the consumption of edible shellfish in occupations over 100,000 years old marks the earliest known systematic use of sea resources. However, the mammals hunted seem limited to the more docile of the larger species or, in the case of more formidable prey, females in advanced pregnancy.

In contrast, hunters of the Late Stone Age made much more efficient use of available resources. Grinding and other new techniques for plant preparation and technological innovations such as the bow and arrow and poisons greatly expanded the range of edible resources within the same habitats. The extinction of many of the big game animals helped stimulate the trend to make more effective use of the remaining resources, producing what R. Klein calls a "more competent" adaptation. The result was a population increase, with more populations coming into contact with one another but not significantly competing because of the narrowness of their realized niches. Such adjacent populations maintained their separate identities through cultural differentiation. One result of this was a limit to the gene flow between populations, which allowed local differences to appear and eventually become emphasized.

This leaves the related questions of when and where the modern Bushman and "Negroid" lines separated (see Figure 13.4). It seems clear that Bushman ancestry can be traced in southern Africa to crania such as Fish Hoek, Boskop, Matjes River Mouth cave, and Otjiseva. These crania combine a small, broad face with a very large cranium having a high, domed forehead and a bulging at the rear of the parietal bones. While they were once considered to represent a separate "race" of "gigantic" Bushmen, it is now clear that they are simply large but very Bushman-like crania, actually within the range of modern Bushman variation. None of these crania seems to have a demonstratively great antiquity.

The resemblance of these crania to the earlier modern sapiens specimens is sufficient to suggest an unbroken line of evolution in southern Africa. By the end of the Pleistocene, the southern part of the continent was inhabited by populations which exhibited more or less Bushman-like features, varying mainly in size, although to some extent also in cranial robustness. This degree of variation in Bushman and Bushman-like populations extends to modern times; as in all populations, archaic skeletal features have not disappeared; although they are rare.

It therefore seems likely that the Bushman and Bushman-like populations of southern Africa evolved locally from more generalized early modern sapiens populations immediately prior to the Holocene. This contention is supported by P. V. Tobias on the basis of independent genetic evidence. The evolutionary changes occurred in the context of the Late Stone Age microlithic technology, resulting in an extreme "gracilization" of the earlier, more archaic features. The technological in-

novations of the Late Stone Age, including the use of efficient long-distance hunting weapons such as bows with poisoned arrows, reduced the necessity for large size and skeletal robustness in hunting populations. Body size reduction as well as many of the other skeletal changes can probably be related to these technological developments in a warm climate. In general, the Late Stone Age, with its microlithic technology and altered subsistence patterns, saw the development of intensive habitat utilization, which narrowed the realized niche ranges and allowed substantive local variation to occur in the post-Pleistocene period.

EAST AFRICA

The late Pleistocene situation in East Africa is very similar to that in the southern part of the continent in that the human fossil sample shows a mixture of crania with varying degrees of "Negroid," Bushman-like, and archaic features. There is good reason to believe that during the late Pleistocene a widespread undifferentiated group occupied sub-Saharan Africa. As in the south, the appearance of marked regional distinctions seems to approximate the end of the Pleistocene.

One of the earliest modern sapiens specimens is the rather securely dated (17,600 years BP) cranium from Lukenya Hill (Figure 13.4, pp. 334-335). The specimen consists of only the frontal and a single parietal, but this is quite sufficient to show several things. First, while the forehead is low, flattened, and receding by modern African standards, it is not outside the living "Negro" range of variation. The top of the nose (nasal root) is flattened, as in many living "Negroes" and Bushmen. Finally, the parietals are markedly bulged outward in a high posterior position. As seen from the top, the vault outline resembles a pentagon—a feature which is supposedly characteristic of Bushmen. In all, one can conclude that the specimen foreshadows both "Negro" and Bushman variation. At the same time, the archaic features resemble earlier African crania. The long and broad frontal and thick supraorbital torus resemble Florisbad, although the Lukenya torus is separated into lateral and central elements by a groove. The point is that elements of continuity with earlier and later samples exist.

That these late Pleistocene East Africans resembled contemporary big-game hunters in other areas

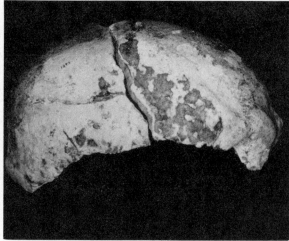

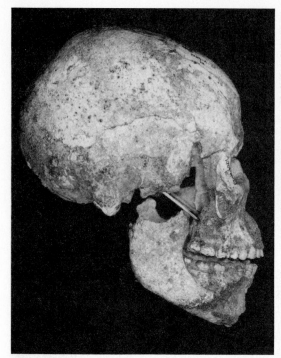

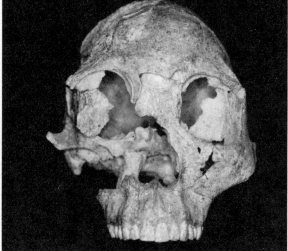

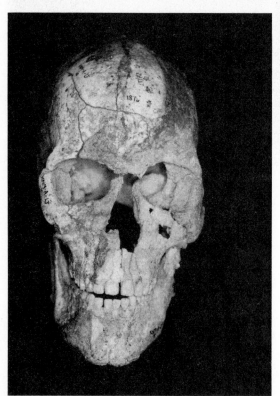

FIGURE 13.4   *Some late Pleistocene and recent African cranial variants. Left (above and below) is the Lothagam specimen, a Late Stone Age cranium. Next above is Lukenya, and below it is one of the early modern East Turkana crania (ER-1793). On opposite page (above and below) is a modern East African cranium, and rightmost (above and below) is a so-called "proto-Bushman" from the Matjes River Mouth cave (cast).*

of the world in their marked size and robustness is suggested by a series of undated but probably early modern specimens from the region surrounding Lake Turkana. To the west, a robust specimen was discovered at Kabua and a second at Lothagam Hill.

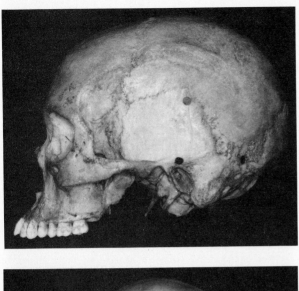
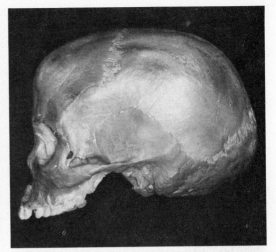
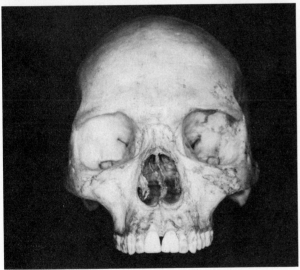
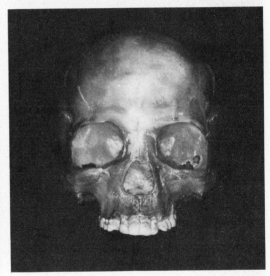

To the east, numerous specimens have been found in the recent ("overburden") layers exposed during excavations of the australopithecine-bearing deposits at East Turkana (Figure 13.4).

The late Pleistocene East Africans form a distinct morphological complex. This may not be a biological complex in the sense that it represents the average for a particular population, but together the crania suggest the morphological forms that were common in the immediate past. The skulls are very large. They are notable for their marked robustness. Cranial thickness is pronounced, but the browridges vary from moderate to absent (the forehead regions tend to resemble specimens from Omo). The occiput is rounded and high, and there

is no nuchal torus. As seen from the top, the outlines of the crania are elongated and oval. The greatest cranial breadth is rather low on the parietals, and there is no parietal bulge. The best-preserved faces are extraordinarily large and broad. The distance between the orbits is great, and the zygomatics are large and flaring. There is a canine fossa.

The dentitions also tend to be very large. The Lothagam posterior teeth are larger than those of Broken Hill. Like the situation in Asia, cranial changes seem to precede changes in the dentition during the late Pleistocene/early Holocene. In all, faces and dentitions of this size would probably not be out of place in the much earlier Omo crania.

The complex is similar to that found in all populations of big-game hunters at the end of the Pleistocene.

The point is that these specimens do not represent a sort of "late-surviving" archaic population in East Africa. They are modern *Homo sapiens*, morphologically transitional between the archaic sub-Saharan sapiens sample and recent gracilized local populations. This early modern sample shows the same degree of variation as the earlier archaic *Homo sapiens* crania, ranging from the thick browridges of the Lukenya specimen (like Florisbad) to the absence of browridges, and sharp orbital margin, in ER-1793 (like Omo/Eyasi). It is probable that these are part of an evolutionary sequence in which the "archaic" features gradually became less frequent and the "modern" features became more frequent. If so, the end products of this are modern East African populations.

EARLY CRANIA FROM OTHER AREAS NORTH OF THE EQUATOR

Crania with a similar mix of features are not restricted to the Rift Valley sites of East Africa. The Singa cranium, from the Sudan, has been indirectly dated to about 17,000 years BP. In this specimen (see Figure 13.5), an archaic frontal region is combined with a Bushman-like posterior region. The cranium is extremely broad, and the parietals are bulged, as in many Bushman crania. In contrast, the frontal region has been described as virtually Neandertal-like, complete with sloping frontal and heavy, rounded, and projecting browridge. While I believe that characterizing Singa as "Neandertal-like" is probably an overstatement, there are some marked resemblances to the archaic *Homo sapiens* cranium from Jebel Irhoud (cranium 1), especially in the frontal bone and general shape of the vault. To the extent that Singa is more modern, it is more like the crania of living Bushmen. Yet I believe it is unlikely that the specimen represents an ancestral Bushman population (as some have suggested) that migrated south to give rise to the living populations.

Indeed, Bushman features remain common in otherwise "Negroid" samples from the late Pleistocene to the present. This fact has led to confusion about the origins of Bushmen, with hypotheses as extreme as migration from North Africa. Arguing

for this possibility, L. S. B. Leakey discussed a cranium from Homa, on the shores of Lake Victoria, with Bushman-like features. Yet two other individuals from the site appear to be "Negroids." As far north as Wadi Halfa, in the northern Sudan, skeletal remains of thirty-six individuals were described as having "Boskop-like" features (i.e., features resembling large Bushmen, such as the recent Boskop cranium from South Africa). Indeed, Coon once described the Jebel Irhoud 1 cranium (Figure 11.3) as a "proto-Bushman."

I doubt that this means either that the "true" origins of the Bushmen are to the north or that recognizable Bushman populations were represented outside of southern Africa at any time. The evolutionary line leading to Bushmen in South Africa is easily traced over the last 15,000 years. When the northern crania with Bushmen-like features were subjected to a mathematical analysis combining measurements of the face and cranium, they consistently showed a close affinity with "Negroids" and not with South African Bushmen. This evidence seems to suggest the widespread occurrence of an undifferentiated ancestral population. In the post-Pleistocene period, the Bushman characteristics became more common in the south, while the "Negroid" characteristics predominated to the north.

"NEGROID" ORIGINS

The African "Negroids," then, seem to have originated north of the Zambezi River. Attempts to find specimens of great antiquity with distinctive "Negroid" characteristics, however, have not met with success. The earliest specimen claimed to show this distinction is from the Iwo Eleru rock shelter in Nigeria, dated to about 11,000 years ago. The skullcap (Figure 13.5) differs from the crania of living Nigerians by its pronounced browridge, sloping forehead, and angled occipital bone. In other words, it has the same appearance as the East African sample discussed above; like those specimens, it suggests "Negroid" affinities overlain by more robust features.

The subsequent further gracilization is apparently quite recent. The earliest cranium showing it comes from Asselar, on what was then the border of the Sahara in eastern Mali. The specimen has been dated to about 6,400 years BP, which is recent

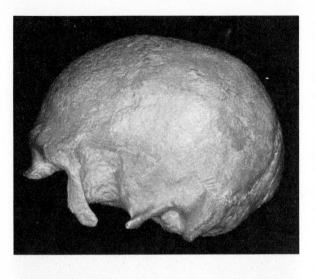

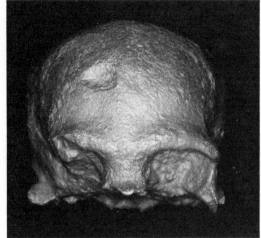

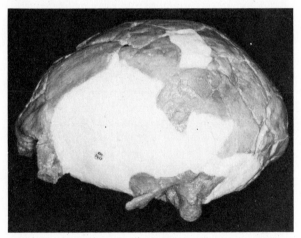

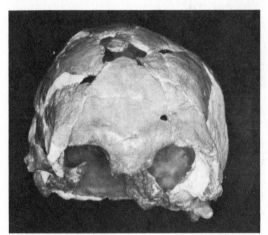

*FIGURE 13.5 Early modern **Homo sapiens** crania from northern and western Africa: Singa (top) and Iwo Eleru (bottom). Both specimens are casts.*

enough to suggest that the changes in selection might be related to the economic change from hunting to agriculture. Asselar is a long cranium with a large face and pronounced alveolar prognathism, which is somewhat obscured by the fact that the upper central incisors were extracted during life. The forehead is high, and there are no brow-ridges. The specimen is actually one of a number of "Negroids" from the Neolithic aged deposits of the Sahara, the area of Africa with the earliest evidence of agriculture and animal domestication outside of the northeast corner of the continent.

Virtually nothing earlier than these specimens shows the combination of gracile features that distinguishes living "Negroids" from the earlier populations. The 6,000–7,000 year old skeletal material at Ishango, in the Khartoum, is characterized by thick bones and large teeth and is thus reminiscent of the earlier material. The mandibles are said to show "Negroid" affinities, as does a much later mandible (4,800 years BP) from near Lake Turkana. The best evidence suggests that the appearance of significant gracilization and animal domestication and/or agriculture are linked; robust but otherwise "Negroid"-appearing populations precede agriculture in East Africa.

In sum, it appears that the distinct gracilization resulting in recognizably modern populations first occurred in the Sudan along the Upper Nile and across the southern border of the Sahara. It is unlikely that the widespread distribution of "Negroids" in sub-Saharan Africa is entirely the result of the much later Bantu expansion, originating in West Africa, since gracilized specimens clearly preceding the Iron Age are known from a variety of East African sites, including Gamble's cave, the first Olduvai hominid to be discovered, and later material from Bromhead's site. Absolute dates are unknown for many of the earlier specimens, but recent work suggests that considerable antiquity is possible for some of them. Before this, local evolution resulting in at least partial gracilization of the earlier populations occurred throughout the continent before the appearance of either iron or agriculture and domestication. In general, the evolutionary trends and the timespan within which they took place closely parallel what occurred in other parts of the world at the end of the Pleistocene, with the evolution of very efficient hunting/gathering societies from the earlier populations of big-game hunters.

NORTH AFRICA

The sample of modern *Homo sapiens* from North Africa is very large but, with a few exceptions, not particularly ancient. The most notable of the earlier material is the newly discovered cranium from Dar-es-Soltane in Morocco. Although the cultural context is not clear, D. Ferembach has proposed that it is associated with a late Levalloisian-like industry that is roughly contemporary with the earlier Upper Paleolithic in Europe. The cranium bears some resemblance to the Qafzeh males from the Levant (Figure 12.6), combining a foreshortened broad face (with a canine fossa) and massive browridges which follow the contour of the orbits but project markedly in front of them. Compared with Jebel Irhoud 1, the face is smaller and less prognathic, but the cranial shape is similar and the robust features are retained. A modern-appearing occipital bone from Témara may be of the same approximate age.

The somewhat later sites of Wadi Halfa (Sudan), Afalou (Algeria), Taforalt (Morocco), and Mechta-El-Abri (Algeria) are all Mesolithic. These samples show a marked degree of similarity, although the

large sample sizes allow the observation of a great deal of morphological variation at each site, only some of which is due to sexual dimorphism.

The North African sample tends to be robust, with many males showing prominent supraorbitals, marked temporal lines, and large jaws and teeth. In general, the crania are long and rather broad; the occipitals tend to be angled; and the faces are medium to small, moderately prognathic, and have broad noses. The North African material does not appear particularly similar to the skeletons from East Africa, discussed above, or to the earlier Sudanese specimen from Singa. On the other hand, there are numerous detailed similarities with living populations in North Africa, and it is probably best to consider the sample as representing a considerably more robust ancestral version of these living groups.

A hypothesis attempting to account for the cranial changes involved in the appearance of modern variants was recently suggested by D. S. Carlson and D. P. van Gerven. Based on their analysis of Nubian crania dating from the Mesolithic (about 12,000 years ago) to the recent, the authors relate observed cranial changes to changes in masticatory function. They propose that the shift to agriculture resulted in a diet of generally softer, better-cooked foodstuffs with much less grit adhering to them. With the need for powerful chewing reduced, there was reduction in the size of the masticatory muscles and the bony areas supporting them (see Figure 13.6). The main morphological consequences involved marked reduction in robustness, a lower, more posterior positioning of the midface, and reduction of the nuchal plane, which led to cranial shortening (and a commensurate increase in height).

Interestingly, the archaic *Homo sapiens* sample from North Africa showed a parallel set of regional similarity to these later samples. D. Ferembach believes that archaic North African *Homo sapiens* populations, such as represented at Jebel Irhoud, gave rise to these later populations through evolutionary changes such as significant facial reduction and expansion of the frontal bone. She suggests that the specific resemblances between the Jebel Irhoud crania and the Mesolithic North African sample indicate that the archaic *Homo sapiens* populations had already developed major geographic differences, corresponding to those which occur to-

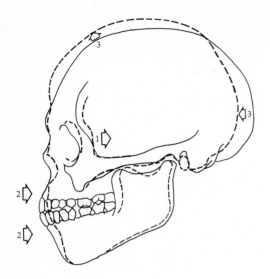

FIGURE 13.6 *A model of facial reduction as a consequence of diminished masticatory function in a Nubian cranial series, after Carlson and van Gerven, 1977. A Mesolithic cranium (solid line) is compared with a historic one (dotted line) about 10,000 years later in time. Arrows show the main average changes, reducing projection of both the face (1) and (2) and occipital region (3) and upward expansion of the vault (3).*

day, and that the transformation from archaic to modern sapiens occurred in many different areas. There are similarities between these explanatory hypotheses, accounting for the evolution of North African archaic populations into Mesolithic populations, and Mesolithic populations into modern ones. It is possible that the past 40,000 years has been marked by a continuous single-directional pattern of cranial and dental change, responding mainly to changing diet, new methods of food preparation, and increasing efficiency in hunting and food gathering.

Upper Paleolithic Europeans

In Europe, the Upper Paleolithic industries are characterized by a shift in manufacturing technique and an emphasis on tools for working bone and wood. The new manufacturing technique involves striking long blades from cores of suitable material, and then using the blades to make specific tools. This technique is more efficient than the prepared core technique since many tools can be made from a single core.

The stone tools, of course, are only a small part of the cultural changes that take place during this period, although the differing styles and the appearance and frequency differences of tool types have been used to define a series of Upper Paleolithic cultural traditions. This series is traditionally arranged in a sequence. However, after seventy-five years of excavation and analysis, three critical questions still remain unanswered (or, put another way, have too many answers). These questions are:

1. Are the industries in eastern and central Europe the same as in the west (i.e., is eastern Aurignacian the same culture as the Aurignacian in France)?
2. Are all the industries truly sequential, or do some overlap in time and perhaps represent different functional variants of each other?
3. If the industries are sequential, do they evolve into each other, or do they represent subsequent replacements reflecting population movements?

In eastern and central Europe, the sequence of cultural evolution in the later Pleistocene begins with the Mousterian-like Szeletian industry, followed by, or in some areas contemporary with, an eastern Aurignacian industry. Later than this is the eastern Gravetian, followed by the last true Upper Paleolithic industry, the Magdelanian.

The archaeological sequence traditionally proposed for western Europe begins with the Chatelperronian (or lower Perigordian), followed by the Aurignacian, Solutrean (in some regions) or Gravettian, and the Magdalenian.

The Chatelperronian (or lower Perigordian), the local transitional industry in France and Italy, appears to have evolved from at least one of the distinct traditions of the preceding Mousterian. However, it is not clear whether the Aurignacian of the west is a distinct industry or a functional variant of the same complex. What was once taken to be a progressive series of industries, each evolving into or being replaced by the next, is now widely considered a single industrial stage in the early Upper Paleolithic exhibiting numerous functional variants and a basic adaptive polymorphism. These variants are referred to as Chatelperrionian, lower Perigordian, or Aurignacian.

The available radiocarbon dates suggest that the earliest Upper Paleolithic sites in eastern and central Europe may be older than their counterparts in the west. While dates in excess of 35,000 years BP seem to be questionable, Szeletian and eastern Aurignacian industries still seem to begin several thousand years before the earliest Upper Paleolithic industry in western Europe. In any event, it appears likely that most, if not all, of the Upper Paleolithic–associated early modern sapiens sample from western Europe is later than the specimens from eastern Europe discussed in Chapter 12.

These parallel (if not related) sequences of tool-tradition changes reflect the more general evolution of the late Pleistocene hunter-gatherers. The evolving adaptive system in Europe came to encompass virtually all of the specific techniques and equipment known in modern hunting populations. These almost certainly included missile systems, tailored clothing, and harpoons. Earlier populations made effective use of the large game animals—mammoths, tundra-adapted oxen, and other large species. As these became rare or extinct, local adaptations shifted to the intensive use of smaller mammals (reindeer, horses, bison) as well as to a more effective use of fish and other water resources. The increasingly efficient habitat exploitation was reflected in the changing morphology of the human populations.

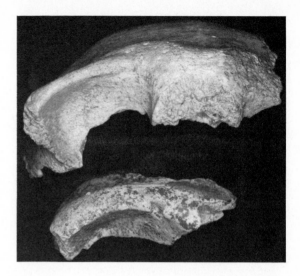

FIGURE 13.7   Comparison of a late Neandertal (Vindija 202, bottom) with an early modern Homo sapiens (Velica Pećina) frontal bone. Both are from Croatia. Note the difference in the browridge form. In the Neandertal, the browridge is continuous and fairly evenly developed. The Velica Pećina morphology resembles many modern Europeans in that the portion of the browridge over the nose is very strongly developed while it weakens considerably over the eyes. The central and more lateral portions of the torus are separated by a groove. Other Vindija supraorbitals are shown in Figures 12.2 and 12.3.

EASTERN AND CENTRAL EUROPE

Mladeč is probably the earliest modern *Homo sapiens* sample from central Europe (Figure 12.8). Slightly later specimens associated with the Aurignacian include the Velica Pećina frontal from Croatia, dated to about 33,000 years BP (see Figure 13.7), some of the Brno crania from Czechoslovakia, and other fragmentary mandibles and teeth. These specimens retain marked cranial robusticity (in the males), although the vaults are higher than in the Neandertals and the browridges show the modern European division into central and lateral elements. Female crania, such as Brno 1, contrast in their gracility, reduction of buttresses and tori, and decreased cranial thickness.

Later in time, the Czech site of the Předmost is associated with the eastern Gravettian (or Pavlovian). Předmost provides one of the largest samples of early modern *Homo sapiens* in Europe. However, its approximate age of 25,000 years BP places it some 10,000 years (or more) after the first appearance of modern people in the region.

J. Matiegka published a detailed, two volume monograph describing the Předmost remains in the 1930s. The detail of the descriptions is fortunate, since the original sample of at least twenty-seven individuals was destroyed at the end of World War II. The material may well represent a single biological population; eighteen of the individuals were recovered from a mass grave formed by a depression lined with mammoth long bones and covered by decorated and colored shoulder blades of this same species, which seems to have been the specialized object of their hunting.

Compared with the European Neandertal sample, the crania are slightly smaller (about 3 percent); the cranial capacity average for eight specimens is 1,467 cc (1,220–1,736 cc). On the average, the crania are shorter and broader, and slightly higher. The greatest difference in a cranial dimension is the 9 percent reduction in occipital breadth. Facial projection varies widely and shows considerable sexual dimorphism.

The adult crania show distinct sexual dimorphism in morphology. Males are characterized by prominent supraorbitals, fairly low foreheads, and large mastoids, while supraorbital development in the females is reduced, foreheads are higher, and the mastoids are small to moderate (see Figure 13.8, p. 342). Metrically, the degree of cranial dimorphism is not different from that found in living populations. Moreover, there is little sex difference in the size and rugosity of the faces.

The Předmost males retain numerous Neandertal-like features, although these are never found together in the same cranium. The posterior of cranium 9 is flattened and bunned. In cranium 18 the supraorbital is extraordinarily projecting and the forehead is quite low. Předmost 3 is particularly reminiscent of Skhul 5 in the development of the browridge, low position of the cranial breadth, and spongy bone development of the cranial base. It differs from the Skhul specimen in that the browridge is divided into central and lateral portions. While all of these features can be found in living Europeans, no living population comes close to matching the Předmost sample in their high frequency of expression.

The Předmost mandibles are characterized by only moderate chin development. In Předmost 3 the ramus begins behind the third molar, while in Předmost 4 it begins just at its back border. Specific features showing sexual dimorphism foreshadow living populations. For instance, male mandibles are deeper, with vertical rami, while in the females the ramus is lower and angled more posteriorly, and the anterior tooth-bearing portion is more prognathic.

The large dental sample shows moderate variation; generally males have larger teeth than females, although there is some overlap. Only at their largest do the teeth approach the maximums reached in the earlier modern sapiens sample. The Předmost sample, as well as others roughly contemporary, shows significant anterior dental reduction when compared to the earliest Upper Paleolithic sample. This reduction seems all the more marked because of the relatively short period of time separating them.

Finally, the conditions of burial resulted in numerous postcrania. The average male height is 64 inches, and the female average is 61 inches. The percentage of sexual dimorphism in height is very small. The Předmost males are the same height as European Neandertal males, while the females are slightly taller than Neandertal females. It would appear that the idea that the early modern sapiens populations were significantly taller than the Neandertals cannot be sustained in central Europe.

Limb proportions at Předmost differ somewhat from the Neandertal condition. The limbs farther away from the body are slightly elongated. Skeletal robustness in the sample is marked. Although no specimen approaches the Neandertal extreme, characteristics of some fall well within the Neandertal range. On the average, however, the relative size of the joint surfaces is reduced. In sum, the Předmost sample combines marked variability with a low level of sexual dimorphism in a Neandertal-sized population. This combination is particularly interesting because the moderate sexual dimorphism and the circumstances of burial make it possible to show that some of the observed variation is not due to sex, time, or the mixture of different biological populations. Thus Předmost provides an indication of the degree of purely individual, or idiosyncratic, variability that can characterize a fossil population. The fact that within this sample individual features overlap well into the Neandertal range is also important. No specimen combines all or even most of the Neandertal-like features, and none could possibly be regarded as a Neandertal. Nonetheless, Předmost fits a model of frequency change for the loss of Neandertal features, expressing these at a lower frequency than occurred in earlier samples and consequently rarely or never in combination.

A scattered set of additional remains date to this timespan, including an incomplete female skullcap from the German site of Stetten and a child's mandible from the Austrian site of Miesslingtal. Both are associated with Aurignacian industries. The

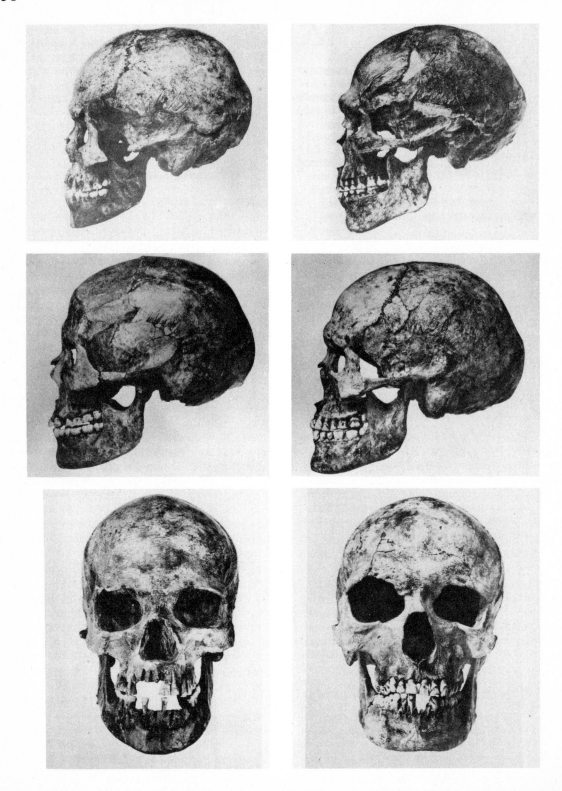

FIGURE 13.8   Some of the better-preserved Předmost crania, after J. Matiegka's 1934 monograph. Females to the left are (top to bottom) crania 4 and 10 and a facial view of 4. Males to the right are crania 5 and 9 (two views).

most complete isolated specimen is the Brno 2 male from Czechoslovakia, a narrow, robust cranium with a low forehead and bunning of the occiput.

THE WESTERN EUROPEAN SEQUENCE: THE EARLIER REMAINS

In contrast to eastern and central Europe, in western Europe only a few remains are clearly pre-Aurignacian. These date to a climatic interlude between stages II and III of the Würm glaciation (see Table 11.1) when there was some glacial retreat and for a short time the climate was moderate. The specimens from Arcy-sur-Cure in France, dated to the earliest Chatelperronian (about 33,000 years BP), consist mainly of teeth. Fortunately, these include some anteriors, which fall within the Neandertal range.

The complete female skeleton (62 inches tall) from Combe Capelle in France was initially reported to derive from Chatelperronian levels. Considerable controversy surrounds this claim, and the real age of the specimen can probably never be clearly established. The cranium is higher and narrower than most Neandertal crania, but the face retains a considerable degree of total facial prognathism. This feature is generally the same across the early Upper Paleolithic of Europe if specimens of the same sex are compared, but the reduction is marked when compared with European Neandertals. Combe Capelle has a more prominent browridge and slightly larger face than the Mladeč 1 female but smaller vault dimensions and less cranial capacity. The mandible is short, vertical, and rather deep, with a vertical symphysis featuring a virtual lack of mental eminence projection. The ramus begins just at the back of the third molar.

The specimens from Grotte des Enfants (Grimaldi) in Italy also seem to be early. The three best-preserved individuals—a male, a female, and a juvenile male—have been interpreted a number of different ways. Early in the century they were

thought to come from the Mousterian layers at the site and were used as evidence of the "coexistence" of Neandertals and modern people. It later became apparent that they were buried into the Mousterian layers from the overlying Upper Paleolithic layers. Their relationship and elements of similarity to the Neandertals were recognized in the 1920s by R. Verneau, who proposed that they represented the most "primitive" (modern) Homo sapiens sample, evolved from Neandertals and ancestral to all living people. However, this interpretation was overshadowed by the idea that two of the specimens were "Negroids," an idea based mostly on the great alveolar prognathism of the juvenile. This is now recognized to have been an artifact of a very faulty reconstruction.

The female and the juvenile male (numbers 5 and 6) are thought to be somewhat earlier than the adult male (number 4), and if the archaeological and faunal associations have been correctly interpreted, all three are later than the (presumed) date for the Combe Capelle female. It should be pointed out, however, that the chronological position of hominids at both sites is problematic. The adult crania are somewhat smaller and markedly less robust than their Mladeč counterparts. Both are well rounded and show reduced supraorbital development, but neither is especially high. The female is notable for her narrow cranial breadth, slightly less than in Combe Capelle and much less than the eastern European females. She is less robust than Combe Capelle in facial and browridge development and in the features of the cranial base. The faces of the Grotte des Enfants specimens are delicate and rather flattened transversely. The female has small, angled cheeks and the adult male somewhat larger ones. Both faces are very short relative to their width.

A third fairly early site in western Europe is Paderborn in Germany. The faceless skull from the site is dated to older than 27,000 years. It is probably contemporary with the Grotte des Enfants specimens. Paderborn is similar to the Mladeč males in size and morphology, although the occiput is somewhat more rounded and the browridges are not as prominent. A multivariate analysis (not including the Mladeč males) placed the specimen closest to the Grotte des Enfants male.

Relatively complete postcranial material was recovered from the burials at Combe Capelle and Grotte des Enfants. In general, the limbs are marked by a reduction in the features associated with muscularity. Shaft diameters and articular surfaces are smaller relative to limb length than in Neandertals. However, in the relative size of the shafts and the articular surfaces, and also in the reduction of midshaft flattening, these early modern Europeans show less reduction than the Near Eastern specimens from Skhul and Qafzeh.

These early modern specimens from western Europe are taller than the Neandertals. Compared by sex, average height is about 8 percent taller; midsex value (average of male and female means) is 66.5 inches (71-inch male average and 62-inch female average). There are some striking differences from the Neandertals in limb proportions; the radius and tibia increase significantly in length relative to the upper arm and upper leg. There is no significant difference from the limb proportions found at Skhul and Qafzeh.

THE LATER REMAINS

There are numerous specimens which date to the later Aurignacian levels in western Europe. Few, however, are complete, and no sample approaches the numbers found at Předmost or Mladeč. These western sites are dated to the Würm III glacial stage, marking a reemergence of cold conditions that were even more severe than the earlier Würm stages. Building on the earlier Mousterian adaptations to cold steppe conditions, the Aurignacian peoples developed effective hunting adaptations based on weapons with projectile points. These included spears, possibly catapulted to greater distances by spear throwers. Bone-working technology proliferated, probably to help replace wood in the prevalent tundra conditions.

Isolated teeth or fragmentary jaws come from the Aurignacian levels at the French sites of Arcy, Castenat and Castelmerle, Fontéchevade, and La Rochette. A relatively large dental sample derives from the Aurignacian and later levels at Isturits in France.

However, the best-known site and the only one with cranial remains of several specimens is Cro Magnon. The stratigraphy and cultural associations suggest that the site dates to the middle of Würm III or later.

The crania from Cro Magnon represent three males and a female (see Figure 13.9). The cranial capacity of the males is quite large (1,636 and 1,730 cc for crania 1 and 3 respectively), and the general dimensions of the crania are correspondingly great except occipital breadth, which is reduced (as in the Předmost sample). Cranium 1, often called "the old man," is high and well rounded, with a rather bulging forehead and little browridge development. In contrast, the cranium 3 forehead is lower and the browridge better developed. The occipital region of cranium 3 is remarkably Neandertal-like, with a prominent bun and cranial flattening above it. The endocast of this cranium also appears to resemble the Neandertals in size and proportions. Cranium 3 is not a Neandertal, but his features confirm the mix of typically Neandertal characteristics in more modern populations. Cranium 4 has even more prominent browridges and extraordinary development of spongy bone at the cranial base, the nuchal muscle attachment area, and the mastoids. However, the back of the cranium is flattened in a very different way from in cranium 3, possibly the result of artificial deformation. The effect of this flattening on the other cranial features is unknown.

The best-known male from the site, cranium 1, is the most gracile and modern-appearing of the three. It is also the only male specimen with a face. The face is very broad (in absolute dimension and in proportion to its height). A number of authors had proposed that tall faces should be associated with long crania, and the Cro Magnon face seemed to disprove this contention. It was thus argued that the loss of the front teeth during life led to facial shortening in this male as the result of resorption of the alveolar bone. However, I do not believe this can account for the facial proportions. Not enough bone could have been lost to cause much reduction in facial height. Historically, this question had importance beyond the true dimensions of a single face, since it was used to support the contention that there were different "races" represented in Europe during the Upper Paleolithic. One of the features thought to distinguish these was the facial height relative to cranial length.

The female (cranium 2) is a smaller, more gracile specimen, which was somewhat distorted and has

FIGURE 13.9   Views of the four crania from Cro Magnon. From top to bottom, these are crania 1, 2, 3, and 4. Only Cro Magnon 2 is female.

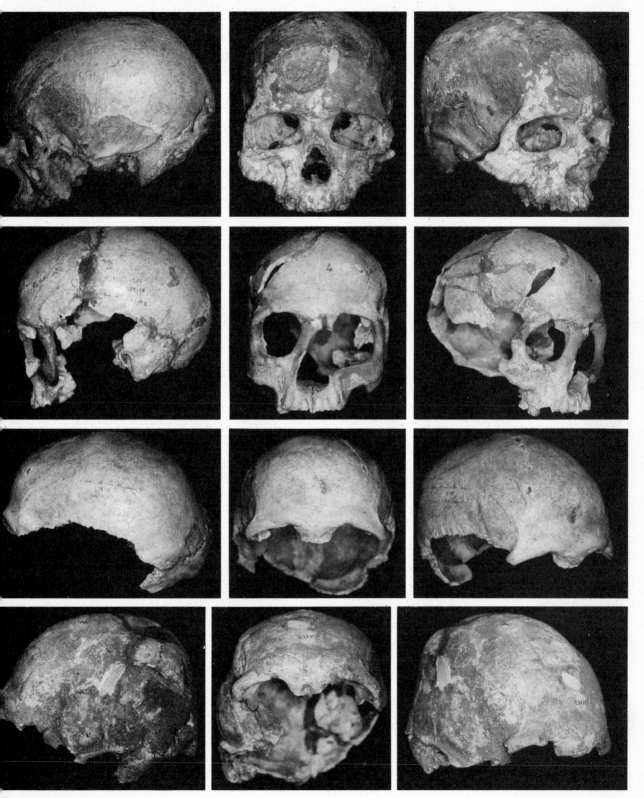

345

not been well reconstructed. As with the Předmost females, sexual dimorphism is better expressed in her cranial vault than in her face, which is almost the size of the Cro Magnon 1 face.

Interestingly, the western European faces differ from contemporaries to the east (but resemble the earlier sample from Mladeč) in their midfacial prognathism (Table 12.1), large noses, and high nasal angles. To this extent, they are more Neandertal-like, although in my view the similarity more likely results from a parallel adaptation to cold conditions than from a closer genetic relationship. Broad faces and large noses with high nasal angles are retained in later European specimens such as Chancelade, and the similarity to the morphology of the cold-adapted Eskimos has been used to suggest an ancestral relation of the former to the latter. Again, it is more likely that this similarity reflects a common response to similar conditions. Würm III was the coldest of the Würm stadials in western Europe.

COMPARISON WITH EUROPEAN NEANDERTALS

It would appear that the earliest modern *Homo sapiens* populations in western Europe were generally taller but less robust than the preceding Neandertals. In eastern Europe, corresponding changes in robustness and proportions occurred without a significant change in height. In both regions, the change in limb proportions was probably the consequence of a more efficient cultural adaptation to the cold and differing activity patterns associated with the use of projectile weapons in intensive big-game hunting.

The early modern *Homo sapiens* crania are, on the average, taller and narrower than but the same length as Neandertal crania of the same sex. While the central projection of the face diminished, the projection of the zygomatics to the sides of the face increased, resulting in flattened cheeks. The facial reduction was partially the result of a smaller maxillary sinus. Consequently, a canine fossa consistently appeared, and the base of the cheeks became smaller and more distinctly angled. The height dimensions of the face were also reduced, while breadths either did not change or in some cases increased. This accentuated the flattening across

the cheeks. More of the facial height reduction occurred in the zygomatics and orbits than in the incisor-bearing portion of the lower maxilla. Both nasal height and breadth reduced, but the breadth reduction was 50 percent greater than the height reduction, making the noses relatively narrower.

Morphologically, the crania retained or expanded basal spongy bone. However, the greatest breadth of the parietals moved to a higher position, and no cranium retained the semi-circular contour (as seen from the rear) that characterized many Neandertals (Figure 9.8). The approximate nuchal attachment area remained about the same. Above it the occipital plane became longer and more rounded.

In the frontal region, many of the early modern specimens have extraordinarily large, projecting supraorbitals; inevitably these are associated with frontals which are no higher or more bulging than in many Neandertals. However, the browridges differ from those of most Neandertals in their division into central and lateral elements by a more or less distinct groove. Only the earliest specimens do not fully conform to this pattern.

The earlier mandibles are rather similar to the latest Neandertal mandibles in their symphyseal area. The symphysis tends to be vertical, and most specimens do not have a prominent chin. The reduction in total facial prognathism is reflected in the decreased mandibular length, and generally but not always the lack of a gap between the last molar and the ramus.

Dentally, the earliest modern Europeans were surprisingly similar to the latest Würm II Neandertals, showing some reduction mainly in the incisors (Figure 11.9). Some reduction also occurred in the anterior mandibular premolar, but the mandibular canines remained about the same size. In view of the marked facial changes, it would appear that, as in the Near Eastern sample, the dentition is conservative.

TIMING AND SOME POSSIBLE CAUSES

A change in function for the incisors is one of the important causal elements in the selection-based hypothesis for the evolution of modern *Homo sapiens* from local Neandertal populations. The viability of such a hypothesis must depend on how credible the cause-and-effect relation is, and on how much time was actually available for the hypothesized evolutionary changes.

The latter is problematic for two reasons. First, the preponderance of males in the northern European Neandertal sample and of females in the early modern sapiens sample plus the problems of precisely dating the latest Neandertals make accurate estimates of how much change was required and the time available for it difficult, if not impossible. Second, a real possibility exists that many of the "marked" changes in osteological features were due more to environmentally and behaviorally influenced differences in growth and development than to actual genetic change. It is possible that there is less genetic difference between the skeletons of Neandertals and early modern sapiens than one would imagine from comparing the form and morphology of the known samples.

If we assume that an average of 20,000 years separates the Neandertal sample from Würm II and the earliest modern sapiens sample, and if we further assume that the entire observed morphological change is genetic, is it reasonable to propose that the observed changes could take place in 1,000 twenty-year generations? The 18 percent reduction in facial height need involve no more than .015 mm each generation, and the average generational change in incisor breadth is so small it could never be measured. Of course, showing that this complex of changes *could* have occurred is not proof that it *did*. However, the fact is that most of the cranial changes can be accounted for by a single functional model based on decreasing anterior tooth use, and that every morphological variant found in the later sample appears at lower frequency in the Neandertals. I believe that the selection hypothesis is more reasonable than one depending on significant amounts of migration from points as yet undetermined "to the east." It cannot be easily dismissed by the contention that there was not enough time for the requisite changes to occur.

SOME IDEAS ABOUT LIFEWAYS

Since the European Upper Paleolithic has its roots in the earlier local Mousterian, the adaptive changes allowed by Upper Paleolithic techniques can be assessed by comparing an earlier and later adaptation to the same area. The Ukraine provides a particularly good opportunity for such a comparison. There Mousterian hunters who were probably Neandertals had been hunting mammoths since at least 75,000 years ago. They evolved the cultural capacity to adapt to a climate that was quite harsh during the peaks of the last glaciation. At the site of Molodova, they built large wood-framed structures, which were covered with hides weighed down or anchored with mammoth bones and heated from the inside. Of the many stone tools found, one of the most common is a large leaf-shaped point that was probably hafted to wood shafts to make a spear for hunting. Other tools include many long scrapers that were used in preparing hides and tools with small notches used for carving and shaping wood. This is one of the many sites where red pigment, probably used for body decoration, has been discovered.

The earliest Upper Paleolithic industries in this area are unknown, but the later Gravettian industries, which correspond to the middle Aurignacian of the west, are important because they contrast the presence of a change in technology with a continuous adaptive pattern. Some 25,000 years ago these Gravettian people hunted the same game and built the same type of structures. Many of the tools that are found perform the same functions. For instance, there is an abundance of scrapers and points. However, these tools are made differently.

The technological innovations that occurred within the early Upper Paleolithic involved two important changes. First, a new technique was developed that eventually replaced the prepared-core technique for producing stone tools. This technique involved "pushing" long, thin, parallel-sided blades off of specially prepared cores of flint or similar material. This gave the people an even finer control over the variety and forms of the tools that were made, and as a consequence many new and even more specialized tools were produced. Second, the technique also allowed much better tools for working wood, bone, and antler to be produced, and additional tools made from these materials also appear. These materials had been used throughout the Paleolithic, but the new techniques for shaping their final form made possible a wider variety of more finely made implements.

Thus the scrapers of the Upper Paleolithic were made on the ends of long blades rather than on the sides of blunter flakes. These could be used more effectively and with more control. Projectile points were thinner and more easily hafted to wood. New tools were developed and older tool forms refined. Woodworking tools became abundant, and bone needles for sewing appeared for the first time.

Yet, when we look for the effect of these industrial changes on the basic adaptive pattern in the Ukraine, it is interesting that it remains largely unchanged. In his analysis of the Ukrainian sites, R. Klein argued that the main effect of the technological changes was to make better use of the same resources. Most of the same tools were made, although differently and more efficiently added, allowing more specialized functions to be performed, we are still dealing with cold-adapted populations, living in wood-framed structures and hunting mammoths.

Klein pointed out that the real adaptive differences can be seen in the range and density of human populations. No Mousterian sites are found north of a latitude of 54 degrees, while Upper Paleolithic sites can be found as far north as within the Arctic Circle. In addition, there are more Upper Paleolithic sites in the areas where earlier, similar Mousterian sites occurred. One must conclude that the primary importance of the new techniques was that they allowed a much more efficient adaptation to the same niche through the use of new and more specialized tools and the refinement of the older technology.

It is important to note that in areas where there is continuity between the Middle and the Upper Paleolithic, these new developments and refinements occurred *after* the appearance of the earliest Upper Paleolithic industries. What Klein describes for the Ukraine is actually the result of at least 10,000 years of cultural evolution *within* the Upper Paleolithic. These changes did not come with the first appearance of Upper Paleolithic industries, but rather evolved after they were established.

CONTINUED CHANGES IN EUROPE

In Europe, the strongest possible case can be made for the continued evolution of modern *Homo sapiens*, beginning with the earliest samples, which retain high frequencies of Neandertal-like characteristics, followed by later samples with lower but still demonstrably present frequencies of the same,

and ultimately culminating in the reduced, gracilized features that characterize living populations. In terms of both cranial and dental features, the earliest modern sapiens sample in Europe is about midway between Neandertals and living Europeans.

Some of the general trends of the Upper Paleolithic continued as the climate once again became extraordinarily cold, shortening the crania and reducing their breadth, while increasing facial projection. At the same time, measures of facial size increase, as does the breadth of the occipital. Various authors have interpreted the differences in skeletal morphology, as well as the differences in culture, to mean that an invasion occurred, bringing with it new people and ideas. One of the more persistent theories comes from studies of the skeleton from Chancelade. The large flaring zygomatics, flat face, and cranial robustness of the Chancelade specimen have been systematically compared with the morphology of living Eskimos, and at one time it had even been suggested that the Europeans of these times (23,000–17,000 years ago) are related or perhaps ancestral to living Eskimos. More recently other authors described this apparent similarity as the consequence of a robust masticatory apparatus superimposed on a European Upper Paleolithic morphology. (The flattened face was already present in earlier Upper Paleolithic samples.) In any event, the "Eskimoid" interpretation ignores the extremely prominent and highly angled nasal bones of this specimen as well as others from this period, such as Barma Grande from Grimaldi. This nasal morphology seems to be a continuing part of the western European cold adaptation throughout the Upper Pleistocene, and the Europeans of this timespan lived during the most severe portion of the last glaciation.

With the end of the last glacial advance, significant changes in subsistence eventually leading to the Neolithic resulted in a combination of gracilization and local differentiation in Europe as elsewhere. The various geographic distinctions, once thought of as the European "races," did not evolve until this period and consequently are extremely recent. In some areas, changes in cranial form were probably more dramatic, and surely more rapid, than at any time in the past. To what extent these changes were the result of different patterns of growth and development is far from clear. The study of European evolution in the Mesolithic and Neolithic periods has only "scratched the surface" of the many relevant problems that must eventually be solved. One sure fact, however, is that this process of gracilization and reduction in the cranium, dentition, and skeleton has continued right up to the present.

While most attention is usually focused on the cranial and dental changes, equally important changes occurred in the postcrania. Measures of robustness in the earliest modern Europeans overlap the Neandertals. Considerable subsequent reduction took place in Europe even before the spread of agriculture and the accelerated changes that followed from it. The early modern populations were, at most, only several inches taller than the Neandertals. The widespread appearance of fairly tall European populations occurred within the last several hundred years.

In sum, the early modern European sample demonstrates the continuity with the earlier Neandertals of Europe and the significant amount of evolutionary change that took place after the Pleistocene. It is the element of continuity which is perhaps the most critical single aspect of this evolutionary sequence.

SUMMARY

A surprising number of parallel or common trends characterize late Pleistocene hominid evolution. These seem tied to an increased efficiency in resource exploitation on a number of different levels. The associated widespread use of projectile weapons and emphasis on big-game hunting resulted in changes in activity patterns that had immediate consequences in postcranial robustness. Both increased anterior tooth use and dietary changes involving both new food sources and improved methods of food preparation and cooking led to reductions in facial size which, in turn, affected cranial changes and changes in tooth size.

At the same time, cultural and genetic differences that had accumulated before the earliest modern *Homo sapiens* populations insured that specific directions of change need not be the same. For instance, it is likely that the same sort of technological and adaptive changes resulted in body size *increase* in western Europe and body size *decrease* in southern Africa. Human adaptation had become specific and efficient enough by the late Pleistocene for morphological changes to be influenced by the finer nuances of adaptive difference. Small body size is an effective heat adaptation in southern Africa, and the widespread use of poisons reduced the need for individual strength and consequently for large robust skeletons. Advantages to the stature increases in western Europe (and other places) may have been tied to effective long-distance stride in following migratory herd animals. This change may have involved little more than redistributing the same body mass found in the stockier Neandertals

along a more linear frame with markedly longer limbs. The large mass in both of these northern forms was part of a cold adaptation, but the distribution of that mass changed with the development of new activity patterns.

Dental changes were similarly widespread and surprisingly uniform. Dental reduction accelerated at the very end of the Paleolithic. While it has proceeded more rapidly in some areas than in others because of cultural and technological differences in diet and food preparation, the direction has been the same. Moreover, the consequences of reduction seem similar. Many of the important differences between the faces and crania of living groups tend to reflect how much dental reduction subsequent to the Upper Paleolithic has taken place. Actually, dental reduction is only one aspect of reduction of the entire masticatory apparatus. Indeed, many workers maintain that the teeth are the last of the masticatory structures to reduce. Continued decrease in anterior tooth loading came as a consequence of technological sophistication. Grinding, roasting, and ultimately boiling had much to do with the decrease in posterior tooth use. The influence of decreased stress during the growth and development of the face seems to have preceded the actual dental reduction that resulted from these changes, and in fact may have been causal. Whatever the case, reduction of facial size and projection has occurred to varying degrees all over the human range. Many groups show associated cranial changes, including reduction in cranial length as smaller nuchal attachment areas and less well developed posterior temporalis muscles allowed a more efficient spherical braincase to appear.

Again, differing adaptations and gene pool differences allow disparate consequences from the same cause. For instance, both Eskimos and some Australian Aborigine groups use their anterior teeth extensively (for a living population). In the Eskimos the resulting facial stress is resisted by a high forehead without substantial supraorbital development, while the Australian aborigines combine a low forehead and marked supraorbital development in response to similar anterior tooth use.

Thus accumulating differences between regions were not all the result of differences in selection. Indeed, many may reflect different but equally effective responses to the same selection acting on different gene pools. Moreover, the role of drift in the accumulating morphological differences that characterize the late Pleistocene should not be overlooked. Effective adaptations allow differently adapted groups to occupy adjacent areas. Numer-

ous cultural mechanisms may act to restrict gene flow under these circumstances, allowing random differences to accumulate. Undoubtedly, different combinations of all these factors underlie the specific recent evolutionary histories of various regions.

Localized regional variation appears late in the fossil record. The marked differences between living Asians and Melanesians may date to not much more than 10,000–20,000 years ago. Similarly, the distinctions between living Bushmen and "Negroes" seem to have no greater antiquity, and the antiquity of the so-called European "races" is much less.

In all, late Pleistocene evolution involved gracilization, reduction, and the appearance of the modern range of diversity. It also involved an acceleration in the rate of cultural and technological change with consequences for morphological evolution that are not yet fully understood.

STATE OF THE ART

When C. Coon wrote in 1963, "The origin of the African Negroes, and of the Pygmies, is the greatest unsolved mystery in the field of racial study," was he correct, or was this yet another instance of misunderstanding the fossil evidence? His own conclusion, that "modern Negroes resulted from a backcross between an original proto-Negro stock and Pygmies," is no less bizarre than most other explanations that have been debated over the past half-century. Needless to say, it remains a matter of controversy.

To begin with, there is a basic disagreement concerning the origins of modern *Homo sapiens* in sub-Saharan Africa. While some recent workers, such as R. Klein and R. Protsch, support an invasion model, others, such as P. Rightmire, P. V. Tobias, and L. H. Wells, see the derivation of modern populatons from early African *Homo sapiens*. The former model makes Negro origins impossible to deal with, given the lack of a known place of origin for the modern population.

Given the contention of an African origin, hypotheses still abound. What probably can be called the traditional view is that Negro origins were a local west-central African phenomenon. It is ar-

gued that during the Late Stone Age, African populations south of the Zambezi were Bushmen. One variation of this theme is the idea that this area was inhabited by a large Bushman form first called "Boskopoid" (after the large, undated Boskop cranium from the Transvaal) and later formally named *"Homo capensis."* L. S. B. Leakey argued that the East African Late Stone Age populations (now recognized as post-Pleistocene Mesolithic populations) were "Caucasoids" of probable Mediterranean origin. This left only West Africa as a place for Negro origins, although for a long time the only solid supporting evidence was the 6,400-year-old skeleton from Asselar, in Mali. Add to this the recent contention that the Sudanese Mesolithic crania from Wadi Halfa are "Boskopoid," descriptions of Singa as anything from Bushman-like to "Neandertaloid," and Coon's interpretation of the early *Homo sapiens* specimens from Jebel Irhoud as "proto-Bushmen," and it is little wonder that Negro origins, or for that matter any other recent substantive evolutionary problem on the continent, could be regarded as a mystery.

Many of the interpretive problems stem from the identification of a so-called "Boskop" race. Boskop itself is a large, thick-vaulted faceless cranium, found in 1913. R. Dart expanded the concept to include other materials in 1923, and by 1937 A. Galloway defined the "type" as a wide-ranging racial group ancestral to living Bushmen. The cultural associations were thought to be Middle Stone Age. Although the cultural associations are now discredited, and many workers have come to realize that there never was a definable "Boskop type," as long as the concept was accepted, the search for "Negro" ancestry was necessarily pushed into the Middle Stone Age. The interpretation of even further removed specimens, such as Singa and Asselar, as "Boskopoid" left neither a reasonable place or anything but a very ancient time for seeking this ancestry.

The argument presented here is that the Bushman/"Negroid" separation is a recent one, probably not extending to much before the post-Pleistocene. Earlier than this, populations were more archaic in appearance and in all areas to some extent combined features of both living groups. This contention essentially parallels conclusions drawn by Tobias, Rightmire, de Villiers, and Wells. It is Rightmire, more than any other worker, who has argued for a more generalized model of "Negro" origins through his demonstration that Leakey's interpretation of "Caucasoid" affinities for the East African post-Pleistocene specimens was incorrect. These specimens associate as "Negroids," and not Bushmen or Mediterraneans. Failure to appreciate this in the past stemmed from a typological view which ignored the normal presence of variability.

Rightmire suggested that the Mesolithic inhabitants of East Africa were recognizably "Negro." Yet their earlier identification as non-"Negro" indicates that these specimens differ from modern populations. My examination of the even earlier Late Stone Age materials from the Turkana area would extend this interpretation into the past, arguing that these earlier specimens, with their robust features associated with big-game hunting, represent forms from which present populations evolved through gracilization. However, the issue will remain unsettled, and the problems of relating East and West Africa cannot be resolved until a comparable series of ancient specimens is discovered in West Africa and better archaeological associations and dating are available for all the materials. Nonetheless, "Negro" origins seem to be anything but a mystery. Reasonable hypotheses regarding the where, when, and why of "Negro" origins seem no better or worse than the hypotheses regarding the origins of other major geographic groups.

FURTHER READINGS

BAKER, J. R. 1968. Cro-Magnon Man, 1868-1968. *Endeavour* 27:87-90.
  Some of the history surrounding the Cro Magnon discoveries.

VON BONIN, G. 1935. European Races of the Upper Paleolithic. *Human Biology* 7:196-221.
  Discussion of the European Upper Paleolithic material, emphasizing the postcrania, which addresses the question of the sample's homogeneity.

BRACE, C. L. 1978. Tooth Reduction in the Orient. *Science*.
  Presentation of the model relating tooth size reduction to technological innovations.

BUTZER, K. W. 1977. Environment, Culture, and Human Evolution. *American Scientist* 65:572-584.
  A general paper considering the relation of environment and adaptation to human evolution, including discussion of some late Pleistocene changes.

CARLSON, D. S., and D. P. VAN GERVEN. 1977. Masticatory Function and Post-Pleistocene Evolution in Nubia. *American Journal of Physical Anthropology* 46:495-506.
  Presentation of the model relating dental and cranial changes in Nubia to masticatory functions.

FRAYER, D. W. 1977. Metric Dental Change in the European Upper Paleolithic and Mesolithic. *American Journal of Physical Anthropology* 46:109-120.
  A discussion of late Pleistocene dental evolution in Europe and its possible cause.

HARRISON, T. 1965. 50,000 Years of Stone Age Culture in Borneo. *Annual Report of the Smithsonian Institution for 1964*, pp. 521-530.
  Niah and the circumstances of its discovery.

JOCHIM, M. A. 1976. *Hunter-Gatherer Subsistence and Settlement: A Predictive Model.* Academic Press, New York.

Detailed presentation of an important model relating human ecology and behavior that can be applied to the later Upper Pleistocene.

JONES, R. 1973. Emerging Picture of Pleistocene Australians. *Nature* 246:278–281.

Review of the recent developments in Australian prehistory.

KIRK, R. L., and A. G. THORNE, EDS. 1976. *The Origin of the Australians.* Australian Institute of Aboriginal Studies, Canberra.

The volume consists of the proceedings of a 1974 symposium on Australian origins. The papers included approach origins through analyses of the Australian and Indonesian fossil material and the distribution of features in living Australian aboriginal populations.

KLEIN, R. G. 1974. Ice-Age Hunters of the Ukraine. *Scientific American* 230(6):96–105.

Comparison of Middle and Upper Paleolithic adaptations of the Ukraine mammoth hunters.

———. 1975. Ecology of Stone Age Man at the Southern Tip of Africa. *Archaeology* 28:238–247.

Focus on the changing adaptive efficiency in a limited region during the later Middle and Late Stone Ages.

RIGHTMIRE, G. P. 1975. Problems in the Study of Later Pleistocene Man in Africa. *American Anthropologist* 77(1):28–52.

Probably the best review and discussion of Upper Pleistocene evolution in Africa.

———. 1979. Implications of Border Cave Skeletal Remains for Later Pleistocene Human Evolution. *Current Anthropology* 20:23–35.

An up-to-date discussion on the importance of these human remains. The paper, and the comments attached to it, illustrate the importance of dating in morphological analysis and outline the particular problems at this site.

RIQUET, R. 1970. La Race Cro-Magnon, Abus de Langage ou Réalité Objective? In *L'Homme de cro-Magnon,* eds. G. Camps and G. Oliver. Arts et Métiers Graphiques, Paris, pp. 37–58.

A thoughtful discussion of the variability in Upper Paleolithic Europeans.

SACKETT, J. R. 1973. Style, Function, and Artifact Variability in Paleolithic Assemblages. In *The Explanation of Cultural Change,* ed. C. Renfrew. University of Pittsburgh Press, Pittsburgh, pp. 317–328.

Sackett presents an alternative to the more typological approach that is common in interpreting the European Upper Paleolithic archaeological sequence, with far-reaching implications for understanding the changing adaptive patterns.

SMITH, F. H. 1976. The Skeletal Remains of the Earliest Americans: A Survey. *Tennessee Anthropologist* 1:116–147.

A comprehensive review of the earliest dated Amerinds and the problems surrounding their interpretation.

STRINGER, C. B. 1979. A Re-evaluation of the Fossil Human Calvaria from Singa, Sudan. *Bulletin of the British Museum of Natural History (Geology)* 32:77–83.

A comparison of the skull to other African earlier sapiens remains.

THORNE, A. G., and P. G. MACUMBER. 1972. Discoveries of Late Pleistocene Man at Kow Swamp, Australia. *Nature* 238:316–319.

Announcement and brief description of the Kow Swamp remains.

VERNEAU, R. 1924. La Race Neanderthal et la Race de Grimaldi; Leur Role dans l'Humanite. *Journal of the Royal Anthropological Institute* 54:211–230.

An early statement of the position of the Grimaldi remains in human evolution.

DE VILLIERS, H. 1973. Human Skeletal Remains from Border Cave, Ingwavuma District, Kwazulu, South Africa. *Annals of the Transvaal Museum* 28(13):229–256.

Discussion of the Border Cave remains and their importance in African evolution.

VLČEK, E. 1967. Morphological Relations of the Fossil Human Types Brno and Cro Magnon in the European Late Pleistocene. *Folia Morphologica* 15:214–221.

Description of the Upper Paleolithic finds, considering the question of whether distinct races were represented in Europe.

WEIDENREICH, F. 1939. On the Earliest Representatives of Modern Mankind Recovered on the Soil in East Asia. *Peking Natural History Bulletin* 13:161–174.

Discussion of the remains from the Upper Cave at Choukoutien and their importance.

———. 1947. Facts and Speculations Concerning the Origin of *Homo sapiens. American Anthropologist* 49:187–203.

Weidenreich's model of *Homo sapiens* origins.

WOO, JU-KANG. 1956. Human Fossils Found in China and Their Significance in Human Evolution. *Scientia Sinica* 5:389–398.

Review of the more recently discovered late Pleistocene Chinese fossils.

———. 1959. Human Fossils Found in Liukiang, Kwangsi, China. *Vertebrata Palasiatica* 3:109–118.

Brief description of the Liukiang cranium.

CHAPTER FOURTEEN

Some Final Comments

 ith the appearance of modern *Homo sapiens* populations, evolution did not cease. To the contrary, evolutionary change has continued up to the present time, and there is every reason to believe it will continue. As in the recent past, the species is characterized by both local changes and widespread trends. Since the end of the Pleistocene, a surprising amount of change has occurred considering the short span involved. Generally, the widespread trends lie in continued gracilization (especially in males) and reduction. Important characteristics that reduce or become less robust are the dentition and related masticatory structures in the face and mandible, skeletal structures supporting strength- or activity-related behaviors, and the expression of sexual dimorphism.

Within these broad directions of change, rates have varied considerably among populations. Thus continent-wide clines for features such as tooth size have been demonstrated for aboriginal Australia, aboriginal America, and Southeast Asia. While the variation is continuous, its range can be very large.

Moreover, other factors have added to the tendency for accumulating local differences. Habitat partitioning resulting from the effective strategies for niche utilization that evolved toward the end of the Pleistocene seems to have led to cultural mechanisms which limit gene flow between adjacent groups that are differently adapted. Drift may have played a role in the additional populational differences that subsequently accumulated. Indeed, for many living populations, a practiced morphologist can often determine an individual's place of origin within a small geographic area (just as a linguist may from subtle differences in dialect).

One of the main characteristics of post-Pleistocene morphological evolution is its speed. Evolutionary rates begin a noticeable acceleration toward the end of the Pleistocene, and the rate of acceleration itself increases throughout the post-Pleistocene. This phenomenon, as much as any other, underscores the positive feedback that exists between cultural change and changes in human morphology. There is every reason to believe that the same processes of gene change in response to the

353

forces of evolution are still taking place. Yet the evolution of human culture has brought us to a point where future evolutionary change may not be predictable from the patterns of the past.

The simplest possible summary of the past 4 million years of human evolution is probably that brains expanded, teeth and faces decreased in size, and a great deal of muscular strength was lost. A more detailed analysis of the fossil material shows that this is not exactly what happened: the changes were not always constant, and a number of other important changes also took place. Nonetheless, as a simplified statement, it probably stands correct. Similarly, the search for causality can be (perhaps) simplified, or discussed in its fullest detail.

Perhaps the best-known attempt by a paleoanthropologist to reduce human evolutionary changes to a single cause was that of F. Weidenreich. He related the reductions in jaws and teeth to growth restrictions resulting from expanding brain size. He argued that all cranial and facial changes were correlated. As the brain expanded, anterior rotation of the face was inhibited, reducing facial prognathism. He felt that the demands of the expanding braincase prevented excess growth of the face and excess development of the teeth. However, the hypothesis of an interdependence between the development of these structures appears to be incorrect.

Another attempt to reduce the evolutionary process to a single cause, and one with an even longer history, is the proposal of neoteny, or fetalization (the retention of ancestral juvenile characteristics by adult descendants). This has been stated in its most recent form by S. Gould, who provided a detailed history of its intellectual origins and development. Gould argued that human evolutionary changes are a consequence of retardation in development. In his view, the retardation itself is the major cause of evolutionary change. Reduction of browridges and of the face, jaws, and teeth is seen as a consequence of retarded growth whereby the ancestral adult condition never appears in the descendants. Expansion of cranial capacity is considered a result of retarded maturation; the brain grows rapidly for a longer period because the time of growth deceleration is retarded. This hypothesis might *seem* to have high explanatory power, especially given the early evidence for delayed maturation in hominids. However, maturational delay occurs earlier in hominid evolution than any of the other changes attributed to retardation. Moreover, the concept, while probably correct in theory, seems to be too general to be explanatory. All evolutionary changes are probably expressed as the retardation or acceleration of localized growth. By explaining everything, the hypothesis actually explains nothing, since ultimately the *reasons* for the specific changes must become the required explanations. For instance, if brain-size expansion results from a retardation of the process stopping brain growth, one would want to know the specific advantages of larger brain size in order to explain this change.

My own attempt to simplify the human evolutionary process reduces to a single concept: culture. The importance of culture may extend to the very point of hominid origins, possibly accounting for the survival of only one of the otherwise successful, widespread ramapithecine species. The consequences of dependence on culture and technology for survival is evident in hominids as early as the australopithecines, expressed in their delayed maturation (with its demographic consequences), neural reorganization, canine reduction and change in function, and possibly also bipedalism. (The australopithecines were bipedal, but the antiquity of this locomotor pattern is not clear.) Continued feedback between culture and technology on the one hand and human morphology on the other is evident in the changes associated with the early evolution of *Homo* and the appearance of *Homo erectus*. Indeed, virtually every important evolutionary development in the Pleistocene seems tied to the interrelated complex of culture, technology, and morphology, even to the point of modern *Homo sapiens* origins and the appearance of intensive big-game hunting using projectile weapons. Once hominids embarked upon the evolutionary path of dependence on culture for survival, there is a certain inevitability to the course of human evolution. Advantageous change came to mean the evolution of more complex cultural behavior.

Increased behavioral complexity in hominids seems to have involved the expansion of neurological prestructuring and subsequently had both neurological and morphological consequences. These consequences, in turn, expanded the potential for further change in the same direction because the directions of effective improvement were limited by past change. The result was continual selection for greater behavioral complexity. In one respect, culture became both the *mode* and the *object* of adaptation.

Yet the underlying basis for cultural change is very different from the basis for morphological change. Morphological change depends on the forces of evolution acting on existing gene pools. It is tied to the past only in that the genetic variation in the gene pool, which provides the basis of future change, is the result of past history and adaptation. Evolutionary change is linear, and is proportional to the strength of evolutionary forces. The greater the amount of selection, the more rapid the change. But Plio-Pleistocene evolutionary changes have not involved adding *more* genetic material. Instead, the genetic material already present has changed. Cultural change, on the other hand, is tied to the past in a very different way. Cultural change is additive and cumulative. What can change depends on what is already known. The reason Neandertals did not invent atomic bombs is not that they were "too dumb," but that too many ideas had yet to be added to the corpus of human knowledge. What this means is that the *rate* of cultural change must continuously accelerate, whereas the *rate* of morphological change can only respond in a linear way, as it has during the post-Pleistocene. Therefore, there must come a time when the former rate exceeds the latter. At some point, it becomes impossible for any individual within a population to learn the entire body of information that is passed from generation to generation.

C. L. Brace has proposed that this occurred toward the end of the Middle Paleolithic. According to Brace, once individuals can learn and utilize only part of the total cultural repertoire, there is no longer selection for widespread individual increases in intelligence. Instead, it is the occasional genius that becomes the important contributor to cultural change. Selection would then act to produce gene distributions within populations that increased the frequency of geniuses, rather than increasing average intelligence. Perhaps this is why there has been little or no substantive increase in brain size since the Neandertals.

The more rapid, and still accelerating, rate of cultural change (when compared with physical change) is perhaps the most important single feature of modern *Homo sapiens*. At the present time, it has become impossible for most specialists to be aware of every significant development in the narrowest of fields, let alone in the broader context of their interests. Technological change occurs so rapidly that innovations become obsolete before they can be produced commercially. In all, there is a growing gap between the changes in human culture and technology and the ability of gene pools to respond to these changes. To a greater and greater degree, the response itself has become cultural. However, this does not mean that human evolution has ceased; gene pools continue to change.

And what of our future? It seems both logical and appropriate to use the context of the past to speculate about our biological future. From my personal point of view, the direction of such speculations is constrained by two convictions which I hold: (1) that there *is* a future to speculate about and (2) that except in the most general sense, its course is unpredictable.

The first point may seem unduly optimistic in a world which measures the strength of nuclear arsenals by *how many times over* the population of another country could be extinguished. Yet it seems that even under the worst of circumstances, a nuclear war would have survivors, and whatever the level of their continued subsistence, the long-term effect would be to alter but not to eliminate future human evolution. A more rational and hopeful view is that there never will be a nuclear war.

Another long-term factor which some suggest could limit the future of the human race is the finite nature of resources on our planet. Yet human prehistory attests to the continued ability of our species to solve its adaptive problems and expand its niche. The fact is that both on our planet and in its immediate vicinity there are literally unlimited sources of energy whose utilization is already possible with current technology, let alone future developments. Optimism in this regard is a virtual certainty, and I believe that the strongest case can be made for the lack of any potential limitation due to diminishing energy and resources. Serious discussion is already underway regarding the construction of orbiting factories using solar energy and built from the moon's mineralogical resources. This is only the first step in what has been contemplated by way of utilizing the resources of our solar system.

In the future, biological change will be even more directly tied to technological change, and this places a limitation on specific predictions of our biological future which I believe is insurmountable—the possibility of predicting future technological innovations. One of the best examples of this is the now famous turn-of-the-century prediction that at the then-current rate of equine population expansion, New York City would be under 25 feet of horse manure by 1975. The ability to foresee technological developments must depend on knowing what technological developments are possible, and this knowledge *in itself* is the "discovery." Once it is known that a technological innovation is possible, the innovation will occur as the result of a greater or lesser amount of dogged effort.

It is easy to predict the development of pocket-sized battery-operated sophisticated computers, or the use of holography in accurately recording and experimenting with alterations in shape and form, because such developments are already technologically feasible, although not yet economically so. The key point is that they are *developments* and not *innovations*. Neither was foreseen by the many sophisticated science-fiction writers of the 1930s because they depended on innovations that had not yet occurred. Of the literally hundreds of earlier stories, books, and movies that dealt with the possibility of a space voyage to the moon before the fact, only one—a comic book story—predicted that the event would be televised around the world and that the first footsteps on the earth's satellite would be observed by millions. How reasonable and commonplace the TV picture seemed when it happened, and yet it was not predicted even a few years before the event, when it was already technologically feasible. The lack of foresight by the professional predictors is understandable in a developing technology such as ours in which the technologically feasible strains the imagination and the theoretically possible boggles the mind.

Biological speculations, in this context, have been mild and conservative. Will people become more intelligent, or less so? Both have been predicted and, in fact, projected on the basis of current gene pool changes. Will humans lose their third molars? all of their teeth? little toes? the appendix? Again, these changes have been predicted, and perhaps they will occur, but at present there is no way of knowing.

What makes these speculations conservative is the increasing likelihood that humans will ultimately be able to control the exact course of biological change through the direct manipulation of genetic material (a sort of directed mutation) or the addition of new and biologically unique genetic information through recombinant DNA. Serious discussions of these possibilities are just beginning, and the view that widespread directed genetic alteration will never be advantageous or economically feasible is probably incorrect.

If the future is not actually predictable, at least there is every reason to believe it will be interesting.

FURTHER READINGS

Berry, A. 1974. *The Next Ten Thousand Years*. Mentor, New York.

    The optimistic alternative.

Brace, C. L., and P. E. Mahler. 1971. Post-Pleistocene Changes in the Human Dentition. *American Journal of Physical Anthropology* 34:191-204.

    One of the few attempts to account for post-Pleistocene change in an evolutionary context. (Also see the Carlson and van Gerven reference in Chapter 13.)

Ferembach, D. 1974. Les Hommes de l'Epipaleolithique et du Mesolithique de la France et du Nord-Ouest du Bassin Méditerranéen. *Bulletin et Mémoires de la Société d'Anthropologie de Paris*, Serie 13, 2:201-236.

    An argument for continuous evolutionary change.

Gould, S. J. 1976. *Ontogeny and Phylogeny*. Harvard University Press, Cambridge.

    The retardation hypothesis, immersed in a general historical discussion.

Hunt, E. E., Jr. 1960. The Continuing Evolution of Modern Man. *Cold Spring Harbor Symposium on Quantitative Biology* 24:245-254.

————. 1961. Malocclusion and Civilization. *American Journal of Orthodontics* 47:406-422.

    Two papers discussing continuous post-Pleistocene evolutionary changes.

Kahn, H. 1961. *On Thermonuclear War*. Princeton University Press, Princeton.

    The pessimistic alternative.

LEACH, G. 1970. *The Biocrats.* McGraw-Hill, New York.
   On the implications of genetic alterations.

WADE, N. 1977. *The Ultimate Experiment: Man-Made Evolution.* Walker, New York.
   While focusing on gene splicing and its implications, the book discusses the many potentials of directed evolutionary change in our species that are now (or almost now) state of the art.

WEIDENREICH, F. 1941. The Brain and Its Role in the Phylogenetic Transformation of the Human Skull. *Transactions of the American Philosophical Society* 31:321–442.
   The hypothesis of correlated change attributed to brain size expansion.

———. 1945. The Brachycephalization of Recent Mankind. *Southwestern Journal of Anthropology* 1:1–54.
   Discussion of post-Pleistocene cranial changes.

Bibliography

The references presented here are supplementary to those that follow each chapter. Some are more complete or technical presentations of materials referenced in chapters, while others relate to points raised in the text discussions. This bibliography is designed to allow further research and readings on both an introductory and a more advanced level. It is arranged in seven categories.

1. Catalogues: these relate the basic information on human fossils—discoverer, associations, date, parts represented, references to descriptive and analytical publications, location of the remains, and availability of casts.
2. General: references to the broad aspects of human evolution not included in the chapter bibliographies.
3. Descriptive: basic descriptions of the most important fossil remains.
4. Edited collections: volumes of readings mainly concerning human paleontology.
5. Archaeology, geology, and dating: specific relevant references ranging from general presentations to detailed analyses of important problems.
6. Evolutionary models and relationships: references particularly concerned with the evolutionary process and specific evolutionary relationships in the hominid fossil record.
7. Topical: references to interpretive problems and procedures.

CATALOGUES

OAKLEY, K. P., and B. G. CAMPBELL. 1977. *Catalogue of Fossil Hominids*, Part I: Africa, rev. ed. British Museum (Natural History), London.
———, and T. I. MOLLESON. 1971. *Catalogue of Fossil Hominids*, Part II: Europe. British Museum (Natural History), London.

———. 1975. *Catalogue of Fossil Hominids*, Part III: Americas, Asia, Australia. British Museum (Natural History), London.
PROTSCH, R. 1978. *Catalog of Fossil Hominids of North America*. Fischer, Stuttgart.

GENERAL

BOULE, M. 1923. *Les Hommes Fossiles*. Masson, Paris.
BRACE, C. L., and M. F. A. MONTAGU. 1977. *Human Evolution*, 2nd ed. Macmillan, New York.
BRACE, C. L., H. NELSON, and N. KORN. 1971. *Atlas of Fossil Man*. Holt, Rinehart, and Winston, New York.
CAMPBELL, B. G. 1976. *Humankind Emerging*. Little Brown, Boston.
CONSTABLE, G. 1973. *The Neanderthals*. Time-Life, New York.
COON, C. S. 1963. *The Origin of Races*. Knopf, New York.
———. 1965. *The Living Races of Man*. Knopf, New York.
DAY, M. H. 1977. *Guide to Fossil Man, rev. ed.* University of Chicago Press, Chicago.
HOWELL, F. C. 1965. *Early Man*. Time-Life, New York.
HOWELLS, W. W. 1973. *Evolution of the Genus Homo*. Addison-Wesley, Reading.
JOLLY, C. J., and F. PLOG. 1976. *Physical Anthropology and Archaeology*. Knopf, New York.
KEITH, A. 1925. *The Antiquity of Man, rev. ed.* 2 vols. Lippincott, Philadelphia.
———. 1931. *New Discoveries Relating to the Antiquity of Man*. Williams and Norgate, London.
VON KOENIGSWALD, G. H. R. 1976. *The Evolution of Man, rev. ed.* University of Michigan Press, Ann Arbor.
KRAUS, B. S., R. E. JORDAN, and L. ABRAMS. 1969. *Dental Anatomy and Occlusion*. Williams and Wilkins, Baltimore.
LEAKEY, L. S. B. 1961. *Adam's Ancestors*, 4th ed. Harper & Row, New York.
———, and V. M. GOODALL. 1969. *Unveiling Man's Origins*. Schenkman, Cambridge.
LEAKEY, R. E. F., and R. LEWIN. 1977. *Origins*. Macdonald and Janes, London.
LE GROS CLARK, W. E. 1964. *The Fossil Evidence for Human Evolution*, rev. ed. University of Chicago Press, Chicago.

Phenice, T. W. 1972. *Hominid Fossils: An Illustrated Key.* W. C. Brown, Dubuque.

Pilbeam, D. 1972. *Ascent of Man.* MacMillan, New York.

Poirier, F. E. 1977. *Fossil Evidence: The Human Evolutionary Journey.* Mosby, St. Louis.

Romer, A. S. 1966. *Vertebrate Paleontology,* 3rd ed. University of Chicago Press, Chicago.

Swindler, D. R., and C. D. Wood. 1973. *An Atlas of Primate Gross Anatomy: Baboon, Chimpanzee, and Man.* University of Washington Press, Seattle.

Tobias, P. V. 1971. *The Brain in Hominid Evolution.* Columbia, New York.

Weidenreich, F. 1946. *Apes, Giants, and Man.* University of Chicago Press, Chicago.

Werth, E. 1928. *Der Fossile Mensch.* Borntraeger, Berlin.

DESCRIPTIVE

Anderson, J. E. 1968. Late Paleolithic Skeletal Remains from Nubia. In *The Prehistory of Nubia,* ed. F. Wendorf. Southern Methodist University Press, Dallas, Vol. 2, pp. 996–1040.

Angel, L. 1972. A Middle Paleolithic Temporal Bone from Darra-I-Kur, Afghanistan. *Transactions of the American Philosophical Society* 62(4):54–84.

Arambourg, C. 1963. Le Gisement de Ternifine I. Archives de L'Institut de Paléontologie Humaine. *Mémoire* 32:37–190.

———, and P. Biberson. 1956. Fossil Human Remains from the Paleolithic Site of Sidi Abderrahman (Morocco). *American Journal of Physical Anthropology* 14:267–290.

Behm-Blanke, G. 1960. Altsteinzeithliche Rastplätze im Traveringebiet Taubach, Weimar, Ehringsdorf. *Alt-Thüringen* 4:1–245.

Billy, G. 1976. Les Hommes du Paléolithique Supérieur. In *La Préhistoire Francaise,* ed. H. de Lumley. Centre National de la Recherche Sciéntifique, Paris, Vol. 1, pp. 595–603.

de Bonis, L., and J. Melentis. 1977. Les Primates Hominoides du Vallésien de Macédonie (Grèce). Étude de La Machoire Inférieure. *Geobios* 10:849–885.

———. 1977. Un Nouviau Genre de Primate Hominoide dan le Vallésien (Miocène Supérieur) de Macédoine. *Comptes Rendus de l'Academie des Sciences,* Série D, 284:1393–1396.

Boule, M. 1913. *L'homme fossile de La Chapelle-aux-Saints.* Mason, Paris.

———, and H. Vallois. 1932. L'Homme Fossile d'Asselar. Archives de l'Institut de Paléontologie Humaine, *Memoire* 9:1–90.

Bowler, J. M., A. G. Thorne, and H. A. Polach. 1972. Pleistocene Man in Australia: Age and Significance of the Mungo Skeleton. *Nature* 240:48–50.

Brain, C. K. 1970. New Finds at the Swartkrans Australopithecine Site. *Nature* 225:1112–1118.

Broom, R., and J. T. Robinson. 1952. *Swartkrans Ape-Man.* Transvaal Museum Memoir 6, Pretoria.

———, and G. W. H. Schepers. 1950. *Sterkfontein Ape-Man Plesianthropus.* Transvaal Museum Memoir 4, Pretoria.

Broom, R., and G. W. H. Schepers. 1946. *The South African Fossil Ape-Men, the Australopithecinae.* Transvaal Museum Memoir 2, Pretoria.

Brothwell, D. R. 1960. Upper Pleistocene Human Skull from Niah Caves. *Sarawak Museum Journal* 9:323–349.

Chang, Kwang-chih. 1962. New Evidence on Fossil Man in China. *Science* 136:749–60.

Chia, Lan-po. 1957. Notes on the Human and Some Other Mammalian Remains from Changyang, Hupei. *Vertebrata Palasiatica* 1:247–252.

Chiu, Chung-lang, Gu, Yü-min, Zhang, Yin-yun, and Chang, Shen-shui. 1973. Newly Discovered Sinanthropus Remains and Stone Artifacts at Choukoutien. *Vertebrata Palasiatica* 11(2):109–131.

Clark, J. D., K. P. Oakley, L. H. Well, and J. A. C. McClelland. 1947. New Studies on Rhodesian Man. *Journal of the Royal Anthropological Institute* 77:7–32.

Coppens, Y. 1966. An Early Hominid from Chad. *Current Anthropology* 7:584–585.

Dart, R. A. 1925. *Australopithecus africanus:* The Man-Ape of South Africa. *Nature* 115:195–9.

———. 1948. The Adolescent Mandible of *Australopithecus prometheus. American Journal of Physical Anthropology* 6:391–409.

———. 1957. The Second Adolescent (Female) Ilium of *Australopithecus prometheus. Journal of the Palaeontological Society of India* 2:73–82.

Day, M. H., R. E. F. Leakey, A. C. Walker, and B. A. Wood. 1976. New Hominids from East Turkana, Kenya. *American Journal of Physical Anthropology* 45:369–436.

Day, M. H., and T. Molleson. 1973. The Trinil Femora. In *Human Evolution,* ed. M. H. Day. *Symposia of the Society for the Study of Human Biology* 11:127–154.

Dubois, E. 1922. The Proto-Australian Fossil Man of Wadjak, Java. *Koninklijke Akademie Wetenschappen te Amsterdam* 23:1013–1051.

———. 1924. On the Principal Characters of the Cranium and the Brain, the Mandible and the Teeth of Pithecanthropus erectus. *Koninklijke Akademie Wetenschappen te Amsterdam,* Series B, 27:265–278.

Fraipont, J., and M. Lohest. 1887. La Race Humaine de Neanderthal ou de Canstadt en Belgique. *Archives de Biologie* 7:587–758

Gorjanovic-Kramberger, D. 1906. *Der Diluviale Mensch von Krapina in Kroatien: ein Beitrag zur Paläoanthropologie.* Weisbaden, Kriedel.

Gramly, R. M., and G. P. Rightmire, 1973. A Fragmentary Cranium and Dated Later Stone Age Assemblage from Lukenya Hill, Kenya. *Man* 8:571–579.

Heim, J. L. 1976. Les Hommes Fossiles de la Ferrassie. Vol. 1. *Archives de l'Institut Paleontologie Humaine Memoire* 35:1–331.

Henri-Martin, G. 1923. L'Homme Fossile de La Quina. *Archives de Morphologie Générale et Experimentale* 15:1–253.

Howell, F. C. 1969. Remains of Hominidae from Pliocene/Pleistocene Formations in the Lower Omo Basin, Ethiopia. *Nature* 223:1234–1239.

———. 1978. Hominidae. In *Evolution of African Mammals,*

eds. V. J. Maglio and H. B. S. Cooke. Harvard University Press, Cambridge, pp. 154-248.

HUGHES, A. R., and P. V. TOBIAS. 1977. A Fossil Skull Probably of the Genus *Homo* from Sterkfontein, Transvaal. *Nature* 265:310-312.

JACOB, T. 1975. Morphology and Paleoecology of Early Man in Java. In *Paleoanthropology: Morphology and Paleoecology*, ed. R. H. Tuttle. Mouton, The Hague, pp. 311-325.

JELINEK, J., J. PALIŠEK, and K. VALOCH. 1959. Der Fossile Mensch Brno II. *Anthropos* 9:17-22.

KLAATSCH, H., and O. HAUSER. 1910. Homo Aurignacensis Hauseri, ein Paläolithischer Skeletfund aus dem Untern Aurignacien der Station Combe-Capelle bei Montferrand (Périogord). *Praehistorische Zeitschrift* 1:273-338.

VON KOENIGSWALD, G. H. R. 1957. Remarks on *Gigantopithecus* and Other Hominid Remains from Southern China. *Koninklijke Akademie Wetenschappen te Amsterdam*, Series B, 60:153-159.

———. 1968. Observations on *Pithecanthropus* Mandibles from Sangiran, Central Java. *Proceedings of the Koninklijke Akademie van Wetenschappen, Amsterdam*, Series B, 71:1-9.

LEAKEY, L. S. B. 1935. *The Stone Age Races of Kenya.* Oxford University Press, Oxford.

———, and M. D. LEAKEY. 1964. Recent Discoveries of Fossil Hominids in Tanganyika: At Olduvai and Near Lake Natron. *Nature* 202:3-9.

LEAKEY, M. D., R. J. CLARKE, and L. S. B. LEAKEY. 1971. New Hominid Skull from Bed I, Olduvai Gorge, Tanzania. *Nature* 232:308-312.

LE GROS CLARK, W. E., K. P. OAKLEY, G. M. MORANT, W. B. R. KING, and C. F. C. HAWKES. 1938. Report of the Swanscombe Committee. *Journal of the Royal Anthropological Institute* 68:17-98.

LEROI-GOURHAN, A. 1958. Etude des Restes Humains Fossiles Prouvenant des Grottes d'Arcy-sur-Cure. *Annales de Paléontologie* 44:87-148.

DE LUMLEY, H., and M. A. DE LUMLEY. 1971. Découverte de Restes Humains Anténéandertaliens Datés du Debut Riss à la Caune de l'Arago (Tautavel, Pyrénées-Orientales). *Comptes Rendus de l'Academie des Sciences*, Série D, 272:1739-1742.

DE LUMLEY, M. A. 1972a. L'Os Iliaque Anténéandertalien de la Grotte du Prince. *Bulletin du Musée d'Anthropologie Préhistorique de Monaco* 18:89-112.

———. 1973. Anténéandertaliens et Néanderthaliens du Bassin Méditerranéen Occidental Européen. Etudes Quaternaires, Memoire 2.

LYNCH, T. F., and K. A. R. KENNEDY. 1970. Early Human Cultural and Skeletal Remains from Guitarrero Cave, Northern Peru. *Science* 169:1307-1309.

MACINTOSH, N. W. G. 1967. Fossil Man in Australia. *Australian Journal of Science* 30:86-98.

MATIEGKA, J. 1929. The Skull of the Fossil Man "Brno III" and the Cast of Its Interior. *Anthropologie* 7:90-107.

———. 1934. *Homo předmostensis fossilni člověk z Předmosti no Moravě I. Lebky.* Nákladem Česke Akademie věd a Uměni, Prague.

———. 1938. *Homo předmostensis fossilni člověk z Předmosti no Moravě II Ostatni časti kostrové.* Nákladem Česke Akademie věd a Uměni, Prague.

MORBECK, M. E. 1975. *Dryopithecus africanus* Forelimb. *Journal of Human Evolution* 4:39-46.

OVEY, C. D., ED. 1964. The Swanscombe Skull. Occasional Papers of the Royal Anthropological Institute, No. 20.

PATTE, É. 1955. *Les Néanderthaliens.* Masson, Paris.

———. 1962. *La Dentition des Néanderthaliens.* Masson, Paris.

RAK, Y., and F. C. HOWELL. 1978. Cranium of a Juvenile *Australopithecus boisei* from the Lower Omo Basin, Ethiopia. *American Journal of Physical Anthropology* 48:345-366.

SAUSSE, F. 1975. La Mandibule Atlanthropienne de la Carriére Thomas I (Casablance). *L'Anthropologie* 79:81-112.

SCHWALBE, G. 1901. Der Neanderthalschädel. *Bonner Jahrbücher*, No. 106, pp. 1-72.

SERGI, S. 1944. Craniometria e Craniografia del Primo Paleanthropo di Saccopastore. *Richerche de Morfologia* 21:733-791.

———. 1948. Il Cranio des Secondo Paleanthropo de Saccopastore. *Palaeontographia Italica* 42:4-164.

———. 1974. *Il Cranio Neandertaliano del Monte Circeo (Circeo 1).* Accademia Nazionale dei Lincei, Rome.

SMITH, F. H. 1976. A Fossil Hominid Frontal from Velika Pećina (Croatia) and a Consideration of Upper Pleistocene Hominids from Yugoslavia. *American Journal of Physical Anthropology* 44:127-134.

THOMA, A. 1967. Human Teeth from the Lower Paleolithic of Hungary. *Zeitschrift für Morphologie und Anthropologie* 58:152-180.

———. 1969. Biometrische Studie über das Occipitale von Vertesszöllös. *Zeitschrift für Morphologie und Anthropologie* 60:229-241.

THORNE, A. G. 1971. Mungo and Kow Swamp: Morphological Variation in Pleistocene Australians. *Mankind* 8:85-89.

TOBIAS, P. V. 1966. A Re-examination of the Kedung Brubus Mandible. *Zoölogische Medeelingen* 41:307-320.

———. 1973. New Developments in Hominid Paleontology in South and East Africa. *Annual Review of Anthropology* 2:311-334.

TRINKAUS, E. 1976. The Morphology of European and Southwest Asian Neandertal Pubic Bones. *American Journal of Physical Anthropology* 44:95-104.

———. 1978. Dental Remains from the Shanidar Adult Neandertals. *Journal of Human Evolution* 7:369-382.

VALLOIS, H. V. 1941. Nouvelles Recherches sur le Squelette de Chancelade. *L'Anthropologie* 50:165-202.

———. 1956. The Pre-Mousterien Mandible from Montmaurin. *American Journal of Physical Anthropology* 14:319-323.

———, and G. BILLY. 1965. Nouvelles Recherches sur les Hommes Fossiles de l'Abri de Cro-Magnon. *L'Anthropologie* 69:47-74, 249-272.

VERNEAU, R. 1906. *Les Grottes de Grimaldi.* Vol. II, Anthropologie. Monaco, pp. 1-212.

DE VILLIERS, H. 1972. The First Fossil Human Skeleton from South West Africa. *Transactions of the Royal Society of South Africa* 40:187-196.

VLČEK, E. 1969. *Neandertaler der Tschechoslowakei*. Verlag der Tschechoslowakischen Akademie die Wissenschaften, Prague.

———, and D. MANIA. 1977. Ein Never Fund von *Homo erectus* in Europa: Bilzingsleben (DDR). *Anthropologie* 15:159–169.

WANG, LING-HONG, HAN, KANG-XIN, and HSU, CHUN-HUA. 1975. Australopithecine teeth associated with *Gigantopithecus*. *Vertebrata Palasiatica* 13:81–88.

WEIDENREICH, F. 1936. The Mandibles of *Sinanthropus pekinensis*: A Comparative Study. *Palaeontologia Sinica*, Series D, Vol. 7, Fascile 3.

———. 1937. The Dentition of *Sinanthropus pekinensis*: A Comparative Odontography of the Hominids. *Palaeontologia Sinica*, New Series D, 1 (Whole Series 101): 1–80.

———. 1941. The Extremity Bones of *Sinanthropus pekinensis*. *Palaeontologia Sinica*, New Series D, 5 (Whole Series 116).

———. 1943. The Skull of *Sinanthropus pekinensis*: A Comparative Study on a Primitive Hominid Skull. *Palaeontologia Sinica*, New Series D, 10 (Whole Series 127).

WEINERT, H. 1939. *Africanthropus njarasensis*. Zeitschrift für Morphologie und Anthropologie 38:252–308.

WELLS, L. H. 1947. A Note on the Broken Maxillary Fragment from the Broken Hill Cave. *Journal of the Royal Anthropological Institute* 77:11–12.

———. 1951. The Fossil Human Skull from Singa. *Fossil Mammals of Africa* 2:29–42.

WOLPOFF, M. H. 1979. The Krapina Dental Remains. *American Journal of Physical Anthropology* 50:67–114.

WOO, JU-KANG. 1964. Mandible of *Sinanthropus lantianensis*. *Current Anthropology* 5:98–101.

EDITED COLLECTIONS: PRIMARY PALEOANTHROPOLOGY

BORDES, F. 1972. *The Origin of* Homo sapiens. UNESCO, Paris.

BRACE, C. L., and J. METRESS. 1973. *Man in Evolutionary Perspective*. Wiley, New York.

COPPENS, Y., F. C. HOWELL, G. L. ISAAC, and R. E. F. LEAKEY. 1976. *Earliest Man and Environments in the Lake Rudolf Basin*. University of Chicago Press, Chicago.

HEBERER, G. 1965. *Menschliche Abstammungslehre*. Fischer, Stuttgart.

HOWELL, F. C., and F. BOURLIERE. 1963. *African Ecology and Human Evolution*. Aldine, Chicago.

HOWELLS, W. W. 1962. *Ideas on Human Evolution: Selected Essays 1949–61*. Harvard University Press, Cambridge.

ISAAC, G. L., and E. R. MCCOWN. 1976. *Human Origins: Louis Leakey and the East African Evidence*. Benjamin, Menlo Park.

VON KOENIGSWALD, G. H. R. ED. 1958. *Hundert Jahre Neanderthaler*. Böhlau, Köln.

KURTH, G. 1968. *Evolution and Hominisation*, rev. ed. Fischer, Stuttgart.

LEAKEY, L. S. B., and J. and S. POST. 1971. *Adam or Ape*. Schenkman, Cambridge.

TUTTLE, R. H. 1975a. *Paleoanthropology: Morphology and Paleoecology*. Mouton, The Hague.

———. 1975b. *Primate Functional Morphology and Evolution*. Mouton, The Hague.

WARREN, K. B. 1951. *Origin and Evolution of Man*. Cold Spring Harbor Symposia on Quantitative Biology 15. Science Press, Lancaster.

WASHBURN, S. L. 1961. *Social Life of Early Man*. Viking Fund Publication 31. Aldine, New York.

———. 1963. *Classification and Human Evolution*. Aldine, New York.

———, and P. DOLHINOW. 1968–1978. *Perspectives on Human Evolution*. 4 vols. Holt, Rinehart and Winston, New York.

ARCHAEOLOGY, GEOLOGY, AND DATING

BADA, J. L., and P. MASTERS HELFMAN. 1976. Application of Amino Acid Racemization Dating in Paleoanthropology and Archaeology. In *Datations Absolues et Analyses Isotropiques en Préhistoire; Méthodes et Limites*, ed. J. Labeyrie and C. Lalou. CNRS, Paris, pp. 39–62.

BEAUMONT, P. B., and J. C. VOGEL. 1972. On a New Radiocarbon Chronology for Africa South of the Equator. *African Studies* 31:65–90, 155–182.

BINFORD, L., and S. BINFORD. 1969. Stone Tools and Human Behavior. *Scientific American* 220(4):70–84.

BINFORD, S. R. 1968. A Structural Comparison of Disposal of the Dead in the Mousterian and the Upper Paleolithic. *Southwest Journal of Anthropology* 24:139–154.

BORDAZ, J. 1970. *Tools of the Old and New Stone Age*. Natural History Press, Garden City.

BORDES, F. 1961. Mousterian Cultures in France. *Science* 134:803–810.

BUTZER, K. W. 1971. *Environment and Archaeology*, rev. ed. Aldine, Chicago.

CHARD, C. S. 1975. *Man in Prehistory*, 2nd ed. McGraw-Hill, New York.

CLARK, J. D. 1970. *The Prehistory of Africa*. Praeger, New York.

COLE, S. 1963. *The Prehistory of East Africa*. MacMillan, New York.

COLES, J. M., and E. S. HIGGS. 1969. *The Archaeology of Early Man*. Penguin, Middlesex.

COX, A., G. B. DALRYMPLE, and R. R. DOELL. 1967. Reversals of the Earth's Magnetic Field. *Scientific American* 216(2):44–54.

CROWELL, J. C., and L. A. FRAKES. 1970. Phanerozoic Glaciation and the Causes of Ice Ages. *American Journal of Science* 268:193–224.

EWING, M. 1971. The Late Cenozoic History of the Atlantic Basin and Its Bearing on the Cause of the Ice Ages. In *Late Cenozoic Glacial Ages*, ed. K. Turekian. Yale University Press, New Haven, pp. 565–574.

HAHN, J. 1973. Das Aurignacien in Mittel- und Osteuropa. *Acta Praehistorica et Archaeologica* 3:77–107.

HOPKINS, D. M. 1973. Sea Level History in Beringia During the Past 250,000 Years. *Quaternary Research* 3:520–540.

HOWELL, F. C. 1966. Observations on the Earlier Phases of the European Lower Paleolithic. *American Anthropologist* (special publication) 68 (part 2, no. 2): 83–201.

ISAAC, G. L. 1972. Chronology and the Tempo Change During the Pleistocene. In *Calibration of Hominoid Evolution*, eds. W. W. Bishop and J. A. Miller. Scottish Academic Press, University of Toronto Press, Edinburgh, pp. 381–430.

———. 1976. Plio-Pleistocene Artifact Assemblages from East Rudolf, Kenya. In *Earliest Man and Environments in the Lake Rudolf Basin*, eds. Y. Coppens, F. C. Howell, G. L. Isaac, and R. E. F. Leakey. University of Chicago Press, Chicago, pp. 552-564.

JELINEK, A., ET AL. 1973. New excavations at the Tabun Cave, Mt. Carmel, Israel, 1967-1972: A preliminary report. *Paléorient* 1:151-183.

KLEIN, R. G. 1969. *Man and Culture in the Late Pleistocene.* Chandler, San Francisco.

———. 1975b. The Relevance of Old World Archaeology to the First Entry of Man into the New World. *Quaternary Research* 5:391-394.

KRIEGER, A. D. 1964. Early Man in the New World. In *Prehistoric Man in the New World*, eds. J. D. Jennings and E. Norbeck. University of Chicago Press, Chicago, pp. 23-81.

LAPORTE, L. F. 1977. Paleoenvironments and Paleoecology. *American Scientist* 65:720-728.

LEAKEY, M. D. 1971. Olduval Gorge, Vol. III. Excavations in Beds I and II, 1960-1963. Cambridge, London.

MARTIN, P. S. 1973. The Discovery of America. *Science* 179:969-974.

McINTIRE, A., ET AL. 1976. The Surface of the Ice-Age Earth. *Science* 191:1131-1137.

MISKOVSKY, J.-C. 1976. Les Changements Climatiques Durant le Pleistocène et l'Holocène Autour de la Méditerranee (Europe). In *Chronologie et Synchronisme dans la Préhistoire Circum-Méditerranéenne*, ed. G. Camps. CRRS, Paris, pp. 20-49.

MÜLLER-BECK, H. 1966. Paleohunters in America: Origins and Diffusion. *Science* 152:1191-1210.

OAKLEY, K. 1955. Fire as a Paleolithic Tool and Weapon. *Proceedings of the Prehistoric Society* 21:36-48.

RONEN, A. 1976. The Skhul Burials: An Archaeological Review. In *Les Sépultures Néandertaliennes*, ed. B. Vandermeersch. CNRS, Paris, pp. 27-40.

DE SONNEVILLE-BORDES, D. 1963. Upper Paleolithic Cultures in Western Europe. *Science* 142:347-355.

VALOCH, K. 1968. Evolution of the Paleolithic in Central and Eastern Europe. *Current Anthropology* 9:351-390.

———, ed. 1976. *Les Premières Industries de l'Europe.* CNRS, Paris.

VANDERMEERSCH, B., A. M. THILLIER, and S. KRUKOFF. 1976. Position Chronologique des Restes Humains de Fontéchevade. In *Le Peuplement Anténéandertalien de l'Europe*, ed. A. Thoma. CNRS, Paris, pp. 19-26.

WALKER, A. C. 1972. The Dissemination and Segregation of Early Primates in Relation to Continental Configuration. In *Calibration of Hominid Evolution*, eds. W. W. Bishop and J. A. Miller. Scottish Academic Press, Edinburgh, pp. 195-218.

EVOLUTIONARY MODELS AND RELATIONSHIPS

AIGNER, J. S. 1976. Chinese Pleistocene Cultural and Hominid Remains: A Consideration of Their Significance in Reconstructing the Pattern of Human Biocultural Development. In *Le Paléolithique Inférieur et Moyen en Inde, en Asia centrale, en Chine et dans le sud-est Asiatique*, ed. A. K. Gosh. CNRS, Paris, pp. 65-90.

AVIS, V. 1962. Brachiation: The Crucial Issue for Man's Ancestry. *Southwest Journal of Anthropology* 18:119-148.

BILSBOROUGH, A. 1972. Cranial Morphology of Neanderthal Man. *Nature* 237:351-352.

BIRDSELL, J. B. 1957. Some Population Problems Involving Pleistocene Man. *Cold Spring Harbor Symposia on Quantitative Biology* 22:47-69.

BRACE, C. L. 1973. Sexual Dimorphism in Human Evolution. In *Man in Evolutionary Perspective*, eds. C. L. Brace and J. Metress. Wiley, New York, pp. 238-254.

BRIGGS, L. C. 1968. Hominid Evolution in Northwest Africa and the Question of the North African "Neanderthaloids." *American Journal of Physical Anthropology* 29:377-386.

BROTHWELL, D. 1975. Adaptive Growth Rates Change as a Possible Explanation for the Distinctiveness of the Neanderthalers. *Journal of Archaeological Science* 2:161-163.

BROWN, W. L., and E. O. WILSON. 1956. Character Displacement. *Systematic Zoology* 5:49-64.

BRYAN, A. 1969. Early Man in America and the Late Pleistocene Chronology of Western Canada and Alaska. *Current Anthropology* 10:339-365.

CARTMILL, M. 1974. Rethinking Primate Origins. *Science* 184:436-443.

CLARKE, R. J., and F. C. HOWELL. 1972. Affinities of the Swartkrans 847 Hominid Cranium. *American Journal of Physical Anthropology* 37:319-336.

COLLINS, D. 1969. Culture Traditions and Environment of Early Man. *Current Anthropology* 10:267-316.

COURSEY, D. G. 1973. Hominid Evolution and Hypogeous Plant Foods. *Man* 8:634-635.

DAHLBERG, A. A. 1963. Dental Evolution and Culture. *Human Biology* 35:237-249.

DART, R. A. 1953. The Predatory Transition from Ape to Man. *International Anthropological and Linguistic Review* 1:201-218.

DRENNAN, M. R. 1956. Note on the Morphological Status of the Swanscombe and Fontechevade Skulls. *American Journal of Physical Anthropology* 14:73-83.

ECKHARDT, R. B. 1972. Population Genetics and Human Evolution. *Scientific American* 226(1):94-103.

FEREMBACH, D. 1972. L'Ancêtre de l'Homme du Paléolithique Supérieur Était-il Néandertalien? In *The Origin of Homo sapiens*, ed. F. Bordes. UNESCO, Paris, pp. 73-80.

———. 1973. L'Évolution Humaine au Proche-Orient. *Paléorient* 1:213-221.

FRAYER, D. W. 1973. *Gigantopithecus* and Its Relationship to *Australopithecus. American Journal of Physical Anthropology* 39:413-426.

———. 1976. A Reappraisal of *Ramapithecus. Yearbook of Physical Anthropology 1974* 18:19-30.

———. 1978. *Evolution of the Dentition in Upper Paleolithic and Mesolithic Europe.* University of Kansas, Publications in Anthropology 10.

GARN, S. M. 1963. Culture and the Direction of Human Evolution. *Human Biology* 35:221-235.

GENOVÉS, S. 1967b. Some Problems in the Physical Anthropological Study of the Peopling of America. *Current Anthropology* 8:297-312.

GREENE, D. L. 1970. Environmental Influences on Pleistocene Hominid Dental Evolution. *Bioscience* 20:276-279.

GREENFIELD, L. O. 1972. Sexual Dimorphism in *Dryopithecus africanus*. *Primates* 13:395-410.

HEMMER, H. 1969. A New View of the Evolution of Man. *Current Anthropology* 19:179-180.

HENNIG, W. 1966. *Phylogenetic Systematics*. University of Illinois Press, Urbana.

HOWELL, F. C. 1952. Pleistocene Glacial Ecology and the Evolution of "Classic Neandertal" Man. *Southwest Journal of Anthropology* 8:377-410.

――――. 1972. Recent Advances in Human Evolutionary Studies. In *Perspectives on Human Evolution*, Vol. II, eds. S. L. Washburn and P. Dolinow. Holt, Rinehart, and Winston, New York, pp. 51-128.

HRDLIČKA, A. 1937. Early Man in America: What Have the Bones to Say? In *Early Man*, ed. G. G. MacCurdy. Lippincott, Philadelphia, pp. 93-104.

KAY, R. F. 1977. The Evolution of Molar Occlusion in the Cercopithecidae and Early Catarrhines. *American Journal of Physical Anthropology* 46:327-352.

KINZEY, W. G. 1974. Ceboid Models for the Evolution of Hominoid Dentition. *Journal of Human Evolution* 3:193-203.

VON KOENIGSWALD, G. H. R. 1954. Pithecanthropus, Meganthropus, and the Australopithecinae. *Nature* 173:795-797.

――――. 1973. *Australopithecus, Meganthropus*, and *Ramapithecus*. *Journal of Human Evolution* 2:487-492.

LARNACH, S. L., and N. W. G. MACINTOSH. 1974. A Comparative Study of Solo and Australian Aboriginal Crania. In *Grafton Elliot Smith: The Man and His Work*, eds. A. P. Elkin and N. W. G. Macintosh. Sydney University Press, Sydney, pp. 95-102.

LIVINGSTONE, F. B. 1962. Reconstructing Man's Pliocene Pongid Ancestor. *American Anthropologist* 64:301-305.

LOVEJOY, C. O. 1970. The Taxonomic Status of the "Meganthropus" Mandibular Fragments from the Djetis Beds of Java. *Man* 5:228-236.

MAYR, E. 1963. *Animal Species and Evolution*. Belknap, Cambridge.

――――. 1974. Behavior Programs and Evolutionary Strategies. *American Scientist* 62:650-659.

McHENRY, H. 1975. Fossils and the Mosaic Nature of Human Evolution. *Science* 190:425-431.

OXNARD, C. E. 1975. The Place of the Australopithecines in Human Evolution: Grounds for Doubt? *Nature* 258:389-396.

PILBEAM, D., and S. J. GOULD. 1974. Size and Scaling in Human Evolution. *Science* 186:892-901.

RENSCH, B. 1960. The Laws of Evolution. In *The Evolution of Life*, ed. S. Tax. University of Chicago Press, Chicago, pp. 95-116

RIGHTMIRE, G. P. 1975. New Studies of Post-Pleistocene Human Skeletal Remains from the Rift Valley, Kenya. *American Journal of Physical Anthropology* 42:351-370.

ROBINSON, J. T. 1953. *Meganthropus*, Australopithecines and Hominids. *American Journal of Physical Anthropology* 11:1-38.

――――. 1954. The Genera and Species of the Australopithe-

cinae. *American Journal of Physical Anthropology* 12:181-200.

――――. 1955. Further Remarks on the Relationship Between *Meganthropus* and the Australopithecines. *American Journal of Physical Anthropology* 13:429-445.

――――. 1963. Adaptive Radiation in the Australopithecines and the Origin of Man. In *African Ecology and Human Evolution*, eds. F. C. Howell and F. Bourliere. Viking Fund Publication in Anthropology 36:385-416.

――――. 1966. The Distinctiveness of *Homo habilis*. *Nature* 209:957-960.

SANTA LUCA, A. P. 1978. A Re-examination of Presumed Neandertal-like Fossils. *Journal of Human Evolution* 7:619-636.

SARICH, V. M., and A. C. WILSON. 1967. Immunological Time Scale for Hominid Evolution. *Science* 158:1200-1203.

SCHALLER, G. B., and G. LOWTHER. 1969. The Relevance of Carnivore Behavior to the Study of Early Hominids. *Southwestern Journal of Anthropology* 25:307-341.

SIMONS, E. L., and D. PILBEAM. 1965. Preliminary Revision of the Dryopithecinae (Pongidae, Anthropoidea). *Folia Primatologia* 3:81-152.

SINGER, R. 1958. The Boskop "Race" Problem. *Man* 58:173-178.

SPUHLER, J. N. 1959. Somatic Paths to Culture. In *The Evolution of Man's Capacity for Culture*, ed. J. N. Spuhler. Wayne State University Press, Detroit, pp. 1-13.

STEWART, T. D. 1950. The Problem of the Earliest Claimed Representatives of *Homo sapiens*. *Cold Spring Harbor Symposia on Quantitative Biology* 15:97-107.

SWEDLUND, A. C. 1974. The Use of Ecological Hypotheses in Australopithecine Taxonomy. *American Anthropologist* 76:515-529.

THOMA, A. 1962. Le Déploiement Évolutif de l'Homo sapiens. *Anthropologia Hungarica* 5:1-111.

――――. 1964. Die Enstehung de Mongoliden. *Homo* 15:1-22.

――――. 1975. Were the Spy Fossils Evolutionary Intermediates Between Classic Neandertal and Modern Man? *Journal of Human Evolution* 4:387-410.

TINBERGEN, N. 1960. Behavior, Systematics, and Natural Selection. In *The Evolution of Life*, ed. S. Tax. University of Chicago Press, Chicago, pp. 595-613.

TOBIAS, P. V. 1966. The Distinctiveness of *Homo habilis*. *Nature* 209:953-957.

――――. 1969. The Taxonomy and Phylogeny of the Australopithecines. In *Taxonomy and Phylogeny of the Old World Primates with Special Reference to the Origin of Man*, ed. B. Chiarelli. Rosenburg and Sellier, Torino, pp. 277-315.

――――. 1972. Recent Human Biological Studies in Southern Africa, with Special Reference to Negroes and Khoisans. *Transactions of the Royal Society of South Africa* 40:109-133.

TRINKAUS, E. 1973. A Reconsideration of the Fontechevade Fossils. *American Journal of Physical Anthropology* 39:25-35.

VALENTINE, J. W., and C. A. CAMPBELL. 1975. Genetic Regulation and the Fossil Record. *American Scientist* 63:673-680.

WASHBURN, S. L. 1960. Tools and Human Evolution. *Scientific American* 203(9):63-75.

――――. 1968. On Holloway's "Tools and Teeth." *American Anthropologist* 70:97-101.

————, and V. Avis. 1958. Evolution of Human Behavior. In *Evolution and Behavior*, eds. A. Roe and G. G. Simpson. Yale University Press, New Haven, pp. 421–436.

Washburn, S. L., and R. Ciochon. 1974. Canine Teeth: Notes on Controversies in the Study of Human Evolution. *American Anthropologist* 76:765–784.

Washburn, S. L., and F. C. Howell. 1960. Human Evolution and Culture. In *Evolution after Darwin: The Evolution of Man*, ed. S. Tax. University of Chicago Press, Chicago, pp. 33–56.

Washburn, S. L., and C. S. Lancaster. 1968. The Evolution of Hunting. In *Man the Hunter*, eds. R. B. Lee and I. DeVore. Aldine, Chicago, pp. 293–303.

Weidenreich, F. 1938. *Pithecanthropus* and *Sinanthropus*. *Nature* 141:376–379.

Wells, L. H. 1969. *Homo sapiens afer* Linn.-Content and Earliest Representatives. *South African Archaeological Bulletin* 21:138–150.

Wolpoff, M. H. 1971. Competitive Exclusion Among Lower Pleistocene Hominids: The Single Species Hypothesis. *Man* 6:601–614.

————. 1971b. Is the New Composite Cranium from Swartkrans a Small Robust Australopithecine? *Nature* 230:398–401.

————. 1971c. Vérteszöllös and the Presapiens Theory. *American Journal of Physical Anthropology* 35:209–216.

Woo, Ju Kang. 1960. The Unbalanced Development of the Physical Features of *Sinanthropus pekinensis* and Its Interpretation. *Vertebrata Palasiatica* 4:17–26.

TOPICAL

Bassett, C. A. L. 1972. Biophysical Principles Affecting Bone Structure. In *The Biochemistry and Physiology of Bone*, ed. G. H. Bourne. Academic, New York.

Behrensmeyer, A. K. 1975. The Taphonomy and Paleoecology of Plio-Pleistocene Vertebrate Assemblages East of Lake Rudolf, Kenya. *Bulletin of the Museum of Comparative Zoology* 146:473–578.

Blanc, A. C. 1961. Some Evidence for the Ideologies of Early Man. In *The Social Life of Early Man*, ed. S. L. Washburn. Viking Fund Publication in Anthropology 31:119–136.

Brain, C. K. 1976. Some Principles in the Interpretations of Bone Accumulations Associated with Man. In *Human Origins: Louis Leakey and the East African Evidence*, eds. G. L. Isaac and E. R. McCown. Benjamin, Menlo Park, pp. 97–116.

Eccles, J. C. 1977. *The Understanding of the Brain*. McGraw-Hill, New York.

Endo, B. 1966. Experimental Studies on the Mechanical Significance of the Form of the Human Facial Skeleton. Japanese Faculty of Sciences, University of Tokyo, Section 5, 3:1–106.

————. 1973. Stress Analysis on the Facial Skeleton of Gorilla by Means of the Wire Strain Gauge Method. *Primates* 14:37–45.

Garn, S. M., and W. Block. 1970. The Limited Nutritional Value of Cannibalism. *American Anthropologist* 72:106.

Geertz, C. 1964. The Transition to Humanity. In *Horizons of Anthropology*, ed. S. Tax. Aldine, Chicago, pp. 37–48.

Genovés, S. 1954. The Problem of the Sex of Certain Fossil Hominids, with Special Reference to the Neandertal Skeletons from Spy. *Journal of the Royal Anthropological Institute* 34:131–144.

Hallowell, A. I. 1961. The Protocultural Foundations of Human Adaptation. In *The Social Life of Early Man*, ed. S. L. Washburn. Viking Fund Publication in Anthropology 31:236–255.

Hardesty, D. L. 1972. The Human Ecological Niche. *American Anthropologist* 74:458–466.

Hewes, G. W. 1973. Primate Communication and the Gestural Origin of Language. *Current Anthropology* 14:5–24.

Hockett, C. F., and R. Ascher. 1964. The Human Revolution. *Current Anthropology*, 5:135–168.

Holloway, R. L. 1969. Culture: A Human Domain. *Current Anthropology* 10:395–412.

Ivanhoe, F. 1970. Was Virchow Right About Neandertal? *Nature* 227:577–579

Jacob, T. 1972. The Problem of Head-hunting and Brain-eating Among Pleistocene Men in Indonesia. *Archaeology and Physical Anthropology in Oceania* 7:81–91.

Kuhn, T. S. 1970. *The Structure of Scientific Revolutions*, 2nd ed. University of Chicago Press, Chicago.

Kummer, B. 1965. Das mechanische Problem der Aufrichtung auf die Hinterextremität im Hinblick auf die Evolution der Bipedie des Menschen. In *Menschliche Abstammungslehre*, ed. G. Heberer. Fischer, Stuttgart, pp. 227–248.

Lancaster, J. B. 1975. *Primate Behavior and the Emergence of Human Culture*. Holt, Rinehart, and Winston, New York.

Lee, R. B. 1968. What Hunters do for a Living, or How to Make Out on Scarce Resources. In *Man the Hunter*, eds. R. B. Lee and I. DeVore. Aldine, Chicago, pp. 30–48.

Le May, M. 1975. The Language Capacity of Neanderthal Man. *American Journal of Physical Anthropology* 42:9–14.

Lenneberg, E. 1967. *Biological Foundations of Language*. Wiley, New York.

Lieberman, P. 1975. *On the Origins of Language*. MacMillan, New York.

Livingstone, F. B. 1969. Evolution of Quantitative Characteristics Which Are Determined by Several Additive Loci. *American Journal of Physical Anthropology* 31:355–362.

Marshack, A. 1972. *The Roots of Civilization*. McGraw-Hill, New York.

Mayr, E. 1969. *Principles of Systematic Zoology*. McGraw-Hill, New York.

Montagu, M. F. A. 1976. *The Nature of Human Aggression*. Oxford University Press, New York.

Musgrave, J. H. 1971. How Dextrous Was Neanderthal Man? *Nature* 233:538–541

Popper, K. R. 1962. *Conjectures and Refutations*. Basic Books, New York.

Premack, D. 1976. *Intelligence in Ape and Man*. Halsted, New York.

Rak, Y. 1978. The Functional Significance of the Squamosal Suture in *Australopithecus boisei*. *American Journal of Physical Anthropology* 49:71–78.

RUMBACH, D. M., ED. 1977. *Language Learning by a Chimpanzee: the LANA Project*. Academic Press, New York.

STEWART, T. D. 1949. The Development of the Concept of Morphological Dating in Connection with Early Man in America. *Southwestern Journal of Anthropology* 5:1-16

ST. HOYME, L. E., and R. T. KORITZER. 1971. Significance of Canine Wear in Pongid Evolution. *American Journal of Physical Anthropology* 35:145-147.

TELEKI, G. 1973. *The Predatory Behavior of Wild Chimpanzees*. Bucknell University Press, Cranbury.

TIGER, L., and R. FOX. 1966. The Zoological Perspective in Social Science. *Man* 1:75-81.

WALKER, A. C. 1976. Functional Anatomy of the Oral Tissues. In *Textbook of Oral Biology*, eds. Shaw, Capuccino, Meller, and Sweeney. Saunders, Philadelphia.

WEINER, J. S. 1955. *The Piltdown Forgery*. Oxford, London.

WHITE, T. D. 1977. *The Anterior Mandibular Corpus of Early African Hominidae: Functional Significance of Shape and Size*. University Microfilms, Ann Arbor.

———. 1978. Early Hominid Enamel Hypoplasia. *American Journal of Physical Anthropology* 49:79-84.

WOLPOFF, M. H. 1973. Posterior Tooth Size, Body Size, and Diet in South African Gracile Australopithecines. *American Journal of Physical Anthropology* 39:375-394.

———. 1974. Sagittal Cresting in the South African Australopithecines. *American Journal of Physical Anthropology* 40:397-408.

———. 1976. Multivariate Discrimination, Tooth Measurements, and Early Hominid Taxonomy. *Journal of Human Evolution* 5:339-344.

———. 1978. Some Implications of Relative Biomechanical Neck Length in Hominid Femora. *American Journal of Physical Anthropology* 48:143-148.

ZINGESER, M. R. 1968. Cercopithecoid Canine Tooth Honing Mechanisms. *American Journal of Physical Anthropology* 29:205-214.

Index

H

I

M

About the Author

MILFORD H. WOLPOFF received his B.A. and Ph.D. at the University of Illinois, Urbana. He taught anthropology at Case Western Reserve University and the University of Illinois and currently is Professor of Anthropology at the University of Michigan. He has done research in Asia, Europe, Africa, Australia, and North America. He is a fellow of the American Association of Physical Anthropologists and the American Anthropological Association. He is the author of numerous papers and book reviews, and has written *Metric Trends in Hominid Dental Evolution* and (with William R. Farrand, Richard W. Redding, and Henry T. Wright III) *An Archaeological Investigation on the Loboi Plain, Baringo District, Kenya.*

A Note on the Type

The text of this book was set in Palatino, a type face designed by the noted German typographer Hermann Zapf. Named after Giovanbattista Palatino, a writing master of Renaissance Italy, Palatino was the first of Zapf's type faces to be introduced to America. The first designs for the face were made in 1948, and the fonts for the complete face were issued between 1950 and 1952. Like all Zapf-designed type faces, Palatino is beautifully balanced and exceedingly readable.

This version of Palatino was composed via computer-driven cathode ray tube by Lehigh-Rocappi from input provided by Random House, Inc.

Printed and bound by R. R. Donnelley & Sons Co., Crawfordsville, Indiana.